30 Sept. 1974

For Ben and Nancy,

It took me two years
to read through the manuscript
of this oversized set, so I really
don't expect you to plow through it
too. My critique ran to 234
pages, and I am thinking of
publishing it separately. That
would make the series truly
endless, though it seems that
way without my help.

With love,

Noel

P.S. Yesterday I was finally
named Editor of the Bulletin
of the ASOR, in which I published
my first article 27 years ago
(under Albright's direction). He was
Editor for almost 40 years.

EPHESIANS

THE ANCHOR BIBLE is a fresh approach to the world's greatest classic. Its object is to make the Bible accessible to the modern reader; its method is to arrive at the meaning of biblical literature through exact translation and extended exposition, and to reconstruct the ancient setting of the biblical story, as well as the circumstances of its transcription and the characteristics of its transcribers.

THE ANCHOR BIBLE is a project of international and interfaith scope: Protestant, Catholic, and Jewish scholars from many countries contribute individual volumes. The project is not sponsored by any ecclesiastical organization and is not intended to reflect any particular theological doctrine. Prepared under our joint supervision, THE ANCHOR BIBLE is an effort to make available all the significant historical and linguistic knowledge which bears on the interpretation of the biblical record.

THE ANCHOR BIBLE is aimed at the general reader with no special formal training in biblical studies; yet, it is written with the most exacting standards of scholarship, reflecting the highest technical accomplishment.

This project marks the beginning of a new era of co-operation among scholars in biblical research, thus forming a common body of knowledge to be shared by all.

William Foxwell Albright
David Noel Freedman
GENERAL EDITORS

Following the death of senior editor W. F. Albright, The Anchor Bible Editorial Board was established to advise and assist David Noel Freedman in his continuing capacity as general editor. The three members of the Editorial Board are among the contributors to The Anchor Bible. They have been associated with the series for a number of years and are familiar with its methods and objectives. Each is a distinguished authority in his area of specialization, and in concert with the others, will provide counsel and judgment as the series continues.

EDITORIAL BOARD

Frank M. Cross   Old Testament
Raymond E. Brown   New Testament
Jonas C. Greenfield   Apocrypha

THE ANCHOR BIBLE

EPHESIANS

Introduction, Translation, and
Commentary on Chapters 1–3
by

MARKUS BARTH

1974

DOUBLEDAY & COMPANY, INC.

GARDEN CITY, NEW YORK

ISBN: 0-385-04412-7
Library of Congress Catalog Card Number 72–79373
Copyright © 1974 by Doubleday & Company, Inc.
All Rights Reserved
Printed in the United States of America
First Edition

PREFACE

Among the more recent commentators on the epistle to the Ephesians, three are outstanding: J. A. Robinson because of his sensitivity to the singular message of this letter, T. K. Abbott as a patient philologist who leaves no stone unturned, and H. Schlier who combines imaginative references to the ancient history of religions with deep theological penetration of the biblical text. Within the triangle formed by the work of these men and their learned predecessors, I have moved and felt at home while writing this book.

To interpret a part of the Bible is to have a conversation with its author —whether or not his name is known—and to participate in the dialogues which informed him and were stirred up by him. An exegete listens and responds above all to the voice of the Bible itself. He realizes that this voice also reflects whispers and thunders heard in the culture of the ancient world and that it has produced many echoes during the almost two-thousand-year history of the synagogue and the church. In turn, the expositor is surrounded and influenced by noises and sounds produced in his own time. While he tries carefully to listen to the past, he also has to respond daringly in terms of the present world. Two examples may elucidate the particular task that confronts a student of Ephesians today.

One: This epistle says things about the peace between Israel and the Gentiles, and about the relationship between Israel and the church, which have no equal in the New Testament and yet clarify and summarize what all apostolic writings appear willing to say. The testimony of Ephesians on these topics made it necessary for me to scrutinize with special care all implicit and explicit references to the Bible of Israel, to read extensively in Jewish apocalyptic, Qumranite and rabbinical literature and to formulate propositions that go beyond the Statement on the Jews pronounced by Vatican Council II.

Two: Some expositors consider the letter to the Ephesians a post-apostolic document. They see in it an introverted glorification of the church, which forgets the centrality of the Messiah Jesus, neglects the church's mission to the world, and falls victim to those thought-patterns of nascent Gnosticism which teach that individual souls are saved by a flight out of this world. The criticisms directed against Ephesians especially by R. Bult-

mann and E. Käsemann made it imperative to face squarely the dialectical
relationship between the devotional prayers and hymns of this letter, its
missionary and ethical exhortations, and its possible borrowings from ancient religious, cultural, and moral trends.

The exposition of Ephesians through the ancient Greek fathers and in
the Orthodox churches of today has received less attention than it deserves. But the exegetical tradition of the western church was given as
careful a hearing as time and space allowed. This tradition ranges from
Irenaeus and Jerome over Thomas Aquinas and the great reformers, to
the fateful cleavage between Roman Catholic and Protestant interpreters
in the post-Reformation periods. It culminates in the resumption of a common quest in our time. Often I was able to learn more from Catholic
scholars than from those Protestant colleagues who had become uncritical
of their own presuppositions and methods.

Just as the Talmudic and Midrashic writings do not pretend to offer
final solutions to the puzzles of biblical texts, but introduce students and
masters alike to the process of asking for truth, wisdom, and obedience, so
in this volume not one but several interpretations are offered for each section of Ephesians—and sometimes even for single words and phrases.
Though I could not and would not hide where I stand at present, my intention was to enable every reader of the Bible, not just scholars, to draw
their own conclusions step by step. I should like to urge them, with the
help of the material and the reflections collected here, to press for deeper
insights, more solid results, and better formulations.

Readers for whom this two-volume work on Ephesians is too thick and
some of its arguments too technical and detailed may refer to the table of
Contents in each volume and to the topical Index (II) at the end of the
second volume for particular COMMENTS and themes of more interest to
them than the philological NOTES. While I intended to present nothing else
than an aid to a literal, historical, and critical understanding of the text and
of its author's intention, I did not want to block the road to a comprehension that is more than merely rational. An exact interpretation of a liturgical document such as Ephesians must necessarily reproduce the appeal
made by its author to the heart of his reader. Thus this commentary has become an invitation to listen to a message pronounced in God's name, and to
understand it not only as a product of a bygone era but also in contemporary terms. For instance, if some readers should feel inclined to join in the
singing suggested in Eph 5:19, they would certainly reveal thereby their
perception of the historical intention and the literal sense of this epistle.

I am grateful to many persons for their help during the preparation of
these pages. The necessary research, and the attempt to publish its results
in the form of a commentary, could not have been undertaken and carried
through without the continuous stimulation, wise counsel, corrections and

suggestions which I received from Professor David Noel Freedman. Among the staff at Doubleday & Company, especially Sallie Waterman and Robert W. Hewetson have shown a subtle and congenial comprehension of all problems of style and substance. The academic community of Pittsburgh Theological Seminary has made many contributions: through President Donald G. Miller and Dean Gordon E. Jackson I was granted a sabbatical leave in 1967–68 to begin the full-time study of Ephesians, and later they accorded me all possible help to facilitate its completion. In seminars, eager students offered their feelings, findings, and ideas for translation and interpretation. Candidates for the ministry and for the degree of Master or Doctor worked with me and for me in the library, checked references and have often come out with useful or daring suggestions: William Rader (whose doctoral thesis on Eph 2:11–22 was finished too late to be quoted in this commentary), Roger Cragun, Rose Moehrke, Waldir Berndt, Archibald Woodruff and Robert Macdonald deserve special credit. Colleagues in the biblical field gave me their critical assessment of novel expositions made possible by recently discovered materials and the restudy of earlier known data. As devoted and untiring secretaries and typists, Mrs. C. Rader in Basel and Mrs. B. Ali, Mrs. E. Eakin and Mrs. D. Dick in Pittsburgh succeeded in transforming my longhand scribble and corrections into clear typescripts. Outstanding among all helpers and incomparable in the breadth and depth of her assistance was and is my wife, Rose Marie. Her contribution not only to my work but also to my life is reflected in the intensive discussion of the passage describing husband and wife, Eph 5:21–33.

Pittsburgh, Pennsylvania
Spring 1972

P.S. All references to the Bible, the Dead Sea scrolls, and the Apostolic Fathers have been checked by a gracious group of students in Basel. The Topical Index was prepared by my assistant in Basel, David S. MacLachlan from Toronto. Still, the responsibility for undiscovered errors lies with the author.
Basel, Switzerland
Summer 1973

CONTENTS

EPHESIANS 1–3
TRANSLATION WITH NOTES AND COMMENTS

PRINCIPAL ABBREVIATIONS

I Versions of the Bible

ASV	The American Standard Version, 1901
JB	The Jerusalem Bible. New York: Doubleday, 1966
KJ	The King James, or Authorized Version of 1611
LXX	The Septuagint, ed. E. Rahlfs. Stuttgart: Württembergische Bibelgesellschaft, 1935
MT	Masoretic (Hebrew or Aramaic) Text of the Old Testament
NEB	The New English Bible. Oxford University Press / Cambridge University Press, 1970
NTTEV	Good News for Modern Man: The New Testament in Today's English Version. New York: American Bible Society, 1960
Pesh.	The Peshitta, a fourth- or fifth-century Syriac version of the Old and New Testaments
RSV	The Revised Standard Version, 1946, 1952
RV	The Revised Version, 1881
SegB	Segond Bible, rev. ed. Geneva: Maison de la Bible, 1964
Symm.	Symmachus' version of the Old Testament, in Greek, late second century A.D.
Theod.	Theodotion's version of the Old Testament, in Greek, second century A.D.
Vulg.	The Vulgate, Jerome's Latin translation of the Bible, late fourth century A.D.
ZB	Zürcher Bibel, Zurich: Zwingli-Verlag, 1935

Note: When in the RSV and other versions the numbering of verses differs (e.g. by one digit) from that of the Greek New Testament text, the numbers of Nestle's Greek text are used.

II Series, Journals, and Frequently Quoted Monographs

AB	The Anchor Bible. New York: Doubleday, 1964–
AER	American Ecclesiastical Review. Washington
AFAW	Annalen der finnischen Akademie der Wissenschaften. Helsinki
AnBib	Analecta Biblica. Rome: Pontifical Biblical Institute
ANET	*Ancient Near Eastern Texts Relating to the Old Testament,* ed. J. B. Pritchard. 2d ed. Princeton University Press, 1955

ANS	Auslegung neutestamentlicher Schriften. Zurich: EVZ
ARW	Archiv für Religionswissenschaft. Leipzig and Freiburg
ASNU	Acta Seminarii Neotestamentici Upsaliensis. Lund: Gleerup
ATANT	Abhandlungen zur Theologie des Alten und Neuen Testaments. Zurich: Zwingli
BBB	Bonner Biblische Beiträge. Bonn: Hanstein
BDF	F. W. Blass and A. Debrunner, tr. and rev. of 9th–10th German ed. by R. W. Funk, *A Greek Grammar of the New Testament and Other Early Christian Literature.* University of Chicago Press, 1961. References to sections
BEvTh	Beiträge zur evangelischen Theologie. Munich: Kaiser
BHTh	Beiträge zur historischen Theologie. Tübingen: Mohr
BhZAW	Beihefte zur Zeitschrift für die alttestamentliche Wissenschaft. Giessen (1896–1934) and Berlin: Töpelmann, 1936–
BhZNW	Beihefte zur Zeitschrift für die neutestamentliche Wissenschaft und die Kunde der älteren Kirche. Giessen (1923–34) and Berlin: Töpelmann, 1936–
BiRes	Papers of the Chicago Society of Biblical Research. Amsterdam: North-Holland Publishing Co., 1956–
BiST	Biblical Studies. London: SPCK
BiTod	The Bible Today. Collegeville, Minnesota
BJRL	The Bulletin of the John Rylands Library. Manchester
BWANT	Beiträge zur Wissenschaft vom Alten und Neuen Testament. Stuttgart: Kohlhammer
BZ	Biblische Zeitschrift. Paderborn
CAK	*Christus, das All und die Kirche,* by F. Mussner, Trierer Theologische Studien 5. Trier: Paulinus-Verlag, 1955, repr. 1968
CBQ	The Catholic Biblical Quarterly. Washington
CD	Covenant of Damascus
Christus	*Christus und die Kirche im Epheserbrief,* by H. Schlier, BHTh 6, 1930, repr. 1966
ConcTM	Concordia Theological Monthly. St. Louis, Missouri
CNT	Commentaire du Nouveau Testament. Neuchâtel / Paris: Delachaux
ConNT	Coniectanea Neotestamentica. Lund: Gleerup
CRCO	*Corpus Reformatorum, Calvini Opera.* Brunswick: Schwetschke, 1863–1900, repr. New York: Johnson, 1964. References to columns
CTh	Cahiers Theologiques. Neuchâtel / Paris: Delachaux
CV	Communio Viatorum. Prague
DB	*Dictionnaire de la Bible,* ed. F. Vigoroux, 5 vols., Paris: Letouzy, 1895–1912; suppl. vols., ed. F. Pirot, 7 vols. to date, 1928–
DFKP	*Die Form der katalogischen Paränese,* by E. Kamlah, WUNT 7, 1964

EBP *Ephesians, Baptism and Pentecost,* by J. C. Kirby. McGill
    University Press, 1968

EcuR Ecumenical Review. Geneva

EE *The Epistle to the Ephesians: Its Authorship, Origin and Pur-*
    pose, by C. L. Mitton. Oxford: Clarendon Press, 1951

ÉHPR Études d'Histoire et de Philosophie Religieuses. Paris

EJ *Encyclopaedia Judaica,* 10 vols. (A–L). Berlin: Eschkol,
    1928–34

EJb Eranos Jahrbuch. Zurich

ERE *Encyclopedia of Religion and Ethics,* ed. J. Hastings. 13 vols.
    New York: Scribner's, 1908–27

ET Expository Times. Aberdeen / Edinburgh

ETL Ephemerides Theologicae Lovanienses. Louvain: Gembloux

EuG *Der Epheserbrief und die Gnosis,* by P. Pokorný. Berlin:
    Evangelische Verlagsanstalt, 1965

EvTh Evangelische Theologie. Munich

FBK P. Feine, J. Behm, and W. G. Kümmel. *Introduction to the*
    New Testament. Nashville: Abingdon, 1965

First Peter *The First Epistle of St. Peter,* by E. G. Selwyn. London:
    Macmillan, 1947

FRLANT Forschungen zur Religion und Literatur des Alten und Neuen
    Testaments. Göttingen: Vandenhoeck

GeistLeb Geist und Leben. Würzburg

GMG *Der Gott "Mensch" in der Gnosis,* by H.-M. Schenke. Göt-
    tingen: Vandenhoeck, 1962

GNT *The Greek New Testament,* eds. K. Aland, M. Black, B. M.
    Metzger, A. Wikgren. Stuttgart: American Bible Society,
    1966

HbNT *Handbuch zum Neuen Testament,* 21 vols. Tübingen: Mohr,
    1911 ff.

HCNT *Hand-Commentar zum Neuen Testament,* ed. H. J. Holtz-
    mann, 4 vols. Freiburg: Mohr, 1889–91

HDB *Hastings Dictionary of the Bible,* eds. F. C. Grant and H. H.
    Rowley. Rev. ed. New York: Scribner's, 1963

HE *Historia Ecclesiastica,* by Eusebius of Caesarea

HMyRel *Die hellenistischen Mysterienreligionen,* by R. Reitzenstein,
    3d ed. Leipzig: Teubner, 1927

HR History of Religions. Chicago

HSNT *Die Heilige Schrift Neuen Testaments,* by J. C. K. von Hof-
    mann. 11 vols. Nördlingen: Beck, 1868–86

HTR Harvard Theological Review. Cambridge, Massachusetts

HUCA Hebrew Union College Annual. Cincinnati

Hymnen *Frühchristliche Hymnen,* by G. Schille. Berlin: Evangelische
    Verlagsanstalt, 1965

IB *The Interpreter's Bible,* 12 vols. Nashville: Abingdon, 1951–
    57

ICC *International Critical Commentary.* Edinburgh: Clark, 1899–

IDB   *The Interpreter's Dictionary of the Bible*, 4 vols. Nashville:
               Abingdon, 1962
IKZ   Internationale kirchliche Zeitschrift. Bern
ITQ   Irish Theological Quarterly. Maynooth
JBL   Journal of Biblical Literature. Philadelphia and Missoula
JbLW   Jahrbuch für Liturgiewissenschaft. Münster: Aschendorff
JE   *Jewish Encyclopedia*, 12 vols. New York / London: Funk &
               Wagnalls, 1901–6
JES   Journal of Ecumenical Studies. Pittsburgh and Philadelphia
JJS   Journal of Jewish Studies. Manchester
JNES   Journal of Near Eastern Studies. Chicago
JQR   Jewish Quarterly Review. London / Philadelphia
JR   Journal of Religion. Chicago
JSS   Journal of Semitic Studies. Manchester
JThC   Journal for Theology and the Church. New York: Harper
JTS   Journal of Theological Studies. London
KEKNT   *Kritisch-exegetischer Kommentar über das Neue Testament*,
               ed. H. A. W. Meyer, 16 vols. Göttingen: Vandenhoeck,
               1832–
KT   Kleine Texte, ed. H. Lietzmann. Berlin: De Gruyter
KTH   Kirchlich Theologische Hefte. Munich
LSLex   H. G. Liddell and R. Scott, *A Greek-English Lexicon*
               (1843), 9th ed. Oxford: Clarendon Press, 1940, repr. 1953
LUA   Lunds Universitets Arsskrift. Lund: Gleerup
LuthW   Lutheran World. Geneva
MNTC   The Moffat New Testament Commentary, 17 vols. New York:
               Harper, 1928–50
Nestle   *Novum Testamentum Graece*, 25th ed., eds. E. Nestle and K.
               Aland. Stuttgart: Württembergische Bibelanstalt, 1963
NovT   Novum Testamentum. Leiden
NRT   Nouvelle Revue Théologique. Louvain
NTA   New Testament Abstracts. Weston, Massachusetts
NTAbh   Neutestamentliche Abhandlungen. Münster: Aschendorff
NTD   Das Neue Testament Deutsch, 12 vols. Göttingen: Vanden-
               hoeck, 1932–
NTF   Neutestamentliche Forschungen. Gütersloh: Bertelsmann
NTS   New Testament Studies. Cambridge
OTTh   *Old Testament Theology*, by G. von Rad. 2 vols. New York:
               Harper, 1962, 1965
Pauly-Wissowa *Real-Enzyklopädie der classischen Altertumswissenschaft*, ed.
               A. Pauly (1839 ff.), rev. G. von Wissowa et al. (1894 ff.),
               1st series, 24 vols., 1894–1963; 2d series, 9 vols., 1914–67;
               12 suppl. vols., 1903–70. Stuttgart: Metzler
PG   Patrologia Graeca, ed. J.-P. Migne. Paris: Migne. Refer-
               ences to columns
PL   Patrologia Latina, ed. J.-P. Migne. Paris: Migne. References
               to columns

PRE   *Realencyklopädie für protestantische Theologie und Kirche,* 18
           vols. Leipzig: Hinrichs, 1877–88
PRJ   *Paul and Rabbinic Judaism,* by W. D. Davies. London:
           SPCK, 1955
PSM   *Paul and the Salvation of Mankind,* by J. Munck. Richmond,
           Virginia: Knox, 1959
1Q   Dead Sea Scrolls from the first cave
1QGenApocr. Qumran Genesis Apocryphon
1QH   Qumran Hodayoth (Hymns of Thanksgiving)
1QM   Qumran Milḥama (War Scroll)
1QpHab   Qumran Pesher on Habakkuk
1QS   Qumran Sereq (Manual of Discipline)
1QSb   Qumran Benedictions
1QTest   Qumran Testimonia
1Q27   Qumran Book of Mysteries
4Q   Documents from the fourth cave, etc.
QuNT   *Qumran und das Neue Testament,* by H. Braun. 2 vols.
           Tübingen: Mohr, 1966
RAC   Reallexikon für Antike und Christentum, ed. J. Hoops, 7 vols.
           to date. Stuttgart: Hiersemann, 1924–
RB   Revue Biblique. Paris
RecB   Recherches Bibliques. Louvain: Desclée
RelgS   *Die religionsgeschichtliche Schule,* I, by C. Colpe, FRLANT
           78, 1961
RGG   *Religion in Geschichte und Gegenwart,* 3d ed., 6 vols. Tü-
           bingen: Mohr, 1957–62. References to columns
RHPR   Revue d'Histoire et de Philosophie Religieuses. Strassbourg
RivBib   Rivista Biblica. Brescia
RQum   Revue de Qumrân. Paris
RSPR   Revue des Sciences Philosophiques et Religieuses. Paris
RSR   Recherches de science religieuse. Paris
SaNT   *The Scrolls and the New Testament,* ed. K. Stendahl. New
           York: Harper, 1957
SbHA   Sitzungsberichte der Heidelberger Akademie der Wissen-
           schaften. Heidelberg
SBM   Stuttgarter biblische Monographien. Stuttgart: Katholisches
           Bibelwerk
SbPA   Sitzungsberichte der Preussischen Akademie der Wissen-
           schaften, Berlin
SBT   Studies in Biblical Theology. London: SCM, and Naperville:
           Allenson
SBU   Symbolae Biblicae Upsalienses. Supplement Litteratur, Svensk
           Exegetisk Arsbok, Lund: Gleerup
ScEccl   Sciences Ecclésiastiques. Montreal
ScotJT   Scottish Journal of Theology. Edinburgh
SNT   *Die Schriften des Neuen Testaments,* 2 vols., ed. J. Weiss, 2d
           ed. Göttingen: Vandenhoeck, 1907, 1908

SNVA   Skrifter utgitt ar Det Norske Videnskaps-Akademie. Oslo
ST   Studia Theologica. Lund
StB   H. L. Strack and P. Billerbeck, *Kommentar zum Neuen
              Testament aus Talmud und Midrasch,* 6 vols. Munich:
              Beck, 1922–61
STK   Svensk Teologisk Kvartalskrift. Lund
SUNT   Studien zur Umwelt des Neuen Testaments. Göttingen: Van-
              denhoeck
TB   Theologische Blätter. Leipzig and Bonn
TF   Theologische Forschung. Hamburg: Reiche
ThNT   *Theology of the New Testament,* by R. Bultmann. 2 vols.
              New York: Harper, 1951, 1955
TLZ   Theologische Literaturzeitung. Halle and Berlin
TQ   Theologische Quartalschrift. Munich, Freiburg, Tübingen
TSK   Theologische Studien und Kritiken. Hamburg, Gotha, Leipzig,
              Berlin
TT   Theology Today. Princeton
TTK   Tidsskrift for Teologi og Kirke. Oslo
TTS   Trierer theologische Studien. Trier
TTZ   Trierer theologische Zeitschrift. Trier
TU   Texte und Untersuchungen. Berlin: Akademie-Verlag
TWNT   *Theologisches Wörterbuch zum Neuen Testament,* eds. G. Kit-
              tel and G. Friedrich, 8 vols. to date. Stuttgart: Kohlham-
              mer, 1932–
TWNTE   *Theological Dictionary of the New Testament* (same work as
              above but tr. into English by G. W. Bromiley, 7 vols. to
              date. Grand Rapids: Eerdmans, 1964–
TZ   Theologische Zeitschrift. Basel
Unity   *The Unity of the Church in the New Testament,* by S. Hanson.
              Uppsala: Almqvist, 1946
VD   Verbum Domini. Rome
VigChr   Vigiliae Christianae. Amsterdam
VT   Vetus Testamentum. Leiden
VTS   Vetus Testamentum Supplements. Leiden: Brill
WA   Weimarer Ausgabe of Luther's Works. Leipzig and Cologne:
              Böhlau, 1883–
WAATNT   Wissenschaftliche Abhandlungen zum Alten Testament und
              Neuen Testament. Neukirchen
WBLex   Walter Bauer, *A Greek-English Lexicon of the New Testa-
              ment and Other Early Christian Literature.* Tr. from the
              rev. Germ. ed. by W. F. Arndt and F. W. Gingrich, Chicago
              University Press, 1957
WMANT   Wissenschaftliche Monographien zum Alten und Neuen Testa-
              ment. Neukirchen
WoDie   Wort und Dienst, Jahrbuch der Theologischen Schule. Bethel
              bei Bielefeld

WUNT	Wissenschaftliche Untersuchungen zum Neuen Testament. Tübingen: Mohr
WZKM	Wiener Zeitschrift für die Kunde des Morgenlandes. Vienna
WZUH	Wissenschaftliche Zeitschrift der Universität. Halle
ZAW	Zeitschrift für die alttestamentliche Wissenschaft. Giessen and Berlin
ZEE	Zeitschrift für evangelische Ethik. Gütersloh
ZKT	Zeitschrift für katholische Theologie. Innsbruck
ZNW	Zeitschrift für die neutestamentliche Wissenschaft und die Kunde der älteren Kirche. Giessen and Berlin
ZRG	Zeitschrift für Religions- und Geistesgeschichte. Erlangen
ZST	Zeitschrift für systematische Theologie. Gütersloh
ZTK	Zeitschrift für Theologie und Kirche. Tübingen

Note: Titles of ancient Greek, Hellenistic, Latin, and Talmudic writings are abbreviated usually after the pattern used in LSLex, TWNT, StB, or the Loeb editions.

III OTHER ABBREVIATIONS

AT	Altes Testament, Ancien Testament (OT)
Bab	Babylonian
Bh	Beiheft (Supplement)
C.E.	Christian Era (=A.D., after Christ)
ch.	chapter
diss.	Unpublished doctoral dissertation
Fs	Festschrift (anniversary volume, in honor of, etc.)
Hb	Handbuch (handbook, manual)
lit.	Literal, word-by-word translation which appears to render the Greek exactly but may not express its meaning
MS, MSS	Manuscript, manuscripts
N.F.	Neue Folge (New Series)
N.S.	New Series, nouvelle série
NT	New Testament, Neues Testament, Nouveau Testament
OT	Old Testament
par.	and parallel passages (e.g. in Matthew or Luke)
qu.	question
(ref.)	by reference only, original text not consulted
repr.	reprint(ed)
var. lect.	*varia lectio* (variant reading of some Greek NT manuscripts)

Note: For works cited by author's name only throughout both volumes, see Bibliography I, Commentaries and Special Studies, at the back of either volume. If not found there, they will be found in the bibliography to the section in which the reference occurs. Sectional Bibliographies 1–16 appear at the back of volume 34, Sectional Bibliographies 17–22 at the back of volume 34A.

1 ¹ From Paul who by God's decision is apostle of the Messiah Jesus, to the saints (in Ephesus) who are faithful to the Messiah Jesus. ² Grace and peace to you from God our Father and the Lord Jesus Christ.

³ Blessed is God the Father of our Lord Jesus Christ. He has blessed us in Christ with the full spiritual blessing of the heavens. ⁴ As [we confess]

> Before the foundation of the world he has chosen us in Christ
> to live by love [standing] holy and blameless before him.
> ⁵ He has predesignated us through Jesus Christ to become his children
> according to his favorable decision
> ⁶ so that the glory of his grace be praised
> which in his beloved son he has poured out upon us.
> ⁷ Through [the shedding of] his blood
> we possess freedom in him, forgiveness of our lapses.
> Such are the riches of his grace
> ⁸ which in all wisdom and prudence he has lavished upon us.
> ⁹ He has made known to us the secret of his decision
> —for he has set his favor first upon Christ
> ¹⁰ that he should administer the days of fulfillment—
> "All things are to be comprehended under one head, the Messiah,
> Those in heaven and upon earth—under him!"

¹¹ As resolved by him who carries out all things after his will and decision, we [Jews] were first designated and appropriated in the Messiah. ¹² We, the first to set our hope upon the Messiah, were to become a praise of God's glory. ¹³ You [Gentiles] too are [included] in him. For you have heard the true word, the message that saves you. And after you came to faith you, too, have been sealed with his seal, the promised Holy Spirit.

> ¹⁴ He is the guarantee of what we shall inherit
> [to vouch] for the liberation of God's own people,
> to the praise of his glory.

¹⁵ Therefore, after hearing of the faithfulness [shown] among you to the Lord Jesus and (of the love) toward all the saints, I, for my part, ¹⁶ never cease to give thanks for you. When mentioning you in my prayers ¹⁷ [I ask] that the God of our Lord Jesus Christ, the all-glorious Father, give you the Spirit of wisdom and revelation so that you may know him ¹⁸ [. I ask] that he illumine the

eyes of your hearts so that you may become aware of the hope to which he is calling you, what glorious riches are to be inherited among the saints, 19 and how exceedingly great is his power over us believers. For that mighty strength is at work 20 which God has exerted in the Messiah when

> He has raised him from the dead.
> He has enthroned him at his right hand in the heavens
> 21 above every government and authority,
> power and dominion, and any title bestowed,
> not only in this age but also in the age to come.
> 22 He put everything under his feet
> and appointed him, the head over all, to be head of the church.
> 23 She is his body, full of him
> who fills all things totally.

2 1 You [Gentiles], especially, dead as you were in your lapses and sins . . . 2 in the past your steps were bound by them [. You were] following [the inspiration of] this world-age, the ruler of the atmosphere, that spirit which is now at work among the rebellious men. 3 In the past all of us [Jews], too, followed these ways. In our own fleshly passions, we did whatever our flesh and our thoughts decided. As much as the rest of mankind we were by nature under the wrath [of God]. 4 But

> God who is rich in mercy
> —for he loves us with all his love—
> 5 just because we were dead in our lapses
> has made us alive together with the Messiah.
>   By grace you are saved!
> 6 For he has in the Messiah Jesus
> raised and enthroned us together in the heavens.
> 7 In order to prove throughout the ages to come,
> through the goodness [shown] to us in the Messiah Jesus,
> how infinitely rich is his grace.
>   8 By grace you are saved, through faith!

This [was] not out of your own doing—it is a gift of God— 9 not [as a reward] for works lest anyone boast about himself. For

> 10 God himself has made us what we are.
> In the Messiah Jesus we are created
> for those good works which God has provided
> as our way of life.

11 Remember, then, that in the past [and] in the realm of flesh you, the Gentiles—called The Uncircumcision by those who call themselves The Circumcision, that handmade operation in the realm of flesh . . . 12 [Remember] that at that time you were apart from the Messiah, excluded from the citizenship of Israel, strangers to the covenants based upon promise. In this world you were bare of hope and without God. 13 But now you are [included] in the

realm of the Messiah Jesus. Through the blood of the Messiah you who in the past stood far off have been brought near. [14] For [we confess]

> He is in person the peace between us.
> He has made both [Gentiles and Jews] into one.
> For he has broken down the dividing wall,
> in his flesh [he has wiped out all] enmity.
> [15] He has abolished the law [, that is, only] the
> commandments [expressed] in statutes.
> [This was] to make peace by creating in his person
> a single new man out of the two,
> [16] and to reconcile both to God
> through the cross in one single body.
> In his own person he has killed the enmity.
> [17] Indeed when he came he proclaimed good news:
> "Peace to you who are far and peace to those near!"
> [18] Through him and in one single Spirit
> the two [of us] have free access to the Father.

[19] Accordingly you are no longer strangers and sojourners, but you are fellow citizens with the saints and members of the household of God. [20] You are built upon the foundation of the apostles and prophets, the keystone being the Messiah Jesus himself. [21] The whole construction, fitted together in him, grows in the Lord into a holy temple. [22] In him you, too, are being built together so as to be a dwelling of God in the Spirit.

3 [1] For this reason I, Paul, the prisoner of the Messiah Jesus for the sake of you Gentiles . . . [2] surely you have heard that I was given God's grace in order to administer it to you. [3] As I have briefly written above, the secret was made known to me by revelation. [4] Correspondingly, by reading [this] you are able to perceive how I understand the secret of the Messiah.

> [5] In other generations it was not made known
>   to the Sons of Men
> as it is now revealed through the Spirit
>   to his holy apostles and prophets:

[6] In the Messiah Jesus [and] through the gospel, the Gentiles are joint heirs, members in the same body, fellow beneficiaries in all that is promised. [7] Through the gift of God's grace which was given me—for his power is at work—I was made a servant of the gospel. [8] I, who am less than the least of all saints, was given the special grace to announce to the Gentiles the good news of the unfathomable riches of the Messiah [9] and to make all men see how the secret is administered [by the Messiah] that was hidden from the ages in God the creator of all things: [10] The manifold wisdom of God is now to be made known through the church to the governments and authorities in the heavens. [11] This is the design concerning the ages which God has carried out in the Messiah Jesus, our Lord. [12] In him and because of his faithfulness, confidently we make use of our free access [to God]. [13] Therefore I ask [God] that you do not lose heart over the tribulations I suffer for you. For they are your glorification.

14 For this reason I bow my knees before the Father 15 from whom each family in heaven and on earth receives its name: 16 Rich as he is in glory may he grant that through his Spirit you be fortified with power [to grow] toward the Inner Man 17 [i.e.] that through faith the Messiah may dwell in your hearts. Stand firm on the root and foundation of love. 18 May you be strong enough to grasp together with all the saints what is the breadth, the length, the height, the depth, 19 and to know the love of Christ though it surpasses knowledge. May you become so perfect as to attain to the full perfection of God.

20 To him who by the power exerted in us
   is able to outdo superabundantly
   all that we ask or imagine—
21 Glory to him in the church and in the Messiah Jesus
   from generation to generation,
   for ever and ever! Amen.

4   1 Therefore I beseech you, prisoner in the Lord['s service] as I am, to conduct yourselves as men worthy of the vocation to which you were called. 2 Be altogether humble and gentle. Patiently bear one another in love. 3 Take pains to maintain the unity of the Spirit through the bond of peace.

4 One body and one Spirit,

just as there is one hope to which you have been called.

5 One Lord, one faith, one baptism,
6 one God who is Father of all,
   he is over all, through all, and in all.

7 The gift of the Messiah is the measure after which grace was given to each of us. 8 Therefore he says,

"When he ascended to the height
he captured a catch of prisoners,
he gave gifts to men."

9 What else does the term "he ascended" imply except that he also descended down to the earth? 10 He who descended is the one who ascended far above all heavens in order to fill all things.

11 He is the one who appointed
   these to be apostles and those to be prophets,
   some to be evangelists and others to be teaching shepherds
12 to equip the saints for the work of service
   for building the Messiah's body
13 until we all come to meet
   the unifying faith and knowledge of the Son of God,
   the Perfect Man,
   the perfection of the Messiah who is the standard of manhood.

14 No longer are we to be babes, tossed by waves and whirled about by every doctrinal gust, [and caught] in the trickery of men who are experts in deceitful scheming. 15 Rather by speaking the truth in love we shall grow in every way toward him who is the head, the Messiah. 16 He is at work fitting and joining the whole body together. He provides sustenance to it through every contact according to the needs of each single part. He enables the body to make its own growth so that it builds itself up in love.

17 Now in the Lord['s name] I say and insist upon the following: No longer conduct yourselves as do the Gentiles in the futility of their mind. 18 Intellectually they are blacked out. Because of their inherent refusal to know [God] and of the petrifaction of their hearts, they are excluded from the life of God. 19 In their insensitive state they have given themselves over to debauchery in order to do all filthy things and still ask for more. 20 But you have not become students of the Messiah this way— 21 assuming you have ever listened to him and been taught in his school. Just as [the instruction] is,

> Truth in Jesus!
> 22 You strip off what fits your former behavior,
> the Old Man rotting in deceitful desires.
> 23 Instead you become new in mind and spirit
> 24 and put on the New Man created after God['s image]
> in true righteousness and piety.

25 Therefore put away the lie. Every one shall speak the truth to his neighbor for we are members of one body. 26 If you are angry yet do not sin. The sun must not set on your temper. 27 And do not give an opportunity to the devil. 28 The thief shall no longer go on stealing. To the contrary, he shall work hard and honestly with his own hands so that he may have something to share with the needy. 29 No foul talk whatsoever shall pass your lips but [say] what is right for meeting a need constructively so that it will do good to the listeners. 30 And do not grieve the Holy Spirit of God [for he is the seal] with which you have been marked for the day of liberation. 31 Every kind of bitterness, passion, anger, shouting, cursing shall be taken away from you, together with any [other sort of] malice. 32 Be good to one another. Be warm-hearted. Forgive one another just as God has forgiven you in Christ.

5 1 Therefore, as [God's] beloved children be imitators of God2 and walk in [the way of] love, just as [we confess]

> The Messiah has loved us
> and has given himself for us
> as an offering and sacrifice
> whose fragrance is pleasing to God.

3 Yet as is fitting for saints, fornication and filth of any kind, or greed must not even be mentioned among you, 4 neither shameless, silly, ribald talk. These

things are improper. Instead, [let there be] thanksgiving! 5 For you had better keep this in mind: No fornicating, filthy, or greedy man, that is, no one who worships an idol, has an inheritance in the kingdom of God's Messiah. 6 Let no one deceive you with shallow words. It is because of these things that the wrath of God comes upon the rebellious. 7 Therefore do not associate with them. 8 For in the past you were darkness, but now in Christ you are light. Conduct yourselves as children of light 9 for the fruit of light consists of everything that is good, righteous, and true. 10 Find out by experience what is pleasing to the Lord 11 and have nothing to do with those fruitless deeds done in darkness. Much more disprove them [by your conduct] 12 for it is shameful even to mention the things that happen in secret. 13 [Only] by the light are all reprobate things revealed. 14 All that is revealed is light. Therefore he says,

> "Awake you sleeper,
>   rise from the dead,
>   the Messiah will shine upon you!"

15 In sum, watch carefully how you conduct yourselves—not as fools, but as wise men. 16 Redeem the time for these days are evil. 17 Therefore do not be senseless but [learn to] comprehend what is the will of the Lord. 18 In particular do not get drunk with wine—that is profligacy—but be filled with the Spirit. 19 Talk to one another in psalms and hymns and spiritual songs. Sing and play to the Lord from your heart. 20 In the name of our Lord Jesus Christ give thanks always and for everything to God the Father.

21 Because you fear Christ subordinate yourselves to one another— 22 [e.g.] wives to your husbands—as to the Lord. 23 For [only] in the same way that the Messiah is the head of the church

> —he, the savior of his body—

is the husband the head of his wife. 24 The difference notwithstanding, just as the church subordinates herself [only] to the Messiah, so wives to your husbands —in everything. 25 Husbands, love your wives, just as [we confess]

> The Messiah has loved the church
>   and has given himself for her
> 26 to make her holy by [his] word
>   and clean by the bath in water,
> 27 to present to himself the church resplendent
>   free from spot or wrinkle or any such thing
>   so that she be holy and blameless.

28 In the same manner also husbands owe it [to God and man] to love their wives for they are their bodies. In loving his wife a man loves himself. 29 For no one ever hates his own flesh, but he provides and cares for it—just as the Messiah for the church, 30 because we are the members of his body. 31 "For this reason

A man will leave his father and mother
And be joined to his wife,
And the two will become one flesh."

32 This [passage] has an eminent secret meaning: I, for one, interpret it [as relating] to Christ and the church. 33 In any case, one by one, each one of you must love his wife as himself, and the wife . . . may she fear her husband.

6 1 Children, obey your parents because of the Lord; for this is right.

2 "Honor your father and mother"

—this is a basic commandment and contains a promise—

3 "in order that it shall be well with you
and you may live long in the land."

4 And fathers, do not provoke the wrath of your children, but bring them up the way the Lord disciplines and corrects [you].

5 Slaves, obey your earthly lords with fear and trembling, as whole-heartedly as [you obey] the Messiah. 6 Do not imitate people who seek to please men by putting on a show, but do God's will from the bottom of your heart, as slaves of Christ. 7 Render your service with fervor—as [a service] to the Lord, not to men. 8 Be aware that the same good which a man performs—be he slave or free—this he will receive from the Lord. 9 And lords, act the same way toward them. Stop using threats. Be aware that in heaven the same Lord is [ruling] over them and over you: he who fosters no favoritism.

10 For the remaining time become strong in the Lord, that is, by the strength of his power. 11 Put on God's [splendid] armor in order to be able to stand firm against the schemes of the devil. 12 For we are wrestling not with blood and flesh, but with the governments, with the authorities, with the overlords of this dark world, with the spiritual hosts of evil in the heavens. 13 Therefore take up God's [splendid] armor so that you are able to put up resistance on the darkest day, to carry out everything, and to stand firm.
14 Stand firm now

"Girded with truth around your waist,
clad with righteousness for a cuirass,"

15 steadfast because the gospel of peace is strapped under your feet. 16 With all [this equipment] take up faith as the shield with which you will be able to quench the fire-missiles of the evil one. 17 Take salvation as your helmet and the sword provided by the Spirit, that is, the word of God.
18 In the Spirit pray at all times through every kind of prayer and petition. To this end stay awake in persevering intercession for all the saints, 19 especially for me [. Pray] that the word may be given to me to open my lips and in high spirits to make the secret known [by proclaiming] the gospel. 20 For this

cause I am an ambassador in chains [. Pray] that I may become frank and bold in my proclamation. For this I must be.

21 In order that you, too, may have knowledge about me and the state of my affairs . . . Tychicus, our dear brother and faithful servant in the Lord, will make known to you all [matters of this kind]. 22 For this very purpose I have sent him to you, that you may know of our situation and that he reassure your hearts.

23 Peace to the brothers, love, and, above all, faith from God the Father and the Lord Jesus Christ. 24 Grace with all who love our Lord Jesus Christ, in eternity.

INTRODUCTION

Ephesians is among the greatest letters under the name of the apostle Paul. Though it has but six rather short chapters and is written in an often painfully ponderous style, it conveys weighty doctrines, warm exhortations and, above all, an urgent invitation to praise God. For a long time Ephesians has been overshadowed, especially in Protestant quarters, by Paul's epistles to the Galatians and Romans. Among the historical-critical scholars of the nineteenth and twentieth centuries, the questions of its authenticity, its place in the history of religion, and its function in the formation of the catholic church have been more intensively discussed than its message. But wherever the mystery of Christ's body and of the unity of its members is considered more important than the issues raised by historical criticism, and where devotion and liturgical worship are preferred to the creation of new theories, Ephesians is still read and used with enthusiasm. Is there a way to reconcile the scientific eros of critical scholars with the passionate love of this letter's less critical readers? We believe that a sober, careful, and critical probing into its peculiarities will not destroy but serve the purpose for which this epistle was written originally.

In the opening sections of this Introduction, some stylistic, form-critical, historical, literary, and doctrinal features of Ephesians will be pointed out. They offer a first glimpse at the character and contents of the epistle as a whole, but also prepare the way for the discussion of the authenticity of this letter to be taken up in sections V and VI. After mentioning the places and dates that must be considered for fixing the origin of Ephesians, and after discussing some problems connected with the transmission of the text, the Introduction will turn to a description of the structure and purpose of this epistle, and end with some information on the form of the commentary that is to follow. The specific materials and arguments collected in the verse-by-verse NOTES and in the COMMENTS are essential for considering any historical, literary, and theological questions with regard to the epistle, while the judgments found in the introductory sections claim no more than preliminary validity.

The following thesis will be proposed for consideration: The apostle Paul himself wrote the epistle to the Ephesians from a prison in Rome toward the end of his life. Paul addresses not the whole church in Ephesus but only the members of Gentile origin, people whom he did not know personally and who had been converted and baptized after his final departure from that city. The strange diction occasionally found in Ephesians stems from hymns and other traditional materials that are quoted in this epistle much more frequently and extensively than in the earlier writings of Paul. Ephesians represents a development of Paul's thought and a summary of his message which are prepared by his undisputed letters and contribute to their proper understanding.

I Vocabulary and Style

More than eighty words not found in other Pauline letters occur in Ephesians. They are called *hapax legomena*. Four among them are found exclusively in the LXX; sixteen outside the LXX only; thirty-eight are met nowhere else in the NT; five have not yet been traced in any Greek document of the pre-Christian period,[1] but many of them do occur in the writings of the Apostolic Fathers[2]—thus creating the impression that Ephesians was written in the post-apostolic age. In all Pauline letters the special topics treated, the peculiar opponents confronted, and the unique situation at hand, find their reflection in the vocabulary chosen for addressing this or that church. Even Romans and I and II Corinthians contain a hundred *hapax legomena,* respectively. Philippians contains about fifty, Galatians more than thirty words that are unique in the Pauline corpus. The Apostolic Fathers have incorporated in their style and vocabulary no more elements from Ephesians than from the undisputed Pauline writings.

The occurrence of *hapax legomena* is matched in Ephesians by the absence of some favorite Pauline words. E.g. the readers are never directly addressed as "Brethren" (though they are called so, 6:23); no reference is made to "many"; the Jews are frequently mentioned and play a decisive role in the argument of the epistle—but they are never called "Jews"; the salvation of men is never described by the verb "to justify"; Paul's preferred word for time (*chronos*) is missing. Instead of mentioning "Satan," the epistle speaks of the "devil." As with the *hapax legomena,* the special topics treated and accents set may explain such differences.

Frequently where the same vocabulary is used in Ephesians as in the main Pauline letters (the so-called homologoumena—esp. Galatians, I and II Corinthians, Romans, Philippians), the meaning of given words appears to be different. Especially the nouns "mystery," "stewardship," "church," "inheritance," "possession," "fullness," and the verbs "to sum up" and "to save" seem to have lost their original Pauline sense. As a possible explana-

---

[1] R. Morgenthaler, *Statistik des neutestamentlichen Wortschatzes* (henceforth *Statistik*) (Zurich: Gotthelf, 1958), pp. 175–80, cf. pp. 44–49; Percy, pp. 179 ff.
[2] See, e.g. E. J. Goodspeed's *Index Patristicus,* repr., Naperville, Ill.: Allenson, 1960.

tion, it may be that Paul took up the specific meanings of given terms which prevailed among those addressed by him at the time. Certainly he did not carry with him a dictionary containing inflexible definitions of key words. There is no reason to assume that he was limited to one possible meaning for a given noun or verb, or with an understanding of the gospel that he had formed at an earlier period.

In Ephesians the occurrence of verbs stands in an extraordinary relationship to the employment of nouns. Most Pauline letters contain fewer verbs than nouns. But in Ephesians the ratio of verbs to nouns is 231:158, against 139:202 in Galatians and 363:377 in Romans.[3] But the liturgical style of Ephesians, also a hymnodic tradition which is to be discussed in the next section, may explain this surprising feature.

Many interpreters deem the epistle's style distinctly un-Pauline. Frequently synonyms are employed; they are with preference combined by a genitive construction[4] or the conjunction "and," (e.g. 1:19). There are pleonastic expressions such as "the holy Spirit of God" (4:30). Abundant attributes are added to nouns or pronouns—either in the form of participles and adjectives, or by the insertion of nouns in the genitive form, or by nouns preceded by the preposition "in." Relative clauses are liberally interpolated into statements that appear loaded enough without them. Indirect questions are a favorite stylistic means.[5] Some sentences wax not only extremely long—artistically composed long clauses may be beautiful —but they are, if judged from a formal, syntactical point of view, downright clumsy.[6]

Percy has presented the most exhaustive description of the style peculiar to Ephesians.[7] He has shown that precisely the same style is characteristic of such passages in the homologoumena in which Paul employs the language of prayer and adoration (e.g. Rom 8:38–39; 11:33–36), and of all the Thanksgivings which except in Galatians are found at the beginning of Paul's letters. So many extended parts of Ephesians consist of prayers and aim at magnifying the oneness of God in the unity of the church, that the whole document may be called a combination of prayers (cf. I Thess 1:2 – 3:16; also Col 1:2–23; Philip 1:3–11). Little wonder, then, that everywhere in Ephesians a diction and style are found that are typical of

---

[3] Morgenthaler, *Statistik*, p. 164.

[4] Percy, pp. 188–89, explains the genitives as genitives of quality or possession. They serve to express a spiritual principle or an attribute. The nouns on which the genitives are dependent are meant to bring to light "the greatness or glory of the concept expressed in genitive form." It may well be that Percy is right in attributing to the genitives a role which is not usual in Greek but dominant in Hebrew. There the full sound and form is retained for what in Greek, Latin, English, German has the derivative genitive status, while an alleviated, "construct" form is used for the noun preceding the genitive.

[5] 1:18–19; 3:9, 18; 5:10, 17.

[6] Esp. 1:3–14; 3:1–7; 4:11–16. The translation of these passages which is given below has dissolved these monster sentences into smaller units.

[7] Percy, pp. 179–252.

synagogue and church prayers. Hieratic traditions outside the Jewish and Christian communities are tainted by similar linguistic traits; liturgical diction has a tendency toward the archaic, clumsy, and unctuous. E. Haupt[8] calls this style "lyric" and finds it divergent from Paul's usual dramatic formation of clauses. It might be better termed hymnodic, for the author of Ephesians gives not only explicit encouragement to "talk to one another in psalms and hymns" (5:19), but he uses or himself composes many a hymnic prayer.

Observations concerning the language and style of Ephesians suggest the following conclusion:[9] The peculiar substance of Ephesians required a specific style. Since a large part of the content is a public prayer to God, the diction of the epistle resembles that of contemporary Jewish and some pagan prayers and of the extant examples of the prayers of Paul. Thus, the vocabulary and style of Ephesians neither demonstrate nor preclude Pauline authorship.[10]

II HYMNS AND TRADITIONAL MATERIAL

In the wake of form-critical studies applied to the whole of the OT and NT, criteria have been tested and collected for discerning in the Pauline letters quotations or borrowings from non-Christian and Christian teachings, confessions, pareneses (exhortations), hymns, and liturgical formulae. The questions whether and in what measure the ethical admonitions of Eph 4–6 are dependent upon traditions that precede the date of the writing of Ephesians will be treated in the comments on the hortatory passages. The focus of the following is on the possible presence in Ephesians of hymns and confessional formulations. The occurrence of catechetical or didactic materials will be discussed at a later stage.

Hymns, fragments of hymns, or confessional formulae borrowed from various sources have been discerned in the following passages of Ephesians: 1:3–14, 20–23; 2:4–7, 10, 14–18, 20–22; 3:5, 20–21; 4:4–6[8], 11–13; 5:2, 14, 25–27.[11] How have they been discovered in the maze of their context? Criteria for sorting out quoted material taken from other sources have been gathered in a short list by E. Stauffer.[12] Recently they

---

[8] Haupt, p. 55; cf. E. von Dobschütz, *Kommentar zu den Thessalonicherbriefen* (Göttingen: Vandenhoeck, 1909), p. 43.

[9] Cf. Percy, pp. 200 f.; Schlier, p. 22.

[10] A. Q. Morton and J. McLeman, *Paul, the Man and the Myth* (New York: Harper, 1966), pp. 35–36, have arrived at a firm denial of authenticity, on the basis of their linguistic studies. But the criteria fed into their computer appear too arbitrarily chosen to yield reliable results.

[11] See BIBLIOGRAPHY 1; cf. fn. 1 to 1:3–14.

N.B. The works listed in this and succeeding sectional bibliographies will be cited by abbreviation, often the author's name only, in the section specified in the parenthetical subheading.

[12] E. Stauffer, *New Testament Theology* (London: SCM, 1955), pp. 338–39. A briefer enumeration of recognition marks is presented by G. Bornkamm in RGG, II, 1003, lines 14–17.

have been refined and regrouped, notably by G. Schille.[13] The following is an excerpt from Stauffer's and Schille's findings, occasionally augmented by further observations.

1. Some special conjunctions like "as," "for," "because," and "therefore" occur at the beginning or the end of a quote (e.g. in Rom 9:16, 18; 10:9; 11:34; I Cor 2:16; 11:23; 15:3; II Cor 10:17; Eph 1:4).

2. The name of Him who is praised is frequently absent when it would be expected. Instead of the name the formula of acclamation, "He is the one who" or the simple relative pronoun "Who," or "in Whom," "through Whom," etc., are found[14]—even at the risk of losing grammatical congruence with the context (e.g. I Tim 3:16; Col 1:15–20).

3. Specific deeds of God or Christ are with preference described either by the (aorist) participle of a verb, or by relative clauses. Not only explicit final or consecutive clauses beginning with "in order to," or "so that," but also infinitives or the preposition "for," or "toward," coupled with a noun, are forms frequently used for describing the purpose and result of God's action (Eph 1:14 ff.; 4:12).

4. Those who benefit from God's mighty acts speak in the first person plural: "For us . . . we through him" (I Cor 8:6), "God our Father" (I Cor 1:3).

5. A concern for brevity is reflected by the omission of the article before key terms (I Tim 3:16). But this interest yields often to that of precision or pleonasm which finds its expression in synonyms, genitive appositions, baroque repetitions (Eph 1:4–14).

6. *Hapax legomena* reveal that the author quotes from a tradition that makes use of other vocabulary than he is wont to employ when he formulates his own thoughts (Philip 2:6–11; Eph 3:5).

7. The text may easily and naturally be divided into cola, lines of similar or equal length which contain a consistent number of beats, perhaps of syllables, too.[15]

---

[13] *Hymnen*, pp. 16–20, 47–50; see also M. Rese, *Verkündigung und Forschung* 15 (1970), 85–87.

[14] In OT ascriptions of praise to God, usually the active participle of the verb is employed. See e.g. Ps 103:3–5, lit. "the one who forgives . . . the one who heals . . . redeems . . . crowns . . . satiates"; Amos 4:13, lit. "the one who forms . . . creates . . . makes known . . . makes . . . treads."

[15] In adding the syllable count to the more frequently observed regularity of up-beats, J. Schattenmann, *Studien zum neutestamentlichen Prosahymnus*, Munich: Beck, 1965 (ref.), and N. Kehl, *Der Christushymnus Kol. 1, 12–20*, SBM 1, 1965 (see esp. the rear inside cover of the book) may have gone to an extreme. Indeed, in the analysis of Hebrew poetry, the count of syllables is a useful procedure which is more reliable than the stress counting. But it is a risky procedure if employed to correct or improve a text supposedly corrupted by prosaic interpolations. The deviations from cola of exactly identical length or syllable number may frequently have been intended by the author or final editor himself and need not demonstrate the corruption of a given passage. While Greek poetry is often composed of completely regular cola, the same is not necessarily true of the Hebraizing NT hymns. It appears that Debrunner's warning of the way chosen by Lohmeyer—see their articles cited in BIBLIOGRAPHY 1—has been thrown to the winds. R. Schütz, "Die Bedeutung der Kolometrie für das NT," ZNW 21 (1922), 161–84, quotes on p. 172 the ancient philologist

8. Elements of careful structure distinguish the piece in question. Not only parallelism of members is discernible, but also a division into stanzas consisting of two, three or more cola, and an opening or concluding key word, or a summary statement. The end may take up the beginning, "*Ring-Komposition*," or other chiasmic features may be obvious.[16]

To these formal criteria a number of elements are added that pertain to the contents of a given passage. The following features are said to reveal that a given text has hymnic or confessional character:

9. The text offers a summary of the message of Christ, the so-called kerygma, but shows no concern for historical accuracy.

10. The cosmic extension of God's or Christ's role is emphasized. Liberal borrowings from pagan mythology are made in order to communicate Christ's cosmic role in a language that is understood by men of the Hellenistic world.

11. The content of a given passage interrupts the context. The preceding or following verses fit or allude to only a small section of it. A larger or smaller portion of the quote overlaps the main line of thought and is superfluous for the argument at hand. The theology of the biblical author who uses a traditional formulation is sometimes contradicted by the original intent and content of the formula. The author may have added glosses to the quoted text in order thereby to suppress a theological tendency contrary to his own (see e.g. Col 1:18a).

It is evident that at least the last-mentioned three criteria, but perhaps many more, too, are not beyond serious doubt. They presuppose that the Bible interpreter knows beforehand, from sources other than the given text, what is historically accurate, whence and whither the movement of thought in the context flows, and which theology is proper or improper to the respective biblical authors. Scholars who push the reconstruction of hymns have so far been unable to avoid questionable methods. Many of them have to excise alleged "glosses" from the texts at hand. They arrive at one or another "original" hymn for which there is no exact literary evidence outside the OT and NT text at all, or only some evidence of a considerably later time. But the extreme risks and steps necessary in trying

---

Suidas' definition of a *kolon:* "A colon is a line which contains a complete thought [or sense, *ennoia*]." This definition offers no encouragement to reconstructing the supposedly "original" lines of a hymn and their length by counting syllables and excising overhanging parts.

[16] Sometimes such a ring-composition which begins and ends with the same word, phrase or idea, is called an *inclusio* (inclusion). Inclusions are frequent in the Psalms, as M. Dahood's interpretation in this series shows (AB, vols. 16, 17, 17A). John Bligh, however, seems to have carried the case too far and in spite of himself to have shown the limitations of the argument, when he seeks to demonstrate that Paul in the most personal of his epistles used the most intricate chiasmic methods (see *Galatians in Greek,* University of Detroit Press, 1966, and *Galatians,* London: St. Paul Publications, 1969).

to discern the presence of traditional materials in Paul,[17] with the concomitant danger of reducing the creativeness and originality of the apostle's thought and diction, are not sufficient reasons to neglect the problems posed by the possible presence of hymns, confessional statements, and liturgical fragments. Paul quoted the Bible of the Jews and also the words of Jesus and the early church (I Thess 4:15; I Cor 7:10; 11:24–25; 15:3–4; cf. Acts 20:35). In Eph 5:14 the same quotation formula introduces a non-biblical text as that employed in Eph 4:8 for a Bible citation. In I Cor 11:23; 15:3, Paul states explicitly that he makes use of tradition.

As an example of his use of another sort of liturgical tradition we mention the reference to the blood of Christ and to forgiveness in Eph 1:7. Though the blood and forgiveness are but rarely mentioned in the Pauline writings,[18] they were fully endorsed in his thought.

As long as Paul was considered an entirely independent witness (on the basis of texts such as Gal 1:11–12), who might correct but certainly not subscribe to or agree with the teaching and preaching of Christians (esp. Judaeo-Christians!) converted before him, those generalizing or specific elements of Ephesians that bear the mark of Christian tradition appeared clearly to speak against the authenticity of the epistle. But since it has become obvious that in the uncontested Pauline epistles frequent use is made of pre-Pauline formulations, the abundant occurrence of traditional elements in Ephesians reveals but a gradual, not an essential, difference from other Pauline epistles. Whether many or few, faithfully reproduced, liberally glossed, or newly formed hymns and confessional fragments occur in Ephesians, their presence can no longer be treated as a cogent argument against Pauline authorship. In the detailed exegesis of the hymnodic Ephesian passages the question will be taken up as to whether or not they must be considered pre-Pauline. Stanley considers it almost certain that all

---

[17] E.g. in the reconstruction by Bultmann of the kerygma of the Hellenistic church, in his *ThNT*, I, 63–164. This kerygma and that church were probably not uniform units. For details of Paul's relation to tradition see e.g. A. M. Hunter, *Paul and His Predecessors*, rev. ed., London: SCM, 1961; K. Wegenast, *Das Verständnis der Tradition bei Paulus und in den Deuteropaulinen*, WMANT 8 (1962), 35–120; recently H. Conzelmann, *An Outline of the Theology of the New Testament*, New York: Harper, 1969; J. P. Sampley, *And the Two shall Become One Flesh*, NTS Monograph Series 16, Cambridge University Press, 1971. E. Käsemann, "Ephesians and Acts," in *Studies in Luke-Acts*, Fs P. Schubert, eds. L. E. Keck and J. L. Martin (Nashville: Abingdon, 1966), p. 297, follows in the footsteps of E. J. Goodspeed when he calls Ephesians "a mosaic composed of extensive as well as tiny elements of tradition." Käsemann does not ascribe to Paul the skillful "selection and ordering of the material" made in this epistle.

[18] "The blood": in Eph 1:7; Rom 3:25; 5:9; I Cor 10:16; 11:25, 27; cf. Acts 20:28; "forgiveness," a favorite term of Luke's: in Eph 1:7; Col 1:14; Rom 4:7; cf. Rom 3:25; Acts 13:38; 26:18. For a specific discussion of the origin and relevance of such Pauline borrowings from tradition see E. Käsemann, "Zum Verständnis von Röm. 3:24–26," ZNW 43 (1950–51), 150–54, repr. in *Exegetische Versuche und Besinnungen*, I (Göttingen: Vandenhoeck, 1964), 96–100; J. Reumann, "The Gospel of the Righteousness of God," *Interpretation* 20 (1966), 432–52; C. H. Talbert, "A Non-Pauline Fragment in Rom. 3:24–26," JBL 85 (1966), 287–96.

Christological hymns in the NT were composed before Paul's letters were written, i.e. before about A.D. 50.[18a] It may be observed that the vocabulary of Ephesians is strange to Paul particularly in those passages which contain hymns or other traditional material.

III   HISTORICAL AND LITERARY RELATIONS

A   The Writer and the Addressees

If the title *To the Ephesians* (or some longer version of this) prefixed to the epistle and the majority of Greek MSS containing Eph 1:1 are considered reliable sources of information, then Ephesians was directed to the Christian congregation in Ephesus, a city that was once outstanding among the harbors and trade centers of Asia Minor. (Except for a short revival in the fourteenth century, Ephesus gradually lost all importance as the mouth of the Kaystros River gradually filled with silt and the harbor decayed. The hometown of Heraclitus with its most famous temple of Artemis eventually became ruins.) According to Acts 18:19–21; 19:1–20; 20:1, 31, the apostle Paul had founded the church, had worked extensively among Jews and Gentiles, and had found friends and associates in Ephesus.

But there is a dilemma which appears to compel the student of Ephesians to make a difficult choice. If Paul himself wrote this epistle, then it could hardly have been addressed to Ephesus. Or if it was really written for the Ephesians, then Paul was most likely not its author. The following reasons seem to leave the reader only with this disturbing choice:

1. According to Eph 1:15; 3:2–3; 4:21, the author does not personally know the congregation, and its members don't know him either. They have only heard of one another and are dependent upon what is told or written of them.

2. No references whatsoever are made to specific conditions or events in the city or church of Ephesus. Other Pauline letters contain allusions to concrete, often unique occurrences that have taken place between the author and the addressees, or among the recipients, or between them and their Jewish or Gentile environment. But Ephesians says nothing specific of the church in Ephesus. It speaks of the universal church, and the polemics found in 2:8–9; 4:14; 5:6 do not reflect a specific local heresy.

3. Only Gentile Christians are addressed in this epistle.[19] Their incorporation into Israel, the elect people of God, is one of the main topics of the epistle. But it seems inexplicable that Paul should have no word for the Jewish Christians of Ephesus.

[18a] D. M. Stanley, CBQ 20 (1958), 173–91.
[19] 1:11–14; 2:1–3, 11–22; 3:1; 4:17–19; 5:8.

4. No personal greetings from Paul or his associates, e.g. from Timothy, are attached to the parenetic (exhortatory) part of the epistle. Should the "holiness" of an apostle (cf. 3:5) be demonstrated by his total neglect of, and unconcern for, specific events and personal relations?

5. The final blessing (6:23–24) is warm enough. But if compared with the ending usually found in the Pauline letters, it has an impersonal flavor and bears the mark of majestic distance. The third person plural, *them,* replaces the direct address, *you,* which prevails in the letters whose Pauline origin is uncontested.

6. According to a few very important MSS[20] the words "in Ephesus" do not belong in 1:1. When Paul's letters were collected, these words may well have been interpolated by copyists or editors who assumed that this epistle needed as distinct an address as the other Pauline letters. But the autograph may have been conceived as an encyclical to be read in several churches as were I Peter (1:1), James (1:1), perhaps also I John. Or it may have been, just as the epistle to the Hebrews, a meditation or speech prepared for occasional or general use.[21]

7. The author of Ephesians seems to speak of the apostles as if they were dead and buried, and at the same time occupying a rank high above the congregation. Together with the prophets, the apostles are called the "foundation" of the church (2:20). They are designated as "holy" (3:5). So they seem to belong at the same time to the dim past and to a superior high rank.

8. The controversy between Jewish Christianity and the Hellenistic or Pauline understanding of faith which fills the Pauline letters and led to the elaboration of the justification-by-faith doctrine, appears not to be continued in Ephesians. Instead, it seems presupposed that this issue belongs to the past and is victoriously settled. Therefore, the epistle has been ascribed to the post-apostolic age.

On the other hand, (a) Ephesians was directed to only one group in the Ephesian congregation. If this group consisted of recently baptized Gentiles, or if the letter is addressed to Christians in cities that were never visited by Paul, it can be easily explained why Paul does not know the addressees personally, and why the recipients of the letter know Paul only by what they have heard or read. (b) Paul himself calls all Christians "saints" or "holy." Gal 1–2; II Cor 3 and 10–13 and other passages show that he had an extremely high notion of the apostolic ministry. (c) And it is a prejudice to make a repetitious pounding upon justification the decisive mark of authenticity. Why should Paul not, toward the end of his ministry, have elaborated upon an irenic presentation of the peace established by Christ between Jews and Gentiles?

[20] See Note on "in Ephesus" in 1:1.
[21] See 1:13; 2:1–2, 11–22; 4:17–19; also COMMENT XIV on 1:3–14.

Yet another argument against Pauline authorship is that Ephesians repeats, or presents in variations, many of the issues and topics dealt with
in the main bulk of Pauline epistles, especially Colossians. Should one and
the same author, a man like the ingenious and impulsive Paul, repeat himself to the extent that Ephesians repeats Pauline letters? It may be that
he did not intend to present a new version of his gospel to those addressed
in this epistle. The so-called dependence of Ephesians upon the Pauline
corpus may be explained as easily by the intention of Paul to sum up the
gist of his message and exhortation, as by the slavish dependence of an
imitator upon the master.

It has further been argued that the readers of Ephesians could understand the unique image of the broken wall in Eph 2:14 only if it is an
allusion to the destruction of Jerusalem in A.D. 70. It is certainly not
impossible that a post-Pauline author characterized by a cruel and malicious heart might ascribe the greatest blessing to that dreadful catastrophe,[22] but detailed exegesis of the verse in question will reveal that
many alternatives exist for explaining the imagery of the *wall*. Not all
things that might possibly be construed as an allusion to a contemporary
event are necessarily an intended reference to it. Eph 2:14 is no absolute
proof that Ephesians was written after A.D. 70, and, therefore, by an author
other than Paul.

The observation and exploitation of parallels between Ephesians and
contemporary religious literature may yield more information on the
writer and the recipients of Ephesians than do arguments built upon
individual verses or statements only. Ephesians may contain either allusions to, partial endorsement and variations of, or polemics against,
teachings that are found in Gnostic circles, in the Qumran community,
and in several NT writings. All these groups of literature have been
summarily called Hellenistic or syncretistic. But instead of a generalizing discussion of the relationship of Ephesians to Hellenism and syncretism, what follows is a survey of outstanding examples from each of the
groups mentioned. We begin with a religious movement whose influence
upon Ephesians is most difficult to demonstrate; then we proceed to considering more obvious literary parallels, including the role of the OT in
this epistle.

B Gnosticism

It was F. C. Baur's opinion that Ephesians belonged in the latter part
of the second century because of its dependence upon Gnostic thought.[23]

---

[22] Though S. G. F. Brandon, *The Fall of Jerusalem and the Christian Church* (London:
SPCK, 1957), p. 216, explicitly states that the author of Ephesians "is able . . . to refrain
from any exultation over the fall of Israel."
[23] *Paulus der Apostel Jesu Christi* (Stuttgart: Becker & Müller, 1845), p. 436; cf. idem,
Die christliche Gnosis, Tübingen: Osiander, 1835. For literature pertinent to the question of
Gnosticism in Ephesians see BIBLIOGRAPHY 2.

Since his time much labor has been invested in discovering, describing, and understanding Gnosticism and its traces in the NT. W. Bousset, R. Reitzenstein, E. Norden, R. Bultmann, H. Jonas, H. Schlier, and E. Käsemann are the best-known contributors to this effort. The materials discovered at Chenoboskion in Egypt shortly before the caves near the Dead Sea began to yield their treasures have given renewed impetus to the continuation and evaluation of research in these fields. Books and articles by G. Quispel, D. J. Dupont, R. McL. Wilson, R. M. Grant, H. J. Schoeps, W. Schmithals, C. Colpe, H.-M. Schenke, and P. Pokorný are based upon the material available before *and after* the new finds, and they permit us to assess the possible relationships between Ephesians and Gnosticism with more accuracy than was available to F. C. Baur and his early followers.

Ephesians is often understood either as Gnosticising, or as outspokenly anti-Gnostic, or as both at the same time.[24] On the other hand, there are many commentaries, monographs and essays on Ephesians that push the problems of Gnosticism aside altogether; among the many definitions of Gnosticism, there is one which uses this term exclusively for the designation of the great second-century systems of Marcion, Valentinus, Basilides, the Barbelognostics, the Ophites and their later versions—however early some traditions of Simon Magus and the *falsely so-called gnosis* of I Tim 6:20 may be dated. It is today commonly accepted that Ephesians is not dependent upon any of the classical Christian-heretic Gnostic systems. But no agreement exists as yet regarding the question whether or not specific elements in Jewish Wisdom literature and apocalyptic books, in Philo, in Matt 11:25–29; Col 1:15–20, and also in the Johannine and the unquestioned Pauline writings deserve to be labeled Gnostic, or proto-Gnostic. It is not impossible that before the second century, maybe even before the Christian era, several proto-Gnostic elements had been combined to form the pattern of a religious world view, and found expression in fabulous myths. If not the full-blown myth of the Aion-Prime-Anthropos, at least several of its constitutive features may have been known to the author of Ephesians. The Qumran literature contains traces of proto-Gnostic thought.

The discussion of specific possible points of contact and controversy between Ephesians and Gnosticism has to be left to the comments upon those verses that seem most likely to prove a close relationship. But some preliminary remarks are appropriate at this place.

[24] M. Albertz, *Die Botschaft des Neues Testaments,* I, 2 (Munich: Kaiser, 1952), 168, speaks of the "Gnostic-anti-Gnostic character" of Ephesians. Schlier and Käsemann emphasize dependence upon, and correction of, Gnosticism with the same vigor. If, with Pokorný, Ephesians is understood as being a line-by-line refutation of Gnosticism, then this epistle is ascribed a polemic intention which makes it similar to the explicitly polemical part of Colossians, i.e. 2:4 – 3:4. The irenic character which actually distinguishes Ephesians from Colossians is then only a façade.

Just like Gnosticism, so also Ephesians speaks emphatically of knowledge.[25] In both Ephesians and Gnosticism, knowledge is a gift from
above; it reveals what was hidden; it is conveyed by a dramatic narrative; its purpose and power are redemptive; it joins the knower with the
deity; he who possesses it follows a distinct way of life. According to a
summary given by H. Jonas,[26] Gnostic knowledge offers those initiated into
its mysteries unknowable things: the secret of existence and the nature of
salvation as narrated in myth; the combination of myths into a great system; the opening of a way for the soul to ascend out of this world; secret
rites, formulae, and other means that contribute to the journey. By knowledge the initiate is transformed, for when he recovers his true being through
it, he experiences his apotheosis.[27]

Even a superficial perusal of Ephesians will convince the reader that
this letter has little, if anything, in common with such Gnostic teaching.
Ephesians does not reveal an unknown God who is distinct from the
creator of heaven and earth, but rather the mystery of God the creator
(3:9). In place of knowledge of the Self, or of abysmal existence under
powers that keep earthly men separate from God, the crucified and raised
Jesus Christ's work for Jews and Gentiles forms the center of all teaching.
The obstruction of hostile powers is not an exciting topic of its own—
however high their location, however vicious their attacks. No way is
shown for the individual to escape the obligations of life on earth; rather
those already raised and enthroned in heaven, that is, the elect of God,
are held to be God's showpiece on earth (2:7). To fulfill this function
they are to do good works, to love one another, and to fight bravely during
the present evil days. Rather than in individual perfection and salvation,
the *raison d'être* of the church is this: that the knowledge of *all* may grow
(3:18–19; 4:13), that the wisdom of God be imparted, and the message
of peace be spread to all who don't know and acknowledge it yet (3:10;
6:15, 19–20).

But if knowledge in Ephesians has a Christocentric, ethical, and missionary character which is not present in Gnostic descriptions of saving
knowledge, there may still be many other features establishing a close
link between Ephesians and Gnosticism. A description of terms such as
mystery, revelation, fullness, principalities and *powers* will be found in
the NOTES and COMMENTS on the passages where they occur; here we shall
only take up the key question connected with the possible relationship between Ephesians and the Gnostics.

The supporters of a Gnosticizing interpretation of Ephesians are con-

---

[25] See the passages mentioned in COMMENT X on 1:3–14.
[26] *Gnostic Religion*, pp. 284–85.
[27] In COMMENT XVI on 1:3–14 the initiation rite will be described in more detail.

vinced that both Ephesians and Gnosticism presuppose and unfold the doctrine of the Aion God and Prime Man, i.e. of a head, a cosmic body, successive problematic emanations, many dispersed members. Gnosticism as well as Ephesians are assumed to reflect the same "myth of the Redeemed Redeemer" who descends from on high and reascends in order to gather his members, the souls of men, to himself. Both supposedly deal with heavenly syzygies (copulations of male and female partners) which are to be re-enacted on earth—though asceticism in one case, marriage in the other may be propounded as the suitable way of re-enactment. Close parallels are seen in a certain negative attitude toward the world and a sincere trust in the sacramental mediation of salvation.

To give an example: in the so-called Naassene Sermon, a distinctly Gnostic document presented in secondary form by Hippolytus,[28] at least four elements are present that are also found in Ephesians: (1) the idea that the spiritual man is a superindividual being; (2) the conception of a cosmic body; (3) the reference to a head on whom life depends; (4) the motif of growth.[29] In following R. Reitzenstein's reconstruction of the Iranian mystery of redemption and other precedents,[30] H. Schlier,[31] E. Käsemann,[32] and H. Conzelmann[33] have based their understanding of the head-body image and the concept of salvation upon the Gnostic notions that are believed to underlie Ephesians. While Schlier has given up his earlier belief that the great Gnostic influence upon Ephesians is hardly reconcilable with Pauline authorship, Käsemann and others still consider it a decisive argument against the authenticity of Ephesians.

Is it at all possible that the apostle Paul himself knew and endorsed as much of Gnosticism as the author of Ephesians supposedly did? If W. Schmithals is right in his daring reconstruction of the doctrine and motives of Paul's antagonists, then the apostle himself had to deal not only with diverse groups of so-called Judaizers, wild enthusiasts, and immoral libertines, but also with distinctly Gnostic misinterpretations of his message which blended some seemingly contradictory beliefs. Schmithals goes so far as to suggest that Paul's own writing occasionally became the victim of Gnostic thought. He considers the verses II Cor 3:17 and 5:16 glosses

---

[28] *Refutatio omnium haeresium* (henceforth Hippol.) v 7:3 – 9:9. R. Reitzenstein, *Poimandres*, pp. 83–98, attempts to reconstruct the original text. R. M. Grant, *Gnosticism*, pp. 105–14, offers its main parts in English translation. The Naassenes flourished around the middle of the second century A.D. The following list reproduces the comparison made by Pokorný, EuG, pp. 53–54.

[29] Parallel statements are found in Eph 4:13–15 and Hippol. v 7–8; Eph 1:23; 4:15; cf. Col 1:17 and Hippol. v 8; Eph 1:23; 4:15; cf. Col 1:18; 2:19 and Hippol. v 7, 8, 13; Eph 4:15; cf. Col 2:19 and Hippol. v 7. Some, but not all, of the Hippolytan passages may not have been a part of the pre-Christian Gnostic document. They may have to be ascribed to Christian editing of the original Sermon; see, e.g. the quote from Eph 3:15 in Hippol. v 7.7.

[30] *Das iranische Erlösungsmysterium;* W. Bousset, *Hauptprobleme.*

[31] In *Christus* and in his commentary.

[32] *Leib und Leib Christi.*   [33] In his commentary.

inserted by a Gnostic hand in Paul's pure Gospel![34] A controversy between Schlier and Käsemann[35] regarding the spread of the head-body imagery over the letters ascribed to Paul puts Käsemann on the side of Schmithals. Käsemann held that not only in the deutero-Pauline epistles to the Colossians and Ephesians but also in Romans and I Corinthians the Gnostic idea of the *Ur-Mensch* is the ground of the elaborations upon the body of Christ. If this is true, then Paul himself was able to and did use Gnostic notions for preaching the Gospel.

The conclusion to be drawn for the authorship of Ephesians is obvious: Even if Ephesians is Gnostic or anti-Gnostic, it may well have been written by Paul himself. Even those who believe that they have sound historical reasons for an early dating of Gnosticism and for finding traces of it spread over the NT are thus prevented from using the late origin or suspect character of Gnosticism as an argument against the epistle's authenticity.

But the most recent research in Gnosticism leads us still further.[36] C. Colpe and H.-M. Schenke put Bousset's and Reitzenstein's assumption in question. They destroy the notion that at Paul's time there was *one* Iranian mystery of redemption available, expressed in the myth of a god, called "Man," who appeared in the form of a messenger to save, to enlighten, and to gather up the dispersed souls. Too many such men or Prime-Anthropoi make their appearance in literature such as the Naassene Sermon, the Apocryphon of John, Poimandres, and the Essence of the Archontes to be simply combined in one figure or one system which might be called The Redeemed Redeemer Myth. The Prime-Anthropos and the Redeemer figures have not been identified earlier than in the system of Mani (who died shortly before A.D. 300). Therefore, it is Mani who deserves the credit for creating or shaping out of several earlier independent mythical notions and tales the myth mentioned. Neither Paul nor John nor a deutero-Paulinist author of the first century could have used this more recent Gnostic myth. Bultmann's, Schlier's, and Käsemann's theory —saying that the head-body image of Colossians and Ephesians is Gnostic and entails a Gnosticizing notion of salvation—is therefore "to be bidden farewell. . . . Our exegetical and historical conscience compels us to do so."[37] Most likely Reitzenstein's Iranian Myth of the Prime Man was never widely spread and known—except perhaps in the imagination of

---

[34] *Gnosticism in Corinth;* see also his essays on Galatians, Philippians, Thessalonians, and Rom 16:17–20 in *Paul and the Gnostics;* his book, *Das kirchliche Apostelamt;* and his essay, "Zwei gnostische Glossen im Zweiten Korintherbrief," EvTh 18 (1958), 552–73.

[35] See fns. 31 and 32 above.

[36] Among the books directly relevant for Ephesians are esp. Colpe, RelgS, and Schenke, GMG. See also Colpe, BhZNW 26 (1960), 172–87. The following is in the main a report on Schenke's findings.

[37] Schenke, GMG, p. 155.

some scholars. The earliest solid trace of the complete myth is found in Mani's ingenious construction.

The labors and results of C. Colpe and H.-M. Schenke have been preceded by the works of specialists like D. J. Dupont,[38] G. Quispel,[39] R. McL. Wilson.[40] Their common tendency is, individual distinctions notwithstanding, to explain second-century and later Gnosticism as a result of extreme and decadent Jewish notions rather than as a beautiful flower grown on the bush of pure Iranian religion. Such interpreters of Ephesians and Colossians as E. Percy,[41] S. Hanson,[42] N. A. Dahl,[43] F. Mussner,[44] P. Bénoit,[45] G. Kuhn,[46] H. Hegermann[47] had always warned of an unwarranted early dating of Gnosticism. They suggested that biblical, Apocalyptic, Sapiential or Philonic Jewish teachings and notions rather than the Gnostic myth be used as a key for explaining the puzzling, supposedly Gnostic, features of Ephesians and Colossians. See COMMENT VI on 1:15–23 for details regarding the head-body imagery and the concept of fullness.

Pokorný[48] proves to be fully acquainted with the recent developments of Gnostic research, yet he aspires to make the best possible use of the theories which Bultmann, Schlier, and Käsemann constructed upon the basis of Bousset's and Reitzenstein's understanding of Gnosticism. None of them treated Ephesians and Colossians as an expression of Gnosticism pure and simple. They recognized that the timeless myth was but the form of a content, a means of communication, but by no means the essence of the gospel. The biblical authors wanted to speak of historical events and decisions; and above all, of the coming and the death of Jesus Christ, the nature of faith and new life. The scholars mentioned above observed that the Gnostic spatial and substantial dualism of spirit and matter was exchanged in the deutero-Paulines for an ethical dualism of decision. Christian ethics excluded the libertinism of Gnostics—and according to Schmithals the Gnostic asceticism and legalism as well.

Now, according to these scholars, the result of the overwhelming influence of Gnosticism upon Colossians and Ephesians, and of the several corrections added to Gnostic thought forms, was the formation of a high-church and sacramental church ideology; and they felt unable to consider

[38] *Gnosis*, see esp. pp. 419 ff., 440, 446.
[39] *Gnosis als Weltreligion;* idem, EJb 22 (1953), 195–234; cf. idem, EvTh 14 (1954), 474–84.
[40] *Gnostic Problem;* cf. his review of Schmithals' *Gnosis in Korinth* in ScotJT 15 (1962), 324–27.
[41] E.g. p. 165.   [42] *Unity*, pp. 68 f., 87, 116, 159 f.
[43] "Adresse und Prooemium des Epheserbriefes," TZ 7 (1951), 241–64.   [44] CAK.
[45] "Corps, tête et plérôme dans les épitres de la captivité," RB 63 (1956), 5–44, esp. 6 f., 17, 33. Cited henceforth as "Corps, tête."
[46] "Der Epheserbrief im Lichte der Qumrantexte," NTS 7 (1960–61), 334–46, esp. 339, 342.
[47] *Schöpfungsmittler*, pp. 91 ff.
[48] EuG; idem, "Soma Christou im Epheserbrief," EvTh 20 (1960), 456–64; idem, ZNW 53 (1962), 160–94.

such ecclesiasticism genuinely Pauline.[49] Pokorný, however, is not willing to follow their lead. He elaborates only and exclusively upon the polemics against Gnostic thought, and the theological result of his research stands in radical opposition to an ecclesiology that detaches the church from the intent of the so-called Social Gospel, i.e. from the saints' political, cultural, economic responsibility for the problems that plague the world. According to him, Ephesians forbids the church to aim only at the salvation of individual souls instead of pressing for communal life and service. God must not be confined to the atmosphere above the earth and the secret sphere of the cult. Rather the crucified Lord is in the center, he who is Lord over all that is created! The sacraments must not be used as an escape hatch. What counts is sociological reality and ethical responsibility. This is Pokorný's summary of Ephesians.[50] For him this letter is the banner of what formerly would have been labeled a low-church conception, and what today may be called a Church-and-Society, or a Theology-of-Revolution approach to Ecclesiology.

While earlier Gnosticizing interpreters of Ephesians were unwilling to accept Pauline authorship because of the high ecclesiology of this epistle, Pokorný believes that Paul cannot have written this document because the catastrophic distortion of ecclesiology which Ephesians seeks to correct belongs to a period after the apostle's death. However, neither the horror of the alleged Gnosticism nor the jubilation over the supposed anti-Gnosticism of Ephesians offers a real proof for or against apostolic authenticity. Since there is no agreement yet in sight regarding what is and is not Gnostic, and which features and dates are definitely to be attached to the concept of Gnosticism,[51] the conclusion is inescapable that the Gnostic discussion has in no way yielded solid evidence about the author.

From the pagan, heterodox Jewish, and Christian-heretic Gnostic movements we turn now to a Jewish group by which the author of Ephesians may have been influenced. Since he was most likely a Jew himself such influence is far from impossible. Perhaps the character and weight of a Jewish background will make a more decisive contribution to identifying the author.

C   Qumran

The Qumran materials discovered since 1947, also some earlier known literature that belongs to the same group, contain thoughts on predestination and election, on the conflicting spirits of light and darkness and the

[49] See sections V–VI of the Introduction, and COMMENT XVI on 1:3–14, below. An exception regarding Pauline authorship is made by Schlier. Schlier's changed attitude coincided, so it seems, with his conversion to the Roman Catholic church.
[50] EuG, passim.
[51] Koester, HTR 58 (1965), 280, lists in a concise manner some of the open questions. The Messina Conference of 1966 has taken definite steps toward clarification; see Bianchi.

corresponding spiritual warfare of man, on the meaning of the present eschatological time, and on the unity and special role of the house or people of God which run parallel to those of Ephesians. Further, there is a remarkable common interest in the Qumran materials and Ephesians in the disclosure of God's secret(s) and in the heavenly inheritance allotted to God's beloved.[52] Scholars who are willing to speak of Gnostic influence even where there is no trace of the Redeemed Redeemer find in the dualism, the predestinarianism, and the hermeneutics (i.e. the concepts of revelation and interpretation) of Qumran distinct traces of Gnosticism.

Among the many possible points of contact between Qumran and Ephesians that will require discussion in the course of our commentary, we have selected the term *mystery,* or *secret,* as holding a prominent position. Whether or not it has Gnostic origin and meaning, this term plays a decisive role in the recognized Pauline writings, in Ephesians and Colossians[53] and in the Qumran literature. The secrets of which the Qumran community speaks concern God's plan and predetermination regarding three realms: (1) the order of the universe, that is, of heaven, earth, angels, stars;[54] (2) the nature, destiny, history, especially the salvation of man[55] (a clear distinction between cosmological and soteriological mysteries is not always plain[56]); and (3) the kingdom of iniquity or of Belial.[57]

The secrets of God are contained in the words of the servants of God, the prophets. Their revelation is granted through the Spirit[58] to the Teacher of Righteousness,[59] and through his Scripture interpretation also to the presiding priests, elders, and instructors of the Community. Inspired Bible exegesis is a new revelation added to the former revelation that was granted to God's servants.[60] It is the conviction of this group that because the last time is at hand, the hidden meaning of the earlier revelation is now revealed. Not every one can know God's mysteries—just the faithful. Therefore, awareness of the final revelation is a privilege of the faithful community, that is, the congregation of Qumran.[61]

Among the features common to Ephesians and Qumran, the following appear most important: Revelation is concentrated upon one person— Jesus Christ here, the Teacher of Righteousness there. There are no mediating agencies of revelation, as dreams, visions, parables, angels, star constellations—except the Spirit. The unity of the former and the present ser-

---

[52] For literature see BIBLIOGRAPHY 3.
[53] The passages are listed in COMMENT IX on 1:3–14.
[54] 1QH I 11 ff.; 1QS x 3–4, xI 3–4.
[55] 1QS III 13 – IV 26; 1Q27; CD II 2–13, III 18–19.
[56] 1QH I 13, 21, XIII; 1QpHab VII 5, 8, 14; 1QS IV 6, XI 15–22.
[57] 1QH v 36; 1Q27 I 2–3; 1QM XIV 9; cf. II Thess 2:7; Rev 17:5, 7.
[58] 1QH XII 11–12.
[59] 1QH II 13, IV 27, v 25, VII 27, IX 23, XI 16; 1QpHab VII 5–8.
[60] See esp. Betz, *Offenbarung und Schriftforschung.*
[61] 1QS III 13, IX 16–19; 1QH VIII 11; 1QM III 9, XIV 12–14, etc.

vants of God is proven by the submission of the present generation to the Bible and its exposition. The recipients of the revelation are conscious of living in the last time in which God grants a knowledge exceeding that of any preceding age; by their knowledge they are distinct from the ignorant threatened by extinction. But God's secret will which is now revealed pertains not only to the people of God, but also to the spiritual, angelic or demonic powers of the whole world. To share in the mystery means to be ethically engaged: unity, faithfulness, truth, humble submission, courage are among the most important features of a conduct fitting the elect.

But there are also noteworthy differences. Qumran speaks of (several, or many) secrets—Ephesians (and Colossians) only of one secret. The Teacher of Righteousness receives the revelation of cosmic, historical, eschatological secrets, while Jesus Christ is the secret in person. Qumran thrives upon salvation through knowledge which is reserved for the true remnant of Israel, while the secret revealed in Christ has a specific content: Gentiles are inserted into God's people; the revelation of this secret must be made known everywhere, by its first recipients as well as by the whole congregation.[62] Therefore the concentration upon Jesus Christ, the emphasis placed upon the common heirdom of Jews and Gentiles, and the obligation to spread the contents of revelation universally form major distinctions between Ephesians and Qumran.

An analogous comparison might be made between Ephesians and the mysteries mentioned in I (Ethiopic) Enoch and in the Apocalypses of Baruch and Ezra. These writings speak of the mysteries of the cosmos, of the sun, the stars, the appointed times, and they proclaim their connection with God's secret plan for mankind in general, and especially with his will regarding the last days and the final judgment. Both are in God's hand, cosmos and salvation. Cosmology, soteriology, and eschatology are treated as strictly theological disciplines. While an arbitrary disclosure of the secrets is impossible or prohibited, God conveys to his servants and to all his elect the knowledge of the correspondence of the first and the last things, of the destiny of the cosmic elements and of God's faithful people. A formerly hidden and finally appearing Son of Man or Messiah plays some role among the secrets of the end-time, but his appearance is transitory. He is one among many eschatological features and figures.

The comparison of statements about God's mystery or mysteries rules out the possibility that Ephesians depends directly upon Qumranite theology or Jewish apocalyptic books. It is more likely that Ephesians, Qumran and the Apocalypses are all offshoots of some common base. Among the traditions which each of them takes up in its own way, the classic imagery of the prophet who stands in God's council and is informed of his

---

[62] Eph 3:3–10; 6:19–20.

(secret) plans and decisions is eminent.[63] Only a chosen man of God gifted with special wisdom is able to reveal the hidden meaning of dreams,[64] books, events.

But there are also other features that may bespeak a connection between Qumran and Ephesians. E.g. the hymnic style of Eph 1:4–14, etc., resembles the diction of the Hodayoth,[65] and the parenetic tradition underlying Eph 4:17 ff. is akin to Qumranite exhortation;[66] also the spiritual warfare described in Eph 6:10 ff. is rich with parallels to the War Scroll (1QM) and to a part of the Rule of the Sect.[67] Even if there are always differences of style and contents in the company of striking similarities, the possibility exists of either a direct dependence of Ephesians upon Qumran, or an indirect relationship that may be explained by a common tradition.

Should this connection prove anything for or against Pauline authorship of Ephesians? J. Murphy-O'Connor[68] believes that Ephesians must be ascribed to an amanuensis of Paul who had come from the ranks of the Essenes and was working under Paul's direction. But this conclusion is not stringent. For the unquestioned Pauline letters reveal that Paul himself was able and willing to use a language and to express thoughts that were also characteristic of Qumranite authors before him, as for example the proclamation of God's righteousness by which totally sinful man is made righteous (Rom 3:21–31, etc.), the imagery of the fight and the weapons of light and darkness (Rom 7:6–25; 13:12), the dualistic language and content of II Cor 6:14–7:1, also some traits of Paul's hermeneutics.[69] Ephesians in toto is neither in form nor in substance any more closely related to Qumran than are other key passages in undisputed Pauline writings. Therefore the obvious resemblance of this epistle to Qumranite diction and theology permits us to assume an early date of Ephesians, but fails to make a decisive argument for the identity of its author.

D   New Testament Books

The epistle to the Colossians is the document which has by far the closest similarity to Ephesians, and a comparison of the two epistles, together with an evaluation of the elements that connect and distinguish them, will be given in the Introduction to Colossians (AB, vol. 34B). A detailed comparison of Ephesians with each letter of the whole Pauline cor-

---

[63] Amos 3:7; Isa 6:8; I Kings 22:18–22; cf. Job 15:8.
[64] Gen 40:5–13; 41:1–45; Dan 2, esp. vss. 18–19, 27–30, 47.
[65] J. M. Robinson, BhZNW 30 (1964), 194–235.
[66] S. Wibbing, "Die Tugend-und Lasterkataloge im NT," BhZNW 25, 1959.
[67] Esp. 1QS III 13 – IV 26; Kuhn, NTS 7 (1960–61), 345; idem, TWNTE, V, 298–300.
[68] BiTod 18 (1965), 1201–9 (ref.).
[69] Johnson, HTR 48 (1955), 157–58; Schulz, ZThK 56 (1959), 155–85; Braun, ZThK 56 (1959), 1–18; Ellis, NTS 2 (1955–56), 127–33, esp. 131 ff. See also Braun, QuNT, I, 167–240; II, 165–80, and the essays concerning Paul in Stendahl, SaNT, pp. 157–82.

pus (especially with Philippians and the Pastoral Epistles) as well as with other NT books (I Peter, Acts, Hebrews, the Gospel and the Revelation of John in particular) is found in the works of T. K. Abbott, E. J. Goodspeed, C. L. Mitton, and others. The coordination in print of the texts resembling one another (sometimes in striking detail) offers a helpful synopsis and shows distinctly that the most substantial, extensive, and impressive parallels to Ephesians are—if Colossians is bracketed out for the time being—found in three NT writings: I Peter, Hebrews, and the Fourth Gospel. Only to these books shall attention be drawn at this point, but later in the NOTES and COMMENTS on individual passages of Ephesians, many other parallel texts will require observation and evaluation.

I Peter bristles with parallels to Ephesians. In recent years they have been exhibited so often that there is no need to present the case anew in detail,[70] and some summary remarks will suffice. As to their *Sitz im Leben*, both Ephesians and I Peter are often considered addresses belonging to the administration of baptism.[71] There is an amazing agreement in the vocabulary used,[72] in the structure,[73] and in the descriptions of the former pagan conduct,[74] of the descent, the resurrection, the ascent, the rule of Christ over the powers,[75] and the building and growth of the spiritual house of God.[76] A ring of joy in redemption and salvation, in God's call, in the promised inheritance, and in the people of God, however much suffering is to be endured, permeates both epistles.[77] I Peter is written as an encyclical. Ephesians may well have a similar ecumenical purpose. Both show ample traces of a theology like Paul's, but neither uses the word "to justify."

However, there are also some remarkable differences which reveal that

---

[70] Cf. C. L. Mitton, EE, pp. 176–96, 280–315; idem, "The Relation of I Peter and Ephesians," JTS, N.S. 1 (1950), 67–73; Percy, pp. 292–93, 433–40; Gaugler, pp. 5–6; Selwyn, *First Peter*, pp. 365–460; J. Coutts, "Eph 1:3–14 and I Pet. 1:3–12," NTS 3 (1956–57), 115–27; J. B. Souček, "Das Gegenüber von Gemeinde und Welt nach dem ersten Petrusbrief," CV 3 (1966), 5–13.

[71] See COMMENT XVI on 1:3–14 for a discussion of the role of baptism in Ephesians. In I Peter, vs. 4:11 appears to contain the last sentence belonging to the liturgical speech. See for I Peter, esp. R. Perdelwitz, *Die Mysterienreligionen und das Problem des I Petrusbriefes*, Giessen: Töpelmann, 1911. M. E. Boismard, "Une liturgie baptismale dans la Prima Petri," RB 63 (1956), 182–208; 64 (1957), 161–83, discusses the theories regarding a baptismal *Sitz im Leben*. According to F. L. Cross, *First Peter: A Pascal Liturgy*, London: Mowbray, 1954, the epistle belongs in a wider liturgical frame. His findings are, in turn, disputed by T. C. G. Thornton, "I Pet.—A Pascal Liturgy?" JTS 12 (1961), 14–26, and C. F. D. Moule, "Nature and Purpose of I Peter," NTS 3 (1956–57), 1–11.

[72] E.g. Eph 1:4; I Peter 1:20: "foundation of the world"; Eph 1:14; I Peter 2:9: "possession"; Eph 2:20–21; I Peter 2:5: "cornerstone," "stones"; Eph 4:27, 6:11; I Peter 5:8: "devil"; Eph 4:32; I Peter 3:8: "warm-hearted"; Eph 5:18; I Peter 4:4: "profligacy"; Eph 5:22; I Peter 3:1: "your own husbands"; Eph 6:13–14; I Peter 5:9, 12: "withstand," "stand"; Eph 6:14 JB; I Peter 1:13: "buckled around your waist," in literal translation.

[73] Coutts, NTS 3 (1956–57), 115–27, compares the Blessings found at the beginning of the two epistles. He discovers in each three subdivisions or stanzas, praising the Father, the Son, the Spirit respectively. Mitton, EE, p. 185, draws attention to the sequence of hope, inheritance, power of God, resurrection of Christ in Eph 1:18–20; I Peter 1:3–5. The parallelism of content and structure of kerygmatic and parenetic material is most carefully presented and commented upon by Selwyn, in *First Peter*, pp. 64–115.

[74] Eph 2:1–2; 4:17–19; I Peter 1:14, 18.   [75] Eph 1:20–21; 4:9; I Peter 3:18, 21–22; 4:6.
[76] Eph 2:21–22; 4:12; I Peter 2:2, 5.   [77] Selwyn, *First Peter*, pp. 39–40.

at least a slavish dependence of one author upon the other's script is out of the question. Eph 2:5 speaks of "resurrection with" Christ, I Peter 1:3 of "rebirth by" Christ's resurrection. Eph 3:5 knows only of revelation by the Spirit in the recent time to apostles and NT prophets; I Peter 1:11–12 refers to the revelation given by the Spirit to the OT prophets. According to Eph 2:19 (cf. 2:12), *stranger*ship has an evil connotation: It is the Gentiles' status before their naturalization in God's people—a status now overcome for good. In I Peter 1:1; 2:11 precisely those elect, redeemed and sanctified are "strangers" on earth. The author of Ephesians prays that "Christ may dwell in the hearts" of the Christians, and he speaks of the "Inner Man" (3:16–17). The writer of I Peter admonishes the elect to "sanctify Christ in their hearts" and he mentions "the hidden man of the heart" (3:15, 4). Eph 4:7 rejoices in the "grace given to each one"; I Peter 4:10 treats of the "gift of grace" that is "taken." Following Eph 4:15–16, 5:30 the Christians are members of the body of Christ; I Peter 2:5 never speaks of the body, but calls the saints "living stones" in the spiritual house.

If only criteria were available for determining which one of two documents as similar and as subtly different as Ephesians and I Peter came first! Then it might be possible to derive from the possible dependence of one text on the other additional knowledge about the date, and perhaps about the author, too, of the secondary script. But unfailing criteria are not yet available.[78] And even if they were at hand, they would help but little in locating the author of Ephesians, for the date and author of I Peter are still hotly disputed. A. Harnack believed he had sufficient reason to proclaim that the apostle Paul had written both the epistles to the Ephesians and I Peter.[79] Theodor Zahn attributed the common features to the hands of the common author or editor Silvanus.[80] A majority of interpreters assume that I Peter is dependent upon Ephesians;[81] but among others B. Weiss[82] and J. Moffatt[83] are convinced of the opposite. Again, new horizons are being opened up by form-critical research: Both Ephesians and I Peter are considered dependent upon

---

[78] Cf. e.g. the discussions about the priority of Matthew over Mark by W. R. Farmer, *The Synoptic Problem*, New York: Macmillan, 1964, and about the priority of Ephesians over Colossians by J. Coutts, "The relationship of Ephesians and Colossians," NTS 4 (1957–58), 201–7. After the literary dependence of Matthew upon Mark and of Ephesians upon Colossians seemed for many decades to be assured, alternatives have to be considered again. Similar problems exist between I Peter and James, and between Jude and II Peter 2.

[79] *Die Briefsammlung des Apostels Paulus* (Leipzig: Hinrichs, 1926), pp. 11, 13, 14; idem, *Die Entstehung des Neuen Testaments und die wichtigsten Folgen der neuen Schöpfung* (Leipzig: Hinrichs, 1914), pp. 64–76.

[80] *Introduction to the New Testament* (London: Clark, 1909), II, 176–78.

[81] As observed by Mitton, EE, pp. 183–97.

[82] *Der Petrinische Lehrbegriff* (Berlin: Schulze, 1855), pp. 425–34.

[83] *Introduction to the Literature of the New Testament*, 3d ed. (Edinburgh: Clark, 1918), pp. 382, 383.

similar Christian doctrinal (or confessional) and parenetic codices or traditions.[84] These epistles contain variations on themes that are older than either document.

Some stronger, some weaker theories about this relationship are available—but that is all we can really say. Actually I Peter exhibits even more as yet insoluble problems than Ephesians. If Ephesians is an unknown, how can it be explained by an unclear relationship to another, greater unknown? Only the name of Silvanus and the reference to Babel in I Peter 5:12–13 may be taken as eventual clues pointing to a secretarial author and to Rome as the place of origin. Mitton has taken the trouble to compose a list of the viable alternatives,[85] but his conclusions are not convincing, in spite of his astute argument.

The same is true of Souček's and Pokorný's attempts at reconstructing the history of Pauline theology in Asia Minor.[86] They assume that after Paul had labored as a missionary in the towns of Asia, his work was compromised by the development of Jewish-Gnostic heresy. Ephesians, they say, was written by an admirer of Paul with the purpose of restoring the apostle's honor and influence. But the heresy grew more dangerous and persecutions increased. Therefore the book of Revelation, written under Domitian, suppressed the name and any knowledge of Paul. The epistle of James and II Peter 3:15–16 demonstrate a prevailing negative attitude toward the founder of the Asian churches. Not earlier than at the time of Trajan, I Peter sought to give back to the Asian churches some of Paul's thoughts; for this purpose its author made use not only of Romans but of Ephesians, too. To Ignatius, finally, belongs the credit for restoring the authority of the apostle Paul. Though this story is lucid and moving, it cannot serve as evidence for its presuppositions, that is, the dates and unknown authors assumed for Ephesians and I Peter. The conclusion is inevitable: The comparison of Ephesians and I Peter has so far not contributed to establishing the date and author of Ephesians.

But should other NT books more readily open a door to the mystery? Ephesians contains distinct points of contact with the epistle to the Hebrews

---

[84] P. Carrington, *The Primitive Christian Catechism*, Cambridge University Press, 1940; Percy, pp. 439–40; Selwyn, *First Peter*, pp. 17–24; FBK, p. 258.

[85] Mitton, EE, p. 177: (a) If it were proven that I Peter was written by the apostle Peter and made use of Ephesians, then the epistle to the Ephesians had to be accepted as Pauline. (b) If I Peter is written by Peter, and if it is used by Ephesians, then Ephesians "will be almost certainly post-Pauline." For "it is incredible that Paul, writing Ephesians immediately after Colossians, should incorporate several echoes from I Peter, whereas in the earlier epistle no such echoes appear"; cf. Mitton, EE, p. 197. (c) If I Peter was written after Peter's death, and if it is dependent on Ephesians, then Ephesians "may be either Pauline or post-Pauline." (d) If I Peter was written after Peter's death, and if it can be proven to precede Ephesians, then the post-Pauline origin of Ephesians is established.

Because he considers Ephesians dependent primarily on Colossians, and because I Peter reveals no acquaintance with Colossians, Mitton decides against the codex theories of Carrington and Selwyn, and for the priority of Ephesians over I Peter. On the lines of his alternative (c) he passes the verdict, Ephesians is non-Pauline.

[86] Souček, CV 3 (1966), 9; Pokorný, EuG, pp. 17–18.

and the Gospel and Epistles of John.[87] Ephesians shares with Hebrews and John the special interest in Jesus Christ's so-called pre-existence and cosmic function;[88] in the flesh and blood of Christ;[89] in the intercessory character of Christ's sacrifice;[90] in the perfection of God's work of salvation and revelation; in the realization of eschatological promises;[91] and finally in the role of the Spirit for revelation and worship.[92] In all of these writings the effect of God's work upon his chosen is described by the verb to *sanctify*,[93] and the priestly imagery of *free access to God* or an equivalent expression is emphatically used.[94] By the description of the spiritual temple of God which is now being built, or of the spiritual worship now offered, a certain polemic against the transitory glories of the stony temple and its cultus is made explicit.

Other elements connect Ephesians with Hebrews only, or with the Gospel of John only. The first include the references to Christ's ascension, to his passing through the heavens, and to the proclamation of peace.[95] There may also be a parallelism between the "approach to the perfect man" mentioned in Ephesians 4:13 and the notion of the migrating people of God that dominates the whole of Hebrews.[96] But the parallelism is not too close; for Ephesians has only a negative evaluation of strangership, while Hebrews teaches that God's people are by nature strangers on earth.[97] Abbott lists about fifteen words or phrases found exclusively in Ephesians and Hebrews. But it is impossible to derive a conclusion regarding the literary priority of one document or the other from such observations.

A comparison of parallels in Ephesians and the Gospel of John offers no more help. Certainly in these two writings the love and the will of God, the election by God, the contrast of light and darkness, the relevance of knowledge, the connection of disobedience and wrath, the doctrine of purification by the word,[98] and the unity of the church are proclaimed

[87] See B. W. Bacon, *The Gospel of the Hellenists* (New York: Holt, 1938), 370 ff.; Abbott, xxviii–xxix; A. Jülicher, *Introduction to the New Testament* (London: Smith, 1904), pp. 143–44; Percy, pp. 441–42.

[88] Eph 1:4–10; John 1:1 ff.; I John 1:1; Heb 1:1–4. The question of Philonic or Wisdom influence will be discussed in the interpretation of Col 1:15–20 in AB, vol. 34B; see also COMMENTS VI and X on 1:3–14, below.

[89] Eph 2:14–16; Heb 9–10; John 1:14; 6:51–58; 19:34; I John 4:2; 5:6.

[90] Eph 2:13–18; 5:2; Heb 7:25; 12:24; John 17; I John 2:1.

[91] Eph 1:7; 2:5–10; 4:13; Heb 1:1–2; 2:10; 3:1–6; 5:9; 6:4; 10:14–17; 11:39–40; John 4:34; 17:4; 19:30; 5:21, 25–27; 11:24–26; cf. COMMENT IX on 1:3–14, below.

[92] Eph 1:17; 2:18; 3:5; John 4:24; 14:17, 26; 15:26; 16:7, 13; Heb 3:7; 6:4; 9:8; 10:15; most important is 9:14.

[93] Eph 5:26; cf. 1:1, 4; Heb 2:11; 10:10, 14, 29; 13:12; John 17:17, 19.

[94] Eph 2:18; 3:12; Heb 4:16; 7:25; 10:22; 12:22; John 14:6.

[95] Eph 2:17; 4:8–10; Heb 2:9–10; 4:14–16; 6:19–20; 9:11 ff., 24; 10:5 ff., 19 ff., according to Schlier, pp. 137–38.

[96] W. Marxsen, *Introduction to the New Testament* (Philadelphia: Fortress, 1968), pp. 87–88; cf. I Peter 1:1; 2:11.

[97] E. Käsemann, *Das wandernde Gottesvolk*, 2d ed., Göttingen: Vandenhoeck, 1957.

[98] Eph 2:2–3; John 3:36; Eph 5:26; John 15:3.

much more energetically and beautifully than in any other part of the NT. Also there is a common emphasis put upon the inclusion in God's people of others besides the Jews.[99] But none of these features nor their number are sufficient to prove a literary dependence one way or the other. They are most likely to be explained by a common, possibly oral, tradition which influenced several NT authors. Whether it is wise to reckon with the existence of diverse theological "schools"[100] exerting influence comparable to that of medieval or modern Western academies, theological faculties, or scholarly fashions, is not yet sufficiently ascertained.[101]

Can the tradition in question be described in more detail and, perhaps, dated also? Should it be labeled "Hellenistic Theology"? If it could be proven that it was developed and flourished after Paul's time only, and if, in addition, it could be ascertained that Paul himself by his writings could not possibly have created such a tradition—then the non-Pauline origin of Ephesians would be sufficiently established. But these preconditions have not been met as yet. Indeed, there is a common element in Hebrews, in the Gospel and Epistles of John, in Ephesians, and notably also in the speech of Stephen contained in Acts 7, the substance of which is the spiritual temple and worship. This type of theology is remarkably different from the theology of the early Jewish-Christian congregation on the one side and Paul's theology on the other. But nothing is contributed to its dating and definition by calling it Hellenistic, for in and outside Judaism a spiritualization of cultic concepts was in full swing even before Paul became an apostle.[102] Philo of Alexandria was a master in the art of reaffirming the value of external, historical cult: He elaborated upon its spiritual and timeless meanings! Even if R. Bultmann and his predecessors and followers were right in assuming that Paul was preceded by a complete "Kerygma of the Hellenistic Church,"[103] Ephesians should not be treated as a fake jewel in the crown of the apostle's works. If there was a firm Hellenistic theology in existence before Paul or at Paul's time at all, Ephesians ought to be treated as its noblest exponent.

But too little is as yet known or proven. The dates of Hebrews and John's Gospel and Epistles are highly controversial. These writings may stand in a very complicated and distant relationship to Ephesians, but except that

---

[99] Eph 1:11–14; 2:11–22; 3:6; John 4:4–32; 10:16; 11:52; 17:20–21; also 21:11. See Kirby, EBP, pp. 166–68, for additional parallels.

[100] Cf., e.g. K. Stendahl's *The School of St. Matthew* (Uppsala thesis), Lund: Gleerup, 1954, and the frequent references found in Introductions to the NT to a Jerusalem, Johannine, or Pauline school.

[101] The academic procedure and influence of Hellenistic philosophical and rhetorical schools, of rabbinical academies, and of the sages of Qumran do not automatically demonstrate similar developments among the Christians of the second half of the first century. See in vol. 34A the NOTES on 4:20–21 and COMMENT III on 4:17–32.

[102] H. Wenschkewitz, *Die Spiritualisierung der Kultusbegriffe, Tempel, Priester und Opfer im NT*, Angelos Bh 4, Leipzig: Pfeiffer, 1932.

[103] Bultmann, ThNT, I, 63 ff., 187–89.

they offer interesting parallels of vocabulary, thought-form and message, they make no contribution to identifying the author of Ephesians. Their authors may have known nothing of Ephesians; or the author of Ephesians may have known nothing of either of them.

It is time to turn to more commonly accepted presuppositions, and their possible implications for dating Ephesians and tracing its author.

E   The Old Testament

While a direct or indirect historical, literary, or oral-tradition connection between Ephesians and Gnosticism, Qumran, I Peter, Hebrews and John cannot be demonstrated with ultimate certainty, it is sure beyond the slightest degree of doubt that the author of this epistle knows the OT and makes use of it. Ephesians contains not only quotes from the OT;[104] it also makes some comments upon the cited texts that reveal the author's hermeneutical methods and his specific understanding of given formulations.[105] In addition there is a host of allusions to OT texts.[106] Of course the reader is not confronted with the whole of the OT or each part of it, e.g. with all the books that after the Exile, in the intertestamental and tannaitic (i.e. earliest rabbinic) periods, in the Roman Catholic or in Protestant churches were considered canonical, or with an immaculate rendition of a Hebrew or Aramaic text. The OT of which Ephesians makes use was mediated to the epistle's author through the worship in which he participated and through his education—in the form in which it was used in Palestine or the diaspora, in an ancient form, in the Targums, or in the LXX or another version. The author's hermeneutics were influenced by rabbinic, Philonic, Qumranite, apocalyptic, or early Christian methods of interpretation. But whichever canon, text, exegetical and homiletical method the author used, he certainly relied upon the help which the OT added to the understanding of his message.

The reader of Ephesians would be left to the wildest guesswork if, without the aid of the OT, he had to explain what might be meant by Jesus' title, "the Christ" (the Messiah); by the designation of his death as an "offering and sacrifice" of "pleasing odor" (5:2); by verbs such as to "elect," to "raise," to "reveal," to "be subject"; by nouns such as "covenant" and "peace," "grace" and "fear." Only a total lack of concern for the obvious dependence of Ephesians upon the OT people, history,

---

[104] 4:8; 2:17; 5:31; 6:2–3; only the first is introduced by a quotation formula.
[105] 1:20–23; 2:13–17; 4:8–11, 25–27; 5:31–32; 6:3–4.
[106] They abound in the description of God's armor (6:14–17) but they are in a less obvious way also spread over the whole epistle. Maurer, EvTh 11 (1951–52), 168, has counted forty-two OT parallels and allusions. It is easily possible to arrive at a much higher figure. Who can tell how many OT passages were in the author's mind when he wrote of God's love, of the people of his possession, of redemption, inheritance, and worthy conduct?

and literature would permit a commentator to spend his time exclusively roaming the fields of Hellenism, Gnosticism, Qumran, or NT books.

Still, to take the unquestionable traces of OT thought in Ephesians seriously does not mean one should be blind to the problem of Gnostic influence upon Ephesians. Maurer discusses two ways in which the presence of both OT *and* Gnostic influences may be explained: Either we are dealing with OT materials corrupted by Gnostic thought, or OT materials are being used to correct corruptions introduced by Gnosticism.[107]

At any rate the presence of OT references, the way in which they are made and commented upon, and the results aimed at or attained may contribute to answering the question: Could the same author who used the OT extensively in Galatians and Romans also have written Ephesians?[108] The hermeneutical method and the exegetical results of Ephesians might be so different from those of Galatians and Romans as to exclude the same author, or so slavishly copied as to suggest an imitator of small mental capacity. If, however, agreements and disagreements with the recognized Pauline letters are no greater than those existing between individual recognized letters (e.g. Galatians and Philippians), then the use of the OT in Ephesians yields no evidence against Pauline authorship.

At any rate, the study of the OT in Ephesians is important. If the OT influence upon the author is so strong that Gnostic influence can be discarded, then the term "in Christ" must to some extent be explained according to the lead given by the formula "in Abraham."[109] Then the concept "head" may rather reflect the ancient Hebrew and rabbinic notion of corporate personality and tribal unity than form an early version of the Manichean Aion-Prime-Anthropos myth.[110] Then the notion "body" might be Old-Testamental and free from mythical hints regarding a fall and dispersion of members of the upper light-world.[111] Then the law is not ascribed to a God other than the Father of Jesus Christ (that is, not to a mischievous creator or his demonic powers). Then it is not invalidated because of its origin. Then revelation and saving knowledge have to be understood against the background of Hosea, Jeremiah, Ezekiel,[112] rather than only from their meanings in Gnosticism. Then

---

[107] Maurer, EvTh 11 (1951–52), 167 ff.

[108] For literature pertinent to Paul's use of the OT see BIBLIOGRAPHY 4. Except the essay by Maurer in EvTh 11 (1951–52), 151–72, no recent special discussions on the use of the OT in Ephesians as a whole have come to my attention. But there exist several essays on the use of the OT in Ephesians 4:8–9 and 5:31–32; see in vol. 34A COMMENTS V on 4:1–16 and VI on 5:21–33.

[109] Gen 18:18 is quoted in Gal 3:8.

[110] Pokorný, EuG, pp. 60–61, refers for an explanation of the image of the head to II Sam 19:12–13; Hosea 1:11; Isa 42:1–9; Exod Rabba 40:3.

[111] A. M. Dubarle, "L'origine dans l'Ancien Testament de la notion paulinienne de l'église corps du Christ," in *Studiorum Paulinorum Congressus Internationalis Catholicus 1961*, AnBib 17–18, I (1963), 23–40.

[112] See, e.g. W. Zimmerli, *Erkenntnis Gottes nach dem Buche Hesekiel*, ATANT 27, 1954; J. L. McKenzie, "Knowledge of God in Hosea," JBL 74 (1955), 22–27.

the bridegroom-bride imagery used for Yahweh's relationship to Israel rather than the Gnostic idea of heavenly syzygies and their earthly re-actualization are decisive in explaining Eph 5:22–33. As we consider the text in more detail, it will become clear that Gnosticism and the OT are certainly not fighting on an equal level and with equal arms for the honor of serving as a key to Ephesians. All the odds favor the OT, which is explicitly cited, while Gnosticism has to be artificially reconstructed and antedated to have a chance in determining Ephesians.

Only a few preliminary remarks regarding the use made of the OT in Ephesians are appropriate at this place. An explicit quotation formula is found only in 4:8 and 5:14. Its wording is "He says." In the first passage it introduces a canonical text,[113] in the second an apocryphal citation, or more likely, a fragment of a Christian hymn. More often quotations appear without any introductory formula. Among the uncontested Pauline letters, I Thessalonians, Philippians and Philemon are notable for their lack of any explicit OT quotations. In Romans, Galatians and elsewhere (as in Matthew, Luke, John) citations introduced by "for it is written," "as it is written," or by similar phrases, are often used, but the preferred Philonic and rabbinic formula "he says," or something similar indicating speech rather than writing, is also employed.[114] The equally widespread custom of quoting Scripture without any preparation for a quote is followed in Eph 1:20, 22; 4:25; 5:31 and in II Cor 3:16; 10:17; 13:1; 15:32. Apocryphal texts are formally announced as quotations in I Cor 2:9; 15:45.[115] Smaller or greater deviations from the Hebrew and LXX texts of the OT are found in all Pauline letters, but these may be due less to carelessness than to a liturgical form of the text, or an edition of the LXX different from the versions on which present editions of the LXX are based.

Everybody using the OT for quotations or allusions will (consciously or not) live by a canon within the canon. Certain OT books or parts will play a greater role than others, some will be completely omitted. In Ephesians about seventeen references to the Pentateuch—mostly to Exodus and Deuteronomy—are matched by thirty to the Prophetic books—about half of the latter to Isaiah. In eleven cases material from the Psalms is utilized; in ten others from the Wisdom books of the LXX. Through the addition of interpretive comments, one Psalm, one Genesis, one Isaiah, and one Exodus or Deuteronomy text are given special emphasis.[116] The ratio among quoted, alluded to, and commented upon OT elements is different in each Pauline homologoumenan—but not so greatly different as

---

[113] In a form that corresponds neither to the Hebrew of the MT nor to the LXX.
[114] E.g. Rom 9:25; 10:21.
[115] Cf. Luke 11:49; I Tim 5:18b; James 4:5; John 7:38; Jude 14. Perhaps also Gal 2:16 and Rom 3:20.
[116] Eph 2:13–17; 4:8–11; 5:31–32; 6:2–3.

to forbid common authorship. Different situations and topics require different selections from the OT and diverse emphases.

Allusions to the OT serve various purposes in various books. They may be made to glorify the person or to explain the way of Jesus; to describe the formation and essence of God's people; to repeat, illustrate or enhance imperatives for personal and communal conduct; or, to serve as a polemic or apologetic tool against Jewish or pagan detractors of the Gospel and against Christian heretics. In Ephesians there is no trace of an apologetic use of the OT. In the kerygmatic, or rather hymnic, parts of the epistle the OT serves to describe God's relationship to his beloved Son and people. It is an instrument for explaining the significance of Jesus Christ's death, exaltation, and gifts. OT temple, planting, and marriage imagery is used to describe the church. From 4:25 to the end of the epistle the author rejoices in drawing from the ethical exhortations of legal or Wisdom texts.

In Barnabas' and Justin Martyr's times and later, the OT became an apologetic tool to prove the verity or superiority of Christian "gnosis" (saving knowledge). Apologetics has also been suspected as underlying and motivating the use made of the OT by Paul, Luke, Matthew, and other NT writers. Since Ephesians cannot possibly fit into this alleged pattern, it may be necessary to re-examine the whole apologetic hypothesis in the light of this epistle.

The main purpose of the use of the OT in Ephesians appears to be this: The demonstration of the oneness and sameness of the God who called first Israel, then the Gentiles. The Messiah promised to Israel has come for the benefit of Israel and the nations, and by OT quotes the Gentiles are encouraged to live as members of the one people of God. Thus the OT does not serve a literary or philosophical, but rather a practical and personal-communal purpose. It is evidence and stimulus for oneness, unity, communion under the rulership of the Messiah. This motivation and purpose are not strange to Rom 3; 4; 9–11; Gal 3–4. In the undisputed Pauline epistles the OT is a living voice telling Jews and Gentiles how to believe in Christ and to live together in peace—neither to one's own glory nor at his fellow man's expense, but "for the praise of God's glory" (cf. Rom 15:7–13; Eph 1:6, 12, 14).

The usefulness of the OT is dependent upon the hermeneutics applied to the interpretation. Ephesians is by no means freer than the homologoumena from occasionally pressing certain words or features of a given text,[117] or from traits of spiritual (allegorical or apocalyptic) interpretation.[118] The difference from pagan and second-century and later Chris-

[117] Cf. e.g. Eph 4:9–10 with Rom 10:6–7; Gal 3:16. Isa. 57:19 appears originally to speak of Jews in Palestine and Jews in exile. In Eph 2:13, 17 the Jews in exile have become stand-ins for the Gentiles.

[118] Cf. Eph 5:32 with I Cor 9:9–10; 10:4; Gal 4:21–31.

tian allegory is equally visible in Ephesians and other Pauline letters: Proper allegory uses the concrete items of a text as tinder to be inflamed by the Spirit. The historical and literary elements are relieved of historical and literal meaning and given a purely spiritual, timeless, abstract, scientific or moral sense. Once when Paul explicitly sets out to *allegorize* (in Gal 4:24), his interpretation is not really allegorical. For in Gal 4:21–31[119] his exegesis moves from the concrete of the past to the concrete of the present. Equally the mystery contained according to Eph 5:32 in Gen 2:24 does not override and suppress the original text's reference to man and woman; see Eph 5:33. The author of Ephesians perceives in the concrete contents of the text a hitherto hidden dimension. Some would call this perspective the *sensus plenior*.[120] It may be wiser to retain the concept of "typological interpretation," which fits other OT excursus in other Pauline letters. More than once, e.g. in 2:13, 17 and 4:8–10, the OT exegesis found in Ephesians reflects traces of rabbinic commentation and goes beyond or corrects its results. Though the hermeneutics of Ephesians is at times keen and full of risks, it is no wilder, no poorer, no more flat, but also no less tradition-bound and critical of Jewish interpretation than Paul's own exegesis.

Judging from the use made of the OT in Ephesians, therefore, it may still be concluded, *nil obstat* against the traditional assumption that Paul wrote this epistle. On the other hand, however, no more positive proof of his authorship can be derived from this argument than from those previously discussed.

IV DOCTRINAL CONSIDERATIONS

It does not take much trouble to discover exactly the same message and exhortations in the major part of Ephesians as in the other letters that carry Paul's name.[121] The same can be said, with slightly less emphasis, of the relationship discussed above between Ephesians, I Peter, the Gospel of John, I John, and Hebrews.[122] However, Ephesians stands even closer

---

[119] As esp. the words, "as then . . . so also now" (4:29) reveal.

[120] For a summary discussion of the sensus plenior, see R. E. Brown, *Sensus Plenior*, Baltimore: St. Mary's Seminary Press, 1955; idem, "The Sensus Plenior in the Last Ten Years," CBQ 25 (1963), 262–85; J. Schmid (BZ 3 [1959], 161–73) would deny its applicability to the Pauline Scripture interpretations.

[121] I and II Timothy and Titus might, however, be excluded. J. Knox, *Chapters in a Life of Paul* (Nashville: Abingdon, 1959), p. 19, calls Ephesians "so thoroughly Pauline though not composed by Paul." K. L. Schmidt, art. *"kaleō,"* etc., in TWNTE, III, 511, considers Ephesians "wholly Pauline in substance." S. G. F. Brandon, *The Fall of Jerusalem*, p. 216, describes this letter as "an epitome of the great Apostle's teaching." The theological relationship between Ephesians and Acts is discussed by E. Käsemann, "Ephesians and Acts," in *Studies in Luke and Acts:* Fs P. Schubert, eds. L. E. Keck and J. L. Martin (Nashville: Abingdon, 1966), pp. 288–97. C. Masson points out doctrinal differences, even contradictions, between Ephesians and Paul.

[122] See Introduction, III D.

to Paul's preaching and teaching—not merely because of the sometimes literal identity of given formulations, phrases, and sentences (which might be ascribed to an imitator), but because of identical subtle accentuations found in passages of Ephesians that possess original wording. God's grace alone, even overflowing grace, is the cause, the nerve, the means of salvation from sin and death.[123] The death and resurrection of Jesus Christ who is at the same time the Son and Wisdom of God and the true man and second Adam, is the core of God's self-revelation, of man's liberation, and of the message entrusted to the apostle for the benefit of the whole world.[124] Jews and Gentiles are joined together to be one man, one people of God, one body—even the body of Christ.[125] The life they have, all unity they share, all knowledge they receive and convey to others, also all acts of faith and obedience are due to the Spirit who works in them. Unlike the OT in which only a chosen few had special gifts, the saints in Ephesus are *all* charismatics according to Paul, and each of them lives and does his service because of the gifts of grace (*charismata*) he is given.[126] The division and pride based upon the physical circumcision and the separation of the elect people from those that are not God's people is no longer valid.[127] A new ground, order, and way of life is open to all men: the manifested, outgoing love of God, the inclusion and participation in Christ crucified and risen, the reconciliation and peace brought by the Messiah, the energy of the Holy Spirit, the ecumenicity of the church that is being built. On this foundation rests the exhortation to walk worthily according to the sum and criterion of all the commandments, love.[128]

In Ephesians, these general areas of agreement are expanded by additional elements in which Pauline doctrine is further developed, and some original contributions are made as well. Unique formulations are created and accents are added.[129] And not only this—but in some passages the impression is created that the author of Ephesians deviates as far from Paul as to come out with flat contradictions of the apostle's teaching. The doctrinal distinctions include the following items:

[123] Eph 1:6–8; 2:4–8; II Cor 9:14; Rom 4:4–5; 5:2, 17–21.
[124] Eph 1:19–22; 2:13–17; 4:8–10; 6:19–20; Rom 1:16–17; 5:12–21; 15:15–16; I Cor 1:18; 2:2, 9–16; 15:11–22, 44–49.
[125] Eph 1:11–14; 2:15; 3:6; 4:3–6, 15–16; Rom 1–5; 9–11; 12:5; I Cor 10:16; 11:3; 12:12–28; Gal 3:27–28; 6:16; Col 1:18, 27; 2:19.
[126] Eph 1:13, 17; 3:16; 4:7, 11–12; Rom 8; 12:6–13; I Cor 12:3–11, 28–31; 14; Gal 3:2, 5; 5:22–25; 6:1.
[127] Eph 2:11–18; 11:7–13; Rom 2:14–29; 9:25–29; Gal 2:3–5, 11–21; 6:11–16.
[128] Eph 4–6; Rom 5:5; 12–15; Gal 5:14 – 6:2; I Cor 3–4; 13.
[129] Mitton, e.g. EE, pp. 16–24, enumerates the following: the concept of the Universal Church; the plea for unity; the pairing of apostles and prophets; the relation to God ascribed to Christ in working out reconciliation and in appointing the ministers of the church; the relevance of the death of Christ; the treatment of the Jew-Gentile controversy; the silence about the second coming of Christ which is matched by the eloquence on his descent to Hades; the utterances on marriage and children; and the evaluation of circumcision. But at the same time Mitton warns against careless use of arguments derived from special doctrines.

1. Most commentators, including those accepting the authenticity of Ephesians,[130] observe that Ephesians places increased emphasis upon the so-called cosmic role of Christ.[131] In the Pauline corpus only Colossians, and in the whole of the NT only the book of Revelation (but also the Little Apocalypse Mark 13 par.), stress this function even more.

2. Instead of continuing the frequent Pauline utterances about house, local or district churches, Ephesians and Colossians follow the lead given in earlier Pauline epistles by Gal 1:13; I Cor 15:19; Philip 3:6 and use the word "church" as a designation for the universal church.[132]

3. While in I Cor 12:21 the head of a body is treated as a member among others, and while in Rom 12:5 Christ is not called the head of the body, Ephesians and Colossians expand an idea hinted at already in I Cor 11:3. In Ephesians and Colossians Jesus Christ is called the head of his body, the church. And not only this, he is also called the head of all things, the whole created universe.[133]

4. The church's function is now described not only in terms of its worship of God, its service to its members, and its mission among Jews and Gentiles. Rather, by its faith and love, in its obedience and suffering, it also has a ministry to fulfill among all creatures, especially the principalities and powers. Hints of such an extended cosmic ministry are certainly contained in Gal 6:15; 5:17; Rom 8:19–23. In James 1:18 the church is called the first fruits of all creatures. But only in Eph 1:4; 2:1–7; 3:10; 6:12–20 is the very essence of the church directly identified with her stance before, her service to, and if need be her resistance against, all angels and demons, all periods and spirits that shape, represent, or terrorize the world.

5. These powers are mentioned with disturbing frequency and given greater attention than they have received in earlier epistles.[134]

6. II Cor 5:18–20 and Rom 5:10 focused on the reconciliation of men *to God*. Certainly in the context it was shown that this reconciliation bears fruit in the unity, peace, love, and order that determine the ethics of the congregation. But in Eph 2:14–16 the reconciliation with fellow man, i.e. the reconciliation of Jews with Gentiles and vice versa, is

[130] See esp. L. Cerfaux, *Le Christ dans la théologie de Saint Paul*, 2d rev. ed., Paris: Du Cerf, 1954, Eng. tr. *Christ in the Theology of St. Paul*, New York: Herder, 1966; idem, *The Church in the Theology of St. Paul*, New York: Herder, 1959 (a rev. ed. of the original, *La théologie de l'église suivant Saint Paul*, appeared in 1965, Du Cerf, Paris); idem, "En faveur de l'authenticité des épîtres de la captivité," in *Littérature et théologie Pauliniennes*, ed. A. Descamps, RecB 5 (1960), 60–71.

[131] Eph 1:10, 22–23; 4:10; cf. Col 1:15–20; I Cor 8:6; Philip 2:10–11.

[132] Cf. Rom 16:1, 4, 16; I Cor 1:2; 7:17; 11:16; 16:1, 19; II Cor 8:18; 11:28, etc., with Eph 1:22; 3:10, 21; 5:23–32; Col 1:18, 24. In Col 4:15–16, however, a house and a local church are denoted by the same term.

[133] Eph 1:22–23; 4:15–16; 5:23; Col 1:18; 2:10; cf. the NOTES on these verses, here, and in AB, vol. 34B, also those on Eph 1:10.

[134] Rom 8:38–39; 13:1–7; I Cor 2:8; 6:2; 15:25–28; Philip 2:10–11.

mentioned before the reconciliation with God. The socio-ethical dimension of peace has major emphasis.

7. In the classical epistles of Paul, the images of building, of planting, of growing, and of a bride loved by the bridegroom are used occasionally, but never in conjunction with one another. In Eph 2:20–22; 3:17; 4:12, 15–16; 5:22–33 they are either intermingled or greatly expanded.

8. Justification of the godless by Jesus Christ by grace, by faith alone, is among the central topics of Galatians, Romans, Philippians, and distinctly alluded to in the Corinthian correspondence.[135] But the verb "to justify," does not occur in Ephesians. The noun "righteousness" is used in ethical context only.[136] The comprehensive term "to save" takes in 2:5, 8 the place of the manifold Pauline utterances on justification and sanctification.

9. The futurist-eschatological ring of "salvation" in Rom 5:10; 8:24 seems to have been forgotten in Ephesians. God's past action is now described by this word. Also hints concerning the mysteries of salvation—mysteries which in the present are only intimated through the gospel and only partially disclosed to faith—have yielded to statements about a fully revealed mystery.[137] The judge coming to "judge the world"[138] appears to have become the "savior of the body," i.e. of the church only (5:23).

10. If in I, II Thessalonians; I Cor 7; and Philip 4:4–8 ethical admonition was completely oriented toward the coming Lord, the *Haustafel* of Ephesians[139] seems to confirm the shift away from Pauline parenetics. Lists of principles or casuistry seem now to require compliance. A virtuous life appears to be substituted for the ethical attitude of a man who lives in the ambiguity of a stranger facing his heavenly home, as Moses faced the promised land.[140] Even when Paul in Rom 13 preaches submission to the Roman authorities, his demand appears not to have reached as high a degree of acculturation and adaption to Hellenistic mores, especially to Stoic ideals and common respectability, as does Eph 4:25– 6:9.[141] Though Paul did speak of a fruit and order of the Spirit (Gal 5:22–23, 25), the transition from "grace" to "good works" in Eph 2:5–10 appears much too simple and easy to have been written by the undoubted author of Galatians.

This list could be continued. Special emphasis could be laid upon a

[135] E.g. I Cor 1:30; II Cor 12:9.
[136] Eph 4:24; 5:9; 6:14; cf. Rom 14:17; II Cor 6:14; 9:9; Titus 3:5; cf. Philip 4:8; etc.
[137] I Cor 1:18; 2:7; 13:12; II Cor 2:14 f.; Rom 1:16, compared with Eph 1:9; 3:5.
[138] I Thess 4:16; II Thess 1:7–10; II Cor 5:10.
[139] I.e. the catalogue describing the right conduct of husband and wife, parents and children, masters and slaves, Eph 5:21 – 6:9.
[140] II Cor 5:1–10; 6:1–10; Philip 3:20.
[141] Cf. "the quiet and peaceable life, godly and respectful in every way," recommended in I Tim 2:2.

possible determinism developed out of Paul's utterances on election in Rom 8–9; upon a Hellenistic or Gnosticizing intellectualism revealed through the balance in which statements on knowledge stand against utterances on faith; upon a wide body of superstition and myth suggested by the references to angelic or demonic powers and to the devil, the prince of the air; upon an unholy ecclesiasticism ushered in by the cosmic role ascribed to the church; and upon a flat bourgeois moralism corresponding to the neglect of the near parousia.[142] But the examples given are sufficient to justify the question of whether Ephesians is a consistent development of Pauline ideas or whether the deviations from Paul are so weighty, compact, and original that they can only be credited to a person other than the apostle.

Outstanding among these elements is a supposed change in theology: Ephesians gives the church a preponderance over other topics which is without parallel in other letters of the corpus Paulinum, except the Pastoral Epistles. E. Käsemann is the strongest exponent of this opinion. He observes that in Ephesians the main interest of the author is focused upon the church, while in the apostle Paul's genuine writings Jesus Christ stands in the center.[143] This transition from Christ to the church is considered the decisive mark of "Early Catholicism" for in this early form of Roman traditionalist, apologetic, legalist, ceremonial, moralist churchmanship, Christology has been almost completely turned into, and displaced by, ecclesiology. Unlike F. C. Baur and others, Käsemann does not locate and date this change in the post-apostolic age. Rather he is convinced that the transition occurred during the lifetime of the apostles. Not only I Clement, Ignatius' epistles, and the Shepherd of Hermas (to mention but a few "Early Catholic" documents) but also the works of Luke, the Gospel according to Matthew, the Pastoral Epistles and with them Ephesians are considered examples of this development.[144]

It cannot be denied that in Ephesians the church has as prominent a

---

[142] See Bultmann, ThNT, II, 175–80. Cf. also M. Barth, *The Broken Wall* (Philadelphia: Judson Press, 1959), pp. 17–26. K. and S. Lake, *An Introduction to the New Testament* (New York: Harper, 1937), pp. 148–49, note that in Ephesians the church (a) is the extension of the incarnation of Christ, (b) contains the embodiment of the virtues embodied in Christ, (c) leaves but little room for the parousia.

[143] E. Käsemann, "Das Interpretationsproblem des Epheserbriefes," TLZ 86 (1961), 1–8, esp. 3; idem, "Paulus und der Frühkatholizismus," ZTK 60 (1963), 75–89. In his latest utterance on Ephesians, contained in *Jesus Means Freedom* (Philadelphia: Fortress, 1970), pp. 89–90, Käsemann states, "Here the Gospel is domesticated . . . Christology is integrated into the doctrine of the church. The head is present only with and through the body. Christ is the mark toward which Christianity is growing, no longer in the strict sense its judge. The church as the real content of the gospel . . . pushed itself into the foreground so that Christ's image above it faded into the image of the founder."

[144] H. Küng, "Der Frühkatholizismus im NT als kontroverstheologisches Problem," TQ 142 (1962), 285–324, has positively, though perhaps not without irony, reacted to this new Protestant view of the historic development: Now finally, he claims, a Protestant (i.e. Käsemann) gives up the former claim that the NT canon supported exclusively the Protestant view of the church; now Catholicism is freed from the charge of being the result of a lapse from the teaching of the apostolic period; now, indeed, both Catholicism and Protestantism can feel equally justified on a biblical basis; even in the NT all ways lead to Rome.

place as in I Peter 2:5–10; Matt 16:18, and I Tim 3:15c. But this fact alone cannot suffice to exclude Pauline authorship. Only if it were infallibly ascertained that under no circumstances and in no wise whatsoever did the apostle Paul ever occupy himself with things other than the worldwide judgment of Christ, even the justification doctrine, could he be held innocent or incompetent of an ecclesiastic theology. Yet Paul's theology may not have consisted of one fixed dogma or set of dogmata based upon an absolute principle. It may have been an instrument and method which changed with the changing people, times, necessities, and opportunities met by the apostle. Certainly those doctrinal differences between Ephesians and the homologoumena that have been mentioned so far can be explained as results of a late stage of theological development reached by the apostle himself. Still, they could just as easily be ascribed to an author of Ephesians other than Paul.[145]

At any rate, now the question must be faced whether there are solid reasons to maintain or reject the authenticity of Ephesians.

V THE PROBLEM OF AUTHORSHIP

The tradition of the church affirms that Ephesians was written by the apostle Paul. All Greek MSS that contain Eph 1:1 and 3:1, the early translations of Ephesians, and some of the titles prefixed to the epistle mention Paul as the author. And this textual evidence is confirmed by those orthodox and heretical voices from the first two centuries that mention Ephesians or quote from it.

Traces of a possible acquaintance with Ephesians are found in the Apostolic Fathers, in Gnostic heretical teachings, among the church Fathers at the turn from the second to the third century, and in the Canon Muratori.[146] Ignatius' remark to the Ephesians (XII 2), saying that Paul "in every epistle makes mention of you in Christ Jesus" may be considered an indication of his acquaintance with Ephesians. If the Apostolic Fathers[147] incorporated elements of Ephesians in their writings then certainly they considered the epistle apostolic, i.e. Pauline. However when no more than certain phrases are used that are also found in Ephesians, the Apostolic Fathers need not necessarily have been dependent upon this letter. They may have drawn from a tradition of doctrine, exhorta-

---

[145] Especially in works of the Catholic scholars F. Prat, L. Cerfaux, P. Benoit listed in BIBLIOGRAPHY 12, the idea of a development of Paul's teaching is unfolded. The question whether some distinct teachings of Ephesians so flatly contradict the homologoumena that a common author is excluded will be discussed below in section VI.

[146] A convenient collection and reproduction of most of the relevant texts is found in Westcott, pp. xxv–xxxii.

[147] E.g. I Clement 36:2, 59:3; Barnabas II 1; Ignatius *Ephesians* XII 2 (?); *Smyrnans* I 2; *Trallians* XI 2; Polycarp *Philippians* I 3, II 1, X 2, XII 3; *Didache* IV 9–11; Shepherd of Hermas *mandates* III 1, 4; X 2:2; *similitudes* IX 13:5, 7; 17:4–5. (Henceforth cited as I Clem.; Barn.; Ign. *Eph.*, *Smyrn.*, *Trall.*, etc.; Polyc. *Phil.*; *Did.*; Herm. *mand.*, *sim.*, etc.)

tion, diction that had earlier also influenced the author of Ephesians. Therefore their testimony for Pauline authorship would be valid only if a common dependence on the same traditions could be ruled out completely.

The first clear evidence of canonical rank and apostolic origin attributed to Ephesians is found among Gnostic heretics.[148] Their witness is
corroborated by Clement of Alexandria,[149] Origen,[150] Irenaeus,[151] Tertullian,[152] the Canon Muratori and later voices: Paul wrote this letter
and it was addressed to Ephesus. The similarity between its teaching and
diction and the other Pauline epistles, especially Colossians, but also First
Peter and the Johannine Writings, may have then contributed to the unchanged judgment of 1700 years of biblical scholarship. Both the apostolic
origin and canonical rank of Ephesians were left unquestioned by the
early church fathers, the medieval scholars, the reformers, and countless
conservative Bible readers of more recent centuries.

But during the Reformation a few facts were pointed out that made
learned students of Ephesians aware that there were some problems. In
1519 Erasmus drew attention to the stylistic idiosyncrasies of Ephesians,
a first signal that anticipated later developments. In 1790 W. Paley was
still able to observe that the authenticity of Ephesians did not appear to
have ever been disputed. However, two years later E. Evanson showed
reasons why the contents of the epistle contradict its address. L. Usteri in
1824, W. M. L. de Wette in 1826 and 1843, and finally F. C. Baur in
1845 were the first to collect weighty arguments against Pauline authorship. During the second half of the nineteenth century more observations and data were added, in the face of stiff conservative resistance. By
the beginning of the twentieth century, the most vocal German scholars,
along with a considerable number of their French, British, and American
colleagues, had accepted the verdict that Ephesians is not authentically
Pauline but the product of an unknown student and admirer of the
apostle.

Today, four schools of thought can be distinguished, and we outline
them here. Most of the outstanding men participating in the struggle have
to be listed by name only; a description of their individual contributions
would lead too far.[153]

---

[148] Marcion, Basilides, Valentinus (or a Valentinian like Ptolemaeus), the Ophites. See
Tertullian *adversus Marcionem* v 11, 17; Hippol. v 7–8 (136, 146, 156, ed. H. G. L.
Duncker), vi 3 (284 D), vii 25 (370, 374 D); in vi 34 (285 D) Eph 3:14–18 is freely
quoted as Scripture. See also Irenaeus *adversus haereses* i 8:4–5, v 2:3 (ed. A. Stieren,
1848–53).
[149] *Paedagogus* i 18; *stromata* iv 65.
[150] *Contra Celsum* iii 28 (xviii 273, ed. C. H. E. Lommatzsch, 1831–48), ed. H. Chadwick
(1953), 145–46.
[151] *Adv. haer.* i 3–4, 8:4; v 2:36.
[152] *De praescriptione haereticorum* 36; *de monogamia* 5.
[153] Works pertinent to a critical assessment of the question of authorship are listed in
BIBLIOGRAPHY 5.

1. In their introductions to the New Testament, their commentaries on Ephesians, or in monographs and essays, the following have affirmed Pauline authorship: Abbott, Asting, Gaugler, Grant, Harnack, Haupt, Hort, Klijn, Michaelis, Percy, Robinson, A. Robert and A. Feuillet, Roller, Sanders, Schille, Schlier,[154] Schmid, Scott, Westcott, Zahn.

2. Another group of authors suggests that Ephesians is based upon an original script dictated or written by the apostle Paul, and that the original document has been augmented by interpolations of an editor. Or they teach that Ephesians owes its existence to an impulse or outline given by Paul. Albertz, Benoit, Cerfaux, Goguel, Harrison, Holtzmann, Murphy-O'Connor, Wagenführer belong to this group.

3. Unable to accept Paul as the author are Allan, Beare, Brandon, Bultmann, Conzelmann, Dibelius, Goodspeed, Käsemann, J. Knox, W. L. Knox, Kümmel, K. and S. Lake, Marxsen, Masson, Mitton, Moffatt, Nineham, Pokorný, Schweizer, J. Weiss.

4. The lack of conclusive evidence is observed by Cadbury,[155] Jülicher, McNeile,[156] Williams.[157] These men refrain consciously from passing any judgment for or against authenticity.

The last group is the smallest, but it may well be the most prudent. The wise reticence shown by its members cannot be equated with an attempt to ignore or dodge the issue. The scholars in question consider the arguments of all the other schools as inconclusive; they hold that Ephesians can be properly exegeted without a pronounced opinion regarding its author. Indeed, even if the historical accuracy of the word "Paul" in Eph 1:1 and 3:1 is left open, enough serious problems of interpretation remain to be solved, and work on them alone may lead to relevant results.

The main arguments against Pauline authorship[158] fall into four groups. (a) Vocabulary and style. (b) Similarity to, perhaps literary dependence upon, Colossians. (c) Historical and literary relationships. (d) Theological distinctions. We repeat, the problems belonging to group (b) which pertain to the special relation between Ephesians and Colossians will be presented in the Introduction to Colossians in AB, vol. 34B. The arguments of groups (a) and (c) are probably more objective than those of the last group (d), which makes it all the more surprising that they are no longer considered decisive.[159] The heaviest weight is today attributed to

---

[154] In his commentary, pp. 22–28; but in his book *Christus*, p. 39, note, Schlier called the endorsement of Pauline authorship "cumbersome."

[155] NTS 5 (1958–59), 91–102. H. Chadwick, "Die Absicht des Epheserbriefes," ZNW 51 (1960), 145–54, argues similarly.

[156] In *An Introduction to the Study of the New Testament*, 2d ed. rev. by C. S. C. Williams (Oxford: Clarendon Press, 1953), pp. 168–69.   [157] Ibid., pp. 165–75.

[158] E. J. Goodspeed, *The Key to Ephesians* (University of Chicago Press, 1956), p. v, enumerates twenty-one of them. Other scholars have contributed additional reasons.

[159] So, e.g. Käsemann, RGG, II, 519. But Kümmel, FBK, p. 254, still attributes to them "the highest degree" of forceful witness against authenticity. Yet he, too, finds that solely the theology of the epistle makes Pauline origin "completely impossible."

the elements belonging to group (d), the difference between the theological contents of Ephesians and those epistles whose authenticity is undisputed.

Those denying Pauline authorship have drawn different pictures of the pseudonymous writer. Either his theology is said to "strictly contradict" Paul;[160] or both his agreements and disagreements with Paul receive equal emphasis;[161] or he is believed to reclaim genuine Pauline intentions from distortion.[162] Goodspeed, Käsemann, Marxsen, Pokorný pay the unknown author high tribute because of the originality of his thought, the creativity of his mind, and his art of systematic arrangement. Most supporters of pseudonymity assume that the writer of Ephesians was Jewish-born, but deeply influenced by Hellenistic, perhaps Qumranite or Gnostic, ideas.

In following a suggestion made by Weiss,[163] Goodspeed has ventured farther out than anyone else in attempting to identify the name of the author, his methods, his motives, and his location:[164]

Inspired by the collection and edition of church letters in Rev 1–3, by the publication of the book of Acts, and by his own unlimited admiration for Paul, the former runaway slave Onesimus, after his ascension to the bishopric of Ephesus, decided to seek, gather, and edit all the letters of Paul. At the start of his project he knew only the epistles to the Colossians and Philemon; but he set out to visit and search the places of Pauline activity mentioned in Acts, and soon enough the strongboxes of local churches yielded the manuscripts he was hoping to find.

Onesimus proceeded to assemble the diverse parts of the Pauline corpus, and the collection was made ready for publication. But an introduction to the collected writings of Paul was still missing. Onesimus decided to write it himself, and to let it fulfill the same function which Rev 1 has in relation to Rev 2–3, or the Prologue of John in relation to the whole Gospel. The introduction was to contain the sum and the highlights of the apostle's thought. By using numerous quotations from the Pauline epistles, especially from Colossians (but not from I, II Timothy and Titus), the author wished to show his indebtedness to Paul. Thus Onesimus' introduction took on the form of a mosaic composed from parts of the genuinely Pauline letters. The date of its composition would be around A.D. 90; the place of origin, Ephesus; the name eventually attached to the document was *To the Ephesians*.

In the later years of his life Goodspeed wrote of his own theory, "It fills

---

[160] Kümmel, FBK, p. 255.

[161] Käsemann, RGG, II, 519.

[162] E. Schweizer, "Die Kirche als Leib Christi in den paulinischen Antilegomena," TLZ 86 (1961), 241–56; repr. in *Neotestamentica*, pp. 293–316.

[163] *History of Primitive Christianity*, I, 150; II, 684.

[164] *An Introduction to the New Testament* (University of Chicago Press, 1937), pp. 222–39; *Key to Ephesians*, pp. xiv, xvi.

my eyes with tears."[165] Indeed this story of the genesis of Ephesians is rich with emotional undertones, and it offers solutions to many questions that were often considered unanswerable. Not only a plausible *Sitz im Leben,* a motivation, a location, and a date for Ephesians are presented, but, in addition, the origin of the Pauline corpus and the interrelation between Ephesians, Acts, Revelation, and John are all "explained."

But the beauty and comprehensiveness of the theory are not sufficient to demonstrate its validity. It should be pointed out: (a) Indeed, Ignatius made mention of an Onesimus, bishop of Ephesus.[166] But there is no evidence that this Onesimus was the same man as Paul's protégé, of whose life but a tiny section is known through Paul's epistle to Philemon and through Col 4:9. (b) In no canonical list, nor in any of the ancient codices, is Ephesians found at the suitable place for an introduction, i.e. at the head of the Pauline corpus. (c) It is difficult to assume that the author of Ephesians knew Acts—or else he would hardly have contradicted Acts[167] as flatly as he does.[168] (d) Since Onesimus was most likely of Gentile origin, he could not have been the author of Ephesians, for the writer of this epistle reveals by his thorough acquaintance with Israel's Bible and with Philonic, rabbinical, apocalyptic or Qumranite methods of Scripture interpretation that he was a Jewish Christian.[169] For these reasons it may be necessary to strip a great number of purely conjectural, if not fantastic, elements from Goodspeed's theory. But the possibility remains that Ephesians is either a fitting introduction or a competent summary of Paul's teaching.[170]

The theory that a secretary (*amanuensis*) or editor of the apostle gave the epistle its present form can be spelled out in several variants, dependent upon the measure of freedom attributed to the associate or admirer of Paul. (a) The secretary may have taken down verbatim what Paul dictated. (b) He may have made notes of the substance of Paul's utterances and thoughts, and then have reproduced them by using his own diction. (c) The apostle may have added revisions and corrections to a draft sketched by the secretary. (d) Paul may have authorized the man to write in his name without asking to see the result, hence without giving his final approval. (e) During or after Paul's lifetime an associate

---

[165] *Key to Ephesians,* p. xv.

[166] Ign. *Eph.* i 3; ii 1; vi 2.

[167] According to Acts 18:19–21; 19:1 ff.; 20:20–21, 31 Paul dwelt several times, for several years in Ephesus and he worked at this place among Jews and Gentiles.

[168] In Eph 1:15; 2:11 ff.; 3:2–3; 4:17 ff., 4:21; no more is reflected than a hearsay acquaintance between Paul and the Ephesians. Paul addresses Gentile Christians only—as if he had nothing to say to the Jewish Christians in Ephesus.

[169] Kümmel, FBK, p. 257; Käsemann, RGG, II, 520; Pokorný, EuG, p. 24; see esp. Eph 4:9–10; 5:31–32; 6:2–3, 14–17.

[170] Mitton, EE, pp. 262 f., believes that Ephesians stands in the same relationship to the genuine Pauline letters as the Gospel of John to the Synoptics: it brings the hidden into the open.

of Paul may have written the letter without proper authorization, though to the best of his ability and in the sense of his master. (f) A man not personally connected with Paul may have used genuine Pauline material (epistles, notes, or dicta) for fabricating Ephesians. Instead of one secretary, editor, or plagiarist, in each case several may have been at work. Also a combination of several of the possibilities is not excluded. In some aspects the origin of Ephesians may be analogous to the work of the Deuteronomist, to the editing of the book of Isaiah, to the writing of the epistle to the Hebrews, or in more recent times, to the composition of a papal encyclica or private letter, or of a presidential speech. Though in one or another form the secretarial theory seems to solve many puzzles, it is too variegated, too vague, and too little supported by specific historical or literary facts to recommend itself as the final solution. Existing analogies can illustrate a theory but not demonstrate it.

Many of the conservative scholars who maintain that Ephesians is authentically Pauline are by no means less critical and solid in their approach to the Bible than their more radical opponents. While even most traditionalist commentators frankly admit that there are linguistic, historical, and doctrinal problems, they point out the ambiguity of the criteria so far applied to the question of authenticity, and the inconclusiveness of arguments such as those presented earlier in sections I–IV. If the maxim "innocent until proven guilty," *in dubio pro reo,* is applied here, then the tradition which accepts Paul as the author of Ephesians is more recommendable than the suggestion of an unknown author. The burden of proof lies with those questioning the tradition. The evidence produced by them is neither strong nor harmonious enough to invalidate the judgment of tradition. Although it cannot be definitely proven that Ephesians is genuinely Pauline, nevertheless it is still possible to uphold its authenticity.

In the following section an argument will be produced which more than others favors the authenticity of Ephesians and encourages the reader to understand the letter on the basis of its Pauline origin.

VI   A CRITERION OF AUTHENTICITY

If Ephesians contained not only doctrines that continue and develop the known teachings of Paul, but also doctrinal elements that strictly contradict the apostle's own teaching, then it would be practically impossible to consider Paul its author. Among the unique elements of Ephesians the following are outstanding:

1. The extensive use made of liturgical diction is but the shell of a solid

but surprising kernel. All deeds of God, all benefits for men, all responses from God's creatures are judged by one goal and criterion: they should serve to praise God's glory. It appears that this epistle explicitly supports the Calvinistic *soli Deo gloria*. In the recognized Pauline letters the elements of prayer, praise, and joy are not completely absent,[171] but the equation of theology with doxology is unique to Ephesians.

2. Unlike I Cor 4:1; cf. 13:2, Ephesians does not speak of many mysteries of God, but just one, the joining of Jews and Gentiles in one body (3:3–6). This mystery, its presupposition and exhibition are described by a peculiar employment and combination of seemingly diverse elements of Wisdom theology.[172] Just as in Wisdom books[173] wisdom has a cosmic role even before the creation of the world, so has Jesus Christ. Just as the same wisdom *saves* men who are taught by her,[174] so Jesus Christ is celebrated as the *savior of his body* (Eph 1:23). Just as again the same wisdom is displayed in practical advice for daily conduct, so the parenesis of Ephesians and Colossians abounds with elements taken from OT Wisdom contexts. There is a distinct emphasis placed upon the reception and communication of knowledge in Ephesians, and we observe the combination of statements on knowledge and on power.[175]

3. The image of the broken wall is as unique in the Pauline corpus as is its interpretation by the abolishment of statutory law (2:14–15). According to Rom 3:31, Paul's message aimed at establishing rather than invalidating the law.[176] Even toward the end of Galatians, Paul takes pains to underline that he supports nothing that would be opposed to the law. He is not an antinomian. But Eph 2:14–15 seems to reveal outright antinomianism.[177]

4. In Ephesians the status of Israel in God's kingdom appears to be described in a way other than in the genuine Pauline letters. (a) According to Rom 11:17; Gal 4:30, the Israel of the present appears to be *cut off* and *thrown out,* Paul evidently believing Gentiles have taken the place of the chosen people. But Ephesians affirms that Israel is the family and people to whom Gentiles were joined when they heard the gospel and received the Spirit. In this epistle Israel is never *far* from God, but rather

---

[171] Eph 1:3–14; 2:18; 3:14–21; 5:18–20; Rom 1:8; 8:31 ff.; 11:33 ff. For more references and literature see above, sections I and II.

[172] In Colossians the selection *and* combination of these elements is still more impressive.

[173] Prov 8:22–31; Wisd Sol 7:17 – 8:1.

[174] Wisd Sol 9:18; 10.

[175] 1:17–21; 3:10, 18–19; 4:13; 6:10–20.

[176] The widely spread opinion, repeated, e.g. in Conzelmann, *Outline of the Theology of the NT,* pp. 160–61, that "Paul does not fight against legalism, but against the law as a whole," is not true to Rom 3:31; 7:12, 14; 8:2–4; 13:9, etc. R. N. Longenecker, *Paul, Apostle of Liberty* (New York: Harper, 1964), pp. 18, 86, 99 f., 125, etc., distinguishes sharply between Paul's stance *for* the law and his fight *against* legalism.

[177] Gal 5:6, 23; 6:15. For a discussion of this issue see COMMENTS VI on 2:1–10 and IV B on 2:11–22.

has been and is the first to be *near* him.[178] (b) Rom 4 and Gal 3 praise the faith of Israel's patriarch, Abraham, and contrast it with the attitude of those Jews who boast of their circumcision and fail to submit themselves in faith to God's righteousness, see esp. Rom 9:30–10:3. The author of Ephesians is aware that the circumcised people are proud of their circumcision (2:9, 11), but he does not ever scold Jewish unbelief. He speaks only of the promise and the covenants given to Israel and of the hope fostered by this people.[179] There are certain remarks in the Pauline corpus which can be exploited for anti-Semitic purposes,[180] the most striking of these to be found in I Thess 2:14–15: . . . "the Jews . . . killed both the Lord Jesus and the prophets, and drove us out, and displease God and oppose all men by hindering us from speaking to the Gentiles that they may be saved—so as always to fill up the measure of their sins. But God's wrath has come upon them at last." The "Israel of God" mentioned in Gal 6:16 has sometimes been understood to exclude the Jews. But the peaceful epistle to the Ephesians, though addressed only to Gentile-born Christians, attests to the peace preached by Christ himself not only to *those far*—the Gentiles—but also to *those near*—the Jews— (2:17). The accents set in Ephesians have been considered a proof that Paul's passionate disputes with Jews and "Judaizers" were a thing of the past when Ephesians was written. But it is true that only if unquestioned Pauline passages describing the unity of Jews and Gentiles[181] were disregarded, the difference between Ephesians and the admittedly Pauline epistles would appear to be so great as to exclude a common author.

5. The charismata enumerated in Eph 4:11 appear to be limited to ministries that are fulfilled primarily by oral testimony, i.e. preaching, prophesying, teaching, counseling, directing.[182] The service done by the so-called laity does not necessarily receive less attention than in Rom 12–13 and I Cor 12. For every church member's service, testimony to truth, daily labor, and missionary responsibility receive great emphasis in Ephesians.[183] But though it is clear that the congregation lives and is ruled by the gifts of grace given to each one of its members, the list of charismata of Eph 4:11 is different from their enumeration in I Cor 12:28–31 and Rom 12:6–9.

6. No reference is made in Ephesians to dying with Christ; but in Paul's epistles this term plays an important role.[184] In Ephesians, it is the resur-

[178] 1:11–14; 2:11–22; 3:6. See also Gal 1:16; Philip 3:3; I Peter 2:9–10.
[179] 1:12; 2:11–22.
[180] But cf. M. Barth, "Was the Apostle Paul an Anti-Semite?" JES 5 (1968), 78–104; repr. in *Israel and the Church*, Richmond: Knox, 1969.
[181] Gal 3:26–29; I Cor 12:12–13; cf. Col 3:11.
[182] D. Y. Hadidian, *"Tous de euaggelistas* in Eph. 4:11," CBQ 28 (1966), 317–21, would add (on the basis, e.g. of Eusebius HE III 37:2–3, v 10:2, and of an observation of W. M. L. de Wette) the writing of Gospels such as Mark's or Luke's.
[183] 1:15; 2:10; 4:12, 15, 25–32; 5:8–13; 6:5–9.
[184] Rom 6:2–5; Gal 2:19; II Cor 4:10; 5:14; Col 2:20.

rection with Christ, combined with the enthronement at his side, that is firmly asserted. While in the Pauline epistles *being with Christ* is an eschatological concept,[185] and especially the resurrection with Christ is a hoped-for future event,[186] Ephesians (and Colossians) builds upon the basis of the saints' completed resurrection and enthronement with the Messiah (2:5–6).

7. Finally the warm admonition to married people found in Eph 5:21–33 is hard to accommodate to the less enthusiastic statements on marriage in I Cor 7.

A feature common to these seven distinctive elements is the open and positive attitude of the epistle to a structured community life. Or, put another way, it is difficult to understand Ephesians as a book containing information and direction regarding individual salvation and perfection. Both the kerygmatic and the parenetic parts of Ephesians show primary concern for the community. There is no individual personal salvation preached in Ephesians which may or must be followed by the demand for social ethics; instead, one new social order, called "peace" in 2:13–17, is established for the benefit of heaven and earth by Jesus Christ. This order is the content of the Gospel.[187] God's glory and man's salvation, Jews and Gentiles, husband and wife, preachers and manual laborers, the building of the church and the mission to the world are unified by Jesus Christ. In 2:10, 15 the work of God is summed up in one brief formula: It consists of the creation of one new man out of the formerly divided two enemies.

Unlike Rom 1:16; 3:21, in Ephesians the gospel is not explicitly called the revelation of God's righteousness. It is named the "gospel of peace," and Jesus Christ himself is the bringer of the good news, even of peace (2:14, 17; 6:15). Therefore God's work is not identified with the salvation of this or that sinful man who may later join the ranks of those individually justified and sanctified, but with the union of formerly separated and opposed persons—this is their salvation, their life and new being. Paul's epistles to the Galatians (esp. chapter 2) and Romans (esp. chapters 7–8), but also II Corinthians and Philippians have often[188] been understood to contain the true information on each and every man's salvation. What Paul had said about "the Jews first, but also the Gentiles," was taken as evidence of the basic equality of all men, whatever their

---

[185] E.g. I Thess 4:17; Philip 1:23; see E. Lohmeyer, "Syn Christo," in Fs *A. Deissmann* (1927), pp. 218–57.

[186] I Thess 4:13–18; I Cor 15:12–56; Rom 6:5; Philip 3:10–11; cf. II Tim 2:18.

[187] Cf. the fitting title and warm content of J. A. Mackay's commentary on Ephesians, *God's Order*.

[188] From Augustine to Luther and Bultmann. But in recent years monographs on Paul have appeared that prepare the way for the necessary correction. E.g. J. Munck, *Paul and the Salvation of Mankind*, Richmond: Knox, 1959; C. Müller, *Gottes Gerechtigkeit und Gottes Volk*, Göttingen: Vandenhoeck, 1964; P. Stuhlmacher, *Gerechtigkeit Gottes bei Paulus*, Göttingen: Vandenhoeck, 1965.

nationality, religion, sex, trade, or age. Indeed, God's gracious judgment passed on the cross and in the resurrection of Christ, the faith in the Messiah Jesus that defies reliance upon individual works of law, and the gift of the Spirit who conveys knowledge of God and unites the believers, are the core and criterion of Paul's preaching and teaching. With good reason the combination of grace and peace, of justification and sanctification, of the great indicative of God's love and the imperative of man's love, were understood as the basis of Pauline ethics. The corresponding Augustinian, Thomist, Reformation, and recent Roman Catholic understanding of Paul has great existential appeal, for it concerns every man, everyone's inability to please God and to attain justification by human, even by religious, efforts. It meets man's need for intervention from the outside. It urges an encounter with the living God. It offers the gospel and faith as means and signs of that encounter. It praises baptism as the instrument of union with Christ and of incorporation into the community of all others saved by grace. It celebrates the Lord's Supper as the God-given way of nourishment and growth in faith and love. It has much to say on both the freedom of each Christian and his responsibility toward brothers and enemies, believers and unbelievers. Whoever accepts Paul's message on these terms will admire and honor him as an outstanding Christian existentialist.[189] Others may prefer to depict him as a true pietist whose objectivizing statements are fully understood only when each of them is translated into terms of subjective individual experience.[190]

But the emphasis placed in Ephesians upon the social character of God's work stands in contrast with the individualism of the alleged existentialist Paul. According to this epistle, God's dealings are with Israel and the nations, with the church and the powers of the world, in short, with the whole of creation. Instead of going out to save souls, God establishes his rule and kingship over heaven and earth. All is to be submitted to the king he has enthroned at his right hand. The much-praised peace of the soul looks like a ridiculous mini-achievement beside the peace and order brought to the world. The pangs of the individual's heart mentioned in Rom 2:15; 7:7–25 come from smaller battlefields than the wounds suffered by mankind divided in hostile groups and by the church in the war to be waged against the spiritual powers of the air (Eph 6:10–17). In sum, a political, social, public concept of the working of God's grace appears in Ephesians to substitute for an individual, psychological and existentialist concern in the main epistles of Paul. For a long time, Paul was understood to answer the question which in Luther's phrasing is, "How do I get a gracious God?" or, in the apostle's own words, "Wretched man that

[189] So e.g. R. Bultmann, *The Presence of Eternity,* New York: Harper, 1957; E. Schillebeecks, *Christ, The Sacrament of Encounter with God,* New York: Sheed, 1963.
[190] So e.g. W. D. Davies, PRJ, pp. 88, 197; D. E. H. Whiteley, *The Theology of St. Paul* (Philadelphia: Fortress, 1964), p. 155.

I am! Who will deliver me?" (Rom 7:24). But the question treated in Ephesians is: What, if any, salvation is there for this world? Paulinism of the first sort will be fostered and served by pastors and teachers who, like Luther, are primarily engaged with the cure of souls. They may eventually find their task in the performance of religiously motivated psychotherapy. The understanding of the gospel suggested by Ephesians is different. Ministers of the Ephesian gospel of peace will not forget or neglect the cure of souls, but their concern for individuals will be imbedded in the conviction that they are ambassadors of God's kingdom to the whole world. Their task will be fulfilled in the political and social as well as in personal domains. "The manifold wisdom of God is now to be made known through the church to the governments and authorities" (Eph 3:10).

Is it really true that if not the vocabulary, style, or historic situation, then the theology of the epistle as we have outlined it here "makes the Pauline composition . . . completely impossible"?[191] On the basis of their interpretation of Galatians and Romans, nineteenth- and twentieth-century Protestant Bible interpreters presumed to know what is and what is not Pauline theology: The author of Gal 2 and Rom 7–8 could not possibly have written Ephesians, they said; the divergencies were all too great. A lapse from the high concept of God, the pacifier of the troubled soul that was restless till it found rest in God—even a lapse from the curing of souls into the lower regions of a God who cared as much for the hostile world as to reconcile its hostile inhabitants to one another and to give them a universal mission of peace—this lapse was considered by several outstanding scholars a fact, a catastrophe, and a betrayal at the same time. Supposedly it is the fall from eschatological existence into ecclesiastical organization, disposition, and application of faith and life. This fall led directly to the dungeons of (pre-Vatican II) Roman ecclesiasticism. To this way of thinking, if Ephesians is forgiven its baroque language, its Gnostic elements, its dependence upon Colossians and other letters of the NT, yet it is not forgiven its "Early Catholicism." The image of Paul cultivated among those Protestants does not permit being dragged into any morass, least of all the ecclesiastical. Therefore Ephesians must have been written by an author different from Paul—however conspicuous his admiration and imitation of the apostle was. It is undeniable that Augustine combined in his person belief in the individual soul's beatific vision and uncompromising hierarchic churchmanship. But Paul is not Augustine. The pure gospel preached by Paul, so it was assumed, could never have been adulterated by the place attributed in Ephesians to the church, the powers, the social realities.

The question must be raised whether this understanding of Paul, based

---

[191] Kümmel, FBK, p. 254; cf. Käsemann, RGG, II, 519.

as it is upon selected passages from Galatians and Romans, can claim that
infallibility which among Protestants is denied the Pope and the Papal
Bible Commission, but is *de facto* claimed for "objective," scholarly, historical-critical research. J. Munck[192] has reopened a discussion which
might have followed the attacks of A. Ritschl and others against the exclusive role ascribed to Paul's doctrine of (individual) justification.[193]
From Munck it may be learned that in his main letters Paul does not
fight about principles. The issues of grace vs. law, faith vs. works, freedom vs. slavery, spiritual vs. ceremonial religion[194] are not the heart of
Paul's concern. Rather he struggles for the inclusion, recognition, and freedom of the Gentiles among God's people. The Scandinavian Lutheran
K. Stendahl[195] has taken up this novel approach to Paul. In going with
Munck and beyond him, we observe the following:

Paul's main interest lies in the right bestowed upon Gentiles by God to
be full members of Israel—even before all Israel has turned to the promised Messiah. Paul's concern is with the community of the Jews and
Gentiles—a communion which does not signify in any way the imposition
of one partner upon the other. The law need not be imposed upon the
Gentiles, pagan immorality must not be pressed upon Jews. Christ has
made them one people by ushering in the rule of grace over both. The
problem of mediation between God and man, exemplified by justification
of faith, is not the only subject matter of Paul's theology. Not for proving
a principle, but for the sake of the salvation of the Gentiles Paul is warding
off those opponents who would make circumcision or another law a condition of salvation. The justification doctrine is but a tool in the proclamation
and demonstration of the oneness and unity of Jews and Gentiles in
Christ. All Pauline letters that deal with justification culminate in the proclamation of the commandment of love and in stressing unity. The chapters
Rom 7–8 are in the safekeeping of Rom 1–5; 9–15—those chapters
which describe the Jews' and Gentiles' stance before God and their relationship to one another. Gal 2:15–21 unfolds the justification doctrine in
the face of the threatening break-up of table communion between Jews
and Gentiles at Antioch.[196] A scandalous split in the congregations is
fought against in I Corinthians, Romans, and Philippians. To be one tem-

---

[192] PSM.

[193] A. Ritschl, *The Christian Doctrine of Justification and Reconciliation*, I, New York:
Scribner's, 1900; W. Wrede, *Paulus* (Tübingen: Mohr, 1907), p. 122; A. Schweitzer, *The
Mysticism of Paul the Apostle* (New York: Holt, 1931), pp. 205 ff.; Davies, PRJ, pp. 221–
22, 352; H. J. Schoeps, *Paul* (Philadelphia: Westminster, 1961), pp. 123, 196–97, 215–16.

[194] E.g. E. W. Burton, *The Epistle to the Galatians*, ICC, Edinburgh: Clark, 1921, works
exclusively on these lines.

[195] "The Apostle Paul and the Introvert Conscience of the West," HTR 56 (1963),
199–215.

[196] Cf. M. Barth, "Jews and Gentiles, the Social Character of Justification," JES 5
(1968), 241–67.

ple of God, one body of Christ, one citizenship or colony of heaven on earth, rather than a conglomeration of individual enthusiasts—this is the fruit and proof of the work God did and does for Jews and Gentiles, through Christ and the Spirit. And the same is the nature of the church.

Obviously such an understanding of Paul's main letters is much nearer the contents of Ephesians than an existentialist theology of individual justification and sanctification that had earlier been derived from Paul.

We may conclude that not even faithful followers of Augustine, Luther, and Calvin, or Hegel and Bultmann, may actually possess a true understanding of Paul's theology. Inasmuch as they dispute the authenticity of Ephesians on doctrinal grounds, pointing to irreconcilable theological differences between Galatians, I and II Corinthians, Romans, Philippians on one side, and Ephesians (and Colossians) on the other, they may be exponents of a prejudiced opinion about the essence, the high points, and the breadth of Pauline theology. Ephesians may force extreme Paulinists of all times to revise their prejudices. Certainly the apostle's teaching and preaching was much more politically, socially, ethically oriented than his individualizing and existentialist interpreters have been willing to acknowledge.

This need not mean that henceforth the intimate, personal passages in Paul's writings are to be disregarded. Strictly personal utterances are essential to Paul's theology.[197] But they are neither the only criterion nor the exclusive center of his thinking and writing. Equally the great texts dealing with justification of the godless through faith are by no means to be belittled.[198] Paul was waging a just war against legalistic and enthusiastic distortions of the gospel of God's righteousness.[199] Augustine made splendid use of Paul's arguments in his dispute with Pelagius. The same Pauline passages served Luther well to fight Franciscan and nominalist medieval theology and corrupt church practices. Wesley, Pascal, and Kierkegaard were inspired by them to fight contemporary churchly arrogance, and K. Barth shook up the pride of both theological liberalism and conservatism with their help. But though justification by faith is one among the great insights Paul has contributed to the preaching and belief of Jesus Christ crucified and risen, it is not all that he had to proclaim. The presence or absence of the justification doctrine in a letter bearing Paul's name is not a criterion of authenticity. In the later years of his life Paul

---

[197] They resemble the biblical and Qumran Psalms which use the pronoun "I" to describe sometimes individual, sometimes communal misery, yearning, salvation, bliss. See esp. Gal 1–2; II Cor 1–5; 10–13; Rom 7; Philip 1; 3; Eph 3:14–19; 4:22–24; 6:19–22.

[198] Rom 1–5; 7–8; 9:30 – 10:21; Gal 2:15 – 4:7; cf. II Cor 5 and Philip 3.

[199] A traditional view holds Palestine Jews or Jewish Christians guilty of the opposition to Paul. Munck, PSM, pp. 79–126, puts the blame on super-Paulinist Gentile Christians; Schoeps, *Paul*, pp. 28–32, 197–200, 213–18, accuses diaspora Jews, and Paul's own ignorance of true Judaism; Schmithals, *Paul and the Gnostics*, identifies the opponents with Gnostic legalist enthusiasts.

himself may have become more irenic and willing to emphasize the unity in Christ. The issues that had earlier forced him to write in a polemic style may not have been as pressing toward the end of his life. Certainly the doubts regarding the authenticity of Ephesians are honest expressions of the theological assumptions fostered by some interpreters, and as such they are most revealing. But so far they have revealed more of the interpreters' minds than of a convincing alternative to Pauline authorship.

In view of the insufficient linguistic and historical arguments, and of the prejudicial character of the theological reasons exhibited against Ephesians, it is advisable for the time being to still consider Paul its author.

Some minor arguments against pseudonymity and in favor of authenticity may be added:

1. The book of Revelation does not refer to Paul and seems to prove that in Asia Minor Pauline influence was minimal or non-existent. Whether this book was written in the sixties or nineties of the first century is not known. But its disregard or ignorance of Pauline theology is contrasted by the contents of I Peter. Certainly in a given period the influence of Paul in Asia Minor must have been small. It may therefore be asked, Why should a pseudonymous author of Ephesians have written under the apostle's name if that name did not necessarily assure high esteem?[200]

2. Not though but *because* some typically Pauline words have a slightly different, perhaps unique, meaning in Ephesians, and *because* deviations from a straight party-line Paulinism are indisputable, Ephesians may have to be considered authentic. Only a very foolish plagiarist or editor would have been unaware of the changes, additions, corrections he made. A clever pseudonymous author would have avoided slips of thought, tongue, or pen that might easily have betrayed him. The apocryphal Laodicean letter shows how a silly and timid fool, a mere compiler of undigested quotations, would proceed.[201] The author of Ephesians was a very thoughtful, perhaps even an ingenious man.[202] Paul himself is the man who could best afford to write in a non-Paulinistic way, even under his own name.[203]

[200] See e.g. the judgment contained in II Peter 3:15–16, "Our beloved brother Paul wrote to you according to the wisdom given him. . . . There are some things in his letters hard to understand, which the ignorant and unstable twist. . . ." In the Pseudoclementine literature Simon the Magician appears to be the straw man for Paul.

[201] See M. R. James, *The Apocryphal New Testament* (Oxford: Clarendon Press, 1955), pp. 479–80. For a newer introduction and translation, see E. Hennecke and W. Schneemelcher, *New Testament Apocrypha*, II (Philadelphia: Westminster, 1966), 128–32.

[202] In JB, NT, p. 261, he is called "someone with a genius for creative thinking." Marxsen, *Introduction*, pp. 196–97, praises him for being a master over the materials used by him, for inserting them successfully into the whole of his composition, for utilizing them not just for citation but for making original statements of his own. P. Benoit, "L'unité de l'Église selon l'épître aux Éphésiens," in AnBib 17–18 (1963), I, 57–58, and A. Feuillet, *Le Christ sagesse de Dieu* (Paris: Gabalda, 1966), p. 276, affirms that a plagiarist would not have understood Paul so well.

[203] See NOTE on "in Ephesus" in 1:1 for a discussion of whether or under what conditions it can be assumed that Paul wrote this letter to Christians in the city of Ephesus.

3. The clear structure and beautiful unity of the epistle, the force with which decisive points are made, and the warmth of devotion and concern, above all the grandeur of the praise given to God on the ground of the love he has demonstrated to enemies and strangers—these elements reveal the hand of a genius and master. Turning the first point on its head: if this admirable wise man and teacher should have been somebody other than Paul, he might well have left in Asia Minor some smaller or larger traces. But there are no traces left that would lead to a theological giant different from Paul. Certainly no one among those named John in the NT can be considered the author of Ephesians.

4. Though Paul was capable of writing or dictating letters in boiling wrath, with cynical irony, or in the midst of streaming tears,[204] his occasional outbursts of temperament did not oblige him to explode all the time. It may be wishful thinking but it is by no means impossible that—just as it is true of good wine—*the old one is milder*.[205]

Most likely Bengel[206] is right: in this epistle Paul writes more openly and sublimely than in any one of his previous letters. The NOTES and COMMENTS to follow are made on the basis of the judgment of Robinson who called[207] Ephesians "the crown of St. Paul's writings." But a concession to those questioning the authenticity is necessary: Inspiration, highest authority, and imperishable value can be ascribed to Ephesians even when the epistle is "bereft of its apostolic authorship."[208]

VII PLACE AND DATE

Those modern scholars who dispute the Pauline origin of Ephesians suggest a date for the epistle anywhere between A.D. 70 and 170.[209] As a place of writing they suggest some location in Asia Minor, sometimes the town of Ephesus itself. Among the reasons given for Ephesus are the relation between Ephesians and Colossians, Onesimus' and Tychicus' connection with Ephesus, the acquaintance of Ignatius with the epistle and

[204] Gal 1:6–9; 3:1; 5:12; II Cor 2:4; 11.
[205] Cf. Luther's translation of Luke 5:39.
[206] Commentary, on Eph 3:4.
[207] In the preface to his commentary, p. vii. Benoit, AnBib 17–18 (1963), I, 57, calls Ephesians "a summit, perhaps the summit, of the Pauline work."
[208] So e.g. Mitton, EE, pp. 270–77. Writers such as Mark and Luke and the author of Hebrews have been canonized though they did not bear the names of apostles.
[209] According to Goodspeed, *Key to Ephesians*, p. vii; Pokorný, EuG, p. 13, the allusions to the destruction of the temple in Eph 2:14, 19–22, yield the *terminus a quo*. I Peter or Ignatius (see fn. 147) or Irenaeus, *adv. haer.* v 2:3 give the *termini ad quem*, i.e. the years around A.D. 95, 115, or 170, respectively. But Marxsen, *Introduction*, pp. 187–98, arrives on other grounds at an early date for the pseudonymous work: Since the apostolic tradition is still in flux and not yet firm, the letter belongs to "the immediate post-apostolic period." Mitton, EE, pp. 260–61, 273; Kümmel, FBK, pp. 257–58, and others would place it later. Mitton suggests the period between 87 and 92—because during this period I Peter was composed and made use of Ephesians; Kümmel is ready to admit a date as late as 100, for he believes that though Ephesians and I Peter are dependent upon the same tradition, a direct literary dependence of I Peter on Ephesians cannot be demonstrated.

some resemblances in the contents of Ephesians to Ignatius' message to the Ephesians. Sometimes also a rather nebulous substance called "the general religious climate" (e.g. of syncretism, of proto-Gnosticism or Gnosticism, of post-apostolic ecclesiology) is called to the witness stand for testimony in favor of Asian origin. All of these arguments lack compelling force.

More clues to solving the puzzle of place and date are available to those assuming Pauline authorship.[210] Assuming that Paul was executed in Rome in A.D. 63—after spending two years in a Caesarean prison and two in Rome (partly in prison)—choices for the origins of Ephesians come down to Rome and the years 61–63, or to Caesarea two or three years earlier. If it could be proven that all the four letters from a prison (the so-called Letters of Captivity), i.e. Philippians, Ephesians, Colossians, Philemon, were written from the same place and about the same time, then Ephesus around the middle of the fifties would also have to be considered.[211] Actually the distinctive language and contents of Ephesians and Colossians on one side and of Philippians on the other[212] suggest that Philippians belongs in the neighborhood of Galatians, Corinthians, Romans, while Ephesians and Colossians presuppose some distance of time, situation, and thought-form from Paul's main epistles. Ephesians is surprisingly mellow if compared with the younger Paul's fiery blasts. Rome, about 62, is the best guess for the origin. While no clear proof is available for fixing the date and place of Ephesians here, none among the suggested alternatives rests upon presuppositions and conclusions that are any less debatable.

A postscript to Eph 6:24 indicates that Ephesians was written from Rome. This postscript is too feebly attested to be considered a part of the original document,[213] but its spurious literary authenticity does not exclude that its author was informed by a trustworthy tradition or had come, by thinking of his own, to a sound conclusion.

[210] E.g. J. Schmid, *Ort und Zeit der paulinischen Gefangenschaftsbriefe,* Freiburg: Herder, 1931.

[211] For the hypothesis of an extended captivity of Paul in Ephesus, see G. S. Duncan, *St. Paul's Ephesian Ministry,* New York: Scribner's, 1930; idem, "Were Paul's Imprisonment Epistles Written from Ephesus?" ET 67 (1955–56), 163–66; idem, "Paul's Ministry in Asia—the Last Phase," NTS 3 (1956–57), 211–18; cf. idem, NTS 5 (1958–59), 43–45; W. Michaelis, "Die Gefangenschaft des Paulus in Ephesus," NTF 13 (1925); idem, *Einleitung in das NT,* pp. 211–20.

While in Acts 23:33 – 26:32 and 28:14–31 imprisonments of Paul in Caesarea and Rome are described, there are in the NT no explicit references to an Ephesian captivity. Paul's three years' stay in that city (Acts 19:1 – 20:1), the mention of his fight with beasts in the same place (I Cor 15:32) and of the dangers to his life sustained in Asia (II Cor 1:8–10), permit us to reckon with it. The commentaries on Philippians, esp. on Philip 1:13 and 4:22, show why neither the term *praitōrion* nor mentioning "Caesar's household" is sufficient to exclude Caesarea and Ephesus as places of origin.

[212] See e.g. J. B. Lightfoot, "The Order of the Epistles of Captivity," in *St. Paul's Epistle to the Philippians* (London: Macmillan, 1913), pp. 30–46; Mitton, EE, pp. 107–10; JB, NT, p. 260.

[213] It is found only in the ninth-century Codex Porphirianus and a huge group of minuscule MSS that are dependent upon the Antiochian (or Koine) text tradition.

The same cannot be said of all the textual variations, as the next section will show.

VIII   TRANSMISSION OF THE TEXT

The history of the textual tradition of Ephesians is part of the history of the Pauline corpus as a whole which is too complicated to be narrated in a few paragraphs. See the Introduction to Romans in AB, vol. 33, when it appears. The texts of Ephesians appear not to have had a history of their own.[214] Certainly they do not rest more immediately upon the author's autograph than the copies of copies of other Pauline epistles. No complete text of Ephesians exists without a title. But the title, *To the Ephesians* (or similar) preceding 1:1 is distinctly inauthentic, the work of a collector of Paul's epistles. Since Papyrus 49, the so-called Yale 415 MS,[215] contains only parts of Eph 4 and 5, this newly discovered third-century MS makes no contribution to our knowledge of the beginning of the epistle. It offers novel readings in 5:5, 6, 8; it duplicates previously known variant readings, e.g. in 4:23, 32. But it does not in any major way alter the total picture.

F. W. Beare's judgment on the subject is most optimistic. He writes,[216] "The text of Eph. has been transmitted with exceptional fidelity. There are few variants of importance, and practically no instance in which the true text is in doubt." Some caution against this attitude is appropriate. In the NOTES numerous variant readings will have to be discussed in detail.[217] Eph 1:1, 15; 3:9, 12; 4:6; 5:2, 14, 30; 6:16 are outstanding among the existing problems; the variant readings of these verses imply a change of meaning. Some variants are supported by the third-century Chester Beatty Papyrus (P 46); some by the whole Hesychian Family (H, a group of texts supposedly derived from a complete re-edition of the NT text made in Alexandria, Egypt, ca. A.D. 300); some by individual members of this family such as the fourth-century Codex Vaticanus (B); some by the sixth-century Codex Claramontanus (D) and the ninth-century Codex Boernerianus (G) only;[218] some by the Latin and Syriac versions; some by a com-

---

[214] N. A. Dahl, TZ 7 (1951), 249.
[215] See W. H. D. Hatch and C. B. Wells, "A Hitherto Unpublished Fragment of the Epistle to the Ephesians," HTR 51 (1958), 33–37; also E. Nestle.
[216] IB, X, 608.
[217] Important or well-attested variants exist in the texts of 1:1, 14, 15, 18, 20; 2:4, 5, 8, 21; 3:1, 8–9, 12, 14, 18, 20, 21; 4:6–9, 15, 16, 19, 29, 32; 5:2, 4, 14–15, 17, 19, 20, 23, 28, 30–32; 6:1, 5, 10, 16, 21, 24.
[218] The last two codices mentioned have in common that they contain both Greek and Latin texts. In their readings of 2:11, 20; 4:15 the Latin version has obviously influenced the Greek text. In 1:6; 2:5, 8; 3:1, 21; 4:19, 29; 5:10, 31; 6:1, 6, 12, 19, one of them, or both, occasionally with the support of the Vaticanus, either dissolve broken sentences and establish a better syntax, or seek to clarify by small additions or changes the meanings of ambiguous or rare words. See Robinson, pp. 285–304.

bination of two or more of these groups; some by lonely also-runners. The important variants will be discussed in detail in the NOTES on the verses in which they occur.

At present it is impossible to derive from the composition of variants contained in individual and in mutually dependent textual traditions a clear picture of the development of the text toward its present state, or an image of distinct schools of understanding the message of the epistle. But the textual variants are a great aid in studying early interpretations. They help the modern expositor to realize where there are as yet insoluble problems. Each one of them (as the omission or addition of "in Ephesus" in 1:1, or of the possessive pronoun "of us" in 4:6 shows) may vitally influence the interpretation of the whole epistle.

In sum, the genuine text of Ephesians is as little available as is the authentic meaning of its words, sentences, paragraphs. Nothing but a careful scrutiny of each individual problem can contribute to the best attainable understanding of the whole.

IX   STRUCTURE, PURPOSE, CHARACTER

Ephesians is usually understood to consist of two main parts of about equal length, 1:3 – 3:21 and 4:1 – 6:22. They are held together not only by the address (1:1–2) and the final blessing (6:23–24), but even more by the interrelation of their contents.[219] While the chapters 1–3 are called dogmatic or kerygmatic, the contents of chapters 4–6 are suitably labeled ethical, didactic or parenetic. The proclamation of God's glorious and gracious deed is made in the form of indicatives; the exhortations which follow them often have the form of imperatives. Participles can substitute either for indicatives or imperatives. God's grace is praised as the sole basis of the faith, obedience, love, and unity of men. Since the same sequence is also observed in Paul's letters to the Galatians and Romans[220] and is typical of Paul's thought even when[221] kerygmatic and parenetic elements are intermingled, both defenders and doubters of the authenticity of Ephesians have treated the bipartition as a Pauline trait.

But some modification of this traditional view appears to be under way. C. Maurer[222] has declared Eph 1:3–14 the key to the whole epistle,

---

[219] E.g. Bengel, on 1:3, distinguished from the preamble the *doctrina pathetice exposita* in 1:3 – 3:21, and the *adhortatio generalis et specialis* culminating in the call to *militia spiritualis* in 4:1 – 6:20. The huge majority of Commentaries and Introductions that were consulted for the structural analysis of Ephesians made a similar division and specified it by appropriate subdivisions. JB gives the following titles to the two parts: I. The Mystery of Salvation and of the Church; II. Exhortation.

[220] Gal 3–4; 5–6; Rom 1–11; 12–15.

[221] As in I and II Corinthians, Philippians; cf. Colossians.

[222] EvTh 11 (1951–52), 151–72; similarly, J. T. Sanders, ZNW 56 (1965), 214–32, esp. 230–32; N. A. Dahl, TZ 7 (1951), 262; Schlier, p. 72.

rather than a first subdivision of the first part. Käsemann and with him Marxsen treat the whole of chapter 1 as an independent opening section of the epistle. They believe that it corresponds to the thanksgiving and intercession of the genuine Pauline epistles but that it has much more weight than the usual introductory prayer of Paul. They consider chapters 2–3 a second section which describes the *notae ecclesiae* and is followed by a third section which develops "ethical foundations . . . based on ecclesiology, which in turn is based on Christology."[223] Thus the church rather than the kerygma of Christ is assumed to hold the central place. Kümmel goes even further.[224] What was formerly considered the epistle's kerygmatic first part, that is, 1:3 – 3:21, is now understood as nothing else but an extended epistolary introduction, consisting of praise, intercession, and petition, to which "at once the admonitions are attached." What, then, has happened to the kerygma? According to Dibelius and Kümmel "the usual core of a Pauline epistle is omitted"! However moving and appropriate the exhortation of 4:1 – 6:20, it stands now on a void instead of on the firm basis of the proclaimed gospel. Kümmel concluded that Paul could not possibly be the author of such (disastrous) theology. Maurer was more discriminating. While he acknowledged that in respect to its form Eph 1:3 – 3:21 belongs to the introduction, he held that materially the descriptions of the resurrection of the Gentiles, of Christ's work of unification, and of the apostle's ministry form the essence of the epistle.[225] The way in which e.g. Robinson analyzed the structure of Ephesians looks less than imaginative when it is compared with the observations, imaginations, and evaluations of his modern counterparts.[226] He finds in the whole of Ephesians a balanced treatment of the purpose of God, the mystery of Christ crucified, and the unity of the Spirit. In his commentary the absence of spirited theories is balanced by an openness to details which discourages generalizing judgments.

Indeed the juxtaposition of preaching and teaching (*kerygma* and *didache*), of indicative and imperative, may have had its day. Their undeniable usefulness as hermeneutical tools may be exhausted (as will be shown in COMMENT II on 4:1–16). Their imposition upon a hymnodic or prayerlike document like Ephesians may be as inappropriate as the attempt to measure the beauty of a symphony with a yardstick or a

[223] Käsemann, RGG, II, 217–18; Marxsen, *Introduction*, pp. 194–95.
[224] In FBK, p. 247, following a suggestion made by Dibelius, p. 78; cf. Gaugler, p. 161.
[225] EvTh 11 (1951–52), 152. What P. Schubert, "Form and Function of Pauline Thanksgivings," BhZNW 20 (1935), 25–26, observes in commenting upon I Thess 1:2 – 3:13 may be true of Eph 1–3 also and confirm Maurer's judgment: thanksgiving can substitute for the main body of other Pauline epistles.
[226] On pp. 13–14 of his commentary Robinson subdivides Eph 1:3 – 6:20 into eleven units, without marking any main divisions. But the roles of prayer, of wisdom, of the Gentile's naturalization, and of unity are recognized.

barometer. The division between Gospel and Law which is maintained in the distinction of Preaching and Teaching has so far proven disastrous for the foundation of evangelical ethics. The sequence, God (or Christ) did *this* for you—now you have to do *that* for him, is a ridiculous caricature of the relationship between God's grace and the good works for which man is created, according to Eph 2:5–10. Above all, it is neither Paul's nor the Ephesian letter's intention to relegate God's will and action to a distant past and to let the church or its members take over control of things on earth now. If a traditional view of Ephesians saw in this epistle no more than a description of God's eternal will, of his historic action on the cross and in the resurrection of Christ, and of the foundation, order and mission of the church, it may have missed what this epistle intends to say in particular. For Ephesians speaks pointedly of the present work and revelation of God and Christ, and of the hope for all the world that is yet to be fulfilled.

The structure of Ephesians is actually such as to emphasize the last-mentioned elements as much as the earlier. The verses 1:3–14 are a prologue, or the overture to the whole that follows. The form is that of a benediction, a praise of God in the congregation. The prologue makes clear that not only the believers but all creatures are confronted by the eternal God himself. He, the creator, is also their gracious redeemer. He who was hidden is now revealed. His love is the power by which he embraces Jews and Gentiles. His Spirit is operating in them. And this is not enough: He continues to subject all and everything to the one who is God's will and grace in person, Jesus Christ.

The first part (1:15 – 2:22) describes God's perfect work. Beginning with a reference to the present work of the Spirit, the author turns to speak of Christ's resurrection. Then he proceeds to the resurrection with Christ of men who were dead in sin. Only then does he come to praise Christ's cross and its effect, even the gift of peace to the world divided by hostility. This gift is not an offer but an act of creation. A new man takes the place of hostile mankind. He is a welcome partner and servant of God. He is identified with the church of Jews and Gentiles which is still being built and growing.

The second part (3:1 – 4:24) praises the ongoing work of God's revelation to and through his people. The unique revelation of God's formerly hidden love to Jews and Gentiles corresponds to the commission of the church to make God's "wisdom" known to all the powers that be. To the worship of God by the apostle corresponds Christ's habitation in the hearts of men and their growth in the knowledge of love. To the one God, Lord, Spirit who is confessed corresponds the conduct of a unified and peaceful congregation. Because of the continued gift of spiritual leaders the whole congregation is destined for perfection and growth in the service it renders. Every day the new man created by God is to replace anew the old Adam that tries to re-enslave those redeemed. In this part of the epistle specific emphasis is placed upon the presence of God's revelation, the presence of Christ, the present work of the Spirit. No room is left for a nostalgic yearning for the old classic days of salvation, revelation, religious experience. The God and Christ described in chapters 1–2 are shown to be at work, now.

The third part (4:25 – 6:20) encourages the readers to let their light shine. All that was and is done and revealed to them has but one purpose: to be shown, to be made known by word and deed, by labor and suffering, to their fellow men on earth, and also to heavenly powers that may seek to obstruct them. The gospel is not for private possession and enjoyment; it is for all. No situation in life, whatever one's position in marriage, one's age, or one's social or economic bracket, is an excuse or obstacle preventing the fulfillment of the mission entrusted to the church. All earthly situations, including suffering, are opportunities to be seized for attesting to God's love. It is God himself who provides the equipment to stand one's ground and to proceed on his course.

Common to all parts of Ephesians is the frequent use made of the words "in Christ." *In him* the outpouring of grace was decided in eternity and is carried through in history. *In him* this grace was and is being revealed through the preaching of the word and the building, the order, the suffering of the church. And *in him* each of the church's members is to walk. While the author is able to say many things without mentioning the church, he can say nothing without referring to Jesus Christ. Jesus Christ, in turn, is described as head of the church. But not only this. He is chosen by God to be head over all. Therefore those knowing him cannot reserve him for themselves. He himself equips them as his people, viz. *through the church* (3:10), to be evangelists to the whole cosmos (6:15). The church is but an instrument or lighthouse built for the benefit of all creation. It is not an end in itself, and it is certainly not co-extensive with the reach of God's love and realm of his kingship. Ephesians is a manifesto of the love and mission of God to the world of which God's people are to be the exponents.

Should this presentation of God's love, of the peace brought by Christ, of the unification of all those divided, encompass or exhaust the whole purpose of Ephesians? To judge from the definitions of the purpose of Ephesians found in introductory and interpretive literature some essential points may have been missed. In section V of this Introduction it was stated that E. Goodspeed considered Ephesians a covering or introductory letter written on the occasion of the first collection and edition of the Pauline epistles. K. H. von Weizsäcker[227] understood Ephesians and Colossians as writings composed for countering the competition offered in Asia Minor by the Johannine literature, and for defending Paul against a theology promoted under Peter's name. A similar historical purpose is ascribed to Ephesians by H. Chadwick:[228] a spiritual crisis of post-Pauline Gentile Christianity was to be met by the emphasis placed upon the unity of the church—a unity founded upon the communion of Judaeo-Christian and Gentile-Christian congregations. Another recent thesis, discussed earlier,[229] holds that the crisis was caused by the influx of Gnosticism, and Ephesians intended to meet Gnosticism with Gnosticizing arguments.

Still more definitions of the purpose can be found. Whether or not the Gnostic background and Pauline authorship are endorsed, Ephesians is often treated as an attempt to sum up and to recommend to a later generation the apostle Paul's teaching. E.g. Beare[230] explains the epistle as "a philosophy of religion, which is at the same time a philosophy of history, [developed] out of Pauline materials"; he calls it "the first manifesto of Christian imperialism exhibiting the church as the spiritual empire which must grow." Schlier[231] understands Ephesians as a Wisdom speech, a meditation upon Christ's wisdom which can be ascribed to Paul himself. Ephesians is treated by Beare, Käsemann,[232] Marxsen,[233] and J. L. Price[234] as a tract rather than a letter, though a weak attempt at epistolary form is admitted. Different again is the description of the purpose of Ephesians given by those who see in it a discourse on baptism written for the benefit of newly baptized Gentiles.[235] Some believe that the purpose of Ephesians was to ward off an enthusiastic or mystery-religionlike misunderstanding of baptism.

In some opposition to the host of those engaged in refined literary, historical, liturgical placements of Ephesians stand authors like J. A. Robinson[236] and P. Dacquino.[237] The former declares the summing up and salvation of all things, even of Jews and Gentiles rather than of individual souls, to be the main subject matter of the epistle. The latter stresses the unique function and dignity of Christ in the redemption and life of the

---

[227] *Das apostolische Zeitalter* (Tübingen: Mohr, 1886), pp. 560–65.
[228] ZNW 51 (1960), 145–54; cf. F. Cornelius, "Die geschichtliche Stellung des Epheser-briefes," ZRG 7 (1955), 74 f. (ref.).
[229] In section III B of this Introduction.   [230] IB, X, 604, 607.
[231] Commentary, pp. 21, 22, 28.
[232] RGG, II, 517; 166.   [233] Introduction, section 18:1–2.
[234] *Interpreting the New Testament* (New York: Holt, 1961), p. 464.
[235] E.g. N. A. Dahl, G. Schille, J. Coutts, P. Pokorný, J. C. Kirby suggest this view; cf. W. Nauck, "Epheser 2, 19–22—ein Tauflied?" EvTh 13 (1953), 362–71. See COMMENT XVI on Eph 1:3–14.
[236] Commentary, pp. 7, 14, 27, 75, 78, 101–2, 183.
[237] "Interpretatio epistolae ad Ephesios in luce finis intenti," VD 36 (1958), 338–49.

church—as opposed to the honor attributed to mediating angels. P. Pokorný[238] combines the various purposes ascribed to Ephesians and presents the following list:

Restoration of Paul who was discredited by heresies.
Refutation of a syncretistic, partly Jewish, partly pagan, Gnosticism.
Instruction on the essence of baptism.
Promotion of the unity of a church composed of Jews and Gentiles.
Strengthening of missionary engagement.

The advantage of recognizing many purposes is obvious. An interpreter who is willing to follow the chapters and changing themes of the
epistle from one aspect to another will be more readily receptive to its
actual contents than a systematizing genius who submits all details to one
keen theory. Because Ephesians has many dimensions, it ought not to be
scrutinized under one aspect only—be it its teaching on the church or on
baptism, or its relation to Gnosticism.

Ephesians is certainly not an occasional letter like those written by Paul
to local churches or individuals. Though it has an epistolary beginning and
other traits found also in the body and conclusion of extra-biblical and
biblical epistles,[239] it is not a letter like the others. For there are no traits
at all suggestive of a special acquaintance of the author with those addressed. The reference to their acceptance of the gospel (1:13; 4:20–
21), the gratitude expressed for their faith and love (1:15), the stress laid
on grace alone (2:8–9), and the warning against relapse into pagan conduct (4:17–19), and against submission to flimsy doctrine (4:14), are
kept in such general terms that they might equally fit any Christian congregation. On the other hand, Ephesians does not belong in the family of
those famous literary works which pretend to be letters but actually are
essays composed for the benefit of an educated class of people (like Plato's
or J.-J. Rousseau's). Ephesians does not reveal the literary pretensions or
aspirations of an orator or philosopher. Just like the High-Priestly Prayer
of John 17, it is above all a prayer directed to God—but a prayer prayed
publicly. Those for whom the author intercedes—those Gentiles converted
in Ephesus after Paul's departure—are made witnesses of his prayer and
urged to join in. The purpose of Ephesians is to be heard by both God and
men. Because more often than in any other NT epistle the doctrinal and
hortatory statements are phrased in the form of prayer, Ephesians occupies

---

[238] EuG, pp. 17–21.
[239] F. X. J. Exler, *The Form of the Ancient Greek Letter*, Washington: Catholic University of America Press, 1923; O. Roller, *Das Formular der paulinischen Briefe*, 1933.
The attempt made, e.g. by Robinson, pp. 275–84, to prove that Ephesians is replete with
elements that belong to an occasional letter are not sufficient to overcome the arguments
collected against this opinion by E. Lohmeyer, "Briefliche Grussüberschriften," ZNW 26
(1927), 158–73, repr. in his *Probleme paulinischer Theologie* (Stuttgart: Kohlhammer, n.d.),
pp. 9–29; but cf. G. Friedrich, "Lohmeyer's These über das paulinische Briefpräskript krit-
isch beleuchtet," TLZ 81 (1956), 345–46.

a unique place among those epistles. Both its possible strength and weakness are directly related to the fact that its author aims at doing the best he can for Christians he does not know. He prays for them; no wonder then that the peculiar content and purpose of Ephesians has found its expression in a peculiar form, the language of prayer.[240]

X   AN APPROACH TO THE TRANSLATION, NOTES AND COMMENTS

The most difficult and certainly the decisive contribution which a commentary can make to the understanding of a document written in a foreign language is a pure and simple translation. The Greek texts used in this commentary are the latest available editions of Nestle[241] (1963) and *The Greek New Testament* (GNT) of 1966.[242] Only on rare occasions have variant readings not contained in these editions been taken into consideration.

Among the more recent translations, the New English Bible (NEB) and the English edition of the Jerusalem Bible (JB) were found more helpful and followed more frequently than others. Though for every verse nothing else but an exact translation was intended, several passages will convey the impression of being a rather free version of the original. The NOTES[243] call attention to points at which our translation more or less radically deviates from other versions, ancient or modern. The Greek text of Ephesians is at some places so clumsy, overloaded, ambiguous, and bare of any beauty and comeliness that a slavish English rendition of its wording achieves nothing better than to puzzle, shock, and deter the reader. A literal rendering and the bewilderment caused by its wording are by no means necessary or safe media for confronting the reader with the "scandal of the cross" or the "obstacle" and "madness" of Christ crucified, as mentioned in Gal 5:11; I Cor 1:23—on the contrary, it may prevent him from grasping anything. It is to be assumed that the author of Ephesians (as much as the Deuteronomist, the Chronicler, or the author of some Qumran passages) knew exactly why he embedded liturgical and other traditional phrases in his writing, piled up synonyms, and created sentences that never seem to end. Also the writer of Ephesians may have had a very clear conception of the meaning or meanings that were to be conveyed by words such as "fullness" or "mystery." Perhaps the first readers

[240] Percy, *passim*, esp. pp. 200–2; Schlier, p. 22.
[241] Nestle and Aland, *Novum Testamentum Graece*.
[242] Edited by K. Aland, M. Black, B. M. Metzger, A. Wikgren, and published by American and other Bible Societies, New York, London, Edinburgh, Amsterdam, Stuttgart.
[243] Especially when they begin with the abbreviation "Lit.," meaning a more literal or verbatim rendition is to follow.

of Ephesians had no problem in enjoying and understanding the form and content of the epistle. But a modern reader is a long way from this enviable situation.

With the intention of bringing to light at least one among several possible meanings of a given passage, the following decision was made: In all cases—as e.g. in 1:10, 22b, 23; 4:16—where sheer literalism would communicate either no sense at all or a multiplicity of ambiguous meanings, the translation sets forth that one among the perceivable clear meanings which appears most appropriate to the context. Preference was given to a little thing clearly said over a bigger cluster of mysteries surrounded by nebulae. Consequently the translation offered in the following may frequently be much poorer, though its contents may perhaps be easier to grasp than those of the Greek original. This risk was consciously taken. On the opposite side, where earlier versions seemed to limit the sense of a word or statement in a manner not sufficiently certified by philogical evidence and the context, compromise solutions have been sought.

Following the plan laid out for the Anchor Bible, the NOTES serve the purpose of explaining, in the light of textual variants, dictionaries, grammars, parallels, other versions, etc., why one rather than another interpretation has been chosen. Frequently alternatives are presented that may claim equal, if not superior, validity to the proposed translation. The NOTES will introduce the reader to biblical, philological, historical, exegetical discussions which are related to given words and phrases. They should enable him to participate in this discussion and to form opinions of his own however divergent they may be from those proposed in the text of this book. Neither the offering of new theories nor the imposition of supposedly final answers and results, but the invitation to form a balanced judgment is the goal of the NOTES.

The same pertains to the COMMENTS. They contain a selection of features from the history of exegesis,[244] the history of biblical and non-biblical literature, the history of religions and of the church, that are of special interest. Also they may hint at the relevance which a given word, text, or topic may have for the relationship of the church to Israel, to her mission, to theological thought. Since Ephesians is a theological document it must be explained in theological terms—or else the exposition would not be literal. But it has proven impossible to separate literary and historical from theological interpretation. Rather it is the careful observation of the place and function of a word, a clause, a paragraph in its literary and historical, be it secular or religious, environment which makes the reader aware

---

[244] A survey on the history of interpretation is to be found in J. Schmid, *Der Epheserbrief des Apostels Paulus,* Biblische Studien 22 (Freiburg: Herder, 1928), 1 ff., and in Percy, 1 ff. It is omitted in this Introduction because some of its highlights have already been mentioned, while others will be found in the NOTES and COMMENTS.

of its theological relevance. Theological exegesis is not an "elective," a luxury, or a merely subjective attachment to historico-critical procedures. It is expected that precisely through sober and careful use of critical, literary, and historical procedures, the message of Ephesians concerning faith and life, and the peace and unity granted by Christ, will become more understandable.

EPHESIANS 1–3
TRANSLATION WITH
NOTES AND COMMENTS

I THE ADDRESS
(1:1–2)

1 ¹ From Paul who by God's decision is apostle of the Messiah
Jesus, to the saints (in Ephesus) who are faithful to the Messiah
Jesus. ² Grace and peace to you from God our Father and the Lord
Jesus Christ.

NOTES

1:1 *From Paul . . . apostle . . . to.* The problem of Pauline authorship is
discussed in the Introduction, V–VI; see also IX regarding the question of
whether Ephesians is really an occasional epistle or a treatise given epistolary
form. Since J. B. Lightfoot wrote his excursus on The Name and Office of an
Apostle,[1] an extensive literature on the Jewish, syncretistic, or specifically
Christian origin and nature of the ministry of an apostle has been developed.[2]
A wider and a narrower concept of apostleship—the latter including only The
Twelve and Paul—have to be distinguished. Ephesians presupposes the restricted sense in 1:1 and 3:5; cf. Col 1:24, etc. Those marks of an apostle
which are emphasized in Ephesians will be discussed in COMMENT III on
3:1–13. See also NOTES on 2:20 and 4:11.

by God's decision. This epistle contains more references to the will or decision of God than any other NT book, except the Gospel of John.[3] The translation "decision" rather than "will" is suggested by the contents of Eph 1:3–14,
also by the formula "to do the will."[4] "Decision" here means God's free voli-
tion; "will" might be misunderstood in the sense of a fixed plan or testament.
Ephesians does not support the notion of an impersonal fate or cosmic blueprint that underlies historic events, or of an impersonal and unchangeable divine rule that determines all acts of human obedience.[5] "God's decision" describes an action and manifestation of the One who is living, personal, wise
and powerful. An event in God himself is now revealed. This event is creating
history and requiring obedience.

---

[1] In his commentary on Galatians, 10th ed. (London Macmillan, 1890), pp. 92–101.
[2] StB, IV, 2–4, and K. H. Rengstorf, TWNTE, I, 413–20, derive the NT meaning of the term
from the Jewish institution of the *shaliach* or *shaluach*. In M. Barth, *Der Augenzeuge*, Zollikon:
EVZ, 1947, an original Christian-eschatological meaning is stipulated which depends upon eye-
witnessing the appearances of the resurrected Christ; G. Klein, *Die Zwölf Apostel*, FRLANT 77
(N.F. 59), 1961, and W. Schmithals, *Das kirchliche Apostelamt*, FRLANT 79, 1961, elaborate upon
the role which the concept "messenger" has in Gnostic faith.
[3] Eph 1:1, 5, 9, 11; 5:17; 6:6; cf. 2:3.   [4] Matthew and others *passim;* Eph 2:3; 6:6.
[5] In COMMENT V on 1:3–14 reasons will be given against the assumption that God follows a
fixed plan or program in acts of mechanical execution, and an alternative will be proposed.

the Messiah Jesus. In this translation of Ephesians the Greek word *christos,* commonly translated as "Christ," is always rendered as "the Messiah" when either one of the following conditions is fulfilled: (a) whenever in the Greek text the article (*ho*) is found before *christos;* (b) when *christos* is placed before the proper name "Jesus." (*Ho*) *christos,* or its OT equivalent, the Messiah (of God, of the Lord, cf. John 1:41), was first used as an appellation or title describing the function of Jesus before God and among men. Several elements contributed to this usage. The history of anointed royal, priestly, or prophetic servants of God; prophetic promises and praises of a coming Prince of Peace; cultic celebrations on Mount Zion with appropriate oracles and paeans; and finally, the high-pitched hopes of pious or radical groups in Israel were all understood by the early Christians as culminating and fulfilled in the appearance, the work, the resurrection of Jesus. Many specific meanings—and by no means only clear and harmonious ones—may be included in earliest confessions, as e.g. those ascribed to Peter, "Thou art the Messiah, the Son of the living God" (Matt 16:16); "God made him [Jesus] Lord and Messiah" (Acts 2:36). But soon enough, certainly before Ephesians was written, *christos* became part of Jesus' proper name. Texts that omit the article before "Christ" and have the sequence "Jesus Christ" show this.[6] Passages such as Eph 1:12; 2:12 ff.; 3:6; 4:12 call distinctly for a translation of *christos* which surprises, perhaps hurts, the reader with its Hebrew or Jewish-apocalyptic bite. Ephesians, more than any other NT epistle, will press the point that Gentiles receive no salvation other than the one they share with Israel and receive through the Messiah. It is the salvation first promised and given to this people alone: Israel.

saints. In the Greek translation of the OT, the congregation assembled for worship, the whole people of Israel, and sometimes also the angels are called "saints."[7] In Eph 2:19 the people of Israel, in 3:5 distinct servants of God, are called "holy" or "saint." By using the same designation in 1:1, the author of Ephesians bestows upon all his pagan-born[8] readers a privilege formerly reserved for Israel, for special (especially priestly) servants of God, or for angels. According to the OT the cause of Israel's holiness lies exclusively in God. He alone makes holy[9]—and he uses many means to achieve his purpose. Following Paul, the Gentile Christians' sanctity is dependent upon God's decision to "sanctify" them (I Thess 4:3). But in order to explain why Gentiles, too, are sanctified, Paul adds that sanctification is mediated through the Messiah.[10] The

---

[6] Besides monographs on the names and titles of Jesus and the corresponding sections in theologies of the NT, see esp. Robinson, pp. 6–7, 22–23, 32; BDF, 260:1; Beare, IB, X, 606–7; F. Hahn, *The Titles of Jesus in Christology* (New York/Cleveland: World, 1969), pp. 136–239; M. de Jonge, "The Use of the Word 'Anointed' in the Time of Jesus," NovT 8 (1966), 132–48; W. Kramer, *Christ, Lord, Son of God,* SBT 50 (1966), esp. 203–14; J. J. Meuzelaar, *Der Leib des Messias* (Assen: Van Gorcum, 1961), p. 57; H. Conzelmann, "Zum Überlieferungsproblem im Neuen Testament," TLZ 94 (1969), 881–88, esp. 884. S. Talmon, "Typen der Messiaserwartung um die Zeitenwende," in *Probleme biblischer Theologie,* Fs G. von Rad, ed. by H. W. Wolff (Munich: Kaiser, 1971), pp. 571–88, elaborates on the specific differences between the rabbinical, Qumranite, Samaritan, and Christian attitudes to the Messiah.

[7] E.g. LXX Exod 15:11; 19:6; LXX 23:22; Deut 7:6; LXX Pss 15[16]:3; 21:4, 33:10[34:9]; 88:6, 8[89:5, 7]; Dan 7 (seven times). Also in I Enoch 1:9; 39:1, 4–5; Jub 31:14; cf. the last NOTE on Eph 1:18 and fn. 71 to 2:11–22 for the meaning of "saint" in Qumran.

[8] See Introduction, fn. 19.

[9] Or "sanctifies," Exod 31:13; Ezra 20:12; cf. Isa 5:16; etc. Biblical wordbooks and theologies supply more detailed information.

[10] As summarily stated e.g. in I Cor 1:2, 30; 6:11. In Eph 2:14–19 the peace work and the blessing with peace pronounced by the Messiah is the cause of their inclusion among the "saints."

whole of Ephesians may be understood as a treatise on the ground, the means, the extension, the purpose of sanctification.

(*in Ephesus*). These words are in parentheses because they are missing in the oldest available Greek MS of Ephesians, also in the original script of codices Vaticanus and Sinaiticus,[11] and in the Minuscule 1739 which appears to have been copied from an early text. The parenthesized words were also absent from the texts used by Marcion, Tertullian, Origen, and Gregory the Great. But the Syriac and Latin versions (that go back to the second century) and the vast majority of extant Greek MSS do contain them. Four arguments are used in favor of considering these words authentic: (a) the mention of a place in the openings of genuine Pauline letters;[12] (b) the presence of the words "who are," which in other addresses prepare the reader for the name of a place; (c) the prescript, "To the Ephesians," which is found in all MSS since the end of the second century and may, though certainly not written by the author, contain the result of careful research; and (d) the mission of Tychicus (6:21–22) which according to II Tim 4:12 directed him to Ephesus.[13] But all these arguments are not strong enough to demonstrate the authenticity of the words "in Ephesus." It is much easier to assume that they were inserted for one or more of the four reasons mentioned than that they should have been omitted by careless copyists. In section III A of the Introduction internal reasons, derived from the contents of Ephesians, are enumerated that throw doubt on the assumption that Ephesians was addressed to the whole congregation in Ephesus.[14] As earlier stated, only if Gentile-born members of the Ephesian congregation who were converted and baptized after Paul had left the city for the last time are being addressed in this epistle, can the authenticity of the words "in Ephesus" be upheld.

who are faithful to the Messiah. Lit. "to those being (in Ephesus) and [or, really] faithful in Christ Jesus." Our translation makes smooth reading but it glosses over several as yet insoluble problems of the Greek text. Proposed alternatives are (a) to avoid all syntactical difficulties by reading "who are in Ephesus and faithful in Christ"; (b) to interpret the words "those being and" as

---

[11] Papyrus 46 and the fourth-century codices Vaticanus (B) and Sinaiticus (S) before the latter were corrected.

[12] Except in Rom 1:7 in the reading of the ninth-century codex Boernerianus (G).

[13] Tychicus is also mentioned in Col 4:7–9; Titus 3:12; Acts 20:4.

[14] Following a suggestion first made by Th. Beza and H. Grotius, J. Ussher in his *Annales Veteris et Novi Testamenti* (London: Crook, 1650–54) suggested that the space filled in the majority of MSS by "in Ephesus" was originally left empty. In this case it was Tychicus' task to insert into each one of the copies he carried with him the name of the city he was about to visit. Lightfoot, Hort, Haupt, Robinson, Percy, Schlier have endorsed this view. But by N. A. Dahl, TZ 7 (1951), 241–64, and Kümmel, FBK, p. 250, a weighty objection is raised: There is as yet no evidence of ancient circulars containing a blank space for such a purpose. Also no MS of Ephesians has as yet been discovered that would contain the word "in" but leave a blank for the name of a city. By reference to a partly analogous text-critical problem connected with the absence or occurrence of a name, D. N. Freedman has (by letter) suggested the following analysis of the history of the words "in Ephesus" in Eph 1:1. The autograph perhaps contained the name of another city, county, or province (see the next NOTE under (c) for the possibility of "Asia"); for some reason in an early copy this name was omitted. A later scribe felt that the syntax of the sentence and analogous letter openings of Paul called for a name and he left a blank space hoping that maybe somebody equipped with proper knowledge would one day fill it. Then, a later copyist inserted "in Ephesus" into the lacuna and this reading became eventually generally accepted. The analogous biblical passage is II Sam [LXX II Kings] 4:1, as reconstructed by F. M. Cross, Jr., *The Ancient Library of Qumran* (New York: Anchor Books, 1961), p. 191, n. 45. —Marcion's Laodicean hypothesis will be discussed in the context of Col 4:16 (AB, vol. 34B).

indicative of their sainthood in fact, not only in appearance;[15] (c) to explain the words "those being" as a misreading of the original reading "of Asia" (in Ephesus), since the form and sequence of the Greek letters appear to permit an error of a copyist;[16] (d) to understand "those being" as expressing (mystical) participation in Him who is Being itself (Exod 3:14).[17] None of these alternatives is convincing, however, and a simplifying version appears preferable. Three decisions have been made to arrive at the simplification proposed in the above translation: (a) the Greek conjunction (*kai*) meaning "and," "also," "namely," "even"[18] which is found before the adjective rendered by "faithful" has been omitted; (b) the translation "faithful" has been preferred to "believers"; (c) the phrase "in the Messiah" has been interpreted by "to the Messiah." Each of these decisions requires explication and may have to be overruled if further evidence should prove them untenable.

a) It is unlikely that Paul wanted to distinguish two classes among the Christians, i.e. a "faithful" group from another larger or smaller group that is "holy."[19] Such a distinction would be unparalleled in the Pauline letters. Even the wild Corinthians are called "sanctified" and "perfect" (I Cor 1:2; 2:6). While occasionally Paul presupposes a sharp division between "those outside" and "those inside," between "the unbelieving" and "the faithful,"[20] he has no room for half- or three-quarter Christians. It is probable that here the Greek conjunction "and" has the meaning of "namely." It serves the purpose of explication[21] and may therefore occasionally be omitted in translation if its intent is preserved.

b) The looseness of Hellenistic Greek grammar would here and in var. lect. Col 1:2 permit the translation, "believers in the Messiah Jesus." But this understanding of the text(s) presupposes that at this point Paul (or a Paulinist author) chooses a diction that falls out of the style of the main Pauline epistles. There[22] Paul speaks, to use a literal translation, of faith, of believing, or of a faithful attitude "to" God or Christ, "into" him, or "upon" him. Or he speaks of "believing that" . . .[23] Sometimes[24] he uses the same terms absolutely, i.e. without mentioning to whom faith is related or what its contents are. His references to the faith "of" Christ or "of" Jesus[25] are usually understood to mean faith "in" Jesus Christ.[26] But there are no passages mentioning "faith" or "believing" in which the content of faith is introduced by the preposition "in" with the following dative. Now an imitator of Paul, perhaps even Paul himself, might well deviate from the apostle's regular mode of speech. If so, then the Messiah Jesus is here and in 1:15 as much the subject matter of faith as in

[15] Bengel considers Rom 13:1, Pokorný (EuG, p. 17), Rom 8:28, as parallels.
[16] So R. A. Batey, "The Destination of Ephesians," JBL 82 (1963), 101.
[17] Origen in the *Catenae*; Basilius the Great, PG 29:612-13.
[18] In Greek *kai. See* LSLex, 857-58; WBLex, 92-94; BDF, *passim* (see Index).
[19] In his commentary on the Pauline letters, Ephraem discovers in Eph 1:1 a differentiation between catechumens and baptized Christians.
[20] I Cor 5:12-13; II Cor 6:14-18; Eph 4:17-21, etc.; but cf. Eph 2:13, 17.
[21] Philologists and grammarians call it *kai epexegetikon*.
[22] E.g. Rom 4:3, 17; 10:14; Gal 2:16; some, but not all, pertinent statements are quotes from the LXX.
[23] E.g. Rom 6:8; 10:9; I Thess 4:14   [24] E.g. Rom 1:16; II Cor 4:13.
[25] E.g. Rom 3:22, 25, 26; Gal 2:16; 3:22.
[26] However, Rom 3:3, 26; 5:19; Gal 2:16, 20; Philip 2:8; not to speak of LXX Num 12:7; I Kings (Samuel) 2:35; 3:20; 22:14; Heb 3:1-6; 12:2, suggest a different interpretation; see the first NOTE on 2:8 and the literature mentioned there in fn. 85.

the differently phrased verses Gal 2:16; Rom 10:11; Philip 3:9; etc. But the stereotyped or technical meaning or meanings which the phrase "in Christ" often has in Paul[27] suggests an interpretation which is less prone to fall out of the usual Pauline diction. The result of this grammatical observation is an understanding of faith which is not restricted to the intellectual and emotional attitudes but includes ethics; see COMMENT I.

c) The version "faithful to the Messiah Jesus" is given preference over the literal translation: believers "in the sphere of the Messiah Jesus." The translation must express a warm, personal, active relationship to the Messiah rather than an ambiguous mystical, psychic, or geographical dissolution of all distinctly human and ethical elements in a given atmosphere. Indeed Ephesians will describe the saints as men resurrected and enthroned with Christ and in Christ in heavenly places, 2:6. But their personal salvation and responsibility, even the doing of good works, is by no means excluded by their privileged location, 2:10; 5:8–9; 6:8.

A viable second choice besides the version here offered might be, "who are the Messiah Jesus' faithful people."

2. *Grace and peace . . .* see COMMENT II.

COMMENTS I–II on 1:1–2

I   In Christ

The phrase "in Christ" or a variation of it occurs, within the NT, in Pauline writings only—though the Gospel of John contains some analogies. It is especially frequent in Ephesians. In 1:3–14 alone it is found no less than eleven times. This key term of Paul's theology is a puzzle that has been treated in any number of monographs and excurses.[28] Mythical (Schlier in his commentary), mystical (Schweitzer), existential,[29] sacramental (Bouttier), local (Deissmann), historical and eschatological (Lohmeyer, Neugebauer, Bouttier),[30] juridical (Parisius), and ecclesiastical (Grossouw)[31] interpretations compete for recognition or are grouped together in various selections (Büchsel and most commentators). "It may also be that *en* [i.e. the preposition "in" in the formula "in Christ"] is meant to be instrumental"[32]—specifically when Paul's Greek diction is understood to have been influenced by Hebrew or Aramaic. The impossibility of elaborating a final definition of the meaning of "in Christ" may well have a simple cause: namely that Paul used the formula in more than one sense. Allan misses in Ephesians that deeper meaning which supposedly exists exclusively in the genuine Pauline epistles. Percy[33] arrives at exactly the opposite result when he speaks of "complete agreement with the recognized Pauline epistles." Kümmel[34] observes that only in Ephesians are three specific variants of the formula found: "in Christ Jesus," 3:11; "in Jesus," 4:21; "in the Lord," 1:13. Neugebauer seeks to distinguish between the different mean-

---

[27] And which is obvious in the letter openings Col 1:2; I Thess 1:1; II Thess 1:1; I Cor 1:2; Philip 1:1, not to mention about 150 other Pauline passages.
[28] See BIBLIOGRAPHY 6.   [29] Bultmann, ThNT, I, 327–28; II, 177.
[30] Cf. Gaugler, pp. 15, 262–63; Maurer, EvTh 11 (1951–52), 151–72.
[31] Cf. Bultmann, ThNT, I, 311.   [32] Bultmann, ThNT, II, 177.
[33] Pp. 290–91.   [34] FBK, p. 254.

ings of the variants. When in the Pauline letters reference is made to "in Jesus Christ," the crucified and risen Lord is called to remembrance. When Paul says "in Christ," he puts the emphasis upon the relation between God's Son and the church. Finally, the formulation "in the Lord" is primarily found in hortatory passages and points to the one who commands. More important may be the fact[35] that, in about one-half of the occurrences of the phrase in Ephesians, God is the subject of the decision or action made "in Christ." At least in these passages[36] an instrumental rather than a spatial, mystical or sacramental sense must be accepted. The phrase will be discussed further when the occasion arises.[37] Here it suffices to observe that in all passages[38] the phrase denotes the relationship formed by Jesus Christ between God and God's people, rather than a bond established by faith or sacraments between Christ and individuals only. While Paul frequently speaks of the submission of principalities and powers "to Christ," he never refers to their being "in Christ."

According to Eph 1:1, the saints are inseparable from the Messiah Jesus. Especially in the verses 1:3-14, Paul gives an extensive description of the ground, mode, revelation, extent, and purpose of this relationship. There it becomes apparent that the formula "in Christ" serves equally well to describe (a) God's election before the foundation of the world, (b) God's saving and revealing action in the time of fulfillment, and (c) God's present manifestation and claim in the congregation.[39] The phrase denotes inclusion in the Messiah. Schlier affirms that in 1:1, Paul designates by the words "in Christ" the ground on which, or the sphere in which, the faithful saints live and move. But "ground" and "sphere" must not be understood as impersonal entities.

But should faith on the ground of Christ militate against faith in Christ?[40] Certainly God's people cannot exist in the realm or under the kingship of Christ without faith in Christ. If only Paul is not understood in too limited a sense! As long as faith is confused with men's belief that . . . , or belief in . . . , it may be easily mistaken for a mental or sentimental attitude of credulity however solid. Not even the distinction and combination of *notitia, assensus, fiducia* exhaust its constituent elements. Later passages of Ephesians will show that in addition to credulity, consent, conviction, and trust, many other attitudes and actions distinguish the saints. They have a new life. Their conduct, joy, suffering, hope—and all of these things in their communal manifestation—are their decisive marks. True faith is faithfulness "on the ground of" . . . , or faith "in relation to" . . . ,[41] or in short, faithfulness "to" the Messiah. New life, new being, new creation and existence are not eventual consequences of faith, but its very being. Such faith is the result of the presence of the power of the Messiah. *It came* when *he came,* Gal 3:16, 19, 23, 25. It pertains to all as-

---

[35] Pointed out by Maurer, EvTh 11 (1951–52), 160–62.
[36] Esp. in 1:3–14, except 1:7, 12–13.   [37] See esp. COMMENT V on 1:3–14.
[38] Including II Cor 5:17, as Gal 3:26–29 shows.
[39] Cf. Ch. Bricka, *Le fondement christologique de la morale Paulinienne* (1923), pp. 8 ff. He calls the formula *"in Christ,* le mobile christologique" of Paul's theology (ref.). See also COMMENT V on 1:3–14.
[40] Bultmann, ThNT II, 178, states frankly, "[In Ephesians], in distinction to Paul, 'believe' and 'faith' play a relatively unimportant role."
[41] Cf. the "faith among one another," viz. the "common faith" mentioned in Rom 1:12, and the "faith . . . toward all the saints" mentioned in the shorter variant of Eph 1:15.

pects of human existence. It embraces and determines social relations as much as matters of the heart and of knowledge.[42]

II   The Initial Blessing

The form and content of the words "Grace and peace to you from God our Father and the Lord Jesus Christ" are different from the good wish found in the first lines of Greek letters.[43] The blessing constitutes an independent sentence. The word "grace" is used instead of the usual Greek "rejoice."[44] The Semitic greeting "peace," is added. And "grace and peace" is qualified by the distinctly Christian references to "God our Father"[45] and "the Lord Jesus Christ." Since the same or a similar form of blessing is found not only in the opening of the other Pauline letters but also in I Peter 1:2; II Peter 1:2; and Rev 1:4, it is probable that the combination of the words "grace" and "peace," and a qualification of both through reference to their divine source and Christological implementation was known to practically all Christian congregations. The place and occasion for such a formula was the worshiping assembly.[46] It is still impossible to trace it back to a specific place, e.g. to the Jerusalem, Samaria, or Antioch church, but wherever it originated, the use of the formula by Paul reveals his solidarity with the faith and worship of the churches founded before the beginning of his mission work. Also, it gives the Pauline writings an official and liturgic character.

In the formulation used by Paul (cf. Rev 1:4), the origin or character of "grace and peace" is given more emphasis than the unqualified words "grace" and "peace" bear individually. The giver determines the contents and value of the gift. "Grace and peace" are "from God our Father and the Lord Jesus Christ." In the OT[47] the name "Lord" (*Yahweh*) is frequently used to identify God, i.e. to specify which one among the many persons in heaven and upon earth called *gods* (*elim*, *'elōhīm*) has revealed himself to Israel and is worshiped by his people and true servants. Equally, Paul reproduces a formula which signals in the briefest possible terms who the God is who gives "grace and peace."[48] It is probable that the apostle uses the exact traditional form of blessing when no article is found before God, and when the oppositive "our Father," or "Father" (Eph 6:23), follows immediately upon God. In these cases it is never explicitly asserted that God is "the Father of Jesus Christ."

---

[42] See e.g. Eph 1:15; 3:17–19; 6:1 (longer variant). Bultmann, ThNT, II, 177, calls "in Christ" "Paul's own phrase to denote Christian existence." He continues by affirming that in Eph 1:1 a "set formula" is used which means no more than "Christian."

[43] See Lohmeyer's and Friedrich's essays mentioned in Introduction, fn. 239; the articles on grace and on peace in theological wordbooks; also A. Pujot, "De salutatione apostolica 'Gratia vobis et pax,' " VD 12 (1932), 38–40, 76–82 (ref).

[44] The latter is found in I Macc 10:18, 25, etc.; James 1:1; Acts 15:23; 23:26.

[45] See J. Jeremias, *The Prayers of Jesus*, SBT, 2d ser. 6 (1967), 11–65.

[46] The absence of articles before the nouns, the comprehensive contents, and the evident rhythm of the diction support this assumption. Cf. I Cor 12:13; I Tim 3:16, etc.; also section II of the Introduction.

[47] E.g. at the beginning of the Ten Commandments, Exod 20:2; Deut 5:6; in the story of the divine judgment on Mount Carmel, I Kings 18:36, 39; and in the book of Jonah; cf. H. Rosin, *The Lord is God*, Amsterdam: Netherlandsch Bijbelgenootschap, 1956.

[48] In I Cor 8:5–6 he acknowledges that there are "many who are called gods and lords in heaven and upon earth," but he quotes the confession saying that "for us God is one, the Father . . . and the Lord is one, Jesus Christ." The philosophical concept of monotheism does not fit this confession. G. von Rad, OTTh, I, 210–11, suggests replacing it with "monolatry." But since this term describes a form of polytheism, it is also misleading.

But when Paul makes a slightly independent reformulation[49] he often sets the article before "God" and connects the words "God" and "Father" with the conjunction "and": "The God and Father." On these occasions he either makes it explicit that God is the Father of our Lord Jesus Christ,[50] or he designates him as "our Father."[51] While sometimes God's fatherhood remains undefined,[52] there are several passages in which Paul elaborates upon the ground, the mode, the extension, and the consequences of the attribute "Father." God's father-hood precedes the creation of the world. It is extended to more than just men. Above all, the same breath which proclaims it, confesses also Jesus Christ the Son and his work, often also the Holy Spirit.[53] Only "in Christ" do men be-come God's children (Eph 1:5). Only because of the work of the Spirit do they call upon God as their Father (Gal 4:6; Rom 8:15; cf. Eph 2:18).

Jesus Christ is called "Lord." While in the OT, "Lord" (*'adōnāy;* LXX *kyrios*) substitutes in liturgy and speech for the name of God, Yahweh,[54] the NT formula of blessing uses "Lord" as a title—just as "Messiah" was origi-nally a title, not a name. The formula used for blessing presupposes that "lord" has so wide and general a meaning (just as "god" in the OT) that the noun requires a specification. The addition of the name "Jesus Christ" reveals which among the many lords is meant. The various meanings of the Greek word "lord" reflected in the NT[55] and the influence of the LXX and of Aramaic-speaking congregations upon its usage (see e.g. I Cor 16:22) is too broad a subject to be discussed here.[56]

Among the many relevant open questions raised by the Initial Blessing, one is whether the conjunction "and" between "God" and "Lord" implies that early Christianity, including Paul and some second-century theologians, ascribed grace and peace to the operations of God and of a "second," or "other god," that is, Jesus Christ.[57] The answer can be found in Ephesians in the Great Benediction contained in 1:3–14. There the preposition "in," i.e. the phrase "in Christ," provides an explication of the relationship between God the Father and Jesus Christ which excludes polytheistic notions. In the light of the inter-pretation which that great blessing adds to the Initial Blessing, the word "and" (between "Father" and "the Lord") possesses in the short formula of 1:2 an ex-

---

[49] Or, when he follows another liturgical tradition.

[50] Eph 1:3; II Cor 1:3; 11:31; Rom 15:6; cf. I Peter 1:3.

[51] I Thess 1:3; 3:11, 13; Gal 1:4; Philip 4:20. Perhaps also Eph 5:20 belongs here or in the pre-ceding footnote.

[52] Eph 5:20; I Thess 1:1; I Cor 15:24; Philip 2:11.

[53] Such elaborations are specifically frequent and intensive in Ephesians; see 1:3–5; 3:15–16; 4:6. The beauty of the praise of God's fatherhood in Rom 8 surpasses all other passages. Rom 4 and Gal 3 are especially important for the connection and differences between God's and Abra-ham's fatherhood.

[54] Exod 3:13–15; 6:2–3, etc.

[55] "Lord" is the title given to an owner of slaves or other property (Matt 20:8; Gal 4:1; John 13:16) and to a person who is addressed, as by "Mr.," "Sir" (Matt 25:11; Acts 16:30). "Lord" is also used to exalt potentates; increasingly the title includes the attribution of divine characteristics (Matt 22:43; Acts 25:26). Finally, "Lord" is used for describing a deity in cultic action and con-fession (I Cor 12:3; Philip 2:11).

[56] For an introduction to the enormous literature see the bibliographies in WBLex, 459–61; TWNTE, III, 1039–40. See also e.g. Kramer, *Christ, Lord, Son of God,* and Hahn, *Titles of Jesus in Christology,* pp. 68–135.

[57] Justin Martyr *dialogus cum Tryphone Judaeo* 56, *apologia* I 13 (henceforth *dial., apol.*); Irenaeus *adv. haer.* II 28; Origen *c. Cels.* V 39. In Philo there are precedents and in III Enoch faint parallels to the polytheistic sound of Justin's and Irenaeus' diction. See Hegermann, *Schöpfungsmittler,* pp. 38, 52, 58, 72 f., 76 f., 82–85, 132–35, and H. Odeberg, *Third Enoch, or, The Hebrew Book of Enoch,* Cambridge University Press, 1928.

pository or epexegetical sense, corresponding to the English "namely," or "that is." The origin of grace and peace is in this case God our Father, i.e. He who is revealed, present, active in the Lord Jesus Christ. He is God our Father because he is "God of our Lord Jesus Christ" (Eph 1:17) and Father of his "beloved son" (1:6).[58] Not a dialectic tension (not to speak of polytheism) but —just as in the Lord's prayer—a full identification of "God" with the work of the "Lord," and of the "Father of Jesus Christ" with "our Father" is expressed by the words "God our Father and the Lord Jesus Christ."

The only precedent and parallel by which the essential operative unity of God's and Jesus Christ's blessing can be illustrated is contained in the Law, the Prophets, and the Psalms of the OT. In II Cor 6:18 Paul alludes to passages such as II Sam 7:14; Jer 31:9; and Hosea 1:10, 11:1. In these OT texts the adoption of God's people is attributed to the Sonship of the One chosen by God. In the royal Psalms 2, 72, 89, 110, and 132, descriptions are found of the blessing of God given to God's Anointed and through him to many beneficiaries, i.e. God's people. In Exod 14:31[59] the bold formulation is found, "They believed in God and in his servant Moses." As little as such OT affirmations imply a deviation from the confession of the One God (Deut 6:4–5), are the briefer or longer Blessings of Eph 1 a denial of Israel's God and faith. Indeed there is a difference of rank and honor between the Messiah Jesus and the chosen and anointed servants of God of earlier times. "Here is more than Solomon" (Matt 12:42; Luke 11:31)! But it is a difference within the blessing and confession of the same One God. Cf. the expression "kingdom of God's Messiah" (lit. "of the Messiah and God") in Eph 5:5. When a Jew writes such words he is not thinking of two sovereigns ruling in possible competition; rather through the Messiah installed at his right hand God exerts his own monarchic rule.

Many congregations using the formula quoted in Eph 1:2 may have forgotten that the word "Christ" was originally not part of a name, but a title. It duplicated the title "Lord." But whether used as titles or names, "Christ" and "Lord" are reminders of the ties existing between Jesus, the church, and Israel. In Ephesians Paul shows not only his solidarity with the churches before him, but equally and all the more the unity of the church and Israel.[60]

The gift of the Father and Lord is "grace and peace." The blessing with grace and peace is always imparted to the saints by an authorized man, here by an "apostle." Like Aaron's Blessing (Num 6:24–26), it is not just a good wish or a kind offer of God or a man; rather it is God's deed. "The grace of God is given to you in Jesus Christ . . . He is the peace . . . Let us hold fast the peace with God through our Lord Jesus Christ . . . Grace has become king . . . You are under grace."[61] What is meant by "grace" and "peace"?

---

[58] Cf. Abbott; in John 20:17; Matt 11:25–27; 27:46 this relation is made explicit.

N.B. When, as here with "Abbott," page numbers are not given, the reference is to his work listed in Bibliography I, Commentaries and Special Studies, specifically to the interpretation to be found there of the verse under discussion.

[59] Cf. Exod 4:1, 31; 19:9; II Chron 20:20.

[60] See esp. 2:1–6, 11–22; 3:5, also COMMENT XIV on 1:3–14.

[61] I Cor 1:4; Eph 2:14; Rom 5:1, 21; 6:15. In Rom 5:1 the subjunctive, "let us hold fast the peace" is to be read, following the better MSS.

In the LXX the Greek equivalent of the English "grace"[62] (*charis*) is frequently used to render a Hebrew term (*ḥēn*) which denotes the favor shown by a superior to an inferior. It describes God's love and the steadfastness with which he keeps the covenant. Unlike the parallel concepts, "righteousness," "truth," and "faithfulness," the Hebrew word *ḥēn* is not used to describe the correct bilateral attitude of both covenant partners. It means God's unilateral, specific, personal favor to man. Furthermore, while pardon or amnesty are certainly not eliminated as signs of a sovereign's favor, forgiveness is not the primary connotation or synonym of "grace." Forgiveness presupposes sin. Though forgiveness is strong enough to overcome sin (Eph 1:6-7; cf. 2:1-8) it is subsequent to it. Without sin, there need not be forgiveness. Grace, however, precedes sin in every sense. Grace would exist even if there were no sin.

With this corresponds another observation: grace in its biblical sense is not an alternative to judgment.[63] Rather, through God's righteous judgment his grace and truth to Israel become triumphant.[64] While in the OT Israel and God's elect servants are privileged in experiencing God's grace, Paul employs the same term in most cases to describe God's will, means, and success in incorporating the Gentiles into his people. This is true of all Pauline epistles; it is, however, most pointedly brought to light in Ephesians. Among the commentators J. A. Robinson especially has elaborated this basic aspect and meaning of "grace."[65] The widely spread individualistic understanding of grace, which since Augustine's time has also been heavily loaded with psychological and metaphysical elements,[66] is certainly not true to the specific nuances which this term possesses in Paul, least of all to the intention and testimony of Ephesians.

Equally, "'peace' is an emphatically social concept."[67] It is a gift of God affecting the totality of psychic, physical, personal, familial, economic, and political dimensions of man's life. "Wholeness" has been suggested as another translation. Though one LXX passage, i.e. Hag 2:9, speaks of "peace of the soul," a general observation is possible: According to the Bible "peace" is primarily neither peace of the soul nor escape from earthly conditions and social responsibility. "Peace on earth" (Luke 2:14) is salvation for, not from, the world. In ancient Israel the hope for peace has again and again been concentrated upon a Messiah to come, that is, a "prince of peace" and savior of

---

[62] See theological wordbooks, also Robinson, pp. 121-28, 221-28; Bultmann, ThNT, I, 288-314; T. F. Torrance, *The Doctrine of Grace in the Apostolic Fathers*, Edinburgh: Oliver, 1948; C. Spicq., *Theologie Morale* (Paris: Gabalda, 1965), pp. 451-61); for the OT background, N. H. Snaith, *The Distinctive Ideas of the Old Testament*, 5th ed. (London: Epworth, 1953), pp. 127-30; and K. W. Neubauer, *Der Stamm CHNN im Sprachgebrauch des Alten Testamentes*, Berlin: Reuter, 1964.

[63] As is, e.g. "mercy," James 2:13, or "cancelling of debt," Matt 18:23-35.

[64] See e.g. Ps 43 (*Judica . . .*); cf. Pss 7:8-11; 9:18-20; 35:24; 96:10, 13; Isa 11:4. God's "righteousness" is according to the OT his saving deed, and God's judgments are his way to save. But the author of Ps 143:2 asks to be spared from God's judgment.

[65] See esp. pp. 224-26.

[66] Cf. the meanings of "grace" in the *Corpus Hermeticum* (henceforth *Corp. Herm.*), e.g. I 32; XIII 12, in neo-Platonic philosophy, and in magical rites, see H. Conzelmann, WBNT, IX, 366, for references. On Augustine see D. Ritschl, *Memory and Hope* (London: Macmillan, 1967), pp. 102-40.

[67] Von Rad, TWNTE, II 406; cf. J. Pedersen, *Israel, Its Life and Its Culture*, four vols. in two, 2d ed. (Oxford University Press, 1946), I-II, 263-335; J. J. Stamm and H. Bietenhard, *Das Wort im Alten und Neuen Testament*, Zurich: Zwingli, 1959.

the poor.[68] The references to the "covenant of peace" made with Levi, also the priestly peace blessing, reveal that the anointed priests had a decisive role to play in the establishment, proclamation, and maintenance of peace.[69] In various ways several NT writers attest that now, in Jesus Christ's coming, death, and resurrection, and through the preaching of the gospel in all places, the Messianic peace has finally come.[70] The short blessing of Eph 1:2 states unmistakably that the peace now given comes from that God who has fully revealed his favor and carried out his decision in the Lord Jesus Christ. Ephesians refers to the Messianic peace. This peace is here pronounced to the saints and over them. The rest of the epistle will show that it reaches far beyond the limited number of those who have always been or newly become near to God.

In sum, the terms "grace" and "peace" are related to one another in the same way as covenant and life, and the sense of each extends beyond the individualistic or psychological. The "grace and peace" given through the Messiah includes the Gentiles. Ephesians contradicts Ps 2:9 by omitting any mention of the nations that are "dashed in pieces like pottery." Rather "good news are preached" to the Gentiles; cf. Gal 1:16. Now the promises given to the "outcasts of Moab" (Isa 16:4); now the gathering of the nations on the mountain of the Lord (Isa 2:2–4; Micah 4:1–3); now the mercy of God shown to Nineveh regardless of Jonah's grudge, have become true on a world-wide, unprecedented scale.

[68] Isa 9; 11; 32; Ezek 34; 37; Pss 72:7, cf. 85:8, 10.   [69] Num 25:12; 6:24–26; Mal 2:4–5.
[70] E.g. John 14:27; 20:19, 21; Acts 10:36; Eph 2:13–17; 6:15; cf. 3:6, "in the Messiah Jesus [and] through the gospel."

II THE FULL BLESSING
(1:3–14)

1   3 Blessed is God the Father of Our Lord Jesus Christ. He has blessed us in Christ with the full spiritual blessing of the heavens. 4 As [we confess]

> to live by love [, standing] holy and blameless before him.
> Before the foundation of the world he has chosen us in Christ
> 5 He has predesignated us through Jesus Christ to become his
>   children / according to his favorable decision
> 6 so that the glory of his grace be praised
>   which in his beloved son he has poured out upon us.
> 7 Through [the shedding of] his blood
>   we possess freedom in him, forgiveness of our lapses.
> Such are the riches of his grace
>   8 which in all wisdom and prudence he has lavished upon us.
> 9 He has made known to us the secret of his decision
>   —for he has set his favor first upon Christ
>   10 That he should administer the days of fulfillment—
> "All things are to be comprehended under one head, the Messiah,
>   Those in heaven and upon earth—under him!"

11 As resolved by him who carries out all things after his will and decision, we [Jews] were first designated and appropriated in the Messiah. 12 We, the first to set our hope upon the Messiah, were to become a praise of God's glory. 13 You [Gentiles] too are [included] in him. For you have heard the true word, the message that saves you. And after you came to faith you, too, have been sealed with his seal, the promised Holy Spirit.

> 14 He is the guarantee of what we shall inherit
>   [to vouch] for the liberation of God's own people,
>   to the praise of his glory.

NOTES

1:3. *Blessed is God. . . . He has blessed us in Christ.* One infinitely long, heavy, and clumsy sentence, replete with dependent clauses, excurses, specifications, repetitions, and the like, runs in the Greek text from vs. 3 through to vs. 14. E. Norden called this statement, "the most monstrous sentence conglomeration . . . I have ever met in the Greek language."[1] The diction of the Deuteronomic sermons and of some Qumran passages, also the "Asian" style of rhetoric, offer precedents. In the version given above, an attempt has been made to make visible the distinctness, the beauty, and the sense of the several limbs of the "monster." The unity and structure of the whole will be discussed in COMMENT I.

The verb rendered by "to bless" means in non-Jewish Greek literature "to speak well of," "to praise." The verbs "to thank," "to glorify," "to sing the praises of," "to confess," are appropriate synonyms.[2] In the LXX and other books written by Jews, including the NT, the verb "to bless" has adopted a second meaning which is probably directly derived from the double or reciprocal meaning of the Hebrew equivalent (*bārak*).[3] The blessing which God promises to give Abraham (Gen 12:1–3) and the praise offered by man to God or fellow man (LXX Ps 15[16]:7; Neh 11:2) are described by the same verb. It may also mean, to consecrate things (Exod 23:25; Mark 8:7; I Cor 10:16). In Eph 1:3 a play on words takes place (called among the Greeks *antanaklasis*) which makes use of the two primary meanings of the verb in the LXX, and of the noun, "blessing," in addition. While Jews might have easily appreciated this stylistic nicety, it may have been a puzzle to Greeks unless they had first gotten acquainted, through the Bible, the synagogue, or conversation, with the peculiar use made of the Greek language by Jews. A newcomer to church or synagogue may have mistaken the blessing given by God to man for a praise of man by God. Perhaps in order to counteract such misapprehension the NT writers employ the verbal adjective *eulogētos* to describe God when he is praised by men, but the passive participle *eulogoumenos* to designate men who are blessed by God. Cf. e.g. Luke 1:68 with Luke 19:38! While in classic Greek the verbal adjective denotes a being that is to be blessed, or is praiseworthy, in the vernacular (*koine*) Greek of the Hellenistic time and of the NT, the same form of the verb is fully identified with the meaning of the passive form. It describes one (being) praised or blessed. Just as in the case of the passives "called," "beloved," and "elect," the verbal adjective has become an adjective describing a state of affairs rather than a wish or necessity. The

[1] *Agnostos Theos*, p. 253, n. 1. For the following interpretation see BIBLIOGRAPHIES 1 and 7. An introduction to the Jewish cult is given by I. Elbogen, *Der jüdische Gottesdient in seiner geschichtlichen Entwicklung*, 2d ed. (Frankfurt: Kauffmann, 1924), esp. pp. 14–154, 206–21; StB, IV, 153–88. See also F. Blass, *Die Rhythmen der asiatischen und römischen Kunstprosa* (Leipzig: Teubner, 1905), pp. 40 ff., and E. Norden, *Die antike Kunstprosa*, II, 4th ed., Leipzig / Berlin: Teubner, 1923.

[2] Schlier; J. M. Robinson, in *Apophoreta*. See also W. Schenk, *Der Segen im Neuen Testament*, Berlin: Evangelische Verlagsanstalt, 1968; C. Westermann, *Der Segen in der Bibel und im Handeln der Kirche*, Munich: Kaiser, 1968.

[3] See A. Murtonen, "The Use and Meaning of the Words *lebarek* and *berakah* in the Old Testament," VT 9 (1959), 158–77. Deichgräber, *Gotteshymnus*, stresses the influence of sectarian Palestinian and Hellenistic diaspora Judaism.

Hebrew underlying the double meaning of "to bless" strongly suggests the translation "blessed is" in place of the weak "praised be."[4]

The LXX offers a parallel, and most likely an explication, of the surprising formulation "blessed in. . . ." Of course the phrase "blessed us in Christ" could mean that Christ is the instrument or priestly agent *by* which God gives his blessing (see 2:17), or that his rule is the domain in which blessing is given. But Gen 18:18[5] suggests a more subtle meaning. "In Abraham," who is blessed by God, or in his seed, all nations of the earth will be blessed (LXX) or will bless themselves (MT). Abraham is at the same time the beneficiary, the beginning, the model, and the instrument of the blessing in which all nations are to participate. Probably a similar passive and active, parabolic and dynamic function is ascribed to Jesus Christ in Eph 1:3.

the full spiritual blessing. The Greek can be translated by "all," "every," "every kind," "the whole" spiritual blessing.[6] When the Hebrew equivalent for "all" is used in phrases similar to Eph 1:3 it gives the noun to which it belongs an intensive meaning.[7] The same may be true of the use of "all" in Ephesians: the interpretation has to avoid any shade of doubt that the blessing may be a composite of many parts. There is no hint that God's one full blessing should be split up into several distinct parts.[8] The blessing given "in Christ" and described in the following eleven verses is an indivisible and perfect whole. If any of its many aspects or dimensions[9] were missing, it would not only be incomplete but distinct from the "blessing [given] in Christ." Instead of expressing joy in but one, two, or three feats of God,[10] the author praises the one Christ (4:5) whose oneness is matched by the singleness of the total blessing. The totality of God's gracious manifestation is extolled in the blessing of 1:3–14. This part of Ephesians is a summary of the whole message the apostle wants to give.[11]

For the meaning of "spiritual" see COMMENT II.

of the heavens. Lit. "in the heavenlies." While the heavenly Father, the heavenly Son, heavenly men and angels, the heavenly kingdom and Jerusalem, a heavenly calling and other heavenly things are mentioned in other books of the NT, only Ephesians mentions *ta epourania* (heavenly places, or things). Certainly, Eph 1:3 might be understood as saying, God has blessed, among all the heavenly angels, precisely us, the saints. Then heavenly beings would be either witnesses of God's blessing, or they would be bypassed in favor of men. But since elsewhere in Ephesians the phrase "in the heavenlies" always denotes

---

[4] BDF, 128:5

[5] Quoted in Gal 3:8; cf. Gen 12:3; 22:18; Deut 32:18; Isa 41:8; 51:1–2; Acts 3:25; see also the Midrash GenR 44 (27a).

[6] Cf. WBLex, 636–37, and the various translations given of the Greek word *pās* in 1:8, 21; 2:21; 4:2, 19; 5:3, etc. Schlier's translation of 1:3, "Alles, was Segen . . . heisst [the epitome, the sum of all that is called blessing]" is beautiful.

[7] E.g. 1QpHab VIII 13; cf. Kuhn, NTS 7 (1960–61), 337.

[8] JB enumerates seven, perhaps in the noble intention to "count your blessings." It is more likely that God's one blessing is shown to be complete by having a structure consisting of seven members.

[9] E.g. "election," "forgiveness," "revelation," "glorification," "unification of all things," "sealing," "joining" of Jews and Gentiles, the gift of hope.

[10] As Jews celebrating the Seder sing, *Dajjenu* ["it would have been enough"], after mentioning each of the great deeds of God in the time of the Exodus.

[11] Schlier, p. 72; Maurer, EvTh 11 (1951–52), 151 ff.; Dahl, TZ 7 (1951), 262.

a location,[12] a place is probably meant in 1:3, also. The heavens are either the place from which God blesses, or the storehouse of his blessing, or (cf. 2:6) the residence already granted to the saints. The translation "blessing of the heavens" was chosen in order to leave room for either interpretation. Possible origins and meanings of the term "heavens" are discussed in COMMENT III. In our translation of Ephesians, the plural "heavens" always (except in 4:10) stands for "the heavenly places." The singular "heaven" is used to render the more common Greek term (*ouranos*) which in the NT occurs sometimes in the singular,[13] sometimes in the plural, in Ephesians only in the plural.

4. *As* [*we confess*]. The Greek word (*kathōs*) translated by "as" is frequently used for introducing a comparison; in those cases an explicit or implicit "so also" follows upon it and prepares for the second member of the comparison.[14] But only in a minority of the eighty-four instances of this word in the Pauline literature does it have this sense. On rare occasions[15] the conjunction "as" is causal, or temporal and causal at the same time. More often[16] the conjunction "as" has the function of leading from the author's preceding sentence to a written or oral statement made previously by another person or by the author himself. In these cases, a quotation which is or ought to be known to those presently addressed, is introduced by "as." The vocabulary, style, structure, and contents of Eph 1:4 ff. have persuaded many contemporary scholars that these verses are a quotation from a hymn or confession formed before the composition of Ephesians.[17] For this reason the bracketed words "we confess" have been added to "as." They indicate the literary-technical, i.e. citational, meaning which "as" has here. See COMMENT I.

Before the foundation of the world. Only a falsely literalistic interpreter of the Greek noun (*katabolē*) rendered by "foundation" would insist upon its etymological sense and translation "the throwing-down." The original meaning of the term[18] was probably biological: the throwing of seed; or medical: an attack, e.g. of fever; or astronomical: the birth of a star; and certainly architectural: the laying of foundations.[19] In COMMENT IV reasons will be given why a possible explication and translation of the noun on the basis of Gnostic notions was rejected for the translation.

he has chosen us in Christ. See COMMENT V.

to live by love [*, standing*] *holy and blameless before him.* Lit. "to be holy and blameless before him, in love." The words "by love" or "in love" may belong to vs. 5 rather than to vs. 4. But in 4:2, 16 (and 3:17) the same phrase is found at the end of a sentence. It qualifies the whole preceding affirmation. In 1:4 either God's act of election, or the holy and blameless appearance of

---

[12] I.e. the place of the throne of Christ, 1:20; of the men raised from their death in sin and enthroned with Christ, 2:6; of unspecified principalities and powers, 3:10; of powers hostile to the saints, 6:11–13.

[13] In Matthew especially when the contrast or harmony between "heaven" and "earth" is emphasized, 5:18; 6:10; 11:25; 18:18; 28:18, but not in 16:19; Eph 1:10; Col 1:20; etc. In Luke's writings the plural is rare; in the Johannine writings it does not occur.

[14] So in Pauline writings Rom 1:13; 15:7; II Cor 1:5; 10:7; Eph 4:17, 32; 5:29, etc.

[15] E.g. Rom 1:28; Philip 1:7; cf. Percy, pp. 243–45.

[16] The Pauline use of "as" resembles in this case that of Matthew, Luke, and especially John.

[17] Criteria for discerning hymns and other traditional materials are listed in section II of the Introduction.

[18] See LSLex; WBLex; TWNTE, II, 620–21.

[19] The biological sense underlies Heb 11:10; the architectural, II Macc 2:29.

those chosen by God, or both are qualified by "in love." If the phrase were connected with vs. 5, "love" would determine God's act only, rather than also its effect upon man. Some parallel statements in Deuteronomy on election,[20] also Eph 2:4 and 5:1, suggest that God's love is meant. But other OT passages from the same context,[21] as well as the dominant place of love in the ethical exhortation of Eph 4:22 ff., lend equal weight to the assumption that man's love of God or of his fellow man are both focused upon in this passage. It is not necessary to choose between the alternatives, for in the OT[22] the right covenant relationship between God and man is described by the terms "love," "steadfast love," "righteousness," "faithfulness." As pointed out earlier these terms denote the reciprocal attitude of both covenant partners and also of human partners toward one another. According to Ephesians[23] Jesus Christ is the epitome of both, the chosen one beloved by God and the man loving his fellow man. The reception and the demonstration of God's love among men are as inseparable in this epistle as in I John. The translation of Eph 1:4 must give expression to each of the possible meanings.

Because in later passages Ephesians emphasizes the *life* given by God to those once dead in sins (2:4–6) and the conduct befitting this life, the Greek verb "to be" was rendered as "to live."

The participle "standing" is not found in the Greek text but has been added parenthetically to give full weight to the meaning of "before him," which is easily glossed over. "Before him" denotes the immediate presence of God to man, and the closest proximity of man to God. The image suggests the position and relationship enjoyed by the cream of society at a royal court; by children to their father; by a bride to the bridegroom (see 5:27!), by the priest in the sanctuary or another elect servant of God; or, by a supplicant seeking legal help from a righteous judge. See COMMENT VII and Eph 2:18; 3:12. According to E. Speiser's and M. Dahood's comments (in AB, vols. 1 and 16) on e.g. Gen 6:11; 10:19; Ps 19:15[14], "before him" (Heb. *lepānāw*) means in one biblical tradition as much as "by his will," "at his pleasure." This explanation may also be appropriate to Eph 1:4.

5. *to become his children.* Lit. "for adoption toward him." Special, though linguistically awkward, emphasis is laid on the words "toward him." Apparently other real or imaginary, salutary or catastrophic father-child relationships[24] are excluded by the will of God to make men precisely his and no one else's children. Among the NT writers Paul alone speaks explicitly of adoption. Others speak of the father-child relationship between God and man, but they prefer biological imagery and mention a specific role which the word of God, the Spirit, the resurrection of Christ, or the reception of Christ in faith has in the act of birth or rebirth.[25] Paul's utterances on adoption emphasize the causative and cognitive power of the Spirit[26] and at the same time the juridical-economical implication of adoption: those adopted receive an inherit-

[20] As 4:37; 7:8, 13; 10:15; cf. also I John 3:1.   [21] Deut 5:10; 6:5; 7:9; 10:12.
[22] In Deuteronomy and elsewhere, esp. in Hosea 2:19–20.   [23] 1:6; 3:19; 5:25, 29.
[24] As mentioned e.g. in Eph 2:3; John 8:39, 44; 17:12; I John 3:10; Matt 23:9.
[25] Rom 8:15, 23; 9:4; Gal 4:5; James 1:18; John 1:12–13; 3:5–8; I John 3:9, etc.; I Peter 1:3.
[26] Rom 8:14–16; Gal 4:6; cf. Eph 1:13; not in Rom 9:4 where the adoption of Israel only is listed among other privileges of Israel.

ance.[27] His specific concern is always the inclusion of the Gentiles among the children adopted by God.

his favorable decision. Lit. "according to the favor of his will." Outside of Alexandrian literature, there are but rare traces of the noun "favor." In this translation the Greek noun *eudokiā* has been rendered by an adjective. *Eudokiā* appears nine times in the NT, e.g. in Luke 2:14; eight times in the LXX Psalms; sixteen times in Sirach, and sporadically elsewhere. The meaning of the term includes good pleasure or desire. Far from any idea of arbitrariness, it has warm and personal connotations. When God's good pleasure is mentioned, his willingness and joy in doing good are indicated. The happiness that accompanies a radiant good will is implied.[28] Those singing God's praise (Eph 1:3, 6, 12, 14) are not inventors of joy; but rather by their pleasure in God, they respond to God's pleasure in doing good. Not a grim Lord watching over the execution of his predetermined plan, but a smiling Father is praised. He enjoys imparting his riches to many children.

6. *his grace . . . which . . . he has poured out.* See the description of "grace" in COMMENT II on 1:1–2. In classic Greek the verb *charitoō* translated by "poured out" is found nowhere. In the Bible it appears exclusively here and in Sir 18:14; Luke 1:28. It is a late Greek formation and possesses ambiguous meaning. Here in vs. 6 it occurs after the sophisticated attraction of the relative pronoun "which" (lit. "of which," resuming the preceding genitive *charitos,* lit. "of favor," or "of grace")—a stylistic nicety which could not be made visible in the translation. The Peshitta and Vulgate versions, also Chrysostom, capitalized on the etymology of the verb in question which contains the stem "grace" and an ending often used to express causation. Therefore, they understood it in a causative sense (corresponding to the Hebrew *hiphil*) "to make lovable," or "to fill with grace"; cf. Luke 1:28. Following their interpretation Eph 1:6 deals with the grace by which God made man worthy of his love. A. Bisping[29] declared Eph 1:6 the *locus classicus* of the Tridentine doctrine of infused and inherent grace;[30] to him it seemed to refute for good the Reformers' doctrine of imputed or forensic righteousness. However, there is no philological evidence to demonstrate that the interpretation of Peshitta, Vulgate, and Chrysostom is correct. A literal translation of the whole clause under review has to take its start from analogous Greek and Hebrew idioms:[31]

---

[27] Rom 8:17; Gal 4:1–5; Eph 1:14. G. M. Taylor, "The Function of *pistis Christou* in Galatians," JBL 85 (1966), 58–76, has made an attempt to throw light upon a Roman legal procedure of disbursing an inheritance to the beneficiaries. How is the property of the Father administered and handed out to the adopted heirs? Taylor answers: Paul's imagery in Galatians is an allusion to the institution of a *fidei commissum.* All goods are put into the "trust of Jesus Christ." Christ's trusteeship may be meant by the words usually translated "faith in Jesus Christ." From the totality of inheritance deposited with Christ each one of the adopted sons receives his share.

It is not impossible that the words "through Jesus Christ" in Eph 1:5 refer to the passing of all privileges of sonship through the hands of the Son of God. In this case Paul affirms that already before the foundation of the world the Son was given the *fidei commissum* for the benefit of the many brothers who were to be adopted. See COMMENT XII.

[28] Cf. G. Schrenk, TWNTE, II, 738–51. For the use of "good pleasure" (Heb. *rāṣōn*) in the Qumran literature, see, e.g. E. Vogt, "Peace among Men of God's Good Pleasure," in SaNT, pp. 114 ff.

[29] *Die Briefe an die Epheser, Philipper, Kolosser,* Exegetisches Hb zum NT, II, 2, Münster, 1866 (ref.).

[30] *Decretum de Justificatione* (Sessio VI).

[31] Such as lit. "to love with love," 2:4; "to energize with energy," 1:19; "to call with a call," 4:1; "to comfort with comfort," II Cor 1:4; cf. the English, "to dream a dream," "to die the death."

the Greek uses the cognate expression "begracing with grace," and means exclusively an abundant demonstration of grace; cf. "grace upon grace" (John 1:16).[32]

in his beloved son. Lit. "in the beloved." The term, "the beloved," is a Messianic title. An equivalent, but heavier formulation is found in Col 1:13 where reference is made to the (lit.) "kingdom of the son of his love." In the LXX the passive perfect participle *ēgapēmenos*, which is also used here, occurs as name of the chosen people or their personal representative. In the Blessing of Moses and in Isaiah this participle renders either *Jeshurun* or *yādīd*, i.e. titles or attributes that almost mean "darling."[33] The verbal adjective *agapētos* is in Hellenistic Greek synonymous with the passive participle. In the beginning of LXX Ps 44[45] and in Ps 107:7[108:6] it is used to translate *yādīd*, and elsewhere to express other Hebrew words signifying love.[34] On the other hand, there are also cases in which the term *agapētos*, following an idiomatic meaning of this term in classical and later Greek, renders Heb. *jāḥīd*, i.e. "only [son]," which ought literally to be translated by the Greek *monogenēs*.[35] Thus the originally distinct meanings of *jāḥīd* and *yādīd* became conflated—perhaps because of textual variants in the MSS used by the LXX, perhaps because of misreadings, perhaps in the interest of idiomatic interpretation. In the Synoptic accounts of Jesus' baptism and transfiguration,[36] also in the parable of the husbandmen,[37] the same expression is a distinct addition to, and qualification of, the title "Son." Jesus is not one among those loved by God. He is The Beloved Son. In the time of the Apostolic Fathers[38] "the beloved" appears as a designation of Jesus Christ which need not be supplemented by the noun "Son."

The pouring out of grace *in* the beloved son may be understood in one of three ways. (a) Before the foundation of the world the grace to be given to those not yet created was bestowed upon Christ. (b) The son is the servant enthroned by God, even the instrument by which the saints have now been given grace. (c) The coming, the death, the resurrection of Jesus—in short Jesus himself is the form, the content, the revelation, the transmission of God's overflowing grace. Several Pauline passages[39] support the third among these alternatives. But since it is uncertain whether an exclusive sense is already intimated in Eph 1:6, the translation given leaves open the exact meaning of the words "in his beloved son." Two things do appear certain. The

---

[32] Among the many practical applications of this verse Chrysostom's is a curiosity. Not only juvenation (which supposedly can be derived from the mentioning of the removal of stains and wrinkles in Eph 5:27), but also the gift of fine rhetoric, even of gracious words, was according to him in the apostle's mind.

[33] Robinson, pp. 229–33, whose argument is here followed almost to the letter, mentions as references Deut 32:12, 15; 33:5, 26; Isa 5:1, 44:2; cf. II Chron 20:7; Dan 3:35; Bar 3:37.

[34] I.e. *yakkīr* LXX Jer 38[31]:20; *ahēb*, Zech 13:6.

[35] Gen 20:2; cf. 20:12, 16; Amos 8:10; Jer 6:26; cf. Zech 12:10. In the Alexandrian LXX text of Judg 11:34 "only" and "beloved" are combined; in the Vatican MS alone is the (more correct) translation *monogenēs*, "only," found. See Robinson, pp. 229–30, n. 2, for examples illustrating the idiomatic meaning of *agapētos*.

[36] Matt 3:17 par.; 17:5 par. (except Luke 9:35, but see the variant readings); cf. II Peter 1:17.

[37] Mark 12:6; Luke 20:13.

[38] Barn. III 6; IV 3, 8; Acts of Paul and Thecla 1 (but cf. 24).

[39] Rom 5:15; I Cor 1:4; II Tim 2:1; also the phrase "the grace of our Lord Jesus Christ," II Cor 13:14, etc., and Eph 1:7. See Torrance, *The Doctrine of Grace in the Apostolic Fathers*, pp. 20 ff.

election of men by God and his outgoing grace are inseparably connected with God's warm and personal relation to Jesus Christ. And election cannot be separated from love—or else another election is spoken of than the one discussed in the overture to Ephesians.

7. *Through [the shedding of] his blood.* The text makes a sudden transition from the election before the world's foundation to a specific event, i.e. to Jesus Christ's death on the cross which is also mentioned in 2:14–16; 5:2, 25; Col 1:20. It is unlikely that "blood" refers to the eucharistic cup, but the liturgy of the eucharist may have been the channel through which the congregation became aware of the sacrificial meaning of Christ's blood.[40]

we possess freedom . . . forgiveness of our lapses. The literal translation "we have redemption, forgiveness of our trespasses,"[41] fails to make the reader aware of the boastful assertiveness of each one of the key words used. "We possess" is stronger than the trite "we have." Suddenly men instead of God are the subject of a sentence. A statement about the present rather than a remote past or future is made. The assertion of vs. 7 has a triumphant ring.[42]

"Freedom" is the clear purpose and result of redemption. While in 1:14 the same word is used for a goal yet to be reached, vs. 7 states that what is expected from the future is already at hand. In this verse Paul does not speak of a way to be followed, a function to be fulfilled, or an action to be completed, but of the complete attainment of the ultimate. The peculiar relationship between present and future in Ephesians will be discussed in COMMENT IX.

The choice of "lapses" instead of "trespasses" in the phrase "forgiveness of our lapses" may sound like a belittling of the "trespasses and sins," and of the "decisions of the flesh and of the thoughts" which according to 2:1–3 cause and reveal man's "death." But the apparent mildness of the word "lapse"[43] corresponds to both the original meaning of the Hebrew and Greek terms for "sin," and to the etymology of the Greek synonym which is used in this verse. To sin is to miss the mark or to fall out from the way. The sin of Adam is described in Rom 5:15, 17, 18, 20 by the term "fall." It may stand nearer "misdemeanor" than "felony." Since "trespass" or "transgression" has according to its Pauline definition and usage the specific meaning of violating the law given by God,[44] this term cannot be used for the translation of Eph 1:7 and 2:1–3. The Gentiles addressed in this epistle had not received the privileges of Israel to which the law belongs. "They do not have the law."[45]

---

[40] In section II of the Introduction the specific role of traditional material in Pauline writings is discussed.

[41] Cf. the fifth petition of the Lord's prayer.

[42] In the first script of the Sinaitic and Claromontan codices the present tense "we possess" had been displaced by the future "we shall possess," or "we shall have." This variant avoids many of the problems posed by the triumphalist affirmation of possession. It brings the contents of 1:7 fully in line with 1:14; 4:30. But the more difficult reading is so well attested that even the grave theological problems posed by it have to be accepted as an essential element of Ephesians.

[43] S. de Vries, art. "Sin, sinners," in IDB, IV, 371, defines "trespass" as "individual lapse." Since "transgression" or "trespass" indicates a deliberate breach of law, or a high-handed sin, these concepts are to be reserved for the translation of passages of the Jews' failure to fulfill the law. R. C. Trench, *Synonyms of the New Testament*, repr. of 9th ed. (Grand Rapids: Eerdmans, 1969), pp. 245–47, holds that only a limited number of Scripture passages and biblical interpreters support the definition of *paraptōma* by "sin not of the deepest dye and the worst enormity . . . an error, a mistake in judgment, a blunder."

[44] Rom 4:15: "where there is no law there is no transgression"; cf. Rom 2:23; 5:14; 7:8; also Gal 3:19.

[45] Rom 2:12, 14; 9:4, 30–31; I Cor 9:20–21; Gal 3:19–25.

What they *knew* of God's statutes (Rom 1:32), they knew indirectly, having heard of statutes given to Israel (Deut 4:6). But though they did not "trespass" or "transgress" the limits posed by the law, they still sinned and fell and died, just as Adam did before the Sinai legislation (Rom 5:12–20).[46] From the vantage point of those who now "possess" forgiveness (1:7) and are already raised from death in sins (2:1–6), the sins committed are miserable "lapses." In Ephesians there is no trace of a tragic hamartology (doctrine of sin). As was earlier observed, sin is not the basis or presupposition of grace. Neither is it the foundation upon which theology rests. Its incidental, senseless, wretched character deserves no better than the demeaning term "lapses." Even the plural of this noun (which is always used in Ephesians) appears to make sin a series of pitiable mishaps rather than the grave force it appears to be when Paul discusses sin in the singular.[47] Since occasionally in the undisputed epistles Paul himself speaks of lapses, transgressions, and sins in the plural,[48] the plural used in Ephesians is not a convincing argument against the authenticity of Ephesians.

8. *in all wisdom and prudence.* The position and exact meaning of these words in Greek are much more ambiguous than appears on the surface of the translation. Wisdom and prudence qualify God's action,[49] especially the act of lavishing grace. Several things can be in the mind of the author. (a) He may wish to state that God does not squander grace at random. (b) Wisdom and prudence point out that God adds revelation to the gift of salvation; God's children are not (to use an old simile for grace received in total and absolute passivity) "stones whetted by rain" but are to be aware of their good fortune. (c) Wisdom and prudence are the gift given by God to man to make him behave.[50] Each of these interpretations is supported by parallels in Ephesians. God's own "manifold wisdom" is mentioned in 3:10 (cf. I Cor 2:7). Revelation is emphasized as much in Eph 3 as salvation is in Eph 2. The contents of the "gift" of wisdom are listed in 1:17–18, and in 5:15 the exhortation is found to conduct oneself "not as a fool but as a wise man." Therefore a choice of the first over the third alternative cannot be made nor of the third over the first. In OT diction, "all wisdom" includes both God's own wisdom and the wisdom given to man.[51] The second alternative must not be eliminated either. Certainly the dimension of wisdom and prudence cannot be restricted to the epistemological realm only, for example the imparting of theoretical knowledge.[52] For the knowledge given of God's secret is no theoretical affair.

[46] The mention of "Adam's transgression" in Rom 5:14 is an exception. It may, however, mean his willful "disobedience" (5:19) against a "commandment" (cf. Rom 7:8, 10–11), rather than a transgression of the law. "The law" was given after his fall, with the effect of making sin "accountable" and "trespass abundant" (Rom 5:13, 20).

[47] Rom 3:9, 20; 5:12–13; 6–8 *passim;* 11:23; I Cor 15:56; II Cor 5:21, etc.

[48] Not only in quotations from the OT and traditional Christian formulae (Rom 4:7, 25; I Cor 15:3; Gal 1:4; cf. Eph 1:7; 2:1, 5; Col 1:14; 2:13) but also in formulations and arguments of his own (I Thess 2:16; Gal 3:19; Rom 7:5; I Cor 15:17; II Cor 5:19).

[49] Jer 10:12; 51[LXX 28]:15; Isa 40:28; Ps 104:24; Prov 3:19; cf. Dan 2:20; Rom 16:27. See also the personification and the pairing of virtues and graces, e.g. in Ps 85:10–11. M. Dahood, *Psalms II, 51–100* (AB, vol. 17), NOTE on Ps 85:11, draws attention to the possible mythological background of such pairs.

[50] Exod 31:3; 36:1–2; I Kings 3:9–12, 28; 4:29–30; Prov 2:6; Dan 2:21; Wisd Sol 9:3, 10; Sir 1:1; James 1:5; 3:15; Col 1:9.

[51] LXX Job 26:3; Dan 1:17; Theodotion Dan 1:4.

[52] E.g. Percy, p. 309, n. 66, prefers this limitation.

Wisdom and prudence are the source, the mode, and the result of the out-pouring of God's grace and of revelation.

What is the essence of wisdom?[53] Is there any substantial difference between wisdom and prudence—or are the two terms synonyms (a hendiadys)? In biblical Greek wisdom and prudence are not distinct terms like theoretical and practical reason.[54] Even when the Bible sets earthly wisdom or the wise men of the world in contrast to God's wisdom, no such differentiation becomes apparent.[55] Both words denote the knowledge of how to do something—i.e. the right handling of the right thing at the right moment. Both include the ability to act appropriately in both the epistemological *and* practical realms. The wise man knows how and when to speak; he gives good counsel; he lives up to his gifts; his actions make sense and are successful. For this reason the conjunction "and" between "wisdom" and "prudence" is to be understood as expository. Paul speaks of that wisdom which is operating in prudence.

9. *the secret.* The translation "secret" appears preferable to "mystery." The references made in Ephesians (and Colossians) to the "secret" point to some-thing different from what is meant by "mystery" in Mystery Religions, in Qum-ran, in Gnostic circles, and in ecclesiastical sacramental teaching. See COM-MENT XI.

for he has set his favor first upon Christ. Lit. "according to his favor which he has set forth in him" (cf. 3:11). These words are the beginning of a parenthetical statement which ends with "the days of fulfillment." Two logical connections and corresponding interpretations are possible. (a) The parenthesis may be understood as a comment on vs. 9a, and say as much as: the disclosure of the secret happened through the publication of God's love to and by Jesus Christ, e.g. in his birth, baptism, transfiguration, teachings, miracles, and/or resurrection. The passage would thus contain a hidden reference to the life of Jesus on earth or to specific events during that life. Among the NT epistles, Hebrews contains such references.[56] In Pauline writings, the emphasis placed upon the cross and resurrection overarches the rare allusions made to the birth and the words of Jesus.[57] It would be surprising if suddenly in Eph 1 Paul himself or a pseudonymous writer attributed to the *vita Jesu* a weight which is not seen elsewhere and is explicitly negated in II Cor 5:16, according to some interpreters. It is therefore unlikely that Eph 1:9b–10a alludes to the life of Jesus. (b) More probably the parenthesis serves to introduce the emphatic, comprehensive, and concluding statement contained in 1:10bc.

In its active and its middle forms the verb translated by "he set first upon" possesses a local or temporal meaning which easily leads to metaphorical use. The Greek verb means to set up, to display, to offer as a sacrifice, to propose. It also means to fix, to appoint, to resolve.[58] Among the NT books only the

[53] For the literature on wisdom used here and in COMMENT X see BIBLIOGRAPHY 8.

[54] This differentiation is made by some Greek philosophers, e.g. Aristotle *ethica Nicomachea* VI 1139B–1145A; it is applied to the interpretation of Eph 1:8 by Thomas Aquinas, Bengel, West-cott, Robinson, Gaugler. But cf. LSLex, 1921–22 and 1956. E.g. in Prov 8:12–14 wisdom and prudence are described as co-inherent: "I, wisdom dwell in prudence and I find knowledge . . . I have counsel," etc.

[55] See Isa 29:14; Dan 2; Matt 11:25; I Cor 1:17 – 2:16; James 3:13–18.

[56] E.g. Heb 2:16; 5:7–10; 7:14. Cf. the role of the transfiguration in II Peter 1:16–17.

[57] Rom 1:3; Gal 4:4; I Thess 4:14; I Cor 7:10; cf. Acts 13:23–25; 20:35; I Tim 6:13.

[58] See LSLex 1536.

epistle to the Romans contains the same word. In Rom 1:13 it means to resolve. In Rom 3:25 the viable senses are to foreordain, to appoint, to set forth, or to offer. Therefore, Romans provides no immediate help for the interpretation of Eph 1:9. Neither does the LXX. But the frequent use of the preposition "before" in Eph 1:3-14[59] strongly suggests that a temporal sense is in the foreground. If Christ's title "the first-born"[60] is considered a parallel, then Eph 1:9b intends to say, the same Jesus Christ *in* whom the saints have been elected, *through* whom they were to be adopted, and *through* whose blood they were liberated and forgiven—this Christ is granted God's favor at the head of all creation. In this case Christ is here characterized[61] as the primary and exemplary elect. Election is then, as it were by definition, first and essentially the election of the Son by the Father.[62] See COMMENT V for a more detailed discussion.

The election of men was emphatically described as their designation for a distinct purpose.[63] Equally, the election of Christ is spelled out as his designation for the fulfillment of a commission which is summed up in the following verse. It reveals that this work has temporal, spatial, and political dimensions.

10. *that he should administer.* Lit. "for administration." The translation here proposed is at variance with the versions presented by most of the old and new Bible translations, commentaries and monographs on Ephesians, although H. C. G. Moule comes near it.[64] Philological examinations of the noun *oikonomiā* show that our interpretation is at least as tenable as others, and the context and parallel passages speak strongly in its favor. It pertains specifically to the Christology of the hymnic passage Eph 1:3-14, for it shows that the expression "in Christ" not only designates Christ as an instrument, sphere, or ground, but also pronounces his free and responsible activity in the service of God.

The Greek word that forms the watershed or touchstone is *oikonomiā,* which occurs in Eph 1:10; 3:2, 9. It has manifold meanings that can be sorted into two groups. (a) The noun denotes the duty, occupation, or performance of a manager entrusted with the care of a private estate or city.[65] The same title, *oikonomos,* "steward" or "administrator," which in the early Christian environment was used for an officer in the Serapis sanctuary or in other Hellenistic cultic associations, is in Pauline writings employed for the apostle himself or for

[59] Eph 1:4, 5, 11, 12.
[60] Rom 8:29; Col 1:15, 18.   [61] Just as in Luke 9:35; 23:35; cf. I Peter 1:20.
[62] The ninth-century Codex Porfirianus, the Elzevir edition of the Greek NT, and also Calvin suggest that God's resolution was made "in him," i.e. in the Father himself, rather than that God at the beginning placed his favor upon the Son. This reading and understanding of Eph 1:9 make predestination an absolute decree, if not a whim, of a deity that is in principle solitary. The contents of Eph 1:4-6 pronounce exactly the opposite, and the translation of 1:9 must proceed upon the assumption that the author of 1:3-14 does not contradict himself. God does not make his decision in splendid loneliness. What the Father has resolved to do "in Christ," what he has set upon Christ—this is his will.
[63] I.e. for holiness, adoption, praise (1:4-6).
[64] In his commentary on Ephesians, Cambridge Bible (Cambridge University Press, 1895), pp. 50-51); idem, *Ephesian Studies* (London: Thynnes, 1927), p. 33. The same result is reached by J. Reumann, *"Oikonomia*—Terms in Paul in Comparison with Lucan Heilsgeschichte," NTS 13 (1966-67), 147-67, esp. 164-66; W. Barclay, *The Letter to the Ephesians* (Edinburgh: St. Andrews Press, 1956), p. 98. It is supported by the translations of Eph 1:10 suggested by Schlier; Conzelmann; F. F. Bruce; R. E. Brown (*Biblica* 40 [1959], 74) in opposition e.g. to Dibelius; Masson; O. Michel (TWNTE, V, 152).
[65] So usually in non-biblical Greek, as well as in LXX Isa 22:19, 21; cf. Luke 16:1-8; Gal 4:2; Rom 16:23.

a bishop.[66] (b) The noun can also mean a legal instrument (e.g. revenue), an arrangement, plan, strategy, or magic trick.[67] Evidence for this second sense is derived mainly from papyri. Magical papyri reveal that this meaning had found a way into religious thought or cultic contexts; when the word is found in the environment of metaphysical or liturgical utterances it is best translated by "dispensation."[68] Ignatius uses it apparently in the sense of God's "plan for salvation."[69] In the *Letter to Diognetus* IV 5 it means God's plan regarding nature.

The first meaning is solidly represented in the Bible, and in Pauline writings specifically. But the second is not so well documented. Its occurrence in magical papyri and in the writings of the Apostolic Fathers is not sufficient proof of its endorsement by biblical authors. Granted, Jewish apocalyptic writings and Qumranite literature presuppose that a scheme of salvation exists.[70] This plan is a secret; it consists of mysteries; it is disclosed piece by piece only to selected servants of God; it pertains to the universe and its order as well as to the history of the faithful and the last judgment; it fixes the devolvement of predetermined periods; and it makes the present time more important than any past period.

It is unquestionable that the substance of Eph 1:9–10 is eschatological and that in these verses several terms are used that have a specific, almost "technical" meaning in apocalyptic literature. But can it be demonstrated that apocalyptic determinism is the core of Eph 1:10; 3:2, 9? J. T. Sanders interprets *oikonomiā* in this sense.[71] Others go so far as to use this "un-Pauline" sense for disproving the authenticity of Ephesians.[72] However, at least five reasons speak against this interpretation of *oikonomiā*.

a) If Eph 1:10a meant a fixed plan of God, the text would read "according to [the] *oikonomiā*," and not, as it actually does, "for [the] *oikonomiā*." The author has in mind an uncompleted performance, not a timetable, blueprint, or program.

b) If the plan of God were the contents of the "secret" mentioned in 1:9, or if it were identified with the secret, then this plan ought to be "made known," for 1:9 affirms the secret's disclosure. But no indication is ever given of a revelation of the *oikonomiā*. And even if it were, the revelation of the secret plan might still be a little thing compared with its execution. But in neither 1:10 nor 3:2, 9 is any hint given of the carrying-out of the *oikonomiā*. The reason for this may well be that the noun *oikonomiā* means in itself performance, execution, administration, rather than plan.

---

[66] I Cor 4:1–2; Titus 1:7; cf. I Cor 9:17; Col 1:25; I Tim 1:4; cf. Ign. *Eph.* VI 1.

[67] See LSLex; WBLex.

[68] Or by equivalents such as "order of salvation" or *Heilsgeschichte*. The latter concept has been shifted, again, into the center of discussion by O. Cullmann. Gaugler, pp. 142–43, 233–47, treats it as an essential dogma of Ephesians.

[69] Ign. *Eph.* XVIII 2; XX 1. Cf. Schlier, *Religionsgeschichtliche Untersuchungen zu den Ignatiusbriefen*, BhZNW 8 (1929), 32.

[70] See section III C of the Introduction; also the NOTE on "days of fulfillment" in 1:10, and COMMENTS V, XI, and XIII.

[71] ZNW 56 (1965), 230–31.

[72] E.g. Mitton, pp. 91–94; FBK, pp. 253–54. In section I of the Introduction other words have been listed which supposedly had changed their meaning in a fashion irreconcilable with a common author of Galatians, Corinthians, Romans, Philippians on one side, Ephesians on the other.

c) If Paul is accepted as author of Ephesians then we have no evidence from the LXX or his other epistles that he could be aware, or was aware, of any other meaning of *oikonomiā* besides stewardship or administration. Paul himself would hardly have introduced a completely new sense without any warning. But if Ephesians should be a pseudonymous work produced by an ardent Paulinist, then the author would have been extremely unwise in giving a non-Pauline sense to a well-known Pauline word. More than Paul himself, an imitator would have been faithful to the given sense of a given vocabulary.

d) In the parallel to Eph 1:10, Col 1:25, *oikonomiā* means administration, not plan. According to that text and to I Cor 4:1–2 Paul is given a stewardship. The possibility exists that in Ephesians Christ's function is described by a noun which elsewhere is used for the apostle's work, just as in e.g. Heb 3:1 Christ is given the title "apostle."

e) According to the interpretation of 1:10 by the rest of Ephesians,[73] Christ is an active servant of God rather than a mere instrument or impersonal sphere. The Father's love of the Son; the mediating function of Christ in the adoption of many; the love of Christ for those entrusted to him; the pouring out of his blood; the making and proclamation of peace; the creation of one new man; the access opened to Jews and Gentiles for their approach to the Father; the enthronement in the position of head of the universe and the church; the installation of his many ministers; the life and growth conveyed to his body; the light he makes shine—such descriptions of Jesus Christ show clearly what eminent, active, and responsible functions are given to him.

In short, it is probable that in Ephesians the superiority of Jesus Christ's ministry over that of the prophets, apostles, teachers and other members of the congregation is indicated. He is made The Steward of God. Certainly the author of Heb 3:1–6 would not consider this title noble enough for distinguishing the Messiah's function from Moses'. He insists upon the superiority of the Son of the house over the "manager" (*therapōn*). But elsewhere in the NT the Son *is* called Servant; see e.g. Mark 10:43–45; Philip 2:7. According to Eph 1:10, 22–23; 4:8–10 (cf. 2:20–22), Christ is entrusted not only with the care of God's people, but with the responsibility to rule in God's name over all times, spaces, powers. See COMMENT XII below, and COMMENT V on 1:15–23.

the days of fulfillment. Lit. "of the fullness of times." A discussion of the various meanings of "fullness" will be found below in the NOTE on 1:23 and in COMMENT VI C on 1:15–23. At this point only the concept "fullness of times" is to be elucidated.

References to the *plērōma* of time, of days, of years, and of periods are found in classic Greek writers, papyri, and the LXX.[74] If connected with concepts of time, "fulfillment" means that the end of a period is reached. However, NT parallels to Eph 1:10[75] show that "fulfillment" designates not just an end point, but the dawning of a new period in which God's promise and law (that is, even all that is said in the Scriptures), are fulfilled. The translation "days of

---

[73] I.e. esp. in Eph 1:20–23; 2:13–18; 4:8–12; 5:2, 14, 25–27.
[74] See LSLex; WBLex; in the LXX e.g. Gen 25:24; Lev 8:33; 25:29–30; Num 6:5; cf. Acts 7:23, 30.
[75] Mark 1:15 (cf. Mark 16, the Freer ending); Luke 21:24; John 7:8 (2:4; 12:23, etc.); esp. Gal 4:4.

fulfillment" attempts to do justice to the extension and contents of the end time. See COMMENT XIII.

All things . . . under him! The sentence beginning and ending with these words is probably a quotation. It is the kernel and highlight of the Great Benediction. But why should just vs. 10bc be treated as a citation within the supposedly traditional blessing quoted in 1:4 ff.?

The character, function, and contents of vs. 10bc are similar to those of the so-called oracles that occur again and again in the royal Psalms of the OT.[76] Three surprising elements occur in the two lines containing the quotation, which are novel if compared with vocabulary and contents of the preceding verses: One, the impersonal concept "all things" may be a synonym for the "world" mentioned in 1:4. It certainly replaces in a surprising way the personal pronouns "we " (or "us") which prevailed in vss. 3–9; cf. 11–12, 14; it is also wider than the number of the "saints" addressed by "you" in vs. 13. Two, an implicit allusion to Christ the head or the unifier may have been present in all preceding statements about decisions and events "in Christ." Only now one single verb, rendered in our translation by "to comprehend under one head" makes what was implicit, explicit. There, the plerophoric attribute of "all things," i.e. the words "those in heaven and upon earth"[77] may again be a synonym for "the world." But the distinction between heavenly and earthly beings is indicative of a possible disruption between the realms of heaven and earth which has not so far been mentioned.[78]

These idiosyncrasies of the oracular sentence are spectacular. But they are not sufficient to demonstrate that the whole sentence is strange to the context and may as well be excised as an ill-suited gloss. On the contrary, the verses preceding and following the quotation may intend to interpret the so-called oracle in new terminology. It is probable that precisely because the author of the Benediction fully endorsed the quoted text, he also appropriated it.

to be comprehended under one head. This translation corresponds to the one suggested by JB, also by B. Rigaux and P. Benoit.[79] While philological reasoning alone is not sufficient to justify it, the history of interpretation and theological consequences can contribute to the choice that has to be made among other translations. Three alternatives for interpreting the Greek verb *anakephalaioō,* translated by "comprehending under one head", deserve consideration:

a) In its simple form the verb (*kephalaioō,* without the preposition *ana*) means usually[80] "to divide into chapters," "to give titles," or "to sum up." The

---

[76] E.g. Pss 2:6–9; 89:19–37; 110:1, 4; 132:11b–12; I Sam 8–11; II Sam 7; 23:3; Isa 42:5–9; 55:3; cf. Ps Sol 17:27 ff. The opposite of a king appointed by God through an oracle is a self-made king, or a ruler appointed by the people, e.g. I Kings 1:5, 2:15, etc.; Hosea 8:4.

[77] Cf. Col 1:16, 20.

[78] For a fuller interpretation of the term "all things" see COMMENT V B on 1:15–23.

[79] See Rigaux, NTS 4 (1957–58), 256, and Benoit, AnBib 17–18, I (1963), 65. For an approach to further special literature on the philological problem at hand, the history of interpreting this passage, and the theological implications see BIBLIOGRAPHY 9. C. F. Burney, JTS 27 (1926), 176, offers an explanation of Eph 1:10 which is based on the double meaning of Heb. *rō'š rē'šit* i.e. "head" and "sum."

[80] In Greek literature outside the Bible, see LSLex, 945, cf. 108; in the LXX the simple verb appears only in Sir 35[32]:8, the composite verb, never. In the Theodotion and Quintus Greek versions of the OT the composite occurs in Ps 71[72]:20 and means in its passive form, "being completed."

composite form found in Eph 1:10 occasionally also occurs found outside the Bible, as Hellenistic writers show a tendency to prefer composite to simple verbs—often without aiming at a shade of difference in meaning.[81] In their writings the verb means "to sum up," and the same sense is presupposed in Rom 13:9, Barn. XI; cf. IV Ezra 12:25. For this reason KJ, RSV, NEB, SegB, interpret the word by "to unite."

b) The Peshitta and Old Latin versions, also Vulgate, translate the verb as "renew" (*instaurare* or *recapitulare*), and Tertullian[82] follows this lead. It has contributed to the formation of Irenaeus'[83] elaborate doctrine of recapitulation, and it was taken up by Jerome, Ambrosiaster, and Thomas. These expositors are obviously influenced specifically by the meaning of the preposition (*ana*) prefixed to the verb in question. This preposition can, besides other things, express a repetition or renewal.[84] However, it is completely impossible that in Rom 13:9 Paul intended to speak of a repetition or renewal of the commandments; thus it cannot be proven that Paul was aware of the meaning, "to renew," or that a pseudonymous author of Ephesians could have learned this sense of the verb from Paul. In literature close to the NT, the meaning of "repeat," occurs only once.[85] The repetition, restoration, or recapitulation[86] theory of Irenaeus was originally formed in order to serve as an anti-Gnostic instrument. It was to teach the Gnostics that the works of God the creator, far from being *abolished* by Christ, are brought to perfection by the redeemer.[87] There is no reason to question the appositeness of this doctrine. However, though it is resplendent and appears to be directly inspired by Eph 1:10, the recapitulation doctrine is not necessarily expressed in the second line of 1:10.

It is possible to combine meanings (a) and (b). According to H. Conzelmann,[88] Gnosticism is the very key to understanding this text. Conzelmann offers as a background to Eph 1:4 and 10 the Gnostic ideas of a "fall of the rulers" (or of "wisdom") out of their unity with the deity,[89] the notion of a prehistorical separation of man's soul from the Aion-Father, and mythical tales of the reintegration of man's soul into the world of light. But his interpretation is based upon second- and third-century literary evidence and is therefore not convincing.[90] Another parallel may prove more important. In the context of a hymn on the "reconciliation of all things with Christ," Col 1:20 takes up and explains this reconciliation by a reference to the "making of peace through the blood of the cross." This passage appears indeed to speak of the restoration of

---

[81] Cf. in the NT the identity of the meanings of "to give (oneself)" (*didōmi*) and "to deliver (oneself)" (*paradidōmi*), Gal 1:4, 2:20; but the meanings of "to change" (*allattō*) and "to reconcile" (*katallattō*), Gal 4:20; I Cor 15:51–52; Col 1:20; Rom 5:10; II Cor 5:18–20) are not identical. Morgenthaler, *Statistik*, pp. 160–62, presents a list showing the frequency of composite verbs in the NT.

[82] *Monogamia* 5.   [83] *Adv. haer.* I 3:4, 10:1; III 22:2.

[84] So e.g. in "rebirth," "renewal" (*anagennaō, anakainōsis*), I Peter 1:3; Titus 3:5; but cf. the discussion between Jesus and Nicodemus, John 3:1–8.

[85] In the Protevangel of James 13:1. Repetition is, however, not fully identified with renewal.

[86] The form and etymology of this Latin word appears to be a most literal reproduction of the Greek verb under review.

[87] Cf. the Latin dictum, *Gratia non tollit naturam, sed perficit.*

[88] In his commentary, p. 61.

[89] See NOTE on "foundation of the world" in 1:4 and COMMENT IV.

[90] In section III B of the Introduction other aspects of the Gnostic problem are discussed; the issue will be treated more extensively in the context of 1:22–23; 4:8–10, 13.

a lost unity between heaven and earth, or between all creatures and God.[91] If Col 1:20 is the key to Eph 1:10 then the combination of the two meanings of the Greek verb *anakephalaioō*, which have already been discussed, i.e. "to unite" and "to restore," is the best solution. Yet a third interpretation has throughout the centuries of the Christian church coexisted with the translations and expositions so far discussed:

c) The meaning of the ambiguous Greek verb is to be derived exclusively from the context of Eph 1:10, and is "to make [Christ] the head."[92] According to the context, Jesus Christ is made by God the head of the universe and of the church. With his presence and power he is filling all things (1:22–23). There is no growth except toward him and from him (4:15–16). He is to fill all (4:10). Thus the verb that seems to be inexplicable has been given a new meaning by the author of Ephesians—if only his own later words in the same epistle are permitted to serve as dictionary and commentary. God "makes Christ the head over all." It is certainly hazardous to ascribe to the Greek verb such a novel meaning.[93] Nevertheless, Paul may have been aware of the true etymology and meaning of the word and yet have used it as a suitable indication of matters that were to be unfolded later on.

None of these three interpretations, taken in isolation from one another, is strong enough to be persuasive. But since Ephesians[94] contains no trace of a recapitulation theory, it is advisable not to make use of the second alternative.[95] Thus the first and third choices remain. They have been blended into one in the compromise translation offered above, which holds together the method and the purpose of Jesus Christ's commission: by becoming head he will prove himself as head; by his rulership he is to unite what was divided and hostile. Headship is the means, reconciliation the purpose, of his appointment. The words "all things . . . those in heaven and upon earth" reveal that the rule of Christ is not restricted to his government over men or the church. Angels and other powers are among his subjects (1:21, 23).[96] Thus, this part of the

[91] A sort of "homecoming of the universe" effected by Christ is then the sum of Jesus Christ's commission.

[92] See esp. 1:22–23; 4:10, 15–16, and the parallels to these passages in Colossians. This view is represented already by Chrysostom who maintains, however, at the same time, the meaning (a), "to unite." The strongest champion of the third way of exposition is Schlier, pp. 64 ff; TWNTE, III, 6, 81–82.

[93] Gaugler speaks of "filthy etymology." The derivation of the verb from "head" (*kephalē*) rather than from "main point," "chief topic," "sum total" (cf. LSLex, 944–45; also Heb 8:1) is indeed an unwarranted etymological adventure.

[94] Unlike Rom 5:12–21; I Cor 15:20–22, 44–49.

[95] The exclusion is tantamount to a prohibition of any sort of speculative exploitation of Eph 1:10. (a) This verse (but also 2:12, 4:18; see the Notes there for an interpretation of the verbs "excluded" and "blacked out") is unduly squeezed when it is made to yield evidence for a primordial unity of God and all things—other than the relation confessed by the term "creator of all things," 3:9. (b) Ephesians does not support the related, though contrary, theory which identifies the act of creation itself with a fall or a division; see COMMENT IV. (c) The notion of an ultimate mystical union between God and man, heaven and earth, in which all distinctions vanish cannot be traced in Ephesians; see COMMENT IV A B on 3:14–21. (d) Robinson's opinion (p. 32) that 1:10 is the Christian answer to the Greek philosophers' quest for the One in the Many, and perhaps also the vision of P. Teilhard de Chardin, goes beyond the evidence attainable for an exact interpretation of this verse. But cf. COMMENT V on 1:15–23. The problem of universal salvation is to be taken up in AB, vol. 34B, in connection with the exegesis of Colossians, esp. of Col 1:20; cf. Rom 8:19–22.

[96] Esp. in Colossians, but also in Heb 1:4–14 and Rev 5, the submission of angels to Christ is a main topic.

message of Ephesians has sometimes been summed up by the term "cosmic Christ."[97]

11. *As resolved.* Cf. Isa 46:10.

11–13. *we [Jews] were . . . the first . . . You [Gentiles] too . . .* The congregation of the saints is suddenly no longer described only by the anonymous pronoun "we." It is not an amorphous mass in which each individual may be exchanged for another; rather it has a structure. Christ is its head; the apostle and other servants installed by God address it with authority and are its foundation.[98] Thus there is a vertical difference of authority in the church, and now a differentiation on the horizontal level becomes apparent. A group called "we" is distinct from another group addressed as "you." Though both participate in the same love, election, and grace of God[99] and are *one* body, some were *first* called to constitute God's people, others were added later.

11. *we [Jews] were . . . appropriated.* The Greek original uses a verb (*kleroō*) which meant originally "to cast a lot," or more specifically, "to appoint or designate an officer by lot."[100] When the procedure of using a lot was forgotten, the word assumed the meaning, "to assign something," or in the passive, "to be in possession."[101] Eph 1:11 is the only NT passage where this word occurs. Probably because of its ambiguous meaning, but perhaps also due to careless copying, some ancient MSS and the *Vetus Itala* substitute the better known verb, "we have been called." The references to "calling" in Eph 1:18; 4:1 support this variant but are not a sufficient reason to give preference to the easier reading.[102] The complicated problems posed by the present text must be met, and a choice among three possibilities faces the interpreter:

a) "We had the good fortune to be chosen by God . . . to become a praise of his glory." In this case the election and designation mentioned in 1:4, 5 would be described with a new word suggesting a happy God-sent accident, even the windfall of a fine appointment. Actually, the Peshitta version uses for vs. 11 the same word, "to elect," as it employs in vs. 5. The opposite to such election, as if by lot, is a salvation based upon "works" (2:9). Indeed 1:11 may qualify the election described in 1:4–8. The words "in the Messiah" (lit. "in whom") can refer to the pre-existent Christ, or the Messiah who was secretly always at work in the history of Israel.[103]

b) "We were given a share" (e.g. of land). When this translation is adopted, the words "in the Messiah" refer either to the place[104] in which the share is located, or to the person with whom the property to be handed out is deposited for the time being.[105] In both cases Ephesians would offer an alternative to the Qumran teaching (e.g. 1QH III 22, VI 13; also 1QGenApocr. II 20–21?) according to which the elect receive a share in the property of angels. Or, an

---

[97] See esp. A. D. Galloway, *The Cosmic Christ,* New York: Harper, 1951; this concept will have to be discussed later in detail, esp. in the NOTES and COMMENTS on Col 1:15–20.

[98] 1:1–2, 15, 22–23; 2:20; 3:5; 4:1; 6:19–20.   [99] 1:3–10; 2:1–6; 4:3–4, etc.

[100] E.g. LXX I Kings [I Sam] 14:41; of a living place, *Letter to Diognetus* (henceforth *Diogn.*) v 4.

[101] LSLex 960.

[102] In the Alexandrian MS of LXX Esther 4:11, the reverse exchange has taken place.

[103] Cf. I Cor 10:4; Gal 3:16; I Peter 1:11.

[104] I.e. the body of Christ, 1:23; or the kingdom of the Messiah and God, 5:5; or the building in which Christ is the keystone, 2:20.

[105] If G. M. Taylor's explanation is at all tenable (see fn. 27 at 1:5 for a summary).

allusion may be made to the allotment of the promised land or its portions to Israel, to each tribe and family, or to the special share of Levi (whose apportionment is the Lord).[106] In the LXX the Hebrew concepts of "lot" or "share" on one hand and of "inheritance" on the other, are frequently combined and sometimes simply identified.[107] Similarly in Ephesians[108] and other Pauline epistles the terms "to inherit," "heir," and "inheritance" play a major role.[109] Col 1:12,[110] i.e. the parallel text to Eph 1:11, speaks distinctly of a "part in the share of the saints."[111] To the notion of "blessing" (1:3) such a distribution fits beautifully. The very term, "to inherit blessing," is used in I Peter 3:9. In the interpretation of Eph 1:7 it was shown that the saints are indeed considered "possessors."

But the second translation suggested, "we were given a share," can be improved further by including a reference to the moment of promise which is inherent in the OT parallels. ZB suggests a version which would read in English "We have been made heirs." This interpretation leaves room for further additions to the bequeathed property—as indeed according to 1:14 the Spirit now given is but an "earnest" of the total that is to come. Again, another variant on the same line may also be tenable: among the OT parallels those that describe the Levites' special allotment can be given preference. Then Eph 1:11 is to be translated by "We have been made God's clergy,"[112] and the Christians can be considered a sort of "levitical community."[113] And there is yet another option:

c) "We have been appropriated." Compare JB, "'claimed as God's own." Eph 1:14 contains the OT concept of "God's own people," lit. the "people of possession," or the "people appropriated by God"; cf. Mal 3:17. This expression may well be derived from the covenant formula, "I will be your God and you shall be my people."[114] It points back to the liberation of Israel from Egypt. The redeemer becomes possessor and protector of the redeemed.[115] Israel is made God's property. To attest to this fact OT writers make use of the same imagery for God's taking possession of Israel as for Israel's receiving a share from God. "The Lord your God has chosen you to be a people for his own possession, out of all the people that are on the face of the earth" (Deut 7:6, 14:2). "The Lord's portion is his people, Jacob his allotted heritage" (Deut 32:9). Israel is called "thy people and thy heritage whom thou hast redeemed" (Deut 9:26).[116] Equally, the Qumran community of the faithful understands itself not only as the *recipient* of a special lot from God, but it also *calls itself* God's lot and considers itself bought by God to be his people.[117] When Ephesians mentions God's riches[118] it may certainly consider them the

106 Exod 6:8; Josh 12:7; I Chron 6:46[61] ff.; Deut 18:1–2.
107 Num 18:24; 26:56; 34:14; 36:3; Josh 12:7; 14:2; 19 *passim;* cf. Acts 26:18.
108 1:14, 18; 5:5.
109 Cf. in the Qumran literature 1QS xi 7–8; 1QH vi 13–14.   110 Cf. Acts 20:32.
111 NEB translates Eph 1:11 by "We have been given our share in the heritage."
112 Perhaps a passage in the Codex Justinianus (II 3:38) makes the same assertion.
113 Cf. I Peter 2:5 and Selwyn, *First Peter*, pp. 414–15, 436; Carrington, *The Primitive Christian Catechism*, pp. 14–21.
114 Lev 26:12; Jer 7:23; 11:4; 24:7, etc.
115 See D. Daube, "Redemption," in *The New Testament and Rabbinic Judaism* (London: Athleone, 1956), pp. 268–84.
116 Cf. Exod 19:5; LXX Exod 23:22.   117 1QS ii 2; 1QM i 5, xiii 5, 9, xvii 6–7.
118 In 1:7, 18; 2:4, 7; 3:8, 16.

source out of which the adopted children *receive* an ample share. But it need not exclude the idea of how much God *spends* on making Jews and Gentiles his own property. The concept of "salvation"[119] means redemption from captivity (4:8), liberation (1:7, 14; var. lect. 3:12), snatching from the realm of death (2:1–6). The emphatic references to the power of God that makes God's love and grace irresistible to any opposing powers,[120] make it clear that God is not only able to disburse abundant riches, but that in defeating the enemies and in the salvation of his people he gains a victory for himself. He acquires men so that they may become a demonstration of his glory. In NT times, the verb *klēroō* had the specific meaning "to acquire," "to take possession," "to appropriate," rather than the senses discussed as alternatives (a) and (b).[121] If this meaning should have the upper hand in Eph 1:11, the formula "in the Messiah" denotes the price which was paid for the redemption and appropriation of God's people and is a synonym of the words "through Christ" (2:18), or "through his blood" (1:7).[122]

Still, OT and NT parallels to Eph 1:11 and purely philological considerations do not permit a final decision in favor of any one of these three alternatives. Below, in the second half of COMMENT IX, other arguments will be presented that favor the third option.

The Greek preposition *pro*, "before," which in this verse is translated by "first" occurs three times in 1:11–12. The pith of these verses as well as other Pauline passages,[123] recommends the pointed interpretation given in the translation. Earlier in the benediction the preposition "before" was connected with nouns and verbs to denote the priority of election over creation and of Christ over those yet to be made God's children. There a priority of rank went together with temporal priority. Now, the temporal precedence of "us" over "you" is stated—but without any indication of a difference of rank. The contents of vss. 4–10 and 14 actually prevent any higher or lower stratification inside the congregation of the saints. The identification of "we" with Jews and "you" with Gentiles will be explained in COMMENT XIV; cf. COMMENT VIII.

13. *You [Gentiles] too are [included] in him . . . the promised Holy Spirit*. It is possible to understand vs. 13 in a manner totally different from the one suggested here, for it might be that the reader has to cope with a broken sentence. This would be the case if Paul started out one way, then interrupted himself by forming a parenthesis, and finally started fresh again on the line of the original beginning. A version such as the following would be the result: "In him you, too—after hearing the true word, the message that saves you—[I mean] when you began also to believe in him, you have been sealed . . ." In this case the words "in him" which are repeated in the Greek (though not in our translation) would denote the object of the saints' faith. This assumption is not supported by linguistic parallels. In COMMENT I on 1:1 it was shown that

---

[119] In the sense in which it is used in 1:13; 2:5, 8; 5:23.

[120] 1:19–23; 3:7, 16–20; 6:10–15.   [121] Cf. Bengel and Robinson.

[122] Cf. the formulae "in Christ Jesus," 2:13, 15, 16; "in the blood of the Messiah," "in his flesh," "in one body through the cross," "through him," 2:13, 14, 16, 18; and the references to Christ's sacrificial death in 5:2, 25; Col 1:22; I Peter 1:18–19, etc. In Col 2:14 entirely different imagery is used for describing the effect of Christ's death; Col 2:15 adds an interpretation which stresses the element of victory over hostile powers.

[123] I.e. Rom 1:16; 2:9–10; Acts 13:46: "the Jew first and also the Greek."

Paul is wont to speak of faith or believing "into" Christ, "upon" Christ, etc. not of believing in Christ. A variant translation, respecting the fact that the words "in Christ" do not belong to the verb "believe," suggests that the formula "in Christ" indicates in both cases the place where, or the agent by whom, the sealing with the Spirit was performed: in him you, too—after hearing—[I mean] in him you were sealed after also believing. Such complicated structuring of a sentence (as an anacoluthon) is by no means strange to Paul or unparalleled in Ephesians.[124] But it is not necessary to wrestle with the innate ambiguities of an anacoluthon as long as other explanations of the syntax and a smoother translation are available.

The repeated Greek words *en hō* ("in him") may have different meanings in the first and second half of this verse. The beginning of vs. 13 makes best sense when it is explained as an "ellipsis": the copula, He is, we are, or they are (or another form of the verbs "to be," or "to become"), is usually omitted in Hebrew when simple predications or identifications are made. Classic, Hellenistic, and biblical Greek equally permit the omission of the auxiliary verb.[125] The translation of Eph 1:13a by "You, too, are in him" is therefore grammatically possible. The addition of "included" is suggested by those passages of Ephesians[126] that pronounce the full participation of the Gentiles in all things that God has decided and carried out with his Son and through him (see e.g. 2:1 ff., 13 ff.). The second occurrence of "in him," in vs. 13, marks the start of a new thought, as Paul turns to the application of a seal.

you have heard . . . you came to faith . . . you have been sealed. Distinctive events are listed that characterize the conversion and incorporation of Gentiles into God's people. The enumeration of these events resembles the pattern of early Christian mission reports,[127] but it is shorter than most of them.

the true word, the message that saves you. Lit. "the word of truth, the gospel of your salvation." Similar descriptions of the gospel and its effect are found in other Pauline and NT writings.[128] They may have been coined before Paul started his mission work. See COMMENT XV.

sealed with his seal, the promised Holy Spirit. Lit. "sealed in him with the Holy Spirit of promise." Cf. 4:30. Most commentators on this passage seem to agree that the term "sealing" is an image for baptizing. In COMMENT XVI reasons for and against this view will be compared.

14. *He is.* Lit. "who is." Who is meant by the pronoun "He" (*hos*)—Jesus Christ or the Spirit? If Ephesians were written according to the rules of classic Greek, the pronoun would refer to Jesus Christ rather than to the Holy Spirit. For the noun "spirit" (*pneuma*) is in Greek (just as in English) neuter. How-

---

[124] Cf. e.g. Gal 2:3–5, 6–10; Eph 2:1–5; 3:1–14. Anacolutha in Romans are discussed by G. Bornkamm. "Paulinische Anakoluthe im Römerbrief," in *Das Ende des Gesetzes* (Munich: Kaiser, 1952), pp. 76–92.

[125] BDF, 127–28. Gal 2:15 would in literal translation say "We by origin Jews." The true meaning, however, appears to be "We are by origin Jewish"; cf. Rom 4:14, lit. "those from the law heirs," means "those from the law are heirs."

[126] As 1:3–10; 2:6, 13–18, 21–22; 3:6.

[127] Cf. Acts 8:12–13, 35–38; 10:44–48; 11:14–18; 13:48, 52, etc.; cf. I Thess 2:13; Gal 3:2; Rom 10:14–15; Mark 16:16. The decisive events of a successful mission are ascribed to God. First he sends and equips the messenger, cf. Eph 4:7–11, and finally he puts his blessing upon the acts of preaching, hearing, believing, praying, baptizing—by giving the Holy Spirit. In COMMENT XV passages will be quoted showing that the act of preaching was considered a deed of God.

[128] Col. 1:5; Gal 2:5, 14; I Cor 1:18, 24; II Cor 6:7; Rom 1:16; cf. II Tim 2:15; James 1:18; Acts 11:14, 13:26.

ever, in three closely related Pauline passages no one else but "the Spirit" is called an "earnest,"[129] and in its present context the whole verse (Eph 1:14) serves obviously as a comment on the sealing with the Spirit mentioned in the preceding verse.[130] Therefore parallels and context require that the pronoun "He" refer to the Spirit. This assumption is supported by the variant reading "it" (*ho*, instead of "he," *hos*) offered by Origen, the third-century Ch. Beatty Papyrus (P 46), the codices Vaticanus and Alexandrinus of the Hesychian family (though not by Codex Sinaiticus), and by a number of later Fathers and MSS. Which is the original reading: "it" or "he"? An original neuter would hardly have been later displaced by the masculine relative pronoun. But the substitution of the neuter for the masculine can easily be explained: reasons for a change to the neuter are (a) to avoid the misunderstanding that the reference is to Jesus Christ; and (b) to straighten out or to beautify the syntax which in its original form seemed inappropriate to the Holy Writ. Probably those who changed the "he" to a neuter "it" did not realize that the author of Ephesians had assimilated the gender of the relative pronoun to the gender of the noun "earnest" which follows.[131] "Earnest" is masculine in Greek and the pronoun "he," though denoting the (neuter) Spirit, may be determined by the gender of "earnest." At any rate, the more difficult reading, "he" instead of "it," is better attested. Still one additional possibility is to be mentioned. Eph 1:14 may be a verse that shows in exemplary fashion how the formation of a special grammar for church use began.[132] In church and theological language the Holy Spirit is often and with good reason denoted as a person. The Spirit is respected as "he" rather than as an "it." God in person, not just a nondescript power or feeling, is present and active whenever the Spirit is mentioned. Just as in Eph 1:4 ff. the Father and the Son were praised as persons, so the Spirit is now. Eph 1:3–14 takes up the trinity—in its own terms and not yet in the language required by later controversies. This hymnodic passage is an attempt at a summary praise of God, his love, his work, his presence. Little wonder that later church confessions[133] adopted a similar structure of thought and have corresponding contents.

the guarantee of what we shall inherit. The Greek noun *arrabōn* means in Gen 38:17, 18, 20 a pledge that is to be returned to the owner when the debt is paid in full. Such a pledge is not a part of the payment due but a security for it. To the debtor the value of such a pledge is generally greater than the amount owed. When the same word occurs in Pauline passages[134] it means another business practice in which the first portion of a payment binds both the payer and payee.[135] Papyri quoted by J. A. Robinson show that the first installment was lost if the buyer defaulted on the later payments; if, however, the

---

[129] II Cor 1:22, 5:5; Rom 8:23.

[130] Perhaps in the pre-Pauline hymn or confession to which 1:14 may have belonged it did not refer to sealing. The rhythmic diction of 1:14 appears to reveal the connection of this verse with 1:4–10 rather than with the prose vss. 11–13.

[131] The vss. Mark 15:16; Gal 3:17; Col 1:27 contain such "attractions of the relative pronoun" to the predicative noun. They are a sign of sophisticated rather than poor diction.

[132] According to E. Lohmeyer, *Die Offenbarung des Johannes*, HbNT XVI, 1953, the Book of Revelation signals the same procedure, e.g. in 1:4 which in literal version reads, "Grace and peace to you from the Being and the Was and the Coming."

[133] As formulated in the Apostles' Creed, the Nicene and later confessions.

[134] II Cor 1:22, 5:5; Eph 1:14.

[135] The correct Latin translation would be *arra* rather than *pignus*, despite Vulg.

vendor was unable to deliver the promised goods he had to pay back double the amount of the earnest. For a discussion of the various Jewish, Roman, Athenian, or Hellenistic-Asiatic legal customs underlying the allusion to inheritance, see the commentaries on Gal 4:1–2.[136]

[to vouch] for the liberation of God's own people. Cf. the translation of JB and the discussion by Percy and C. Kruse.[137] Dibelius suggests a paraphrase saying "until the redemption comes which makes us gain our heirdom." The Greek noun peripoiēsis here translated by "God's own people" is understood by Dibelius in the sense of man's taking possession. Once again the choice must be made between the second and third alternatives presented in the NOTE on Eph 1:11. Peripoiēsis indeed has various nuances—not only outside but inside the Bible. It denotes the act of saving or preserving life,[138] of acquiring some good,[139] or the state of possession, i.e. property.[140] A decision for but one of these meanings appears unwarranted. However, if only man's enrichment were focused upon, the breadth of the contents of Eph 1:14 would be reduced. The reference in 1:14a to inheritance ("what we shall inherit") shows sufficiently that man will be enriched. Both verses, Eph 1:11 and 14, add to this a hint that God is gaining something for himself too: a people that praises his glory.[141] In blunt terms: God is not only spending, he is also earning. Man is not only a receptacle that must remain passive; he is also to live actively.

In 1:14 as well as in 1:3–10 a terminology is used for the salvation of Jews and Gentiles which had formerly been reserved for Israel only. But expressions such as the "new" or "true" Israel (that seem to correspond to the "new" covenant, the "new" man, the "New" Testament) are not found in this context or anywhere else in the NT.

COMMENTS I–XVII on 1:3–14

Eph 1:3–14 is a digest of the whole epistle[142] and replete with key terms and topics that anticipate the contents of what follows.

I   The Great Benediction and Its Structure

Verses 1:3–14 form a whole which is best described by the Jewish term "benediction" (berakāh).[143] It is an exclamation of praise and prayer, resembling those pronounced in Jewish synagogues and homes. Tobit 13:1 ff. presents a good example: "Tobit wrote a prayer of jubilation: Blessed is God who lives forever, and his Kingdom . . ." The apocryphal Song of the Three Young Men (29–68) is another illustration. A rhythmic diction that makes use of traditional elements found in the Psalms[144] and reflects at the same time a po-

---

[136] E.g. Burton in ICC.
[137] Percy, pp. 188–89, n. 15; C. Kruse, "Il significato di peripoiēsis in Eph 1,14," RivBib 16 (1968), 465–93 (ref.).
[138] E.g. LXX II Chron 14:12[13]; Luke 17:33; Heb 10:39.
[139] E.g. I Thess 5:9.   [140] E.g. LXX Mal 3:17; I Peter 2:9.
[141] As Jeremiah phrases it (13:11), ". . . that they might be for me a people, a name, a praise, and a glory." Cf. Kruse, RivBib 16 (1968), 465–93 (ref.).
[142] See Introduction, section IX.
[143] See the discussion of hymnology in section II of the Introduction, BIBLIOGRAPHIES 1 and 7 and the discussion of "blessing" in the NOTES to 1:3, including the literature mentioned there in fns. 1, 2.
[144] E.g. LXX Ps 71[72]:18–19.

tential of artistic Greek prose is characteristic of the benedictions preserved in Greek. Short benedictions resemble enthusiastic outbursts.[145] Longer benedictions elaborate on specific topics.[146] In the essays of N. A. Dahl, S. Lyonnet, and J. M. Robinson,[147] the long benediction in Eph 1:3–14 is compared with Jewish *berākōth* of the type found in 1QS xi 2–8. Strong influences of a Jewish form and tradition are convincingly demonstrated. This benediction—at least its more rhythmic parts[148]—may (but need not necessarily) have come to Paul from the living stream of oral, probably liturgical, Christian tradition. It is not attributed to a word of the Lord, to a revelation, to a dream or a vision. The "we"-form of the hymnic parts reveals that Paul is far from presenting in this prayer of praise his private opinion only. He sings to God in the terms and in the midst of the worshiping congregation. But psalm verses like Ps 22:25 make it explicit that precisely the "praise" given in the midst of the congregation comes from God, the Lord.

The contents of the benediction are primarily the grace, the action, the revelation of God. God is the subject of most sentences; even when passive verbs are used—as "we were designated and appropriated," "you have been sealed" (1:11, 13)—a description of God's action is given. The whole benediction resounds with the praise of God's glory. This praise is the purpose of God's work (1:6, 12, 14).

Still, vs. 7 and the prose vss. 11–13 seem to constitute an exception.[149] They mark a transition from objective presentation to personal application: "We possess freedom, forgiveness . . . We [have been] the first to set our hope upon the Messiah . . . We were to become a praise." A distinction between "we" and "you" is made. The sequence of "hearing," "believing," "sealing" is pointed out. The possessive ring to 1:7, but also the reference to "lapses," and finally the concreteness of the utterances contained in 1:11–13 are surprising in their lofty and generalizing context. Events are recalled that took place and are true in the life and history of those addressed in Ephesians. An appeal is made to their experience and awareness. Verses 11–13 appear to explain in terms of subjective experience why the bold statement on possession was made in vs. 7. Certainly this experience is completely dependent upon God's decision and action. Not the amount or quality of men's individual needs, of their receptiveness for the gifts and the revelation of God, or of their feelings about them, but the "riches of God's grace lavished" upon men are the measure of truth, reality, history.[150] Because God is by no means a stingy or begrudging father, men are simply overwhelmed by his deeds. And yet the overwhelming grace does not condemn man to simple passivity. God's decision and action were made *in* the Christ who shed his blood on earth, and who was

---

[145] E.g. Gen 24:27; Rom 1:25, 9:5; II Cor 11:31.

[146] I Macc 4:30–33; II Cor 1:3–4; I Peter 1:3–5. Best known among the NT benedictions is the *Benedictus*, Luke 1:68–79.

[147] Listed in BIBLIOGRAPHY. See also Schille, *Hymnen;* Deichgräber, *Gotteshymnus;* Kirby, EBP, pp. 25–40.

[148] I.e. vss. 4–10 and 14. Gaugler treats all the twelve verses of Eph 1:3–14 as a "hymnic pro-oemium"; others see a hymn in the total sequence 1:4–14. Schille, *Hymnen*, pp. 66–69, has collected the strongest arguments for treating 1:11–13 as a (Pauline) prose interpolation into a pre-Pauline hymn.

[149] Prose interruptions are also found in John 1:6–8, 15, inside the Johannine Prologue.

[150] See also e.g. Ps 112:9; II Cor 9:8–11.

established ruler of heaven *and* earth. An earthly history, i.e. the coming, the death, the rule of Christ and the corresponding experience of the saints, belongs to the revelation of God's eternal good will. The election by God which precedes the creation of heaven and earth, does not wipe out man's history. Following Eph 1:11–13 it makes and shapes *our* and *your* history. The experience of the saints, e.g. (a) their hope, (b) the distinction of groups among them, (c) consecutive events as hearing, believing, sealing, (d) their assurance regarding their possession, (e) the living praise of God by their very existence—all of this belongs to the subject matter, if not of the original hymn, then of the present benediction. God is blessed because his blessing has attained its purpose. It has a palpable result on earth in earthly historical events. Actually, if the blessing were not really conveyed to men, if it had not arrived at its destination—it would not deserve to be called "blessing," and no man would bless God.

But a concession is necessary. If the distinction between objective and subjective parts of the benediction contributes to an elucidation of its contents, it still does not determine its external structure. What are the main subdivisions and topics?

The search for the discovery of the structure of the hymnodic prologue to Ephesians has led to diverse results. Verse 3 is obviously an introduction; in vs. 9 a hitherto unmentioned key word of revelation, *gnōrizō*, "to make known," suddenly appears and may reveal the beginning of a new part. The less rhythmic diction and the distinction of "we" and "you" in vss. 11–13 appear to interrupt the flow of thought. If there is some agreement on these observations, there is yet no unanimity regarding the question whether external or internal, i.e. formal or material criteria, ought to be considered decisive for the demarcation of the subdivisions.

External signs indicating the end or beginning of several stanzas of a hymn have been noted specifically by J. Coutts and J. Cambier.[151] They consider the variations of the formula "to the praise of his glory" in 1:6, 12, 14 a kind of refrain which each time indicates the end of a stanza. By cutting out from 1:3–14 all comments and afterthoughts supposedly added by the hymn's author himself, Coutts succeeds in reconstructing three strophes of equal length. This procedure is arbitrary and forced. It fails to explain why the refrain has a different wording each time.[152] Since vss. 11–13 fall out of the rhythm of the preceding and following verses, the reconstruction of three stanzas of an originally uniform hymn is not convincing. M. Dibelius believes that the relative pronouns, specifically the recurring Greek words "in whom" (1:4, 7, 11 [and 13]), mark the beginning of three stanzas. (In our translation, they are reproduced in four different versions.) N. A. Dahl takes the prepositional expressions that are followed by a relative clause and "limp after" main statements as a sign of the end of a strophe.[153] He considers the six verse units 4–6a, 6b–7, 8–9a, 9b–10, 11–12, 13–14 as that many strophes. The outstanding place given to the participles "he has blessed," "he has pre-

designated," "he has made known" (1:3, 5, 9) permits him to group the whole
into an introduction, four main parts, and a final application. It was mentioned
earlier that JB distinguishes seven blessings. Gaugler, Schille,[154] Käsemann,[155]
and others prefer to speak of only two parts of the prooemium, i.e. the descriptions of God's supratemporal plan, and of its intratemporal execution.[156]
All these attempts at reconstructing strophes and all the criteria applied are
noteworthy. But none of them has proven more convincing than an ingenious
play: A. Debrunner's warning against the trust expressed by Lohmeyer[157]
and others in a regular colometry and the possibility of reconstructing original,
pre-biblical hymns has often been overlooked, but still demands attention.
No incontestable formal criteria have yet been developed for controlling
subjective feelings of the interpreters and for attaining generally acceptable
results. Perhaps very small units were taken up from various traditions (including poems) by the biblical authors and cemented together into larger
hymnodic structures. The latter compositions would then inevitably sound
like larger earlier poems, but they would still be original works. Printing our
translation in separate lines serves to indicate rhythmic speech but cannot
pretend to offer a final solution.

But there are also internal elements in Eph 1:3-14 which may contribute
to discovering its structure. This passage is outstanding not only because of
the frequent occurrence of the preposition "in,"[158] but also because of the
somersaults of the prepositions "from," "before," "into" (or "for"), "through,"
"according to." Some of them are prefixed to verbs, others are found before
nouns. The play with prepositions in which the writer of Ephesians indulges
does not necessarily please every reader.[159] But if it fails to contribute to
the beauty of Greek diction and style—not to speak of modern language
versions of Ephesians—it is still an outstanding mark of all Pauline epistles.[160]
The purpose of the compound prepositions in Eph 1 is clearly discernible.
With the help of prepositions the origin and order of God's decision, the
means and mode of carrying it out, and the goal and effect of its fulfillment
are at one and the same time distinguished from one another and kept together.
The Father's conversation with his Son before the creation; the promise and
hope given to his people before the coming of the Messiah; the charge
entrusted to Christ; the pouring out of Christ's blood; the formation of the
congregation; the gift of the Spirit; the destination of men to be a free people
that praises God; and the unification of the universe under one head—these
eternal, past, present, and future events are carefully knit together. In the
briefest possible manner the various prepositions underline the unity of eternal
destination, historical fulfillment, and expected completion. Each of these elements is given equal weight and is essential to the whole. This internal
structure of Eph 1:3-14 cannot be caught by the discernment of units
formed by successive verses or stanzas. It permeates almost every verse.

Parallel to this observation runs another. While the benediction is from be-

---

[154] *Hymnen*, pp. 67-68.   [155] RGG, II, 519.
[156] Vss. 5-8, 9-11, or 3-6, 7-12, respectively.   [157] TB 5 (1926), 120-25, 231-33.
[158] Eleven times "in Christ" or equivalents; four times (var. lect. six times) with a noun.
[159] In the translation an attempt was made to cover up the all too embarrassing compilations.
[160] For the use of the prepositions in the NT see BDF, 203-40.

ginning to end a praise of God, his love, his deed, his purpose, and his achievement—while it is, in brief, a strictly theological treatise—the word "God" occurs in the Greek text only once, in 1:3. But the passage bristles with references to the fatherly attitude and action of God, to Jesus Christ's function and responsibility for God's people and the world, and, at the beginning and end, to the presence and operation of the Holy Spirit. It has been noted by the majority of interpreters that the benediction has a trinitarian structure which moves from the Father through the Son to the Spirit.[161] In order to give an opportunity for the discovery and enjoyment of this internal structure the translation offered above had to refrain from dissecting the benediction into separate parts corresponding e.g. to the Apostolic and Nicene Creeds. Each subdivision would certainly have obfuscated the unity of God, salvation, and revelation. The relatively sharp division between the work of the Father, of the Son, of the Spirit, which Greek and Latin Fathers attempted or were forced to put into formulae of confession, the Hebrew Paul was unable or unwilling to present to his readers. But see 4:4–6.

II   Spiritual Blessing

Three meanings of the adjective "spiritual," can be distinguished: (a) In the Pauline writings the adjective "spiritual" is sometimes used as an attribute of a person, or of a thing or status belonging to the heavenly world. "Earthly" persons or "fleshly" matters are the opposite.[162] In Eph 6:12 hostile heavenly powers are called "spiritual (hosts)." (b) The adjective may also qualify special (charismatic) gifts of God, including palpable things such as food or drink, whose meaning can be understood and explained, through spiritual[163] interpretation, by inspired men only.[164] (c) Above all, those things or events are called "spiritual" that are a result and evidence of the presence of the Spirit.[165]

The distinction between local, epistemological, and dynamic meanings of the term "spiritual" does not necessarily mean that the predominance of one meaning in a given passage excludes the presence of the two others. However, since in Eph 1:3 the "spiritual blessing" is not explicitly put in contrast to earthly blessings as received by the saints (at, e.g. the time of Moses or the patriarchs) the first among the three senses just mentioned appears not to determine this verse.[166] Elsewhere Paul declares as "spiritual" the law, the manna, and the water given to Israel.[167] It is probable that in Eph 1:3 by "spiritual blessing" is meant that decision, action, and revelation of God which has culminated and been "sealed" when the "Holy Spirit" was given to both Gentiles and Jews (1:13–14; 4:30). How did the nations receive the "blessing" promised to Abraham, and through Abraham to them? When they

---

[161] M. H. Scharlemann, "The Secret of God's Plan," ConcTM 40 (1969), 532–44; 41 (1970), 155–64, 338–46, 410–20 goes so far as to identify the very secret of God's plan (Eph 3:9) with that of the three persons of the Trinity as described in 1:3–14.

[162] Gal 6:1; Rom 15:27; I Cor 3:1; 9:11; 14:37; 15:44, 46.

[163] Or on occasion, allegorical.

[164] Rom 1:11; I Cor 2:13, 15; 10:3–4; 12:1; 14:1; also Rom 7:14; I Peter 2:5.

[165] Eph 5:19; Col 1:9; 3:16; I Peter 2:5; perhaps Rom 7:14.

[166] Chrysostom, Erasmus, Calvin, Bengel, Robinson play out the difference between spiritual and material blessings.

[167] Rom 7:14; I Cor 10:3–4.

were given the Spirit![168] Now they cry, "Abba, Father"; now the secret and wisdom of God is made known to them; now they confess that "Jesus is Lord"; now manifold "spiritual gifts" (*charismata*) are manifest among them.[169] Obviously they offer tangible evidence of God's blessing. This blessing makes history.

"Spiritual blessing," therefore, does not mean a timeless, otherworldly, abstract blessing. Rather it describes changes effected upon and among people of flesh and blood. It means a history, that is, decisions, actions, testimonies, suffering[170] which have been set in motion and are as yet unfinished.

III   Heavens

The Hebrew word used for "heaven" in the OT is always in the plural. This does not prove that all OT writers had one and the same image of the structure of the universe and assumed that there were several heavens forming concentric spheres and lying one over another like the layers of an onion cut in half. But sometimes[171] several heavens are explicitly mentioned. Paul shows in II Cor 12:2 that he is similarly convinced of a hierarchic order among several heavens. The Ethiopic (I) Enoch (20–36) offers a topography of the various parts of heaven. According to Slavonic (II) Enoch (8–10) paradise and hell are found in the same sphere. Several passages of Ephesians[172] reveal that the work of peacemaking and the victory of Christ are not limited to the earth but pertain as well to the heavenly realms and their occupants.[173]

This is not the place to enter a description and discussion of the Celestial Hierarchy of Dionysos Areopagita. But among recent courageous attempts to tackle the problems posed by biblical utterances on the heavens,[174] Schlier's[175] is of special interest. He goes to some length to offer a demythologized, i.e. existential, interpretation of the "heavenly places." These spheres are identified with the transcendental dimension of human life. They mean all that lies beyond man's control, even the threats and challenges to which man is exposed and which force him to ever new decisions, especially to the willingness to fight. In his excursus on the term "heavenly places" M. Dibelius is less certain of their exact sense. He suspects this "hieratic" term was

---

[168] Gal 3:2, 5, 8 and esp. 3:14; 4:6.

[169] Rom 8:15 and Gal 4:6; I Cor 2:9–16 ff; 12–14; Eph 3:1 ff; Gal 5:22–23. The whole chapter (Rom 8) deals exclusively with this topic.

[170] Gal 3:2–5, etc.

[171] E.g. Deut 10:14; I Kings 8:27.

[172] 1:10; 2:2; 4:8–10; 6:12; cf. Dan 10; Rev 12; Jude 6, 9; also Matt 12:25–29. Special interest in events occurring in heaven, or in the several heavens, is displayed in apocalyptic, apocryphal, sectarian and, above all, Gnostic literature. See e.g. *Ascension of Isaiah* xi 22–40. In most cases a direct or indirect influence of astrology has to be presupposed. See F. Cumont, *Astrology and Religion among the Greeks and Romans*, London: Constable, 1912; repr. New York: Dover, 1960; M. P. Nilsson, *Geschichte der griechischen Religion*, II (Munich: Beck, 1950), pp. 256–67, 465–97. For briefer presentations see R. Bultmann, *Primitive Christianity* (New York: Thames, 1957), pp. 146–55; and C. Neugebauer. "The History of Ancient Astronomy," JNES 4 (1945), 1–38.

[173] In COMMENT V on 1:15–23 an attempt will be made to identify the principalities and powers ruling in those realms.

[174] E.g. Karl Barth, *Church Dogmatics*, III:3 (Edinburgh: Clark, 1961), 369–531; H. Traub, TWNTE, V, 497–536; H. Bietenhard, *Die himmlische Welt im Urchristentum und Spätjudentum*, Tübingen: Mohr, 1951; U. Simon, *Heaven in the Christian Tradition*, New York: Harper, 1958; J. G. Davies, *He Ascended into Heaven*, New York: Association, 1958.

[175] *Christus*, pp. 1–18, esp. 6, n. i; Schlier, pp. 45–48.

borrowed for reasons unknown from a non-Christian cult. Schille[176] suggests a Christian (baptismal) liturgy.

While at present any certainty in matters of origin and meaning of this term is not attainable, two things may be pertinent to the understanding of Eph 1. (a) The "heavens" are not to be understood as a locality or space only. As the references to thrones of rulers (1:20, 2:6) and to principalities and powers show, "heavens" is not defined by geographical limits but determined by the exertion of power. In terms of modern physics "heavens" is a field or several fields. It is not limited to an intangible and invisible sphere but it exerts its influence upon life, history, and conduct on earth.[177] (b) "Heavens" is still being misused for disorderly conduct by powers inimical to God and man (6:12). This does not prevent or threaten the right order of heaven which consists in, and will be consummated by, the submission of all powers to Jesus Christ (1:20–23; 4:10).[178]

In sum, the mention of "heavens" in Eph 1:3, just like the attribute "spiritual," has by no means a limiting function. On the contrary, the extension, efficiency, validity, and sufficiency of God's blessing is pointed out. God himself is the source of blessing, and all real or imagined dimensions of creation and of man's existence are permeated and changed by that blessing —the still ongoing rebellion of some powers (6:12) notwithstanding. In COMMENT IV on 2:1–10 and in the exposition of 4:8–10 more will be said on the surprising connotations of the term "heavens."

IV   Creation and Fall

Gnostic documents ascribe the origin of the world to a cosmic fall by which the primordial unity of all things in the All-Father was lost, as the fullness of a first created sphere was destroyed.[179] Just as H. Schlier deemed it possible to explain "heavens" in terms of existentialist philosophy, H. Jonas[180] identified the common denominator of the myths, narrating a cosmic fall, with M. Heidegger's concept of "thrown-ness." Creation and fall are in this case not only contemporaneous, but practically synonymous. A poor light falls on the deity that caused or permitted creation. Tragic love stories and the concomitant conflicts of supernatural powers, including at times Wisdom and stars, explain the miserable human condition. The very existence of man under the law of fate (*anagkē, heimarmenē*) is understood as a curse.

But H.-M. Schenke[181] recently attempted, with the help of both earlier and newly discovered materials, to give a more subtle picture of the various

---

[176] *Hymnen,* p. 68.

[177] The Qumranite anthropology, as it is unfolded in 1QS III 13 – IV 26, and its Pauline counterparts in Rom 7:7–25 and Gal 5:16–25 reveal a clear connection between the spirits, or the Spirit, and the conduct of each man. See E. Kamlah, *Die Form der katalogischen Paränese im Neuen Testament* (henceforth DFKP) WUNT 7 (1964).

[178] Cf. e.g. I Cor 15:24–27; Philip 2:10–11.

[179] Schille, *Hymnen,* p. 70, sums up the opinion of the Gnosticizing interpretation of Eph 1:4 by asserting, "the formula *before the down-thrust of the world* cannot belie the traces of a mythological worldview. The Gnostic creation myth treats of the down-thrust of the Psyche's substance into matter or starts from the thought of the masculine sexual function. Both notions are proper to the concept *katabolē* [down-thrust]." It is to be noted that Schille speaks of "the Gnostic creation myth" as though there were but one.

[180] *Gnostic Religion,* pp. 62–63, 320–40.

[181] GMG.

Gnostic myths and notions of creation. The result of his labors and other recent work on Gnosticism[182] is an end to the all too rash conglomeration and exegetical or existentialist exploitation of Gnostic patterns of belief. The traits of Valentinian Gnosticism especially are so diversified and certainly to a large extent so late that they cannot, and must not determine the interpretation of Ephesians. The OT notion of God the architect, who has "founded" the world "upon the seas" (Ps 24:2), or who has otherwise laid a firm and deep foundation (Amos 9:6; Isa 45:18), rather than Gnosticism, stands behind the terminology used in Eph 1:4.

Indeed, while the word for creation employed in Eph 1:4 has the etymological meaning, down-thrust, Eph 1:4 and its context show no sign whatsoever of a dualistic worldview and a tragic understanding of earthly existence. Not even the distinction of the present from the future aeon (1:21), or the mention of present evil days (5:16; cf. Gal 1:4), would support this assumption. The same God who is "the creator of all things" has now "given grace" and "revealed his secret" (3:3–9). The very verb "to create" is repeatedly[183] used to describe salvation. In Ephesians neither a bad nor a neutral but a good concept of creation prevails throughout. Otherwise the author would not be able to give specific ethical exhortations affecting all realms of life, and to call for the singing of hymns (5:19, cf. 1:3–14), even when "the days are bad" (5:16) and a worse day is looming ahead (6:13). Literary evidence for the notion of a downfall of the world dates from almost one hundred or more years after the composition of Ephesians. What Valentinus and Mani and their respective disciples after them have said of creation is neither presupposed, nor endorsed, nor fought against in this epistle—though Ephesians was used in due time for supporting both Gnostic and anti-Gnostic teachings.

Another observation confirms this judgment. Not earlier than 1:7—and there under the heading of liberation and forgiveness, and by employment of the extenuating term "lapses"—does this epistle speak of men as sinners. Sin is obviously not considered the presupposition of man's election by God. As was earlier observed, God's grace is real before the foundation of the earth and the beginning of earthly or fleshly history. Because of man's sin Jesus Christ's commission to unite and dominate all things (1:10) receives special relevance and requires the special price of his blood. But the love of God for his Son and the inclusion of men in that love are independent of sin. God's creatures are not sinful because they are created. But creation follows upon the election by love and means nothing else but the first realization of the counsel of grace. Sin is a later incident which despite all its seriousness, filth, and deadliness cannot call into question the goodness of creation.[184] God asserts himself, and he confirms his grace not by revoking creation but by creating a new man (Eph 2:15 ff; 4:24).

[182] See BIBLIOGRAPHY 2.   [183] 2:10, 15; 4:24.
[184] Robinson, p. 28, calls sin an "interloper" in the eternal counsel of God.

V   Election in Christ vs. Determinism

The praise of God who elects men by grace (Eph 1:4–5; cf. Rom 11:5),[185] is something other than the proclamation of a principle or axiom of absolute determinism. There are six distinctive reasons why Ephesians cannot be considered the charter for the eternal predestination of one part of mankind for bliss, the other for hell, and a seventh reason which by itself is decisive.

a) The tone of the statements made on God's decision is adoring rather than calculating or speculative. God himself is being praised, not a fate or system above God, or a scheme created by him. No effort is made to construct systems and draw consequences; neither is election balanced by reprobation or rejection.[186] There is no hint of creation for a double destiny of man,[187] and least of all any correlated doctrine regarding the mediating role of the stars, the natural seasons, or the psychic structure of man.[188] According to Eph 1, to speak of election means to speak of God himself, not of dominating or intervening forces. Here Paul describes the single attitude and act of God, i.e. his love and—unlike Rom 9:13, 18—not a double edge of his will, e.g. love and hatred.

b) The election of men is not one among several features of an impersonal omnipotent rule or disposition of a deity over all created things.[189] To the contrary, it is described in strictly personal terms. It pertains exclusively to the relationship of the Father to his children. If no wise human father would treat his children according to a schedule fixed before their birth, how much less would the Father blessed in Eph 1:3–14! The father-child imagery stands in opposition to a thinking based upon the patterns of cause/effect, blueprint/fabrication, and (last) will/execution. It describes solely the love relationship of living persons. Mechanical predetermination calls forth the reaction of marionettes to the wire-pulling artist: there may be blind submission and compliance; there may also be fruitless rebellion or mechanical failure. But election for adoption finds its response in hearing, believing, hoping, loving, praising. In apocalyptical, Qumranite, and rabbinical forms of Judaism, belief in the predetermination of all things and in the special election of Israel played a large role. This faith served well to sustain persecuted communities and individuals in hours of threatening despair. It did not exclude, but paradoxically embraced a warm and personal relation to God. The same is true of the conviction expressed in Eph 1:4 ff. The saints are not subject to the whims of fate or to an anonymous predetermining force. Their election is praised in a language fitting the glorification of the heavenly Father's love.

c) God's relationship to the saints is described in terms which lack orig-

---

[185] See P. Maury, *Erwählung und Glaube*, Theologische Studien 8, Zurich: EVZ, 1940; Karl Barth, *Gottes Gnadenwahl*, Theologische Studien 47, 1936; *Church Dogmatics*, II:2 (1957), 3–506.

[186] As in Calvin's or Beza's doctrines of double predestination. Eph 5:5 treats not predestination but the consequence of the conduct of some church members.

[187] But see 1QS III 13 – IV 26.

[188] As it appears to have been held in Qumran and Colossae.

[189] In the Westminster Confession of Faith 1647, ch. III, double predestination is treated as a subdivision among the absolute decrees of God. It is understood as the specific way in which God applies to man his absolute sovereignty over all things.

inality. The author is dependent on OT statements about election.[190] However, the language used to praise election contains no hint of the author's acquaintance with earlier or contemporary philosophical discussions and his intent to participate in the debates. E.g. the problems of the prime mover, the one and the many, the relationship between being and appearing, the ideal and the phenomenal world appear not to have bothered him. He is satisfied when he can speak of God and Christ in OT terminology. But while OT passages proclaiming election show necessarily a particularist slant in favor of a patriarch, a tribe, a king, or the whole of Judah or Israel, the letter to the Ephesians has a universalist ring. Not only Israel but the nations too are included in God's love, peace, and worship.[191]

d) The eternal election of Jews and Gentiles is not a mystery that must remain hidden. Neither is it a gratuitous corollary to the gospel. God has set a time for making it known through revelation, and special ministers have been appointed to spread it abroad. Therefore, it cannot be suppressed by secrecy or for pedagogical reasons. The gospel is the publication of the secret of election.

e) Election cannot be identified with an event of the remote past or with a timeless divine will. Rather, in Eph 1:4 ff. the election which precedes the time and space of the created world is coupled with deeds effected by God and experienced by men in time and history. God elects not only before the creation of the world but He is and remains the electing God when his grace is poured out, when sins are forgiven, when revelation opens the eyes of man's mind, and when the seal of the Spirit quickens the dead and assembles those dispersed. Again, the same (eternal and present) election is also the future destiny of the saints. They are chosen to live as God's beloved and loving children, and to glorify God publicly by their very existence. Election (just as liberation) is not merely election from . . . , or election by means of. . . . It is completed only when those things have occurred for which God has designated the children he wanted to adopt. In sum, election is an event which is still being fulfilled. The planner of a medieval cathedral may die before his work is completed, but it may nevertheless be completed exactly according to his plans. The author of a book may die yet his work come to life only after his death. God who elects the saints does not die but sees to it in person that his decision is executed. Eph 1:3–14 speaks of neither a testament nor an epitaph but an ongoing dialogue with the living God. The image of the "book of life" in which the names of God's elect are written down is not used in Ephesians.[192]

f) Awareness of God's election is given together with awareness of the forgiveness of sins. Election means resurrection from the dead. It is not derived from the experience that one part of mankind has a holy, happy, or successful life while another appears condemned to frustration and misery. The elect know they have been engulfed by the same death which, because of sin, has come over all mankind.[193] Theirs is not an easy life that invites

---

[190] Deut 7:6–8 may be quoted as an example: "You are a people holy to the Lord your God; the Lord your God has chosen you to be a people for his own possession . . . not because you were more in number than any other people . . . but it is because the Lord loves you."
[191] 1:11–14; 2:1 – 3:6.
[192] But it occurs in Philip 4:3; Luke 10:20; Rev 3:5 etc.; cf. Exod 32:32–33; Ps 69:28; Dan 12:1.
[193] Rom 5:12, 14; 11:32 is reflected in Eph 1:7; 2:1–6, 11–18; 4:17–24; 5:14.

conclusions drawn from alleged freedom from any threat. But they live by hope for final redemption (1:14, 18); they are in prison (3:1, 13; 4:1; 6:20); their days are full of evil because impurity in their own ranks and devilish attacks of superior powers threaten them (5:3–16; 6:10–17). Awareness of election is neither a church steeple from which to view the human landscape nor a pillow to sleep on. But it is a stronghold in times of temptations and trials.[194]

While these six elements distinguish election from determinism, the main feature of Eph 1:3–14 has not yet been mentioned: this passage states that the election of the saints was made "in Christ."[195] The meaning of "election in Christ" is manifold and cannot be comprehended in one definition. For the sentences in which the formula "in Christ" occurs give it several interrelated, but clearly distinct, interpretations:

a) Christ has a passive role in election. He is the epitome of the beloved (1:6), the first upon whom God set his favor (1:9), or briefly, the first elect.[196]

b) As such Jesus Christ is the revelation, or to use Calvin's expression, "the mirror" of revelation. "The secret of God's decision" has been "made known" through the favor which was "set upon Christ" and through the charge with which he was entrusted (1:8–10). In 2:5–6 the resuscitation of the saints from their death in sins is clearly described in terms derived from Jesus Christ's resurrection (1:20). Resurrection from death, together with Christ, is the content of election. Apart from the revelation given in the resurrection of Christ there is no election.

c) Christ is also the means or instrument of election. "Through him" the adoption of many children is to be carried out (1:5); "through his blood" they are liberated and forgiven. God administers and carries out election through Jesus Christ.

d) The commission given to Christ lifts him far beyond the level of an impersonal tool, an intangible sphere, or an agent who fulfills his role mechanically. Rather Jesus Christ's function in election is that of a free, responsible, active agent.[197] Precisely when the death of Christ, seemingly the lowest ebb of his passive role, is mentioned, the epistle makes use of active terms. "He has made both [Gentiles and Jews] into one. For he has broken down the dividing wall, in his flesh . . . to make peace by creating in his person a single new man. . . . he has killed the enmity. . . . he proclaimed good news. . . . He will shine upon you. . . . He has loved us and has given himself for us. . . . He has loved the church and given himself for her to make her holy."[198]

The formula "in Christ" denotes the concentration, summation, revelation,

---

[194] This was the original intention of Calvin's doctrine of predestination. He wanted to give comfort to the dwindling Protestant minorities. See J. Haroutunian, *Calvin: Commentaries,* Library of Christian Classics 23 (Philadelphia: Westminster, 1958), pp. 37–50.

[195] In the closest parallel to Eph 1:4–5, i.e. Rom 8:29; cf. Philip 3:10–11, 21, the connection of election with Christ is essential and expressed by terms indicating *conformity* with the crucified and risen one (see also I Cor 1:26–30).

[196] So I Peter 1:20; cf. Matt 3:17 par.; 11:27; 17:5. See the Note on "the beloved" in 1:6. I Clement is perhaps the earliest extra-canonical witness extant for Ephesians. In 64:1 the statement is made, "God . . . elected the Lord Jesus Christ and through him us for his own people." Thus the election of Christ is at the same time distinguished from ours and connected with it.

[197] The Gospel of John points this out 5:17; 6:70; 13:18; 15:16, 19, "My Father goes on working, and so do I . . . I have chosen you." Compare Christ's role as "administrator" in Eph 1:10.

[198] Eph 2:14–17; 5:14, 2, 25–26.

and execution of God's own decision in one person, that is, the Messiah upon whom the Jews had set their hope (1:12). This mediation of God's gracious decision through one person is analogous to the OT utterances on the relationship between God, Abraham, Israel, and the nations.[199] The function of Moses also offers a precedent and illustration. With this chosen servant God speaks directly. This servant sees God. Through his hands Israel is liberated from Egypt and the law is given. His greatest function is probably as an intercessor for Israel.[200] Finally, there is David. In the books of Samuel and in the (late) prescripts to the Psalms which attribute their composition or meaning to "David," David is cast as the epitome of humiliation and defeat, but also of salvation and exaltation by grace alone. He is the exemplary singer of God's praise when he praises God for salvation from death. Little wonder that Matthew takes such pains to describe Jesus as the "son of Abraham," the "servant of God," the "son of David."[201] The OT figures *in* whom God has elected, blessed, ordered, borne, and saved the life of his people may with Heb 8:5; 10:1 be called a "foreshadowing." Paul himself speaks in an analogous context of a "type of the one who was to come" (Rom 5:14; cf. I Cor 10:11).

In Eph 1 the apostle does not explicitly quote OT texts to undergird or illustrate his statements on God's eternal election or the days of fulfillment. But his diction and doctrine are filled with OT elements and allusions. The biblical figures mentioned and their function in God's dealings with Israel and the nations certainly offer a weighty alternative to a mystical or spheric interpretation of the formula "in Christ."

In COMMENT I on Eph 1:1–2 it was pointed out that this formula describes God's relationship to the congregation of the saints rather than to individuals only. Election "in Christ" must be understood as election of God's people. Only as members of that community do individuals share in the benefits of God's gracious choice.

A conclusion can now be drawn which distinguishes decisively between the election of God as praised in Ephesians and a fatalistic belief in an absolute decree. If the person of Jesus Christ is the prime object and subject, the revealed secret and instrument of God's election, and if he represents all those elected, then all notions of a fixed will, testament, plan, and program of God are not only inadequate but contrary to the sense of Eph 1. Election does not consist of the creation of a scheme which divides mankind into two opposite groups. Much more is it that person-to-person relationship of love which exists in the relation between God and his Son and is revealed only by the events that manifest this relationship. Thus election has nothing to do with a prescription or schedule. God's election is not an *absolute* decree, but is relative to the Son, his mission, death, resurrection. God's love of the Messiah is not legislated or fixed in a book. It is a matter of

[199] Gen 12:1–3; 18:22–33; Deut 32:18; Isa 41:8; 51:1–2. The Talmudic reference to election in Abraham (GnR 44 [27a]) was mentioned earlier.
[200] Exod 3 ff; 14:31; 19 ff; 32:30, 32; Num 14:13–19; Deut 1:37; 3:26; 34:5, etc. See C. Barth, "Mose, Knecht Gottes," in *Parrhesia,* Fs K. Barth, (Zürich: EVZ, 1966), pp. 68–81, for the connection between the ministry of the servant and intercessor.
[201] E.g. 1:1; 12:18–21; 21:9. "Son of . . ." means not only descent but also "the kind of . . ." Character and function of a person are described by the reference to his origin.

God's heart. While a scheme or plan is to be carried out according to the letter, Jesus Christ is not given a detailed job description. Rather he is trusted to act out freely what pleases the Father. To repeat an earlier observation, a god who has fixed every detail beforehand may retire or die. His presence is no longer required. But the Father who will reveal his love and rule through the Son watches over the Son, hears his prayer, sees his agony, raises him from the dead, and pours out the Spirit given to his Son over many. He does not permit the Son's blood to be spilled in vain. Though in form and substance the benediction of Eph 1 closely resembles contemporary Jewish (esp. apocalyptic) utterances, the words "in Christ" and the emphasis laid on Christ's relationship to God and man reveal the unique character of this *Christian* proclamation of eternal election.

Eph 1 bears testimony to the living God, the Father, the Son, and the Spirit. Everything said is personal, intimate, functional. An invitation to fatalism under the scheme of double predestination or another deterministic plan cannot be found here.

VI   Pre-existence

A thorough discussion of the term "pre-existence of Christ," belongs to the exposition of Col 1:15–20.[202] The problem of Christ's pre-existence in *Israel* is posed by Eph 2:12. Pre-existent "good works" are mentioned in 2:10. Only the special contribution of Eph 1:4 ff. to the topic of pre-existence is to be described now.

Several NT key passages that speak of the so-called pre-existent Christ[203] have one common feature: they speak of Christ's (the Logos', the Son's) relation to *all things* (*panta* or *ta panta*), before they describe his special function for men.[204] He is denoted—to use an ambiguous nomenclature which may have to be corrected later—"mediator of creation"[205] before his ministry for the salvation of men is praised. In Eph 1:4–10 this order is reversed. Even before the creation of the world God "has chosen *us* in Christ" (1:4). Christ's cosmic assignment "to comprehend all things under one head" is mentioned only later, in 1:10. In Ephesians the representative function of Christ for mankind and its salvation by God not only precedes the laying of the world's foundations, but actually takes the place of any explicit mention of Christ's participation in the creation of heaven and earth. God

---

[202] Cf. fn. 206 and the text *supra* fn. 262.

[203] John 1:1 ff; 17:4; I Cor 8:6; Col 1:15 ff; Heb 1:3–4; also Matt 11:25–30; Rev 3:14. But Philip 2:6; II Cor 8:9 are exceptions. In these texts Christ's pre-incarnation relationship to men is mentioned without previous reference to his function in relation to "all things." Christ's relationship to "all things" is sometimes (e.g. in I Cor 7:6b; Eph 1:22–23) correlated with his relationship to man—without an explicit reference to pre-existence. F. B. Craddock, *The Pre-existence of Christ in the New Testament*, Nashville: Abingdon, 1968, gives an account of the biblical and non-biblical background of the idea of pre-existence, its use throughout the NT, and its role in the church's creeds, and in modern theological debate. See also F.-J. Steinmetz, *Protologische Heilszuversicht*, Frankfurter Theologische Studien 2, Frankfurt: Knecht, 1969; P. Benoit, "Pré-existence et incarnation," RB 77 (1970), 5–29; R. G. Hamerton-Kelly, "The Idea of Pre-existence in Early Judaism," diss. Union Theological Seminary, New York, 1966 (ref.); idem, *Pre-existence, Wisdom, and the Son of Man*, Society for NT Studies Monograph Series 21, Cambridge University Press, 1973.

[204] This sequence may explain why in dogmatic presentations predestination figures sometimes under the heading of God's (universal) providence.

[205] Cf. Hegermann, *Schöpfungsmittler*.

is "the creator of all things," so it is affirmed in 3:9—and there is no explicit affirmation that all things were created "in Christ" or "through him." Instead, Ephesians asserts more emphatically than John 1 and Heb 1, and as pointedly as Colossians, that Christ unites under his rule and fills all things in heaven and upon earth (1:10, 22–23). What, then, is Christ's role in creation? Eph 2:15 states that it is he who creates "a new man" out of the divided mankind— just as according to John 17:24 it is he who works and prays *ut omnes unum sint*. In Eph 1:4 God's eternal love of his children and Christ's responsibility for them are given priority over the concern for all things.

The pre-existence of Christ as it is proclaimed in Eph 1 does not mean that the author imagined two deities coexisting in eternity first for their own sake,[206] and then, eventually, for the sake of creating a universe. Rather the ground and the source, the reality and the possibility of a future demonstration of God's love of his children is pointed out when God's transhistorical relationship to Christ, and Christ's to God, are mentioned. The eternal concreteness and validity of the full blessing of man is vouchsafed by God's eternal love of the Son. The Son is the eternal reality, and he is therefore the reliable demonstration in history of a love which is not accidental but essential to God. The eternal presence of the Son at the Father's side is the substance and ground of the affirmation that love is of God's essence. Love can by no means be separated from God or be identified with a passing whim, a retractable decision, a historical coincidence.[207] God *is* love—this is the essence of Christ's pre-existence.

In the fashion of the philosophically trained Scholastics, Paul's interpreters have drawn conclusions concerning God's being from the action that took place in Christ before the creation.[208] But the Scholastics were not the first to speak of pre-existence and to make an ontological statement out of doxological and functional descriptions. Jewish Wisdom books call wisdom "God's image" or "technician."[209] This wisdom is eventually identified with the Law (or Word) of God[210] and the Spirit.[211] Its cosmic and soteriological roles are equally emphasized.[212] Though functional terminology prevails, it is also called, in ontological terms, "God's first creature." This means that its pre-existence is temporal rather than eternal. Philo, along with apocalyptic and rabbinic literature, shows the influence of this doctrine and expands it.[213] Paul, however, speaks of eternal pre-existence of the Son;

[206] Among the NT passages, only John 1:1 in the current translation, "the Word was with God, and the Word was God," seems to speak of a static co-existence. The more literal translation, "the Word was [directed] toward God," and the later Johannine reference in 17:5 to the "glory" that was Christ's "with thee [God] before the world was made" correct this impression. Cf. Prov 8 and Wisd Sol 8 regarding the pre-existence of Wisdom.

[207] Cf. P. Althaus, RGG, V, 492, s.v. "Präexistenz Christi." W. Manson, "The Son of Man in Daniel, Enoch and the Gospels," BJRL 32 (1950), 184, prefers the term "pre-mundane election" to "pre-existence."

[208] The axiom *Operari sequitur esse* is prone to eradicate or invite speculative thought. Speculation, in turn, need not necessarily be an evil use of man's mind.

[209] Job 15:7 ff; 28; Prov 8:22–31, esp. 8:30; Wisd Sol 7:22 – 8:1; Sir 1:4–10; 24:9; see BIBLIOGRAPHY 8 and COMMENT X.

[210] Prov 28:4, 7; Ezra 7:25; Bar 4:1; Sir 24:3–9, 23; Wisd Sol 9:1–2; cf. Deut 4:6; Rom 2:20; StB, II, 353 ff.; III, 131; Davies, PRJ pp. 168–73.

[211] Wisd Sol 7:7, 21–25; 9:17.   [212] Esp. Wisd Sol 7–10.

[213] Philonic references are collected e.g. by Hegermann, *Schöpfungsmittler*, pp. 6–88; rabbinic texts, by Davies, PRJ, pp. 147–76; the rabbinic texts dealing with the several pre-existent things are also discussed by A. M. Goldberg, "Schöpfung und Geschichte," *Judaica* 24 (1968), 27–44; cf. Schlier,

the Son is not created. The one God is in all eternity what he is in his relation to the Son.

Of special importance for understanding Eph 1 are not those things eventually considered pre-existent by the rabbis,[214] but the utterances found in apocalyptic writings on the (pre-existent) hidden Messiah who will be revealed, and on the pre-existent heavenly sanctuary or heavenly Jerusalem which will descend and replace the earthly one.[215]

In Jewish apocalypticism, the connection between the pre-existent Messiah and the pre-existent Jerusalem is loose. In Rev 19 and 21 (cf. Eph 5:22–23) they are related as bride and bridegroom. Equally, Eph 1:4–6 combines God's love of the Son so intimately with the election of God's people before the foundation of the world that some interpreters[216] have found in this text not only the doctrine of the pre-existence of Christ, but also a theory of the pre-existent church. It is certainly noteworthy that, in contradistinction to Gnostic myths, Ephesians and other NT Books show no trace of a combination of the pre-existent savior with the pre-existent souls of human individuals.[217] But does it make sense to speak of the pre-existent church?[218]

a) The answer must be affirmative if by pre-existence nothing is meant but the precedence of thought or decision over action or execution. The

---

pp. 49–50 n. 4, and StB, III, 351–55, 435–39. II Bar 17–19; 59 is in certain aspects a parallel to them. Among apocalyptic materials see also: Apoc (IV) Ezra 13:26; Ethiopic (I) Enoch 48:2. Hamerton-Kelly (see fn. 203) examines the complete early Jewish (OT, LXX, Philonic, tannaitic, apocalyptical) material.

[214] In the Talmud tractate *Pesachim* 54a; cf. *Nedarim* 39b, seven things, i.e. the law, repentance, paradise, Gehinnom (hell), the throne of glory, the heavenly sanctuary, and the Messiah are not called pre-created, but pre-conceived in God's thoughts. These (late, and far from generally accepted) rabinical teachings may be a reflection of the Platonic doctrine of the pre-existent ideas, or may be the result of a reasoning that anticipates the Christian Scholastics' endorsement of Aristotelian ontology; see fn. 208.

[215] Ethiopic (I) Enoch 39:7; 40:5; 46:1–6; 48:3–4; 89:73; 90:28–29; Slavonic (II) Enoch 61:2; II Bar 4:26; IV Ezra 8:52; 13:32; cf. John 1:33; Matt 11:25–30; Gal 4:26; Heb 8:5; 9:23; 12:22; Rev 21:2, 10. The primeval origin of the Messiah hinted at e.g. in Micah 5:2; the engraving of Zion in God's own hands mentioned in Isa 49:16; the heavenly archetype of the earthly sanctuary intimated in Exod 25:9, 40; 26:30; 27:8; Num 8:4—such biblical passages may lie behind the later visionary and speculative developments of thought. Eph 2:12 presupposes the pre-existence of the Messiah and/or of his benefits for Israel; see below. E. Sjöberg, *Der verborgene Gottessohn in den Evangelien*, Lund: Gleerup, 1955, discusses extensively the utterances related to the pre-existent Messiah.

[216] Among them Schlier, 49–50, 268 ff. In the literature of the early church, see II Clem. XIV; also Herm. *vis.* I 1:6; iii 4–5 may be relevant.

[217] As U. Wilckens, RGG, V, 492, rightly observes. He quotes as a counter example *Gospel of Thomas* 19, "Blessed is he who was before he was created." In *Corp. Herm.* XI 20 the divine nature of the human soul may include its pre-existence, and a Platonic idea may be reflected.

[218] E.g. in the words of Herm. *vis.* II iv 1, "She was created the first of all things . . . and for her sake was the world established"; cf. II Clem. XIV 1–3. Davies, PRJ, 150 ff., warns against mistaking terms of glorification for mythological or literalist descriptions; they ought not to be used for a mythification of the church. Schoeps, *Paul*, p. 150, lashes out against Paul because he allegedly "for the first time made out of it [the title "God's Son"] a title of dignity and ontological affirmation, and raised it to a mythical level of thought." Davies' warning and Schoep's ire would in this case have to be directed not only against Paul's Chrisology but against the "high ecclesiology" of the apostle as well. Indeed, Hamerton-Kelly, *Pre-existence, Wisdom, and the Son of Man*, pp. 108–12, 156, 185–86, esp. 191–95, suggests that Paul's contribution to apocalyptic and sapiential reflections on pre-existence lies in the field of ecclesiology rather than of Christology. The (incidental!) reference to "Jerusalem above" in Gal 4:26 is considered solid evidence of a genuine Pauline speculation on a pre-existing church or temple, which in turn is linked up with the pre-existent Christ through the pre-existence of the head-body relationship! The Adam-*guf* speculations, which will be discussed in COMMENT VI B to 1:15–23, may be quoted in support of this interpretation of Paul: O. Hofius, "Erwählt vor Grundlegung der Welt (Eph 1:4)," ZNW 62 (1971), 123–28, has shown that in Jewish writings, such as Jub. 2:19 ff. and *Joseph and Aseneth* 8:9, the idea of the election of God's people before the creation is clearly represented. However, the most ecclesiological of Paul's letters, Ephesians, does not unambiguously support Hamerton-Kelly's thesis, least of all in 1:4–5.

conception of an idea antedates its realization. Such pre-existence might be termed noetic. It exists only in the mind. But already the ancient Egyptians' reference to Thought (which may be reflected in a part of Philo's *logos* doctrine),[219] not to speak of John 1:1 ff.; Col 1:15 ff.; Heb 1:3–4; Philip 2:6 ff., forbids such oversimplification. The ontic realm cannot be excluded from the meaning of pre-existence.

b) The answer to the question may be affirmative if by pre-existence of the church not eternity is meant, as is confessed in the praise of the trinity of Father, Son, and Spirit, but a first date and place among the many creatures created by God—as in the Wisdom books ascribed to wisdom, or among rabbis to the law or the heavenly sanctuary. In this case the pre-existence of the church is essentially different from that of Christ, and it might be wise to designate it by a different term.

c) The answer is bound up with an intricate Christological problem if the eternal pre-existence of Christ is explicitly called pre-existence of *Jesus* Christ, i.e. of Jesus of Nazareth, the man, his body, his history.[220] For the earthly, crucified, and raised *body of Christ* is—as the later discussions of the term "body" will show—directly related to, and perhaps identified with, the church. The pre-existence of *Jesus* might necessarily imply the pre-existence of the church. Her pre-existence would then have to be called ontic rather than noetic only.

d) The answer has to be negative if subsequent utterances in Ephesians on the church are taken seriously. The church is the community of those gathered together from dispersion, liberated from wrath and captivity, reconciled after hostility, raised from the dead (2:1–6, 13–18). There is no indication that after the model of Christ (4:9–10)[221] its members have descended before they ascended. The trinitarian creed of the churches ought to be replaced by a quaternitarian confession, which includes the church,[222] if eternal pre-existence were one of her attributes. Actually the church lives because she is eternally chosen by God and given eternal life. Ephesians makes it clear enough that this life is a gift of God. The church's existence is identified with its life. Since life is not a possession the church can hold independently of Jesus Christ's death and resurrection, or without the operation of the vivifying, unifying, and illuminating Spirit, it is not appropriate to Ephesians to speak of the church's pre-existence.

e) A negative answer is finally suggested by the fact that sapiential terminology of pre-existence is often used in the NT[223] for describing Christ's pre-existence, but never for describing the church's pre-existence.

Since Eph 1 does not contain any term equivalent to the cumbersome concept of pre-existence, the interpretation of this chapter ought to be limited to the discussion of "election" and other functional terms. It is doubtful whether Ephesians can serve the construction of a Christian ontology.

---

[219] For Philo's concept of a "second God" see fn. 57 to 1:1–2.

[220] Cf. e.g. the interpretation of K. Barth's Christology given by E. Jüngel, *Gottes Sein ist im Werden*, Tübingen: Mohr, 1967.

[221] Or like the souls in Gnosticizing thought.   [222] Or Mary as her representative.

[223] Schweizer, *Neotestamentica*, pp. 110–21, gives access to the pertinent literature. See esp. Feuillet, *Christ Sagesse*.

VII   Holiness before God

Philo of Alexandria[224] lays special emphasis on biblical passages[225] that treat man's "standing before" God or his "drawing near" to God. To stand or walk before God—this is the apex of communion with God, of perfect humanity, of a wise man's conduct, of beatific vision. The epistle to the Ephesians certainly does not promote the individualistic ideal of perfection which is sought by Philo. But the position of man "before God" which is sketched in 1:4 and more fully described later, is by no means less elevated than that envisaged by the Jewish middle-Platonist.

The adjective "holy" contains a strong priestly element, as seen in the NOTE on *saints* in 1:1. The attribute "blameless" alludes to the indispensable quality of sacrificial animals (Exod 29:1, 38; Lev 22:19–26); perhaps also to the exclusion of cripples from priestly office (Lev 21:17–23; cf. II Sam 5:8). However, in Ephesians holiness and blamelessness are not results of the physical, moral, or social past of some persons. Rather they are the intention, promise, and gift of God to people who have been worse off than bodily, moral, or mental cripples. They were "dead in sins" and have been "resurrected" (2:1–6). In 5:25–27 the self-offering of Christ is shown to be the means by which men are pronounced clean; the status given to the church is not only called "free from spot or wrinkle, . . . holy and blameless" but also "resplendent." Thus the element of the majestic, beautiful, and pleasant is added to priestly qualifications. In the immediate context of 1:4, i.e. in 1:5, 7, 14 several other aspects are placed in the foreground. 1:5 mentions the father-child relationship established by adoption; 1:7 speaks triumphantly of the (legal) possession of release from captivity and of forgiveness; 1:14 combines the familial and juridical elements by referring to an inheritance. In later contexts, biological, architectural, political imagery will be added to complement the priestly term found in 1:4.[226]

VIII   The Praise of God's Glory

The three similar, though slightly varied, references to the purpose of God's decision and work, that is, to the "praise of his glory"[227] in Eph 1:6, 12, 14, are without exact parallels in the LXX and NT.[228] It is unlikely that the mention of the "praise of God's glory" is no more than a superfluous ornament, a brief *bᵉrakāh* (blessing) within the great benediction, or a refrain. If it were so the wording scarcely would change each time. The author of the benediction— whether it was Paul or an unknown Christian before or after his time—wanted

[224] Esp. in *de posteritate Caini* 23–31, but see also *de Abrahamo* 107–76; *de migratione Abrahami* 132–33; cf. G. R. Goodenough, *By Light, Light; The Mystic Gospel of Hellenistic Judaism* (Yale University Press, 1935), p. 152. See also the second NOTE on Eph 5:10.

[225] Such as Gen 17:1; 18:22–23; Deut 5:27.

[226] For information on sanctity and sanctification see esp. R. Asting, *Die Heiligkeit im Urchristentum*, Göttingen: Vandenhoeck, 1930; and K. Stalder, *Das Werk des Geistes in der Heiligung bei Paulus*, Zürich: EVZ, 1962. While Asting (pp. 7–17) may rely too credulously on manaistic notions of ancient religions, Stalder (pp. 101–30) builds upon the OT concept of holiness and shows that sanctification is the overarching topic of Paul's Theology. See the discussion of the term "perfect" in COMMENT VII C to 4:1–16.

[227] See the literature mentioned in the exposition of the Thanksgiving, below in fn. 72 to 1:15–23, esp. G. H. Boobyer, *Thanksgiving and the Glory of God in Paul*.

[228] Though I Chron 16:24–27; Philip 2:11 bear some resemblance.

to make clear that not only the root and means of God's decision and work are located in God himself but also their purpose.[229] In Cor 8:6 this is crisply stated in the terms of a pre-Pauline confession. "From him [i.e. God the Father] are all things and we [exist] for him." This does not mean that God wants ultimately to praise himself. Self-laudation is according to Paul (Rom 2:17–29) a caricature of the word and essence of "praising." God wants to be praised by the children he has adopted. It is their bliss which he seeks. So long and intensively does he shower grace on them that finally they cannot help but sing paeans to his splendid grace. His joy and pleasure in doing good is only fulfilled when they show themselves utterly pleased. Therefore he does not act like a tyrant who suppresses the freedom of his subjects and yet likes nothing better than sycophants praising his generous gifts. The praise God's people are to give is the enthusiastic applause and cheers of captives who have been given freedom (1:7, 14, 3:12). Among others, Psalms 66; 68; 105–108, are songs of such praise. In Eph 5:19–20 (cf. 3:16–17) the readers are admonished never to cease giving thanks. According to I Cor 10:31; Rom 15:6, eating and drinking and all other human actions, including abstention, are to serve the praise of "God's glory." More is suggested than the singing of hymns only, or the saying of grace at table.

The Greek word used for "praise" has a very secular, certainly not a liturgical ring. According to the strange formulation of 1:12 the saints are not just to say, recite, or sing, but "to become [lit. to be] a praise of God's glory." Three tenuous parallels to this surprising statement are found. Isa 62:7 says, "He [the Lord] establishes Jerusalem and makes it a praise in the earth"; Deut 26:19 asserts, "[The Lord] will set you high above all nations that he has made, in praise and in fame and in honor"; and Jer 13:11 affirms the expectation "that they might be for me a people, a name, a praise and a glory." While Eph 1:6, 14 did not say explicitly who was to give praise to God's glory,[230] 1:12 makes it unmistakably clear that here as much as in Deuteronomy, Isaiah, and Jeremiah Israel is meant. This people was destined not only to give praise but "to be a praise." The similarity and shades of difference of the various forms of diction may well correspond to those of "bringing honor" and "being an honor" to one's family, profession, city, or country. He who *is* a praise is characterized by more than just occasional outbursts of enthusiasm or by martyrdom once bravely endured. His total existence in good and evil days, from the cradle to the grave, his strength and his weakness are included. Following Eph 1:12 God has decided that the Jews should be minstrels of God not solely in special hours, places, actions, sufferings, but through their very existence—be it in the promised land or in exile, in positions of honor as held by Joseph and Daniel, or in the predicament of Jeremiah and Jonah. The etymological interpretation given to the name "Judah" in Gen 29:35 is employed for a play on words by Paul in Rom 2:17–29: it is the destiny of the Jews to "praise the Lord," and

---

[229] Boobyer, *Thanksgiving*, pp. 78–87, on the basis of II Cor 4:13–18. Boobyer assumes that in the Pauline churches "probably special liturgical thanksgiving was practiced for glorifying God." I Cor 14:16; II Cor 1:20; Rom 15:5 ff.; Gal 1:22–24 exclude the restriction of such a practice to Pauline churches: "The churches of Judaea . . . praised God on my behalf."

[230] Some Psalms (e.g. 103:1–18, 20–22) would suggest that angels as well as men, faithful servants as much as crushed enemies of God, are in question.

much more, to "be praised by him." The authors of the Books of Chronicles and e.g. Ps 136 have the same destination of Israel in mind. By its singing, shouting, dancing, moaning, in the face of the pitfalls of sin or misery, but equally under the shower of the mercies of God, Israel is appointed to be a witness to God and a light among the nations, "my chosen people, the people whom I formed for myself that they might declare my praise."[231] What Eph 1:12 denotes as the privileged function first entrusted to Israel, is according to other passages of the same epistle[232] the promise and task given to the church composed of Jews and Gentiles.

IX   The Presence of the Future

The great benediction, Eph 1:3–14, contains elements that are seemingly paradoxical and mutually exclusive. A scholar trusting form-critical or traditio-historical procedures might ascribe them to different traditions imperfectly collated. A rationalist will despair of finding any sensible logic at all. Certainly cheap attempts at harmonization are to be avoided by all means. Precisely those elements that stand in dialectical tension, or perhaps seem to contain outright contradictions, may be essential to the message of Ephesians.

This epistle proclaims the presence of eternal salvation. Gifts that according to other parts of the NT had been expected by Christians and Jews for the end-time only are announced as present possessions. Yet Ephesians speaks also of unfulfilled promises and hopes, the full fruit of redemption that is not yet obtained. Technical theological language of recent decades has distinguished "realized eschatology" from "futurist eschatology."[233] Both were combined in Ephesians, as much as in John.

The conviction that the ultimate promises are now fulfilled and that the promised goods are already in the hands of the elect is attested by 1:7, "we possess freedom, forgiveness." The emphasis placed on the present by this translation is supported by many other passages of Ephesians. The "secret" of God's decision *is now* made known; the advent of the Messiah Jesus has ushered in the "days of fulfillment"; the saints have already been "raised" from the dead and "enthroned in heavens"; they have been "saved"; "the wall" of enmity between man and fellow man, also between God and man, has been "broken down" and the "proclaimed peace" is a present reality. "Confidently we make use of our free access [to God]."[234] This epistle likes to play out the

---

[231] Isa 43:20–21. In the LXX: "[the people] that I acquired [or, saved] that they might tell my miracles." Cf. Isa 42:1, 6; 43:12; 49:6; I Peter 2:9; Acts 2:11.

[232] 1:6, 14; 2:7; 3:10; 6:15, 19–20; cf. 5:8; Philip 2:15.

[233] An access to the respective facts, problems, and main literature is given by A. Schweitzer, *The Mysticism of Paul the Apostle;* O. Cullmann, *Christ and Time,* Philadelphia: Westminster, 1964; *Salvation in History,* London: SCM, 1967; P. Minear, "The Time of Hope in the NT," ScotJT 6 (1953), 337–61; W. G. Kümmel, *Promise and Fulfillment,* Naperville: Allenson, 1957; Schmithals, *Gnosticism in Corinth.* A combination of both is found in Ephesians e.g. in Bultmann, ThNT, II, 175 ff.; P. L. Hammer, "A Comparison of *klēronomos* in Paul and Ephesians," JBL 79 (1960), 267–72; P. Stuhlmacher, "Erwägungen zum Problem der Gegenwart und Zukunft in der paulinischen Eschatologie," ZTK 64 (1967), 423–50; F.-J. Steinmetz, "Parusie-Erwartung im Epheserbrief?" *Biblica* 50 (1969), 328–36. P. Tachan, "Einst und Jetzt im NT," diss. University of Göttingen, 1968 (see report in TLZ 95 [1970], 75–77) believes that the emphasis given (esp. in Eph 2) to the contrast between "then" and "now" stems from an ancient sermon pattern.

[234] 1:9–10; 2:5–6, 13–18; 3:12. In the Greek text of 3:12, the same word, "we have," or "we possess," occurs as in 1:7.

contrasts between those past and irretrievable things that "have been" (or "were") and are "no more." "Now" is a glorious period: the time of new "creation," of "the new man," of "good works."[235] The jubilation over the great change that is already effected is so exuberant that the second coming of Christ (see e.g. Col 3:4), his so-called *parousia*, is only hinted at but never fully unfolded. But see the NOTES on 2:20 and 4:13 and COMMENT VI C 2 on 2:11–22; VII on 4:1–16.

The enthusiasm about the glorious present cannot be declared absolutely un-Pauline, or anti-Pauline. It is supported by several statements made in unquestioned Pauline letters, and it is found in the rest of the NT.[236] But the behavior of the overenthusiastic Corinthians, also the polemic against men like Hymenaeus and Philetus who claim that "the resurrection has already taken place" (II Tim 2:17–18), are apt to show where full satisfaction with the present might lead. Has Ephesians given cause for, or fallen victim to, an overemphasis on the present? What about the future?

The same great benediction which is suspected of unbridled enthusiasm because of 1:7 receives a corrective in 1:14.[237] The Spirit is "the guarantee of what we shall inherit." The "liberation of God's own people" is vouchsafed but is still lying in the future. With the Spirit "you have been marked for the day of liberation" (4:30). Indeed, all the saints are heirs (3:6), but they have not yet received all the riches coming to them. An equal number of Ephesians passages support realized eschatology *and* the future coming of salvation. Despite their present installment upon heavenly thrones (2:6) the saints are admonished to behave so that they "may live long in the land" (i.e., on earth; or in Ephesus if the variant reading of 1:1 is accepted).[238] A distinction is made between this age and the age or generations to come.[239] The evil spirit is still, even *now*, at work among the rebellious, and a merciless war of evil hosts is waged against the saints.[240] Therefore "hope" stands beside faith and love[241] —a hope that looks forward to, and is dependent upon, a filling, building, growing, and attaining that is far from being completed.[242] An explicit reference to the last judgment is not missing.[243] Passages containing the preposition "for" (*eis*) and expressing the purpose of God's decision and action are too

[235] 2:1–6, 10, 11–13, 15, 19; 3:5, 10; 4:14, 17, 22–24, 28; 5:8; cf. Col 1:21–22, 24, 26; 3:7–8. Colossians uses the words "now" and "formerly" (or "in the past; at that time"), but not the emphatic, "no more." Schlier suggests that the frequent allusions in Ephesians to the past, i.e. a condition which exists "no more," have their reason in the recent conversion of those addressed. Neophytes are supposedly in greater danger of backsliding than veterans.

[236] E.g. Gal 1:4; 4:4; 6:15; II Cor 3:18; 5:17; 6:2; I Cor 3:22; cf. Col 1:13; Luke 4:18–21; Acts 2:17–21. Especially the connection between the (realized) eschatology of Ephesians and that of the Gospel of John (e.g. 5:25; 11:25–26) has often been noted.

[237] Schille, *Hymnen*, p. 69, speaks of a "theological gap" here. Though on p. 16 he asks, "Who would quote a passage foreign [to his own theology]?" he elaborates on pp. 18, 59, 71, 104, 107 on the hard clash between the theology of the hymn quoted, and the theology of the interpretive remarks added by the biblical author. Such explicatory or corrective remarks are in most recent German parlance called *Interpretamente*. Schille contradicts himself when he treats at the same time 1:14 as a part of the pre-Pauline hymn *and* as correction of the quoted hymn; compare p. 67 with pp. 104–7.

[238] Schille, *Hymnen*, p. 68: instead of leaving people in heavens where the baptismal hymn (or baptism itself, compare p. 57 with p. 103) has placed them, "the author sees men on this earth (4:9 f; 5:5 etc.)." See also Pokorný's above mentioned (Introduction, section III B) understanding of the polemic of Ephesians against Gnosticism.

[239] 1:21; 2:7; 3:21.   [240] Eph 2:2; 6:10–17.

[241] 1:15–18; 4:4; cf. I Thess 1:3; 5:8; I Cor 13:13; Col 1:3–4.

[242] 1:23; 2:22; 3:19; 4:10, 13, 15–16. See COMMENTS VI C 2 and VII on 2:11–22.

[243] 6:8–9; cf. 5:5–6.

frequent to be enumerated. All of them reveal an openness toward the future which is not only a trait of human self-understanding, but based upon God's own will and deeds.[244] The comprehension of all things under the one head, Christ (1:10), is not yet accomplished. The saints have not yet come to meet the "Perfect Man" (4:13).

In the light of such statements the "possessive" assertion of 1:7, "we have freedom, forgiveness," may well have to be qualified by an expression such as that found in Heb 6:4: the saints have "tasted the heavenly gift." C. H. Dodd's correction of his early phrase "realized eschatology" by "eschatology in the process of realization"[245] may lack linguistic beauty and clarity but it is preferable to the extreme interpretations of Ephesians that fail to take note of any futurist eschatological traits. H. Schlier[246] is probably right in summing up the available evidence by saying, "Ephesians knows of a concrete eschatology." The gift of God's "full" blessing (1:3) contradicts this judgment as little as the blessing given to patriarchs precludes the extensive history of Abraham, Isaac, Jacob. The use made of inheritance terminology proves that Paul follows in Ephesians the same lines of eschatological thought as he does, for example, in Rom 8.

But P. L. Hammer[247] disputes this point. He believes that in Ephesians a different concept of heirship prevails: while Ephesians looks supposedly only to the future (!), Paul speaks of the past and present; see especially Gal 3:18. And while in Paul Christ is at the same time the heir, the contents, and the means of our inheritance (so that we are his fellow heirs right now in history), in Ephesians the joint heirdom is shared between Jews and Gentiles, and the existence of the church points to a transhistorical realization of inheritance. This differentiation makes Ephesians at the same time less Christocentric, more ecclesiastical, *and* more futurist-eschatological than the Pauline homologoumena.

However, the Great Benediction in Eph 1 and passages like 2:5–6, 15–22 do not support Hammer's argument and opinion. Since election and adoption of the saints are clearly said to be "made" in Christ, and since the Christians are called possessors of freedom, resurrected from the dead, enthroned in heaven, free servants, a temple of God, and a light that shines, the Christological center and the historical realization of the eschatological work and gift of God are asserted at least as vigorously as in any other Pauline epistle.

The various meanings and accents of the present and futuristic eschatological utterances are treated in the NOTES to 1:7, 14, 2:5–6, 20, 4:13 and in COMMENT IV on 2:1–10, IV C 2 and VII on 2:11–22; VII on 4:1–16. But one aspect of the issue at hand has yet to be mentioned. How are the present and the future held together? Is it more than man's temporality that requires, or his wishful thinking that reckons with, the perfection to be attained tomorrow? If only man gained something by having a future, he might have to ask himself whether he has dreamed up the future for his own consolation. But if God

---

[244] Cf. I. de la Potterie, "L'emploi dynamique de *eis* dans Saint Jean et ces incidences theologiques," *Biblica* 43 (1962), 366–87.

[245] Cf. *The Interpretation of the Fourth Gospel*, 2d ed. (Cambridge University Press, 1954), p. 447, with *The Parables of the Kingdom* (London: Nisbet, 1935), p. 51, etc., but see also p. 189.

[246] Schlier, p. 292.   [247] JBL 79 (1960), 267–72.

himself wanted and created the future for his own sake, man's hope would have a more solid foundation.

In Ephesians God is not only praised for the benefits and riches (as grace, freedom, forgiveness, inheritance) he gives to man. He is also "blessed" because of that which he acquires for himself. In a NOTE on 1:11 it was shown how the verb "be appropriated" has probably anticipated what in 1:14 is explicitly affirmed and what is underscored by the three references to the praise of God's glory (1:6, 12, 14). An acquisition made by God is simultaneous with the handing out of an inheritance to man. By God's decision, revelation, and action, events take place which in the past, present, and future are beneficial to more than man only. They also contribute to God's own property and honor.[248] It is he who acquires Israel *first*, and later creates out of Jews and Gentiles together his own people. He gives the Messiah the task and power to fill all (1:10).[249] His own dominion is to be carried to triumph (I Cor. 15:25-28). It is his glory that resounds in the praise of more and more of his creatures. Therefore not only man's benefit but also God's majesty itself is at stake in all that God wills and does, in the things promised and already realized—but also in those still outstanding. Therefore the prooemium of Ephesians affirms that "in Christ" a deployment and increase of God's power, possession, and honor is taking place. God gains a people for himself! God's glory will be praised!

The very term "blessing" in 1:3 bears this out. For by the act of blessing, a person does not only effectively increase the life, power, property of others; he also exerts and increases his own power.[250] E. Gaugler refers in his exposition of Eph 1:3 to this primitive notion of mana, and believes that it is completely overcome in Eph 1. This may not be the case, for not only man but God himself has an interest in completing the work of salvation and revelation. Moses is not ashamed in his intercession for Israel to make an appeal to God's own "ability" to carry out his work.[251] God's honor might be put in question if he stopped protecting and forgiving Israel. His people, his property, and therefore the cause of God himself is at stake. Frequent in the OT are appeals to God "for his name's sake." Equally, Eph 1:3-14 shows that in God himself—not in man's need or misery—is the ultimate cause of election, grace, adoption, and other demonstrations of good will toward man. Many of the prayers of Moses and the Psalmists sound almost unbearably anthropomorphic, and the same is true of some undertones of the father-child imagery in Eph 1. But even in their anthropomorphic diction these passages reveal that man's salvation is secured in God himself, that God deserves praise for his own sake, and that God himself shapes not only the past and present, but will equally shape the future. These texts do not speak of a paradox or a dialectic tension for its own sake, nor of a special trait of some mysterious faith. It is in the nature of God that at the present time and in the future the work will be carried out which God resolved to do in the Messiah. God is the creator of aeons and generations. Jesus

---

[248] Cf. D. Ritschl, *Memory and Hope* (New York: Macmillan, 1967), p. 98.
[249] See COMMENT XIII.
[250] Pedersen, *Israel* I, 182-213, II, 437-52; G. van der Leeuw, *Religion in Essence and Manifestation* (Gloucester: Smith, 1967), pp. 408-9.
[251] Num 14:15-19; Deut 9:25-29.

Christ who was, is, and will come is the thread running through all times. He holds them together.

While in I Cor 15:35–54; II Cor 5:1–10; Rom 8:23 and elsewhere the final fulfillment of God's will and man's hope is described in terms that seemingly refer to individual men, e.g. to their body, it is characteristic of Ephesians to announce the future liberation of "God's own people" (1:14, 4:30). Does this mean that the egotism of a collective has taken the place of the yearning of individuals for their personal salvation? The danger of a threatening group-egotism is effectively met by one ever present concern in this epistle: the church will not find the way to its freedom and perfection in a flight from the world, in detachment from those who never heard the gospel, or in hiding from the powers ruling the world. The saints are as much the congregation elect for eternal salvation, as they fulfill a missionary task among all men and powers. The seeming delay of the last eschatological events cannot be explained, as O. Cullmann has shown, without pointing to the as yet unfulfilled mission of the church.

X   Wisdom and Knowledge

In his references to wisdom[252] Paul presupposes and endorses what was emphasized in canonical and apocryphal OT books. Wisdom is proper to God the creator. It is also given to the craftsmen who built the ark. It is the gift from above which lets a sovereign rule wisely and a judge pass righteous sentences. For everybody it is the guide that lets him choose right conduct and behavior.[253] Very often wisdom is identified with, or set parallel to, the "power" of the Spirit of God.[254] It is also called a "way," especially the way prepared by God for men.[255] Hence it became a synonym for the law.[256] This wisdom is at the same time the architect of God in the act of creation and the only trustworthy teacher and savior of man.[257] Of some chosen persons it is said: "They were saved by wisdom" (Wisd Sol 9:18). The opposite is true of others, including giants: "God did not choose them . . . so they perished because they had no wisdom" (Bar 3:26–28). Wisdom is the assurance of immortality.[258] Wisdom may also have a theoretical or a scientific bent. This is apparent when it denotes intimate knowledge of the cedar and the hyssop, the beasts, the birds, the reptiles, the fish.[259] By wisdom God imparts "unerring knowledge of all that exists, to know the structure of the world and the activity of the elements . . . both what is secret and what is manifest."[260] Wisdom's theoretical bent is apparent when it is put to use in artfully composed catalogues or lists of

---

[252] Cf. the NOTE on 1:8 and BIBLIOGRAPHY 8.
[253] For OT references see M. Noth and D. W. Thomas, *Wisdom in Israel*, pp. 225 ff; also, below the NOTE on "the Spirit of wisdom" in 1:17.
[254] Jer 10:12; 51 [LXX 28]:15; Job 11:7; 12:13; Wisd Sol 7:25; I Cor 1:17 ff.
[255] Job 28:23–27; Prov 3:17; 4:11; 9:6; Bar 3:13, 20, 23, 27.
[256] The biblical references for the equations of wisdom and law, wisdom and Spirit are given above in fns. 210 and 211.
[257] Wisd Sol 7:22, 24; 8:6; 10:1 – 11:14. See also COMMENT VI.
[258] Wisd Sol 6:17–20; 8:13, 17; see also Eph 6:24 following Eccles 7:12 "wisdom preserves the life of him who has it."
[259] I Kings 4:33[5:13].
[260] Wisd Sol 7:17–21. In 7:22 an ontological reason for this is given: because wisdom is the architect or fashioner ("technician") of all things (cf. 8:6; 14:2), it is the competent "teacher" of their structure, nature, variety, cycles.

creatures or forms of behavior. But even in these cases wisdom is practical knowledge or practical reason, for it serves to exert and to demonstrate dominion over animate and inanimate creatures; it enables the wise man to use the idiosyncrasies, e.g. of the ant, the viper, the leopard, the vine, and the cedar as striking images for describing good or wicked human conduct and destiny. Together with lists and parables, fables belong to the forms in which the message of wisdom is communicated. "You filled the earth with parables and riddles" (Sir 47:15).

Ephesians shows ample traces of the influence of Wisdom traditions. Such traces are not limited to those verses in which the word "wisdom" occurs, or in which readers are told to conduct themselves as "wise men" rather than "fools."[261] The ethical exhortations especially of 4:17 ff. and 5:21 – 6:9 are replete with formal and material elements of wisdom teaching. Large portions of the Sermon on the Mount, the parables, also the epistle of James make similar use of form and content of wisdom teaching. But Ephesians contains no elements reflecting those features of wisdom tradition sometimes called "mythological." In this epistle wisdom is not personified, not called pre-existent, not made the subject of a dramatic journey downward toward mankind, and homeward to God away from this inhospitable environment.[262] In COMMENT VI it was noted that several NT books make use of the vocabulary and imagery of traditional personifying utterances on Wisdom in order to describe in the highest possible terms Jesus Christ's relationship to God, the world, and man.[263] Ephesians is not among those books. A puzzling combination of a high wisdom-Christology and of wisdom-moralizing is characteristic of Matthew, I Corinthians, Colossians, perhaps James, too—but not of Ephesians. Despite H. J. Holtzmann's and H. Schlier's suggestions[264] this epistle ought therefore not to be called an example of "theosophy" or "wisdom-discourse." Ephesians cannot possibly be compared to Job 28; Prov 8–9; Wisd Sol 7–10; Bar 3:9 – 4:4; Sirach, or other encomia on wisdom. The wisdom in which God decides and acts, and the wisdom he gives to men do not overshadow the praise of Jesus Christ crucified and risen.

All the more noteworthy is the great emphasis placed in this epistle upon knowledge. The noun "knowledge"[265] occurs as frequently as the verb "to know."[266] The verb "to make known" belongs in this context. It is used six times[267] and appears to be (when God is the subject) a synonym of "to reveal."[268] Little wonder that, together with the church, knowledge has been considered the main topic of Ephesians,[269] and that positive or polemic connections between Ephesians and Gnosticism have been intensively discussed.[270]

Three groups of statements on knowledge may be discussed: (a) God imparts

---

[261] 1:8, 17; 3:10; 5:15.

[262] As e.g. in Prov 8–9; I Enoch 42. The meaning of the ambiguous term "personification" is interpreted in different ways e.g. by Ringgren, Davies, and Wilckens.

[263] See esp. John 1:1–18; Matt 11:16–19, 25–30; I Cor 1:17–2:16; Col 1:15–20; Heb 1:1–4.

[264] Holtzmann, pp. 216–18; idem, *Lehrbuch der Neutestamentlichen Theologie*, II (Tübingen: Mohr, 1911), 271–74; Schlier, pp. 21, 28.

[265] *Gnōsis*, 3:19; *epignōsis* 1:17; 4:13; understanding (*synesis*) 3:4.

[266] 3:19; 5:5; 6:22; cf. 1:18; 6:8–9, 21; "to understand" 5:17.

[267] 1:9; 3:3, 5, 10; 6:19, 21; cf. "to teach" 4:21.

[268] Cf. 3:5a with 3:3, 5b, 10; 1:17; the noun "revelation" is found in 1:17; 3:3.

[269] K. and S. Lake, *Introduction to the New Testament* (New York: Harper, 1937), p. 149.

[270] See section III B of the Introduction.

knowledge by revelation.[271] (b) The apostle, the congregation, and the Messiah above all, are given knowledge, wisdom, or understanding.[272] (c) The apostle and congregation are equipped to make known to all men and powers what was formerly hidden.[273]

Utterances on the gospel or the word of truth preached by Christ and heard, believed, and communicated by the congregation[274] contain the same three accents. Knowledge comes from God. It is first given to specific servants of God who are called apostles and prophets. From there it goes to the congregation. In turn, the congregation is but a lighthouse[275] or a trading post. What it receives it is to pass on for the benefit of all who are not its members. The events of receiving and imparting knowledge are intimately intertwined. No one can claim to have knowledge unless he lets the received light shine before others. The only demonstration of knowledge consists of its public attestation.[276] Earlier it was observed that this view contradicts the esoteric concepts of knowledge fostered in Qumran and by Gnostics. But as in those circles ignorance is inseparable from perdition and corruption, so is it in the case in Eph 4:17–19, 22. Knowledge and salvation are inseparable. The "true word" that "you have heard and believed" is the gospel that "saves" you (1:13). To quote, again, Wisd Sol 9:18: "Men . . . were saved by wisdom."

The topic knowledge is also touched upon or more extensively treated in other main epistles of Paul.[277] Three things stand in opposition to knowledge: the former hiddenness of God's secret; ignorance of God, or man's refusal to know God, which may pretend to be ultimate wisdom; a puffed-up conceit of Jews or Christians. The specific depth of Paul's concept of knowledge becomes apparent wherever he declares that man's knowledge of God is dependent upon his "being known by God."[278] Paul shares with the OT and most NT writers an understanding of knowledge which lifts this concept far beyond the merely epistemological and intellectual level.[279] R. Bultmann[280] has shown that not only acknowledgment and recognition but a whole way of existence and behavior is described by this word—as exemplified especially by the use of this term for the mutual sexual relation between man and woman (Gen 4:1, 19:8, etc.) and by the role ascribed in the OT to the knowledge of God.[281]

---

[271] 3:3, 5; cf. 1:17; 3:10; 5:13–14.

[272] 1:18; 3:4, 18–19; 4:20–21; 5:5, 8, 15, 17. The "teaching" mentioned in 4:21 is a further parallel. Eph 4:13 may, as the exegesis of this verse will show, refer to that knowledge of which the Messiah is both subject and object. In the OT the wisdom of the king and judge is exemplary for the wisdom of everyman, Isa 9:6; I Kings 3; Ezek 28:2–6, 12—or else the Wisdom books would not have been ascribed to King Solomon.

[273] 3:8–10; 5:19; 6:15, 19.   [274] 1:13; 2:17; 4:21; 6:15, 19.

[275] The circumscription of knowledge by imagery taken from the nature, effect, use of light is spread in many cultures and languages including the OT and NT. Compare the role of light in theophanies. In Ephesians this imagery is used several times; see 1:18; 3:9; 5:8, 9, 13 f.

[276] See 2:7 and COMMENT V on 2:1–10, regarding the juridical imagery which Paul occasionally employs.

[277] E.g. Rom 1:19–32; 2:18–23; 15:14; I Cor 1:5; 2:6–16; 8:1–3; 13:2, 12; II Cor 8:7; Philip 3:10; Philem 6; Colossians passim.

[278] Gal 4:9; I Cor 8:2–3; 13:12; cf. Matt 11:27; John 10:14–15.

[279] Unless I Cor 1–2 and Eph 3:19 fight a Gnostic conception of knowledge (as suggested by W. Schmithals), these passages might contain explicit caveats against identification of knowledge of God with Greek or Hellenistic notions of knowledge.

[280] In his article on knowledge in TWNTE, I, 689–719; cf. 115–21.

[281] Esp. in Hosea, Jeremiah, Ezekiel. See e.g. W. Zimmerli, Erkenntnis Gottes nach dem Buche Hesekiel, ATANT, 27 (1954); J. L. McKenzie, "Knowledge of God in Hosea," JBL 74 (1955), 22–27.

Knowledge of God is "to have God for a husband";[282] cf. Hos 2:16; Jer 31: 31–34.

Ephesians certainly means by knowledge a similar existential relationship between God and man as found in other OT and NT books. But while, e.g. in Colossians, the element of an ever growing and deepening acknowledgment and recognition of God is in the foreground, the main emphasis of Ephesians lies in the continuous receiving and spreading of knowledge. Not just the saints but all the world is to share in the fruit of its light.

How can knowledge be so important and become so inseparably tied to salvation?

The character and effect of knowledge is dependent upon what is known. It is the secret of God now revealed which, according to Ephesians, makes the present and future the scene of the gift and outreach of ever greater knowledge. The present is the time in which the secret of election, of grace, of liberation, of inclusion of the Gentiles into God's people, is no longer locked away. Through men chosen by God the saints have heard and learned that which all the world is to know, i.e. the decision of God to "comprehend all under one head, the Messiah" (1:10). What good would be done by knowledge of a god who had decided against caring for his Son and any dealings with his creatures? Or a knowledge restricted to the awareness of man's alienation, man's need, or man's potential for higher aspirations? Or who would sing God's praise if God had made his gracious decision and carried out his plan—without making it known to the beneficiaries of his goodness? Knowledge is inseparable from salvation because it is awareness of the covenant between God and man established in Christ. No one can "enjoy God"[283] without knowledge; for salvation without joy and jubilation would not be true liberation.

According to the rabbinic tract *Pirke Aboth* III 19 the revelation of God's creative act is an even greater proof of God's love than the act of creation itself! Indeed, in the whole Bible the connection between election and revelation is very close. Because Abraham is chosen, God does not hide his plans before him (Gen 18:18–19). The same is true of the prophets.[284] With epiphanies, God elects and appoints his servants for the salvation of his people (Exod 3; Isa 6; Amos 3, etc.). The apocalypticists Ezra and Baruch receive the revelation of the things to come on the ground of their election. The author of Eph 1:4–8 might well be accused of wild speculation, of transcending the limits of human history and knowledge, of groping for things that no man can know. But because his thinking and writing harken back to revelation and knowledge given from on high, his detractors may have a hard time. They have to fight God and his revelation rather than only Paul. The reference made in 1:4 to election *before* "the foundation of the world" is explained in 1:9 as a result of revelation. Under the impact of the knowledge imparted to him and to the congregation, the author could not keep silent about a decision made by God "in Christ." It is revelation that forced Paul to say what God had decided—long before Israel and the Gentiles ever heard of God and before God's decision was carried out in the coming of Jesus Christ and the work of the Holy Spirit.

[282] To use a formula orally communicated by Rabbi M. Kaplan.
[283] In the sense of the Westminster Catechisms, Question 1.
[284] See e.g. Amos 3:3–8, esp. 7; Jer 23:18; Isa 41:27; 43:10.

After the revelation of God's secret, knowledge of the secret is no longer a mere possibility or choice. And it is more than an intellectual perception. Knowledge is a gift of God which makes man lead that new life to which dead people have been raised at the price of Christ's blood and in the company of the risen Lord.[285] Eph 1:17 mentions in the same breath the Spirit, wisdom, revelation, and knowledge. The practical knowledge of God taught by Ephesians is indeed a spiritual matter dependent on revelation and ultimately identical with wisdom. The teaching of Ephesians on these matters is so distinctly dependent on OT tradition and NT Christocentric reflection that it does not make sense to derive it from Qumranite, Philonic, or Gnostic so-called "parallels." In the next COMMENT this view will be tested by studying another concept: *mystērion*.

XI   Mystery or Secret?

In section III C of the Introduction the relationship between the concepts of "mystery" fostered by the Qumran community and Jewish apocalypticists on one side, and by Ephesians on the other, has been discussed at some length. Reasons were shown why at about the same time Vogt, Coppens, Rigaux, Cerfaux, Brown, Kuhn, Braun, Mussner[286] arrived at converging results: an immediate dependence of Ephesians on Qumranite and apocalyptic literature cannot be demonstrated. But all documents in question, including Ephesians, may well be various offshoots from a tradition that dates back to the classic and the late prophets of Israel and emphasizes the indivisible revelatory, cosmic, soteriological, and eschatological traits of God's will and action. Undoubtedly in Ephesians traditional elements have been used selectively. However, they were melted into a whole which apparently constitutes something novel and original. The substitution of one "mystery" for many, the Christocentric description of The Mystery, the inclusion of Gentiles into the elect people, and the need of world-wide publication have been noticed as the main marks of distinction between Ephesians and other documents that deal with mysteries.

One question has so far neither been posed nor answered: what did the author intend to say when he used the Greek word *mystērion* for describing the will, the revelation, and the work of God?

Among the Greeks this term apparently had at first an almost technical meaning. It denoted a secret rite subject to the *disciplina arcani*. What must not be exposed to profanation by being divulged was called a mystery. The "mystery" rites and religions owe their name to this meaning.[287] From this narrow sense a wider meaning was derived: any secret thought or matter could be called a mystery. In the latest (apocryphal) parts of the Greek OT, the word is

---

[285] Cf. John 17:3 "This is eternal life: to know thee, the one true God, and him whom thou hast sent, Jesus Christ."

[286] See BIBLIOGRAPHY 3.

[287] For a careful examination of the meager source material available for the reconstruction of the trends of various Mystery Religions, see F. Cumont, *The Oriental Religions in Roman Paganism*, Chicago: Open Court, 1911; and G. Wagner, *Pauline Baptism and the Pagan Mysteries*, London: Oliver, 1967. Wagner's book is apt to fulfill the same function as C. Colpe's, *Die religionsgeschichtliche Schule*, I, FRLANT 78, 1960. An uncritical resort to "parallels" between the NT on the one hand, Mystery Religions and Gnosticism on the other (whether seen as separate movements or as coinherent), as exemplified by H. Lietzmann's commentary *An die Römer*, HbNT, 8, 4th ed., Tübingen: Mohr, 1933, and H. Conzelmann's treatment of Ephesians, is no longer considered solid, scientific historical exegesis.

used with both meanings. There are rare illusions to the initiation rites of Mystery Religions. While they are abhorred in Wisdom of Solomon,[288] Philo ventured to describe the history of Israel's salvation after the pattern of just such a religion.[289] More frequently *mystērion* denotes in the late parts of the LXX the secret of a king or friend that must remain enclosed in the heart of the one who knows about it.[290]

Ignatius speaks in Gnosticizing fashion of "three crying mysteries" of revelation.[291] The Greek fathers[292] use "mystery" or correlated terminology increasingly as a designation for the sacraments of the church, i.e. in the narrow (technical) sense of the Greek noun. Tertullian compared, contrasted, and yet, in formal regard, equated baptism with the military oath of the Roman soldiers (which was called *sacramentum* and bore distinct marks of a religious initiation).[293] Since his time *mystērion* or *sacramentum*, became the technical term for describing baptism, the eucharist, and other essential sacred rites of the church. Eph 5:32 was often understood to yield the proof text: the union of husband and wife . . . *Sacramentum hoc magnum est* (Vulg.).

Does the NT really use the term mystery in this sense? It indeed shows acquaintance with something similar to mystery cults. This is proven by allusions made to the cult or the rites celebrated by the Colossians (Col 2:6–18), to symposia in pagan sanctuaries (I Cor 10:20), to events in the congregations addressed in Rev 2–3, also to the rule of the animal from the abyss (Rev 13). Thus "mysteries" in the technical sense were not only known to the Christians of the NT time, but even enticing to some of them. Yet the respective religious and cultic practices are never explicitly called "mysteries." Also, there is no evidence the first-century Christians called their liturgy or rites a *mystērion*. Bornkamm[294] is right in affirming that in the NT the word *mystērion* has nothing to do with the mystery cults of antiquity. While Eph 5:32 poses special problems to be discussed in the context of Eph 5, in all other verses of this epistle, perhaps of the whole NT, the noun *mystērion* distinctly signifies a "secret" rather than a rite or a cultic religion. Also it is impossible to demonstrate that at any place in the NT it signifies an insoluble puzzle or incomprehensible—and yet believed—mystery, though the English translation "mystery" may suggest this meaning. To avoid confusion with such a puzzle the term "secret," has been chosen in our translation.[295]

---

[288] Wisd Sol 14:15, 23; cf. 12:5.

[289] Philo plays extensively with the idea that the history of God with Israel constitutes a Mystery; cf. Goodenough, *By Light, Light;* Hegermann, *Schöpfungsmittler*, pp. 26–66.

[290] Tobit 12:7, 11; Sir 22:22; 27:16, 17, 21; II Macc 13:21; cf. Judith 2:2.

[291] Ign. *Eph.* XIX 1. See the books of Schlier and Bartsch mentioned in BIBLIOGRAPHY 2. But cf. also D. Daube, *"Tria mystēria kraugēs,"* JTS 16 (1965), 128–29.

[292] For references see Goodspeed's *Index Partisticus* repr. Naperville, Ill.: Allenson, 1960. H. Kraft, *Texte zur Geschichte der Taufe,* KT 174 (1955), pp. 24–29, has collected examples from the time of the emperor Constantine and later; see also T. Paponstati, *Ta mystēria tēs ekklēsiās mēs* (*The Mysteries of Our Church*), Athens: Apostolike Diakonin, 1953. (*Mystēria*=seven sacraments.)

[293] A. Kölping, *Sacramentum Tertullianum,* Münster: Aschendorff, 1948; C. Mohrmann, *"Sacramentum* dans les plus anciens textes chrétiens," HTR 47 (1954), 141–52; G. Bornkamm, art. *mystērion* in TWNTE, IV, 802–28.

[294] Bornkamm, TWNTE, IV, 824.

[295] 1:9; 3:3, 4, 9; 6:19; also Col 1:26–27; 2:2; 4:3. See esp. Abbott, pp. 15–17, 174, and Scharlemann, "The Secret of God's Plan," ConcTM 40 (1969), 532–44; 41 (1970), 155–64, 338–46, 410–20.

This understanding of *mystērion* is corroborated by the predicates added to the noun in Ephesians and Colossians. *"He has made known to us the secret of his decision." "The secret was made known to me by revelation." "I understand the secret of Christ . . . to make all men see how the secret is administered." "An eminent secret meaning—I, for one, understand it. . . ." "To make known the secret." "The secret that was hidden . . . is now revealed* to the saints." "God decided *to make known* what are the riches of the glory of this secret . . . *to make* the secret *known . . . to speak out* the secret of the Messiah."[296] All Ephesian and Colossian verses that contain the noun *mystērion* convey the information that it is now "revealed," "known," "understood," and frankly "spoken out." In all cases a noetic or cognitive event is mentioned. This event is always the same, disclosure. If the noun were used to describe a ritual, a thing, a plan, then other predications would be appropriate, e.g. the *mystērion* was kept, completed, repeated, celebrated.[297] Or an invitation might be found to keep it guarded, to protect it from profanation, to respect its unfathomable depth. But no such statements are made in Ephesians. This epistle discusses the time and the conditions created by the *disclosure* of the formerly hidden (3:3–11). The people chosen by God are given—together with the revelation, knowledge, and understanding of the "secret"—the task to divulge it. Ephesians shares with other NT books precisely the same idea. The secret (*mystērion*) has now been revealed and is to be further revealed: "To you has been given *to know* the secrets of the kingdom." "Many prophets and righteous men longed *to see* what you see, and did not *see* it, and to *hear* what you *hear*, and did not *hear* it." "Nothing is *covered* that will not be *revealed*, or *hidden* that will not be *known. What I tell you in the dark, utter in the light; and what you hear whispered, proclaim* upon the housetops."[298]

While Ephesians and Colossians speak of one *mystērion* only, there are in other epistles some references to a plurality of mysteries. They concern Israel, the resurrection, evil[299] or other unspecified matters.[300] However, not only in the letters considered deutero-Pauline[301] but probably also in I Cor 2:1[302] and certainly in I Cor 2:7 Paul speaks of one, single, comprehensive "secret of God." The "mystery of iniquity" (II Thess 2:7) may never be revealed and understood—yet the history of "God's secret" is its disclosure! Jesus Christ is the essence and contents of the revealed secret (Col 2:2). "Christ

[296] All these quotes are from the verses listed in the preceding footnote. Matt 3:11 par.; Mark 4:11 par.; I Cor 2:1 (with GNT—against Nestle, Vulgate, etc.—the reading *mystērion* is in this verse to be preferred to *martyrion*, "testimony"); I Cor 2:7; 13:2; 14:2; 15:51; Rev 17:5, 7 speak equally of a "revealed" *mystērion*.

[297] Rev 10:7 states "The *mystērion* of God is completed." It is probable that in this passage, in a fashion corresponding to Philo's interpretation of certain events of *Heilsgeschichte* (perhaps also to II Thess 2:7; I Cor 4:1; I Tim 3:9, 16), *mystērion* does not mean "secret" but a plan, a mode of action, or an event.

[298] Matt 13:11 (a variant reading and the parallel text Mark 4:11 have "the secret" instead of "the secrets"); 13:17; 10:26–27; cf. Eph 3:3–10; 6:19.

[299] Rom 11:25; I Cor 15:51; II Thess 2:7; cf. the mysteries of a star constellation and of the woman sitting on the beast (Rev 1:20; 17:5, 7). The secret meaning of a Scripture text mentioned in Eph 5:32 belongs most likely to these several mysteries.

[300] I Cor 4:1; 13:2; 14:2. Equally it is asserted in Ephesians 3:8–10, 18–20 that the riches and the love of Christ, the manifold wisdom and power of God the creator are beyond man's grasp, understanding, imagination, petition. See the exposition of 3:8 ff., 18 f.

[301] Besides Ephesians and Colossians also I Tim 3:9.

[302] See fn. 296 for the textual problem posed by this verse.

among [or in] you, the Gentiles" (Col 1:27) is its manifestation in person. While in I Cor 1–2 and 15 Jesus Christ's crucifixion and resurrection are placed in the foreground (and in Colossians, the hope), in Ephesians the accent is set upon the rule of Christ over all powers in heaven and on earth, and upon the creation of a new man by the peace made between Jews and Gentiles and God. In all cases Jesus is proclaimed the Messiah. His secret is this: before the creation in God's counsel, during the historic fulfillment of God's decision, and at the consummation of God's will, he includes in himself a great people. His power over all powers guarantees their salvation.

Why is this comprehensiveness of the Messiah called a *mystērion?* One may speak of the many mysteries of creation, the universe, the relation of spirit and matter, or of energy. There are anthropological mysteries belonging to such questions as, what constitutes humanity, life, existence, the soul, a community? Again, the church is to herself a mystery and she fosters the mysteries of its sacraments, of the priesthood and laity, of the sermon and faith—not to speak of the mysteries of evil and of suffering. For theological inquiry the trinity, the two natures of Christ, the justification of the sinner, and many other things will forever remain mysteries. By calling a thing mysterious man manifests an appropriate awe of a condition, a relation, or an event which remain, temporarily or of necessity, beyond the grasp of scientific explication, outside manipulation by technological means, and certainly high above all dogmatic and creedal definitions. The inexplicable, or at least, the as yet unexplained and uncontrolled, is for man a mystery. Paul is human enough to be aware of the inexplicable depth of the riches, wisdom, knowledge, judgments, ways of God (Rom 11:33). In Eph 3:19 it is explicitly stated that acknowledgment of Christ's love surpasses knowledge. The several mysteries (plural!) of which Paul speaks he never attempts to dissolve—except an exegetical mystery such as that of Gen 2:24 (see Eph 5:32).

But the one *mystērion* of God, even the "secret" of God, is for Paul far from unknowable. It is known by revelation and is to be made known all over the world. Certainly he has the highest respect for the revelation and gospel entrusted to him—but it is respect caused by knowledge rather than by ignorance and incompetence. No *disciplina arcani* prevents him from disclosing in Ephesians things which far surpass the visions of Ezekiel. The "secret" of which he speaks can therefore not be identified with a mystery wholly or partly, always or temporarily, actually or intentionally shrouded in a cloud bank. He does not engage in paradoxical logic or glossolalia. Plain, frank, sober, courageous talk, though tinted with characteristics of the diction of prayer, is the way he speaks of God's secret. In short, when he speaks of one *mystērion,* then he means a mystery that is revealed; all he has to say is based on the manifestation of the formerly hidden.

The one mystery no longer exists in hiding. It cannot be the mystery of creation, the trinity, the incarnation, the justification, the church, the world and its powers. For each one of those mysteries and many more are revered but not disclosed, or revealed and yet remain concealed, or offered to faith and knowledge and yet not understood. In all these cases the questions "Why?"

and "How?" ultimately remain unanswered. The reason, the method, the techniques, the operation remain in the dark; up to the last day man will have but fragmentary knowledge of them (I Cor 13:12). But in Ephesians Paul speaks he uses the word *mystērion* he has in mind a fact, not a method; an event, not a cryptic reason or operation. The fact and event he mentions is this: the one *mystērion* has been revealed, therefore it must be made known everywhere. Now it is as public and plain as the gospel; or rather, the gospel *is* its disclosure (6:19)!

This is the secret that is finally revealed to the saints: God loved them before the creation. He loves them despite their sins and death. He loves them notwithstanding the former division of Jews and Gentiles. He loves them with the intention that they praise his glory. Man did not know this love; the powers did not. But God did. It was God's secret because it was hidden in his heart, identified with his own being, his whole self. Now it has been laid bare. The whole, true God is no longer hidden and unknown. His very heart is opened.

When a lover confesses to his beloved his secret love, he does not reveal a method or technique. Rather he reveals himself, he opens his heart, and in so doing he delivers and gives himself to the beloved. The secret revealed is his innermost heart. He is essentially and totally for the other and makes known that he never wants to be without or against the beloved. Even so and much more God reveals himself when he reveals his secret. It is God himself by whom Jews and Gentiles were brought together, by whom even hostile powers are brought under control. Above all, everything that they are in, with, and through Christ, is not just a passing whim of God. It is his revealed secret. They have no reason to suspect, or to ask for, a true deity behind or above the revelation who might be different from the revealed God. Or else God would have kept something hidden from them. But through the salvation now experienced they have access to God himself (2:18; 3:12). God has not just revealed this or that of his identity, or—as Greek oracles did—one or another thing that was to happen or to be done. He has revealed HIMSELF. This is the meaning of the references to The Secret that is disclosed (cf. the last NOTE on 2:4).

XII   Christ the Administrator

The title "administrator," "steward," or "manager," which belongs to Jesus Christ if the above translation and NOTE on 1:10 be tenable, is not commonly used as a designation of Christ. The title seems to sound too secular to be appropriate for liturgical or theological use—though in I Cor 4:1; Col 1:25, it occurs in religious context and is applied by Paul to himself. Of course what fits the servant may seem unfit for the master. Still, in COMMENT V evidence was given showing that Jesus Christ's role in God's election, in his work of salvation, and in the shaping of a people that praises God, might be suitably summed up precisely by this term. The title "administrator" poses Christ (in

303 1:18; 4:18; 5:14; 6:12.

analogy to the placement of the kings of Judah and Israel) immediately under God the ruler and owner of all things; at the same time, it reveals his superiority over all other servants of God. Using different nouns, but aiming at the same goal, passages such as Heb 1:1–4; 3:1–6 elaborate on the same distinctions. However, while the OT kings are regents on God's behalf (Pss 2:2; 72:1 ff.; 110:1; cf. Eph 5:5), no specific role is ascribed to the shedding of their blood. Their reign is restricted in time and space. Priests and prophets reveal the limit of the kings' power. Christ unites all offices in his own person, and he is administrator of the whole will of God over all creation.

Can it be imagined that Paul himself[304] changed the application of the steward-imagery as drastically as is indicated by the contrast between Eph 1:10 and I Cor 4:1; Col 1:25? Paul himself combines in I Corinthians utterances on the (one) mystery of God with the mention of (many) mysteries. With equal ease he could make the transition from a human administrator like himself to Christ the arch-steward.[305] This procedure may be labeled a Christological concentration. It is certainly in line with Paul's own theology—though shifts in the other direction are not excluded, as a comparison of the statements on the church's foundation in I Cor 3:11 and Eph 2:20 reveals.[306] Christ's role in God's election shows that the position of a son entrusted with the stewardship over all possessions and the administration of all plans and decisions of the master is a fitting image to describe Christ's unique honor and responsibility.

XIII   Days of Fulfillment

The phrase *plērōma tōn kairōn,* lit. "fulfillment of times,"[307] rendered in our translation "days of fulfillment" (1:10), has as its background the idea of consecutive periods of history which are to be crowned and completed by an era surpassing all previous periods. Sometimes, e.g. in Isa 11; Matt 19:4–8; Rev 22, the belief was expressed that the end-time would fully restore the primeval conditions of paradise. Except by the use of the verb "to create" for God's first and final action, however, Ephesians shows no interest in developing a recapitulation theory.[308] But history is understood as something different from a haphazard conglomeration of events, from a meaningful cyclical or an ultimately meaningless recurrence of better and worse events. According to this epistle, history makes sense because it moves, or rather, it has already moved, to an apex. That moment is—now!

Apocalyptic writers and the Qumran community[309] took up an element of those prophets[310] who spoke of "that day" or "those days" on which God

---

[304] See fn. 72 to 1:3–14.

[305] Similarly in I Peter 2:25 Christ is called "the shepherd and bishop," the existence of many shepherding bishops notwithstanding. Cf. the use of "apostle" in Heb 3:1.

[306] Cf. John 8:12; 9:5; 12:46; Acts 26:18 where Christ is the light, with Matt 5:14; Acts 13:47; Eph 5:8 where the Christians have become light. In John 17:18 apostolicity is attributed to the disciples as much as to Jesus, but the priority of Jesus is maintained.

[307] See the literature listed in fn. 233; also J. Marsh, *The Fulness of Time,* New York: Harper, 1952; J. Barr, *Biblical Words for Time,* SBT 33, Naperville: Allenson, 1962; Stalder, *Das Werk des Geistes,* pp. 240–57.

[308] See the NOTE on "comprehended under one head" in 1:10, and COMMENT VI A on 2:1–10.

[309] E.g. LXX Dan 2:21; 4:34; 7–12; Apoc (IV) Ezra 4:37; 1QS I 14; III 23; IX 12–14, 18–21; 4 QpPs 37 I 9; 4QpHosea b I 9, 12.

[310] As Hosea 1:11; LXX Amos 4:2; 5:18; Joel 2:1; 3:1, 18 etc.; cf. Acts 2:17–21.

would prove true to the promises made to his chosen, and to the threats made against his and his people's enemies. Many rabbis joined in this eschatological expectation.[311] Instead of dealing with the several periods preceding the time of redemption, heterodox and orthodox teachers sometimes lumped together the whole of history into two aeons. The present, old, evil aeon was to give way to the coming era. When Paul speaks of "days of fulfillment" he alludes to a notion widespread, though not universally accepted, among the Jews of his time. Some Gentiles were equally hopeful after reading Vergil or the *Sibylline Oracles*. But Ephesians fails to acknowledge that pagans possess realistic hopes. According to this epistle, those uncircumcised, had been "bare of hope" (2:12). For Paul the only hope worth mentioning is that set upon the Messiah (1:12). Christ is not one among several important eschatological events. Nothing but his advent brings and shapes the new time and its benefits.

If the pre-history of the term "days of fulfillment" and Christ's creative role for that time were ignored, an important element not only of Eph 1:10 but of Pauline theology would be overlooked. Time is not an automatically moving production line on which this or that concrete object or event may find its place. The OT, apocalyptic, Qumranite, rabbinic, and Pauline concepts of time agree in considering time as something that is always formed and filled by a specific content or person. There are the times of the patriarchs, the exodus, the Sinai legislation, the conquest of the promised land, the kings, the exile, etc. Thus time is never a neutral ground, stage or platform on which anything or everything might happen. Instead, time is created and maintained for the elect servants of God and filled by specific deeds of God. The various periods that are eventually listed in one or another timetable are the effect rather than the presupposition of God's and his servants' actions. No time "works itself out," or "works out Christ."[312] According to Ephesians Christ alone "administers" the final days. *He* works them out. He is depicted as the one who was to make them dawn (cf. 5:14). He shapes, fills, uses, masters, extends, concludes them.[313] The days of fulfillment are Christ's time, however "evil" are some of the present days (5:17; 6:13).

A clear distinction between two eras—with the time before Christ's coming

---

[311] For references, details, and differentiations see StB, IV, 799–1015; G. F. Moore, *Judaism*, 3 vols. (Harvard University Press, 1954) I, 270 f; II, 375–95; Davies, PRJ, pp. 36 ff.; J. Bonsirven, *Paulestinian Judaism in the Time of Jesus Christ* (New York: Holt, 1964). pp. 163–225.

[312] As F. C. Synge and H. Schlier suggest.

[313] Gal 4:4 ("When the time had fully come, God sent forth his Son," RSV) seems at first sight to say the opposite. The appointed time appears to have come before the Son is sent. However, in that context the period created by the promise to Abraham is said to overarch the period created by the law given to Moses (Gal 3:15–22). Both the all-inclusive era of promise and the shorter era of law have the same *terminus ad quem*. Their end is called the "coming of the seed" (3:19); the "coming of faith" (2:23, 25); the coming of the "fullness of time," i.e. the "sending of the Son" (4:4). Paul uses the analogy of a "date set by the father" (4:2). This shows that the gift of the promise to Abraham, of the law to Israel, of the Messiah and of faith to both Jews and Gentiles form and fill the respective periods of history. In his interpretation of Galatians Luther, WA, LVII, 29–39, interprets Gal 4:4 boldly by saying *"Ubi Deus misit filium suum venit plenitudo temporis . . . Missio filii fecit tempus plenitudinis* [When God sent his Son the fullness of time came . . . The sending of the Son brought about the time of fullness]," not vice versa. Stalder, *Das Werk des Geistes*, pp. 251–52, reads to the same effect: "Gal 4:4 does not mean, *Because* the moment has come, the Son was sent but exclusively, When the fullness of time had come, . . . The mission of the Son makes that time to be the special time." In Rom 5:12–21; Gal 1:4; Col 1:13 and other passages, Paul makes similar distinctions between the eras of Adam, of evil, of darkness on one side and of Christ on the other. There is no neutral or empty time. Time is always constituted by its contents.

a period of law and curse, and the time after, a period of gospel and bliss[314] —is not the sum of Paul's teaching. Already Abraham lives out of the promise and is justified by faith (Rom 4:9; Gal 3:6). The law given through Moses is "spiritual" and "given for life" (Rom 7:10, 14)[315]—even though the deadly curse threatened by the law became effective through the law because of sin (Rom 7:7–12; Gal 3:10–13). David lives in the time of Mosaic law, but praises the man whose sins are forgiven (Rom 4:6–8). Thus the bygone era, understood as a period of years or centuries, cannot exclude the influence of the new era upon it. Equally, the presence of the new aeon cannot erase all traces of the old: the "mystery of iniquity" is not precluded (II Thess 2:7). If dates dictated or prohibited the presence of certain conditions, the mutual overlapping of the two aeons[316] would constitute a paradox. Since it is always God who gives a period its essence and character, faith in God—wherever and whenever found—attests to the presence of the new aeon. Equally, unbelief seeks to continue the duration of the old.

According to Eph 1:10 the time of fulfillment is entrusted to the hands of Christ. Inasmuch as he "fills all" (1:23; 3:19; 4:10), the days of fulfillment are present. The ongoing process of comprehending all "under one head" is the content and sense of these days.

XIV   Jews and Gentiles

The verses 1:11–13 contain distinct statements made about us ("we") and about "you." Who are those who speak of themselves in the first person, and who are the ones addressed?[317]

a) In the Pauline letters the distinction between "we" and "you" is natural wherever the apostle and his co-workers, or the apostle alone, is speaking in a somewhat majestic or pontifical way, addressing the members of a congregation.[318] Paul employs the manner of speech characteristic of princely utterances. It survives still, e.g. in papal decrees and letters.

b) Another reason for the "We"-style is equally plain. When Paul quotes,

---

[314] This view is classically represented by A. Nygren's commentary on Romans (London: SCM, 1955), esp. pp. 16–26.

[315] Despite its harsh words about the obsolescence and senility of the first covenant and its institutions, the epistle to the Hebrews states, "To us the gospel is preached just as to them [i.e. the Fathers] . . . To them the gospel was first preached" (4:2, 6; 8:13). Gifts of the new era are tasted now, but already Abel, Enoch, Noah, Abraham, Isaac, Jacob, Joseph, Moses and many others were saved by faith (6:4; 11:4–40). Paul's references to Gen 15:6 and Hab 2:4 express exactly the same conviction.

[316] Of which P. Minear speaks in the essay mentioned in fn. 233, and to which O. Cullmann's frequent references to the "tension" between the "already now" and the "not yet" seek to do justice.

[317] T. Zahn, Introduction to the New Testament, I (London: Clark, 1909), 508–9; R. E. Wilson, "We and You in the Epistle to the Ephesians," in Studia Evangelica, ed. by F. L. Cross, TU 87 (1964), 676–80; E. Peterson, "Die Kirche aus Juden und Heiden," in E. Peterson Theologische Traktate (München: Kösel, 1951), pp. 239–42; G. Dix, Jew and Greek, London: Dacre, 1953; Mitton, EE, pp. 225–28. In his earlier mentioned essay (ZNW 51 [1960], 145–54) H. Chadwick places special emphasis upon the abiding role ascribed to the Jews in the whole of Ephesians. See also Benoit, AnBib 17–18, I (1963), 57–77; Meuzelaar, Der Leib des Messias, pp. 20–58, esp. 54 ff. An identification of those called "we" in Eph 1:11–12 with the Jews is opposed by e.g. Percy, pp. 266–67, n. 16; Bieder, TZ 11 (1955), 334; Cambier, ZNW 54 (1963), 91–95; Gaugler, p. 52.

[318] See e.g. in I Thess 1:2; II Cor 1:4–24; 3:2a; 4:12. P. Schubert, BhZNW 20 (1939), 17–21, discusses the antithetical style characteristic of Pauline thanksgivings. The juxtaposition of "we" and "you" is according to him not a literary or oratorical device as among Cynic and Stoic orators, but "the direct expression of the epistolary situation" (p. 20).

or alludes to given confessional or hymnic formulations,[319] a reference to "we," "us," or "our" is a characteristic feature and almost standard. When Paul resumes his own teaching, he returns to the address, "you." Occasionally[320] variant readings reveal the copyist's intention to avoid a seemingly inexplicable transition from "we" to "you," from "our" to "your," or vice versa.

c) In decisive passages of Ephesians, however, the change between "we" and "you," "our" and "your," indicates something other than the pitting of apostolic authority against a disconsolate or unruly congregation, or an appeal to a common Christian creed, or a cavalier, unnecessary, and meaningless change of diction: as observed earlier, those addressed in Ephesians are all of Gentile origin.[321] They have been "apart from the Messiah, excluded from the citizenship of Israel, strangers to the covenants . . . bare of hope and without God" (2:12). These formerly hopeless people are distinct from other men who have equally been "under the wrath [of God]" (2:3), but were privileged to be the "first to set" their "hope upon the Messiah" (1:12). While the latter call themselves "The Circumcision" because of a "handmade operation," the former are called "The Uncircumcision" (2:11). In 2:17 (cf. 13), one of these two groups is called "those who are far," the other, "those near." 2:19 speaks of recently naturalized citizens, or newly adopted children who are now among the saints as members of God's household. Five times[322] the first group is called "the nations" or "the Gentiles"; in 2:12 the second group is explicitly identified as "Israel." It is emphatically asserted that Gentiles have now been made fellow heirs, fellow members, fellow beneficiaries in an heirdom, a body, and a promise that were established already before any Gentiles were given access to it (1:18c; 2:19; 3:6). Gentiles now partake of Israel's privileges and possess the same rights and titles as were formerly reserved for the Jews only.

This does not mean a superiority of the Jews over the nations, or any qualitative distinction. Paul describes the situation of the Jews before God as no better than that of the Gentiles. The Jews have been "dead" through "lapses and sins," caught in "fleshly passions," drawing upon themselves "the wrath of God"—just as have the Gentiles (2:1–3). In 2:11–19 the distinction created by circumcision between Jews and Gentiles is recognized, but its permanent character is denied. The Jews live as much as the Gentiles from God's election and love only. If God had not exerted his power over them to resurrect the dead, they would still be as dead as the Gentiles were. The salvation of Jews and Gentiles is "by grace" alone (2:4–10). Thus a full solidarity in both sin and grace joins Israel and the nations. The peace made between these two constituents of the human race, and between both and God (2:13–17), constitutes and reveals this solidarity.

However, solidarity and peace do not prevent Paul from discussing priority and posteriority. Just as in Rom 1:16, so also in Ephesians, Paul calls election and salvation by grace events that concern "the Jew first and [also] the Greek." In his undisputed letters Paul has special words sometimes for the Jews, some-

---

[319] As in I Cor 16:22; II Cor 1:2; perhaps also Eph 1:3–10, 14; see section II of the Introduction.
[320] E.g. in Eph 1:13, 19; II Cor 3:2b; Gal 4:6.   [321] 2:1–2, 11–12; 3:1; 4:17–19.
[322] 2:11; 3:1, 6, 8; 4:17.

times for the Gentiles.[323] Ephesians as a whole is a document destined for Gentile-born Christians only.

The remarks made in 1:11–13 on Jews and Gentiles contain three features that call for special attention.

a) In 1:13 it is stated that the Gentiles (i.e. the pagan-born readers of Ephesians) "heard and believed the gospel" and received the Spirit. A similar explicit mention of the conversion of the Jews is not found in 1:11–12. No doubt, the context 1:3–10, 14 makes clear that the Jews described in vss. 11–12 are "in Christ"; they are members of God's people. But "in Christ" they are God's people for a specific reason which does not equally apply to the Gentiles: We, "the first to set our hope upon the Messiah" (lit. "in the Messiah" or "in Christ") "were to become a praise of God's glory" (1:12). These words imply that even before their baptism the Jews were (unlike the Gentiles [2:12]) not apart from the Messiah but held together by him to whom they were looking forward. Already without baptism they belong to the Messiah. The urgency with which (according to Acts) John the Baptist, Peter, and Paul called Israel to accept the gospel, repentance, baptism, and the Holy Spirit[324] is not belied by Eph 1:11–12. The absence of a reference to gospel, faith, and baptism in Eph 1:11–12 provides at best an *argumentum e silentio* which must not be exploited. Yet it is remarkable that Paul sets the *recent* conversion of Gentiles through the gospel in contrast to the hope and destiny that were *previously* given to the Jews! Later passages in Ephesians will throw further light on this distinction.

b) The name "Jews," added in parentheses in our translation, occurs nowhere in Ephesians. Its absence cannot be explained by the fact that in a document received under Paul's name there was no need to identify the "we" by "Jews," for in his other letters Paul uses the noun or adjective *Ioudaios*.[325] In Ephesians the designation of the Israelites "to become a praise of God's glory" (1:12) may be an etymological substitution for the name "Jew."[326] In Paul's ears—though hardly in those of the recipients of Ephesians—the very name "Jew" may have evoked the mental image of a man who offers God the praise that is due him. "The churches in Judea that are in Christ . . . glorified God" (Gal 1:22–24). This passage shows that not all the Jews but only the Jewish-Christian congregations were giving God the glory due to him. "Not all from Israel are Israel" (Rom 9:6)—every radical prophet of Israel would agree with this hard judgment of Paul, for the prophets grieved long before him about the facts underlying it. In Ephesians, however, not the factual stance of *many* Jews but the common hope and destiny of *all* Jews are under consideration. The vocation of Israel remains true even when many Jews

---

[323] In Rom 2:17–29; Gal 2:14–21 Jews are addressed; in Rom 11:13 ff.; Gal 3:1 ff., esp. 8, Gentiles only.

[324] Acts 2:38; 13:24; 20:21.

[325] Emphatically Gal 2:14–15, "If you are a Jew . . . We are Jewish by birth . . ."; Rom 2:17, "If you call yourself a Jew . . ."; 3:1–2, "What advantage has the Jew? . . . Much in every way"; 9:4–5, "They are Israelites, and to them belong the sonship, the glory, the convenants, the giving of the law, the worship, and the promises; to them belong the patriarchs, and of their race, according to the flesh, is the Messiah." In most of the about twenty other references to "Jews" in the Pauline epistles, Jews and Gentiles (or, and Greeks) are mentioned in the same breath.

[326] In COMMENT VIII, it was shown how on the basis of Gen 29:35 Paul exploited the etymology of the term *Judah*.

belie the contents and meaning of the term "Jew." Because of Paul's pain over the factual shortcoming of many Jews (Rom 9:1–3), the blunt term "Jew"= "He who praises God," may have been omitted from Ephesians. While pointing out to the Gentiles the priority of the Jews, the apostle did not want to give rise to any sort of Jewish boasting. In Eph 2:9 he strictly excludes the possibility that any man boast of his achievements before God or fellow man.

c) The references to Israel's "first" in 1:11–12, and to its dismal opposite: the Gentiles' "past,"[327] might look like a superfluous, if not mischievous, harking back to a state of division and enmity which is "now" gloriously overcome (2:13–22; 4:4–6). Why such reminders of the bright or dreary "past"—when the contents and consequence of the gospel of Jesus Christ are the beginning of a new aeon? The old is "no more"! And inasmuch as it still exists, it is to be "stripped off" and "disproven"![328] All men are called to "keep" and to "meet" nothing but "unity."[329] What good can therefore be achieved by bringing up a past status or past events?

Three answers are suggested by the context: (a) On the plane of history Israel's temporal priority over the Gentiles mirrors the eternal priority of God's love for and in Christ, over the actual carrying out of his decision in the history of all creation. Only if Gentiles are willing to accept the priority of the Jews can they respect God's eternal superiority. I John 4:20–21 states that God is not loved unless the brother is loved. According to Ephesians the prototype of this "brother" is the Jew. (b) The precedence of Israel's election over the incorporation of Gentiles into God's people reveals that the time between the creation of the world and the coming of Christ is not void of the presence of God and the performance of his will. Certainly those days were but preliminary. The secret now revealed was still hidden, but the time between creation and Christ was nevertheless a time filled by "covenants," viz. by the "promise" of covenant renewal (Eph 2:12). Even before the days of fulfillment had dawned, God proved his love. This excludes notions such as those held in Gnostic circles that creation, or the law, or the very time and transience of all flesh ought to be attributed to a god or to powers other than the strong and rich Father of Jesus Christ. (c) If Israel's election were revoked or no longer mattered, Gentiles would have reason to doubt whether the election in Christ which now manifestly includes them is solid, irrevocable, eternal. But Paul reminds them of the privilege granted to Israel. By pointing to Israel, he shows that God is a lord who not only gives a promise, but keeps it. Israel is as by definition a community of hope and destined to God's praise (1:12).[330] Through Israel's history God has proven himself true to his promise and faithful to his elect. Without knowing of God's self-revelation through Israel and without accepting the demonstration given of God's essence and existence through Israel, Gentiles cannot believe in the same God.[331] Eph 1:11–13 agrees with John 4:22, 42: the salvation brought by "the savior of the world" is "the salvation" that comes "from the Jews."

[327] Eph 2:1–2, 11–12, 19; 4:17–19.   [328] 2:13, 19, etc.; 4:22; 5:11.
[329] 4:3–6, 13.
[330] Cf. e.g. Rom 1:2; Acts 23:6; 24:15; 26:6; 28:20; also Heb 4 and 11.
[331] Differences of accentuation that distinguish Ephesians from Galatians and Romans will be mentioned in the exegesis of 2:11–22.

XV   The Saving Word of Truth

In Eph 1:13 the three nouns, "word," "truth," and "salvation" are found in close and related succession. This is not the place to outline the long, fascinating, and complicated history of these three nouns in the ancient Orient, the Hellenistic world, the OT and NT, the apocryphal, sectarian, and rabbinic writings.[332] But one question deserves some comment: how can the apostle identify the "word" preached by men of flesh and bone, with "the truth"? In other words, how can he ascribe to preaching that saving function which according to John 14:6 only Jesus Christ himself, following John 8:32 only truth, possesses?

Paul esteems the words spoken by Christ's messengers far more highly than man-made narrations, speculations, expositions, and exhortations. The preached gospel is the means by which God himself reveals his righteousness (Rom 1:17). It is God who reveals his Son in the person and work of his messenger (Gal 1:16). "God is appealing through us" (II Cor 5:20). In II Cor 13:3 Paul asserts "Christ speaks in me," and in I Cor 2:12–15 he ascribes his knowledge, understanding, and teaching of spiritual things to the Holy Spirit. To the same Spirit he attributes prayer (Rom 8:15, 26). In I Thess 2:13 Paul thanks God for people who have accepted the apostle's preaching as the "word of God." Thus according to Paul God is the speaker in all speech related to God. On this ground must be interpreted all statements about the saving power of the gospel.[333]

In I Peter 1:11; 3:19 the self-manifestation of Christ is dated back to the times of the prophets and the days of Noah. According to Heb 2:3 Jesus Christ (the incarnate [Heb 2:14–16]) was the first to preach "salvation." In Luke 4:43; Mark 1:38, Jesus Christ declares that preaching is the very purpose of his mission. The gospels are replete with examples of how Jesus of Nazareth exerted power by his words: people wondered or became silent; they were healed, forgiven, dismissed "in peace"; storms were stilled and demons expelled. Just as Paul in Gal 1:6–7; Mark 1:1 speaks of the gospel "of" Jesus Christ. This gospel includes good news "about" Jesus the Messiah (Rom 1:1, 3), but it is above all the good news which Jesus Christ himself is, ushers in, and proclaims.[334] Just as in Acts 10:36, by allusion to Psalm and Isaiah texts, Christ is epitomized as "the word sent by God" through whom peace was announced, so also Eph 2:17 sums up his ministry, "when he came he proclaimed good news: 'Peace to you who are far and peace to those near!'" In this epistle the "apostles," "prophets," "evangelists," "teacher-shepherds" by whom the word is preached are his appointees (4:11). Their message is in 1:13 called "the true word that saves."

The Gnostics knew also of one or several apostles who conveyed holy words imbued with saving power.[335] The power of regenerating, enlightening,

---

[332] For all three concepts see the articles published in theological dictionaries of the Bible. For "word" see esp. the commentaries on John 1:1; "salvation" will be briefly discussed in the context of Eph 2:6, 8; Paul's concept of "truth" stands very near that of "salvation," perhaps even in the colloquial formulae "I say the truth," and "to speak the truth" (Rom 9:1; Eph 4:25).

[333] As Eph 1:13; Rom 1:16; I Cor 1:18, 24.

[334] For an extended discussion of Mark 1:1 see W. Marxsen, *Der Evangelist Markus*, FRLANT 67 (1959).

[335] See esp. W. Schmithals, *Das Kirchliche Apostelamt*, FRLANT 79 (1961).

and saving which is ascribed to the *logos,* e.g. in *Corp. Herm.* XIII 18–22, is by no means smaller than the power attributed by Paul to the gospel (Rom 1:16; Eph 1:13). The formal parallelism between Paul's and Gnostic statements about the "word" can as little be denied as parallelisms in the notions of grace and knowledge. But analogies are not demonstrations of dependence. If there is any interdependence between Ephesians and Gnosticism then the dates of the documents in question speak decisively for the priority of Ephesians. Also the contents and function of the "word" are so different that a dependence of Paul upon the concept of the *hieros logos* (myth, cultic formula, magic word, etc.) appears excluded. Jesus Christ crucified and risen, the peacemaker between "those far" and "those near," rather than a combination of creation- fall- and redemption-myths, is the contents of the gospel. No cultic or psychic magic is implied. Knowledge of Christ (or the Son's knowledge? 4:13) is the ultimate goal—not knowledge of the self, i.e. of its divine origin, tragic fall, dire imprisonment, potential liberation by whispered word or secret rituals. The acknowledgment of God includes the salvation of total man and all the moaning creatures, not just the liberation of the soul from the captivity in the mortal body. Finally, as stated in section III B of the Introduction, the "true word" is not to be kept secret in the confines of an esoteric group. It is to be announced to all the world (6:19–20).

XVI   Sacrament or Seal?

A last issue raised by the great benediction of Eph 1:3–14 is to be faced now. Is or is not the "seal of the Spirit" mentioned in 1:13 the sacrament of baptism? A series of monographs on baptism[336] provides ample material for facing the alternatives. In the following, arguments for and against such an equation will be presented under the letters (A) and (B) respectively.

A

1. The book of Acts shows, and almost every NT book explicitly presupposes, that people who "had heard the gospel" and "believed it" were baptized and thereby became members of God's people. Since Eph 1:13–14 means by "sealing" an event following upon such hearing and believing, i.e. an event that assures men of their forthcoming inheritance and redemption as "God's own people," this text appears to speak of baptism.[337]

[336] K. Barth, *Church Dogmatics,* IV:4 (1969); G. R. Beasley-Murray, *Baptism in the New Testament* (New York: St. Martin's, 1962), pp. 171–77; Bousset, *Hauptprobleme der Gnosis* (Göttingen: Vandenhoeck, 1907), pp. 286–89; J. Daniélou, *Bible et Liturgie* (Paris: Du Cerf, 1951), pp. 76–96; F. J. Dölger, *Sphragis, eine altchristliche Taufbezeichnung,* Paderborn: Schöningh, 1911; A. Erhardt, "Christian Baptism and Roman Law," in *The Framework of the New Testament Stories* (Manchester University Press, 1964), pp. 234–44; W. F. Flemington, *The New Testament Doctrine of Baptism* (London: SPCK, 1948), pp. 66–68, 75; O. Heggelbacher, *Die christliche Taufe als Rechtsakt,* Freiburg, Switzerland: Universitätsverlag, 1953; G. W. H. Lampe, *The Seal of the Spirit,* London: Longmans, 1951; E. Maass, ARW 21 (1922), 241–86; B. Noack, "Das Zitat in Epheser 5, 14," ST 5 (1951), 52–64; J. Thomas, *Le Mouvement Baptiste en Palestine et Syrie,* Gembloux; Duculot, 1935; cf. also M. Barth, *Die Taufe—ein Sakrament?* Zürich: EVZ, 1951; N. A. Dahl, "Dopet in Efeserbrevet," STK (1945), (ref.). The most recent intensive discussion of the role of baptism in Ephesians is found in Kirby's monograph, EBP, pp. 150–61.

[337] The opinion of E. Barnikol—see "Das Fehlen der Taufe in den Quellenschriften," WZUH 6 (1956–57), 1–18—that earliest Christianity did not practice baptism has remained insulated.

2. In the cults of the environment surrounding Israel and the church, but also in the biblical descriptions of Jewish and Christian liturgies, there are ample evidences of one or another cultic sign. By a symbolic, i.e. effective (or "mimetic magic") action, a man was made a member and marked as a member of the community in question. Such a "sign" established and expressed[338] ownership, domination, and protection. The religious custom of applying a sign or seal on a person may be derived from commercial and juridical practices, e.g. the marking of cattle or slaves. But it is not impossible that the reverse process took place: religious practices and meanings penetrated the so-called secular spheres. At any rate, the purpose of sealing is to establish an especially close connection, to authenticate this relationship, and to make it public. In other cases, the gift of a seal includes the conveyance of divine, human, or demonic power.[339]

Eph 1:13 appears to yield a clear sense if it is thus understood. God's blessing is a power imparted to the saints. They are now God's agents, perhaps his clergy.[340]

3. In Gen 17:11 circumcision is called a "sign." In Rom 4:11 Paul connects the same term with the function of a "seal."[341] In Barnabas IX 6—and since the fourth century A.D. in rabbinical writings[342]—circumcision is explicitly called a "seal." A plain identification of the OT concept of "sign" with the legal term "seal" has now taken place.[343] Because in post-NT times circumcision was called a seal, the conclusion was drawn that in the NT, too, baptism is called by the same name. Is this conclusion warranted? Indeed, in Col 2:11 circumcision and baptism are correlated. The *Odes of Solomon* XI 1–3 call the (Christian?) initiation ritual a circumcision (of the heart). Therefore it is argued that wherever in the NT the verb "to seal" or the noun "seal," occurs, baptism is meant.[344] Also, in post-NT literature there is no lack of evidence for describing baptism by the term "seal."[345] No alternative would appear to be left—"sealing" in Eph 1:13 must mean baptism.

4. Early Christianity may be classified among the several baptismal movements that sprang up in and around the Jordan valley between 100 B.C. and A.D.

---

[338] In the Bible e.g. Gen 4:15; Exod 13:9, 16; Lev 19:28; 21:5; Deut 6:8; 11:18; 14:1; Ezek 9:4; Ps Sol 15:6, 9; Rev 9:4; 13:16–17; 14:1. A mark worn by the worshipers of Mithras is mentioned by Tertullian *de praescriptione* 40.

[339] The meaning of a key, ring, and seal given to a vice-regent or deputy is illustrated, e.g. by Gen 41:42; Isa 22:22; Esther 3:10; Matt 16:19. See also John 6:27; Rev 7:2; 9:4 and WBLex, 804.

[340] Cf. part (c) of the NOTE on "we [Jews] were . . . appropriated" in 1:11.

[341] "Abraham took the sign of circumcision as a seal of the righteousness by faith."

[342] See StB, IV, 31–33; Lietzmann, *An die Römer*, HbNT, 8, 1933, on Rom 4:11; F. J. Dölger, *Sphragis*, pp. 149 ff. If—as in Kirby, EBD, p. 154, the date of Jewish and Christian references to circumcision as a seal is totally neglected—then it is easy to consider "seal" in Eph 1:13; 4:30 a reference to a Christian circumcision, that is, to baptism.

[343] The LXX had not yet translated the Hebrew "sign" (*ōth*) by the Greek "seal" (*sphragis*), and in Rom 4:11 both terms possess still a distinctive meaning.

[344] The *Odes of Solomon* (henceforth *Od[s] Sol*) is a collection of Gnosticizing hymns from the second or a later century A.D.; see *Die Oden Salomos*, ed. W. Bauer, KT 64 (1933). NT references to a "seal" are found especially in Eph 1:13; II Cor 1:22; Rev 9:4. Cf. also the anointing mentioned in II Cor 1:21; I John 2:20, 27; which alludes to the anointing of priests, kings, prophets in Exod 28:41; 29:7; I Sam 9:16; 10:1; 15:1, 17; Isa 61:1, etc.

[345] The first such evidence is found in second-century documents: II Clem. VII 6; VIII 6; Herm. *sim.* VIII 6:3; IX 16:3–6; 17:4. In *Acts of Thomas* 131 baptism is *expressis verbis* called "seal." Later, esp. Augustinian references, revealing an increasing influence of juridical thought patterns, are collected and discussed by O. Heggelbacher, *Die christliche Taufe.*

300.[346] The Qumran community,[347] John the Baptist and his disciples,[348] the Ebionites,[349] and the several syncretistic groups by or for whom the *Sibylline Oracles*[350] and the *Odes of Solomon*[351] were composed—these and other religious associations set great store on baptism. Those *Odes of Solomon* which may be labeled "initiation hymns," praise above all the enlightenment, the rebirth, the gift of life, the restoration of God's image.[352] Since similar things are ascribed to baptism in the NT, and are found also in Ephesians, the identification of seal and baptism in Eph 1:13 appears natural. Those scholars who consider the washings practiced among Jewish heterodox groups and/or the proselyte baptism introduced by the orthodox Jewry, as too insignificant to explain the role of baptism in early Christianity, can still draw on the Mystery Religions. If not a Jewish, then a pagan rite may have been imitated by the Hellenistic Christian practice and teaching of baptism. At any rate, the prevailing religious "climate" of Ephesians supports a sacramental interpretation of 1:13.

5. Allusions to baptism and some baptismal hymns have been discovered throughout this epistle.[353] If 1:13 alludes to the beginning of Christian life made in baptism, then the positive hints about the necessity to grow (2:21, 4:15–16), and the warnings against overestimating the present possession[354] appear sensible and well placed. H. Schlier[355] assumes that references to the eucharist in 5:20, 29 and to marriage in 5:22–23 close the sacramental cycle.

The equation seal=baptism has had a decisive influence upon the interpretation of the whole epistle. Among the consequences derived from this equation, four are outstanding:

a) The complete section 1:3[or 4]–14 may require an exposition determined by the key given in vs. 13. If 1:13 describes baptism, the whole benediction is perhaps a confession or hymn belonging to the liturgy of baptism.[356]

b) The baptismal-liturgical proem of Ephesians, in turn, can throw light upon the character and purpose of the whole epistle. Like I Peter,[357] Ephesians may *in toto* be a meditation or address composed for the newly baptized. And why should it not include some necessary warnings against a Gnosticizing misapprehension of the nature and meaning of the initiation and regeneration ritual?[358]

[346] So J. Thomas, *Le Mouvement Baptiste;* cf. Schille, *Hymnen,* pp. 62, 80, 85.
[347] 1QS III 4–12; v 13; CD x 10–11.
[348] John 1; 3; 4:1–2; Matt 3; Acts 19:1 ff. etc.; Josephus *ant.* XVIII 5:2.
[349] Described and glorified, on the ground of the Pseudo-Clementine literature, e.g. by H. J. Schoeps, *Theologie und Geschichte des Judenchristentums,* Tübingen: Mohr, 1949.
[350] IV 165 ff; cf. VI 4–7; VI 84.   [351] Esp. IV:7–8; VIII:15; XIII:1–3.
[352] Schille, *Hymnen,* pp. 63 ff., 76 ff., 96 ff. attempts to distinguish between initiation hymns and baptismal formulae in these Odes. But the connection between both should not be questioned. The baptism described, e.g. in *Corp. Herm.* IV 6 ff. is according to Pokorný, EuG, p. 108, "fundamentally identical" with the initiation of *Corp. Herm.* XIII.
[353] Only in 4:5 baptism is mentioned by name. But in 1:18, 20–23; 4:22–24, 30; 5:8–13, 14, 26 baptismal language or baptismal songs are being discovered.
[354] As seen, e.g. in the contrast between 1:7 and 1:14; see COMMENT IX.
[355] Schlier, pp. 249–50; 252–80.
[356] So esp. J. Coutts, NTS 3 (1956–57), 124–27. See also E. Käsemann, on the parallel passage Col 1:15–20, "Eine frühchristliche Taufliturgie," in Fs R. Bultmann (1949), pp. 133–48; translated in *Essays on New Testament Themes,* SBT 41 (Naperville: Allenson, 1964), 149–68.
[357] As a whole, or only in the first part 1:1 – 4:10.
[358] A baptismal understanding of the whole epistle appears first to have been timidly suggested by W. Lueken, SNT, II, 2d ed. (1908), p. 362, and by Percy p. 447; also by Dahl, Nauck, Coutts in their essays mentioned earlier. Schille, *Hymnen, passim,* Pokorný, EuG, pp. 17–21, and Kirby, *passim,* have endorsed and fortified this view. The Church of Scotland's *Interim Report of the Special Commission on Baptism,* I (Edinburgh, 1955), 5, goes even further: every page

c) The baptismal character of the whole of Ephesians, again, may serve to demonstrate that Ephesians is authentically Pauline. It may explain the liturgical diction and style; the lack of personal acquaintance between Paul and those addressed (1:15; 3:3–4); the absence of all personal greetings. If Paul wrote Ephesians from afar as a baptismal exhortation for the benefit of recently converted Christians, then he could not have known the readers.

But much more important than such literary and historical consequences is a doctrinal result.

d) There may exist a close, partly positive, partly polemical, relationship between the utterances on baptism made by Ephesians and by Gnostics. In observing this connection, traditional convictions about Christian baptism may be strengthened or questioned. P. Pokorný ventures to reconstruct the original, pre-Christian, Gnostic mystery rite.[359] Ascetic exercises at the beginning, and an exhortation and hymnic thanks offering at the end, form the frame for the two main elements of the cultic act: revelation and transformation. "Revelation" by communication of secret tradition includes (1) self-presentation of the god "Man," (2) information regarding man's captivity in matter which, however, does not preclude his original consubstantiality with the deity, (3) enlightenment concerning the ascent (of the soul) into heaven and reunion with the Heavenly Man, (4) the awakening-call. The "transformation," supported by the consumption of wine, includes (1) an ecstasis that numbs the senses and the will and produces a death-like state, (2) the awakening, rising, and ascending into a heavenly sphere, (3) incorporation of man into the body of the androgynous highest god, an event which is symbolized by putting on new garb.

While Pokorný is convinced that Christian "baptism is opposed to the Gnostic initiation,"[360] Schlier,[361] Schille[362] and others attribute to Ephesians a doctrine on baptism which in many aspects closely resembles Gnostic ideas. Christian baptism is described as a re-enactment of Christ's death and resurrection, i.e. as a death, a burial, a resurrection and ascension into heaven that take place "with him" (2:5–6). Baptism is considered the moment of forgiveness by God and reconciliation with God; here new life, faith, and enlightenment are given to man; here occurs the incorporation into the body of Christ. "What happened there, on the cross, potentially, has now happened actually, through baptism . . . In baptism, God made us good."[363] If indeed, the term "sealing"

---

of the NT supposedly refers to baptism. But Schlier (p. 212, n. 1) who in his commentaries on Galatians (in KEKNT, 7, 13th ed. 1965) and on Ephesians displays greatest enthusiasm for the various miraculous effects of baptism, shows a wise restraint: baptism alone is *not* the key to understanding Ephesians.

[359] EuG, p. 110; material showing the influence of Gnosticism upon Christian baptismal liturgies of the second and later centuries is found among the sources elaborated upon by P. I. Lundberg, *La typologie baptismale*, ASNU 10 (1942); cf. also C.-M. Edsman, *Le baptême de feu*, ASNU 9 (1940), pp. 134–99.

[360] EuG, p. 109.   [361] Schlier, pp. 69–70, 73, 80, 111–12, 117, etc.

[362] *Hymnen*, pp. 34, 43, 57, 103.

[363] Schlier, pp. 109, 117. Main passages outside Ephesians that are drafted to support this high view of baptism are Gal 3:27; I Cor 4:11; 12:13; Rom 6:3–5; Col 1:13; Titus 3:5. Besides Gnostic sources, the meager available information on Mystery Cults is drawn upon for establishing the similarity. A justification for mixing Gnostic and Mystery Cult sources is found in the fact that many among the earliest Gnostic elements found expression in the Mystery Religions—a presupposition which has not yet been sufficiently verified.

in Ephesians does refer to baptism and also signifies a Gnosticizing understanding of that rite, then saving power to the highest degree must be attributed to baptism, even to baptism alone.

Adherents of such baptismal teaching are certainly not blind to differences which coexist with the similarities. Jesus crucified in history is unlike the timeless Redeemed Redeemer. The creation of "a single new man out of the two formerly divided men" (2:15) is different from the reunion of the soul with the deity of which it always formed a part. An ethical dualism demanding ever new decision replaces the metaphysical dualism and a false security. The Gnosticizing and perfectionist contents of Eph 1:7 are protected from misuse by the futurist aspect of perfection presented in 1:14.[364] But once baptism is ascribed the function of the Gnostic "seal," the differences count for little if compared with the central fact, that is, the assumption that all blessings of God are channeled and conveyed through baptism.

The high doctrine on baptism sketched above is, however, not dependent upon the enthusiastic support it receives from the Gnostic school of NT interpreters. In many decisive issues such Roman Catholic, Anglican, Lutheran, and Reformed exegetes as were not afflicted with the Gnostic fever have come to exactly the same conclusions.[365] For even before Gnostic parallels to the rite of sealing by initiation were found, Eph 1:13 was understood as a praise of baptism.

Is there any alternative to this widespread interpretation? The rich possibilities it offers to sacramental theology are certainly not sufficient proof of the literary and historical accuracy of the equations, sealing is baptizing, the seal is baptism.

B

All evidence for the identification of "sealing" adduced from known literature and the history of religions dates from the second century and later. Rom 4:11 and Barn. IX 6 may or may not prove that in oral rabbinic teaching circumcision was called a "seal" as early as the first century. But as Paul's line of thought in Rom 4 is original, so his choice of vocabulary may be also. The syncretistic *Odes of Solomon,* the Shepherd of Hermas, II Clement, not to speak of the materials assembled in the *Pseudo-Clementine Homilies,* are all close to one hundred years later than Ephesians. Even if Ephesians should be deutero-Pauline, it would still antedate second-century and later literature by too many decades to permit linguistic and theological dependence. The grouping of Christianity among the baptismal movements may amount to a *petitio principii.* Equally dubious is the placement of Eph 1, or 1–6, into a liturgy of baptism. There is many another *Sitz im Leben* outside the sacrament. Indeed, several NT passages may treat baptism without using the very word, baptism. But

---

[364] A reference to Schille's emphasis on this point (pp. 68–69) has already been made.

[365] Examples from each of the four groups are: R. Schnackenburg, *Baptism in the Thought of St. Paul,* New York: Herder, 1964; G. W. H. Lampe, *The Seal of the Spirit,* 1951; Kirby, EBP, pp. 123 ff. (based on his studies in Jewish liturgy esp. of the Festival of Weeks); the section on baptism in Luther's Cathechisms; O. Cullmann, *Baptism in the NT,* London: SCM, 1950; the Church of Scotland's *Interim Report* mentioned in fn. 358.

there are also passages that speak of "baptism" and "baptizing" and have no direct reference to the baptism performed in the churches.[366] Eph 1:13 cannot with certainty be claimed for the first of these two groups. On the contrary, it is certain that this verse attributes "salvation" to the "gospel" rather than to "sealing"; cf. Rom 1:16. According to Eph 1:14, 4:30, the act of "sealing" is not an *earnest* of the future inheritance, but it is the "Spirit" himself who guarantees the final liberation.

If the spiritual "seal" is not to be associated with baptism, then what does it signify?

A host of NT utterances on the Spirit provide an answer. There are many Pauline passages that mention the gift and the reception of the Spirit. The Spirit produces a witness of a special sort: the congregation. He evokes the confession "Jesus is Lord," and he inspires the prayer "Abba." Manifold manifestations that constitute the life of the congregation, and rich "fruit" determining every member's daily conduct are ascribed to him.[367] In all these operations the work of the Spirit is "God's authentication of the Gentile converts."[368] According to the book of Acts[369] such authentication takes place and is recognized when Jews or Gentiles begin to praise God and his mighty deeds in the astonishing form of "speaking in tongues." Whenever they are "filled with the Spirit," apostles and other servants of God are enabled frankly and boldly to deliver their testimony.[370] Paul mentions the same tongue-loosening, witness-producing function of the Spirit. He fought the Spirit-drenched and Spirit-drunk Corinthians' enthusiastic loquaciousness (I Cor 14); but he did not distrust the Spirit as such (Gal 3:2, 5). He ascribed his own teaching and preaching exclusively to him.[371]

Since, according to Eph 4:7–8, 11 the gift of the exalted Christ, i.e. the Spirit, provides the congregation with men equipped for the preaching, teaching, and counseling ministries, the "sealing with the Spirit" mentioned in 1:13 may well mean the opening of the hearts and lips of the saints to render testimony. In this case the "seal" they bear is the fact that they glorify God, confess Jesus as Lord, edify and exhort one another by hymns, and become witnesses to out-

---

[366] Mark 1:8b; 10:38–39; Luke 12:50; perhaps also I Cor 12:13, refer to Spirit- and death-baptisms.

[367] Gal 3:2, 5, 14; 4:6; 5:22–23; I Cor 12:3, 7–11; II Cor 3:3; 11:4.

[368] Robinson, p. 35; he defines the "seal" by "their [the Gentile Christians'] foretaste and their security of the fulness of blessing in the future." Gaugler, p. 197, explains Eph 4:30 by stating "The Spirit is the form in which you received the seal."

[369] E.g. 2:4, 11; 10:44, 46; 19:6.

[370] Acts 2:4, 14 ff.; 4:8, 31; 6:3; 7:55; 9:17; 11:24; 13:9. In Luke 4:18 Jesus' own preaching is ascribed to the same Spirit. According to Matt 10:20; Luke 24:49; Acts 1:8; John 15:26; 16:13–15 the Spirit was promised to give the disciples of Jesus the wisdom, courage, power, and joy to speak.

[371] I Cor 2:4, 13; Rom 15:19. Obviously there is some difference between three seemingly equal events: (a) the clarity of an apostolic sermon and letter; (b) the many languages heard at the day of Pentecost (Acts 2 and perhaps in Cornelius' house, too, Acts 10:46; 11:17; cf. 15:8); and (c) those unintelligible exclamations or noises that were made in the Corinthian assembly. But a common denominator is present. In each case the decisive event after the preaching and hearing of the gospel is a tangible and surprising proof given of God's nearness, not the performance of the rite of baptism. God demonstrates his approval of the assembled saints, and his power over them, by making prophets out of a variety of older and younger people (Acts 2:17), of a few wise and noble men but much more of the despised and ignoble (I Cor 1:26–28). Certainly baptism is requested and administered in recognition of, or preparation for, the reception of the Spirit. But the gift of the Spirit and its consequences, rather than baptism alone, is the final proof of God's blessing (Acts 2:38; 10:44; 15:8; Gal 3:2, 5; I Cor 2:15; 12:3, 13; II Cor 5:5).

siders. Since the proclamation and confession of Jesus, the Lord, or of the Father, Son, and Spirit, are essential to baptism, the "seal of the Spirit" would include the administration of this rite. But the sealing need not be restricted to the moment of baptism. It would rather consist of a continuous flow of strength from God to man—the perpetual or ever new giving of strength, wisdom, courage, joy, and the right words. Sealing with the Spirit is in this case equal to "supplying the Spirit." In Gal 3:5 and Phil 1:19 Paul uses the verb and the noun "supply," which originally meant to make financial provisions for theatric performances. The act of "sealing" or "supplying" is as little completed, and as much dependent upon continuous renewal, as that of "filling" with the Spirit (Acts 4:8, 31, etc.).[372]

It may be asked, why should Paul use the term "sealing" in Eph 1:13 and II Cor 1:22 if he meant to say the same as in other passages with the less ambiguous verbs "to give," "to receive," "to supply," "to fill"? The possible connection between II Cor 1:22 and 3:2–3 provides an answer. While a "gift" may be handed out and received between two persons in private, a "seal" presupposes, or aims at, an impact upon a third party. Sealing takes place in order to establish a public event, that is, to prove authority or authenticity for public benefit. Paul's apostlehood was obviously challenged among the Corinthians. Unlike Jewish sh*eluchim (delegates from the Sanhedrin, a synagogue, or a family) he could not produce letters proving his authority, let alone a badge. His reply to the Corinthians is "You are yourselves our letter . . . that anybody can see and read, and it is plain that you are a letter from Christ . . . written not with ink but with the Spirit of the living God."[373] The reference to the "seeing" and "reading" of this letter by "anybody" manifests the public purpose and function inherent also in the act of "sealing with the Spirit."

Applied to Eph 1:13 this means: the sealing with the Spirit has a specific beginning but it still continues. It enables the saints to do things they would not do of their own resources: to participate in the praise of God's glory (1:6, 12, 14); to make known God's wisdom to the powers (3:10); to carry abroad the news of peace (6:15); to wield the sword of the Spirit which is the word of God (6:17). Such sealing by the Spirit is much more than assurance of personal salvation, and more precious than individual peace of mind. It makes God's chosen men troubadours before God for the joy of the whole world. On earth they now demonstrate God's praiseworthiness and his good will toward all creatures in heaven and upon earth—"to prove throughout the ages to come, through the goodness [shown] to us in the Messiah Jesus, how infinitely rich is his grace" (2:7). They are God's seal upon the earth—just as is Jerusalem, according to the prophecies on Zion contained in the book of Isaiah.[374] Those sealed are an exhibition of God's love and power. Theirs is a mission. No danger exists that people entrusted with so great a commission will not also

---

[372] The Greek tense used in Eph 1:13 is an aorist "you have been sealed." This tense, above all in the indicative form, denotes—except in the rare cases when it occurs in proverbial utterances (gnomic aorist)—a unique, complete, past action. The aorist seems to preclude the interpretation offered above. But as little as the aorists "he has blessed us," "he has chosen us" in 1:3–4 will be used to prove that God has ceased to bless and to choose after a given moment, ought the sealing to be considered as restricted to one instant only in man's life.

[373] II Cor 3:2–3, JB.   [374] See esp. von Rad, OTTh, II, 155–169.

personally enjoy the seal and benefit from it—whatever burdens and suffering it implies.

Such observations may offer an alternative to the restrictive and narrow interpretation which identifies the seal with baptism only. But they do not yet suffice to disclose all the dimensions of the term "sealing with the Spirit." When Luke,[375] and with him Paul in the passages mentioned, ascribe to the Spirit the power to call forth prophetic speech,[376] they follow a precedent set by classic prophets[377] and almost canonized during later periods:[378] the Spirit of God is primarily defined as the "Spirit of prophecy." He makes man speak to God, in the name of God, about God. However, in the Gospel of John and the Pauline writings the Spirit's function is not only prophetic. His presence may be recognized by events other than sudden outbursts of clear or obscure speech. (1) The Spirit has a place and function before God the Father. He is counselor or advocate, and he knows all things.[379] (2) He is the one through whom God creates and renews life; therefore man's new birth and resurrection are attributed to him.[380] (3) He gives knowledge of God and Christ, and he effects understanding of the Scriptures and of the message of Christ and the apostles.[381] (4) In his hands are not only the intimate relation to God the Father manifested in prayer, but also the gift and criterion of conduct and works performed among believers and non-believers.[382] Because of the Spirit there is forgiveness, faith, hope, patience, endurance, freedom, love[383]—i.e. in all cases considerably more than baptism.

Ephesians is especially eloquent in ascribing many functions to the Spirit. Through the Spirit God's secret is revealed; God's wisdom is known; joint access to the Father is given to Jews and Gentiles; strength is given to the inner man; the unity of the congregation is established; numerous ministers are appointed; the building and growth of the congregation continues; the church members are inspired to converse in the language of hymns; consistency of prayer is assured.[384] All utterances in this epistle on the demonstrations of God's power and the carrying out of God's decision may be considered descriptions of the operation of the Spirit.[385] Most works of the Spirit go far beyond the enrichment or edification of individual persons. They pertain to the life of the community or to a function to be fulfilled by chosen persons in a public service. Consequently, the working of the Spirit is always such that it is seen and perceived by many—whether they be Jews, Gentiles, or Christians and whether they are credulous, skeptic, or antagonistic to the gospel, its

---

[375] In Acts *passim*. I Peter 1:11–12; II Peter 1:21; II Tim 3:16 belong in this context too.

[376] Besides "speaking," "prophecizing" and "speaking in tongues" Luke uses the verb "to speak up" (*apophtheggomai* in Acts 2:4, 14), a term used among the Greeks for referring to the speech of wise men, cf. Acts 26:25, but also of oracle-givers and other inspired persons; see WBLex, 101.

[377] Micah 3:8; Hosea 9:7; Isa 42:1; 61:1.

[378] Zech 7:12; Joel 2:28; Num 11:25; cf. I Sam 10:10; Rev 19:10; 22:6.

[379] John 14:16, 26; 15:26; 16:7–11, 13; I Cor 2:10; Rom 8:26.

[380] John 3:5; 6:63; 20:22; I Cor 12:13; 15:44–45; II Cor 3:6, 17–18; 5:5; Titus 3:5; cf. Luke 1:35. In Heb 6:4–5 the possession of the Spirit is identified with the tasting of the new aeon.

[381] John 14:26; 16:8–11; I Cor 2:10–16; 10:3–4; II Cor 3:17.

[382] Rom 8:2–10, 15–16; Gal 4:6; 5:16, 22–25; 6:1.

[383] John 20:22–23; Gal 5:5; II Cor 3:17; 4:13; Rom 8:23, 26, etc.

[384] Eph 1:17; 2:18; 3:5, 16; 4:7–16; 5:18–19; 6:18.

[385] E.g. in 1:19–20; 3:7, 20. Cf. the statements on God's "energy," or on the execution of his plan by the Spirit in Gal 2:8; 3:5; I Cor 12:6–7, 11; Col 1:29. An equation suggests itself saying, the Spirit is the demonstration of God's power and presence.

ministers, or the congregation.[386] Occasionally Paul refers to miracles,[387] more often, especially in II Corinthians, to the suffering endured by him or the congregation under the protection of God's strength.

Thus the Spiritual sealing of Eph 1:13 may signify many other things besides the gift of oral confession and witness. The words "you have been sealed" can be paraphrased in the following way: you have been reborn, i.e. resuscitated with Christ; you have begun to know God and to sing his praise; you have been given an open door to approach God in the company of former adversaries; you have experienced a unity worth keeping; a foundation was laid under your feet that anticipates the growth of a fine building. So numerous are the manifestations and so rich is the essence of the *seal* imprinted upon the saints. All later chapters of Ephesians unfold the meaning of the spiritual "seal." Paul may have considered it sufficient in 1:13 to use the cryptic term "sealing" because he wanted at this point only to announce things which would be clarified later.

In sum, in the light of Ephesians, of the whole Pauline corpus, and of the entire NT, it is not advisable to limit the meaning and act of sealing exclusively to the rite of baptism. Sealing is the designation, appointment, and equipment of the saints for a public ministry—a ministry which includes the power to understand, to endure, to pray, to sing, and to live in hope.

In the line of Jewish apocalyptic teaching, and above all because of the eschatological contents of Eph 1:14, the verb "sealing" must also be understood as denoting "eschatological preservation."[388] But preservation may again be misunderstood in the sense of a private and personal interest of the soul. The ministerial, missionary, evangelistic character of "sealing" should not be permitted to lose its radiance. The seal is a light kindled to the glory of God and the benefit of the whole world.

XVII   Conclusion

As was stated earlier, 1:3–14 is a summary of the whole epistle to the Ephesians. Decisive among the theological insights conveyed by this passage are the following:

a) The ground and origin, but also the purpose and highest achievement of all speech about God is the praise of God. Theology is doxology—or else it fails to speak of that God who through acts of abounding goodness revealed himself as the loving, faithful, liberating Father. Thus a theologian cannot help being a happy man as long as he sticks to his proper task, for theology cannot commence with a discourse on man's sin, captivity, alienation, or insatiable need; rather it has to deal with God who loves and redeems men even though they have lapsed into sins and fallen into death.

b) The manifestation of God in his many acts of election, creation, salvation, and revelation have an origin, a center, a unity. It is not conditioned by the limits of space and time characteristic of the phenomenal world. Neither is it timeless, spaceless, absolute, or general—as is the world of ideas or pure forms. To the contrary, God's love and its manifestation have a specific location and

[386] E.g. Gal 2:7–9; Luke 2:52; Acts 2:7–13; I Peter 2:12.
[387] Gal 3:5; II Cor 12:12.   [388] So Schlier, p. 72. See for this dimension COMMENT IX.

occasion. In Eph 1 the following specifications are given: the mutual relation between the Father and the Son; the plenipotence given to The Beloved to administer God's kingdom; the sacrifice of Jesus Christ for the sake of man; the seal of Christ, i.e. the Spirit, who determines the life, the mission, and the safety of those who acknowledge him. In place of determinism or double predestination stands the living Jesus Christ—he who is one and the same before creation, in his manifestation on earth, and in the completion of his work.

c) The decision of God regarding his Son's ministry and the work of God carried out in the same Christ and through the power of the Spirit are now praised by both those who had hoped for the Messiah before his coming and those who had no hope at all. All are now given to know the very heart of God. They confess that before creation, in the course of subsequent historic periods, and in the consummation of all things there is no other God, and no other will and wisdom of God, but the one now revealed in Jesus Christ. The unification of Jews and Gentiles in the common praise of God and the common mission among all creatures demonstrates on earth the overflow of the riches of God's grace. Not only the insiders but together with them all creatures in heaven and upon earth are destined to be submitted to Christ.

d) The saints are given and already possess the full blessing promised by God. By the same token, all present possession is but an earnest of greater things yet to come. For God's work is not yet over, his revelation not yet exhausted. As God himself was present when he poured out his grace in Christ, so he is and will be present to carry through and crown his work of liberation for all. The church lives from that grace, and it is equipped to attest to that grace, that was and still is active, and that will be proven even more triumphant in the future.

III INTERCESSION, A PRAISE OF GOD
(1:15–23)

1   ¹⁵ Therefore, after hearing of the faithfulness [shown] among you to the Lord Jesus and (of the love) toward all the saints, I, for my part, ¹⁶ never cease to give thanks for you. When mentioning you in my prayers ¹⁷ [I ask] that the God of our Lord Jesus Christ, the all-glorious Father, give you the Spirit of wisdom and revelation so that you may know him ¹⁸ [. I ask] that he illumine the eyes of your hearts so that you may become aware of the hope to which he is calling you, what glorious riches are to be inherited among the saints, ¹⁹ and how exceedingly great is his power over us believers. For that mighty strength is at work ²⁰ which God has exerted in the Messiah when

He has raised him from the dead.
He has enthroned him at his right hand in the heavens
²¹ above every government and authority,
power and dominion and any title bestowed,
not only in this age but also in the age to come.
²² He put everything under his feet
and appointed him, the head over all, to be head of the church.
²³ She is his body, full of him
who fills all things totally.

NOTES

1:15. *Therefore . . . I, for my part.* Lit. "Therefore I, too."[1] It is typical of Paul to interrupt more general descriptions of God's relation to the church and the world with references to himself.[2] These references are not just a rhetorical device. Rather they express a high apostolic self-consciousness which has its root in the function entrusted to the apostle by God. In II Cor 3 Paul goes so far as to compare his ministry with that of Moses and to ascribe to his own task a surpassing glory. His special function was to announce the incorporation of the Gentiles into God's people.[3]

[1] Cf. "You, too" (1:13); "all of us, too" (2:3); "we too have put our faith in Jesus Christ" (Gal 2:16 NEB).
[2] Cf. Eph 3:1, 13; 4:1; 6:19, 21; Rom 7:24–25; Gal 1:10 – 2:21; II Cor *passim*, etc.
[3] Gal 1:16; Rom 1:5; 15:15–21; Eph 3:5–6 etc.; see esp. J. Munck, *Paul and the Salvation of Mankind*, Richmond: Knox, 1959.

after hearing. Cf. Col 1:4. The problems posed by the hearsay acquaintance between the writer and his addressees are discussed in Parts III A and IX of the Introduction.

faithfulness [shown] among you to the Lord Jesus. See the last NOTE on 1:1 for an explanation of why "faithfulness to" is preferable to "faith in."[4] The parallel verse (Col 1:4) speaks of "your faith," rather than the "faith[fulness] among you." It is unlikely that the version found in Ephesians is a clumsy substitute for "faith of yours," or "your faith."[5] Rather "faithfulness" (or, faith) is hypostatized: it lives, dwells, and is observed among the saints; cf. Rom 1:8, 12; Gal 1:23. The addition of "[shown]" underlines the fact that faith is more than an invisible feeling. In Gal 5:22 "faith" is listed in the catalogue of the fruits of the Spirit and has the character of an ethical attitude.[6] Cf. the next NOTE.

(of the love). These words are missing in the Chester Beatty Papyrus, the Vatican Codex, and the first script of the Sinaiticus, nor are they found in the codices A, P, or in a MS used by Origen. But they are present in all other manuscripts, in the ancient versions, and in the parallel Col 1:4.[7] While Paul thanks God for "faith" only in Rom 1:8, or for "faith and love" in II Thess 1:3; Philem 5, the triad "faith," "love," and "hope" is twice mentioned as reason for his gratitude.[8] The same triad occurs also in other contexts.[9] But this does not demonstrate that the words "of the love" are authentic in Eph 1:15, for it is more likely that some translators and copyists inserted "love" in order to fill a supposed lacuna than that others should have crippled a familiar Pauline triad by willful or incidental omission of one of its parts. Indeed, if "love" belongs in the text of Eph 1 the Ephesian epistle resembles other Pauline writings, and Eph 1:15 is free from ambiguity. In this case faith in the Lord Jesus is at the same time indissolubly connected with, and distinguished from, the mutual love of the saints. Does this mean that "dogmatics" is represented by "faith," and that "love" substitutes for the sum and substance of all "ethics"? The distinction between dogmatics and ethics appears to presuppose that faith equals belief in Christ rather than faithful conduct in the kingdom of Christ. Certainly, the ethical meaning of faith[10] is obfuscated when the necessity is felt to add "love." Paul throws light on his understanding of faith in Rom 1:12, where he mentions the comfort he hopes to receive among the Christians in Rome through the "faith" which they and he have "among one another." Since this mutual "faith" is usually called "love," the copyists interpolating "love" in Eph 1:15 did no wrong. But probably more often than not the word "faith" means faithfulness, i.e. something similar to love, an attitude equally ethical as love. In Philem 5 both "love and faith" are directed to both "the Lord Jesus

---

[4] Cf. Schlier; Gaugler. According to Abbott, p. 25, *pistis en* refers to "that in which the faith rests," unlike *pistis eis* which denotes "that to which it is directed."

[5] Abbott presents late Greek examples for such circumscription and finds it also in Acts 17:28; 18:15; 26:3.

[6] Cf. I Tim 6:11; see, e.g. B. S. Easton, "New Testament Ethical Lists," JBL 51 (1932), 1–12, esp. 11.

[7] The Nestle edition of the NT, also GNT, suggest that they are authentic.

[8] I Thess 1:3; Col 1:4–5; if the words "of the love" in Eph 1:15 are genuine, then Eph 1:15, 18 is the third instance in which the triad occurs in a thanksgiving formula.

[9] I Thess 5:8; Gal 5:5–6; I Cor 13:13; Rom 5:1–5.

[10] Gal 5:22; I Tim 6:11.

and all the saints." The OT contains surprising precedents for using the verb "to believe" or "to be faithful" in relation to both God and to a man at the same time.[11] For these reasons the bracketed words "of the love" should be treated as an interpolation that has two effects: it facilitates the understanding of Eph 1:15, but it narrows down the wide meaning of "faith." However, if the words "of the love" are considered authentic, a simple explanation for their omission in many MSS can be given: a copyist may have made a mechanical mistake by skipping from the Greek article (*tēn*) before "love" to the same article (*tēn*) which follows it.

all the saints. A definite restriction. Paul mentions only faithfulness (and love) shown to the saints, not to the whole of humanity. In Gal 6:10 he exhorts the saints to "do good to all men, and especially to those who are of the household of faith." Similarly, in the OT love, faithfulness, truth, etc. are related primarily to the partners of a specific covenant. Each Israelite is to love God with his whole heart and his "brother" or "neighbor" (including the resident alien) as himself. The distant Egyptians and the hostile Amalekites are not mentioned; and total humanity, e.g. "all flesh," is never called the object of this love. Eph 1:15 contains the same factual limitation. Nobody can love everybody. Christians cannot love (or be faithful to) people whom they don't know or whom God has not joined to them by a special event. See COMMENT III on 4:1–16 for further discussion of the character of love. R. Asting[12] suggests an even stricter limitation to the meaning of the term "saints," in which the apostles, evangelists, and similar officeholders are the sole recipients of the love mentioned in 1:15. When, e.g. Eph 3:5 is compared with Col 1:26, this identification seems possible. But Paul's frequent utterances on mutual love of all the Christians (Rom 13:8–10, etc.) contradict such a discrimination in favor of the clergy inside the church.

16. *to give thanks for you.* See COMMENT II.

mentioning you in my prayers. Cf. NEB. Lit. "making remembrance."[13] To translate *mneian poioumenos* by "remembering" is not sufficient because it suggests a mental act moving backward in time. The biblical notion of "remembering" implies an action, usually of cultic character,[14] which uses the past as a precedent for the present and future time.[15] Since Paul does not know the addressees personally, he cannot "remember" them in the English sense of the word. But he can make use of all he knows of their origin, history, and mode of life (1:13, 15) in order to intercede before God on their behalf. In Eph 1:16

---

[11] Exod 4:31; 14:31; 19:9; II Chron 20:20.
[12] *Die Heiligkeit im Urchristentum*, pp. 174–87, using Col 1:26; Eph 3:5, 8; 4:11–12; Philem 5, 7 as his main evidence.
[13] The same circumscriptive phrase ("*making* remembrance" instead of "remembering") is found in Rom 1:9; I Thess 1:2; Philem 4; cf. the circumscription "making petition" Philip 1:4. Only in I Thess 1:3 the direct verb, "remember," is used. No equivalent is found in Colossians.
[14] E.g. Exod 12:14; I Cor 11:25.
[15] K. H. Bartels, "Der theologische Quellort der Sammlung und ihrer Parole 'Katholische Reformation,'" EvTh 20 (1960), 364 ff, esp. 371–79; P. A. H. de Boer, *Gedenken und Gedächtnis in der Welt des Alten Testamentes*, Stuttgart: Kohlhammer, 1962; B. S. Childs, *Memory and Tradition in Israel*, SBT 37 (1962); N. A. Dahl, "Anamnesis," ST 1 (1947), 69–95; J. Jeremias, *The Eucharistic Words of Jesus* (London: SCM, 1966), pp. 237–55; D. R. Jones, "Anamnesis," JTS 6 (1955), pp. 183–91; J. J. Petuchowski, "Do This in Remembrance of Me," JBL 76 (1957), 293–98; H. Kosmala, "Das tut zu meinem Gedächtnis," NovT (1960), 81–94; J. Pedersen, *Israel*, III–IV, 401–2, 408–11; W. Schottroff, *Gedenken im alten Orient und im Alten Testamentes*, Neukirchen-Vluyn. 1964; G. von Rad, OTTh, I, 242–43.

the Greek words "for you" oscillate between "I give thanks" and "I make mention"; as Pauline thanksgivings in other letters show, they belong equally to both verbs. In our translation they are used twice, thanks "for you" mentioning "you."

17. [*I ask*]. Cf. NTTEV. This interpolation serves the purpose of a smooth translation; indeed, the verb "to ask" or "to make petition" occurs in other thanksgivings.[16] The version "May God give . . . ," is not recommended, because it substitutes wishful thinking for the concreteness and confidence of Paul's prayer. The Greek form of the verb "to give" is probably not an optative suggesting a remote, though desirable, possibility, but a subjunctive. It replaces the indicative after telic conjunctions.[17]

the all-glorious Father. Lit. "Father of glory." This term is probably a liturgical formulation of priestly origin; its roots lie in the OT, and perhaps in Canaanite religious tradition.[18] Since in the OT[19] the glory of God is identified with the splendor characteristic of his appearance, the term "Father of glory" may denote God as the source of the splendor which produces a light in the hearts of men (1:18; cf. II Cor 3:18). Glory and enlightenment are directly correlated in II Cor 4:4, 6. In the same verses Christ is denoted as the image of God. According to Bengel, *gloria . . . est ipse filius Dei.* Cf. Heb 1:3.

the Spirit of wisdom and revelation. Only a long paraphrase could adequately express the meaning of the genitives "of wisdom" and "of revelation." Paul intends to affirm that God's Spirit creates in man a new (human) spirit (cf. 4:23), for the noun "Spirit" is used by Paul with and without an article to denote the Holy Spirit of God. Both the act and the effect of inspiration by God are described wherever this noun occurs—except in Eph 2:2. The result of inspiration is the creation, operation, and demonstration of a new "mind" of man (4:23), the presence of a human spirit, e.g. a spirit "of meekness" (Gal 6:1), or as here "of wisdom and revelation" (Eph 1:17). In turn, this spirit is not only the disposition to learn but also to teach,[20] not only to accept revelation but also to communicate knowledge of the revealed secret to others.[21]

so that you may know him. Lit. "in knowledge of him." The Greek noun used here is a composite of a preposition and the normal word for knowledge

---

[16] I Thess 3:10; Philip 1:4; Rom 1:10; Col 1:9.

[17] Cf. BDF, 369:1; 95:2. The same form is found in II Thess 3:16; Rom 15:5; II Tim 2:25.

[18] Cf. "God of glory," Ps 29:3; Acts 7:2; "king of glory," Ps 24:7; "Lord of glory," I Cor 2:8; "Lord Jesus Christ of glory," James 2:1; "Father of mercies," II Cor 1:3; "Father of the lights," James 1:17. For the Canaanite and other uses of the term "father" see COMMENT III A on 3:14–21 and the interpretation of Eph 4:6.

[19] E.g. Exod 24:16; 40:35; Deut 33:2.

[20] Robinson, p. 38.

[21] Actually, three dimensions of the gift of the Spirit may be discerned: (a) The bestowal of knowledge and understanding of the things revealed by God; (b) The direction and means to live, act, and form judgments according to the insight gained, i.e. to walk in the Spirit (Gal 5:16, 25; Rom 8:13–14; Eph 4–6; esp. 5:15–18). (c) The commission to convey knowledge to others, to be a light in their midst, to spread the gospel which reveals God's wisdom and mystery (Eph 3:10; 5:8–13; 6:14–20).

In I Cor 2:10–16 the identity of the Spirit operative in all of these three dimensions is specifically emphasized. Here Paul speaks only of the Spirit of God, not of man's. See COMMENT III; also COMMENT X on 1:3–14.

(*epi-gnōsis*). The composite noun, as well as the corresponding verb, may denote real, deep, and full knowledge, as distinct from first awareness or superficial acquaintance. Schlier speaks for many earlier commentators when he assumes that Paul asks God to give the saints real and special knowledge. Indeed, among Gnostics full knowledge was reserved for the perfect only.[22] The emphasis placed in Eph 4:18–19 upon understanding the four dimensions of God's wisdom and the love of Christ which "surpasses knowledge" appears to support a translation of 1:17 saying, so that you *fully*, or *really* know him. Cf. I Cor 13:12 RSV "Now I know in part; then I shall understand fully, even as I have been fully understood." However, Robinson has collected evidence pointing in another direction.[23] When Paul uses the shorter term, he probably does not mean imperfect knowledge, but a general knowledge related to anything under the sun. The composite noun and verb serve in his diction to denote knowledge of a particular object or knowledge as contrasted to other ways of discernment. If Robinson is right, the term knowledge makes full sense in Eph 1:17 even without any implication of Gnostic influence.[24]

18. *that he illumine the eyes of your hearts.* In the OT, in Plato and in Philo, in apocalyptic writings, in Qumran, in the Corpus Hermeticum, and elsewhere,[25] light and related terms are used to describe the process of understanding, along with corresponding references to the eyes of the heart. It is grammatically and syntactically possible to consider the beginning of Eph 1:18a a parenthesis which interrupts the main flow of thought from 1:17b to 1:18b. Therefore the passage can be translated "that he give you the Spirit . . .—since you have been inwardly enlightened—so that you may become aware." The perfect passive participle "enlightened" denotes not only an action of God, but a status already created by that action. The action of God might be found in an event resembling Paul's illumination near Damascus, or it might be considered the essence of baptism.[26] The terms "to illumine," "illumination" (or "to enlighten," "enlightenment") are found in Justin Martyr, in the *Odes of Solomon,* and later, where baptism is denoted.[27] But in Pauline diction a blunt identification of enlightenment with baptism is never suggested. The evidence from the undisputed letters of Paul argues against this equation, and except for some interpretations of Heb 6:4, other deutero-Pauline and

---

[22] I Cor 2:10 is apt to be understood as a reflection of this view. Schlier, p. 200, cf. 79, 81, calls the full knowledge, "existential knowledge, that is, experience. It presupposes . . . faith and love and it is their self-explication."

[23] 248–54. He shows that in pre-Alexandrian Greek, the term means discernment or recognition—without implying specific depth or completeness. The information given by LSLex, 627, on the respective verb and noun supports this judgment.

[24] The mention of knowledge in Eph 1:17 is obviously too ambiguous to yield a decision regarding the Gnostic problem. But cf. Introduction III B and COMMENT X on 1:3–14.

[25] E.g. Ps 19:8; Bar 1:12; Plato *republica* VII 519B; Philo *de Abr.* 57; idem *de Josepho* 147; IV Ezra 14:22, 25; 1QS II 3; Corp. Herm. IV 2, X 21, XIII 17, 19; *I Clem* 36:2; 59:3. Jews and Jewish-influenced literature speak of the "eyes of the heart"; Greeks, "of the mind."

[26] A brief participial parenthesis in Col 2:12a makes an explicit reference to "baptism." Equally, the reference to baptism in Rom 6:3–4 has a parenthetical function in the main ethical argument of Rom 6:1 ff.

[27] Cf. Philo *de virtutibus* 179; Justin Martyr *apol.* 1 61:12; 65:1; *dial.* 39:2; 122:1–2, 6; *Acts of Thomas* 132; *Od Sol* XV; R. Ginza II 3 (ed. M. Lidzbarski [Göttingen: Vandenhoeck, 1925], pp. 57–61); Gregory Nazianzus *orationes theologicae* 40:3–4; Pseudo-Clementine *homilies* VII 8; Clement of Alexandria *paed.* I 6; *Catechismus Romanus* II 2 qu. 3, 38, etc. Whether the third-century Roman interpretation of Heb 6:4 and 10:32, which equates enlightenment with baptism, really corresponds to the sense of these passages is not certain.

non-Pauline letters of the NT do not point to this equation either.[28] Only if an explicit allusion to *baptism* were made in Eph 1:18[29] would this verse actually serve as evidence for or against the assumption of the Pauline origin and authenticity of Ephesians. An alternative to a formally parenthetical and materially sacramental understanding of 1:18a is offered by another view of its place in the syntax of the whole sentence 1:15–21[23]. Gaugler suggests that the verb "give" in 1:17 has two objects: "the Spirit" and "the illumined eyes." It is indeed possible from a purely grammatical point of view[30] to consider specifically the "eyes" of the saints as the recipients of illumination. But whether there be one object or two, the emphasis of the text is on the creative function of the Holy Spirit. Not only a (human) spirit of wisdom and perfection, but also eyes, i.e. enlightened inner eyes, comparable to the circumcision of the heart (Rom 2:29), are then denoted as the work of the Spirit. In our translation the perfect tense of the participle "enlightened" appears to be neglected, but the preceding verse should prevent such a misunderstanding. Just as the giving of the Spirit is continued from day to day and from occasion to occasion (cf. Matt 10:19–20; Acts 4:8, 31; 7:55; 13:9, etc.), so the illumination of man (or of his inner eyes) which is effected by the Spirit is not exhausted or perfected in one moment only. It is a continuous process.[31]

18–19. *the hope . . . glorious riches . . . exceedingly great . . . power*. The Greek text combines three (indirect) questions: What is the hope? What are the riches? How great is the power? Answers to all are to be received by "knowledge." The text is ambiguous, however, since it either divides the contents of knowledge into three parts—hope, riches, power—[32] or sums up all its contents under the heading of hope, with a subsequent explication of hope by reference to rich inheritance, on the one side, and to the power displayed in Christ's resurrection, on the other. Schlier[33] may be right in opting for the latter alternative. At any rate, placing hope at the beginning shows that Ephesians does not completely forget, neglect, or obstruct futurist eschatology.[34] Nor does it shroud the future in a cloud of mystery—otherwise it would not spell out the contents and basis of hope.

the hope to which he is calling you. Lit. "which is the hope of your calling." Col 1:5 suggests that a "hope deposited for you in heaven" is meant here, and in Col 1:27 Christ himself is called the glorious hope. When the epistles to

---

[28] See I Cor 4:5; II Cor 4:4, 6; Eph 3:9; cf. John 1:9; II Tim 1:10. Schlier supports the opposite conclusion on the basis of Gnostic and Mandaean texts. T. F. Torrance, "Ein vernachlässigter Gesichtspunkt der Tauflehre," EvTh 16 (1956), 437, note, understands Eph 3:9 as a reference to baptism.

[29] It may be added that if a parenthesis were intended at all, vs. 18a would be a broken sentence, i.e., an anacoluthon. To the dative "[to] you" in 1:17 the dative participle, *"to"* those enlightened, would fit better than the accusative found in the Greek text. Absolute participles occur in Paul, e.g. in 2:1; 4:3; Col 2:12; 3:16; Philip 3:16–17. But they do not fall completely out of the syntactic order of the context. See BDF, 458–63; 465–70 on asyndeta, parentheses, and anacolutha in NT diction. Debrunner quotes from Isidor Pelusius IV 28, PG 78, 1080, "Gentiles reproach the Christians' language. It omits connections" (i.e. connecting verbs like "to be," conjunctions, etc.).

[30] Though the Greek article between "illuminated" and "eyes" appears to speak against it.

[31] Cf. 3:18; 4:13, 23. The status before illumination is described in 4:17–19; 5:8, 11.

[32] Bengel, e.g. speaks of elements related to the future, the present, and the past respectively.

[33] Schlier, pp. 81–82.

[34] God's promise is mentioned in 1:13; 2:12; 3:6; 6:2; hope, in 2:12; 4:4; a future inheritance, redemption, or judgment, in 1:14; 4:30; 5:5; 6:9. Cf. COMMENT IX on 1:3–14 and the literature there mentioned; see also COMMENTS VII on 2:11–22 and VII on 4:1–16.

the Ephesians and Colossians speak of hope, the emphasis lies not so much on the mood of the person hoping as on the substance or subject matter of expectation. Hope is for all practical purposes equated with the thing hoped for.[35] The simple verb "to hope," which would express the presence of hopefulness in man, is never used. Only once, in Eph 1:12, is a composite of hoping used: "to be the first to hope." The objective element prevails over the subjective, though the latter is certainly not ruled out. Subjective hope or hopefulness as such is not, however, automatically identified with the gift of the Spirit; see the NOTE on "hope" in 2:12. In 2:18 Paul prays that God grant the saints discernment among the various hopes that are possible. They are to become aware *which* hope is decisive for them. Not any hope or number of hopes, but just "one hope" is held and confessed by the Christians (4:4). Eph 1:18 and 4:4 specify the one prospect as "the hope of your calling," or "the hope to which you have been called." It lies before man but is not simply in him. Since in Paul's epistles[36] it is always God who "calls" men, our translation adds a reference to God who calls. The essence of calling in the NT has been aptly described, e.g. by K. L. Schmidt and H. Schlier.[37] Calling is an act of creation and election; through this act non-being becomes being, not-beloved becomes beloved. In the Pauline letters the instrument of the call is the gospel. But the call is more than an offer: it goes out in the power of God and is effective. Because of it man is placed in a new relationship and on new ground. The call does not end as does an alarm but sounds continually. It determines the present life and requires worthy conduct. While it overcomes past conditions it also opens, and prepares for, a specific future.

what glorious riches are to be inherited among the saints. Lit. "which is the riches of glory of his inheritance among the saints." This statement takes up again the contents of 1:14. Unlike 1:11 it clearly describes the heirdom destined for men: the "saints" with whom the readers of Ephesians are promised their share may be either the angels or Israel.[38] Israel is suggested by 2:19 and 3:6, where Paul speaks distinctly of fellow citizenship and co-inheritance of Gentiles and Jews. Wisd Sol 5:5 registers amazement at the presence of an outcast "among the saints." Do the parallels in Acts 20:32; 26:18 and the boldface type in Nestle suggest that Eph 1:18 alludes to a sacred Jewish text? If so, this text should not be sought in Deut 33:3–4 because the Deuteronomy passage treats the privilege granted exclusively to Israel by the gift of the law! Eph 1:18 resembles closely Col 1:12, "The Father has qualified us to share in the inheritance of the saints in the light." Ephesians and Colossians may make an allusion to a sectarian text, such as 1QS XI 7–8, or to an interpretation of Dan 7:27 which promised the saints on earth a place among the heavenly angels. While it cannot be demonstrated that the author of Ephesians knew the Qumran literature, it is certain that he describes the rela-

[35] Cf. in English the identification of love with the beloved in the line "Me and my true love shall never meet again."

[36] See I Thess 2:12; 4:7; 5:24; II Thess 1:11; 2:14, etc. A possible exception is Gal 1:6.

[37] K. L. Schmidt, art. "calling etc." (*kaleō*) in TWNTE, III, 487–501; H. Schlier, Der Ruf Gottes GeistLeb 28 (1955), 241–47 (ref.); Schlier, 82–84. See also W. Bieder, *Berufung im Neuen Testament*, ATANT, 38 (1961), and COMMENT II on 4:1–16 for a further discussion of the nature and effect of calling.

[38] See the references in fn. 7 to 1:1–2. Schlier opts for the angels, and Qumran texts such as 1QS IX 7–8; cf. IV 22; 1QSa I 9, 12–13; 1QSb IV 23 support this interpretation.

tionship between Israel and the Gentiles in terms that are analogous to the Qumran conception of the relationship between the elect sons of Zadok and the angels. Cf. 2:19, 3:6, and COMMENT XIV on 1:3–14.

19. *how exceedingly great is his power . . . that mighty strength is at work.* Lit. "what is the exceeding greatness of his power . . . in accordance with the energy of the force of his strength." At this point the style typical of Ephesians is displayed at either its worst or its best, certainly in most exemplary fashion. Four nearly synonymous Greek words are used in succession to describe God's power,[39] and the author adds the noun "greatness," qualified by the attribute "exceeding" (or "overwhelming"). The way in which so many words of similar meaning are combined is not simple, but is complicated by the use of three genitives[40] and the preposition "according to." In our translation an attempt has been made to cover up what appears quaint and baroque, and yet to bring forth the intention of the Greek text. The author wants to point out the absolutely unique and superior power exerted by God in the resurrection of Christ. He will speak of other "powers" soon enough, and he is far from underestimating their potential, their actuality, their energy. But these "powers" are outdone by The Power demonstrated in the resurrection. Mighty deeds, i.e. miracles, are sometimes mentioned as counterdemonstrations against historic, religious, or natural forces.[41] "Power" is obviously not considered an evil in itself or an inevitable source of evil. All depends on who exerts it and for what use. Nor is it essentially in opposition to love. The same God whose action is motivated by love alone (1:4, 6; 2:4) shows according to 1:19 the power to carry through the decisions made out of love. Love without the power to overcome its obstacles would be chimeric. The authority of God is distinguished by its substance, love.[42]

19–20. *over us believers . . . in the Messiah.* This passage establishes a direct connection between the resurrection of Christ and the resurrection of the saints; cf. Rom 8:11; I Cor 15:12 ff. In Ephesians the praise of Christ's resurrection by God's power (1:20–23) will be immediately followed by the praise of the resurrection of the saints of Jewish and Gentile origin (2:1–10). Later, in 3:16–20; 6:10–17, the effect of the same power upon the stance of the saints before God and the evil powers will be described. In 3:21 the glory due to God "in the church and in the Messiah Jesus" is one and the same glory. The words, "over us believers" (1:19), indicate that the exertion of the power of God's love affects the saints immediately—though the modes of its effect upon human existence are described only later, in ch. 2.

---

[39] The first (*dynamis*) denotes the ability to accomplish what is planned, promised, or started; the second (*energeia*), inherent (muscular) strength or brute power; the third (*kratos*), power to resist and to overcome obstacles or opponents; the last (*ischys*), the actual exercise of power. Cf. Abbott, p. 31; Beare, p. 637, and the dictionaries. Bengel distinguishes God's *virtus* from his *virtus in actu* and the *actus* itself.

Pairs or double pairs describing God's attributes are frequent in the OT, see, e.g. Ps 85:10–11. God is surrounded and accompanied by (his) almost hypostatized, certainly personified, righteousness and justice, loving-kindness and mercy—as if they were members of his court. God's power in particular is described in many terms, e.g. in Exod 15:6–7; Pss 18:2; 96:6; 144:2; 145:4–7.

[40] Synonyms denoting power are often interconnected through genitive constructions (1:19; 3:7; 6:10); cf. Isa 40:26. The same is true of terms describing will or decision (1:5, 11), the world (2:2), the wall (2:14), the mind (4:23). Cf. Percy, pp. 186, 204.

[41] Matt 11:20–23; 24:29; Gal 3:5; II Cor 12:12; Acts 2:22; 8:13, etc.

[42] Cf. J. L. McKenzie, "Authority and Power in the New Testament," CBQ 26 (1964), 413–22.

20–23. *He has raised him . . . all things totally.* The NOTES on individual verses (1:20, 21, 22, 23) must be preceded by some observations on the form, syntax, structure, contents, and conclusion that hold them together:

a) Form: The four verses bear several of the hymnic traits listed in Section II of the Introduction.[43] But in contrast to other Christological hymns or confessions of the NT,[44] these hymnic verses praise only the resurrection and exaltation of Christ. An explicit reference to his humiliation and death is missing, except perhaps in the clause "raised him from the dead" (1:20). If the passage 1:20–23 is a hymn at all, then it should be called a resurrection psalm.

b) Syntax: While God is the grammatical subject of the statements made in vss. 20–22, in 23 the church is suddenly the subject. Also, for the first time in vss. 22–23 the noun "church" replaces the pronoun "we" which has been used to this point to denote the people of God. In Greek diction frequently, though not always, the end of a sentence contains the apex of the whole; if this rule is applied to 1:20–23, then the ecclesiological statement of 1:23 has more emphasis than the preceding affirmations about God and the Messiah.[45] But it is impossible to bypass the triumphant theology and Christology of 1:19–22 in favor of the ecclesiology of 1:23. The latter is an element tacked on to the whole sentence, rather than its basis or center. Not until 2:1 ff. does the church properly become the focus of attention.

c) Structure: Two parallel pairs—the first consisting of two aorist participles translated by "he has raised" and "he has enthroned"; the second containing two aorist finites, "he put under," "he appointed"—describe what God did to and with the Messiah. These descriptions of God's acts are sandwiched between three different statements that qualify God's action as demonstrations of unique power. The power itself is described with many words in 1:19; the "powers" affected and defeated by it are enumerated in 1:21; the subjugation, called "filling of all things" is stated in 1:23.

d) Contents: These verses are not only reminiscent of OT royal or enthronement psalms, they contain two quotes from them.[46] The praise of the resurrection here will be complemented in Eph 2:14–18 by extended *laudes* of the cross. Among the effects of God's power shown in Christ's resurrection, the church is outstanding, and in 1:23 she is for the first time in Ephesians called Christ's "body." But she is not the only consequence of resurrection:

[43] Dibelius, p. 64, and Schille, *Hymnen*, p. 55, speak of "a sort of hymn," Schlier, p. 86, of a transition "almost into the style of a hymn following the formulation of a traditional confession." Schille omits an intensive discussion of this passage. It does not fit into his categories of Redeemer, Initiation, or Baptismal Hymns.

[44] As Philip 2:6–11; Rom 4:25; I Peter 3:18, 22; I Tim 3:16; cf. Eph 4:9–10; but in agreement with Col 1:18; cf. Gal 1:1; II Tim 2:8.

[45] Gaugler, p. 79 (cf. Käsemann as quoted in the Introduction, Section V), believes that in this hymn "the church is praised, not Christ."

[46] Ps 110:1 in Eph 1:20; Ps 8:7 in Eph 1:22. Scholars representing the Scandinavian Divine-Kingship School, like H. Ringgren, *The Messiah in the Old Testament*, SBT 18 (1956), 19–20, consider Ps 8 a Messianic psalm which reflects the identification of the King with the Prime Man, cf. Ezek 28. The parallels to Ps 8 found in Pss 80 and 89 and perhaps in Dan 7 support this view. In Christian congregations the psalm was certainly understood this way (Matt 21:16; I Cor 15:27; Heb 2:6–9). A difference between Pss 8 and 110 pertains to the time of the submission of the powers. Following Ps 8 they have already been subjected, but according to Ps 110 they are being progressively subjugated under Christ's feet. I Cor 15:25–27 and Heb 2:8–9 cope in different ways with the different statements.

several interpreters of the NT speak of the "cosmic" role of Christ connected with his soteriological and eschatological function.[47] Already in the benediction of Eph 1:3–14, in which the election and salvation of man certainly stood in the foreground, first an allusion to, then an emphatic statement was made about the rule of God extended through the Messiah over all creation and all things (1:4, 10). While in 1:20–23 the drift of thought is clearly toward the church, the same verses first put all emphasis upon the Messiah's cosmic rulership.[48]

e) Conclusion: Verse 23, which forms the end of the hymnic passage, presents serious interpretive problems. The vocabulary used contains the mysterious concepts "body" of Christ and "filling"; and the syntax can be interpreted in a variety of ways. In regard to form, it may be questioned whether the verse is part of a traditional hymn at all, for the relative pronoun at its beginning (translated by "she") has a longer form than is usual in NT hymns (hētis instead of hē; the masculine hos would be normal, as in I Tim 3:16). If Eph 1:23 contains a parallelism of members (i.e. if it juxtaposes the headship over the body and the filling of all) then the parallelism is much more hidden or uneven than in the poetic parallels found in vss. 20 and 22. Actually vs. 23 gives the impression of an afterthought, an added interpretation. If it could be proven that 1:20–22 is a traditional hymn quoted by Paul, then 1:23 may contain a Pauline explication and application. But it is also possible that Paul, while drawing from several pre-Pauline pieces of confession, himself composed the whole passage 1:20–23 and wanted all its parts, including vs. 23, to sound hymnic. As "each" inspired Corinthian "has his psalm," so here Paul too may have aimed at conversing with fellow Christians by means of a new song composed to the glory of the Lord.[49]

21. above. The translation "high above" is tenable and perhaps more in line with hieratic exuberance. It is, however, not necessary. Most frequently a composite adverb, verb, or noun possesses in Hellenistic Greek exactly the same meaning as the corresponding simplex. Cf. "beneath under" Heb 2:8 with "under" Eph 1:22.

every government and authority, power and dominion and any title bestowed. Lit. ". . . and any name named."[50] With all these terms Paul denotes the angelic or demonic beings that reside in the heavens. For the translation English words have been chosen that point to the direct association of these heavenly principalities and powers with structures and institutions of life on earth. See COMMENT V and the literature mentioned there. By referring to names named, that is to "titles bestowed" (cf. Luke 6:13–14), or to deities

---

[47] E.g. A. D. Galloway, The Cosmic Christ, New York: Harper, 1951; F. Mussner, CAK, TTS 5 (1955). See the interpretation of Col 1:15–20 in AB, vol. 34B.
[48] Later, esp. in 2:7; 3:10; 4:7–16; 6:10–20, Ephesians will have reason to speak of the cosmic function of the church. However, the passage 1:20–23 describes God's and his Messiah's world-wide power, not the church's. Regarding the meaning of "fullness" in 1:23, which is sometimes used to prove the opposite, see the NOTES on that verse and COMMENT VI C.
[49] Cf. I Cor 14:26; Eph 5:19; Col 3:16.
[50] Lists enumerating diverse powers that are subjugated are found also, e.g. in Col 1:16, 20b; Philip 2:10; cf. Rom 8:38–39. They appear to take up a form of praise which is as old and honorable as the listing of four or five groups in Ps 103:19–22: "All you his angels, you mighty ones . . . all his hosts, his ministers," and are for this reason not to be considered strange elements in traditional hymns. They may have their origin either in the cult or in Wisdom schools. The NT enumerations of powers are certainly also a result of the apocalypticists' special interest in the angelic and demonic worlds.

cultically invoked or proclaimed (cf. LXX Jer 20:9; 32–39; Acts 19:13), Paul does not intend to imply that the powers possess nominal quality only and are bare of real existence. To the contrary, in the ancient Orient a person's name was often identified with his hidden essence, demonstrated power, and recognized honor.[51] In his writings Paul enumerates names, numbers, functions, and/or honors of heavenly powers in consistent or in varying sequences.[52] He did not aim at completeness: the words "and any title" or "and any name" show that the four groups that are distinguished and listed are not exhaustive. In pagan cults and in magic formulae to mention a superior spiritual power's name causes the deity or demon to listen, to help, or to refrain from doing harm.[53] The NT enumerations of diverse powers appear to reflect pagan practices. But vss. 19–22 do not support cultic magic, for the subjugation of the powers is ascribed to the victory of God's power as exerted in the Messiah's resurrection and enthronement.[54] In Col 2:10, 18, 23, the cultic invocation of "angels" is explicitly denounced.[55] According to Matt 25:24, 44, even the pronunciation of the right name can prove futile.

this age . . . the age to come. Cf. Matt 12:32; Mark 10:30; Gal 1:4 and the apocalyptic and rabbinic distinction of two aeons mentioned in COMMENT IX on 1:3–14. The present aeon is evil, the coming one created by the triumph of God. The main contrast elaborated upon in Ephesians is that between the *past* period of division, sin, hiddenness, darkness, and the *present* time of peace, sanctification, revelation, light.[56] The past and the present, not the present and the future, form the decisive poles. It looks as if the two-aeon scheme mentioned in 1:21 were a relic of a futurist eschatology which does not fit into the "realized eschatology" of Ephesians. If 1:21 is part of a pre-Ephesian hymn, then the unsuitability of the alleged relic is easily explained. However, the (present) "evil days" mentioned in 5:16, not to speak of the coming "evil day" for which 6:13 prepares the reader, and finally the references to the (many!) "ages to come" (2:7, cf. 3:21) and to the "Perfect Man" still to be met (4:13), show that in this epistle no one temporal scheme is proposed or strictly adhered to. Time as such is not an absolute, and its periods are delineated in diverse ways—always in dependence upon specific dominant figures, traits, or events. As stated earlier, Ephesians definitely does not refer only to the past and present, but points just like other NT books (though less emphatically than strictly apocalyptic chapters) to good and evil events that are yet to come.

[51] Paul's usage of the noun "name" and of the verbs "to name," "to call" in Philip 2:9; I Cor 8:5; Rom 15:20; Eph 2:11; 3:15; cf. II Tim 2:19 reveals the same conviction. But cf. the nominalistic undertone apparent in I Cor 5:11; Eph 5:3; Rev 3:1.

[52] Eph 6:12; Col 1:16, 20; 2:10, 15; I Cor 15:24; Rom 8:38–39; Philip 2:10–11; also Rom 13:7; cf. I Peter 3:22 and Revelation *passim*. See below COMMENT V for an attempt at a more exact description of these powers and their function.

[53] From the viewpoint of the history of religions, e.g. Moses' asking for the name of the appearing God, the obsessed man's blurting out Jesus' identity, and all that is done "in the name of the Lord," belong in the context of magic incantation of, and control sought over, a deity (Exod 3:13–17; Mark 1:24; Acts 2:21). Cf. O. Grether, *Name und Wort Gottes im Alten Testament*, BZAW 64 (1934); W. Heitmüller, *Im Namen Jesu*, FRLANT, I 2, (1903), 128–265; H. Bietenhard, TWNTE, V, 242–83. Also the art. *Namenglaube*, in RGG IV, 1301–6. Cf. Ps.-Clem. *hom.* III 36, "to make known the names of angels."

[54] In I Cor 2:8 and Col 2:14–15, to his death on the cross.

[55] Cf. Heb 1:4–14; Rev 19:10; 22:8–9.

[56] 2:1–10, 11–13; 3:3–5; 4:17–24; 5:8.

22–23. *everything under his feet . . . the head over all, to be head of the church . . . him who fills all things totally.*[57] This translation renders the same Greek word (the neutral plural *panta* of the pronoun *pas*, "all") in four different ways. The varying translations have been chosen for reasons of English style and correspond to variations introduced by other translators. But the differentiation may be called into question since it is intended to do more than merely gloss over the repetitious monotony of the original Greek: each translation also suggests a particular interpretation. Certainly Eph 1:22–23 has evoked a multiplicity of expositions. After basically agreeing on the translations of the unambiguous psalm verse quoted in vs. 22a, "He put everything [or, all things] under his feet," the interpreters part ways, as is illustrated by three examples: RSV "[God] has made him the head over all things for the church, . . . him who fills all in all." JB "[God] made him, as the ruler of everything, the head of the Church, . . . him who fills the whole creation." NEB "[God] appointed him as supreme head to the church, . . . him who himself receives the entire fullness of God." Only JB unmistakably affirms Christ's relation to the whole world, together with his rulership over the church. RSV gives no clear indication whether Christ really rules all things (including powers operative outside the church) for the benefit of the church, or is all-decisive exclusively within the church, in all church matters. NEB makes no reference at all to the universe controlled by Christ, but combines RSV's ecclesiastical interpretation with a novel element: God's total presence in Christ (rather than Christ's presence in church or world) is made the sum of Eph 1:23.

All these translations and implicit expositions are tenable on grammatical grounds, and perhaps in the end they converge. But there is one alternative which simply cannot be neglected or belittled: does the end of the passage Eph 1:20–23 only or primarily concern Christ's absolute rule in the church and for the church? Or, is his ecclesiastic rule in and over the church paralleled, perhaps undergirded, by his cosmic headship? At least three arguments must be compared in searching for an answer:

a) The term "all things" (*panta* with and without article) appears sometimes in Pauline writings in references to governments and authorities. In these and in many other cases[58] this term is used to describe God's omnipotence, e.g. 4:6, or the omnipotent cosmic role of Christ, e.g. 1:22a. In Ps 8 the power exerted by God's chosen "man" (that is, by Israel's king) over men, rulers, and enemies, including the realm of nature, is indicated by the reference to the subjection of "all things." Because this psalm is quoted in Eph 1:22 it is probable that the hymn 1:20–23 intends to describe Christ as *kosmokratōr*[59] and to characterize his rule over the *church* as a very specific form of his *universal* (cosmic) power and dominion.

---

[57] Cf. "all things" in 1:10, 11; 3:9, 20; 4:6, 10; 5:13.

[58] Eph 1:21–23; Col 1:16; I Cor 15:24–28. Other biblical and non-biblical, also bibliographical references for the following will be found in COMMENT V B.

[59] In the Hellenistic world this term was used for gods, spirits, emperors or planets. In the NT the title occurs but once, in Eph 6:12, as a name of principalities and powers; see COMMENT IV on 6:10–20. Jesus Christ is according to Ephesians not one among the competing "rulers of the world," but above all of them, 1:21.

b) In the last of its four occurrences in Eph 1:22–23, the plural of *pās* may mean "all men" as well as "all things" for the masculine and the neuter of the formula *en pāsin* (in all) are indistinguishable. If persons are meant— who are they? Most likely only the saints, for references to "all the saints"[60] are frequent in Ephesians, and a variant reading of 4:6 speaks of God the "Father of all . . . over all, through all, and in all *of us*." Verse 23 would then assert not only Christ's total and unquestionable right over "all *things*," that is, all thoughts, movements, actions, and experiences of the saints, but also over all earthly and ecclesiastical potentates (all *persons*).[61] The internal and exter- nal constitution of the church is described in this case: the church is a mon- archy, whatever be the order of the world or the confused state of mind of the persons inside and outside the church.

c) The last two occurrences of the plural of *pas*, i.e. the phrase "all things in all things" (or "persons"), may be equivalent to the classic Greek adverb *pantapāsin*, meaning "all-in-all," "altogether," "wholly." The NEB version of 1:23, which leaves the issue of church- or world-dominion untouched and sug- gests that it is Christ who is being filled, suggests this understanding.

The second of these three arguments is to be considered in the light of the first remarks on the unit (vss. 20–23). It is valid then only when Eph 1:23 is divorced from its context, denied any hymnic character, and perhaps treated as a gloss or interpolation. In that case the narrow, ecclesiastical range of this verse contradicts the cosmic concern revealed in verses 19–22. The third interpretation is supported by Colossians, but it presupposes the passive meanings of the noun "fullness," and the verb "to fill," which will later be demonstrated as mutually irreconcilable and foreign to the context. Ephesians may contain a message different from that of Col 2:9, though not contradictory to it. Only the first interpretation, which explains "all things" as part of a biblical and non-biblical omnipotence formula, corresponds to the thought developed from vs. 19 onward as well as to the original meaning of the psalm quoted in vs. 22 and to the author's pointed interest (shown, e.g. in 1:10 and 4:10) in Christ's universal and cosmic rule.[62] It is unlikely that the enumeration of the cosmic powers in 1:21 and the psalm quotation in 1:22a form only an interlude to be disregarded in the final interpretation of "all things." The interconnection between the cosmic and ecclesiastic dimensions of the Messiah's kingship appears to be the very point Paul wants to make in singing the praise of the resurrected Christ. The church cannot claim for herself a Lord other than the one who is also Lord over the world. "He fills" not only the church but also "all things totally."[63]

22. *He . . . appointed him . . . to be head.* Lit. "he gave him." In political and priestly contexts the Hebrew verb "to give" sometimes has the

---

[60] "all [the] saints" are mentioned in 1:15; 3:8, 18; 6:18; cf. 2:3; 4:13; 6:24 ("all").
[61] At the expense of, and as a warning to, e.g. emperors, popes, bishops, general superintend- ents, secretaries, synods, majorities, etc.
[62] Cf. Col 1–2; Mark 13; Heb 1; Rev *passim*.
[63] For the translation of "in all" 1:23 by "totally" see A. Feuillet, *Christ Sagesse*, p. 288. On the basis of I Cor 12:6; 15:28; Col 3:11 he understands the words "all things in all" to be an equiva- lent to the classic Greek "all in all," or, "wholly" (*pantapāsin*) which does not occur in the NT. Grammatically he is certainly right. But the contexts of I Cor 15:28 and Eph 1:23 advise against the omission of an explicit mention of "all things."

meaning "to appoint" or "to install."[64] The same is true of the Greek verb in Eph 4:11 and probably in 1:22. The narrow meaning "to appoint" does not exclude that both the head and the various ministers of the church are also and primarily gifts of God. By taking the order of the church into his own hands God gives her what she needs; by his (ontic) *gift* her (hierarchical or organizational) *shape* is determined. She is a monarchy in which Christ the king is not only supreme ruler, but also the source of life, the savior, and the unity in person; see COMMENT VI A. Vicars of this head are not mentioned in Ephesians, but the role of prophets and apostles will be pointed out in 2:20; 3:5; cf. 4:11.

22–23. *the church. She is his body, full of him who fills.* Several literal translations vie for acceptance: "(the church) which is his body, the fullness of the one who *fills*"; or ". . . the fullness of the one who *is filled.*" While many translations can be offered, one purpose is clearly recognizable: to describe the essence of the church. Definitions are rare within the NT,[65] but Eph 1:23 contains, in the form of appositions, two definitions of **the** church:[66] she is Christ's body, and she is his fullness. The latter definition is not a second choice or a complement to the earlier, but an explication of it. Because of the close interconnection of the terms "head," "body," "fullness,"[67] the possible origins, meanings, and theological interpretations of these three words will be treated together in COMMENT VI, below. At this point some philological facts should be pointed out that determine the translation of the noun "fullness" and the verb "to fill":

a) According to the information available regarding the classic, Hellenistic, and biblical meanings of the Greek terms *plērōma, plēroō,*[68] the *noun* "fullness" has either an active or a passive sense. It denotes that which fills or completes (also, the act of filling or summing up), or it designates that which is filled up and full, including the sum, the state of being full, or the overflow. Unless the context or clause in which the noun occurs is free from ambiguity, there is no foolproof rule for establishing which of the variants of the active or passive senses is meant. The text and context of Eph 1:23 is at first sight far from clear. The church, or the body of Christ, may be described as a society, event, or power that is filling up a vacancy in Christ; cf.

[64] E.g. I Sam 8:5–6; Lev 17:11; Num 14:4; Isa 42:6. The verb, "to set," "to appoint," occurs in the NT, e.g. in I Cor 12:18, 28; Acts 20:28.

[65] See, e.g. Heb 11:1; I Peter 3:21 for definitions of faith and baptism. The usual Semitic way of describing something is by narration. See, e.g. the description of faith in Rom 4 and Heb 2:17 – 3:6; 11; of baptism in Matt 3 and Acts 8:12–24; 10:44–48; 19:1–6; of the church in Matt 16:15–18; Luke 22:14–30; John 13; 21.

[66] J. Bengel disputes this. According to him the words, "the fullness of him who fills . . ." are a description of Christ, made in the absolute accusative form and harking back to vs. 20. Indeed 3:19; 4:10, 13; 5:18; Col 1:19; 2:9; cf. John 1:14, speak of the fullness of God, of Christ, or the Spirit who fills. Bengel's interpretation greatly facilitates the understanding of Eph 1:23. But it is not permissible to bypass in this manner the philological and theological problems posed by this verse.

[67] Cf. 4:13–16; Col 1:18–19; 2:9 and the common treatment of these three mutually interpretative terms in T. Schmidt, *Der Leib Christi* (Leipzig: Erlangen, 1919), pp. 186–87 (ref.); Benoit "Corps, tête et plérôme dans les épîtres de la captivité," RB 63 (1956), 5–44; the chapter, "L'église plérôme du Christ," in Feuillet, *Christ Sagresse*, pp. 275–319; and in L. Cerfaux, *La Théologie de l'église*, Unam Sanctam 54, rev. ed. (Paris: Du Cerf, 1965), pp. 223–319.

[68] See LSLex, 1419–20, WBLex, 676–78, G. Delling, TWNTE, VI, 283–308. A. Feuillet, "L'église plérôme du Christ d'après Ephés. 1, 23," NRT 78 (1956), 449–72, 593–610; idem, *Christ Sagesse*, pp. 275–319; J. Ernst, *Pleroma und Pleroma Christi*, Biblische Untersuchungen 5 (Regensburg: Pustet, 1970), esp. pp. 105–20.

Col 1:24.[69] Or the church itself may be considered an empty space or vessel that is filled up, or an incomplete structure that is completed by him.[70]

b) Does the *verb* "to fill" help decide the issue? Again, no philological certainty is available. The verb always means "to fill," "to make full" in a spatial and material sense (e.g. to load a ship, fill a cup, pay a bill, man the breastworks, impregnate a woman, etc.), or "to complete," "carry out," "sum up" something abstract. In the NT the object being filled is frequently a Scripture word, a law, a promise, or a prayer. To describe such action, not just the Greek active but sometimes also the middle voice (genus) of the verb is used. In good Greek the middle voice describes the filling of oneself or the act of filling (e.g. of a boat) in one's own interest. There is no doubt about the corresponding meaning of the passive forms. But it is not clear whether in Eph 1:23 the present participle of the verb is middle or passive. And even if it were clear, the fact remains that in Hellenistic, including Pauline Greek, middle forms are sometimes used for the passive and vice versa.[71] Thus the Greek participle (*plēroumenou*) contributes to the ambiguity of 1:23: on linguistic grounds, both translations, "of him who fills all things totally," and "of him who is being filled totally," are equally justified. Just as the noun "fullness" could possess an active or passive meaning, so the verb may be understood in either sense.

Only one thing is clear: if the verb is understood passively, the noun must be taken in its active sense; then the church fills Christ so that he becomes full in all aspects, by the incorporation of all members. Correspondingly, if the verb is used in the middle voice with active sense, the noun has passive quality: Christ who fills all things totally (with himself, or for his own sake) is in a specific way filling the church too. This issue obviously cannot be solved with the help of dictionaries and grammars. Other factors and arguments in reaching a decision are: (1) parallel or substantially related Pauline statements, especially in Ephesians and Colossians; (2) OT themes and Jewish beliefs that may be alluded to; (3) philosophical and religious tenets, and utterances from the Hellenistic environment of Paul; (4) the weight of the reasoning in both old and new interpretations; (5) perhaps also the harmony or disharmony of the conclusion eventually reached with other Christological and ecclesiological doctrines. See the end of COMMENT VI C for a collection of such arguments and a conclusion from the available data.

[69] Instead of Christ, God may be considered the one who is being filled, so, e.g. by Benoit, "Corps, tête," pp. 42–43. This interpretation might correspond to the enrichment of God discussed in part (c) of the NOTE on "We [Jews] were . . . appropriated" in 1:11.

[70] The notion of a complementation of God or Christ by the church is despite its Patristic support passionately disputed, e.g. by Feuillet, *Christ Sagesse*, pp. 275–319. He understands (just as W. L. Knox, *St. Paul and the Church of the Gentiles* [Cambridge University Press, 1939], p. 186, and J. A. T. Robinson, *The Body*, SBT 5 [1952], 68–69) the form of the verb "filling" in Eph 1:23 as passive (pp. 289–92). This passive may well be a *passivum divinum*, saying that God does the filling. Just as according to Col 1:19 God fills Christ, so according to Ephesians Christ fills the church. This way God becomes "all in all" I Cor 15:28. In other words, God's power works in Christ, Eph 1:19–23, but then also in the saints, 2:1–10; 3:16–19. By no means is a filling of God or Christ through the church indicated. Colossians emphasizes more the filling of Christ by God, Ephesians the filling of the church by Christ. But as Eph 1:20 – 2:10 holds the Christological and ecclesiological elements together, so does Col 2:9–10.

[71] E.g. I Cor 10:2 middle for passive; 6:7 passive for middle; see BDF, 307, 314, 316.

COMMENTS I–VII on 1:15–23

I The Structure

Like the preceding section, Eph 1:15–23 has the form of one long sentence. It is easier to describe the various themes, subdivisions, ambiguous elements, and literary forms of this structure than to explain why they are coherent. From giving thanks to God for the faithfulness of the saints (15–16), Paul proceeds to intercede for the gift of the Spirit who reveals the hope, the riches, the power imparted by God (17–19). Among the insights to be given is the perception of God's unique strength (19). This strength is praised by reference to Christ's resurrection and enthronement over all powers (20–21). The passage concludes with the briefest possible description of what Christ, the Lord over all cosmic powers, is for the church: he was made her head and he fills her (22–23). Thus the end leads back to the beginning, a reference to the communion of saints. But while the saints were described at the beginning as being "in Christ," at the end Christ seems to be portrayed as the one who is filling them.

The main units contain thanksgiving, intercession, praise of the resurrection, and a description of the church. The main agents are God, the Spirit, and the Messiah. The apostle, the saints, and the church are mentioned in turn. Whatever "deadness" (1:20) prevailed among them, and whatever the principalities and powers may be or do, the whole world and the saints have been submitted to the special power and care of God which is exerted by the Messiah. Again, the action of God is not limited to the past. Rather the faith, prayer, and community of the saints are related to that God who is still pouring out his Spirit, increasing knowledge, proving his might over all powers, filling the church and the world. The saints are still to attain to an heirdom which lies before them; their faith (and love) cannot be genuine unless it is a hope relying on God who has made a promise, gives hope, and will keep his word.

II Thanksgiving and Intercession

The thanksgivings found at the beginning of the Pauline letters[72] contain a series of more or less regularly recurring elements—though their formulation always varies. The longest thanksgiving is found in I Thess 1–3 where it actually takes the place of the kerygmatic part of the epistle, while no thanksgiving at all is found in Galatians. The end of all thanksgivings and the transition to the respective letter's first topic is always more or less fluid. Paul usually makes immediate transitions to the main subject matter to be taken up. Distinctive elements of the thanksgiving passages are:

a) the principal verb, I "give thanks";[73]

---

[72] G. H. Boobyer, *Thanksgiving and the Glory of God in Paul*, Leipzig: Borna, 1929; T. Schermann, "Griechische Zauberpapyri und das Gemeinde- und Dankgebet im I Klemensbriefe," TU 34 (1910); P. Schubert, "Form and Function of Pauline Thanksgivings," BhZNW 20 (1939); see also C. Westermann, *The Praise of God in the Psalms*, Richmond: Knox, 1965.

[73] Eph 1:16; Philem 4; Philip 1:3; I Cor 1:4; Rom 1:8; or "we give . . . ." I Thess 1:2; 2:13; Col 1:3; or "we are bound to give . . . ," II Thess 1:3; 2:13; or "we are able to give," I Thess 3:9.

b) the temporal and verbal expression, "never ceasing";[74]

c) the naming of the recipient of thanks, "God";[75]

d) the pronominal indirect object, "for you," or "on your behalf";[76]

e) two qualifying participles indicating

  1) the cause of gratitude, "hearing of . . .";[77]

  2) the mode of thanksgiving, "mentioning you in my prayers";[78]

f) a final clause containing the substance of Paul's intercession, "I ask that. . . ."[79]

II Corinthians and I Peter contain a benediction in place of a thanksgiving; Ephesians is the only Pauline letter to combine the two.[80] The juxtaposition of "I" and "you," "we" and "you," "my" (our) and "your," is typical of all Pauline thanksgivings and benedictions. Since God is never directly addressed in these passages with the words of e.g. Luke 18:11, "I thank thee, God," the Pauline thanksgiving ought not to be considered a liturgical form of speech, but a distinctly epistolary trait with a proclamatory and exhortatory bent. It always serves the purpose of introducing a vital theme of the letter in question. It is the merit of Schubert's work to have shown the non-biblical, non-liturgical, but Hellenistic character of the motif of thanksgiving.[81] The Greek noun "thanks" and the verb "to give thanks" are not found in the older parts of the LXX. Not earlier than the time of Ignatius[82] did thanksgiving (*eucharistiā*) become a technical term denoting the Lord's Supper ("Eucharist").

The thanksgiving of Paul marks a notable distinction of the apostle from Moses and the prophets. Though Paul fostered as little as they any illusions about the moral and religious perfection of God's people, and though he proceeds often and quickly from thanksgiving to intercession, he begins all his letters but one with the expression of thanks. More than a trite *captatio benevolentiae* stand behind this method. "Now is the day of salvation" (II Cor 6:2). The mere fact that now Gentiles, however imperfect their knowledge, conduct, and stability, are joined to the congregation that calls upon the Lord is sufficient for Paul to give thanks to God. Unlike those grim preachers who combine their zeal for God with flaming indictments of their congregation, the

---

[74] Eph 1:16; Col 1:9; or "always," Philem 4; I Thess 1:2; Col 1:3; Philip 1:4; I Cor 1:4; II Thess 1:3; 2:13; or "unceasingly," I Thess 2:13; or "always" and "unceasingly" combined, I Thess 1:2–3; Rom 1:9–10; or "night and day," I Thess 3:10; or "first of all," Rom 1:8.

[75] So explicitly in all thanksgivings except Eph 1:16. In this passage, however, God is as distinctly meant as elsewhere, see 1:17. Only in Luke 17:16 are thanks offered to Jesus. But this exception is immediately corrected in Luke 17:18.

[76] Or "all of you," I Thess 1:2; Philip 1:4; Rom 1:8.

[77] Eph 1:15; Col 1:4; cf. 9; "remembering," I Thess 1:3; cf. Philip 1:3; "knowing," I Thess 1:4; cf. "on the ground of . . . ," I Thess 3:9; I Cor 1:4.

[78] Found in all thanksgivings (though at times without the words, "mentioning you," or "making mention of you"), except in I Cor 1:4–5; I Thess 2:13; II Thess 1:2–3; 2:13.

[79] Cf. "whether perhaps," Rom 1:10; "for" with the infinitive of a verb, I Thess 3:10. A final clause is absent in the four passages mentioned in the preceding footnote, but a causal statement, beginning with "because" is substituted for it.

[80] Schubert, "Form and Function," p. 44, considers the thanksgiving superfluous after the benediction in the prooemium. He declares the thanksgiving "a highly conscious effort on the part of the (pseudonymous) author to omit nothing which he considered formally essential in Pauline epistolography." This argument against the authenticity of Ephesians is not convincing. As Paul exercised the freedom to present only a benediction in II Cor 1, and no benediction or thanksgiving at all in Galatians, he or an imitator might certainly have chosen to combine both in Ephesians.

[81] "Form and Function," pp. 122–78, discusses the later Stoic usages of the term, and its role in political, economic, religious, and private life as reconstructed from inscriptions and papyri.

[82] Ign. *Smyr.* VII 1; VIII 1; *Phila.* IV 1; *Eph.* XIII 1; *Did.* IX 1 – X 6; Justin Martyr *apol.* I 65–66; *dial.* 117–18; 14:1 ff.; 70:1, 4.

apostle was unwilling to attest his love of God without affirming his joy over the brethren in faith assembled by God.

But his gratitude is not exhausted by the expression of his feelings or by his enjoyment of the present. The intercession attached to most thanksgivings reveals Paul's realistic estimation of the conditions prevailing among his readers. God's work, the apostle's labor, and the sanctification of the saints have still to be continued. Even when Paul thanks God for riches conveyed, he is not ashamed to speak as a beggar. Praying will always be asking and begging; it is not the end of a dialogue or the final receipt for a benefit given, but depends on God's further presence, response, and help. Moses and the prophets had been intercessors for their people (Exod 32:31–34; Deut 9:25–29; Amos 7:25, etc.). Especially on the Day of Atonement, the high priest's main task was his intercessory appearance before God (Lev 16; cf. Exod 28). By references to his blood, especially in Hebrews, but also in Ephesians 2:14–16, 5:2, Christ's death and eternal ministry are described as an intercessory action. Paul participates in Christ's ministry inasmuch as he does not write as an advocate of God against man, but as man's advocate before God.

Both thanksgiving and intercession have an unknown and unmarked ending. The prayer of Paul has "lost itself in the wonder of the blessing prayed for,"[83] and in this letter no formal ending to the prayer is actually indicated before 3:21. It was said before that the surprisingly peaceful contents of this epistle fit the specific style and diction of Ephesians, and vice versa. Where there is such prayer as in Ephesians there is also peace with fellow men and God.

III   The Inspiration of the Church

LXX passages as different as I Kings 3; Isa 11:2–3; Dan 2; Wisd Sol 7:7, 22, 24, 25; 9:17 show clearly that it is impossible to distinguish sharply between the Spirit or wisdom of God and the spirit of wisdom and understanding found in man.[84] According to Paul, the same Spirit who knows the hidden things of God is also given to the apostle and the congregation in order to learn, to pronounce, and to discern Spiritual things and persons (I Cor 2:9–16). For this reason Paul's intercession on behalf of the saints—in which he asks that God give them the Spirit of wisdom—is not only a prayer for the gift of some charismatic *effect* of the Spirit, e.g. a wise human mind, but a petition for the Spirit *himself*. Paul asks for continuing inspiration of the saints, and Eph 1:17 might equally well be translated, I ask that "God inspire you with wisdom and revelation."

The passage speaks of an inspiration of *all* the saints that is equal to the inspiration of some select and chosen servants of God in Israel and to that of the NT apostles and prophets. The "Spirit of wisdom and understanding" is often mentioned in the OT. God's Messiah is given this Spirit by God;[85] therefore his wisdom is unlike the self-claimed, though awesome wisdom of the prince of Tyre that will fail.[86] Joshua and Daniel received the "Spirit of understand-

---

[83] Robinson, p. 73.
[84] See above the NOTE on 1:8, and COMMENTS VI, X, and XVI on 1:3–14.
[85] Isa 11:2; cf. 42:1; cf. I Enoch 49:3; 62:2; *Test. Judah* XXIV 2–4; *Test. Levi* II 3; XVIII 7. (*Test.=Testament of.*)
[86] Ezek 28.

ing";[87] Bezalel, the craftsman, possesses the divine Spirit of "wisdom, understanding, and skill."[88] The house of David is promised a "Spirit of grace and
compassion."[89] Angels are equipped with the Spirit.[90] Late OT passages
promise that all members of God's people will be given this Spirit.[91] Indeed,
the chosen community of Qumran that understands itself as the remnant and
representative of the true Israel claims for itself the Spirit of "understanding,
insight, wisdom, knowledge, sanctity, unity."[92] Ezra, the apocalypticist, is inspired by the Spirit to dictate twenty-four writings and seventy apocalyptic
books.[93] According to Sir 38:24, 39:6–11, the scribes are filled with the
"Spirit of understanding" and "pour forth words of wisdom." But the term,
"Spirit of revelation" (Eph 1:17) is not contained in the LXX.

Since according to Eph 3:5 only *now* "through the Spirit," has the mystery
of Christ been revealed, the term "Spirit of wisdom and revelation" (1:17)
probably has a specific meaning. Though it alludes to the LXX passages referring to the "Spirit of wisdom and understanding," the added words "and of
revelation," indicate that now even more is given by the Spirit than ever before: ultimate wisdom and understanding related to the disclosed secret of
God. But is not the gift and possession of this Spirit the privilege of the
apostles and prophets of Jesus Christ? Indeed, Eph 3 seems to affirm such a
restriction. And yet, not only does Col 1:26 speak of the "revelation of the
secret" to (all) the "saints of God" (unlike its restriction to prophets and
apostles in Eph 3:5); and not only does Luke affirm[94] that exactly the same
Spirit as was given the apostles is also given or to be given to the whole congregation, but Eph 1:13; 4:30 assert that all the saints are "sealed by the
Spirit," and in 1:17 God is asked to continue granting this gift. The same inspiration as experienced in OT and NT times by the select men from Israel is
now to be received by all the Gentile-born saints. "In Jesus Christ the blessing
of Abraham came to the nations, that we should receive through faith the
promised Spirit" (Gal 3:14).

In COMMENT X on Eph 1:3–14 and in the NOTE on 1:17, it was shown
that the "wisdom" and "knowledge" imparted by the Spirit are not limited to
perception, learning, and theoretical insight, but show the wise man how to
live. It is characteristic that knowledge cannot exist without growth and expansion. A knower remains a learner, and knowledge will always seek to give
others a share in its contents. Therefore "wisdom, revelation, enlightenment,"
when they are *given* to man, do anything but make him passive. They activate
the man who was formerly blind—not only blacked-out mentally and walking
in darkness (4:17–18), but darkness itself, as the keen formulation of 5:8a
asserts. Now he is made "light in the Lord" (5:8b).

In order to acknowledge the unique dignity and authority of the prophets'
and apostles' inspiration, two theses have been formulated and defended in the

---

[87] LXX Deut 34:9; Sus 64 (cf. 45).   [88] LXX Exod 31:3; 35:31.   [89] Zech 12:10.
[90] I Enoch 61:10–11; cf. Jub 40:5. In Rev 1:4; 5:6 angels appear to be identified with the seven
spirits (mentioned in Isa 11:2–3?).
[91] E.g. Num 11:29; Joel 2:28–29; but cf. already Ezek 36:26–27; 39:29. In Acts 2 the fulfillment
of this promise is announced.
[92] 1QS IV 3–5.   [93] IV Ezra 14:37–48.
[94] In Luke 11:13; Acts 11:16; 15:8–9; also in Luke 11:2 according to the reading of Codex Bezae
Cantabrigiensis.

course of the church's history: (a) God's revelation ceased with the death of the last apostle. Illumination rather than inspiration is the mode of the Spirit's action in the post-apostolic times. (b) The inspired testimony given by prophets and apostles is infallible. Neither of these axioms, however, is supported by the statement on inspiration made in Eph 1:17. The "Spirit of revelation" sought by Paul enables the church not only to receive God's revelation through the hands of those who first received it, i.e. the NT prophets and apostles, but also to "make known" to others what was "made known" to the apostles and by them.[95] Whenever the secret of the gospel is made known, then the "revelation" takes place that is characteristic of the time which has *now* dawned. Revelation is not over but continues to be given by God. Further, the apostle hopes and promises to say nothing but the truth (Gal 1:20, 4:16, etc.), and he expects the saints as well in all things always to say nothing but the truth (Eph 4:15, 25).[96] But he also knows that God's chosen men are weak, tempted, fallible. The grace of God, thanks to which there is "no condemnation for those in the Messiah Jesus" (Rom 8:1), is not an automatic protection from further lapses. The men "sealed with his seal, the promised Holy Spirit" (Eph 1:13) have offending brothers in their midst (5:3–13). Waves of false doctrine threaten to toss them around (4:14). Unless inspiration had prevailed over and in spite of devilish temptation and human failing, and unless God had revealed himself even to and through sinners, there would have been no revelation before the advent of Christ (I Peter 1:11), at the time of Christ, or after Christ. Only of him is it said that he resisted the tempter and that there was no sin in him.[97] All other recipients of revelation are and remain fallible men.

The priority, uniqueness, and authority of the revelation given to prophets and apostles cannot be questioned; see Eph 2:20 and 3:5. But restricting revelation to the time of the apostles limits God's freedom to be present and recognized in ever new dimensions of his love (3:18–19) during the generations and periods following the apostolic age (2:7, 3:10). Identifying inspiration with the gift of infallibility assumes a technical operation of the Spirit which negates or destroys the freedom, the responsibility, the diversity, and the weakness of the human vessels filled with God's treasures (II Cor 4:7). It is characteristic of God who gives the Spirit to remain free and to make men free, rather than use them as mechanical tools.

IV   The Resurrection and Enthronement of Christ

Eph 1:20–23 (cf. 4:8–10), sings the praise of Christ's resurrection and exaltation. Almost identical terms are used in 2:1–6 for describing the resurrection and enthronement of the saints: they have been raised with Christ. A future resurrection of men, e.g. of their body, is not explicitly mentioned in Ephesians.[98] Equally, there is no explicit reference to the creation of a new

---

[95] 1:9; 2:7; 3:5, 9–10; 6:15, 19.

[96] He claims to be a truthful witness even in a context where his memory may have slipped regarding details (Gal 1:20). Occasionally he has not only to clarify but sometimes to correct previously made statements, e.g. Rom 1:11–12; I Cor 1:14, 16.

[97] Matt 4; 16:23; John 8:46; I John 3:5; II Cor 5:21; Heb 4:15; 7:26; 9:14.

[98] It is ascribed to God's power, e.g. in I Cor 6:14; 15:12–58; II Cor 5:1; 13:4; Rom 6:4–5, 8; 8:11; Philip 3:21. In Ephesians vss. 6:8–9 come closest to affirming a future judgment according to works.

Though R. Bultmann[111] still represents and uses the methods and thoughts of the history-of-religion school, his intention is to get away from its limitations. He aims at restoring to Christ's resurrection a sense which establishes its true relevance for the first witnesses of resurrection as much as for men of all ages. Resurrection is no longer considered the glorious, though spurious, fate that befalls any respectable Hellenistic hero or deity after death and is therefore to be attributed to Jesus too. Rather, behind the early Christians' mythological belief and diction stood an existential concern which can be fully appreciated and shared by even a modern reader of the Bible.[112] How can man be freed from the merciless control and fear of fate (*heimarmenē, anagkē;* in Christian terminology: law), how can he escape despair or silly attempts to establish his own self, and become hopeful and open for the future? The answer given is: only when a change in his self-understanding is effected, which includes his understanding of God and the world. Such a change cannot possibly be ascribed to an external historical event, not even to the fact that the prophetic teacher from Nazareth, Jesus, died on a cross. But the change does take place when the meaning (*Bedeutsamkeit*) of Jesus' crucifixion is realized. According to Bultmann, exact historical research is unable to prove that on Easter morning a bodily resurrection took place, but it *can* demonstrate that on that day a faith was born in the disciples and a message was formed which gave sense and power to their encounter with the man who was crucified. The disciples became aware and began to proclaim that God himself had met them when they met Jesus, and that God himself acted upon them even through the death of Jesus. Now they realized that they could no longer remain their old selves; they were made free to live as new men. When they attributed this renewal to Jesus Christ's resurrection, their intention was far from seeking to promote a mythology. Rather they wanted to ascribe their faith, their *kerygma,* their new self-hood, only and exclusively to a miraculous deed and gift of God.

Thus Bultmann does not intend (in the fashion of an enlightened, rationalistic, historical scholar) to "eliminate" the resurrection of Jesus Christ. But he understands the resurrection as the God-given interpretation and application of the cross of Jesus to man. Resurrection means that a life of hope, commission, and trust is offered to man, and that all men are challenged to accept it in faith. "Christ has risen into the *kerygma.*"

The advantages of this "interpretation" of resurrection over the attempts of so-called "liberal" theologians to eliminate resurrection altogether are obvious. Cross and resurrection are held together—not as two historical "facts," but as an ambiguous historical event and its true meaning. W. Marxsen's thesis that the resurrection is an "interpretament" of the cross, G. Ebeling's magnification of faith, and S. M. Ogden's attempt to demythologize the cross and the *kerygma* of Christ together with the resurrection[113] are among the outstanding

[111] Esp. in *Primitive Christianity,* London: Thames, 1956; "New Testament and Mythology," in H. W. Bartsch, *Kerygma and Myth,* I (London: SPCK, 1957), 1–44; ThNT, I, section 33.

[112] Bultmann's early student H. Jonas (in the books mentioned in BIBLIOGRAPHY 2, esp. in the last chapter of *Gnostic Religion*) has unfolded the problems of existence that are common to both the Hellenistic and the modern man.

[113] Marxsen, *The Resurrection;* G. Ebeling, *The Nature of Faith,* Philadelphia: Muhlenberg, 1961; idem, *Word and Faith,* Philadelphia: Fortress Press, 1963; S. M. Ogden, *Christ Without Myth,* New York: Harper, 1961.

elaborations of Bultmann's thought. The true meaning of the statement, "God has raised the Messiah from the dead," is then this: it is God who gives faith, i.e. authentic self-understanding. Or, in terms of Eph 2:1-10, the creedal affirmation means: We have been raised and made new men by an act of God's grace, not by our own power.

Many elements of this interpretation may be true. Concerned with the problem of communicating to modern man, Bultmann succeeds in giving some meaning to the resurrection. But it is hard to find in the NT any reference to Christ's resurrection which really states that faith is substituted for fact and that man's understanding of himself, of God, and of the world is the measure of all things. Though the Bultmannian understanding of resurrection purports to be true to the NT, it does not claim to be derived from Eph 1:20-23 and offers no help in understanding this text. For it neglects five things that play a prominent role:

a) OT passages (taken from Pss 8 and 110) are used to describe the mode and effect of Christ's exaltation, just as elsewhere Paul takes up an early confession stating that Christ was raised "according to the Scriptures."[114] Not a free-wheeling but a Scripture-bound understanding of the resurrection's meaning is suggested by the allusion to Israel's Bible.[115]

b) The resurrection and enthronement of Christ are explained as deeds of God that affect not only individual men and their faith,[116] but also principalities and powers, all things, and the church as a whole.[117] A purely individualist and existentialist interpretation of the resurrection is discouraged by all statements indicating its cosmic relevance.

c) The divine demonstration of power over both God's people and the world has an eschatological ring, and takes up apocalyptic and Wisdom motifs which are frequently found in Paul, especially when his thought reflects the apocalyptic and rabbinic scheme of two aeons. Resurrection signals and ushers in a completely new time, i.e. the completion and triumph of God's kingdom, the victory of his creative, preserving, guiding, and saving wisdom, and the fulfillment of all his promises.[118] When the later parts of the OT and the OT apocrypha proclaim the resurrection of the dead, it is not primarily to answer the question: what happens to me after death? Will I continue to exist? Can I attain new being? Rather it is a response to the outcry: will God's righteousness

---

[114] I Cor 15:4; cf. Rom 1:2-4, etc.; Luke 24:26-27, 44-46; Matt 16:21, etc. See esp. C. H. Dodd, *According to the Scriptures*.

[115] E. Schweizer, *Lordship and Discipleship*, SBT 28 (1960), demonstrates that the pattern of humiliation-exaltation (which is common to the life of elect persons such as the patriarchs, David, the Suffering Servant of Isa 53, the righteous man described in Wisd Sol 2-5, etc.) rather than the fate of pagan deities is followed by Jesus, his disciples, the NT's teachings. The contents, character, and intention of the OT texts quoted in NT resurrection passages are discussed in M. Barth and V. Fletcher, *Acquittal by Resurrection*, pp. 48-66. In the NT the faithfulness of God shown to his Son; the validity of the righteousness of the One for Many; the demonstration of the inseparability of heavenly and earthly righteousness; the evidence of God's own presence in history; finally the reason why remembrance and proclamation are appropriate—such essential elements of Jesus Christ's resurrection are brought to light with the help of Scripture quotations and allusions.

[116] The anthropological dimension is at first mentioned in passing (God's power "over us" was demonstrated; "from the dead" he was raised [1:19-20]), then with great emphasis: *you* and *we* are raised with him, saved and created anew (2:1-10).

[117] Cf. I and II Thessalonians; Rom 8:19-22, 31-39; I Cor 15.

[118] Heb 1:8, 10-11 adds to these elements of Ephesians a specific emphasis upon the irreversibility of the changed conditions. The throne of the exalted Messiah will never be shaken, but stands fast in eternity.

heaven and a new earth. However, Christ's past resurrection and present rule from his heavenly throne are not strictly objective "facts" that are by nature divorced from man's present and future. Neither are they mere possibilities that become actual only by, e.g. repetition, meaningful interpretation, or personal experience. Rather, the power by which Christ was raised "is at work . . . over us, the believers" (1:19). Christ was not raised in splendid isolation and detachment from the company and predicament of all those called "dead." The term "the dead" (1:20) includes the saints (2:1, 5). Actually, there are four steps in Paul's discussion of the resurrection of Christ, which in modern discussions[99] comprise the distinction between the supposedly objective and subjective, mythological and existential, cosmic and soteriological aspects of resurrection. Paul begins with the statement that in the resurrection and enthronement of the Messiah the unique, strong power of God is at work (1:19–20), and he ends by praising man's salvation and new creation for good works by grace alone (2:8–10). The four steps connect the praise of power with the praise of grace.

a) By his exaltation the Messiah is placed in control over the principalities and powers (1:20–22a).

b) He is made "head over the church" and "fills her" just as he is "head over all things" and "fills them" (1:22b–23).

c) Gentiles who had been "dead in their sins" and captives of the ruler of the atmosphere, as well as Jews equally "dead" in their fleshly desires and lapses, have been raised and enthroned together with Christ (2:1–6).

d) This evidence of God's grace serves as demonstration and instruction for the benefit of coming aeons, or onrushing demonic powers (2:7).

The salvation received by the saints through God's "power" as demonstrated in Christ's resurrection, is in 1:19–23 inseparably connected with the subjection of the several powers and of "all things" under the feet of the risen Christ. A clear division between the effect of resurrection upon the powers and its consequences for men cannot be made—except at the price of stipulating a grace of God for man which is bare of cosmic relevance. But the love preached in Ephesians is powerful and public rather than a helpless or purely private and internal matter. The "infinitely rich grace" of 2:7 is not without the "exceedingly great power" mentioned in 1:19.[100]

What does Paul mean by his praise of the resurrection of Christ? He certainly does not attempt to dissipate "modern" man's doubts that a dead man can ever come to life again, or his skepticism that a scientifically enlightened man should believe in stories that cannot be tested by biological experiments or legal courts.[101] Nor does he count the resurrection as one among other

---

[99] A bibliography of the longer and shorter treatments of reports on the resurrection given in the Gospels and Acts and of the present-day form-critical disputes cannot be given at this point. Some titles specifically relevant to the *Pauline* doctrine on resurrection are listed in BIBLIOGRAPHY 10.

[100] The Greek text uses the same participle *hyperballon* to describe in these two verses the "greatness of God's power" and the "riches of his grace."

[101] E. Rohde has collected evidence showing that mankind in antiquity was exposed to substantially identical doubts. The early Christian apologetes would not have taken refuge in the bird Phoenix and engaged in other apologetic antics for proving the glory of "paradoxology," unless the majority of their enlightened contemporaries had fostered strong objections against resurrection and after-life. See R. M. Grant, "The Resurrection of the Body," JR 37 (1948), 120–31, 188–208; *Miracle and Natural Law*, Amsterdam; North-Holland Publishing Co., 1952.

miracles.[102] Since the unique power of God is at work in the resurrection, the resurrection is an event without parallel.

But is not the proclamation and the cultic adoration or sacramental celebration of Christ crucified and risen an analogy to the cultic veneration of ancient and Hellenistic dying and rising deities or heroes?[103] The upsurge of the study of Gnosticism since the days of Lidzbarski, Reitzenstein, and Bousset has added the "parallel" of the descending and ascending light-messenger. In some Mystery Religions elements of ancient Eastern religions and of nascent Gnosticism seem to be blended together. It has been assumed that, like the introduction of sacraments in the young Christian movement was in answer to an opportunity or a need represented by contemporary religions,[104] the development of empty tomb tales and/or Easter morning visions into a "resurrection kerygma" corresponded to a market requirement. The Easter stories appear to reveal little more than the construction and adoption of a sensible means of communication shaped by missionary and apologetic purposes. If the unknown Jesus from the tiny Palestinian corner of the Mediterranean Sea was to be believed and proclaimed as Lord and *pantokratōr,* he simply must have risen. There were too many miracle doers, wise teachers, and crosses around to make him outstanding—unless he was also raised and could be revered in the cult as a deity ever present. It is argued that modern man neither wishes nor needs to embrace resurrection in his faith; he can believe in the fatherhood of God, the brotherhood of man, and the infinite value of the human soul without believing in a risen Son of God.[105]

The days of such simplistic exploitation of "parallels" have passed, and historians of religion have become much more reluctant to see dying and rising gods everywhere they look. The earlier mentioned works of C. Colpe and H.-M. Schenke have exploded the myth of a complete, ready-made Gnostic system in which Paul or John wrapped their message in order to make the Christ figure existentially relevant to their contemporaries. M. Wagner's careful collection and evaluation of the meager bits of information available on the Mystery Religions have confirmed F. Cumont's,[106] C. Clemen's,[107] and other scholars' earlier misgivings about Bousset's[108] attempt to explain the Christian *kyrios*-cult as an adaptation to the worship of Hellenistic deities, or H. Lietzmann's[109] and J. Leipoldt's[110] endeavor to find in pagan cults the root of the baptismal dying-rising pattern.

[102] A miracle may be copied by the Pharaoh's court magicians (Exod 7:9–12), by migrating rabbis or sons of a high priest (e.g. Acts 19:13–14), or by Satan and pseudo-apostles (Matt 12:24; Acts 8:9–11, 18–24; II Cor 11:13–14).

[103] As, e.g. shown by the works of Rohde, Leipoldt, Noetscher, Goguel, McCasland, Nikolainen, cf. the early editions of J. G. Frazer, *The Golden Bough,* London: Macmillan, 1894, 1900, 1915. When Marxsen relegates the resurrection of Christ to the realm of the history of religions and actually attempts to ban it from the proper NT proclamation, he reveals himself as a late radical exponent of this school of thought.

[104] O. Casel, e.g. in *Glaube, Gnosis und Mysterium,* JbLW 15 (1941), 155–305; *Die Liturgie als Mysterienfeier,* Ecclesia orans 9, Freiburg: Herder, 1923; F. Kattenbusch, PRE, 19 (1907), 404; A. von Harnack, *Mission and Expansion,* I (New York: Putnam, 1904), 286–88.

[105] See e.g. A. Harnack, *What is Christianity?* New York: Putnam, 1901.

[106] *The Oriental Religions in the Roman Paganism,* Chicago: Open Court, 1911.

[107] *Religionsgeschichtliche Erklärung des Neuen Testamentes,* Giessen: Töpelman, 1909.

[108] *Kyrios Christos* (henceforth cited as *Kyrios*), 4th ed., Göttingen: Vandenhoeck, 1935.

[109] See esp. his interpretation of Rom 6 in HbNT.

[110] *Die urchristliche Taufe im Lichte der Religionsgeschichte,* Leipzig: Dörfling, 1928.

ever be triumphant over the present slaughter of his servants and the seeming defeat of God's cause?[119] The slaying and rising of the two witnesses in Rev 11 is typical of this meaning of resurrection. Its deepest concern is theological, not anthropological. Not just man's salvation, but God's glory is at stake. The answer given in the NT to the cry for a triumphant demonstration of God's righteousness includes an answer to, but does not exhaust, the representative question, "Wretched man that I am! Who will deliver me from this body of death?" (Rom 7:24).

d) The death of Christ is mentioned in Eph 1:7, hinted at in 1:20, extensively interpreted in 2:13–18, and again mentioned or alluded to in 4:9–10; 5:2, 25. But the statements of Ephesians on Christ's death and on his resurrection are, except perhaps in 4:9–10, not as closely combined as in many other NT texts.[120] Therefore it is impossible to consider 1:20–23 an interpretation of the meaning of Christ's death. To the contrary, the proclamation of Christ's resurrection stands at this point[121] on its own. To speak of God and of faith in him means, according to Paul, to speak of "God who gives life to the dead" (Rom 4:17; cf. I Cor 15:13–17; I Sam 2:6). The will and power of God to resurrect the dead is one of his attributes. His ability to cope with sin and death is assured by it. But it is not dependent upon man's fear of death, and it is certainly not to be identified with the ability of man—even if this ability were given by God himself—to explain the "meaning" of death, least of all of Christ's death.

e) The proclamation of Christ's resurrection in Eph 1:20–23 is made in political terms, couched in the political language of OT royal psalms; the term "head" has a distinctly political meaning which is not Greek but Hebrew; see COMMENT VI A. The imagery suggests that the author intends to speak of an event in God's world politics. The existence, constitution, government, and victory of his kingdom are discussed here—rather than just a feature of faith or a disposition of the soul. The political event announced is the enthronement of Christ on high—an enthronement which takes place at the expense of other powers that had been vying for world dominion.[122] Before the (political!) role of Christ's death in terminating the hostility between Jews and Gentiles is unfolded in Eph 2:13–16, it is stated that God gave his Messiah the highest place over all powers.[123] A change of government such as that effected by Christ's enthronement will certainly affect the consciousness and behavior of citizens

---

[119] See the relevant passages listed and interpreted in the works cited in BIBLIOGRAPHY 10 by Branton, Martin-Achard, Nikolainen, Noetscher, Schubert, StB; also monographs such as W. Bousset, *Die Religion des Judentums*, 3d ed. (Tübingen: Mohr, 1926), pp. 202–301; P. Volz, *Jüdische Eschatologie von Daniel bis Akiba*, Tübingen: Mohr, 1934; R. H. Charles, *Eschatology*, 2d ed., London: Black, 1913; E. Käsemann, "God's Righteousness in Paul," JThC 1 (1965), 100–10. The NT connection between resurrection and justification is demonstrated again in works cited in BIBLIOGRAPHY 10, e.g. by Durwell, Lyonnet, Stanley, Vawter. In his commentary on the Psalms (AB) M. Dahood points to Canaanean sources and their possible influence upon Israel (as supposedly demonstrated e.g. by I Sam 2:6) in order to show that there is evidence of belief in afterlife and resurrection not only in the later but also in earlier parts of the OT. But P. W. Lapp, "If a Man Dies, Shall He Live Again?", *Perspective* 1 (Pittsburgh, 1968), 139–56, comes to the opposite result. He maintains that the literature and burial rites of early Israel yield no evidence that pre-exilic Israelites believed in resurrection.
[120] E.g. I Cor 15:3–4; Rom 4:25; Philip 2:6–11; Acts 2:23–24, 31–32; 4:10–11; 5:30–31; Matt 16:21; Rev 1:5–6, etc.
[121] Similarly in Rom 1:4; Gal 1:1; I Cor 15:12 ff; II Tim 2:8.   [122] 1:19–21; 2:6–7; 6:12.
[123] The Messiah is subject only to God's own dominion, I Cor 15:25–28; cf. Matt 28:18.

and slaves who now have a new lord. It would be chimeric and meaningless if it did not produce substantial changes for and in them. But the change made above them and for their benefit precedes all secondary, subjective changes. The author of Ephesians is not familiar with the contrast established by post-Enlightenment philosophy and epistemology between "objective historic" and "subjective" or "existential" events of "historicity." Rather he proclaims the priority and superiority of God's action over man's reaction. By fear or with faithfulness, in amazement, horror, or joy, man responds to the Messiah's establishment. But the Messiah's enthronement precedes the joy of Israel and the fear of her enemies (Ps 2, etc.). Otherwise man's joy and fear might be unfounded, dependent solely upon the ups and downs of the restive human heart as it is described in Jer 17:9.

If these five traits of the resurrection proclamation were present in Eph 1:20–23 only, they might be considered a doctrinal reason against Pauline authorship. But, whether individually or in combination, each of the features mentioned is also represented in uncontested Pauline epistles, especially in Romans and I Corinthians. Ephesians intends more than any other letter to present the gospel as a message of world-wide peace, rather than as the news of the salvation of individual souls only. Just as the cosmic relevance of the cross is described in e.g. Col 2:14–15, so Ephesians emphasizes the political and cosmic relevance of the resurrection, by which a new and good order is established for the whole universe.[124]

V   Principalities, Powers, and All Things

A   Origin and Definition of Powers

In the triumphal procession of a potentate the number and rank of subjugated hostile kings serves to enhance the victor's glory.[125] In Eph 4:8 and Col 2:15 allusions to such a procession are found. The image of a royal court in which servants, supplicants, and defeated foes pay their respect to the ruler is used in Eph 1:20–22. Not only in Philip 2:6–11, as A. Ehrhardt[126] has demonstrated, but probably also in Eph 1 and other Pauline passages the enumeration of the defeated powers makes clear the dimensions of Christ's victory and rule. In the Synoptic Gospels, esp. in Mark 5:1–20, the irresistible authority of Jesus over individual demons, as well as over an agglomeration of

---

[124] See e.g. Gal 6:14; I Cor 2:8; Col 2:14–15; cf. Eph 2:13–16. L. Cerfaux assumes that three stages of Paul's doctrinal development can be discerned: the apostle moves from a Jerusalem-type eschatology in I II Thessalonians; I Cor 15, through his classic period of a theology of passion and of anti-Judaistic polemics in Galatians, Corinthians, Romans, to the cosmic and cultic Christology of Ephesians and Colossians. W. Hahn, *Mitsterben und Mitauferstehen*, ascribes the difference less to a development of doctrine than to the various situations and heresies to be met in various places at different times. The libertinism and enthusiasm of the Corinthians led him to stress the future resurrection with Christ. The legalism and ceremonialism of the Colossian type were presuppositions of the emphasis placed in Colossians and Ephesians upon the present dominion of Christ and resurrection with him.

[125] OT songs of triumph, heavily tinged with mythological elements, such as Isa 14:4 ff. and many Psalms, also oracles of doom, that name one nation after another (see Amos 1–2; Isa 13–19; Jer 37–51; Ezek 25–32; Zech 9), may be considered an analogy. The Gospels' accounts of Jesus' entry into Jerusalem are remarkably different inasmuch as the meekness of the entering ruler and the low estate of the applauding crowds is emphasized (Matt 21:1–6). In Zech 9 and Col 1 both motifs are connected: by his humility or his death Christ becomes victorious.

[126] In EvTh 8 (1948–49), 101 ff.

as many as a legion of demons, is described in picturesque detail. Christ's king-ship according to Paul is manifested by the continuous submission of one op-ponent after the other, death being the "last enemy" to be "swallowed up in victory" (I Cor 15:25–27, 55). Who or what are the other "powers" men-tioned by Paul in Eph 1:21 and in similar catalogues?[127]

Scholarly research has not yet led to results that permit clear definitions of each of the four terms used for their designation in 1:21, or of any other term found elsewhere. Also, it is as yet unknown whether the sequence in which they are enumerated follows an ascending or descending line of rank. Books such as I Enoch (6–36), *Test. Levi* (3:5–8), or Dionysios Areopagita's *Heavenly Hierarchy* contain much information about their hierarchy or internal order, but there is no way to prove that these authors were elaborating on exactly those things presupposed by Paul.[128] Nor is it known why Paul shows no interest in a clear identification of the various groups of powers. Perhaps he assumed that his readers knew exactly what he was talking about, but it is more likely that he did not care to distinguish between the several powers because he wanted to say only one thing: whoever and whatever they are, they are subject to an absolute monarch and possess the relative equality of *subdued* princes. State-ments of the Pharisees, the Qumran community, the Apocalypticists, and the canonical Gospels, agree on the following: all powers—be they good or bad, angels or demons—are under the control of God who has created all. Though the rebellious camp dominated by an evil ruler (called Beliar, or by similar names[129]) seems to put God's universal kingship in question and fights God's heavenly hosts, and though heterodox writings may have prepared the way toward a Gnostic-dualistic world view, no clear-cut dualism is formed and proclaimed. The NT writings describe the obstruction offered by evil powers to the Messiah Jesus, but they emphasize even more that God puts each and all of them under the Messiah's feet. To repeat an earlier observation, no OT passage is quoted as frequently in the NT as Ps 110:1—that oracle which prom-ises the subjugation of those powers.

But does Ephesians reflect the immediate influence of Gnostic or other Hellenistic teaching to a greater degree than the other Pauline letters?

1) Gnosticism of the Valentinian type speaks of up to thirty "aeons" (*aiōnes*) which express and constitute the "fullness" (*plērōma*) of the one perfect pre-existent All-Father Aion.[130] Reference is also made to "the rulers" (*archontes*),[131] a body of heavenly beings sometimes identified as the zodiac or the planets that determine the fate of man with an iron grip. Though Paul speaks in Ephesians of a "ruler of the atmosphere" and "over-lords of this dark world" (2:2; 6:12), in 1:21 he does not use the technical

---

[127] The meaning or meanings of the term "elements" (*stoicheia*) in Colossians and Galatians is not included in the following inquiry. For monographs pertinent to the interpretation of Ephesians see BIBLIOGRAPHY 11.

[128] Bengel explicitly denies the interpreter's competence to come to sharp conclusions. F. W. Beare, IB, X, 635, sees in Paul's list "a certain mockery of the whole elaborate classification."

[129] Eph 2:2; II Cor 6:15; Matt 6:13; 12:24–28; Luke 4:6; John 12:31 etc.; CD IV 13, 15; V 18, etc.; 1QS I 18, etc.; 1QM I 1, 5, 13, etc.; Jub I 20; XV 33; I Enoch 8:1; 9:6, etc.; Rev 12–13; Mar-tyrium Isa 1:8–9; 2:4; 3:11; *Testaments of the XII, passim.*

[130] Ptolemaeus, according to Irenaeus I 1:1–2. See COMMENT VI C 1 for details.

[131] E.g. in the Chenoboskion Script about the *Essence of the Archontes.*

terms "aeons" and "rulers." Therefore, proof is missing for the theory that he is using Gnostic terms.[132]

2) Instead of Gnostic ideas, Paul's vocabulary may reflect the deification of political potentates.[133] He is certainly an exponent of that Hellenistic trend which stems from the westward movement of oriental thought and customs: giving divine titles to earthly rulers! The terms used to describe the powers in Eph 1:21 frequently denote political rulers in legal, financial, and philosophical literature. Assembled military power can also be meant. In Rom 13:1–7 Paul describes the Roman state with one of the terms used in Ephesians and Colossians for principalities and powers; so it is possible that in Ephesians he wanted to call the resurrected Christ the Great-king above all human kings ruling on earth; cf. Rev 19:16. Even when he mentions the *heavenly* dwelling place of the powers and calls them spiritual hosts,[134] he may have thought specifically of their earthly representatives.

3) It is most likely that M. Dibelius, C. B. Caird, G. H. C. MacGregor, G. Rupp, D. E. H. Whiteley and others are right in tracing Paul's utterances on "powers" back to the OT (more specifically, to its latest apocalyptic portions), to Jewish intertestamental apocalypticism and later rabbinical teaching. Qumran, too, showed great interest in the power of good and evil spirits and of the angels:

The idea dates back to the time of the exodus and the Judges that Israel's victories are due to God's own warfare against the hosts of his opponents; see Exod 15 and Judg 5, etc. God proves himself the Lord of hosts. In the historiography, prophecy, and poetry of Israel's monarchic period, the pagan kings, because of their association with their deities, are considered quasi-gods incarnate. Scholars of the Divine-Kingship School hold that also the kings and the judges in Israel were respected as "gods" (Pss 45:6; 82:1, 6; cf. Ezek 28:2, 6, 9). In Dan 7–12 a heavenly Son of Man, the angel Michael, beasts, and princes are mentioned as heavenly representatives of the chosen people and the nations on earth. Rev 1–3 refers to the angels of the several Christian congregations. Every element, every season, as well as the sea, the winds, the rain, and the wells, were eventually understood to be supervised, administered, or represented by angels. Angels communicate God's will to man, e.g. during the giving of the law on Mount Sinai, but they also carry man's prayers to God and are sometimes understood as intercessors; cf. their appearance on Jacob's ladder (Gen 28). Birth and death, health and pestilence are given into their hands.[135]

---

[132] In I Cor 2:8 the word "rulers" has perhaps a demonic sense. But in Rom 13:5 the same term is used in praise of the Roman state. An explicit allusion to astrologic beliefs is contained in the words "zenith" and "nadir" (Rom 8:39), and maybe also in other denominations of angels and powers. But though astrology can be associated with tragic fatalism, there is no evidence that the apostle had in mind the Gnostic tragic dualism which assumed a split in the deity itself. "Aeons" are mentioned in Eph 1:21; 2:7; 3:9–11. Clearly in 1:21, but perhaps also in the later passages, time periods rather than demonic powers are meant. See especially the second NOTE on 2:7.

[133] For the Egyptian and Babylonian ideologies see H. Frankfort, *Kingship and the Gods*, Chicago University Press, 1948. Their possible influence on Israel is discussed, e.g. by S. H. Hooke, *Myth, Ritual and Kingship*, Oxford University Press, 1958; S. Mowinckel, *He that Cometh*, New York: Abingdon, 1956, and other Scandinavian scholars.

[134] As he does in Eph 1:20–21; 2:2; 6:12.

[135] See the indices, s.v. angel, in StB, IV; Moore, *Judaism*, II; R. H. Charles, *The Apocrypha and Pseudepigrapha*, II, Oxford: Clarendon, 1913, for references in Jewish orthodox and heterodox writings.

The contact established during the exile between Israel's beliefs and Iranian doctrines regarding good and evil spirits helped to strengthen elements that were seminally already present in the notion of the holy war and of divine kingship. It appears that in each case the "oriental pattern" mentioned in the preceding paragraph was complemented by a supererogation of earthly phenomena on a heavenly level.

In the time of Jesus and Paul certainly not all the Jews had adopted such beliefs. The ruling class of the Sadducees, and with them probably a substantial proportion of the Jewish people in Palestine and in the diaspora, refused to believe in angels and ghosts (Acts 23:8). Still, some Palestinian Jews were more ready than were many Gentiles to preserve or to adopt picturesque notions that are open to mythical understanding. Even though in the Hellenistic world enlightenment and syncretism were eating away, amalgamating, or reinterpreting what was left of the ancient Egyptian, Greek, and Roman religions, and even though at the same time astrology, mystery cults, popular philosophy, and the deification of great and petty rulers were playing an ever increasing role, in that period Jews began to speak more, not less, of angels and demons, and they considered themselves specialists in exorcism, e.g. Acts 19:13–14. Those (few) who cared enough to ask for a Scriptural ground to the origin and existence of evil powers used Gen 6:1–4 for elucidation; the story of the copulation of the sons of God with the daughters of men was seen a fit answer to disturbing questions about the nature of evil. Not earlier than in the Gnostic use (or misuse) of the same story a fully developed dualistic system came into being. Jewish writers intended at all times to uphold and defend God's absolute monarchy, see e.g. 1QS iii 13 – iv 26.

The canonical Gospels reveal not a little of contemporary Jewish thinking on these matters. Here the spiritual powers opposed to the appearance and work of Jesus Christ are called "demons" (daimonia)[136] or "spirits." Some Jews considered Jesus possessed by such a demon.[137] Obviously justice cannot be done to the Gospels if their accounts are explained as oriental overstatements, superstition, or a supererogation of earthly phenomena. Rather they want to affirm that Jesus exerted on earth power over powers that were beyond human control but controlled men and resisted the word and work of the "Son of Man." According to Ps 8 the "Man" or "Son of Man" who is "remembered" by God is victorious over them.

It is possible[138] that the principalities and powers mentioned in the Pauline epistles include the demons that, according to the Synoptic Gospels, especially Mark's,[139] were expelled by Jesus. They may include also the princes of nations who in Daniel's account have to yield to God's kingship, and the angels of the congregations, of natural events and elements, that following the book of Revelation became witness to the victory of God.

Because of the late, apocalyptic, and distinctly Jewish character of the

---

[136] Lit. "little demons." The Greek word daimōn itself denotes a god or divine power. Paul uses the belittling term for idols (I Cor 10:20–21).

[137] Matt 12:24; John 7:20; 8:48–49, 52; 10:20–21.

[138] As A. Wilder, H. Schlier, C. Maurer, EvTh 11 (1951–52), 165, G. H. C. MacGregor, and others have shown.

[139] G. Aulen's understanding of Paul's doctrine of Christus Victor is confirmed by J. M. Robinson, The Problem of History in Mark, SBT 21, 1957.

Pauline references to principalities and powers, are all such utterances of the apostle to be considered proof that Paul himself fostered mythical beliefs? Is Paul superstitious, or does he only use poetic language? The condescending title of Dibelius' pioneering work (in English it would be "The World of Ghosts in Paul's Belief") has contributed to the current vogue to treat Paul's statements on the powers as irrelevant and therefore either to demythologize or dismiss them. Since no exact opinion can be formed without precise knowledge of what Paul himself may have understood by principalities and authorities, and their subjection to Christ, the question now has to be asked: what and how much does Paul reveal about their essence, history, and function?

The same Pauline epistles which so far have resisted identification of the individual powers do however permit a description of the functions and dimensions which their combined hosts fulfill.[140] (1) Some of them are identified with political (Jewish or Gentile), financial, juridical, ecclesiastical, tribal, etc., potentates who dominate the earth. Therefore, e.g. kings, procurators, senators, judges, high priests, and sheikhs, may be meant. Thus Paul's terminology appears to reproduce in Greek the occasional OT nomenclature of rulers and judges, i.e. "gods."[141] (2) Some Pauline terms are linked so closely with references to death and life, present and future, zenith and nadir, that they appear to denote natural, biological, or historical determinants of human life.[142] (3) The "titles" mentioned in Eph 1:21 may well include such forms of address and proper name as became titles—e.g. papa, or Caesar. Also, such titles as emperor, savior, benefactor, father of the fatherland, duce, belong in this context, and nicknames or symbolic names corresponding to John Bull, Uncle Sam, Deutscher Michel are not to be excluded. (4) Finally, if the "elements of the world"[143] belong in the company of these powers at all, then traditions, doctrines, and practices that concern the application of law in religion and private life are also envisaged.

To summarize, it is probable that Paul means by principalities and powers those institutions and structures by which earthly matters and invisible realms are administered,[144] and without which no human life is possible. The superior power of nature epitomized by life and death; the ups and downs of historic processes; the nature and impact of favored prototypes or the catastrophic burdens of the past; the hope or threat offered to the present by the future; the might of capitalists, rulers, judges; the benefit and onus of laws of tradition and custom; the distinction and similarity of political and religious practices; the weight of ideologies and prejudices; the conditions under which all authority, labor, parenthood, etc., thrive or are crushed—these structures and institutions are in Paul's mind. Van den Heuvel mentions sex, education,

---

[140] See for the following Caird, pp. 20–21; Wilder; Galloway, p. 26; Schlier; Berkhof, p. 34; van den Heuvel; Whiteley, pp. 23, 26, 229–31; also Pokorný, EuG; PG, p. 126; J. Sittler, "Zur Einheit berufen," in New Delhi Dokumente, ed. F. Lüpsen (Witten: Luther Verlag, 1962), pp. 300–11; M. Barth, The Broken Wall, pp. 88 ff., 217–18, 228 ff; idem, Acquittal, pp. 43–48.
[141] Rom 13:1–7; I Cor 2:8; (cf. 6:1–3; Eph 3:15); Ps 82:1; also 86:8; 97:7? The term "lordship" (Eph 1:21; Col 1:16; cf. II Peter 2:10; Judg 8) may specifically mean the economic and social power possessed by land-, factory-, or slave-owning "lords."
[142] Rom 8:38–39; I Cor 15:24–27.
[143] Mentioned in Gal 4:3, 8–9; Col 2:8.
[144] Cf. Diogn. VII 2.

environment; Sittler, politics, economics, aesthetics, ways of living; Pokorný puts emphasis upon including not only natural powers, but also human society, its laws and intellectual traditions.[145] God's creation obviously does not consist of earthly-visible things alone. Just as Gen 1:1 treats the creation of the heavens and the earth, so also in Col 1:16 "invisible things in heavens" are added to those that are tangible. In the latter verse, either both or only the invisible things, are identified with the powers. It is probable that in Ephesians Paul had in mind at the same time both visible, specific governors *and* the invisible authority exerted by them; concrete conditions and manifestations of life *and* the invisible mystery of the psyche; specific legal acts *and* the overarching role of law in general, etc. According to Eph 1:10 both the heavenly and the earthly entities are subjected to Christ. Only when both are affected is the whole creation changed.

Pokorný[146] is not the only scholar to recognize in P. Teilhard de Chardin's unified world view a reflection of the teaching of Ephesians and Colossians. Indeed, a connection is possible between Teilhard de Chardin's Omega Point and the comprehension of all things under one head, the submission of all powers to the Christ, and the movement of all toward the perfection of the One Man.[147] But while the great French scholar had the vision of an ongoing spiritualization of the cosmos and of man, based upon the incarnation of Christ, Paul speaks of a personal rule and revelation of the crucified and risen Christ which cannot be compared to a cosmic or human evolution.

If "principalities and powers" are an outdated expression for what modern man calls the structures, laws, institutions, and constants of nature, evolution, history, society, the psyche, the mind—then there is no reason to reject or eliminate the respective Pauline statements as silly products of superstition. Paul could not know what modern physics, biology, sociology, psychology, anthropology, and cybernetics were to elaborate. The recently coined scientific terminology for describing invisible and visible constants of creation, evolution, change, decay, and destiny was not available to him. But he showed concern for precisely the same fields. He did not despise or exclude the world of creation from his theology. Knowing that God had created heaven *and* earth, and that God "had made all things very good" (LXX Gen 1:31), Paul could not possibly endorse a dualism which ascribed creation to a split in the deity, or to the result of ever deteriorating emanations from the deity. A final dualistic tension between the worship of God and the scientific perception of the phenomena of nature and history, psyche and society, had no room in the mind of ancient Israel's Wisdom teachers, nor in the mind of Paul who took up much of that tradition, as was earlier shown.[148] References to Christ's

---

[145] "Death" is among these powers. But "flesh"—though Paul often personifies it and has even more to say than John about its horrible dominion over man—is never enumerated among the hostile powers. In Johannine and Pauline writings "flesh" has become a technical term denoting the corruption, captivity, guilt of all mankind (cf. Gen 6:12; Isa 40:6). It possesses an evil sense in the NT whenever it is compared with the Spirit, e.g. John 6:63; Gal 5:16–25 (but not in Joel 2:28; Acts 2:17). But it is not a constituent of God's creation, man's psyche, or social life. The corruption of the flesh is an unnatural incident, not a structure of created existence.

[146] EuG, pp. 126–27.

[147] Eph 1:10; 2:20–21; 4:13; not to speak of Col 1:12–20; 2:15; 3:1–4.

[148] The juxtaposition of worldly and divine wisdom in I Cor 1:18 – 2:16; Rom 1:21–23; Col 1–2 has nothing to do with the modern contrast of religion and science. Paul fights in these passages not science and philosophy but man-made religion—in Romans idolatry, in I Corinthians inflated Christian pride.

dominion over principalities and powers reveal Paul's concern for all that is essential in the visible and invisible spheres of creation. Far from being an indigestible burden to "modern" man's credulity or faith, the references show that the immense problems facing modern man are still within the scope of the gospel.[149]

It has been repeatedly stated[150] that the message of Ephesians is concerned less with the salvation of the individual soul than with the peace between man, his fellow man and God, i.e. less with private piety than with the social character of the church and its mission to the world. Now an addition and qualification is due. Ephesians[151] not only describes God's work for a community of brothers and fellow citizens that is to be enjoyed within God's people, but it deals with all dimensions, structures, and institutions of life in the created world. To be human means more than to have self-understanding, to encounter one's fellow man, or to be bound to a community. Man is also in the grip of the powers of nature and history. Though he is called to exert dominion and seems able with the help of progressive science to exert an ever increasing technological control over nature, society, and the psyche, he is also subject, if not victim, to the powers of environment, tradition, heredity, and the rule of majorities or minorities. When Paul speaks of the risen Christ's dominion over the "powers," he thinks of the relevance of God's work for everything that shapes man's life in the created world.

The context of Eph 1:21 serves to attest to the validity of the foregoing arguments:

B   All Things

According to Eph 1:10 (–11?), 22–23,[152] "all things" (Greek *ta panta;* always with the article except when Ps 8:6 is quoted) are the object of Christ's rulership—whether his rule is exercised in creation, redemption, or consummation. In the immediate neighborhood of a reference to "all things" there is also repeatedly found an enumeration of the powers or dominions.[153] While Paul speaks in many other texts of "all (things)" in a general sense,[154] in these specific passages the term "all things" appears to possess a special meaning. It either sums up the previously listed principalities and powers, or it prepares the way for a list to follow. Thus the list of these powers may be considered an authentic interpretation of "all things." In this case "all things" are not identified with the Greek term "the All," or, "the Whole" (*to pān*), which denotes the compact, total universe, including the deities. Neither do "all things" mean a haphazard or chaotic conglomeration of

---

[149] As esp. Wilder has pointed out, see also his *New Testament Faith for Today,* New York: Harper, 1955.
[150] Especially in section VI of the Introduction and in COMMENT XIV on 1:3–14, on Jews and Gentiles.
[151] And, even more so, Colossians; cf. Mark 13 and Revelation.
[152] Cf. Col 1:16–17; I Cor 8:6b; 15:27–28; Heb 1:3–14; Matt 11:27; 28:18.
[153] In the passages just listed, except in I Cor 8:6; Eph 1:10; Matt 11:27; but also in late OT books as e.g. LXX II Esd 19:6[Neh 9:6].
[154] E.g. "All is yours . . . All is permitted to me but not all is useful . . . He will inform you of all" (I Cor 3:21–22; 6:12; Eph 6:21). The accusative "all things" occurs also in an adverbial sense and may mean "totally," e.g. Eph 1:23; 4:15.

objects or events. To the contrary, the term can signify in Pauline writings the world as structured by powerful institutions, forces, and constants that may be divided (as previously shown) into earthly and heavenly, visible and invisible powers.[155] The technical function of the reference to "all things" has already been intimated: it is a means of describing the omnipotence exerted by God or conveyed to Christ and exerted by him.

There are at least two ways to trace the origin of the technical term, "all things," and to explain the specific sense it might possess in the apostle's mind, or in the minds of his first readers.

1. E. Norden[156] has attempted to prove that confessional NT statements about "all things" that are "from, through, toward God"[157] make use of a "Stoic formula of omnipotence." Norden discovered similar formulae not only in Stoic literature, but also in pre-Heraclitic Orphism and in magic incantations. The term "fullness" is at times used to comprehend and describe both the one supreme deity and the wholeness of the created and existing things. An ultimate identity of "the One and the All" (*hen kai pān*) is presupposed in magic practice, in Stoicism, and—despite the recognition of a tragic rupture—in Gnosticism.[158] But Pokorný[159] is not satisfied with a one-sided Greek and Hellenistic derivation. He discusses three aspects of the term, "all things": a general sense which embraces heaven, earth, underworld; a specifically Jewish understanding which includes the present and future aeons; finally a popular Hellenistic notion of all sorts of elements and powers to which life is subject. While an amalgam of meanings is by no means inconceivable in the case of the Hellenist Paul, a more distinct alternative ought not be ruled out yet:

2. When Paul writes of the omnipotence given to Christ he sometimes quotes Pss 110:1 or 8:6, or both, or he alludes to Wisdom passages, especially Prov 8:22–31; Wisd Sol 7:22 – 8:1. While the quoted psalms may or may not contain some analogies to the Divine-Kingship ideology, they have certainly nothing to do with Orphism, later Greek philosophy, or Hellenistic religion. Indeed, the Wisdom texts resemble Stoic utterances on the function of Reason or Word (*nous* or *logos*), but the Israelite Wisdom tradition

---

[155] Equally Plato *Phaed.* 79A, divides the universe into a visible and invisible realm. Catalogues of the many categories of created beings meant by "all things," i.e. of the universe and its parts, are found, e.g. in Ps 148:7–12; Song of the Three Young Men 35–68; Philo *spec. leg.* I 210. In all these cases the blessing of God, viz. the gratitude of man lies behind the composition of the extended catalogues. Philo goes beyond the Three Young Men when his thanksgiving includes not only the righteous servants of the Lord, but also the human race as a whole and the several races, including the groups of women, Greeks, Barbarians, continentals, islanders. In the short list of Philip 2:10 the beings populating the underworld are added; Ps 148:7 mentions explicitly "sea monsters and all the deep" among those praising the Lord.

[156] *Agnostos Theos* (Leipzig: Teubner, 1913), pp. 240–50. See also D. J. Dupont, *Gnosis* (Louvain: Neuvelaerts, 1949), p. 245, etc.

[157] Especially Rom 11:36; I Cor 8:6; Col 1:16–17; Heb 2:10. Eph 4:6 might be added to these passages if the pronoun "you" is considered an inauthentic addition.

[158] Antecedents of this formula are acclamations to Zeus and Isis, such as, "Zeus is all, and that which rules over all" (Aeschylus Fragments 70 N); "Goddess Isis, only one, you are all things" (*Corpus inscriptionum Latinorum*, ed. T. Mommsen [Berlin: Reimer, 1883], no. 3800). For additional references see R. Reitzenstein, *Poimandres* (Leipzig: Teubner, 1904), p. 26; Norden, *Agnostos Theos*, pp. 245 ff; H. Hegermann, *Schöpfungsmittler*, p. 110; N. Kehl, *Christushymnus* SBM 1 (1967), 112–13. Benoit, "Corps, tête," pp. 35–36, offers a selection from Hellenistic texts showing the monotheistic (anti-dualistic) tendency of the *hen-kai-pān* formula. Cf. Sir 43:27, "The sum of our words is: 'He is the all.'"

[159] EuG, p. 71.

antedates by far the various post-Aristotelian schools. Whenever Paul speaks of "all things" he may well intend to cut through the maze of Hellenistic syncretism (although not without making use of its diction) to OT testimonies. Orthodox and heterodox, i.e. rabbinic, apocalyptic, and Qumranite Judaism reveal the same intention. Having no equivalent to the Greek or Latin or English terms "world," or "universe," the Hebrew Bible speaks of "heaven and earth," or simply of "all" (things), e.g. Gen 1:1, 31; Isa 44:24. In order to encompass the whole of creation, the NT often follows this precedent. But the NT also makes use of the Greek terms for "world," or "creation," and occasionally these nouns and the adjective "all" (in the sense of a substantive) are used in the same context and obviously understood as synonyms.[160] The NT affirms as strongly as the OT that God is the undisputed creator, Lord, and ruler of "all things." In this capacity God is not a part, or an element, or one of the powers of the world; nor can he and the world be in any sense declared as ultimately identical. The biblical creed is therefore essentially distinct from pantheistic and Stoic affirmations of the deity's omnipresence and omnipotence.

But there is still another distinction between the Bible and the Greeks of the ancient and the Hellenistic periods: in the Bible one man, and he alone, fully shares in God's omnipotence. His title is "the Messiah," or "Son" or "(Son of) Man"; his function is to reveal and to exert God's own full power over all things. Certainly Stoicism had its wise man who is "king" because he makes proper use of the Reason that holds the world together. But biblical prophecies, hopes, and descriptions point to just one man as God's plenipotentiary. Inasmuch as he is a real man he is unlike the deified Pharaohs who were elevated to the rank of gods in human disguise.[161] But who is he?

Paul was not the first Jew to speak of the delegation of God's power into the hands of one man. E.g. Gen 1:26; Ps 8:6–8; Dan 7 describe the commission of one man with supreme power. The range of thought in the three passages mentioned extends from an etiology of farming and animal husbandry to the vision of an apocalyptic victory over demonic enemies. Between these two extremes a long series of passages might be mentioned that describe man's technical abilities as gifts of God, the wise man's wisdom and prudence, and the saving character and influence of the chosen servants of God. Outstanding among all those texts are the Royal Psalms that praise the king as the paragon of man. He is the one blessed with fertile fields and stables, many descendants, and victory over his enemies.[162] The animals to be domesticated according to Gen 1, have become symbols of the defeated enemies; the soil cultivated, a guarantee of the subjugation of the earth; the posterity promised, an earnest of the everlasting solidity of his throne. Neither Orphism, nor Stoicism, nor Gnosticism gives any reason why and how God's omni-

---

[160] Cf., Eph 1:4 with 1:10; Col 1:15 with 1:16; Rom 8:19–20 with Eph 3:9.
[161] In Ezek 28 the king of Tyre draws God's wrath upon himself because he elevates himself to equality with a god; cf. Gen. 3:5, 22; Isa 14:12 ff.
[162] Isa 11; 53:10–11; Pss 2:8–10; 45; 72:5–11; 110:1, 6; 132:17–18. Cf. the Psalms praising God, the king, e.g. 47:96–99. As Matt 21:16; I Cor 15:27; Eph 1:22; Heb 2:6–9 show, Ps 8 was already in the early church, perhaps before Paul's time, understood to refer to God's Messiah.

potence should be entrusted into the hands of just one man. But the OT utterances on the relation between God and his Messiah, between the Messiah and both Israel and the nations, and also between man and nature, viz. history, offer precedents to NT confessions regarding Jesus Christ. And more than precedents: they are *quoted* by Paul as part of the description of Jesus Christ's omnipotence.

The difference between "all things" mentioned in the Stoic formula and "all things" in Ps 8:6 does not lie in the claim for universality. Each time all and everything *is* meant—though the Bible does not include God among those "things." But the OT is more specific and less sweeping: it means by "all things" political and religious enemies, e.g. the Gentile kings and nations who represented (or were represented by) their respective gods or angels.[163] The OT also mentions specific events, like the growth of olives and barley, the birth of cattle and many children. To "all things" belong also public order, peace, freedom, justice, stability, and all of the other concrete and specific blessings which God grants through the king who is to come.[164] Explicit OT references to social, juridical, economic conditions, and to blossom and seed, sun and rain, rivers and sea, health and growth, fruit and longevity are often specifically beautiful. Both the anthropological-historical and the physical-biological realms are subsumed and held together under the promises given the Messiah.[165]

In conclusion, philosophical axioms and the magicians' disclosure and use of the deity's omnipotence have no original connection with the hope of Israel that God would send a prince of peace. Ovid's and other seers' expectation of a child and prince of peace belong to another context. The transferral of omnipotence to the chosen servant of God, the specific constituents of "all things" in history and nature, the simultaneous demonstration of God's power over men and impersonal things, and the absence of an eventual tragic dualism—features such as these connect Paul's statements about "all things" much more closely with the OT promise than with alleged Greek parallels. If pre-Pauline Christian congregations possessed confessional formulae such as I Cor 8:6b that sounded more Greek than biblical, then I Cor 15:25-27 and Eph 1:20, 22 show that Paul, if not wise men before him, added Scripture references to them. The connection with Israel's hope and call which was thus established had much more than apologetic value. It was an apt instrument to counteract pantheistic notions, to proclaim the historic manifestations of God's omnipotence in one man (the "Perfect Man"; see 4:13), to ridicule magic ways of perceiving and manipulating God's power, and to introduce statements on the ethical responsibility of Christians.

---

[163] Pss 82:1; 86:8-9; Dan 11-12 are examples.

[164] An outstanding description of OT expectation is given by Mowinckel, *He That Cometh*, pp. 65-74.

[165] The distinction between matters religious, political, and natural which is made in modern times is not typical of the Bible. The "cause of God" (Ps 74:22) affects at the same time (as the whole of Ps 74 and e.g. Isa 51:9-11 show), the mythological power of Rahab and Leviathan, the political and military power of Egypt, the historic condition of Israel among the nations, the waters of the sea, and the successive times of many generations.

C Angels and Demons

Are the structures and institutions of human existence identified by Paul as "powers" and "all things" good, neutral, or evil by nature?[166]

1. The "last enemy, death," is among them (I Cor 15:24–27; Rom 8:38). The "overlords of this dark world" are called "spiritual hosts of evil" that must be resisted by the saints under the protection of God's armor (Eph 6:12). They appear willing and able to interfere in a hostile, derogatory way between God and man—or else Paul would have had no reason to proclaim that they are not strong enough to separate the saints from the love of God (Rom 8:38–39). Though they may be considered and respected as "angels," the elements of this world must not be worshiped (Col 2:8, 18). Passages like Gal 4:8–9; I Cor 8:5–6 reveal that these beings who are "non-gods by nature" were formerly, and are still, worshiped by the Gentiles. Thus there is clear evidence in the Pauline letters that principalities and powers belong in the realm, and share the character, of the chief evil "spirit, the ruler of the atmosphere" who is "at work among the rebellious"; cf. 2:2. Does this mean that Paul considered all "powers" evil? If so, the conclusion is inevitable that all power—except God's, the Messiah's, the Spirit's—is evil, and that institutions and structures as such, including *all* things essential to created life, are bad.

2. Not all powers mentioned by Paul have the same evil quality, however. "Life" and "angels" are mentioned in one list (see Rom 8:38), and Paul never suggests that angels and life are the enemies of God or man. To the contrary, each one of the powers is called a "creature" in Rom 8:39, and while the whole of "creation" was "consigned to futility," yet it was not of its own will, and not because it was created this way (Rom 8:20). Futility is its anti-nature, as if it were anti-matter confronting matter. So if at times all kings and rulers of the earth appear to be arrayed against God's Messiah (Ps 2:2), yet there are other times when Melchizedek is called a priest of the Most High (Gen 14:18; Ps 110:4), and when Cyrus is praised as a servant of God (Isa 45). Paul himself extols the beneficial function of the Roman state, calling it an institution established by God. Precisely because the Christians know about the subjection of all existing powers to God, they are conscience-bound to pay their taxes and give officials the honor they deserve (Rom 13:1–7).[167] The royal psalms, whose vocabulary is chosen by Paul to describe Christ's omnipotence, certainly put special emphasis upon the submission of

[166] Assuming that they are identified with astral powers or with the *plērōma* mentioned in Gnostic sources, Schlier (in his monograph on principalities) considers all of them bad. However, in his later work (Schlier, p. 113) he exempts the "neutral" aeons from this summary judgment. Thomas Aquinas (commenting on Eph 6:10–12) teaches that Cherubim, Seraphim, Angels, Archangels, and "Thrones" are always "turning towards God," i.e. are good; that the names "Principalities" and "Powers" are given to both good and evil angels, while the nomenclature "Satan" and "Angels of Satan," indicates that the latter (since their "fall") are always evil. Benoit, "Corps, tête," p. 31, observes that Paul's statements lack clarity, especially regarding the question of whether the powers are neutral, good, or corrupted by man's fall, and in regard to the "moral quality of their submission." Bengel, in his notes on Eph 3:10; I Cor 15:24 (but cf. on Eph 6:12) and with him Robinson, pp. 21, 41, etc., Langton, pp. 129 ff, and others take pains to show that some of the "powers" are good.

[167] Of course under different circumstances Paul would have agreed to the contents of Matt 22:21; I Peter 2:17; Rev 13. In any case the fear and worship owed to God limits the debts and duties owed to Caesar.

all enemies to the one king enthroned by God. But the triumphant affirmation of the king's steadfast superiority over all enemies does not deny his excellence among, and superiority over, his friends and faithful servants also. In Ps 45:7; Heb 1:9 companions of the king are mentioned. In Heb 1:3, just as in the previously quoted Pauline passages, it is asserted that Christ sustains "all things." "All things" are in turn interpreted by a reference to angels. In Heb 1:4–14 a florilegium from royal psalms or similarly understood passages proclaims the superiority of the Son, God, and Lord over the angels. There is thus no reason to assume that all angels were considered evil demons.

Translated into modern diction this means: though many institutions and structures of society are futile, pernicious, catastrophic, deadly, and clearly hostile to the honor of God and the well-being of man, those structures that shape created life by certain constants and laws are not essentially evil. To the good creation mentioned in Gen 1:31 belong also the existence and function of invisible powers. God the king does not have only human servants. Rather a court of beings, seen only by visionaries under extraordinary circumstances, surrounds him and executes his will. Over all these powers, through which God rules heaven and earth, Christ was given dominion. They are among God's creatures as much as all visible and tangible, animate and inanimate things. And they have been created by him equally *good*, as are all things coming from his hand (Gen 1:31).

And yet some of these powers *are* evil. Unlike an apocryphal Jewish tradition,[168] however, Paul does not use the sin and fall of angels to account for this. He differs from the later development of such mythical tales by never mentioning a pre-cosmic or cosmic catastrophe. And in contrast to Qumran,[169] he fails to affirm that God himself created the spirits of light *and* the spirits of darkness. While Ezekiel does not speak about the creation of evil spirits by God, he yet affirms that God "gave statutes that were no good and ordinances through which Israel could not have life" (20:25). Despite all his polemics against the institution and power of the law, Paul never says that the law of God is subject to sin, death, or the flesh. But Paul does speak of the letter (of the "holy" law!) that kills because of the intervention of sin; of dying "through the law" and "to the law"; of a "weakening" of the law by the flesh; and of the subjection of the creation to futility.[170] What he denounces is idolatry, the worship offered to a creature rather than to the creator, to demons rather than God, to non-gods in the place of the Father.[171]

Only because some powers, including the law, are idolized by man have they become evil. The "futility" to which the whole creation, including the principalities and powers, was subjected (Rom 8:20) has to be identified with the folly of idol worship offered by man. Indeed, in Rom 8:19–22 Paul

---

[168] E.g. I Enoch 6; Jub 5:1–2 referring to Gen 6:1–4; cf. II Peter 2:4; Jude 6.

[169] 1QS III 25.

[170] II Cor 3:6; Rom 7:6–12; 8:3–20; Gal 2:19, etc. Whether the subjection of creation to vanity (Rom 8:20) is caused by God or by man's sin is not clear. See the commentaries on Romans e.g. JB, NT, p. 281, n. l.

[171] Rom 1:25; I Cor 10:20; Gal 4:8. A similar warning of idolization of creatures and the statement that "all the nations under the whole heaven" were "allotted to worship and serve . . . the sun and the moon and the stars, all the host of heaven" are found in Deut 4:16–20.

affirms that on the same day that men cease to revere creatures instead of God, the whole creation will be freed; the creation waits with great yearning and pain for this awakening of the free children of God. Thus the sin and captivity of man has more than only psychic, physical, and social consequences: it affects the whole world and seeks to spoil the function of God's good gifts. The very law of God given "for life" becomes a power "for death" (Rom 7:10–11). Through man sin enters the world, and through sin, death (Rom 5:12; cf. I Cor 15:56). Yet not even this plain statement is sufficient to reconstruct a systematic Pauline doctrine of the nature of evil. While *God's* mystery is revealed in the coming of Christ, Paul is not the messenger of a revealed mystery of *iniquity*. He does not explain why, how, or when the rule of Satan and his hosts was established. This omission may be a necessity. He who believes in God has no way to explain, and thereby implicitly to excuse, evil.

But the apostle makes three things clear beyond doubt: the responsibility of man (Rom 1:20; 3:23); the inextricability of man's life from angelic and demonic forces; and the victory given to and by the Messiah over all these powers (Rom 8:31–39). Not only a portion of man, e.g. his capacity for religious beliefs and exercises, but his whole being with its intricate relationships of soul and body, nature and history, self and society, past, present, and future, are affected and changed by the Messiah. The change effected by Jesus Christ's enthronement above all powers certainly affects man's self-understanding, but a new self is a consequence rather than the presupposition of Christ's exaltation.

Paul describes the mode of Christ's victory in various ways. For example, according to Eph 1:10 Christ is from eternity given the commission to be head over all things. Following Col 1:15–16 the presupposition of his victory lies in his role in creation. According to Col 1:20–22; 2:14–15; Eph 2:14–16, the triumph is gained on the cross. In Eph 1:20–23 it is affirmed that Christ's resurrection, enthronement, and present rule over church and world are the means for subjugating the powers. According to Philip 2:10–11; I Cor 15:25–26, the subjection of the powers is still in progress but is pressing toward its consummation. I Cor 15:26–27 speaks of his future total conquest. Rom 8:37 mentions the victory already given to the saints.[172]

Different too are the terms used to describe how the hostile powers are subjugated. Paul speaks not only of their subjugation, but also of their being abrogated,[173] stripped, led in triumphant procession or into captivity; they are made to genuflect; they are pacified or they are reconciled.[174] Most amazing is the use of the terms "pacified" and "reconciled": everywhere except in Colossians[175] Paul has reserved them to describe Christ's work only for man. The difference between God's dominion over the church and over the world is described in the apocryphal, late second-century Acts of John (112) by the words "Father of those [men] under heaven, ruler of

---

[172] Cf. I John 5:6. C. Morrison's book on the powers (SBT 29 [1960], 118, 125, 135) culminates in the statement that the church is the place of the victory over the powers.

[173] See esp. Dahl's arguments against the interpretation of the Greek verb (*katargeō*) as "eliminating" or "annihilating" (*The Resurrection of the Body*, pp. 117–19).

[174] E.g. I Cor 15:24–26; Col 1:20; 2:15; Philip 2:10; Eph 1:22; 4:8–10.

[175] And Eph 2:14?

those [powers] heavenly." Benoit,[176] Cerfaux,[177] Maurer[178] and others speak of the distinction between Christ's love and Christ's power, or between the gift of life to man and naked authority over the powers. No reference is ever made to a justification or sanctification of the powers, or to faith, love, and hope expected from them. Neither, as was observed earlier,[179] does the "in Christ" formula place them into the same intimate relationship to Christ as is enjoyed by the saints.

However, it is only with the help of Colossians that answers can be given to questions concerning the powers that arise from a study of more or less obscure passages in Ephesians.

VI Head, Body, and Fullness

During the past three or four decades an enormous amount of literature has been produced that seeks to analyze the term "body of Christ" which Paul uses to designate the church. Christological questions have been treated less frequently and enthusiastically than the issues of ecclesiology, and the discussion of the "body of Christ" has been given preference over research into about a hundred other NT designations for the church. In the most recent years has the concept "people of God" moved into the foreground. The concept of Christ "the head" is closely, though not always or exclusively, connected with the term "body of Christ."[180] In some key passages the noun "fullness" or the verb "to fill" is essential to the statements on "head" and "body,"[181] and in what follows these three important words will be treated together.

Of the flood of issues raised in the pertinent literature,[182] only the most debated and diverse, albeit partially overlapping, arguments and viewpoints will be presented here. Though the verses Eph 1:22–23 are too short and ambiguous to permit final conclusions, they pose some of the problems which will be dealt with by later passages in Ephesians (and in Colossians).

A The Head

When Paul uses the noun "head" to describe Jesus Christ, he is most likely not inventing a new title; it is also improbable that he gives the metaphor a meaning independent of the many senses attached to respective Hebrew or Greek terms. Of course, its application to Christ may have involved as many changes of meaning as occurred in the title "Messiah." But some connection with a traditional meaning will never be excluded as long as a speaker or writer is concerned with communication. Three possible origins (and corresponding senses) of "head" can be mentioned.

1. In the Hebrew and the Greek OT, just as in other Semitic documents,

---

[176] "Corps," pp. 26–31.   [177] *Théologie de l'église*, p. 284.
[178] EvTh 11 (1951–52), 164–65. Compare COMMENT V C on Eph 5:21–33, regarding different meanings of the verb "subordinate."
[179] See COMMENT I on 1:1–2.
[180] Christ is also called "head of each man" and "head of all things" or "powers," I Cor 11:3; Eph 1:22–23; cf. 1:10; Col 2:10; see esp. the interpretations of Col 1:18.
[181] Eph 1:23; 4:10–16; Col 1:18–19; 2:9; cf. fn. 67.
[182] See BIBLIOGRAPHY 12.

"head" designates a tribal chief, political ruler, or military leader.[183] Once, in
II Chron 13:12, it is stated that God is "at the head" of Israel. In this sense,
"head" implies all functions of rulership, e.g. the role of a savior, a representative, a source and guarantor of unity.[184]

But is the OT concept of "head" sufficient to explain *all* of Paul's utterances
on the head and the body? In the OT there are no explicit hints that the subjects of the head or ruler are considered his "body."[185] A reason for this may
well be that the Hebrew word "head" (*rōsh*) does not only, and perhaps not
even primarily, have a physiological sense. Often it denotes, without being used
as a metaphor, the prime position held by something or somebody, e.g. the
summit of a hill or the rulership over a tribe. In those cases, a body is not
mentioned. But other passages reveal that to the head belongs a body, and that
a body requires a head; thus especially those texts that speak of decapita-
tion,[186] of a good fate or an evil retribution brought "upon the head" of a
man,[187] of a head count,[188] or of the anointing or crowning of a head. The
king of Israel and Judah is in Hosea 1:11 called their "head." The Messiah is
also named the "breath of our nostrils" (Lam 4:20).[189] These manifold idioms
show that the head is considered representative of the whole person or people.
In idiomatic speech, the head is the opposite of the "tail" or "foot."[190] When
the body (or a part of it) is mentioned together with the head, the latter is
always the most important part. In I Cor 12:21,[191] however, Paul refers to
the head as if it were but one member of the body, equally dependent upon
the body's other members as they are upon one another. In that passage the
head is among the many members that contribute to the common life of the
whole body. But when Paul speaks of Christ the head over principalities,
powers, and all things, such mutual dependence is out of the question. Then the
OT political meaning of head is indeed taken up: "He enthroned him . . .
above every government and authority . . . He put everything under his feet
and appointed him head over all" (Eph 1:20–22; cf. Col 2:10). Again, the
same is true of the statement "the Messiah is the head of each man" (I Cor

---

[183] Judg 10:18; 11:8–9, 11; I Sam 15:17; I Kings 21:12[LXX III Kings 20:12]; Job 29:25; Isa
7:8–9; Hosea 1:11[LXX 2:2]; Deut 33:5; Jer 31[LXX 38]:7; Lam 1:5; Ps 18:43. Some LXX MSS
translate occasionally the Hebrew *rōshē* by the Greek words *archē*, "rule," or *archōn*, "ruler": see
the passages from Judges and Hosea, and LXX III Kings 20:12 in the sixth-century Coden Veronensis
(R). Cf. I Cor 11:3: God the head of the Messiah; the husband, the head of his wife; Christ, the
head of each man.

[184] Cf. D. J. Dupont, *Gnosis*, pp. 419 ff, 446 ff, etc.

[185] Passages such as II Sam 19:12–13 in which blood relationship is described by the words
"you are my bone and my flesh" do not prove the opposite. According to Gen 2:23 Adam uses a
similar term in recognizing Eve. The two "become one flesh" (Gen 2:24). Indeed, Paul identifies
"one flesh" with "one body," and the one body thus described is the "body of Christ" (Eph 5:28–
32). Thus the apostle is convinced that already the OT, spiritually interpreted, attests to the head-
body relationship between Christ and the church. But the OT itself never calls God's people, "body
of God," or "body of Abraham," or "body" of a king. Also Eve is never explicitly called, "body
of Adam."

[186] I Sam 17:46, 51; II Kings 10:6.

[187] Evil consequences: I Sam 25:39; II Sam 1:16; I Kings 2:32–33, 37, 44; 8:32; Pss 7:16; 38:4;
Prov 25:22; Joel 3:4, 7; Obad 1:15; blessing: Prov 10:6; 11:26; LXX Prov 10:22; Ezek 16:12, etc.

[188] Num 1:2, 18, 20, 22, etc.

[189] "In the head of a family the family's soul is concentrated," according to Mowinckel. *He That
Cometh*, p. 70. Pedersen, *Israel* I–II, 174, states, "In the head the soul is prominent"; cf. III–IV,
33–41.

[190] Deut 28:13; Isa 1:6; 9:14.

[191] Only in this one passage, but certainly not in Eph 1:22–23; 4:15–16; 5:23; Col 1:18; 2:10, 19!

11:3). The same position of authority is proclaimed in the affirmation that the "head over all" is appointed "head of the church" (Eph 1:22; Col 1:18). Only when in the immediate context the church is called Christ's body is a thought introduced that has no explicit precedent in the OT. It is probable that in these texts Paul has drawn from other sources. What are the origins of his particular thought and diction?

2. In religious or related literature—ranging from Orphic fragments[192] through Plato,[193] Cleanthes' *Hymn to Zeus*[194] and other Stoic philosophers' voices,[195] the Magic Papyri,[196] the Naassene Sermon, and up to early medieval Mandaean documents[197]—the idea is expressed that the whole universe resembles one large human body. Its head is its originator, power source, and life spender: it is the supreme god, called e.g. Zeus or Aion or Reason. The members of this body are, on descending levels, the invisible powers, man, animals, organic and inorganic things. According to this notion Zeus is not only the highest part of the universe, but its very life. Philosophers preferred to ascribe this function to the soul rather than to the head, but both conceptions can also be combined: "The soul of the universe is located in the head."[198] The concept of the Prime-Anthropos and the ultimate identity of the One and the All mentioned before are further expressions of this world view.[199]

It is true that in section III B of the Introduction reasons have been given for excluding second-century and later Gnostic systems from the viable traditions that may have influenced the author of Ephesians. But if Paul could not have known classic Gnosticism he may yet have been acquainted with some elements that preceded it and contributed to its formation. To these elements belong the Orphic and Stoic ideas of the structure of the universe. If the apostle was acquainted with them, then it is most remarkable that he never used the term "body of Christ," to denote the universe or all things.[200] Only the church is called "body of Christ." Also, he never subsumes both God and the universe under the one term "fullness"; Creator and creature remain clearly distinguished (Eph 3:9; cf. 2:10, 15). Nor does Paul assert an ultimate substantial or essential identity of Christ and the church. The use he makes of three other

---

[192] Nos. 167–88, in O. Kern, *Orphicorum Fragmenta* (Berlin: Weidmann, 1922), pp. 201–2.
[193] *Timaeus* 30B–34B.
[194] No. 537, in J. von Arnim, *Stoicorum veterum fragmenta*, I (Leipzig: Teubner, 1903), 119–24.
[195] E.g. Cicero *de natura deorum* I 35, III 9; Seneca *quaestiones naturales de natura deorum* VI 14:1; idem *epistulae* 92:30; 95:52.
[196] E.g. Papyrus Leiden V, in K. Preisendanz, *Griechische Zauberpapyri*, I–II (Leipzig: Teubner, 1928, 1931), I, no. 12, p. 243.
[197] For the Naassene Sermon see the references in the Introduction, section III. Quotes from the Mandaean Books are found, e.g. in Schlier, TWNTE, III, 678. See also *Od Sol* XVII 14–17; *Evangelium Veritatis*, Cod. Jung XVIII 29b–40a; Ign. *Trall*. XI 2.
[198] H. Hegermann, *Schöpfungsmittler*, p. 100; cf. COMMENT VI B 1.
[199] See the discussion of "all things" in the preceding COMMENT, also fn. 158.
[200] However, Theodore of Mopsuestia taught that the apostle made this equation. H. Schlier and E. Käsemann assume that the Gnostic hymns underlying Colossians and Ephesians spoke of the world as Christ's body, and that Paul intended to correct them, esp. by the interpolation of the word "church" into Col 1:18. Still, Schlier, p. 91, goes so far as to say, "In Ephesians and Colossians . . . occasionally the body is [identified with] the All." On p. 209 he affirms (cf. Dibelius, pp. 36, 84) that in Col 2:19; Eph 4:16 the original, i.e. the cosmic meaning of *body* is still recognizable. Mussner, CAK, pp. 65–67, Benoit, "Corps, tête," pp. 29–31; Pokorný, EuG, p. 74; Dacquino, "De Christo," pp. 81–88 (ref.) and others deny that there is any evidence of Paul's intention to make this identification.

images reveals this clearly: the keystone is not identified with the building (2:20–22); the inhabiting power is something other than the inhabited heart (3:16–17); the bridegroom has a bride but is not bridegroom and bride at the same time (5:22–33). Paul's description of Christ's relationship to the body reflects the notion that the head, by permeating the body with wisdom, reason, power, and will, gives the body its life and saves it from destruction.[201] Paul speaks of the body growing from the head (4:16; Col 2:19). He occasionally appears simply to identify Christ and the (life-giving) Spirit (II Cor 3:6, 17).[202] Since in Eph 4:16 the head is said to provide for the body, it is probable that also in 5:29 Paul ascribes to the head the functions of "providing and caring" for the body, and that in 5:23 the head as head is called "savior of the body." But while many of the benefits conveyed from the head to the body (among them the gift of life especially) resemble the beneficial work of Zeus, of the world soul, or of another divine power, great differences cannot be overlooked. Resuscitation of members from the dead, forgiveness of their sins, and love are mentioned in Ephesians but not in hymns to Zeus or philosophical tracts or magic texts. The Pauline restriction of the "saving" function of the head—only the bride is saved! (5:23) and only those who have faith (2:8)—could hardly appeal to Stoics. It must have looked narrow-minded to any universalist thinker who cared for the whole cosmos. On the other hand, Gnostics enjoyed their esoteric participation in knowledge and their individual salvation.[203] But Paul's missionary understanding of the gospel and the church does not permit placing him in their midst. For these reasons it is improbable that by his head-body similes Paul intended above all to make use of, and to appeal to, either pantheistic or esoteric Hellenistic notions of a beneficial cosmic "head."

3. Paul's utterances on Christ the "head" may have been influenced by the knowledge and skill possessed by doctors and anthropologists of his time.[204] When he says "the head fills" the body with its "fullness" (Eph 1:22–23), and the body "grows to" and "from the head" (4:15–16), he may have derived these metaphors from contemporary biology, physiology, or neurology. The same is true if the attribute "savior of the body" (5:23), and the functions of "providing and caring" (5:29), or of "supplying and fitting together" (Col 2:19; Eph 4:16) are also directly or indirectly ascribed to the head. If medical precedents or parallels exist they can contribute to the understanding of Paul. If there are none, a warning is given against overinterpreting the head-body image. Of course, in the pertinent passages Paul might just have followed his own wild imagination; in this case the imagery used would have obscured rather than clarified his thought and intention. However, as an educated man

---

[201] Lightfoot, p. 223, defines Christ's headship inter alia by calling him "the seat of life." Benoit, "Corps, tête," pp. 26–27, speaks of *principe vitale* and *animation*. Cf. G. Martelet, "Le mystère du corps et de l'esprit dans le Christ resuscité et dans l'église," VigChr 12 (1958), 31–53; C. Spicq. *Théologie Morale* I (1965), 82.

[202] See esp. Martelet, p. 52, n. 31. Cf. the close connection between the "one Spirit" and the "one body" in Eph 2:16, 18; 4:4.

[203] Hegermann, *Schöpfungsmittler*, p. 100.

[204] Lightfoot, p. 267; Robinson, p. 104; Benoit, "Corps, tête," p. 27, make more or less moving hints that Paul consulted "Luke the beloved physician" (Col 4:14) in order to receive the amazing detailed and correct physiological and neurological information contained in Eph 4:16 and Col 2:19.

living between the times of Hippocrates[205] and Galen,[206] he could hardly avoid reflecting some views held by the doctors of this time.[207] In Eph 4:16 and Col 2:19 technical physiological terms abound.

What is known of the physiology and neurology contemporary to Paul, and what has been considered relevant for understanding his statements on Christ, the head? Two trends are visible among Greek scientists, and one feature characteristic of Hebrew anthropology deserves special attention. Among the Greeks, Hippocrates (whose findings were further developed by Galen) stands in opposition to the leading Stoics.[208] The two camps may be considered as representative of Plato[209] and Aristotle[210] respectively. The Aristotelian-Stoic group ascribes priority and superiority to the heart rather than to the brain. The positions of Hippocrates and Galen, however, appear to be nearer Paul's and therefore will be sketched briefly here.[211]

Hippocrates writes what he "assumes" (*nomizō*) to be true: the brain is the strongest "power" in man. Long before the muscles it receives the pure dry air which is inhaled through the nose, and it distills from this fresh air its quintessence, clear knowledge.[212] The eyes, ears, tongue, hands, and feet[213] carry out their work according to the discernment (or decision; lit. "knowledge") of the brain. The brain is in command, the members obey. It exerts its

---

[205] Ca. 460–380 B.C. The writings ascribed to him, though not necessarily written by him, date between 420 and 360 B.C. They were completed before the great explosion of medical science in Alexandria which occurred between 300 and 200 B.C. During this century the discovery was made that the motor function of some nerves had to be distinguished from the sensory ("aesthetic") role of others. For Hippocrates' work see ed. E. Littré, *Oeuvres complètes d'Hippocrate*, 10 vols., Paris: Baillière, 1839–61; esp. the Index in vol. X, 814 ff. A later edition was made by H. Kühlewein I–II, Leipzig: Teubner, 1894, 1902.

[206] Ca. A.D. 130–200. In his writings Galen summed up the accumulated progress of knowledge attained between 300 B.C. and A.D. 100. His complete works have been edited by C. G. Kühn, *Medicorum Graecorum Opera, Galenus*, 20 vols., Leipzig: Cnoblochius, 1821–33; see Index in vol. XX, 114 ff. F. Solmson, "Greek Philosophy and the Discovery of the Nerves," Museum Helveticum 18 (1961), 150–67, 169–97 sums up the progress made between the pre-Socratic scholars and Galen. Bibliographic information on the ancient doctors' works has been collected by H. A. Diels, *Die Handschriften der antiken Ärzte*, 3 vols., Berlin: Akademie-Verlag, 1905–7; one volume reprint, Amsterdam: Hakkert, 1970.

[207] About A.D. 30 Cornelius Celsus wrote his multi-volume work *de medicina*, as part of his encyclopedia on all fields of knowledge. These volumes may contain what Paul could have known—though it is unlikely that he was acquainted with them.

[208] See Galen, ed. Kühn, III, 625; V, 213 for broadsides on "Zeno and Chrysippus and their whole troop [or choir, or gang? *chōros*]." Hippocrates *"de morbo sacro*, 16" ed. Littré, X, 390, apostrophizes his opponents by the word "some"; Galen calls them by name.

[209] Esp. *Timaeus* 11 DE, 69–70, 73 DE.

[210] The *Index Aristotelicus* by H. Bonitz, Berlin: Gray, 1870; repr. Darmstadt: Wissenschaftl. Buchgesellschaft, 1955, esp. pp. 386–87, opens the door to the many utterances of the philosopher on medical matters e.g. *de partibus animalium* II 10.

[211] The passages from Hippocrates' treatise on epilepsy, *de morbo sacro* 16–17, ed. Littré, X, 390 ff., and from Galen *de const. artis medicae* and *de usu partium* XII 4, ed. Kühn, which are paraphrased in the following, are those selected and printed in Greek by Lightfoot, pp. 366–67. In exceptional cases parts omitted by Lightfoot have been added. Since, however, Lightfoot reproduced the texts available at his time—i.e. texts which bear occasionally marks of corruption and are practically untranslatable—advantage was taken of the results of text criticism presented in later editions and translations of Hippocrates and Galen. Prof. Felix Heinimann, Basel, has given advice and help in tracing the best critical editions and translations of their works. To the neurologist Alfred Briellmann, M.D., in Basel I owe thanks for elucidating the medical meaning of obscure ancient utterances. But errors possibly retained in the following are not to be ascribed to either of them.

[212] About 430 B.C. Diogenes of Appollonia had elaborated upon the connection of pure air and pure knowledge. To humid air (i.e. humidified air as it is exhaled after its run through the body's muscles is completed) corresponds a putrid knowledge. The connection between atmospheric conditions, life, and thought is in Greek more easily established than in English: the one word *pneuma* ("air, wind, spirit, breath," etc.) embraces all the dimensions mentioned.

[213] I.e. the sensory and the motor parts of the body; a sharp distinction between motor and sensory was made after Hippocrates' time only.

rule by sending dispatches to the seat of awareness (or consciousness; or comprehension; *synesis*), and it is also the interpreter of the messages coming to it
from awareness. Therefore the brain both instructs and interprets. Only the
brain has a "causative" role, and holds first place among all bodily functions of
"perception" (*aistanomai*). Two opinions thus are excluded: (1) the assumption that the diaphragm does the thinking;[214] (2) the belief that the heart is
the seat of reason and the ruler of man. For, says Hippocrates, it is fortuitous
or incidental that mind and diaphragm are denoted by the same word; the heart
which senses pain cannot possibly think at the same time. In sum: according
to Hippocrates the brain is the source of thought and of awareness, and the
ruler and judge of all other things. Pain and other sensations seated here or
there in the body co-operate with the brain, but their powers are secondary.

Galen is much more specific. He writes of things "which we have learned
palpably." He is sure that the brain is the origin of power for all nerves[215]
but admits that "it is still unclear" (1) whether the brain is as much dependent
upon an (as yet unknown) other part of the body, as the nerves are dependent
on the brain; or (2) whether the brain is the very beginner, i.e. "source" of all
other parts. If the latter is true, then nothing in the body is prior or superior to
the brain. In any case Galen is convinced of one thing: that the brain precedes
(and rules? *archē estin*) the nerves. The "intelligent psyche"[216] is sown in the
brain like seed in arable soil. Its offshoot is the spinal "marrow," which in turn
has the function of the stem of a great tree. The nerves branch out from it;
thus "the whole body" receives from the brain, by means of the spinal cord
and nerves issuing from it, "first and above all, motion," then also, secondarily,
"perception" (*aisthēsis*).[217] In sum, the brain or head may be compared to an
"acropolis of the body."[218] It houses those perceptions that are valued highest
by man and are most necessary for him.

Translated into twentieth-century terminology, Hippocrates' and Galen's
neurological doctrine amounts to the following: the head, i.e. the brain, is the
coordinator and integrator of the body's sensations. Thus it is the body's chief
administrator. It not only receives, registers, arranges, and retains messages, but
much more, it also has a causative, almost creative, function: it selects,
evaluates, and steers the sensations of the body communicated to it, and decides on a proper reaction to them. In brief, it could be called a sort of computer, although it differs from factory-made electronic machines in its independence from technicians and other fallible human personnel who have
created it, and also in its creative originality.

Did Paul have these functions of the brain in mind when he pronounced that
Christ, the "head," "fills" his "body," the church? Before an answer can be given
still another alternative is to be mentioned.

---

[214] This theory reflects the derivation of the Greek verb "to think" (*phroneō*), and the corresponding noun "mind" (*phrenes*), from the noun "diaphragm, midriff" (*phrēn*).

[215] Unlike its use in Hippocrates' diction, "power" means in Galen's writings the abstract ability of function, not the ability to give direction. Probably in the wake of Aristotle's concept of po-
tentiality, power is no longer identified with dynamic actual realization, but has dwindled to the
rank of "possibility."

[216] This part of the soul is probably (with Plato *Timaeus* 69–70) distinguished from the passionate and the desiring *psychai* that are seated in the heart and below the navel respectively.

[217] Thus affirming the superiority of the motor over the sensory system.

[218] The image is Plato's. *Timaeus* 70A.

OT and rabbinical physiological and medical ideas stand nearer the views of Aristotle and the Stoics than to Plato and the Platonizing natural scientists. If OT and Talmudic doctrines on man's body possess any uniform conception at all,[219] the following may be called characteristic of "Jewish" physiology:[220] the kidneys and bowels are the seat of the strongest emotions, and the heart is the center of reasoning and will. References are made to the thoughts but not to the brain of man. Among the Hebrews as well as among most people not affected by the analytical skills of western man, each part or member of the body represents the whole. Thus each part is not a portion of a sum, or a factor of the total, nor is the body the composite of so many parts. Rather, each member is the whole body in a specific function. The heart is man who reflects, decides, and goes into action. The eye is man who perceives, desires, or scorns. The head is man who is anointed, or counted, who commands or is defeated, and who is held responsible for his deeds. In all cases, disorder or disease of the respective part or function called for the intervention of a priest rather than a natural scientist.[221] The priests were not doctors or healers, but priestly diagnosis and prescription served to keep the spread of contagious disease under control. According to the OT, the healer *par excellence* is God himself (Exod 15:26; Isa 38).

In his anthropology Paul is certainly no more independent of OT influence than elsewhere. The mutual responsibility of each member of the body, which is called to the Corinthians' attention in I Cor 12, contains not only elements of Stoic oratory but also of OT tribal solidarity. The statements made in Eph 1:18, 3:17, 4:28, about the eye, the heart, the hands,[222] are fully in line with the OT understanding of the diverse members. Also, Paul could and probably did learn from the OT, as was earlier shown, the idea expressed in Ephesians and Colossians (though not in I Cor 12) that the head exerts a one-sided control over all that is subjected to it.[223] But OT conceptuality has proven in-

[219] Since fifteen centuries and uncounted cultural influences are reflected in the OT, and since no less time and acculturation contributed to the contents of the Talmud, a unified and clear-cut "doctrine of man" cannot be expected either of the Bible or the Talmud. Also it ought not to be artificially imposed upon them.
[220] See, e.g. W. Eichrodt, *Theology of the Old Testament*, II (Philadelphia: Westminster, 1967), 231–59; von Rad, OTTh II, 336–56; Pedersen, *Israel*, I–II, 99–181. Information about rabbinical views is accessible through StB II, 447–48; A. Sandler, art. "Medizin in Bibel und Talmud," in *Jüdisches Lexikon* IV, 1 (Berlin: Jüdischer Verlag, 1930), 10–25; S. Tschernokowski, art. "Anatomie," in EJ, II, 775–84; J. Hyrtl, *Antiquitates anatomicae* (University of Vienna, 1835), pp. 92–94. Among the elements of Talmudic thought and diction that may date back to the time of Paul and that he may have learned from his teachers, several deserve mention: (a) The heart, often in combination with the kidneys, is the seat of the psyche. Hardly anything appears to be known or is said about the function of the brain and/or the spinal cord when the steering mechanism of the human body is discussed. (b) Muscles, sinews, ligaments, nerves, blood vessels are not strictly distinguished from another. The noun *gîd* serves to describe every one among the string-like parts of the body. (c) *Bāsār* (flesh) can be used as a designation of the male and the female genital parts. —These examples illustrate both Paul's dependence and independence of rabbinical teaching. Sometimes the role attributed by him to the *head* reflects OT and Platonic teaching, without showing influence of rabbinical ideas. On other occasions he speaks of the heart in a way that combines OT, Aristotelian, and rabbinical elements.
[221] Not earlier than in Sir 38:1–15 is an independent role attributed to the physician. But the same text ascribes to God alone the physicians' eventual success in diagnosis and therapeutics; for "they too will pray to the Lord . . . Their prayer is the practice of their trade" (38:14, 34).
[222] Cf. Rom 3:13–18 concerning throat, tongue, lips, mouth, feet.
[223] The one-sided relationship would be denied by Eph 1:23, if this verse referred to the church filling Christ. But the head-body image has so far—except for its pantheistic version—not given any grounds for that interpretation.

sufficient to explain Pauline utterances on the mode of control exerted specifically over the "body."

Lightfoot leads the groups of those scholars who believe that the Greek medical parallels to Eph 4:15–16; Col 2:19, etc. are sufficiently strong to elucidate what Paul has in mind. Why is Christ called the head of his body, the church? Lightfoot[224] writes, because he is "the inspiring, ruling, guiding, combining, sustaining power, the mainspring of its [i.e. the body's] activity, the centre of its unity, the seat of its life."[225] S. Tromp has shown that in their interpretations of Paul the Greek fathers emphasized the head as the center of the nervous system,[226] while Jerome was more concerned with its rule over the circulatory system and the nerves' motor function.[227] Jerome thus adds the motor to the perceptive functions, but he remains within the limits marked out by Galen. At any rate, a unifying action is ascribed by Paul to the "head" in Eph 1:10. The verbs "to fit" and "to join" together in 4:16 denote the head's operation.[228] All bodily functions of coordination and stabilization take place in the process of growing toward and from the head (4:15–16).

The evidence offered by the medical parallels is sufficiently strong for concluding thus: by his acquaintance with physiological insights Paul could ascribe to the head more than a representative and dominating function. He could attribute to it the power to perceive, to interpret, to coordinate, and to unify all that went on in the body and its several members. Because the head is the "greatest power" of the body, causation and coordination can be ascribed to nothing else. There is but one source, throne, and acropolis of all members, including their movements and perceptions—the head. In other words, by its power the head is omnipresent in the whole body; its relation to the body is as a "dynamic presence." Paul mentions emphatically the "power" working in Christ and the congregation (Eph 1:19–20; 3:16; 6:10; cf. 3:18 "May you be strong enough . . ."), and he speaks of the "indwelling" of Christ (3:17).

The term which Paul seems to prefer to describe the mode of the head's rule over the body is the verb "to fill." "Filling" means both the presence felt by the exertion of power *and* the exertion of power by immediate presence. Presence alone might be static and inoperative. Power alone might be exerted by remote control. The term "filling" appears to be Paul's way of popularizing the insights expressed in more sophisticated terms and described in more colorful imageries by natural scientists of his time. Just like the OT concept of "head," so also the scientists' views suggested to Paul a completely unilateral and irreversible relationship between head and body, or between ruler and subjects respectively. If Christ is the head then he is the "greatest power," the

[224] P. 223. The opposite view is represented, e.g. by E. Lohmeyer, KEKNT 9 (1930), 125 on Col 2:19: "Paul is completely untouched by the sharp physiological observations of hellenic and hellenistic medical science."

[225] Benoit, "Corps, tête," pp. 26–27 comes to the same result when he speaks of Christ the *principe vital, moteur, nourricier,* and of the *animation* effected by him. Wikenhauser, 179 ff. derives similar definitions from the concept "body of Christ." Pius XII, arts. 28–29, states that Christ is creator, head, sustainer, and redeemer of his mystical body.

[226] According to Chrysostom XI, nerve energy flows from the head through the body, whose organs are operated and coordinated by the head. The Holy Spirit is identified with this nerve energy.

[227] See also Richard of Mediavilla in his Commentary on the *Liber Sententiarum* II d 13, art. II, qu. 1 (ref.).

[228] See in vol. 34A the NOTES on this verse and on the parallel Col 2:19.

"source," the "beginning" or the "rule" (*archē*), the "acropolis" of all members. Thus it is impossible to assume that they "fill" him. He alone "fills" them.

Yet there also are gaps and differences that exist between the conceptions of Paul and the physicians of his time. Paul speaks of the head, not the brain. He uses no terms equivalent to the "nerves."[229] While he uses architectural, botanical, or biological metaphors, and while the concept *archē* ("beginning," or "rulership") occurs in Col 1:18, he does not speak of a "source," "offshoot," "stem," or, "tree," nor does he distinguish between motor and sense faculties. No parallels have as yet been traced in the books of scientists to the statements in Eph 5:23, 29; 4:15–16 and Col 2:19 about the capability of the "head" to "save," "provide for," "care for" or "sustain" the body. But one analogy may be important: a literal translation of Eph 4:16 and Col 2:19 would read, "from it [the head] the body grows." The astonishing idea of "growth *from* the head" can eventually be reconciled with Galen's image of the source, the arable land, the offshoot, the stem, the tree. But instead of describing the nervous system, Paul speaks of the gift of life, thus attributing more to the head than doctors ascribed to the brain. How is this difference to be explained?

A choice among three alternatives is to be made: (1) either Paul omitted from, or added to, contemporary medical views whatever best fitted his argument; (2) or the verses Eph 5:23, 29; Col 2:19 are not to be counted among the texts that use the image of the "head"; (3) or all physiological texts that have been discussed as "parallels" to Ephesians and Colossians are to be discounted as a means of interpretation.

Were Lightfoot and his followers too careless in disregarding the second and third of these alternatives? While the total Christology of Ephesians and Colossians[230] certainly implies the doctrine that Christ "inspires" the church and is the "seat of its life" (cf. "the breath of our nostrils," Lam 4:20), the adduced medical texts do not mention this function of the head.

Therefore the physiology of Paul's time cannot possibly be considered an open sesame or *passe partout* to all mysteries of the head-body imagery in the captivity letters. It may, however, serve a necessary and partial function in that the doctors' findings stand much nearer Paul's intention than the pantheism or panentheism of the Orphic, Stoic, or Gnostic sources. The medical "parallels" offer a viable alternative to the Gnosticizing interpretation of the head-body image. They provide a background to those elements in Paul's teaching which cannot be explained on the ground of OT and Jewish conceptions. They guard against a Christology and ecclesiology which would ultimately identify the One with the All, the head with the body, Christ with the church. They do not contradict OT head imagery, but are together with OT notions used to describe the authority, unifying power, and presence of Christ in the church. When used as elucidating parallels they are not only less disruptive of his theological

---

[229] If in Eph 4:16; Col 2:19 he had spoken of nerves rather than of "contacts" and "ligaments," the parallel to Hippocrates' and Galen's findings would be much more impressive. Or did he mean the nerves—albeit with a diction that reveals the layman who sooner or later stumbles when he attempts to delve into technical matters? Below, in the interpretation of 4:16, it will be shown that Paul does not intend to designate specific persons as power lines through which the head rules the body.

[230] See e.g. Eph 4:7–13; Col 3:3–4.

intention than Stoic or Gnostic influence would be, but they contribute forcefully to the recognition of the structure, government, unity, and life of the
church which is the purpose of Ephesians. The image of Christ, the head of the
body, denotes his authority over the church, his power exerted in the church,
his presence to the church, the unity of the church, and the coordinated operation of all its members.[231] It means that the church, his body, is privileged to
grow "with the growth of God" (Col 2:19c).

B   The Body

When Paul[232] calls the church a "body" (*sōma*) or "the body of Christ"[233]
he always means a living body.[234] The body is either the totality of its members, or man's external being as distinguished from his soul or mind, or a
simple designation of the whole man corresponding to the English term "person."[235] Just like any man, Christ is one body having many members.[236] Quite
frequently Paul means by "body of Christ" (or "his body"; or "my body") the
physical body of Christ which was crucified. This is sometimes made clear
either by the combination of the words "body" and "blood," "body" and
"flesh," or by the substitution of "flesh" for "body."[237] Just as "my body" can
be a synonym for the pronoun, I, "his body" is occasionally a synonym for
"him."[238]

"Man does not have a body, he is body."[239] The reference which Paul
makes in I Cor 15:3–4 to the death, burial, and resurrection of Christ reveals
that he is as much convinced of Christ's bodily resurrection on the third day
after the crucifixion as he is of the future physical resurrection of all the dead
saints (I Cor 15:12–57, esp. vss. 35–50). While he affirms that "flesh and
blood cannot inherit the kingdom" of God, he is yet convinced that the present
"physical body" will be transformed into a "spiritual body" (I Cor 15:44,
50).[240] Because "body of Christ" often denotes the crucified and raised body

---

[231] Schlier, p. 90, arrives at practically the same result though he endorses fully the Gnosticizing interpretation of Ephesians. According to him, the term "head" means (a) that Christ and
the church belong together, (b) that the church is subject to him, (c) that she grows from and to
him, (d) that she is his form of manifestation to the world, (e) that the unity of her members is assured. Unless Schlier had actually disregarded or contradicted the evidence of the Gnostic texts
with which he wanted to work, he could not have come to these conclusions.
[232] See BIBLIOGRAPHY 12 for the literature discussed in the following.
[233] I Cor 6:15–17; 10:17; 12:12–27; Rom 12:4–5; also I Cor 11:24, 29?; Eph 1:22–23; 3:6; 4:4,
15–16; 5:28–30; Col 1:18, 24; 2:19; 3:15.
[234] Homer uses *sōma* to describe a corpse, as have later writers; see Luke 17:37; Acts 9:40; Matt
27:58, and other NT texts.
[235] T. Schmidt, p. 5. See, e.g. I Cor 12:12; I Thess 5:23; I Cor 5:3; Rom 7:22–24; Rev 18:13.
[236] In I Cor 12:12, Paul speaks probably of Jesus Christ's physical body.
[237] I Cor 10:16; 11:24–25, 27; Rom 8:3; Col 1:22; Eph 2:13, 14, 16; cf. I Peter 2:24; Heb 10:10,
20. "Body" (or, "flesh") "and blood" of Christ denote specifically Christ's sacrificial death as the
eucharistic words and John 6:51–59 show. In an anthropological sense these terms are elsewhere used
for describing living men, e.g. Matt 16:17; Gal 1:16; I Cor 15:50.
[238] Rom 6:12–13; 12:1–2, etc. See Bultmann, ThNT, I, 194–201.
[239] Bultmann, ThNT I, 194; cf. the English terms "somebody," "nobody," "everybody." Bultmann is, however, not to be followed when he seeks to prove, ThNT I, 192–203, that man as
"body" means only and primarily man in his capacity to be an object to himself, i.e. to possess
self-consciousness. Man as body includes also man's factual relationhip to fellow man and the
world, i.e. his body is his total history, not his "historicity" only.
[240] Stalder, *Das Werk des Geistes*, p. 57, is probably right in understanding by "spiritual body"
a body not constituted of Spirit substance, but fully corresponding to and directed by the Spirit. See
also COMMENT II on 1:3–14.

of Christ, some interpreters of Paul are unwilling to consider the church's designation, "body of Christ," a metaphor.[241] They insist upon the physiological and historical effect of resurrection: by this event Jesus' physical body was transmuted into a spiritual one without losing contact with the world of matter and time. While the head of that body is hidden in heaven, and assures and supplies life to the body (Col 3:3–4), its members are the saints on earth and in heaven. They are the church. The church is in this case much more than "called" the body: she *is* it. And Christ himself is then not only the head of the church, as if he were its most noble and indispensable part, but he himself is head *and* body.[242] The conclusion appears inevitable, that "the church is Christ"—certainly not instead of him (the body cannot live without the head and does not displace it!) but together with him, as his complement or extension. The Gospel of John seems to support the same idea with another image: Christ is the vine, the disciples are the branches (John 15:1, 5). Thus Christ is not only the stem but also the branches and the fruit. Does Paul actually preach that in some sense "the church is Christ," an embodiment ("incorporation") of the incarnate Logos, an extension of the incarnation,[243] an expansion of his fullness over the world, *quasi altera Christi persona*, or *veluti alter Christus?*[244]

A. Schweitzer considered no riddle of Pauline theology as puzzling as that of the body of Christ.[245] But a reference to mysticism and use of the term "mystical body" do not contribute to its clarification.[246] When mysticism means that a mystery is respected which is impenetrable to sheer reasoning, it has its legitimate place in theology. But the dissolution of personal distinctions and the fusion of the one with the whole, and vice versa, which at times are characteristic of mystic thinkers, are certainly not the intent of Paul's utterances on the "body of Christ."[247]

The history of recent scholarly attempts to elucidate this mysterious term

---

[241] T. Schmidt, pp. 206–17; E. Schweizer, *Das Leben des Herrn in der Gemeinde und ihren Diensten*, Zürich: EVZ, 1946; Goossens; Mascall; Mussner; J. A. T. Robinson; Thornton; Cerfaux, *Église*, pp. 271–304; R. Schnackenburg, *The Church in the New Testament* (New York: Herder, 1965) pp. 165–76; Benoit, p. 11, place special emphasis upon the interrelation of the incarnation, crucifixion, resurrection of Christ and the essence of the church. Though they distinguish between special characteristics of the physical, the raised, the mystical body of Christ respectively, they insist upon their ultimate identity. Cf. J. Havet, "La doctrine du corps du Christ," in *Littérature et théologie pauliniennes* (Louvain: Desclée, 1960), pp. 185–216, esp. 187. The decisive texts quoted for the identification are I Cor 10:17 and 12:12–13.

[242] So, e.g. Robinson, p. 43; Schlier, p. 91; Conzelmann, p. 63. A Feuillet, pp. 275–319, is among those who reject this conclusion.

[243] Nygren, pp. 92–96; J. A. T. Robinson, pp. 49–55; Pius XII, arts. 54–55. Scholars such as H. de Lubac, *Histoire et esprit* (Paris: Aubier, 1950), esp. pp. 363–73, and R. P. C. Hanson, *Allegory and Event* (Richmond: John Knox Press, 1959), p. 194, find traces of an extended incarnation doctrine in Origen.

[244] See, e.g. Pius XII, pp. 218, 231. E. Gaugler, "Die Kirche in biblischer Sicht," *Kirchenfreund* 71 (Zürich, 1937), 97–103, 113–20, esp. 117–19, has collected and critically reviewed corresponding Roman Catholic utterances.

[245] *Mysticism of Paul the Apostle* (New York: Holt, 1931), p. 116.

[246] See, e.g. the contrasting information contained in R. Otto, *The Idea of the Holy* (London: Oxford University Press, 1957); W. James, *The Varieties of Religious Experience* (London/New York: Longmanns, 1902), pp. 379 ff.; E. Underhill, *Mysticism* (New York: Noonday, 1955), pp. 71–124; not to mention the various descriptions and assessments of mysticism offered by A. Deissmann, Bousset, Reitzenstein, Schweitzer, W. R. Inge. Dibelius, p. 65, sees in Ephesians a step from individual and esoteric to ecclesiastical mysticism. Cf. BIBLIOGRAPHY 16 and COMMENT IV B on 3:14–21 for the pertinent literature and the main alternatives.

[247] Benoit, pp. 21, 29; Pius XII, arts. 86–87.

has been repeatedly told.[248] The following alternatives are outstanding:

1. Paul may have borrowed a metaphor current in philosophy and rhetoric in which the organization and unity of a city or state were compared to the human body. The unifying function was attributed either to the stomach, the head, or something else.[249] Among others F. Mussner considers this background sufficient to explain the Pauline use of the image, though he admits that the apostle develops it beyond its original meaning.[250] The rhetorical sense of the body parable certainly yields strong support for the Pauline emphasis upon the unity of church members. In secular imagery however, the head—or any other organ of the body—is merely the noblest or most important part or function of the body, and not its very life, let alone the "savior of the body." If it was Paul's intention to underline the (horizontal) unity of the church members as much as their (vertical) union with the head, then he needed more than the popular simile of the body politic. It appears that he shared with his readers a higher, fuller, and deeper estimation of the head than that attributed to it by philosophers and orators.

2. Since about 1925, when Bultmann published a pioneering essay on the Mandaeans, German exegetes especially have, on the basis of the work done by Reitzenstein and Bousset,[251] drawn on the parallels between the diction and contents of Ephesians and Colossians on the one side, and of Gnostic doctrines on the other.[252] The "complete harmony of Ephesians with Hellenistic and Gnostic writings"[253] is said to be clear specifically, though not exclusively, in the description of the relation between head and body. As has been frequently mentioned in other contexts, it is held that Ephesians presupposes the Gnostic notion of the Aion, Prime-Anthropos, Redeemer-Revealer figure who constitutes one huge body—the head being the deity, the body the world.[254] Again, an alteration of this image by Ephesians (and Colossians) is not denied, for in (deutero-) Pauline teaching only the church, and not the world, is called Christ's body.[255] But a majority of Scandinavian, British,

---

[248] See, e.g. O. Linton's splendid report on ecclesiological studies. Brief surveys on successive interpretations of the body-image are found, e.g. in Best, pp. 83 ff.; J. A. T. Robinson, pp. 55 ff.; also M. Barth, "A Chapter on the Church, the Body of Christ," *Interpretation* 12 (1958), 131–56.

[249] Esp. in I Cor 6:15–17; 12:12–27; Rom 12:4–5 Paul may be dependent upon a fable like that told by Menenius Agrippa *Livy* II 32:8–12. The body metaphor occurs frequently in ancient literature; see, e.g. Plutarch *Coriolanus* 6; Seneca *epistulae* 95:52; earlier: Plato *resp.* v 464B (cf. VIII 828D); Aristotle *politica* I 1253A. See further references in W. L. Knox, "Parallels to the New Testament use of *sōma*," JTS 39 (1938), 243–46; idem, *St. Paul and the Church of the Gentiles*, pp. 159–63; Schlier, p. 91; Schweizer, *Neotestamentica* p. 292, n. 169; 306 ff.; J. J. Meuzelaar, pp. 150–55. In Seneca *de clementia* I 5:1, II 2:1; Tacitus *annales* I 12–13, the person who stands at the head of the community, represents its unity, and decides over its welfare, is compared to the head. A collection of Greek materials is also contained in W. Nestle, "Griechisch: APRAGMO-SYNE," in *Griechische Studien* (Stuttgart: Hannsmann, 1948), pp. 374–86 (ref.).

[250] CAK, pp. 132–40. The majority of monographs listed in BIBLIOGRAPHY 12 reject this thesis.

[251] See the literature on Gnosticism listed in BIBLIOGRAPHY 2.

[252] Bultmann, "Die Bedeutung der neuerschlossenen mandäischen und manichäischen Quellen für das Verständnis des Johannesevangeliums," ZNW 24 (1925), 100 ff.; idem, ThNT, I, 178–79; Schlier; Käsemann; Wikenhauser, pp. 232–401, esp. p. 279; Conzelmann, p. 63. Pokorný is the most outspoken non-German advocate of this interpretation.

[253] Schlier, *Christus*, p. 48.

[254] As earlier mentioned in his interpretation of Col 1:19, and especially of 2:9, Theodore of Mopsuestia understood Paul to say, "the world is Christ's body"; Schlier, p. 209, finds this meaning of "body" included in Col 2:19, but also corrected: The church is hidden in creation. The world-body and the church-body are according to Schlier two aspects of the same thing; Paul stresses in Eph 4:16 and in Col 2:19 the church aspect.

[255] See fn. 200.

French, and American biblical scholars have rejected a Gnostic explanation for the concept "body." In section IV B of the Introduction it was shown that C. Colpe and H.-M. Schenke[256] have in recent years completely ruled out any dependence of the Ephesian and Colossian head-body concept upon Gnosticism. The Chenoboskion finds of Gnostic texts enabled them to prove that the god Aion, the Prime-Anthropos, and the Redeemer-Revealer occur only in separate sources (or strata of sources), and were originally distinct mythical figures. They were melted into one person no earlier than in Mani's system toward the end of the third century. Therefore, however late in the first or second century Ephesians may have been written and to whomever the epistle is ascribed, it cannot have used the final (third-century) Gnostic concept of the Prime-Anthropos body upon which the arguments of Bultmann and his followers rest. Together with any dependence on Gnosticism, the assumption is also to be ruled out that Ephesians teaches an ultimate identity of the deity and its body, i.e. of Christ and the church. As stated before, this epistle never affirms that the church is Christ.[257] Rather, the church is called the "new man created in him" and "by him." She is his bride, his beloved (2:15, 5:22–33). Thus she is always his partner. Therefore this epistle is not dependent upon, or in full harmony with, Gnosticism.

3. The implications of the term "body," like those regarding the "head," may at least in part be based upon OT notions. The possible background of the body-of-Christ concept was first suggested by T. Schmidt in 1919. L. Deimel took up the challenge in 1940, and he was followed by the Scandinavians Percy, Hanson, Dahl. Later the same hypothesis was elaborated upon in various ways by Thornton, Goossens, J. A. T. Robinson, Benoit, Cerfaux, Dubarle, Quispel, Schoeps, and others.[258] Certainly it had to be recognized that the OT does not contain the concept "body" in a sense corresponding to its Christological and ecclesiastical meaning in the Pauline writings, but the OT or Semitic notion of "corporate personality"[259] appeared sufficient to solve two riddles at the same time: the meaning of the "in Christ" formula, and the sense of "body of Christ."[260] Christ was understood to fulfill the role of the patriarchs, kings, and other representative figures in whom each Israelite saw incorporated

[256] Cf. Hegermann, Schöpfungsmittler, pp. 155 ff.

[257] Identification is forcefully rejected, e.g. in Mystici Corporis, arts. 86–87, and by Benoit, pp. 21–22. But it is suggested by Od Sol. xxxi:8 ff; xxxvi:1–8; cf. 1QH ii 1–5. Cf. Schille, Hymnen, p. 84, "The initiated himself now becomes the revealer and gathers his own through his word and redeems them. At this place the early Christian congregation was unable to follow. It had to protest energetically"; cf. pp. 51–52. Many OT psalms introduce the praise of salvation from death by the words "In David." David is probably mentioned as the prototype of the rescued, but he does not take the place of the redeemer.

[258] E.g. T. Schmidt, pp. 245 ff.; Deimel, pp. 139 ff.; Percy, Leib Christi, pp. 38–43, 50; Percy, pp. 69, 108–13; ZNW 43 (1950–51), 191–93; Hanson, pp. 65–70, 87, 114–16, 159–60; Dahl, pp. 224–27, 268, 325; Thornton, chs. 9–10, esp. pp. 298–303; Benoit, p. 11; Cerfaux, Église, pp. 305–19; Quispel, EJb 22 (1953), 195–234, esp. 223 ff.; H. J. Schoeps, Theologie und Geschichte des Judenchristentums (Tübingen: Mohr, 1949), p. 99; Urgemeinde-Judenchristentum-Gnosis (Tübingen: Mohr, 1956), pp. 24, 42, 49; M. Meinertz, Theologie des NT, II (Bonn: Hanstein, 1950), 156; Hegermann, Schöpfungsmittler, p. 153; E. Schweizer, Neotestamentica, pp. 374–85, 305, 310; Best, passim.

[259] As developed in the wake of Pedersen's psychologic and sociopsychologic approach to the mysteries of Israel, Its Life and Its Culture, I–IV; also by H. W. Robinson, "The Hebrew Concept of Corporate Personality," BhZNW 66 (1936), 49–62; T. W. Manson, The Servant Messiah, Cambridge University Press, 1953, and others.

[260] The parallel use of the term "one body in Christ" and "body of Christ" in Rom 12:5 and I Cor 12:27 and the concurrent references to the "body of Christ" and the being "in Christ" in Ephesians and Colossians suggest that both problems are mutually inherent. Earlier it was observed that the meaning of the Pauline formula "in Christ" may be influenced, e.g. by the OT promise of the blessing given to many nations "in Abraham" (Gen 12:3; 18:18; Gal 3:8).

his own life, history, and salvation. Soon enough links were discovered in the intertestamental period to give substance to the somewhat abstract idea of corporate representation by an individual. Either Philo's doctrines of the heavenly man and the world as body;[261] or rabbinic and apocryphal concepts of Adam, the vessel of the souls;[262] or Wisdom speculations,[263] or extensive interpretations of the image of God (Gen 1:26–27);[264] or the concept of the heavenly city;[265] or a combination of several of these elements have been understood as a key to Paul. At a later stage, these elements contributed to the formation of the Gnostic myth. Indeed to a large extent Gnosticism can be explained as an offshoot from Samaritan and other Jewish heterodox soil, which was watered by streams of vulgarized philosophy, astrology, Platonism, and which finally developed the fruit displayed by the great systems of Valentinus, Basilides, and Mani. However, the question must be asked: Did perhaps Ephesians and Colossians anticipate a Gnosticizing interpretation of certain OT and Jewish elements that contributed to the formation of classic Gnosticism? A positive answer is suggested by many features of the language and contents of Ephesians and Colossians—yet not by the term "body of Christ" or by the role which this concept plays in Paul's utterances on baptism, the Lord's supper, and marriage.[266] If Paul had called the church the people, tribe, or family of Christ, the OT derivation of his language would be evident. But when the church is designated as his "body," a term is used that is foreign to the OT and must stem from another source.

4. E. J. Rawlinson[267] has attempted to prove that the key to the body-of-Christ utterances is Paul's sacramental, especially his eucharistic, theology as represented by I Cor 10:16–17. In Comment XVI on Eph 1:3–14 other scholars have been mentioned who, mainly on the ground of I Cor 12:12–13, attribute to baptism the creative power of forming the body or implementing it by the incorporation of new members. The breaking of the bread, the participation in the body of Christ, and the essence or existence of the faithful as one body are so closely linked together that not only a revelatory and proclamatory, but also a causative function appears to be ascribed to the eucharist (and/or to baptism). However, in Ephesians the Lord's Supper is never explicitly mentioned, though it is certainly presupposed. Only if 2:13–16 were understood as an excursus on the Lord's Supper and not on the cross, would it be necessary to connect the body of Christ, the church, and the new man directly with the eucharistic body. Baptism is explicitly mentioned in 4:5, but neither this verse nor the possible implicit reference to baptism in the verb "sealing" (1:13) is sufficient evidence for stating that the origin of the body-of-Christ concept must be sacramental.

[261] See Pokorný, p. 59, for a summary and references.
[262] E.g. Exod Rabb. 40:3. See W. D. Davies, PRJ, pp. 36–57, and R. Jewett, *Paul's Anthropological Terms*, pp. 239–45, for a collection and discussion of the available material.
[263] E.g. Quispel, EJb 22 (1953), 195–234, esp. 202 ff.
[264] Cf. J. Jervell, *Imago Dei*, FRLANT N.F. 58 (1960), 197–213; Schenke, GMG, pp. 72–93, 121–43.
[265] So esp. Cerfaux, *Église*, pp. 306–12.   [266] I Cor 10:16–17; 12:12–13; Eph 5:22–33.
[267] Rawlinson, pp. 225 ff; cf. T. Schmidt, pp. 201–5; Cerfaux, *Église*, pp. 224–26; C. O'Grady, "The Church the Body of Christ in the Theology of Karl Barth and in Catholic Theology," ITQ 35 (1968), 3–21, esp. 15–17; idem, *The Church in the Theology of Karl Barth* (Washington: Corpus Books, 1968), pp. 258–65, esp. 264. The concept of sacramental incorporation is fully unfolded, e.g. by Mascall, pp. 77–200, and the Church of Scotland's *Interim Report on Baptism*, I, 5, 16, 26 ff, 53.

5. C. Chavasse[268] has focused attention upon Eph 5:22–33: through love bridegroom and bride become "one body" or, in the terms of Gen 2:24, "one flesh." Man's love of "his own body" is considered an analogy to the love he owes his wife. Love of one's wife is, in turn, identified with love of the self. The Genesis text describing the union of husband and wife is understood allegorically; Paul interprets it to describe Christ's relationship to the church.[269] There are many OT precedents for describing the covenant between God and Israel with metaphors from the realm of courtship and marriage, and for measuring matrimonial fidelity by the yardstick of God's faithfulness to man.[270] Other "parallels" are found in the celebration of the *hieros gamos* in ancient Near Eastern cults and in the myths of syzygies endorsed by some Gnostics.[271] But these problems will have to be faced in the interpretation of Eph 5:22–33 and not before. For the present context only one thing is important: the epistle to the Ephesians contains in its fifth chapter a comment on the term "body of Christ" which makes its meaning dependent upon the love of Christ shown in his self-offering on behalf of man. Why and how were men made "his body"? Not simply because he is "head" in the OT sense of ruler, but because he has established his rulership by no means other than love and sacrifice. Without love and without the historic event of the cross there would be no body and no members of Christ. Gnosticism treats the ingathering of dispersed members through the descending and ascending Redeemer, but the Redeemer is not a historic figure and he does not die; his body is restored rather than created. Ephesians treats the "creation of a single new man" and of "becoming one flesh" (2:15; 5:31). Only with the death of Christ did this body, the bride of Christ made of Jews and Gentiles, come into being, just as according to Paul Eve was made "one flesh" with Adam only through their union.[272] If it took a love so unique as that proven by Christ in his death (5:25) to create his body and to make Christ and the church "one flesh," then Paul could not derive the body image from literature that does not speak of the love shown on the cross, i.e. from the OT, Gnosticism, or Jewish intertestamental Adam and Wisdom speculations. Thus it becomes clear why principalities and powers or "all things" are never called Christ's body, though he is their head.[273] Neither can the church be considered an extended or expanding incarnation: for though Christ's incarnation is the presupposition of his death, only the death of Christ is the means and moment of the church's formation. In Eph 2:13–16 precisely this is affirmed. Paul has in this case neither derived the term "body" (of Christ) from any source nor applied it to a new object. Rather he has created it to interpret the creative effect of Christ's death.[274] But still another aspect of the term "body" deserves consideration.

[268] Cf. Odo Casel, "Glaube, Gnosis und Mysterium," JbLW 15 (1941), 290–91.
[269] Eph 5:28–32; cf. I Cor 6:16–17.
[270] Hosea, *passim;* Jer 2:2; 31:32; Isa 54:5–8; Ezek 16; 23; cf. the rabbinical and Christian allegorical interpretation of the Song of Songs.
[271] Cf. Schlier, *Christus,* pp. 60–75; Schlier, pp. 264–76.
[272] Paul is not alluding in the authentic text of Eph 5:30 to Gen 2:21–23, i.e. to the creation of Eve from Adam's rib and the hailing of Eve as "bone of my bones, flesh of my flesh."
[273] Heb 2:16, "For it was not the angels that he took to himself; he took to himself the descendants of Abraham," cf. JB.
[274] As E. Schweizer in his essays on the Church, the Body of Christ, has affirmed.

6. K. Barth[275] and E. Schweizer[276] explain the term "body of Christ" in a functional sense. It expresses not only the church's dependence upon, and connection with, Christ, her life and savior, but also her commission in and toward the world. Indeed, in Hebrew anthropology the soul is the life kindled by the Spirit which God gave (Gen 2:7); and man's body is the public *manifestation* of the life that is in man. In fn. 189 references to the close connection between head and soul were quoted. Paul himself calls Christ not only "the head" but also "the life" of the church (Col 3:3–4), and consequently ascribes to the head not only the dominion over, and integration of, the body, but also its sustenance (Eph 4:16; 5:29; Col 2:19). Therefore his designation of the church as the "body of Christ" can and must make it possible to interpret this phrase as meaning that the church is the *manifestation of Christ to the world*.[277] Käsemann[278] went only so far as to call the church in Ephesians "the sphere of Christ's ubiquity and at the same time the instrument of his omnipotence." Schlier[279] has been more specific: "The church is the body of Christ which through the Spirit presents itself on the cross and in heaven." Less cryptic is another formulation of Schlier's:[280] "The church is the mode of the head's appearance in the cosmos." W. Robinson writes, "The Church is Christ manifested in the flesh,"[281] and L. Cerfaux gives one chapter the title, "L'église, manifestation du mystère du Christ."[282] Common to these interpretations of the term "body of Christ" is (1) their dynamic character (as indicated by the terms "mission" and "manifestation"), (2) the understanding of the church as an activity of Christ, and (3) the inclusion of the world in the definition of the church. According to these descriptions the church exists only inasmuch as an event takes place—the miracle of the living Christ's self-revelation to the world.[283] When Christ is the subject of any statement seeking to define the church, and when the world is included in her definition as both the field and the necessary beneficiary of the blessing bestowed upon her, then justice is done to "Christ" the "head": now Christ's headship over the world no longer

[275] *Church Dogmatics*, IV:1–3, esp. IV:1, pp. 664–65. Cf. O'Grady, *The Church in the Theology of Karl Barth*, pp. 262–63.
[276] "The Church as the Missionary Body of Christ," NTS 8 (1961), 1–11; Gabathuler, esp. pp. 144–49, follows Schweizer's lead. Cf. also Käsemann, *Perspectives*, pp. 105–8 and esp. 117, and R. A. Batey, *New Testament Nuptial Imagery* (Leiden: Brill, 1971), p. 35. The latter defines the meaning of "body of Christ" by calling the church "the visible locus of Christ's personal presence in history at the level of human experience and activity."
[277] According to J. Luzzi, "Solidaridad del soma tou Jristou," *Ciencia y Fé* 16 (Buenos Aires, 1960), 3–45; cf. 15 (1959), 451–73, the church is the external manifestation of the person of Christ himself (ref.).
[278] RGG, II, 518.
[279] In H. Schlier and P. Warnach, *Die Kirche im Epheserbrief* (Münster: Aschendorff, 1949), p. 88.
[280] Schlier, p. 94.
[281] *The Biblical Doctrine of the Church* (St. Louis: Bethany, 1948), p. 101.
[282] *Église*, pp. 293 ff. Formulations such as those just quoted are explicitly rejected, e.g. by Percy, *Leib Christi*, pp. 17, 50; Best, p. 188; Deimel, *passim*. Though Meuzelaar, pp. 148, 156, 172 lays major emphasis upon the practical (i.e. ethical as opposed to ontological) meaning of the term "body of Christ," he appears unwilling to take seriously the missionary aspect of unity of Jews and Gentiles in the one body, see pp. 17–18. But Schweizer, *Neotestamentica*, pp. 292, 314, 323–29, states plainly, "As Christ's body the church is the place at which Christ seeks and serves the world. . . . Even in the utterances about the body of Christ, God himself and his march through the world are at the center of interest. . . . It is just in his body, the church, that Christ is permeating the world."
[283] Cf. the interpretation of wisdom and knowledge in COMMENT X on 1:3–14. In Best's excellent book, p. 182, the cosmic dimension of the body-of-Christ metaphor is sorely neglected and flatly denied.

stands in tension with his being head of his body, the church (1:22–23). The servant function of the body is brought to light, and an ontology of the church will never be sought apart from, or at the cost of, the description of the church's activity in the world. The church will seek to live "for the world," rather than segregate herself from the world, at its expense, or for its subjugation. Now she cannot consider herself as an end in herself, and will desist from claiming identity with Christ. Christ is "in" the church and the church is "in" him and "with" him (Rom 8). But her greatest honor is to be his covenant partner, that is, a distinct person who is loved by him, and who serves the demonstration of his love to the world.

A concluding definition of the church, the body of Christ,[284] would combine the arguments found in the last two points. The church is the self-manifestation of the crucified and risen Jesus Christ to all powers, all things, all men. "For his own sake" and/or "with his own self" he fills the church in order to reach all creatures.[285] She is proof and manifestation of the living Christ who is "enthroned at God's right hand in the heavens" (1:20), that is, who shows the authority and strength which was given to him to live and make alive, and who demonstrates his presence on earth, as will be shown in 4:7–12.

More will be said about the church later when Ephesians mentions the cross and resurrection, the Spirit and spiritual gifts, and the worship, building, and growth of the church. It will also be indispensable, once again,[286] to speak of the people of God as composed of Jews and Gentiles. The metaphor "body of Christ" is complemented by those that suggest a building, a plantation, a bride, and many others.[287] The additional metaphors strengthen the body-of-Christ image where it is deficient or correct it where it is prone to over or mis-interpretation. The body metaphor does not monopolize the discussion and perhaps does not even have a supreme position. The term "people of God" may be clearer and more comprehensive, though it is less apt to emphasize the presence of God. But the preliminary definition of the church just given may suffice to interpret the term "his [Christ's] body" in Eph 1:23. The essential role ascribed in this definition to Christ, to his self-manifestation, to mission, and to the world is certainly preferable to the obscure term "mystical body." Also, this definition avoids the dangerous reference to the "mystery of the church" which tends to replace the concern for the manifested "secret." With it are excluded any reliance upon individual status, habitus, or salvation, and every collective egotism or imperialist presumption of the church and her members.

A concluding survey on the meanings attributed to the noun "fullness," and the verb "to fulfill" will serve to test the findings regarding "head" and "body." It may appear unfeasible to pair a non-Gnostic meaning for the Pauline terms "head" and "body" with a Gnostic sense of "fullness," but only an unprejudiced approach to the special problems posed by this term can lead to any judgment in this matter.

---

[284] Another summary of definitions is given by Schlier, p. 279.
[285] See the philological discussion in the NOTE on "filling" in 1:23, esp. on the middle genus of the verb found in the Greek text.
[286] Cf. the NOTE on "appropriation" in 1:11 and COMMENT XIV on 1:3–14.
[287] P. Minear enumerates close to one hundred; cf. J. R. Nelson and L. Williamson.

C Fullness

The noun "fullness"[288] occurs six times in the uncontested Pauline epistles
and equally often in Ephesians and Colossians.[289] While the reference to
"the days of fulfillment" (lit. "fullness of time") in Eph 1:10 corresponds to
the similar concept in Gal 4:4, it has often been assumed that the other
Ephesians and Colossians passages presuppose a mystical or mythical (Gnostic?) sense which is different from the meanings proper to the noun in I
Corinthians and Romans: Ephesians and Colossians speak of a fullness of
God, of Christ, or of the church, which seems to have but one NT parallel,
John 1:16: "From his fullness we have taken grace upon grace."[290] The context of the Johannine passage refers to the *logos,* i.e. to Jesus Christ, the Son
of God, who dwells among men, and to the revelation of his glory—that glory
of the Father which is full of grace and truth (John 1:14). While in the Pauline homologoumena the verb "to fill" seems to present no problems beyond
those posed by its meanings in LXX, some of the Ephesian and Colossian passages present a special puzzle.[291] If the noun and the verb in Ephesians and
Colossians had a sense totally disconnected from, or contradictory to, that
found in the other Pauline writings, this might be considered an argument
against the authenticity of these two particular epistles of captivity.[292] But it
is possible that in both epistles Paul took up a key word familiar to his readers
and let it come back at them with a modified content. Percy,[293] in turn, is
convinced that Paul himself developed and unfolded the meaning of this term,
and that there is no reason to credit the Ephesians (though perhaps the Colossians)[294] with attributing a special technical meaning to "fullness" or "filling."
We repeat what appears certain: Colossians places emphasis upon the filling of
Christ by God, Ephesians upon the filling of the church and all things by Christ;
still, neither of the two epistles excludes what is specifically emphasized by the
other.[295]

The two alternatives for interpreting the history and meaning of "fullness"
and "filling" that are presented here already have been encountered in the

---

[288] Cf. COMMENT XIII on 1:3–14 and the NOTE on the active and passive senses of fullness in
1:23. See also BIBLIOGRAPHY 12.

[289] I Cor 10:26, what fills the earth (Ps 24:1); Gal 4:4, the time of fulfillment; Rom 11:12, 25,
the full number of Jews and Gentiles; 13:10, fulfillment or sum of the law; 15:29, abundance of
Christ's blessing; Eph 1:10, days of fulfillment; 1:23, the church filled by Christ; 3:19, the saints
filled by God's fullness; 4:13, the perfection (lit. "fullness") of the Messiah; Col 1:19, the fullness residing in Christ; 2:19, the fullness of the deity residing in Christ; cf. Ignatius' opening in
his letters to the Ephesians and to the Trallians.

[290] Lightfoot, p. 329, explains this coincidence by the fact that the Gospel of John was written
for the same readers as Ephesians.

[291] The contents of Eph 5:18 ("filled with Spirit"); Col 1:9 ("filled with knowledge"); 1:25
("fulfilling the word of God"); 4:17 ("fulfilling a service"), correspond to analogous NT and
Pauline usages, except that the term "fulfilling the Scripture" is missing. The latter idiom is also
absent from Hebrews, I Peter, the Pastoral and Johannine epistles, and Revelation. But the "filling
of all things" and "of the saints" mentioned in Eph 1:23; 3:19; 4:10; Col 2:10; 4:12 has no NT
parallels.

[292] Mitton, pp. 94–97, considers the difference a fact—but in Ephesians only, not in Colossians.
Therefore he denies authenticity to Ephesians but maintains it for Colossians.

[293] Percy p. 78; he refers to Rom 15:14, 29.

[294] See G. Bornkamm, "Die Häresie des Kolosserbriefes," TLz 73 (1948), 11 ff.; repr. in *Das
Ende des Gesetzes* (Munich: Kaiser, 1952), pp. 139–56, esp. 139–44.

[295] According to the interpretation of Feuillet and others; see fn. 70.

sections on head and body: the Gnostic (or anti-Gnostic) origin and the root in the OT and Jewish theology have to be taken up again. It is possible that there exists a connection between "fullness" and the "dividing wall" mentioned in Eph 2:14, or between fullness and the principalities and powers in 1:21, etc. How Gnostic and OT elements could be combined is revealed by the references which Gnostic writers make to OT texts.[296]

1. In Gnostic writings, especially of the Valentinian school,[297] the term *plērōma*, "fullness," plays an important role. It has acquired the nature of a technical term and occupies a key position in the special vocabulary used to describe the mysteries of the cosmos, the soul, and redemption. Actually, there is more than just one concept of *plērōma* which the Colossians, Ephesians, Paul, and the Valentinians might have inherited from a common source or tradition and transmuted to serve their respective purposes. No fewer than seven versions of the Gnostic concept have been counted among the Valentinians alone.[298] These or other meanings are shifted around in kaleidoscopic fashion,[299] and only a selection is to be mentioned here:

Plērōma is the totality of divine attributes, powers, manifestations (Mind, Truth, Logos, Life . . . Sophia, a total of thirty) that emanate by means of copulations (*syzygies*) from Aion, the Forefather, and Depth. These emanations are personified; they are called Aions. *Plērōma* is (a) the name of their group as a whole.[300] The associated heavenly Aions stand opposite the lower sphere or power realm of Void (*kenōma*) or Deficiency (*hysterēma*), just as the Platonic ideas stand opposite the phenomenal world, the spiritual realm to the material, light to darkness, the good to the bad. The lower sphere originated as a result of the unholy passions of Wisdom which resulted in abortion. Out of elements from the aborted sphere the Demiurge eventually created the material world; the latter is dominated by the world rulers (*archontes*) or the law. The crisis in the *plērōma* to which the material world owes its existence finds ontic expression in a personified Boundary or Fence (*horos*) which now forms an impenetrable wall between the *plērōma* and the world of *hysterēma* or *kenōma* in which man lives.[301] *Plērōma* has thus (b) become the name of a geographical place which originally was perfect and good but was eventually disturbed by Wisdom's misbehavior. But new emanations occur

[296] Esp. to Gen 1:26–27; 3:1–13; 6:1–4.

[297] See, e.g. Irenaeus *adv. haer.* I 1–5; 11:1, 3, 5; III 11:1; Hippol. VI 29–34; Clement of Alexandria *excerpta ex Theodoto* 32–33, 42; Origen *in Ioannem* XIII 4. Among the Chenoboskion documents, esp. the Barbelo-Gnostic *Apogryphon of John* and the *Gospel of Truth* are important primary sources of information that permit a check on the picture of the heretics offered by the church fathers. For a summary discussion of these materials see, e.g. H. Jonas, *Gnosis und spätantiker Geist*, I, 2d rev. ed. (Göttingen: Vandenhoeck, 1954), 362–75; *The Gnostic Religion*, pp. 40–47, 179–205; Kehl, pp. 109–24. The most important recent books on Gnosticism are found among the monographs listed in BIBLIOGRAPHY 2. Grant, *Gnosticism*, pp. 163–81, offers a translation of some of the texts describing the system of the Valentinian Ptolemaeus.

[298] Jonas, *Gnostic Religion*, p. 178.

[299] Perhaps the diverse Valentinian *plērōma* doctrines originated with Cerinthus. Cerinthus in turn may or may not have been influenced by the Colossian heresy or an equivalent movement. Again, the Naassenes and Ophites developed different concepts of *plērōma*, as Lightfoot, pp. 107–13, 330–39, observes.

[300] Hippolytus' Docetics (VIII 9–10) speak of "the plērōma of the entire aions."

[301] Schlier's interpretation of the dividing wall (Eph 2:14) is determined by his collection of manifold Gnosticizing or Gnostic utterances on this cosmic wall; see *Christus*, pp. 19–26; Schlier, pp. 124–33.

forming Christ, the Holy Spirit, and the Lower Wisdom (*achamōth*), so that now the dividing wall is penetrated. The lower world, created so miserably, is offered redemption by the appearance of a new Aion, Jesus, "the perfect fruit of the *plērōma*." He leads the human spirits[302] that were imprisoned in matter back into the *plērōma*. The *plērōma* becomes the "bridal chamber" in which Jesus is married to Sophia, and the spirits to the angels. *Plērōma* is thus (c) also the sphere and fact of man's salvation which is effected by his reunion with his divine origin.[303] However, occasionally *plērōma* is also (d) a designation of individual Aions!

It is obvious that these mythological, cosmological, angelological, and soteriological meanings are far more specific than the earlier mentioned magic and Stoic concepts,[304] and also than the Ophite understanding of *plērōma*.[305] Before and after the development of the Valentinian systems *plērōma* could also designate (e) the "One and All," the deity and man in their mutual interdependence and totality.[306] In some Gnostic thought only—but apparently not in Marcion's and Basilides' theology, cosmology, and soteriology—*plērōma* had attained the key position just described. In brief, it may have denoted the spiritual dimensions of being, especially the angelic/demonic background of human existence, fall, and redemption.[307]

The explicit references of Gnostic writings to Ephesians and Colossians demonstrate that the Gnostics intended to elaborate on Paul's discussion of *plērōma*. But their pretension of being inspired by Paul does not prove Paul's acquaintance with, or dependence upon, one or another of the manifold senses of *plērōma* they unfold. There is no evidence that before the second century A.D. *plērōma* was used in the technical or mythological sense it possesses in Gnostic literature. Even if there were absolutely no other way to explain Ephesians and Colossians except as the oldest historical evidence of the Gnostic meaning or meanings of *plērōma*, the historical presuppositions of Käsemann, Schlier, Pokorný and others would remain contestable. Cf. section III B of the Introduction.

This need not mean that the great effort spent over the Gnostic interpretation of the Pauline antilegoumena has been in vain. For it has shown that in Hellenistic Greek the word *plērōma* may well mean something specific, e.g. a spiritual force as opposed to a gaping void or deficiency, an ontic presence which operates and is experienced in powerful actions and events, a force

---

[302] Not "souls," for soul and spirit are distinguished: "Sophia is called Spirit, the Demiurge, Soul," Hippol. VI 34:1. Similarly in I Cor 15:44-46 the "psychic man" is identified with the created fleshly man. According to Gnostic teaching only the spirit of man, i.e. the spiritual or inner man, is of divine origin and nature, and will be reunited with the deity.

[303] The Docetic heretics described by Hippolytus consider Christ the product of all aions and identify the salvation of the perfect Gnostic with his participation in the *plērōma*. In the *Pistis Sophia*, "revelation" of the mystery and of the *plērōma* on one side, and the act of "perfecting in every *plērōma*, in every perfection, and in every mystery" on the other are parallels; perhaps they are identified. Once Mary is called "the *plērōma* of all the *plērōmata* and the perfection of all the perfections." For references see e.g. Lightfoot, pp. 338-39.

[304] See COMMENT V B.

[305] Among the Peratae, a sister movement of the Naassenes, the totality of the three spheres of the universe, i.e. the uncreated, the self-creating, and the created spheres, including their three gods, Words, Minds, and Men, is comprehended in the three natures of "Christ." Col 1:19; 2:9 is understood to treat the "fullness" of all these three assembled in Christ. Hippol. V 12.

[306] *Corp. Herm.* XII 15.

[307] This way the term is explained by Schlier, pp. 96-99, and Pokorný, pp. 70-76.

of perfection overcoming the imperfect, a pre-cosmic or trans-cosmic essence that is manifested in human life, history, salvation, perhaps also in abounding riches that can be shared by many without loss of substance. In their own way the Gnostics may have tried, a century after Paul and later, to specify what Paul himself had taken up from a pre-Gnostic tradition and formulated with the suggestive Greek terms "fullness" and "fulfill."

Nevertheless they contradicted him at decisive points. Paul gives no hint—least of all in Philip 2:6–11—of God's deprivation by an event connected with the origin of the *plērōma;* neither does he intimate a reconstitution of the one God by the work of redemption. Yet Gnostic sources speak of a rupture in the deity and an impairment of divine unity by the loss of substance that accompanies the emanation of Aions, the disorder in their ranks, and the building of a cosmic wall, behind which the Demiurge, the world rulers, law, matter, and death go about their miserable business. According to the Gnostics, the reconstruction of the *plērōma* by the emanation of a new Aion, and the ingathering of the dispersed light or spiritual elements among mankind is an event by which the deity itself is restored.[308] The redeemer has to go out from the *plērōma* and leave it behind in order to become man's savior and later return to the heavenly sphere.[309] The threatening dualistic element which was inherent—above all—in the Gnostic concepts of *plērōma* is absent from Paul. The alternative to the Gnostic interpretation of Ephesians and Colossians will show why dualism found no place in Paul's teaching.

2. An essay by G. Münderlein[310] has become the outstanding manifesto for an interpretation of *plērōma* which is based upon the OT and equates it with the concepts of the *shekina* (glorious presence), spirit or wisdom of God. Benoit, Cerfaux, Feuillet, Meiklinger, Meuzelaar, Ernst, Kehl, and others have been working along the same lines. According to the OT the "glory" of God "fills" not only the house of God[311] but also the earth.[312] Jeremiah (4:12) speaks of a wind (spirit) of judgment that is "filling," or full of, something. Wisd Sol 1:7 describes the Spirit of the Lord who "fills the world," "holds all things together," and "knows what is said." Ps 119:64 praises the "steadfast love" of God of which "the earth is full"; Ps 48:10 extols the "name" and "praise of God" that "fill" the ends of the earth. Jer 23:23–24 caps all these statements by the bold assertion that God, whether he is near or far away, "fills" (in person) "heaven and earth." Benoit[313] considers these utterances parallel to the Stoic affirmations of God's ubiquity. Indeed, a certain resemblance cannot be denied—as long as it is noted at the same time that there is no identification of the One and All, nor any mutual dependence between them. Not immanence but the marvelous appearance and work of God the creator, the judge, and the redeemer is praised in the OT. While several sapiential statements on wisdom do resemble the Stoic doctrine of *logos* or *nous* (word, spirit, reason), in later Jewish theology a terminology prevails

---

[308] Jonas, *The Gnostic Religion*, pp. 40–46.   [309] Gabathuler, p. 99.
[310] NTS 8 (1962), 264–76. Münderlein takes up a suggestion made by S. Aalen.
[311] Isa 6:1; Ezek 43:5; 44:4; Hag 2:7.
[312] Isa 6:3; Ps 72:19. See H. U. von Balthasar, *Herrlichkeit*, III 2, Einsiedeln: Johannes, 1967.
[313] Pp. 35–36, in following Dupont, *Gnosis* (see BIBLIOGRAPHY 2).

that marks a distinction from philosophical axioms: God's name or the *shekina* is the means by which the majestic creator and judge proves himself present among his creatures.[314] The praise of the dynamic self-presentation or appearance of God, rather than the observation of a static universal presence, lies at the core of Jewish theology.

In the OT passages just quoted, God's presence and manifestation are always described by a form of the verb "to fill" or by the adjective "full"—but never by the noun "fullness." In the OT this noun is never used to denote an action or attribute of God, but occurs to designate the creatures that "fill" the earth[315] and the sea.[316] In I Cor 10:26 Paul quotes one of these passages, Ps 24:1. He reveals his acquaintance with Wisdom and rabbinic literature, while paralleling Philo's thought,[317] when he leans upon the dynamic character of the verb "to fill" and lets this dynamism determine the meaning of the noun "fullness." Certainly he differs from OT usage in using the noun to describe the essence, glory, power, and presence of God or Christ. But as long as OT ways of thought are considered relevant, the noun means the miracle, process, and the event of filling—not (as in Gnosticism) a sum of attributes, a sphere, a locality. Thus Paul has probably understood "fullness" in line with OT thinking. "Fullness" is the result of a one-sided movement: God fills his house or the earth with his presence, so that his "fullness" resides at the chosen place and manifests itself with power. By his authorization, various creatures fill the dry land and the sea; again this includes the notion of dominion, and of the dynamic presence. Therefore, if the puzzling term "fullness" in Ephesians and Colossians has any roots in OT theology and diction, it must mean the act by which God makes his power and presence felt.

It appears likely that in Ephesians and Colossians a function is attributed to Christ and the church which OT passages ascribed to the house of God, for the metaphor of indwelling and the building imagery is applied to both Christ and the church, his body, in connection with *plērōma* statements.[318] Münderlein[319] considers *plērōma* in Pauline diction an attribute of God, i.e. a circumscription of the Holy Spirit; R. Fuller[320] calls *plērōma* a *kyrios* name.

---

[314] Cf. I Kings 8:16; Sir 24:4, 8, 11; I Enoch 49; more references in StB, II, 314–15; Moore, I 371, 434 ff. Regarding the *merkabah* mysticism and the resemblance between the Merkabah and its perception by vision on one side, and the Gnostic *plērōma* and the ascent of the soul on the other, see G. Scholem, "Judaism and Gnosticism," *Dartmouth College Comparative Studies Center Report* (Hanover, N.H.: Dartmouth College, 1966), pp. 139–45, esp. 142. See also G. Scholem, *Major Trends in Jewish Mysticism*, New York: Scholem, 1946.

[315] Pss 24:1; 50:12; 89:11; 104:24; Jer 8:16; 47:2; Ezek 12:19; 19:7; 30:12; 32:15; cf. the verbal description of their "filling the land" (Gen 1:22, 28; 9:1, 7). According to Ps 80:9 "the vine" brought by God from Egypt "fills the land."

[316] Pss 96:11 98:7; I Chron 16:32. Those LXX passages that call creatures the *plērōma* of the earth, i.e. that which "fills" the earth, repudiate a restriction which Lightfoot, pp. 323–26 imposed upon the meaning of *plērōma*. He had obviously not considered the evidence of the LXX when he stated, "It is objectionable to give an active sense to *plērōma* under any circumstances," p. 326.

[317] According to Philo the *logos* is filled by God, but—in contrast to the Stoics—the world is not God and does not comprehend God in itself, *migr. Abr.* 179. God contains all things in himself but is contained in none, for he is "full of himself," self-sufficient, while other things are poor, lonely, and void. Thus God himself is the one-and-all, *legum allegoriae* I 44; cf. *de somniis* I 182–85. He conveys to the *logos* the incorporeal powers of creation, dominion, legislation, mercy, etc. by which the *logos* directs the universe, *somn.* I 62; cf. *de fuga et inventione* 94–105. See Feuillet, p. 290.

[318] Col 1:19; 2:9; Eph 2:10; 3:17–19; 4:16; etc.

[319] NTS 8 (1962), 272.

[320] *The Foundation of New Testament Christology* (New York: Scribner, 1965), pp. 215–16.

He and Münderlein declare baptism and transfiguration the decisive events of Christ's election by the divine *plērōma*. Indeed, the inhabitation of the *plērōma* in Christ means no less than God's presence and operation in Christ; the dwelling of Christ in the saints (or of the Spirit in the house of God that is now the congregation) is to be identified with Christ's full and real presence in his body, the church. In turn, through the church God reveals his presence to the world; Christ is to fill all things totally, not just the church. In all cases, the *plērōma* appears in Ephesians and Colossians to designate God in a specific action and manifestation. *Plērōma* may therefore be considered a synonym of the name, the glory, the Spirit, or the *shekina* of God. Not an unmoved essence, a static nature, a dormant attribute or quality, but the gift of God's self in revelation, salvation, self-presentation is then meant.[321] In this case the notion that God or Christ may be filled by the church is absurd. Wisdom permeates all creation[322]—not vice versa. According to the OT, to medical science, and to Paul, the head's relationship to the body is a one-way affair: the body does not contribute to the life of the head, but the head is its life. Equally the "filling" proceeds from God to Christ, from Christ to the church and world, not vice versa. This is the sum of the matter— if the OT alternatives to the Gnostic meanings of *plērōma* are taken seriously at all.[323]

It is now appropriate to make a summary of the arguments presented so far, and to decide upon one among the viable interpretations of Eph 1:22–23. It might have been superfluous to discuss all the alternatives regarding "head," "body," and "fullness"—if the three terms had not appeared in mutual connection in Eph 1:22–23, and if 1:23 had not given rise to divergent interpretations. The viable meanings of the noun "fullness" especially, and the lack of certainty regarding the active, middle, or passive sense of the form of the verb "to fill" has opened the way for the following three expositions:

1. The church fills or completes Christ.
2. The church is filled by the same Christ who also fills all things.
3. The church, filled by Christ, fills or penetrates all things.

Out of these three choices five could be made if (with Eph 3:19; Col 2:9, but against the evidence of Eph 4:10) God rather than Christ is meant by him who "fills" church and world. But since Eph 1:22–23 describes the relationship of Christ, the head, to the church, to his body, and to all things, rather than the relation between God, the saints, and the world, at this point only the three alternatives will be discussed. The three may yet be reduced to two. Does Ephesians teach that the church is filling, i.e. implementing, Christ, and at the

---

[321] Münderlein; Hegermann, pp. 105–6; Kehl, p. 125; Meuzelaar, pp. 138–42.

[322] Wisd Sol 1:6–7; 7:24–27.

[323] The approach to Paul via OT and Jewish sapiential and rabbinic theologoumena obviously does not possess one advantage offered by the Gnostic road: the mysterious identity of the "broken wall" (2:14), and the connection made between Christ's "descent" and "ascent" with his "filling all things" (4:8–10), are not explained simultaneously with the puzzles of *plērōma*. But it is the Valentinian *plērōma* doctrine and Schlier, not the epistle to the Ephesians, that have concatenated the *plērōma* and dividing-wall concepts. In 2:14 there is no reference either to fullness or to filling; in 4:10 only the verb "to fill" occurs, but not the noun *plērōma*. Colossians speaks extensively of "fullness" and "filling" without ever referring to a wall. Schlier ingeniously superimposes a Gnostic world view upon Ephesians. A similarly creative imagination can be observed in Pokorný's attempt to capitalize upon the *anti*-Gnostic character of Ephesians. The text of Ephesians itself, however, appears to be manhandled either way.

same time filling, i.e. permeating and eventually dominating, the world?[324] Or does the epistle speak of Christ who—by divine appointment—fills the church and the world in an irreversible and unique way? Though the term "body of Christ" has a dimension that includes the missionary church-world relationship, the following discussion will focus on the Christ-church relation which, together with the Christ-world relation, forms the main topic of 1:22–23.

The issue is posed by Lightfoot[325] and others,[326] who are not impressed by the cloud of witnesses who attest to the implementation of Christ by the church. Commenting on Col 1:19, Lightfoot states that the understanding of "*plērōma* as referring to the church (comp. Ephes. I. 22), though adopted by several fathers, is unsuited to the context and has nothing to recommend it." Not all of Lightfoot's reasons for this stance are persuasive; he could not know as much about Gnosticism as modern scholars do, and he might have made better use of the OT. But his viewpoint is still strongly defended by many.

Since scholars continue to be divided into two camps, one supporting Lightfoot and one against him, it may be best to hear their testimony as if given before a court.

1. The scholars who tackle Eph 1:23 with the aid of lexica and grammars are divided for the reasons presented above in the NOTE on this verse. But the philological arguments for one or the other side cancel each other out, and testimony from other quarters is called for.

2. The interpreters who argue from the parallels to Eph 1:23 in Ephesians and Colossians have at hand a majority of statements in which the noun "fullness" and the verb "to fill" are used to describe God who fills Christ, or to point out that God or Christ is the one who fills church and world.[327] The primary emphasis laid by Colossians on Christ as the vessel of God's fullness is complemented (though not contradicted; see Col 2:9) by the stress laid in Ephesians upon the church and the world as recipients of God's fullness. But a minority of passages in Ephesians, esp. 1:23; 4:13, appear to suggest that the epistle to the Ephesians contains an element not found in Colossians: the cosmic function of the church exerted in her implementation of Christ and her penetration of all things. Certainly Ephesians stresses ecclesiology in a way unparalleled by Colossians, but whether this specific emphasis is really contained in the texts using the words "fullness" and "to fill" is not certain. Those texts make good enough sense when they are understood to speak of God

---

[324] So, e.g. all ancient versions (the Syriac, Latin, Bohairic, Sahidic, etc.) except the Peshitta; also Origen *Catenae* VI 133–34; Chrysostom PG 62, 26; Jerome PL 26, 464. Calvin writes on Eph 1:22, "Indeed, the greatest honor of the church consists in this: The Son of God considers himself somehow imperfect unless he be joined with us ... This happens not because of a defect or want ... All the more his goodness is apparent." J. A. T. Robinson, pp. 41–45, 88, 150, "Christ still waits for completion ... The Church is the completeness of the Christ ... As the Church grows, he grows"; cf. Prat, I, 357–58; II, 341–43; Abbott, 48; Fowler, 294; K. Barth, *Church Dogmatics*, IV:2, 625–26. Soiron, p. 144, writes, "Christus und die Kirche sind also ein Individuum ... mit der Bestimmung, alles in allen zu umfangen, also die mystische Einheit, die Christus mit seinem Leib, der Kirche, verbindet, auf das ganze All auszudehnen, die Incarnation Verbi divini in kosmischem Umfang zu verwirklichen." See also Augustine *tractatus in I Ioannis* I; *enarrationes in Psalmos* XVII 51 XC 2.1.

[325] P. 225, cf. his explanation of the head-body relationship on pp. 223, 264–67.

[326] E.g. H. Grotius; Bengel; Haupt; W. Lueken, SNT; Percy, *Leib Christi*, p. 50 n. 93; Meuzelaar, pp. 123–24; Hegermann, p. 152; Feuillet, 287–92.

[327] Col 2:10; Eph 3:19; 4:10; Bengel adds Eph 4:13; 5:18; John 1:14, 16.

and Christ as the persons who perform the filling—without implying that the church in turn has the task or power to fill Christ or the world. Since it is possible but not certain that Ephesians may promote this particular doctrine, the issue cannot be decided upon the ground of parallels in Ephesians and Colossians.

3. The scholars who refer to parallels in the Pauline homologoumena and other biblical books assume that, e.g. in I Cor 12:12, Christ is denoted as the whole body, including the head, just as in John 15:1, 5, he is the whole vine, the branches included. Wherever the coming, person, and dominion of the Messiah are described he is shown to be God's Anointed for the benefit of a great people; without them the Messiahship is an unfulfilled promise. The fulfillment of the Scripture texts that refer to him involves gathering the Jews to himself and incorporating the Gentiles into God's people. Therefore the people incorporated into his realm "fulfill" the Messianic kingdom, and implicitly the Messiah himself. The "saints of the Most High" in Dan 7 are given as the very meaning and interpretation of the "Son of Man" who was seen by the visionary; Adam is incomplete without Eve; Paul speaks of "filling up what is lacking in Christ's afflictions" (Col 1:24): these parallels to an eventual Ephesian doctrine of Christ's complementation by the church are impressive. Biblical texts do contain the promise and the announcement of fulfillment, saying: the Messiah is not the Messiah, and he cannot, will not, be the Messiah without his people. There may be references to *logos*, to Wisdom, to the Son, etc., without an immediate connection with the people of God, but the title of the Messiah, also of the Son of Man, is empty unless it includes a kingdom on earth. His kingship is not exerted over a void, but rather he is king over many citizens. Still, the possible harmony of an interpretation of Eph 1:23 with an element of the teaching of the Pauline homologoumena and other biblical texts cannot prove beyond any doubt that an implementation of Christ by the church is really attested in 1:23. A majority of expositors may be inclined to choose this interpretation, but a minority points out that the verse's evidence itself is inconclusive.

4. The evidence presented by the specialists in OT studies and in intertestamental Wisdom, Philonic, apocalyptic, sectarian, and later rabbinic theology is clear: it is God who fills his house and the earth with his glory, power, and presence. Though his creatures are given the freedom to fill the earth, they cannot fill the creator. The notion that the house of God, because it is filled by God, will in turn fill the earth, is not supported by their evidence. The term "head" so obviously means (in the references quoted by these scholars) "ruler" that no "body" need be mentioned in the context. If the relation between the Messiah and his people is spelled out, it is his election and appointment by God for the people that is stressed; it is never stated that God's people "make" their king or implement him. He, the appointed, "is" their life, they do not "make" him their breath (Lam 4:20). The patriarchs and chosen servants represent the totality of God's people, the offspring that is to be born, and the redemption that is to be experienced. But they are not constituted or complemented by the coming generations, or by the many whom they represent. Despite all elaborations on Adam, Enoch, the Son of

Man, and Wisdom, the *uni*lateral relationship which exists between God's glory, name, Spirit, *shekina* on one side, and Israel, the nations, and all creatures on the other, is never questioned. Indeed, it is affirmed that God not only demonstrates but also widens his power by choosing Israel, by making this people his possession, by inspiring it to praise his glory among the nations. The confession of the "One God" affirms that he is the "Lord" over Israel and all the world. Wisdom plays before God (cf. Prov 8:30c lit.), permeates all things, elects to dwell in Israel, and elicits a response in the knowledge and prudence of wise men. The one Spirit of God conveys many gifts or spirits to men. The covenant relationship is only fulfilled when man's faithfulness, truth, righteousness, and steadfast love correspond to God's love, but the covenant partners are not mutually complementary. To the majesty of God's gifts comes the answer of man's praise. Man is chosen to contribute to God's glory among his creatures, and God himself as creator, lover, lawgiver, and judge, is most personally involved in the history of this glorification; nevertheless Hebrew and other Jewish sources fail to affirm a complementation of God or God's Messiah by his people. God is and God fills all in all. Thus the evidence of this group of witnesses amounts to a resounding "Nay."

5. The material offered as evidence by scholars in the fields of comparative religion, that is, in Orphism, Stoicism, magic texts, and especially Gnosticism, has the opposite effect. Monistic and dualistic systems, whether by means of esoteric restrictions or universalist claims, assert an ultimate identity of the "One and All." Without the body or all things, the head or the One would not be divine. The One and the Many stand in mutual need of each other. After suffering a rupture and crisis, the deity becomes whole by the completion of its saving work. Thus the Gnostic interpretation of Ephesians suggests that the implementation of Christ by the church be affirmed. But the force of this Aye is somewhat subdued by the fact that the Gnostic systems in question date to the second century and later, which throws serious doubt over the admissibility of their testimony. In addition, the majority of Christian churches have so far treated the Christian Gnostics as heretics.

6. The information gathered from the medical science of Paul's day does not explicitly mention an act of "filling" performed either by the head or the body. Obviously Paul attributed much more to Christ, the head, than doctors did to the brain. If their metaphorical description of the operation of the brain and the nerves was popularized by Paul's use of the verb "to fill," then Paul understood them to say, the head fills the body with powers of movement and perception and thereby inspires the whole body with life and direction. But Paul could not derive from the physicians the opposite notion that the body in any sense fills the head, for there is no evidence of an analogous medical doctrine. While he speaks of the body's growth and upbuilding, he never mentions a growth, upbuilding, or implementation of the head. The evidence available from the adduced medical sources favors rejecting the proposition that the church complements Christ.

Can a judge, jury, or the public come to a fair verdict when faced with such weighty but contradictory evidence? Certainly a counting of noses and a majority vote cannot decide the issue. The session of the court may have to be continued *ad infinitum*. But there is one important reason for deciding in favor of those who deny the implementation of Christ by the church: while the OT is quoted in the context of Eph 1:23, i.e. in 1:20, 22, and frequently throughout the epistle, citations of the speculative and ambiguous Gnostic sources are never made. Paul was a Jew, and even though when seen through the unfriendly eyes of the Ebionites and others he resembled the Samaritan magician Simon (the supposed Arch-Father of all Gnostics), he remained a rabbinical Jew. Like other Jews influenced by orthodox or apocalyptic tides of his time, he never gave up his faith in the One God. A tragic rupture in the deity, a repair of that rupture by a reconstitution of the deity itself, that is, by the return of the elect among the creatures, was beyond the scope of his thought. Neither should he be praised or condemned for a great or miserable feat of syncretism.[328]

In sum, it is most unlikely, and certainly not proven by Eph 1:23, that Paul believed in an implementation of God or the Messiah by the church. He who does the filling is God or Christ. That which is filled by God is Christ, the church, or all things—never God. And that which is filled by Christ is the church and the world. There is no explicit statement affirming that the church fills Christ or the world.

In Ephesians and Colossians fullness and filling denote a dynamic unilateral relationship: the revelation of God's glory to the world through Jesus Christ; the power exerted by God in Christ and in the church for the subjection of the powers and the salvation of all mankind;[329] the life, growth, and salvation given by Christ to his body; or, in brief, the presence of the living God and his Messiah among his chosen people for the benefit of all creation.[330] If there is a cosmic role ascribed to the church in Ephesians then it is as servant.[331] She is to manifest the presence of the loving and powerful God.[332] Not God, Christ, or the Head, but solely the body of Christ, that is, the house of God, the church, is "to grow."[333] Any notion of world dominion by the church is missing, but the church is equipped to do a "work of service" and to "stand against," and "resist," the attacks of evil powers.[334] The idea is lacking that one day the church will fill or replace the world.[335] Assurance is given that Christ is filling all things[336] and that the saints will attain or will be filled with, all of God's and the Messiah's fullness.[337]

Yet another hint is appropriate. Some commentators and dictionaries[338]

---

[328] E.g. Benoit, p. 44, lauds Paul for producing "a synthesis of incomparable depth" of Old Testament and Stoic elements, and Schoeps condemns the apostle for the same.

[329] According to Aristotle *pol.* IV 1290B–1291B the *plērōma* of a city consists not just of the total of its inhabitants but of the total of necessary services rendered. Following Philo *somn.* I 62, God fills the *logos* with powers.

[330] Fullness is therefore not to be considered an attribute of either the church or the world, as done, e.g. by Conzelmann, p. 64. He defines *plērōma* as "the possibility of the world to come in the church to its own fulfillment . . . The world is not being by-passed but mastered . . . Here is an approach to genuine secularism on the lines of faith in the creator."

[331] In Eph 2:7; 3:10; 6:10–20, the cosmic role; in 4:12 its fulfillment by service is described.

[332] Cf. Y. Congar, *Jésus-Christ* (Paris: Du Cerf, 1965), p. 152.

[333] 2:21–22; 4:15–16; cf. 4:13.   [334] 4:12; 6:13–14.

[335] She is obviously not a rubber balloon inserted into a water tank and inflated long enough to expel all water from the tank.

[336] 1:23; 4:10.

[337] 3:19; 4:13.

[338] E.g. LSLex, 1426; Lightfoot, pp. 323–24; B. Rigaux, NTS 4 (1958), 237–62, esp. 248; Meuzelaar, pp. 133, 139. See also the literature mentioned in the second NOTE on 3:19.

observe that "fullness" and "fill" may mean "perfection" and "make perfect." There is a distinct Greek noun (*teleiōsis*) and verb (*teleioō*) for denoting perfection, but in Eph 4:13; Col 4:12[339] nouns or verbs formed from the stems *plēr* and *tel* ("fill" and "perfect") are used in the same verse, perhaps as synonyms. The translation of Eph 3:19 below will reflect the possible synonymity. Since "perfection" and the adjective "perfect" are cultic terms, it may well be that the same is true of "fullness" and "filling." Certainly the OT concept of "filling" God's house with the glory of the Lord, the "indwelling" of God's fullness in Christ (mentioned in Col 1:19; 2:9), and the Pauline description of the church as God's or the Spirit's "temple," suggest a connection between fullness, filling, and cultus. Also, the days of fulfillment (Eph 1:10) might have a ceremonial undertone, see e.g. Luke 1:23, which need not contradict their eschatological character. Further inquiry on the cultic *Sitz im Leben* may add evidence which is in favor of the understanding of "fullness" and "filling" proposed in this COMMENT.

VII   Conclusion

In Eph 1:15–23 Paul continues to radiate his joy: the benediction of 1:3–14 is followed by a jubilation. In quick steps Paul moves from thanksgiving for faith and love to the intercession for inspiration of knowledge and hope, to the description of God's unique power and its demonstration in Christ's resurrection. In the second half of this section Christ's omnipotent role over all powers is described as the presupposition of his rule by love over the church. Concerns common to all these steps are the expansion of God's glory, the demonstration of God's presence, the penetration of all things by God's power, the special election of the church. Just as in 1:3–14, Jesus Christ is the agent and the revelation, the proof of God's movement toward his creatures. Again, the Spirit is mentioned explicitly and special statements are made about the church. In chapter 2 the author will concentrate upon the origin, purpose, composition, and growth of the church.

[339] Only in the reading of Papyrus 46 and the Koine texts; see also the texts quoted from *Pistis Sophia* by Lightfoot, pp. 338–39. The "bond of perfection" mentioned in Col 3:14 may belong in this context.

IV SALVATION BY RESURRECTION
(2:1–10)

2 ¹ You [Gentiles], especially, dead as you were in your lapses and sins . . . ² in the past your steps were bound by them[. You were] following [the inspiration of] this world-age, the ruler of the atmosphere, that spirit which is now at work among the rebellious men. ³ In the past all of us [Jews], too, followed these ways. In our own fleshly passions we did whatever our flesh and our thoughts decided. As much as the rest of mankind we were by nature under the wrath [of God]. ⁴ But

God who is rich in mercy
—for he loves us with all his love—
⁵ just because we were dead in our lapses
has made us alive together with the Messiah.
By grace you are saved!
⁶ For he has in the Messiah Jesus
raised and enthroned us together in the heavens
⁷ in order to prove throughout the ages to come,
through the goodness [shown] to us in the Messiah Jesus,
how infinitely rich is his grace.
⁸ By grace you are saved, through faith!

This [was] not of your own doing—it is a gift of God—⁹ not [as a reward] for works lest anyone boast about himself. For

¹⁰ God himself has made us what we are.
In the Messiah Jesus we are created
for those good works which God has provided
as our way of life.

NOTES

2:1. *You [Gentiles], especially, dead as you were* . . . The Greek conjunction (*kai*) translated by "especially" might as well be interpreted by "and" or "also," but here as in 2:5 a more dramatic translation fits better. In 2:5 Paul's logic resembles that of Gen 8:21. Not "although" but "because man's heart contrives evil from his infancy," the Lord will never again curse the earth. Thus the opening of Eph[1] may be understood as saying, "Just because you were dead . . ." Still another version of 2:1 is grammatically possible: "Of all people, just you . . ." The less loaded interpretation need not rule out the special accents in the alternatives.

Paul opens a new paragraph by naming a new subject which belongs under the affirmations of 1:19–23. In 2:1–6 Paul points out that not only the Messiah but also many men—"you" and "we"—have been raised from death and exalted by God's unique power. Therefore the vocabulary used in 2:6 closely resembles that of 1:20. In COMMENT XIV on 1:3–14 it was suggested that those addressed in Ephesians, i.e. "you," be identified as "Gentiles." In 2:1–3 a distinctive description of "your" dominion by evil and "our" fleshly conduct is given. It culminates in the assertion of "our" solidarity with "the rest of mankind" (lit. "the others"). "The others" are designated in I Thess 4:13 as people "bare of hope." Precisely the same characteristic is given of the Gentiles in Eph 2:11–12. Therefore the insertion of "[Gentiles]" in vs. 1, and of "[Jews]" in vs. 3 is appropriate. In 2:1–5 the procedure of 1:11–14 and, in sharply reduced form, of Rom 1:18 – 3:31 is repeated. After the Gentiles' and the Jews' conditions are described separately, a final statement comprehending Jews *and* Gentiles sums up their common predicament.

Verse 1 is a broken sentence,[2] containing no subject and no verb. Only vs. 5 shows what Paul was setting out to say: it is God who made you, the dead men, alive. The intervening statements of vss. 2–4 broaden the affirmation to come by describing the cause, mode, and evidence of man's death, by including Paul and other Jews among the dead, and by extolling God's motivation for raising them.

dead . . . in your lapses and sins. The translation "lapses" is explained in a NOTE on 1:7 and in COMMENT IV on 1:3–14. In section II of the Introduction the role of traditional formulations was mentioned, to which Eph 2:1 may belong. It is most unlikely that by using two different words for sin Paul intended to distinguish between different sorts or modes of failure. "Lapses and sins" appear to be a hendiadys. In 1:7 and Col 2:13 the author speaks of "forgiveness of lapses," in Col 1:14 of "forgiveness of sins." In Rom 5:12–21 the singulars of both nouns are used interchangeably, i.e. as synonyms; in Rom 4:25; I Cor 15:3 the same is true of their plurals.[3] In regard to the meaning of the term "dead" which in the Bible is often used for denoting spiritual death,[4] see COM-

---

[1] Equally in 1:15; 6:19; cf. 3:1; 4:1 where in our translation other conjunctive words or phrases are used.

[2] Haupt; von Soden, p. 118; J. A. Robinson; Dibelius; Schlier, and others comment in slightly different ways on the anacoluthon in Eph 2:1–5.

[3] Abbott, p. 39, describes and criticizes attempts such as Augustine's *ad Lev. questiones* 20, to distinguish between *desertio boni*, "lapse," and *perpetratio mali*, "sin," or between an evil mental conception of disposition and the concrete sinful deeds. As stated earlier, the etymological meaning of both Greek terms is practically identical. And the same term "sin," which in Plato's writings denotes the defective nature of man, describes in Aristotle a devious individual act. For references see G. Stählin and W. Grundmann, TWNTE, I, 296–302. A third noun, trespass, or transgression (*parabasis*) denotes in Pauline writings willful violation of a law (Rom 2:23; 4:15; 5:14; Gal 3:19; cf. trespasser Rom 2:25, 27; Gal 2:18; James 2:9, 11). As stated earlier (on Eph 1:7) in Pauline diction, strictly speaking, only Jews can be accused of "trespassing" because only they have been given the law, but cf. Rom 5:14. "Lapses" and "sins," however, are common to Jews and Gentiles.

[4] Ps 30:3; 33:19, etc.; Jonah 2:6; Job 5:20; Luke 15:24, 32; I John 3:14; John 5:24; Rom 5:12–21; I Cor 15:21–22; Eph 2:1, 5; Col 2:13; Rev 3:1–2.

MENT III below. The death "in lapses and sins" attributed to Gentiles is a result of Adam's sin.[5] It is to be distinguished from the death of the Jews effected by means of "the law";[6] from the death of Jews and Gentiles "with Christ";[7] from the daily exposure of the apostle "to death";[8] from the "conformation with" the crucified and risen Lord;[9] and from the state of being "dead in Christ."[10] It is also distinct from death "to sin" and "to the law."[11] The preposition "in" [before "lapses"] has as wide a meaning as Hebrew b^e ("in," "by," "at," "from," "during," etc.); cf. the formulae "in Christ," "in the law." "Lapses and sins" are at the same time the cause, the instrument, the manifestation, the realm, and the consequence of death. Though the translation "through your lapses and sins" sounds better, it would restrict the meaning of "in" to an instrumental sense.

2. *in the past your steps were bound by them*[. *You were*] *following* [*the inspiration of*]. Lit. "[the sins] in which you formerly walked according to." These words explain the formula "dead in lapses and sins." In typical Semitic fashion a brief historic reminder in narrative form takes the place of a definition. To live a certain life is to follow a given path.[12] In the OT God opens up such a way by preceding his people in a pillar of smoke and fire; the law he gives them is a "directive" to walk on that way.[13] Qumran capitalizes on "the way of the Lord in the wilderness" and equates the sectarian Rule with the right way.[14] Pharisaical teaching is largely halachic, i.e. concerned with conduct. Jesus calls upon his disciples to "follow" him, and the apostolic teaching and preaching is called the "way."[15] Perhaps on the basis of Ps 34:12–22[16] the doctrine of the Two Ways was developed which is alluded to in Matt 7:13–14 and was taken up by Christian writers of the second century.[17] Paul uses the verb "to walk" more frequently in Ephesians than in any of his other epistles, yet this term was at all times a favorite of his. He learned to use it in rabbinical rather than in Greek schools, and always employed it as a metaphor, i.e. in the ethical sense which is foreign to Greek usage. This verb does not occur in the Gospels and Acts, but is prominent in the Johannine epistles.[18] Instead of denoting an aimless promenading or strolling about, in Paul and the Johannine epistles the verb means a choice of steps on a given ground in a given direction. In Eph 2:1 the ground is formed by "lapses and sins"; in 2:10

---

[5] I Cor 15:21–22, 44–29.
[6] Gal 2:19; 3:21; I Cor 15:56; II Cor 3:6–7; Rom 7:1, 4, 10–11; cf. 2:12.
[7] This is a unique past event according to Gal 2:19; Rom 6:5–6, 8; Col [2:11] 3:1; II Tim 2:11; cf. II Cor 5:14–15.
[8] II Cor 4:10–12; Philip 1:20–21.
[9] Gal 4:19; 6:17; I Cor 15:49; Rom 8:29; Philip 3:10–11, 21.
[10] I Thess 4:16.
[11] Rom 6:2, 6; Gal 2:19.
[12] See S. V. McCasland, "The Way," JBL 77 (1958), 222–30; F. Noetscher, *Gottes Wege und Menschenwege in der Bibel und Qumran*, BBB 15, 1958 (ref.).
[13] See, e.g. G. Östborn, *Tora in the Old Testament*, Lund: Boktryckeri, 1945.
[14] Isa 40:3; 1QS VIII 13–16; IX 18–21; X 21.
[15] E.g. in Acts 9:2; 18:25–26; 19:9; 24:14; cf. I Cor 4:17.
[16] See G. Klein, *Der älteste christliche Katechismus und die jüdische Propagandaliteratur* (Berlin: Reimer, 1909), pp. 137–38.
[17] Barn. XVIII–XX; *Didache* I–VI.
[18] Paul's and John's use of the term is most likely influenced by LXX passages as IV[II] Kings 20:3; Prov 8:20; Eccles 11:9. But it is also possible that only the rabbinic *halacha* determined the Greek use of the verb for ethical conduct. Cf. H. Schlier, *Der Brief an die Galater*, KEKNT 7, 13th ed. (1965) 247–48.

by "good works provided" by God.[19] A dialectic contrast between location and direction is indicated in II Cor 10:2–3: While walking "in the flesh" man is not to walk and fight "according to the flesh." Eph 2:2 designates the world or its ruler as the one who gives direction or who inspires.[20] For a smooth translation, the interpolation of the words "the inspiration of" is suggested by the word "spirit" in the context.

this world-age. Lit. "the age of this world." The first of the Greek terms (*aion*), here translated by "age," denotes originally eternity, time, or time span. It has a long philosophical and religious history which culminates about 200 B.C. with the worship of a god Aion in Alexandria. The Hebrew term '*ōlām* developed in an analogous way. Perhaps under Persian,[21] certainly under Jewish influence, *aion* received a spatial connotation and became almost equivalent with "world" (*kosmos*).[22] Rabbis and apocalypticists spoke of "this age" and called its opposite "the age to come"; cf. Eph 1:21.[23] For them the term '*ōlām* included the meaning of "world."[24] Since Aion is the name of a Hellenistic deity and Paul speaks[25] of the "god of this age," it is not impossible that in Eph 2:2 Paul thinks of a personified world-age, that is, of the world-age in person, a personal antagonist of God's good creation and of God himself. Perhaps this term ought therefore to be capitalized and written, World-Age. "World-Age" is certainly used as one of the names or titles of the devil who is described at greater length by the following words: "the ruler of the atmosphere," and "that spirit which is now at work." The English term "atmosphere" with its many meanings is the best translation for the Greek words *exousiā tou aēros* ("dominion of the air"). Elsewhere in Ephesians[26] the author speaks explicitly of the "devil" or the "evil one," but he never calls him "Satan," "Beliar," or "Destroyer."[27] Since the *hapax legomena* "Destroyer" and "Beliar" in the Corinthian letters do not disprove the authenticity of those epistles, the titles "devil" and "evil one" in Ephesians do not prove its spuriousness either, though they do not occur in the undisputed epistles; see the NOTE on 4:27. The term "ruler" is used of the devil in the Gospel of John: he is called "ruler of this world"; while his work is still going on, he is nevertheless about

---

[19] Elsewhere "wickedness" (II Cor 4:2); "futility of mind" (Eph 4:17); fornication, impurity, etc. (Col 3:5–7), are mentioned on one side; "newness of life" (Rom 6:4); "love" (Eph 5:2); "Christ" (Col 2:6); "wisdom" (Col 4:5) on the other, as the soil or confines of man. In I John 1:6, 7; 2:11; II John 4; III John 3–4 "darkness," "light," or "truth" form the realm in which man walks.

[20] Instead of the world, the devil, or the evil spirit, some NT passages name other determinants of man's way: man (I Cor 3:3); the flesh (II Cor 10:2–3; Rom 8:4; also 8:1 var. lect.); cf. the commandments (II John 6); the tradition of the elders (Mark 7:5).

[21] See M. Zepf, "Der Gott Aion in der hellenistischen Theologie," ARW 25 (1927), 225–44 (ref.). The Iranian deity Zrvan may have influenced Egyptian and Jewish thought. Zrvan is god of time *and* space.

[22] H. Sasse, TWNTE, I, 203–4. The role which the All-Father god Aion and his emanations, the Aiōnes, played in second-century Gnosticism, was discussed in COMMENT VI C 1 on I:15–23.

[23] See also I Cor 1:20; 2:6, 8; 5:10; 7:31; II Cor 4:4; Rom 12:2; cf. Gal. 1:4; Col 1:13. In I Cor 3:18–19 "age" and "world" appear to be used as synonyms. The obliteration of a sharp distinction between space and time corresponds to a feature of twentieth-century physics. But Bengel's differentiation between the more external *world* and the more "subtle" *age* may still be true to the Greek words in question.

[24] IV Ezra 8:1, etc.

[25] Once only, in II Cor 4:4! Cf. the Johannine passages mentioned in fn. 28.

[26] 4:27; 6:11, 16.

[27] As Paul does in I Thess 2:18; II Thess 2:9; I Cor 5:5; 7:5; 10:10; II Cor 2:11; 6:15; 11:14; Rom 16:20.

to be thrown out and judged.[28] There are three ways to explain the function of the noun "spirit" in Eph 2:2.

a) It may be an expository apposition either to the remote noun "world-age," to "ruler," or to "atmosphere."[29] One of these or all three are then marked as energetic, in their own way inspiring "spiritual" forces. Correspondingly, the "hosts" of the devil, or "of evil," are called "spiritual" beings (6:12), and in the Gospels demonic powers are sometimes named "spirits."[30] The "energy" of God's unique power shown in the resurrection of Christ (1:19–20) and God's "spiritual blessing" (1:3) are opposed to the affectiveness of the evil "spirit" and overpower it.

b) Or "spirit" may be understood as a third name for the devil, complementing the preceding titles "world-age" and ruler of the atmosphere."[31] In that case the compilation of the enemy's names in Rev 12:9 (great-dragon, arch-serpent, devil, satan, deceiver), or his trinitarian manifestation as dragon, animal from the sea, and animal from the earth (Rev 13), would be parallels—a satanic counterfeit of the Messiah's titles as they are compiled in Rev 2:1, 8, 12; 5:5–6, etc., also in e.g. Isa 9:6 and John 1:35–51.

c) Finally, if "spirit" is understood as an apposition to the preceding noun only ("atmosphere," lit. "dominion of air"), it may qualify the air as a substance that is breathed in by man and poisons his thoughts and actions.[32] In this case the devil would be denoted as the ruler who poisons the atmosphere, producing a devastating stench or killing in the manner of the aftereffect of atomic explosions or industrial air pollution. Athanasius' ascription of the "purification of the air" to the crucifixion of Christ[33] fits both this imagery and reality. The different translation possibilities reveal various dimensions of the devil's character and means of operation; they are not mutually exclusive and are not contradictory. For the OT and other religious backgrounds to the satanology displayed in Eph 2:2, also for details concerning the realm, the means, the time, and the history of the devil's power, see COMMENT II.[34]

the rebellious men. Lit. "sons of disobedience." The Greek contains a Semitism which is reflected in such English idioms as "son of a gun" or something worse. Specifying an origin in this way (son of) takes the place in briefest nar-

---

[28] John 6:70; 8:44; 12:31; 13:2, 27; 14:30; 16:11.
[29] Various syntactic combinations are e.g. suggested by J. Schmid, Dibelius, Percy, p. 216 n. 6.
[30] Matt 8:16; 10:1; 12:43, etc.
[31] This would still not justify the identification of the present description of the devil with the "spirit of the world" mentioned in I Cor 2:12, or the homiletically effective combination of the first and last devilish titles by the German word *Zeitgeist* and the blunt equation of *Zeitgeist* with the devil himself which Schlier, pp. 104–5 suggests. But it rules out the ascription of evil on earth to matter and finality only. The cause, means, and effects of evil are in their own way just as spiritual as are those of God's blessing, revelation, and salvation, cf. Abbott. A precedent of contrasting an evil spirit with the Spirit and work of God is found in the Qumran Scrolls, esp. in 1QS III 13 – IV 26. But although it is possible (and in the light of II Cor 6:14 – 7:1 probable) that Paul "combated ideas such as emerge in the Scrolls and used these very ideas in the service of the gospel" (W. D. Davies, "Paul and the Dead Sea Scrolls: Flesh and Spirit," SaNT, pp. 157–82, esp. 180), the terminology of Eph 2:2 (also of 4:27) is too distinct from Qumran to permit the final assertion of Paul's dependence on Qumran. See H. Braun, QuNT I (1966), 216, 218–19.
[32] For the role of "air" breathed in, see COMMENT VI A on 1:15–23.
[33] *De incarnatione* 25.
[34] The intrinsic operation ("energy") ascribed to God's and the devil's powers is discussed by K. W. Clark, "The Meaning of *energeō* and *katargeō* in the New Testament," JBL 54 (1935), 93–101.

rative form of characterization by an adjective,[35] or an outright definition. It shows that the attribute is original and innate to a person, not just incidental. Disobedience is the main sin of man whenever, as in the OT and NT, God is manifested as the rightful and commanding personal Lord who has to be heard and followed. Nonconformity to an idea, principle, or fate is not discussed in the Bible. Disobedience is not only a lack of compliance with the revealed will of the living God, but active rebellion, which is why "the rebellious men" was chosen as translation. Compare Isa 30:9 RSV, Eph 2:2 JB. While in 2:2 only the Gentiles are called rebels against God, in 2:3 those born as Jews are included: "all of us [Jews], too, followed these ways." In other Pauline passages Jews as well as Gentiles, in brief, "all men," are designated as rebels.[36] Perhaps the object of rebellion in Eph 2:2 is not only God, his Spirit, his law, or a specific commandment,[37] but all of this lumped together and revealed by disobedience to Jesus Christ, or to the gospel preached by his apostles (Rom 10:16). Faith and obedience interpret each other (Rom 1:5; 16:26; II Cor 10:5; cf. I Peter 1:22, etc.).[38] In the epistle to the Hebrews[39] unbelief and disobedience are the same, and Paul comes close to equating them.[40] I Peter 2:8 and 4:17[41] distinctly treat disobedience to the word and the gospel, Heb 3–4 disobedience and disbelief in the gospel preached to the fathers. Since Eph 2:2 speaks of a manifestation of the devil *now*, it is probable that the Gentiles' rejection of the gospel of Jesus Christ is in the foreground of the apostle's thought, rather than their pre-Christian immersion in idolatry and immorality.[42] All rebellion against God and his commandments is bad enough, but rebellion against the revealed gospel is outright devilish.

3. *In the past, all of us [Jews], too, followed these ways . . . As much as the rest of mankind.* The relative pronoun translated by "these ways" is masculine or neuter. It refers more likely to the Gentile-born "rebels" than to the remote "lapses" of vs. 1. The author demonstrates at the beginning and end of vs. 3 the full solidarity of the Jew with the Gentile under sin, death, and wrath. But according to 1:4–13; 2:5–22; 3:6, companionship in sin is far outdone by solidarity under grace. In the form of a confession of guilt the author takes up what many a prophet since Amos had to preach to his people, or to say to God in prayers of intercession: not only the Gentiles but Judah and Israel as well are under God's judgment (Amos 1:2 – 2:16). Just as the Gentiles' conduct ("walking") was the cause and evidence of their death in sin, so is the conduct of "all" Jews. The reference to "all" includes the Jewish Christians, and among them, Paul. Precisely when he claimed to have been most faithful to the "traditions of the Fathers" (Gal 1:13–14) did he ravage the church of God;[43] of all people those who boast of possessing the law are reminded that they

---

[35] Cf., e.g. Isa 57:4; Prov 31:2; John 8:44; I Thess 5:5; Eph 2:3; 5:8; Col 3:6 var. lect.; II Peter 2:14.

[36] Rom 3:23; 10:21; 11:30–32; 15:31. In Isa 30:9; Heb 4:6, 11; cf. Barn XII 4, Jews are meant, in Heb 11:31, Gentiles only.

[37] See Isa 36:5; 63:10; Deut 1:26; 9:23; 21:18; Rom 1:30; II Tim 3:2.

[38] Cf. Gen 15:6 with 26:5.   [39] 3:12, 18–19; 4:2, 6, 11.

[40] Rom 2:8; 10:21; 15:31; cf. Acts 14:2; 19:9. In WBLex 82 this identification is called "greatly disputed." See also E. Grässer, *Der Glaube im Hebräerbrief* (Marburg: Elwert, 1965), p. 69.

[41] Cf. 3:1, 20.   [42] But cf. 4:17–19; I Thess 1:9; Rom 1:18–32, etc.

[43] Cf. Philip 3:4–8.

have been given the law because *they* need instruction, are thieves, adulterers, temple robbers, a shame to God's name (Rom 2:17–24). The Greek verb used by Paul for their behavior (lit. "to dwell," "to conduct oneself") is different from the one used for the Gentiles in 2:2, but its meaning is synonymous.[44] Life and conduct are conceived of as a *way*.

In our own fleshly passions, we did whatever our flesh and our thoughts decided. A more literal translation would read "[among the Gentiles all of us Jews, too, walked inside the confines of our fleshly passions] acting out the willful decisions of the flesh and the thoughts." Instead of the devil who was described as leader and ruler of the Gentiles in 2:2, "the flesh" is mentioned twice as the power determining the Jews. See COMMENT II.

by nature under the wrath [of God]. Lit. "by nature children of wrath." The Greek term "by nature" is as ambiguous as its English translation,[45] and has led interpreters to a concept of original sin which included natural depravity or a corruption of nature itself; see COMMENT II for alternatives. The indictment of the Jews contained in Eph 2:3 is very sharp; cf. I Thess 2:15–16. It cannot be denied, however, that such prophets as Amos, Hosea, Jeremiah, and Ezekiel spoke in even blunter terms about Israel's rebellion and sin. Since in so doing they are good Jews rather than anti-Semites, the same can be true of Paul; cf. the essay on this topic mentioned in fn. 180 to the *Introduction*.

4–10. God who is rich in mercy . . . has provided as our way of life. G. Schille[46] has sought to elucidate the anacoluthic and doublet character of vss. 1–3, the use of the conjunctions "but" and "accordingly" (in vss. 4 and 11; in the latter verse our translation has "then"), the hymnodic diction of vss. 4–7, 10 and the prose interlude of vss. 8–9. The result is a reconstruction of a pre-Pauline hymn. He calls it an "initiation hymn" and distinguishes four stanzas of equal length, containing three almost isometric cola. Stanza I (vss. 4ab, 5a) sings of God's mercy toward the dead; II (vss. 5b–6) takes up salvation and describes it after the pattern of the Christological formula in 1:20; III (vs. 7) points out the public announcement of God's action; IV (vs. 10) concludes with an ethical admonition. Verses 8–9 are considered a prosaic Paulinist interpretive interpolation.[47] The translation given above roughly follows Schille's suggestions but does not presuppose uniformity of the length of stanzas and cola. Two brief exclamations mentioning grace (2:5c, 8a) interrupt the "we"-form of the rest by the sudden change to "you." These interruptions would be beautifully explained if they were liturgical responses of the celebrating priest to the singing of the congregation, or Pauline comments upon a traditional hymn. Especially in the latter case all the elements in vss.

---

[44] Robinson; Schlier. In James and I Peter the second verb is exclusively used. It has exactly the same ethical implications as the first. See also the first NOTE on 4:22 regarding the respective nouns.

[45] See R. M. Grant, *Miracle and Natural Law* (Amsterdam: North Holland, 1952), pp. 4–18, and discussions of Natural Law, as e.g. E. Wolf, *Das Problem der Naturrechtslehre* (Karlsruhe: Müller, 1955), pp. 11–106, where no fewer than nine definitions of Nature and nine of Law are listed and illustrated that have played a role in the legal, philosophical, theological and political history of the West.

[46] *Hymnen*, pp. 53–60.

[47] J. T. Sanders, ZNW 56 (1965), 214–32, esp. 218–19 proceeds even more radically. He proposes that an earlier three-line hymn consisting of vss. 4–5 was treated by the author of Ephesians in the manner of an OT proof text and paraphrased in vss. 6–7 by borrowings from 1:20–21.

5–7 and 10 that seem strange in Paul's theology[48] could be ascribed to a church theology which Paul feels free to quote (cf. I Cor 15:29) while nevertheless adding certain correctives. However, some caveats are appropriate. Though the Qumran Hodayoth and the *Odes of Solomon* contain "initiation songs," it is doubtful whether this "form" (*Gattung*) was simply endorsed by Christian congregations or Paul. Eph 2:4–10 may describe the miracle or experience of conversion or baptism, but the passage does not explicitly say so. Even without imitating or creating a liturgy for a specific purpose Paul was capable of lifting his voice and using his pen for liturgical and poetic diction.[49] In a NOTE on the end of vs. 5 it will be shown that the statements on "grace" in vss. 5 and 8, if judged by standards of style, contain elements just as novel as vss. 4–5a, 6–7, 10. If vss. 5c and 8–9 have distinctly Pauline contents in spite of some surprising features, vss. 4–7, 10 might be Pauline as well. It appears best to maintain the literary unity of 2:1–10 but to acknowledge that it combines—just as the prologue to John's Gospel and the Benediction in Eph 1:3–14 do—poetic and prosaic utterances.

4. *rich in mercy—for he loves us with all his love*. An allusion is made to OT passages such as Exod 34:6 and Deut 7:7–9 that speak of the riches of God's mercy, the motivation of his action by love alone, and the identity of God in his essence and his manifestation. The frequent allusion to the "riches" of God is a peculiarity of Ephesians.[50] An elaboration upon the blessedness of the poor[51] might correspond to it beautifully, but is not found in this epistle. Those granted God's mercy are dead in sins, 2:5, not just poor. A poor man may still cry and beg; he has the God-given right to be granted *sedāqāh* (meaning "righteousness" in the OT; "charity," "giving alms" in Matt 7:1 and rabbinic literature). But the dead have neither right nor hope, and yet God's riches are such that he calls the dead to life. Mercy (*eleos*) is the LXX and NT translation of the OT term *hesed*. The RSV rendering of this noun is "steadfast-love" and suggests that *hesed* is the stable and loyal way in which God keeps the covenant. The KJ version "loving-kindness" may still be preferable because it conveys the meaning "undeserved mercy" or "prevenient grace."[52] Though

---

[48] I.e. the omission of a reference to "dying with Christ" (cf. Col 3:1; Rom 6:3–8); the proclamation of completed resurrection which contradicts the testimony of Thessalonians, Corinthians, Philippians, Romans; the strong emphasis upon *good works*.

[49] Rom 8:31–39; 11:33–36; cf. Eph 1:3–14, etc.

[50] See 1:7, 18; 2:7; 3:8, 16: also Col 1:27; 2:2 and, in the uncontested Pauline epistles, Philip 4:19; Rom 2:4; 9:23; 10:12; 11:33. Statements about the enrichment of the saints are found in I Cor 4:8; II Cor 8:9.

[51] As present in the "theology of poverty" reflected e.g. in Exod 21:2; 22:25–27; 23:10–11; Deut 15:1 ff, etc.; Amos; Jer 22:13–17; Ps 72:2–4, 12–14; in the final identification of the "poor" and "humble" (*'᷃ni* and *'ānāw*) in the Psalms—exemplified by the change of words and meaning occurring between Pss 37:11; and 74:19, 21; 9:12; Pss 10:17; 147:6; 149:4 and 74:21; 86:1–2; in the designation of all Israel or its faithful remnant as "the poor," Isa 41:17; 49:13; 1QH v 20–22; xviii 14; 1QM xi 9, 13; xiii 14; in the praise of the poverty of the Messiah (Zech 9:9), or of the Teacher of Righteousness, 1QH 1, 13–14, 16, 18, or of all those indigent, Sir 10:30; in the expectation of the blessing still to be inherited, Isa 61:1–3; Ps 113:7–8; *Test. Judah* xxv 4; Jub 23:19; 4QpPs 37 iii 10–11; 1QpHab xii 3, 6, 10; Matt 5:3; Luke 4:18; James 2:1 ff, etc. See e.g. H. Birkeland, ANI *und* ANAW *in den Psalmen* (Oslo: Dybwad, 1933), pp. 1–118. F. M. Cross, Jr., *The Ancient Library of Qumran* (Garden City, N.Y.: Doubleday, 1958), pp. 61–62, 182–83; M. Dibelius, HbNT 10, 10th ed. (1959), pp. 37–44; H. W. Beyer, TWNTE, II, 81–93; E. Bammel, TWNTE, VI, 885–915, and commentaries on Gal 2:9 and II Cor 8–9.

[52] JB translates, "kindness," or "tenderness." The relationship to covenantal terminology is discussed in the JB note on Hosea 2:22[19]. N. Glueck, *Hesed in the Bible*, New York: KTAV, 1968, probably overemphasizes the legal (covenantal) character of *hesed*. *Hesed* is kindness shown beyond a stipulation or requirement; i.e. beyond the call of duty. Often the noun describes the relationship of parties not bound by legal or contractual claims.

"love" belongs in Deuteronomy to the covenant terminology, Ephesians does not make use of specific covenant language. In this epistle the father-child relationship between God and man, which is first praised in 1:4 ff., supersedes the contracted covenant bond and its legal implications as much as it does in Rom 8. An extensive literature[53] exists which describes the difference between the love of God and the Christians on one side, human friendship and spiritual or carnal eros on the other. But in the Bible the distinction between the pertinent terms (*agapē, philiā, erōs*) is not always as sharp as that made by its interpreters.[54] At any rate, Eph 2:4 treats the love of God as motivated by neither the attractiveness of his (dead!) human partners nor a weakness in his own nature. For his own sake God showers love upon man (Deut 7:6–9). This love is manifested through the love of the Messiah, who out of love delivers himself into death for man's sake.[55] It is also manifested by God's power to give life to his beloved children and make them "resplendent" (lit. "glorious," 5:27) by their "enthronement in heaven" (2:6). The price paid by God's love was already hinted at in 1:7 and will be extensively described in 2:13 ff.: it is the blood of Christ. The power and effect of "all" of God's "love" is praised in 2:4–10. If "all the love of God" is manifested in the resurrection of the dead, then the very heart of God is now revealed; cf. COMMENT XI on 1:3–14 regarding the revealed "secret." There is no suspicion that God might be different in nature from the powers or attributes disclosed in Christ; cf. COMMENT XI on 1:3–14. God is in essence what he manifests in action, and vice versa; cf. Exod 3:14. The revelation of his name counteracts nominalism. It is God's nature to love and to act out of love—"for his name's sake," as the OT untiringly repeats.

5. *just because we were dead.* In vss. 1–3 the pronouns "you" and "we" denoted Gentiles and Jews respectively. In vss. 4–5 the pronouns "us" and "we" describe in hymnic form the saints of Jewish *and* Gentile origin as a community. The translation of the Greek conjunction *kai* by "just" (or, "precisely") has been discussed in the first NOTE on 2:1.

in our lapses. Lit. "in the lapses." The first three verses of chapter 2 have shown that the author is speaking about the sins and lapses of *all* saints— whether they followed the devil or succumbed to "the evil impulse." In the Greek text the article before "lapses" refers to the failures mentioned in 2:1, 3. If 2:5a were really part of an unchanged pre-Pauline hymn, reference would probably be made to either "lapses" (without the article) or "our lapses" (*paraptōmasin hēmōn*, instead of *tois paraptōmasin*).[56] Variant readings substitute "bodies" for "lapses" (cf. Rom 7:24, 8:11); or they speak of "sins" instead of "lapses"; or they add "sins" to "lapses," in imitation of 2:1; or they mention "lapses" and "desires" (cf. 2:1, 3). No change of meaning results from these variations.

made us alive. Sometimes in the LXX, and in the majority of cases in the

---

[53] Ranging from A. Nygren's to C. Spicq's works on *agapē*.
[54] The same is true of the respective verbs: the LXX only, not the NT, uses *eros* and *eromai.* See COMMENT V D on 5:21–33.
[55] Eph 5:2, 25; Gal 2:20.
[56] Among the criteria for discerning such hymns are counted today the absence of articles before key words, and the presence of the pronoun, "we," or the possessive form, "our"; see section II of the Introduction.

NT, the verb "to make alive" is a synonym of "to raise" from the dead.[57] But the first verb may also mean "to keep alive" or "to preserve life,"[58] and the second means normally "to arouse from sleep," "to lift up a sick person," or "to raise to the throne." An association with the gift of spirit or life, or with the vivification of a dead person, is not naturally inherent in either verb. Paul's contemporaries were as little prepared as men of later generations to accept talk of resurrection from the dead as a generally acceptable form of discourse.[59] But the Bible proclaims that the Spirit gives life not only in the first creation but can also give it again to a dead man.[60] When the two verbs mentioned above are used to denote resurrection their proper interpretation requires the addition of "the dead" or "from the dead." See COMMENT III.

together with the Messiah. The preposition "together with" has a double meaning at this point, and connotes the combination of Jews and Gentiles in common resurrection, and their resurrection with Christ.[61] The variant reading, together "in" the Messiah, and also the safely attested formula "in the Messiah Jesus," at the end of vs. 6, prohibit the exclusion or neglect of the first sense; Jews and Gentiles are, if at all, raised in communion.[62] Resurrection is personal only inasmuch as it is also a social event. Certainly Pauline texts[63] state emphatically that no man will be raised except with Christ, by Christ, like Christ. But it belongs to the specific message of Ephesians that no person's resurrection takes place without his fellow man. Here resurrection is, by definition as it were, co-resurrection. Ezek 34 and 37 aptly illustrate what is meant here: the dispersed sheep will be gathered by the one good shepherd, whose appearance effects the union of separated Israel and Judah. All this is seen in the form of a vision of dramatic resurrection achieved by the blowing "wind." The puzzling double meaning of the verb in Eph 1:10, translated above by "comprehending under one head," is in 2:5-6 made clear by this reference to resurrection. To have this man, God's Messiah, for a head, means to have breath in one's nostrils (Lam 4:20) and to be united out of dispersion and division.

By grace you are saved. A variant reading, sufficiently backed by MS evidence to deserve some consideration, has "by whose grace . . ." The variant obliterates the parenthetical character of the interjection in the majority of MSS, but it cannot bridge or explain the sudden transition from the pronoun

---

[57] IV[II] Kings 5:7; Ps 70[71]:20; perhaps also II Esd[Ezra] 9:8-9; 19[Neh 9]:6; certainly in John 5:21; 6:63; Rom 4:17; 8:11; I Cor 15:15, 22, 36, 44-45; II Cor 3:6; I Peter 3:18; Eph 2:5.

[58] Judg 21:14; Job 36:6; Eccles 7:12; probably also Gal 3:21; I Tim 6:13 var. lect.

[59] The NT itself points to the basic disbelief, e.g. of the disciples (Mark 9:10; Luke 24:22-23, 37-41); of the Sadducees (Acts 23:8); of Greeks such as the Athenians (Acts 17:18, 32).

[60] Cf. I Cor 15:45; II Cor 3:6; John 6:63; I Peter 3:18. In the background are OT passages like Gen 2:7; Ps 104:30. In these texts Spirit has more than only an anthropological meaning.

[61] Schlier; monographs on dying and rising *with Christ*, as E. Lohmeyer, "Syn Christo," in Fs A. Deissmann (Tübingen: Mohr, 1927), pp. 218-57; W. T. Hahn, *Mitsterben und Mitauferstehen mit Christus*, I. Gütersloh: Bertelsmann, 1937; D. J. Dupont, *Syn Christo; l'union avec Christ suivant S. Paul*, Bruges: Abbaye de Saint-André, 1952; B. McGrath, "*Syn*-Words in Paul," CBQ 14 (1952), 219-26; E. Schweizer, "Die Mystik des Sterbens und Auferstehens mit Christus bei Paulus," EvTh 26 (1966), 239-57; R. C. Tannehill, *Dying and Rising with Christ*, Berlin: Töpelmann, 1967, tend to emphasize more the eschatological, mystical or anti-mystical, than the social character of the resurrection with Christ.

[62] The notion of the inclusiveness of the first and last Adam (I Cor 15:22, 45, etc.) may well underlie the ease with which Paul proceeds from Christ's to the saints' resurrection. Cf. J. Coutts, NTS 4 (1957-58), 205.

[63] E.g. I and II Thessalonians; I Cor 15; Rom 6:4-11; 8:11, 17; II Tim 2:11; Eph 5:14.

"we" (cf. our, us) to "you." No matter which reading is chosen, the clause still has the character of an antiphon. Because it addresses the believers, it is more appropriate to a leader of worship than to the congregation. See COMMENT II on 1:1–2 in regard to "grace." Mitton considers vss. 8–9 "the most effective summary we have of the Pauline doctrine of salvation by grace through faith."[64] Verse 5c is a foretaste of that summary, but it appears to be couched in most un-Pauline diction: the verb "to save" replaces Paul's characteristic term "to justify."[65] The perfect tense of "to save" in Eph 2:5, 8 replaces the present, future, or aorist tenses found elsewhere in Pauline literature.[66] While the combination of "grace" and "faith" in 2:8 is no more redundant than other Pauline statements on justification "by faith," "in Christ," "in his blood,"[67] the combination of salvation and faith is typical of the Synoptic Gospels and James,[68] not of Paul. James polemizes against misusing the formula, "saved by faith alone"—but this phrase does not occur in Paul. In the undisputed Pauline writings the term "to save" most frequently describes future, eschatological salvation in the last judgment (Rom 5:9; 10:8–9, etc.), though it is also used to denote the personal experience of the saints who hear, accept, and confess the contents of the gospel (I Cor 1:18, etc.). Yet in Eph 2:5, 8 (cf. 5:23) a completed deed of God and its result are described by "saved." The use of the same verb for a past and future event corresponds fully to the diction of LXX where salvation means either future redemption, for which an Israelite yearns with prayer and hope, or a completed past action of God in favor of either his people or an individual.[69] Were it not for the "realized eschatology"[70] of Ephesians with its parallels in undisputed Pauline writings, especially in II Cor 6:2, the perfect form "saved" in 2:5, 8 might be considered a proof either of the non-Pauline origin of the whole of Ephesians, or at least of the "hymn" 2:4–7, 10. Indeed, despite their Pauline contents the two interspersed responses 2:5, 8 are less in line with Paul's habitual diction than the rest of the hymn! However, Paul was not duty bound always to speak about justification. As he spoke on distinct occasions of perfected, past, ongoing, and future justification and sanctification,[71] so also he was free to speak of completed "salvation," not just of its present progress or future attainment. The absence of the preposition "with" (or "together") before "saved" is not to be taken as a denial or correction of the social character of the Jews' and Gentiles' common salvation, as the next verse shows.

6. *in the Messiah Jesus raised and enthroned us together in the heavens.*

---

[64] EE, p. 155.

[65] In the Pauline writings the verb "to justify" is used 27 times, to which ought to be added 57 occurrences of "righteousness," 7 of two related nouns, and 7 others containing the adjective "righteous" in a related sense. There are 29 appearances of "to save," 18 of "salvation," and 12 of "savior." See Morgenthaler, *Statistik*, pp. 89, 147. Among the sermons and speeches of Paul reproduced by Luke, only one (Act 13:38–39) contains an explicit reference to the justification doctrine which is unfolded in Galatians, Philippians, Romans, I Cor 1:30.

[66] The future is preferred by Paul, see Rom 5:9–10; 9:27; 10:9, 13; 11:14, 26; I Cor 3:15; 5:5, etc. The present is found in I Cor 1:18, cf. 21; II Cor 2:15; the aorist (connected with "in hope!") in Rom 8:24; cf. II Tim 1:9; Titus 3:5.

[67] E.g. Rom 3:24, 26, 28; 5:9; I Cor 6:11; Gal 3:17.

[68] Matt 9:22; Mark 10:52; 16:16, etc.; James 2:14.

[69] E.g. Deut 33:29; Ps 56[57]:3; Isa 10:20.   [70] See COMMENT IX on 1:3–14.

[71] "Justified" in the perfect tense: Rom 6:7; I Cor 4:4; in the aorist: Rom 4:2; 5:9; 8:30; I Cor 6:11, etc.; in the present and future: Rom 2:13; 3:24, etc., and always (except 3:6?) in Galatians. Regarding "sanctification" see I Thess 5:23; Rom 15:16; I Cor 1:2; 6:11; 7:14; Eph 5:26. The same variety is found in the tenses of, "to reconcile" (Rom 5:10; II Cor 5:18–20).

These words both repeat and give puzzling interpretation to the contents of vs. 5ab. They are repetitious, for "raised" is a synonym of "made alive." The Jews and Gentiles benefit in common rather than as individuals, and both groups receive God's gift "in the Messiah" only, i.e. with him, through him, like him, not in competition with, or apart from him.[72] The same verse is interpretative, however, because it makes no reference to "death in lapses," adds the "enthronement in heavens," and complements the Messiah title with the name "Jesus." Verse 5a told from what, how, by, and in whom the saints were saved; vs. 6 likewise refers to the modality ("raised," "together," "in the Messiah"), but adds an indication of why this salvation took place. Verses 7 and 10b say more about the purpose, vss. 8–10a more about the cause and modality. The formula "in the Messiah Jesus" will recur in 7 and 10. Just as the words "in Christ" describe the cause, modality, place, and purpose of salvation so does this formula. For attempts to explain the meaning of "enthroned" see COMMENT IV.

7. *in order to prove.* The verb used here, as well as the corresponding noun "demonstration" or "proof," are favorites of Paul.[73] Both verb and noun were used by the Greek writers, and on rare occasions in the LXX, for any sort of omen, indication, display, or exhibit. But they also possess specific legal and scientific meanings. In the juridical realm, they denote not only the information of an indictment against someone, but also the actual proof of his guilt or innocence.[74] See COMMENT V for a discussion of the lawsuit imagery in which the term "prove" belongs.

throughout the ages to come. The Greek words might as well be translated, "among the attacking [hostile] aeons." The opinions of interpreters are sharply divided here:[75] the verb translated by "to come" can possess a neutral meaning pointing to something which comes, or turns up, without any malicious intent, but sometimes it possesses the specific connotation of a malicious surprise attack. The noun *aiōnes* ("ages" or "aeons") may mean no more than any stretch of time. Unless there is a qualifying attribute, it is not clear whether the speaker or writer has an evil or a good age in mind.[76] Earlier it was shown that according to the Bible *no* time or age is actually neutral; each time is shaped and filled by its specific content. But the same term had a religious meaning even before Paul's time, and was to play a great role in the Valentinian Gnosis.[77] Certainly the technical second-century Gnostic meaning of *aiōn* cannot

---

[72] Cf. Rom 6:3–11: in this passage the formulae "into Christ," "into his death," "like Christ," "with Christ," "through the glory of the Father" are finally (at the end of vs. 11) summed up by the term, "in the Messiah Jesus."

[73] See Rom 2:15; 3:25–26; 9:17 (quoting Exod 9:16); 9:22; II Cor 8:24 (verb and noun! Cf. Plato *leg.* XII 966B); Philip 1:28; cf. I Tim 1:16; II Tim 4:14; Titus 2:10; 3:2; Heb 6:10–11.

[74] LSLex, 558; WBLex, 262. W. G. Kümmel, *"Paresis und endeixis. Ein Beitrag zum Verständnis der paulinischen Rechtfertigungslehre,"* ZTK 49 (1952), 154–67, however, argues against the applicability of this meaning to the interpretation of Rom 3:25–26.

[75] A neutral, temporal understanding of the phrase was accepted from the traditional interpretation, e.g. by Robinson, p. 52; Dibelius, HbNT 12, 2d ed. 1927, 51 Sasse; TWNTE, I, 205–6; Percy, p. 259 n. 5. JB refers to Ps 22:30–31; 48:13; 71:18; 78:5–6; 102:18. The opposite interpretation, taking "aeons" for another name of the principalities and powers mentioned in Eph 1:21; 2:2; 3:10; 6:12, was suggested by R. Reitzenstein, *Das Iranische Erlösungsmysterium* (Bonn: Marcus, 1921), p. 236, then taken up, e.g. by Schlier; Jonas, *Gnostic Religion,* pp. 54–55; Dibelius; Conzelmann; Schille, *Hymnen,* p. 57.

[76] Cf. Eph 1:21; 2:2; 3:9, 11, 21; 6:12 var. lect.

[77] See the NOTE on *world-age* in 2:2, and COMMENT VI C 1 on 1:15–23.

possibly be drawn upon for interpreting Eph 2:7, but some explicit statements made in Ephesians about the relevance of God's work and the church's existence for the principalities and powers offer the possibility that this verse speaks about the confrontation between the church and the powers: Christ "fills all things" (including the powers) and "the church" (1:23). According to 3:9–10 the mystery hidden for "ages" (*aiōnes*) is now being revealed "through the church to the governments and authorities in the heavens." In 6:12–13 the attack of "the overlords of this dark world" against the saints is mentioned. Thus there are sufficient parallels to 2:7 in Ephesians that mention a function which the church is to fulfill among angelic or demonic powers.[78]

But an equally weighty series of passages in Ephesians suggests that the *aiōnes* in 2:7 have a temporal meaning only. The distinction discussed earlier between the present and the coming *aiōnes* (1:21), the parallel, if not synonymous, use of "ages" and "generations" (3:5, 9, 21; Col 1:26); the eternity formula "for ever and ever" (lit. "the age of the ages," or "the aeon of the aeons" (3:21), stands opposite the angelic-demonic understanding.

A decision for one of the two competing interpretations should not be made arbitrarily because elements of both are supported by the context. As shown in COMMENT V B on 1:15–23 the powers enumerated in 1:21 signify the invisible yet real structures, institutions and traditions of creaturely life. The age of the Caesars, the age of the Holy Roman Empire including its medieval and Napoleonic revivals, also the ages of the Reformation, colonization, Enlightenment, revolution, etc. belong among those "powers." Even successive generations and diverse families are not neutral age-groups but sometimes confront one another with bitterness. Each raises its claims for uniqueness, worthiness, respect, if not worship. Ages, generations, families, etc. precisely in their untouchable value and worth, or their equally intangible depravity and wickedness, are according to Eph 2:7 destined to perceive the evidence which God gives of his grace, through the goodness shown to the saints.

The translation "ages" was chosen in order to preserve the concrete, specific, and historic aspect of God's grace and the church's function. The angelic-demonic dimension of the "ages" does not show in the translation given, but will be made explicit in 3:10. When Eph 2:7 and 3:10 are read together, Ephesians need no longer be suspected of supporting a superstitious cosmology; yet the reader is warned not to neglect the spiritual dimensions of human existence to which the epistle points. Both verses completely exclude the notion that the church is concerned only with the cure and salvation of individual souls, and has nothing to do with the rising and falling, good or evil structures, institutions, and powers of individual and social, psychic and political life. A paraphrase of Eph 2:7 might go so far as to read "God will prove . . . his grace . . . to the Ciceros and Neros of tomorrow."

through the goodness [*shown*] *to us*. The Greek noun "goodness" occurs in the LXX, above all in the Psalms. Only in a minority of cases does it denote

---

[78] Further removed passages are I Cor 2:6–7; I Peter 1:12; not to speak of apocryphal and apocalyptic notions such as the fight over Moses' body mentioned in Jude 9, or the "angels of the churches" addressed in Rev 2–3.

human kindness; mostly it is a summary description of God's love and mercy. Paul usually describes by this noun God's love of men,[79] but occasionally, when alluding to Greek catalogues of virtues, he means by it a human attitude.[80] The formula "[God's] goodness upon Israel" occurs in *Ps of Sol* 5:21[18]. Not because of some virtuous behavior by the saints but only for his own name's sake does God give evidence of his grace to the world by showing goodness to his chosen people.

8. *through faith*. Verse 8 overlaps the parallel antiphon of vs. 5b with two new elements: in Greek the article is added to "grace," and the words "through faith" appear. Are the changes a proof of the interpolative character of vss. 8–9?[81] Again, this is possible, but proves nothing about the authorship of Ephesians or of this passage. The Pauline substance of these verses is uncontested even when Ephesians is ascribed to a pseudonymous author: the capital epistles of Paul explain the meaning of the words "through faith." Twice[82] Paul alludes to a Habbakuk text for clarifying what faith and its effect are. But he quotes Hab 2:4 in a version that corresponds to neither the MT nor LXX.[83] The Greek OT speaks of man "righteous by my [God's] faithfulness," the Hebrew of him who is "righteous by his [own] faith." Paul omits the pronouns "my" and "his" for reasons hard to define. (a) It may be that he understands the passage to refer to God's faithfulness.[84] (b) He may also, just as does the epistle to the Hebrews, have Christ's faithfulness in mind; he ascribes to the obedience and love of Christ toward God and man a decisive role in justification.[85] (c) Finally, he may intend to speak of

[79] Rom 2:4; 11:22; cf. Titus 3:4; the corresponding adjective "good" is found in Rom 2:4; cf. I Peter 2:3; Luke 5:39. The Apostolic Fathers, e.g. I Clem 9:1; 14:4; II Clem xv 5; *Diogn.* IX 1–2, 6; Ign. *Magnesians* X follow his example.

[80] Aristotle *eth. Nic., passim;* Philo *legatio ad Gaium* 73; Plutarch *de Demetrio* 50:1; *de Galba* 22:7. In the NT see Gal 5:22; II Cor 6:6; Rom 3:12; Col 3:12. The adjective "good" is used in Eph 4:32, also in I Cor 15:33 in a quotation from Menander. The quote demonstrates Paul's ability in ethical contexts to make use of the formulations of Greek philosophers, poets, orators. Cf. also the Cleanthes quote in Acts 17:28. The catalogues of virtues will be discussed in COMMENT VIII on 4:17–32; see also BIBLIOGRAPHY 19 in vol. 34A.

[81] See the NOTE on 2:4–10. Schille, *Hymnen*, p. 58, holds that the "gloss" (vss. 8–9) has the purpose of redressing the possible damage done by the all too rampant mythological contents of vss. 6–7: "The mythology is straightened out."

[82] In Gal 3:11 and Rom 1:17.

[83] Variant readings of Heb 10:38 reveal that at least some copyists had become aware of a possible inaccuracy.

[84] Rom 3:3: "Should their perfidy abrogate God's faithfulness?" Cf. the exclamation "Faithful is God," I Thess 5:24; II Thess 3:3; I Cor 1:9; 10:13; II Cor 1:18, and the synonymous use of the terms "faithfulness," "righteousness," "truth of God" in Rom 3:3, 5, 7.

[85] Heb 2:17; 3:2, 5–6; 12:2; Philip 2:8; Rom 5:19; Gal 2:20; Eph 5:2, 25. Cf. Gal 2:16, 20; 3:22, 26; Philip 3:9; Rom 3:22, 26; Eph 3:12; 4:13; also II Tim 3:15?—i.e. those passages that either contain a superfluous doublet by combining "faith of the Messiah Jesus" with man's "believing in" him, or that correlate Christ's and the Christians' faith. In the latter case the formula, from "faith to faith" (Rom 1:17) would contain more than empty rhetoric. See E. Lohmeyer, "Gesetzeswerke," ZNW 28 (1929), 177–207; repr. in *Probleme paulinischer Theologie* (henceforth cited as *Probleme*) (Stuttgart: Kohlhammer, n.d.), pp. 31–74: "Faith of Jesus Christ" is "the Pauline antithesis to service of the law. It is a genitivus subjectivus for through Christ comes faith; it is a genitivus objectivus for faith is directed toward Christ; and it is a genitivus qualitativus for Christ is this faith" (p. 74). The issue was raised first by J. Haussleiter, *Der Glaube Jesu*, Erlangen/Leipzig: Deichert, 1891; then by G. Kittel, "Pistis Jesou Christou bei Paulus," TSK 79 (1906), 419–36; A. G. Herbert, "Faithfulness and Faith," *Theology* 98 (1955), 373–79; T. F. Torrance, "One Aspect of the Biblical Confession of Faith," ET 68 (1956–57), 111–14; E. Fuchs, "Jesus und der Glaube," ZTK 55 (1958), 170–85; P. Vallotton, *Christ et la Foi*, Geneva: Labor et Fides, 1960; R. N. Longenecker, *Paul Apostle of Liberty* (New York: Harper, 1964), pp. 148–53; H. Ljungmann, *Pistis* (Lund: Gleerup, 1964), pp. 38–40. To the arguments compiled by these authors ought to be added a reference to the indispensable function of the faithful Abraham (Gal 3:9) and of a faithful OT king or priest for the salvation of Israel and the blessing of the nations. A discussion of the "faith of Christ" is also found in K. Kertelge, *Rechtfertigung bei*

the faith of the saints (cf. Eph 1:1, 15, 19, etc.). It is impossible to exclude any one of these three senses from the interpretation of the word "faith" in Eph 2:8. Of course the last meaning appears to be the easiest, but the continuation of vs. 8 shows that Paul was aware of the danger that his readers might think only of man's faith and misapprehend this faith as a work. If Paul calls "faith" a "gift of God" at all, he cannot intend to overlook the fact that God who gives faith is himself faithful and proves his loyalty to the covenant by the gift of his beloved, obedient, and loving Son. By the only way to keep a covenant, i.e. "through faith," God, the Messiah, and Jews faithful as Abraham are joined together (Gal 3; Rom 4). In Eph 2:8 as much as in Galatians and Romans, Paul wants to affirm that the Gentiles are saved in no other way. The "faith" by which "you are saved" would be no good if it were not first shown by God himself and then begun and completed on earth by Jesus Christ (cf. Heb 12:2).

This [was]. The neuter pronoun "this" may refer to one of three things: the "grace," the verb "saved," the noun "faith." It is Augustine's merit to have pointed out that the *gratia gratis data* includes the gift of "faith" to man.[86] Faith is not a contribution of man to salvation, least of all a meritorious contribution.[87] A true believer will never boast that his coming to faith, his solid stance in faith, and his (ethical) demonstration of faith[88] are of his own doing. "Faith came"—its exemplary anticipation by the faithful Abraham notwithstanding (Gal 3:6–9)—when the "promised seed," i.e. the Messiah Jesus, "came" (Gal 3:19, 23, 25–26). The Messiah is not only the confirmation and fulfillment of all "promises of God," he is also the epitome and means of man's "Amen" to God (II Cor 1:20). In consequence the anti-Pelagian teaching of Augustine—that not only grace itself, but also man's acceptance of grace is a gift of God—corresponds fully to Paul's preaching. Still, the pronoun "this" in Eph 2:8 need not have the restricted (anti-Pelagian) meaning. It may also refer to the eternal election by grace and the "outpouring" of grace mentioned in 1:4–8, and to the preaching of the "true word, the message that saves" (1:13).

not of your own doing—it is a gift of God—9. not [as a reward] for works. Lit. "not of yourselves . . . not from works." The insertion of negations to underline positive statements is a stylistic element appropriate to a polemic setting. This style-form is more abundantly used in the Gospel and First Epistle of John, and in the disputes aired in I Thessalonians, Galatians, Corinthians, Romans, James, Hebrews than in other NT books. Explicit nega-

---

Paulus (Münster: Aschendorff, 1967), pp. 162–66, and in J. Bligh, "Did Jesus Live by Faith?", *Heythrop Journal* 9 (1968), 414–19, esp. 418–19; G. E. Howard, "Christ the End of the Law," JBL 88 (1969), 331–37, esp. 335. Entirely new light has been thrown on this issue by the essay of G. M. Taylor in JBL 85 (1966), 58–76, which was summarized above in fn. 27 on Eph 1:5. See also M. Barth, "The Faith of the Messiah," *Heythrop Journal* 10 (1969), 363–70.

[86] E.g. *de dono perseverantiae* 2.

[87] Faith is therefore *not*, as occasional early Jewish (e.g. the opponents mentioned in the Epistle of James) and the later Tridentine polemics suggested, to be understood as a work which substitutes for all the works of obedience required by God; see StB, III, 562–66, and H. Denzinger and A. Schönmetzer, *Enchiridion Symbolorum*, 34th ed. (Freiburg: Herder, 1965), no. 1533 (older eds. no. 802.). The love in which faith is working out is the fulfillment not the annulment of all commandments (Gal 5:6, 14; Rom 13:8–10), etc.

[88] Of which Paul speaks, e.g. in Gal 2:16; Rom 13:11; I Cor 16:13; Col 1:23; Gal 5:22; Rom 1:12; Eph 1:15.

tions rarely occur in the peaceable epistle to the Ephesians, and amazingly seldom in Philippians and Colossians, though the latter are not lacking sharp polemics.[89] The exclusion of a meritorious character of "works" does not mean that all human activity in obedience to God is condemned. For the relation of the "works" here condemned to the "good works" mentioned in 2:10, see COMMENT VI.

lest anyone boast about himself. Paul warns or accuses Gentiles, Jews, Christians, friends and opponents alike—though for different reasons. "No flesh shall boast [about itself] before God!" (I Cor 1:29). Occasionally he substitutes for *kauchaomai,* "boasting," the verb *physioumai,* "to be puffed up," or he uses both together as synonyms.[90] Equally, the active perfect of *peithō: pepoitha,* "to put one's confidence in" means almost the same thing in Pauline diction.[91] The notion that a man "dead in lapses and sins" should take pride in himself because he possesses worldy wisdom or the law, and is circumcised, is excluded just as much as certain Christians who brag about their superior knowledge or ritual perfection. The bragger is man in revolt against God, and a tyrant over his fellow man. But he who boasts of God and accepts his own weakness gives God the glory he is due, and he will be praised by God. Instead of stressing his own and demanding other people's bodily circumcision, his heart will be circumcised (Rom 2:25–29). Because "circumcision, that handmade operation" (2:11) is mentioned in the context of Eph 2:9, it is obvious that circumcision, boasting about it, or imposing it upon the Gentiles, are among the "works" which are denied saving power. How should anyone brag of such works?

10. *God himself has made us what we are. In the Messiah Jesus we are created.* The translation "made us what we are" is J. Moffatt's. Lit. "we are his [and no one else's!] work."[92] The Greek noun (*poiēma*) used here has often, esp. in the LXX, the same general meaning as the other better known word for "work": *ergon* which occurs in both vss. 9 and 10c. But *poiēma* can also bear the connotation of a "work of art" (so JB), especially a poetic product, including fiction.[93] The addition of the verb "created" to *poiēma* in vs. 10 reveals that a creative act could be, but was not always or necessarily, associated with it. Eph 2:10 speaks distinctly of divine creation, not fiction. The work of God done in Christ or by Christ is not only the first and final work of God. It is, as the Gospel of John and the epistle to the Hebrews explicitly state, a perfect work,[94] i.e. God's masterpiece. Later passages in Ephe-

---

[89] Negations are found in Eph 1:21; 2:8–9; 3:5; 4:20, 26, 30; 5:5, 17–18; 6:6–7, 9, 12. If Philippians is undoubtedly Pauline and yet almost lacks the literary feature of negative juxtapositions to positive statements, then Ephesians and Colossians are not neccessarily inauthentic because the frequent negations typical e.g. of Galatians and Romans are absent from them.

[90] Gal 6:4, 13; I Cor 3:21; 4:6–7, 18–19; 5:2; 8:1; 13:4; II Cor 10:17; Rom 2:17, 23; 5:2, 11; 11:18; cf. 3:27; 4:2; Col 2:18. To be "puffed up" always had a bad overtone, "boasting" most often—except when done "in God," "in the Lord," "in Christ," "of weakness," "in hope": Gal 6:14; I Cor 1:31; II Cor 10:17; 11:30; 12:9; Rom 5:2, 11. Only a fool (e.g. Paul intentionally making a fool of himself in II Cor 11–12) would be proud of other things. The negative and positive Pauline utterances on boasting are anticipated by Jer 9:23–24, a passage to which the apostle refers in II Cor 10:17.

[91] II Cor 1:9; Rom 2:19; cf. Luke 18:9. Cf. Bultmann, ThNT, I, 242–43.

[92] While Robinson, p. 156, comments, *"Workmanship* is a little unfortunate," this strange term is still used in the RSV.

[93] Starting from Eph 2:10, L. Williamson has aptly summarized the whole message of Ephesians under the title *God's Work of Art,* Richmond: CLC Press, 1971.

[94] John 4:34; 17:4; 19:30; Heb 2:10; 5:9; 12:2.

sians, 4:7, 11–13, 15–16, will show that completion of the work done in Christ includes not only the activity of God, Christ, and the Spirit but also the mission, conduct and action of the saints. See COMMENTS I on 1:1–2; V and XII on 1:3–14 for the formula "in Christ," and COMMENT VI on 2:1–10 for the relation between God's creative activity and man's works.

for those good works. The preposition *epi* here translated by "for," usually means, if connected with the dative, "on," "above," "on the ground," or "at the time of." But there are some instances where it indicates the purpose, goal or result of an action.[95] The term "good works" is, contrary to an opinion widely spread among Protestant interpreters,[96] solidly founded in undisputed Pauline writings. These works have nothing to do with "works (of law)" by which Paul's opponents sought to secure their justification; see COMMENT VI B and C. Good works are neither a basis or means of salvation (or justification), nor simply a desirable goal, but the gift of God provided for those saved from death.[97]

which God has provided as our way of life. Lit. "which God has prepared beforehand so that we walk in them." The Greek original uses the sophisticated rhetorical device of the attracted relative pronoun. The verb "has provided" refers again to all that was decided upon by God before the foundation of the world (1:4–10), probably also to the pre-existence of the beloved son. In his interpretation of 2:10, Chrysostom speaks of a "road" prepared by God. On this highway built by God the commandments of God are fulfilled. Those walking on it rejoice in the law of God because it is spiritual, righteous, and good. From the beginning it was the sole purpose of the law to point out, or to direct the chosen people to and upon, this way.

COMMENTS I–VII on 2:1–10

I   The Structure

The anacoluthic verses 2:1–3 describe the Gentiles' and the Jews' common captivity in death prior to the demonstration of God's grace. They are followed by the hymnic contents of 4–10 praising the salvation by resurrection with Christ, the task of the church vis-à-vis the world, and her preparation for good works. The hymnic part is interrupted by vss. 8–9, which in the form of an excursus combine the praise of *sola gratia* with polemics against those who would boast of themselves and their own works. In the NOTE on 2:4–10 reasons have been presented for this formal and material subdivision of the section under review.

[95] E.g. Wisd Sol 2:23; I Thess 4:7; Gal 5:13; II Tim 2:14; WBLex, 287; BDF, 235:4.

[96] See among the latest, e.g. Schille, *Hymnen*, pp. 54, 58, who considers the reference to "good works" in 2:10 an un-Pauline trait, contrary to Pauline opinion as formulated in 2:8–9, and therefore a product of a *Gemeinde-Theologie* which was still fettered by Jewish notions of "righteousness by works."

[97] See e.g. Bengel and Robinson; also Schille, *Hymnen*, p. 59, despite his just quoted negative attitude to "good works." Not only in the epistle of James which is reputedly anti-Pauline because of its emphasis on works, but also in I Peter—the non-Pauline NT epistle that shows the strongest Pauline influence—the "doing of good" (works) is very much emphasized. W. Brandt "Wandel als Zeugnis nach dem 1. Petrusbrief," in *Verbum Dei manet in aeternum*, Fs O. Schmitz (Witten: Luther-Verlag, 1953), pp. 10–25; and J. H. Elliott, *The Elect and the Holy*, NovT Suppl. 12 (Leiden: Brill, 1966), pp. 179–82, speak in their interpretation of the concept *anastrophē* (conduct, which is related to *peripateō*, to walk, in Eph 2:10, etc.) of a *Lebensführung*, that is, a "way of life" which is a testimony to God in a pagan environment.

II   The Realm of the Evil One

The commander of the atmosphere described in 2:2 is a monarch,[98] his realm an absolute monarchy. He is called "devil" in 4:27; 6:11, "the evil one" in 6:16. In a NOTE on 2:2 other names were listed which are used by Paul and other NT writers to designate him. Though he is often mentioned in the Bible, it is impossible to derive an ontology, phenomenology, and history of Satan sufficiently complete to create a "satanology" which in the slightest measure corresponds to the weight of biblical "theo-logy."[99] Some hints only are to be given here which may contribute to an understanding of the most Satanic verse in Ephesians, i.e. 2:2. Surprising things are said about the devil's location and history, and about his mode of operation:

As to place, the reference to the "atmosphere" or air is repeated in 6:11–12. The devil and his hosts reside "in the heavens"—a localization that may have been made possible by OT allusions to Satan's operation before God's throne, by the distinction of several heavens mentioned earlier, and by Jewish apocryphal teachings.[100] According to Matthew, John, and Revelation[101] the devil's obstruction to God is brought to an end when he is thrown out; one day he will be confined to everlasting torture. But before this happens he still makes his power felt, and he is more active against Jesus, his disciples, the church, than against anybody else. It may be that such Christian sects as the second-century Naassenes and Ophites offered him respect and worship precisely because of the enormous power which he exercised throughout the history of mankind, from Adam to the present. It was never customary to ascribe to the devil only the locality of, and dominion over, the lowest of the three levels of the universe that are distinguished by some among the ancient peoples, e.g. in Phil 2:10.

H. Schlier[102] surmises that just as in second-century Gnosticism, so also in Ephesians the devil's realm was imagined to lie between God's heaven and the earth, forming a dividing wall. He explains this wall by reference to *horos*, i.e. that "limit" which kept man separated from the *plērōma* of divine *Aiōnes* and from access to their origin, the All-Father.[103] By combining Eph 2:2, 14–16 and 4:8, Schlier concludes that according to Ephesians, Christ's victory consists of his breaking through the hostile wall from above and

---

[98] Cf. 6:11–12; Matt 12:24–26; John 12:31, etc.; Rev 12–13. According to Luke 4:6 the ruler of this realm is aware that his power is not absolute but derived: "it is given to me [by God]."

[99] See J. Kallas, *The Satanward View*, Philadelphia: Westminster, 1965; M.-E. Boismard, "Satan selon l'ancient testament et le nouveau testament," *Lumière et Vie* 15, St. Alban-Leysse, 15 (1966), 61–76 (ref.). Apocalyptic books and Qumran literature contain a much more pronounced satanology than the biblical books; see Braun, QuNT, pp. 216–17, for Qumran. H. A. Kelley, *The Devil, Demonology and Witchcraft*, New York: Doubleday, 1968, represents recent attempts at demythologization. Just as in Jewish apocalyptic, rabbinical, and sectarian circles, so in the NT the role of the evil one is—due to dualistic influence of Persian origin?—either described in political and religious terms, or the devil is specifically described as the seducer of man, the prosecutor before God's court, or the executor of punishment. Cf. StB I, 136–49; G. F. Moore, *Judaism* I, 406–7; 478–83; II, 340–43.

[100] See e.g. Job 1–2; I Kings 22:19–21; Zech 3:1–3. In *Test. Benj.* III Satan is called an "airy spirit"; cf. Philo *de gigantibus* 6; *de plantatione* 14; II (*Slav.*) *Enoch* 38:9; *Ascension of Isaiah* VII 9; X 29; StB IV 501–35, esp. 515–16 for the residence of the demons in the air; see also COMMENT II on 1:3–14.

[101] Matt 12:25–27; John 12:31; 13:27; 14:30; 16:11; Rev 12:8–9; 20:10.

[102] *Christus*, pp. 18–26; Schlier, on 2:2 and esp. 2:14. Schlier's main proof-texts stem from the Valentinian Gnosis, the Odes of Solomon, and Mandaean writings.

[103] As was shown in COMMENT VI C 1 on 1:15–23.

returning to the God who sent him—a return in which liberated human souls were permitted to ascend with him to heaven. This concatenation of passages in Ephesians with the conceptuality of Valentinian teaching and the Odes of Solomon is ingenious enough, but because of the date and the different content of the writings quoted by Schlier, it is also less than solid. After all, what is gained by replacing the subterranean location of the devil with a supramundane realm? According to Schlier it elucidates the image of the "broken wall" (2:14). But in Eph 2:15 that wall is not identified with the devil or his realm but with the "law," and while the final destruction of the wall is explicitly stated, Eph 2:2 asserts that the devil is still ruling "now." Unless Schlier could prove that devil and law are identified by Paul and that the abrogated law is still valid now, his argument is not consistent. Christ's descent "down to the earth" (4:9) adds additional evidence against Schlier: the author of Ephesians did not make use of one world view only. The enemy to be conquered by Christ is not only in the air, but also in the lowest places of the earth. Christ had to overcome Satan, and the church has to resist him wherever he is active, whether in heavenly places, on earth, or in subterranean hideouts. High *and* low places are equally threatened or dominated by the evil one.

As to the time and history of devilish activity, Eph 2:2 agrees on at least one thing with the Gospels and Revelation: The devil is "now at work."[104] Whenever the adverb "now" is used elsewhere in Ephesians, it is to proclaim the present time as the day of salvation. The author has identified the past with ignorance, darkness, deceit (3:5–10; 4:17–19; 5:8), and yet according to Eph 2:2 the devil is working "now"; according to 6:12–16 he operates against the church from outside; following 5:5–6 he is active also inside the church, cf. II Cor 11:14. A punitive role is attributed to him over false Christians in I Cor 5:5; 10:9 (also 11:30?). Obviously it is precisely the demonstration of God's presence and power which makes the devil react with unheard-of outbursts and counter-demonstrations of his presence. The end-time is a time of devilish tribulation, not of an easy victory (cf. the last petition of the Lord's Prayer).

The mode of the devil's operation, according to 2:2, is spiritual. Ephesians gives no reason to associate the devil more intimately with matter, materialism, or the sensual realm than with lofty religious, political, or moral ideas. According to 2:3 the subjection of the "passions" and the "thoughts" of the Jews to the "flesh" have the same devastating result as the subservience of the Gentiles to the devil in 2:2. Bodily *and* mental desires have been corrupted. The term "flesh"[105] as such denotes nothing evil. In the OT and NT

---

[104] Cf. the stories of Jesus' temptation; of Peter's well-meant recommendation that Jesus spare himself; of the demons crying out against Jesus' activity; of the suspicion that Beelzebub or demons operate in Jesus; of Judas the traitor. To these stories correspond the apocalyptic visions of Matt 24 par.; II Thess 2; Rev 12–13; 20.

[105] See Bultmann, ThNT, I, 239–46; Davies, PRJ, pp. 17–35; idem, "Paul and the Dead Sea Scrolls: Flesh and Spirit," in SaNT, pp. 157–82; K. G. Kuhn, "New Light on Temptation, Sin and Flesh in the New Testament," SaNT, pp. 94–113; R. Meyer and E. Schweizer, art. *sarx*, TWNTE, VII, 98–151. A. Sand, *Der Begriff Fleisch in den paulinischen Hauptbriefen*, Biblische Untersuchungen 2, Regensburg: Pustet, 1967, seeks to derive the Pauline concept immediately from the OT, without essential qualification by rabbinical or other Jewish interpretations. Cf. also fn. 145 to COMMENT V on 1:15–23.

"flesh" describes the muscles of the body, the pudenda, meat used for sacrifice or food, the complete man (including his soul and spiritual activities), and finally animals, procreation, descendants, and relatives. When only man is meant, "flesh and blood" are sometimes mentioned together. Because all of this is created by God, it is far from being "neutral." Instead of being neither good or bad, it is, just as are all other creatures of God, "very good."[106] Thus "flesh" often has a positive meaning.[107] But "all flesh had corrupted their way," and God's good creature, man, is now under the condemnation and "wrath" of God.[108] Occasionally Paul and John come close to using "flesh" in that evil sense which has been attributed to the body and matter in Platonizing philosophy and religion, especially in Gnosticism and Manicheism. But the NT writers do not follow dualistic tendencies in a completely Hellenistic way, for they include highest intellectual and devout religious performances under "flesh," and they praise Christ for coming "in the flesh." Thus their awareness of corruption comprehends a wider realm than the sphere of matter and finiteness only, and they proclaim that in assuming flesh the Son of God did not hide but manifested the glory and love of God (Rom 8:3; John 1:14, etc.). While Paul does not seek an escape from life "in the flesh" but continues "in faith," he does warn of conduct or knowledge "according to the flesh."[109]

In Eph 2:3 "flesh" is used in its worst possible sense. Though flesh is never listed among the principalities and powers, in its dominion, outreach and internal corruption it is worse than the most wicked of them. Just as the Devil according to 2:2 worked spiritually in man, so the flesh corrupts not only the physical existence, bodily needs, and sensuality of man, but is as dominating a power as his thoughts. Its works—including religious works such as supposedly meritorious abstinence, imposed circumcision, soul-saving festivals (Galatians and Colossians)—are as much opposed to the operation and fruit of the Spirit (Gal 5) as the devil himself. In Eph 2:3 Paul may have in mind the "evil impulse" of which rabbis began to speak in his time.[110] While the Gentiles' sins can at least be attributed to the external influence of the Devil, the failure of the Jews is caused, according to Eph 2:3, by that wickedness which resides and is triumphant in man himself. In Col 3:5 all men, Jews and Gentiles alike, are urged to kill evil desire.

Still, Paul does not condemn impulses, "desires" and corresponding actions as if they were evil in themselves. The Stoic ideal of *ataraxia*, i.e. of an existence free of any passions, is far from the rabbis' and the apostle's minds.[111] It appears that the description of the Jews' evil conduct is explicable solely on the ground of the meanings which flesh, desire, and will are given in Rom 7–8. The distinction of Jewish and Gentile sin by reference to the

---

[106] Gen 1:31; J. Barr, in HDB, p. 299.   [107] E.g. in Gen 2:23–24; Isa 40:5; Ezek 21:5.
[108] Gen 6:3, 12; Isa 40:6; Eph 2:3. In almost all passages that set flesh and Spirit in opposition, "flesh" has an evil connotation, see, e.g. Rom 8:2–13; Gal 3:3; 5:16–23; John 6:63; but cf. Rom 1:3–4.
[109] Gal 2:20; II Cor 5:16; 10:2–3; Phil 1:22.
[110] Coutts, p. 204; Moore, *Judaism*, I, 479–96.
[111] E.g. in I Thess 2:17; Philip 1:23, Paul speaks in a positive way of his "desires." In Col 3:5 "desire" is qualified by the adjective "evil"; it is obviously not evil by nature as is Augustine's *concupiscentia*. Only when desire is combined with sin and rebelling against the forbidden coveting (Rom 1:24; 6:12; 7:5, 7–11; 13:9, 14; cf. John 1:13; I John 2:16), it becomes a means and manifestation of sin and death. Cf. Bultmann, ThNT, I, 223–27.

flesh and devil respectively, and the equal condemnation of both, is reminiscent of Rom 1:18 – 3:23 and Gal 2:15. The Gentiles, who do not have the law, are exposed to the same judge and judgment as those who were given the law (Rom 2:12; 5:12–14, 20–21).

Does this mean that all men are sinners by nature, that it is natural and essential for man to sin? The formulation, "by nature under the wrath of God" (Eph 2:3), appears to suggest a positive answer. But the term "nature" (*physis*) is far from being easily explained and correctly understood. In Pauline writings at least four variant meanings of *physis* can be discerned. The concept "by nature" might mean (a) in the natural order of things; (b) in reality, as opposed to error or fiction; (c) voluntarily, as opposed to being forced by external laws; (d) determined by birth, tradition, or fate.[112] Only the last of these fits the context of Eph 2:3. This verse corresponds to such confessions of lifelong sin against God as are found, e.g. in Ps 51:5; Jer 3:25; Job 14:6. The first variant is excluded because Paul is not a Manichean, and while the second and third make good enough sense they suggest ideas not essential to the argument at hand. Paul is most likely speaking about a status that has come into being because of man's historic defaulting and is now characteristic of both Jewish and Gentile existence before God. The "nature" mentioned here has the same relation to the created essence of man as the incidental and unnatural has to the normal and natural. There is no hint of a fall of nature, or of a timeless fallenness, but there is full consciousness of the historic corruption of the flesh.

In their commentaries on Ephesians, Chrysostom, Jerome, (in other contexts Augustine[113]) but also Thomas and Calvin have elaborated upon the contrast of the "nature" mentioned in 2:3 to the "grace" praised in 2:5, 8. For them the juxtaposition of "nature" and "grace," perhaps to a lesser degree also the formula "children of wrath," attest and confirm the doctrine of "original sin," understood in the sense of a sinful quality and state which is passed on from generation to generation. However Eph 2:3 certainly does not assert that because of their procreation and a physical transmission of the poison of sin, even babies are condemned. Paul speaks here about adults and to adults; babies can be included only in a derivative way. The position and function which the term "by nature" possesses in 2:3 are totally unlike the role of "grace" in 2:5, 8. "Children of wrath" is a Semitic idiom for condemned and cursed men, not a reference to babies. The necessary confession of sin and the declaration of mankind's solidarity under the righteous wrath of God must not be identified with the fabrication and promotion of a doctrine of innate sin—in Eph 2:1–3 as little as in Rom 3:10–18, 22–23, 5:12–21. The distinctive description of Gentiles and Jews is free from the sweeping affirmation of man's "natural" depravity. Not a human doctrine, but the experience of God's "wrath" is the occasion for Paul's statement, cf. Rom 1:18.

In the Bible the "wrath" of God, in turn, does not represent the intemperate outburst of an uncontrolled character. It is rather the temperature of God's

---

[112] Variant (a) is supported by Rom 1:26–27; 11:21, 24; I Cor 11:14; (b) by Gal 4:8; (c) by Rom 2:14–15; (d) by Gal 2:14; Rom 2:27. The history of the interpretation of Eph 2:3 is described by J. Mehlmann, "Natura filii Dei," AnBib 6 (1957) (ref.).
[113] Especially in his anti-Pelegian writings, e.g. PL xxxiii 767–70.

love,[114] the manifestation of his will and power to resist, to overcome, to burn away all that contradicts his counsels of love. According to Gal 3:13 the full "curse" with which God threatened the trespasser was poured out upon Jesus alone so that those threatened by it might be saved. Curse is infinitely worse than wrath.[115]

While, in sum, the rule of the evil one over man is for Paul an undeniable fact, the apostle never goes so far as to say that man is evil by nature. What evil he suffers and what wretchedness he experiences has come to him from the devil, from the flesh, under the wrath of God. Evil is incidental, not essential. It is disorder, not order. It is an entr'acte, not the beginning and not the end. This is not to belittle the hold of evil over man—but it is to show that even its worst exponent, the devil, cannot stand up against God or dominate his creatures forever.

This is made apparent by Paul when he speaks about the fruit of the devil's and the flesh's dominion: The fruit of man's sin is man's "death" (Rom 6:23)! "You . . . we were dead in our lapses" (Eph 2:1, 5), separated from the "life of God" (4:18). There is no glory in the realm of the evil one, least of all for those or among those who fear, serve, or worship him.

III From Death to Life

Ephesians stands out among the other Pauline epistles by the way in which salvation is identified with the already accomplished feat of the resurrection of the saints. In Galatians, Philippians, Rom 1–5, 9–11, the saving act of justification has been so forcefully presented that to this day in western theology those Pauline statements became neglected which put the death-life sequence as much into the foreground as do the Gospel of John and the mainstream of eastern theology.[116] Forgiveness of sins—of which Paul but rarely speaks—became the heart of the message, whereas "newness of life" (Rom 6:4) should be at least as essential to it. Indeed, in Ephesians "forgiveness" has been mentioned—the glorious undertone of 1:7 cannot be forgotten—but in 2:1–10 resurrection and new life are dramatically glorified. What is meant by the death and by the resurrection mentioned in this section?

Those caught "in lapses and sins" are called "dead" (2:1, 5). Does this mean physical death?[117] If it were intimated that the Jews and Gentiles are worthy of death and destined one day to meet their just reward, then Eph 2 ought to be understood as referring to physical death and its anticipation in diseases and suffering of all kind (cf. I Cor 11:30). In that case the appropriate act of salvation would consist of a reduced punishment or amnesty rather than resurrection. But Paul affirms that "dead" people have been "raised" (2:5–6). He speaks of more than threatening death and promised resurrection for he refers to a death and resurrection that have already taken place! It seems that he uses the terms "dead" and "raised" in a metaphorical way in

---

[114] Schlier, p. 109, "His wrath does not exclude his mercy but presupposes it."

[115] The "curse" falls according to Deut 27–29 upon those only with whom God before has made the covenant and to whom the law is given.

[116] As Gal 2:19–20; II Cor 3–5; Phil 1; Rom 6–8.

[117] See for the following Gen 3:3; Deut 30:15–20; Rom 1:32; 5:12; 6:23.

order to speak of "spiritual" death and "spiritual" resurrection. The problem posed by his diction is to explain what might be meant by "spiritual." Are spiritual death and resurrection in any sense less concrete, actual, even physical, than the bodily death and resurrection which wait for man in the future?

Biblical parallels elucidate the diction chosen in Eph 2:1–6. While Israel lives in division, enmity, sin, she is compared to a "valley full of bones; there was no breath in them; they were clean cut off" (Ezek 37:1, 5, 11). Paul says the same of the Gentiles: "They are excluded from the life of God" (Eph 4:18) and therefore "dead" (2:1). In either case it is presupposed that physical life is still in those who are described as "dead." Those "dead in trespasses" still have a bodily life, for they live in "fornication, impurity, passion, evil desire" (Col 2:13; 3:5–7). A voluptuous widow is called "dead even while she lives" (I Tim 5:6). "You have the name of being alive, and you are dead" (Rev 3:1). It is assumed that such people can still hear the reveille, "Awake, you sleeper, rise from the dead" (Eph 5:14). Precisely when the Prodigal Son "lived it up" he was considered "dead" by his father (Luke 15:24, 32). These are hardly oriental overstatements or exaggerations, for already the Psalms identify a life in disease, sin, captivity, alienation, or under defeat by enemies, as a life in the realm of "death" or in *Sheol*.[118] The man forsaken by God and delivered to the powers of evil is already *in* the realm of death (Ps 22). Deadness of this sort was at least as real and certainly a much more dreadful experience to a Jew than physical death.

It is not because of biological or philosophical and moral analysis that biblical authors speak of a death that is due to sin (Rom 5:12, 6:23; I Cor 15:56).[119] Rather, there is a prophetic tone present in all the passages just quoted. In some texts[120] it is made explicit that the finding of God, the judge, or the effect of his law are the basis for the judgment of death. Much more frequent are passages in which death and resurrection are affirmed in the same breath. "O Lord, thou hast brought up my soul from Sheol . . . We have passed from death into life . . . He was dead and is alive again."[121] The statement that the Ephesians were "dead" is therefore neither rhetorical only, nor a kind of moral *post-mortem*. It is equivalent to the confession of many a psalmist and the pronouncement of the Prodigal Son's father: as it is being proclaimed only after the salvation of the dead and lost man, it must be called a *post-resurrectionem*. Only in the light of the reality of God's resuscitating power can the reality of man's former death be recognized.

When was life given to the saints? While the text of Eph 2:5–6 contains no explicit information on the date and place of their resurrection, parallels from Pauline and non-Pauline writings may provide a specific answer:

a) The same resurrection which according to Eph 2:5–6 has taken place

---

[118] E.g. Pss 31:12; 88:3; 143:3; Isa 38:10–20; for details and parallels in Near Eastern religions see C. Barth, *Die Errettung vom Tode* (Zurich: EVZ, 1947), pp. 91–122; also M. Dahood; commentary on the *Psalms*, AB (vols. 16, 17, 17A).

[119] I Tim 5:6 would be an exception if this passage spoke of death like a "barbarian's philosophy calling dead those who . . . have subjected their mind to the psychic passions" (Clement of Alexandria, quoted by Abbott pp. 40–41).

[120] E.g. Rom 1:32; 5:19; 7:10–11; I Cor 15:56; Gal 2:19.

[121] Ps 30:3; Jonah 2:6; I John 3:14; Luke 15:24, 32.

once, in history, and completely (this is the meaning of the Greek aorist used here) "with Christ," "in Christ," "together," is in Col 2:12 called a resurrection "through faith." Is therefore the hour in which faith is born the hour of resurrection? Is faith in itself the miracle of new life given from above? "I live in faith" (Gal 2:20)! Indeed in Gal 2:16b and Rom 13:11 Paul is probably speaking of that hour, as he also uses the aorist tense of believing. In Eph 2:5–6 he may therefore have in mind the moment of enlightenment or conversion. But Paul, who according to Gal 1:13–16 (cf. Acts 9:22, 26) knew at least as much as others about the relevance of the hour of crisis, never called his Damascus experience, or anybody else's analogous conversion, a resurrection—though for him it meant the beginning of a new life, and though he equated the character and value of enlightenment with the act of creation (II Cor 3:17, 4:6, 5:17). Though in Ephesians he speaks to believers and mostly about believers rather than about a worldwide resurrection of the good and the evil,[122] the absence of any reference to faith in vs. 6 is noteworthy; not before vs. 8 will the missing element be added. A resurrection due to faith or a resurrection of faith does not appear to be in Paul's mind.

b) There are commentators on Ephesians, especially of the Gnosticism-oriented school,[123] who place the moment of the saints' resurrection in their baptism. Schille e.g. is convinced that in 2:5–6 baptism is identified with the saving deed of God and the journey of the soul into heaven. This understanding of the sacrament may well have been fostered by the Corinthians, and Paul fights it in I Cor 10:1–13 and in other passages of his Corinthian correspondence where he counters their excessive enthusiasm. It was probably the doctrine of Hymenaeus and Philetus (II Tim 2:17–18), of Menander and others,[124] and it is always repudiated. Twice when Paul speaks explicitly of "baptism" he calls it a burial with Christ (Rom 6:3–4; Col 2:12): "By [viz. in] baptism we [viz. you] have been buried" (rather than raised). Those who are baptized have died to sin with Christ and trust that they will be raised with him. It has been assumed that in Col 2:12 not only the burial but also the resurrection with Christ is ascribed to baptism.[125] John 3:5 and Tit 3:5 may or may not identify rebirth with the event or immediate effect of baptism,[126] but in Ephesians no word is said of regeneration. Rather a resurrection and enthronement corresponding to Christ's are described; nobody would speak of Jesus Christ's rebirth or ascribe to Jesus' baptism his regeneration and exaltation! Thus the reasons for imposing a sacramental interpretation upon Eph 2:5–6, or upon the whole context 2:4–10, are insufficient.[127]

[122] According to R. H. Charles, *Eschatology*, 2d ed. (London: Black, 1913), pp. 449–50. Paul spoke only of a resurrection of the righteous. But I, II Thessalonians; II Cor 5:10 etc., put this opinion into question.

[123] As Schlier, pp. 109 ff.; Schille, *Hymnen*, pp. 57 f.; see also the names and arguments discussed in COMMENT XVI on 1:3–14.

[124] Cf. II Thess 2:2; Justin Martyr *apol.* i 26:4; Irenaeus *adv. haer.* i 23:5.

[125] See COMMENT V C on Eph 4:17–32 and the commentary on Col 2.

[126] It is more likely that both passages speak of baptism with the Spirit, cf. I Cor 12:13. Spirit-baptism, in turn, is according to Mark 1:8 and Acts far from identical or simultaneous with water-baptism. If both are distinct at all, water-baptism cannot mean or convey resurrection.

[127] Though the sacramental exposition can be supported by "parallels" from Mystery Religions and Gnosticism, and though it lives on, e.g. in the Benedictine consecration ritual.

c) As much as Christ's crucifixion has for Paul a representative character and includes the death of every man "with Christ,"—whether he is a believer or not[128]—so Christ's resurrection may be proclaimed as a representative, comprehensive event. But while Paul says, "if one has died for all, then all have died" (I Cor 5:14), he never says the same of resurrection. In his resurrection Jesus Christ is *primus inter pares,* "the first-born among many brethren," who is to be followed by one man after another.[129] The death and resurrection of Christ are events of such different character that their validity for others and the participation of others in them cannot be described by the same formula. Paul does not postulate that the representative crucifixion of the whole world with Christ (Gal 6:14) entails the automatic resurrection of all men on Easter Day. The resurrection is but a beginning and includes as yet only those elected.[130]

d) When in Eph 2:5–6 Paul speaks of our resurrection "with Christ," he probably means the same event which in Eph 1:13 is called, "sealing with the Spirit." "The Spirit gives life" (II Cor 3:6). Resurrection is in this case the cause and beginning of that courageous witness to God's mighty deeds which is extensively described in Acts; of that gathering into a wondering, loving, suffering community which forms the church; of that gift of forgiveness, knowledge, patience, hope, steadfastness which marks a true Christian. It is the fact and willingness to be conformed to the image of the crucified and raised Son of God. Obviously the Corinthians and other enthusiasts were not satisfied with these features. They expected, sought, found, and managed much more than the mentioned sober features and demonstrations of new life: e.g. ecstatic speaking in tongues; liberty from any and all moral restrictions; high-flying and deep-searching omniscience and wisdom; mystic sweet individual communion with God and Christ; strictly personal perfection; superiority over weak and retarded fellow Christians; zeal for highest honors and names; experience of individual strength; absence of all traits of weakness; absolute security on the basis of baptism; not to speak of boisterous, luscious banquets in the company of Gentiles.[131] Just as Paul recalls the Corinthians to sobriety, so he gives in chapters 4–6 of Ephesians a description of the new life which is surprising for its almost pedestrian character. The Thessalonian epistles exhort the saints to work hard instead of yielding to laziness. Following Philippians, the citizens of heaven accept suffering and humiliation gladly and with patience; they hold out in waiting for the coming Lord. Romans urges the saints to show exemplary loyalty to the officials of the Roman Empire. The Pastoral Epistles bristle with appeals for reasonableness and sobriety. According to Revelation precisely those already "raised" to the honor of "kings and priests" are recognized by their faithful testimony and martyrdom on earth. Ephesians makes clear that the life given to Jews and Gentiles formerly "dead in lapses and sins" is comparable to the life given to Israel with its redemption from Egypt, the house of slavery

---

[128] Gal 2:19; 6:14; Rom 5:6–8; II Cor 5:14.   [129] Philip 3:21; Rom 8:29; Col 1:18.
[130] A collection and discussion of all pertinent Pauline passages on the death and resurrection of Christ and with Christ is contained in M. Barth, *Die Taufe ein Sakrament?* (Zürich: EVZ, 1951), pp. 264–306; see also the literature in fn. 61.
[131] I, II Cor *passim.*

and death. They are a people liberated from captivity and death. They remain the migrating people of God. They seek to attain a perfection which is not yet theirs (Eph 4:13; Heb 11). However, because of their resurrection with Christ, Jews and Gentiles live together and thus are witnesses of peace for the benefit of the whole world (rather than consumers of private peace and perfection as e.g. promised by Mystery Religions and later Gnostic groups). Their life is called "new life" (Rom 6:4), "life of God" (4:18). All the subsequent parts of Ephesians spell out the essence of that life. The life given is a self-demonstration of God the creator. When Abraham was "called" and life was awakened in his and Sara's dead bodies, "God who raises the dead . . . called non-being into being" (Rom 4:17–18). The resurrection act of which Paul speaks in Eph 2 no longer pertains only to a future, promised Messiah. The call to rise is extended by, and still heard from, the Messiah who has already come and has been raised: "Awake you sleeper and rise from the dead, the Messiah will shine upon you" (5:14). After God is described as creator in 2:10, the same attribute will in 2:15 be given to the Messiah.

IV Enthronement in Heaven

What is meant by the mysterious statement, "he has enthroned us in the heavens"? It is certainly even more puzzling than the reference to a resurrection already achieved. A "gift of God" (2:8) additional to the gift of life can hardly be meant. For unlike Luke 24; Acts 1; John 20, Paul does not consider the resurrection and the ascension (enthronement) of Jesus successive and separate events.[132] For this apostle Christ's enthronement above all powers, including death, is the essence of his resurrection from the dead, not its aftermath. Correspondingly the enthronement of the saints reveals the substance of the life given to them rather than an honor or effect beyond that life. What is the resurrection life, if it is a life characterized by sitting on a throne in the heavens?

a) A bodily removal from earth, a disappearance from sight as may be ascribed to a journey into an upper sphere[133] or to an "ascension of the soul,"[134] cannot be meant.[135] For the people addressed in Ephesians live "in Ephesus" (1:1 var. lect.), or in whatever country or "land," they hope to fare "well and live long" (6:3). All the more reason why the topological character of the statement, "enthroned in the heavens" comes as a surprise. It is not unique in the NT.[136] According to the Gospels the mother of the sons of Zebedee, or John and James themselves, asked for special seats in

---

[132] Paul speaks either only of the resurrection of Christ (Rom 1:4; 4:24–25; 6:4–5; 8:11 etc.), or exclusively of his exaltation and heavenly enthronement (Phil 2:9; Col 3:1 etc.). When he combines both in the same text (I Cor 15:12–26; Rom 8:34), he does not add distinctive statements on the cause, date, meaning, or effect of either one. What Luke reports of Paul's sermons before Jews and Gentiles (Acts 13:30, 37; 17:31, etc.) confirms the evidence of the Pauline Epistles.

[133] Cf. the biblical legends of Enoch's, Moses', Elijah's end, or the various traditions of Mary's "conclusion of her earthly course."

[134] "Himmelfahrt der Seele." Schlier, Schille and others draw upon Gnostic and Philonic texts for illustrating the meaning of Eph 2:6. Since the Platonistic distinction of the soul's origin, worth, and destiny from the body's depravity and final elimination is not taken up and supported by Ephesians, Eph 2:6 must be explained without the aid of the alleged (Platonizing Gnostic) "parallels."

[135] See 1:7, 11–14, 15–18; 2:20–22, not to speak of the ethical chapters 4–6.

[136] See for the following Matt 20:20–28 par.; II Cor 5:1–2; I Thess 4:17; Acts 7:55–56; Rom 8:34; Heb 1:3; 12:22–23, etc.

the heavens. Once, so it is affirmed in Matt 19:28, the twelve disciples were assured that they would obtain them. According to Paul, "the saints will judge the world" presumably after they are "taken up" in the "clouds . . . to meet the Lord" in the "air." Jesus Christ is enthroned at God's right hand, or he stands there to plead as an advocate for the saints. The reference to Christ's own "descent," his "ascent," and his function of "filling" (4:8–10) is, at least in its metaphorical form, unmistakably topological. It appears necessary to conclude: if Christ's disappearance from the earth and his present location presupposes a spatial transfer, then the enthronement of the saints in the heavens mentioned in 2:6 cannot mean anything essentially different. However, there is an alternative.

b) When the principalities and powers were subjected to Christ's feet (1:20–22) they remained located in the heavens according to Eph 3:10; 6:12. The change forced upon them came from their new overlord, and affected their function rather than their location. While Rev 12 speaks of their dislocation, Ephesians stresses only the new relation between the power of God, Christ, and the principalities. Equally the verb "to enthrone" and references to honors and privileges connected with enthronement are sometimes used in the Bible without implying a necessary dislocation. When the kings described in the royal psalms are raised to their thrones, they become something rather than go somewhere. If the idea of lifting up is combined with enthronement at all, then it makes visual the greater stature and honor of the ruler and/or the position of his throne above the level of his subjects. By his exaltation the king is not definitely dissociated from those living on earth;[137] the king who sits "at God's right hand" (Ps 110:1) is a king who rules on earth, not a king removed from the earth. The "right hand of God" mentioned in the Psalms is the same "hand" or "outstretched arm" of God with which God performs mighty deeds on earth,[138] and is not limited to geographical spheres outside earthly time and space. The throne of God upon which the Messiah is seated is the "throne favored by the Lord."[139] Zion is its location, and Zion is a place on earth. God is as present among his chosen and at his elected place as he is in heaven.[140]

The heavenly places in which the saints are enthroned according to Eph 2:6 may therefore be the places elected by God for the manifestation of his presence, glory, and power. "Heavens" is in this case not an absolute locality inhabited by God, and eventually by principalities, powers, and the saints.[141] Rather, it is the sphere formed by him who fills and determines it. It is the

[137] As stated previously, in the OT the verb "to raise" means occasionally the making of a king or other leader, before it is combined with "from the dead" and receives the technical connotation of resuscitation, see e.g. Judg 2:16, 18; 3:9, 15; Deut 18:15, 18; cf. Acts 2:32–36; 13:22–23. Saul is said to have surpassed in stature all the people (I Sam 10:23). In the Gospel of John, the verb "to lift up," cf. "to glorify," means at the same time Jesus Christ's elevation on the cross and to heavenly glory (3:14; 8:28; 12:32, 34; cf. 7:39; 12:23; 16:14).
[138] Exod 15:6; Ps 18:35; Isa 51:5, 9; 52:10; 63:5, etc.
[139] Ps 45:6; I Chron 28:5; 29:23; II Chron 9:8; cf. 13:8. H. Frankfort, *Kingship and the Gods*, pp. 341–42.
[140] Num 7:89; I Sam 4:4; 6:2; Isa 24:23; 52:7, etc. E.g. Ps 11:4 states unmistakably the simultaneous presence of God on earth and in heaven: "The Lord is in his holy temple, the Lord's throne is in heaven." See Dahood's discussion of this and similar passages that relate the earthly to the heavenly temple. Not even an anti-temple statement such as Isa 66:1, "Heaven is my throne and the earth is my footstool," intends to negate God's presence among his chosen.
[141] Cf. the analogous argument regarding "time" in COMMENT XIII on 1:3–14.

dynamic starting point of God's saving action.[142] Heaven or heavens is
where God is with his power and salvation. Heavens is also where dominating
powers and men entrusted with royal dignity are found. Because the saints
are assembled with God who has been and still is present in their midst,
they are "in the heavens." Thus the throne or thrones suggested by the verb
"enthroned" are to be understood as a metaphor denoting the privileges,
honor, authority, and function given to the saints. They are given a position
at the least equal to David's, and are no one's servants except God's. They
are free men[143]—free from death (2:5) and captivity (4:8); free to be
witness to the coming ages (2:7); free to live worthily (4:1) and to do good
works (2:10); free to approach the Father (2:18); free for a brave fight
against onrushing enemies (6:10–17).[144] They enjoy all the privileges of "kings
and priests."[145] They are, to speak with I Peter 2:9, "a royal priesthood."

Thus their resurrection from the dead is not a restoration to their previous
lives, but the gift of unprecedented honor and, as vss. 7 and 10 will show,
of a great and responsible task, too. The closest Pauline parallel to the
enthronement mentioned in 2:6 is probably Philip 3:20 NEB: "We . . . are
citizens of heaven." Cf. Eph 2:19–22, "You are fellow citizens with the
saints . . . a dwelling of God." By "saints" (as was earlier observed) not
only Israel but also the angels in heaven might be meant.[146] The question
of the date and mode of the saints' naturalization, viz. enthronement, in
heaven was discussed in the preceding COMMENT: the sealing with God's
Spirit contains the answer.

A distinction between ideal and phenomenal, potential and actual, spiritual
and bodily enthronements[147] corresponds in no wise to the contents of
Eph 2:6. Paul was not a Platonist, and indeed he surpasses the hopes of
Jewish apocalypticists. According to Ephesians the saints are closer to heaven
and more firmly established there now than theater-goers who have reserved
tickets in their pockets and wait for admission. Cf. the NOTE on "free access"
to 2:18.

V   God's Cosmic Lawsuit, the Church, and the World

The imagery used by Paul in Ephesians is predominantly cultic, political,
sociological, and biological. On one occasion, i.e. when he employs the term

---

[142] H. Traub (following K. Barth, *Church Dogmatics*, III:3 [1961], 432–33) in TWNTE, V, 514,
520–22.

[143] Readers of Paul acquainted with Stoic philosophy may have been reminded of the Stoic
equation of a wise and free man with a "king." Perhaps Paul's ironic suggestion to the worldly-wise
Corinthians, "Without us you have become kings! Would that you really had become kings so that
we might be fellow kings with you" (I Cor 4:8) implies an allusion to the Stoic metaphor.

[144] The Greek terms "freedom" or "to liberate," also a reference to "authority" or "full power"
(*exousia;* "all is allowed" I Cor 6:12; 10:23) given to the saints do not occur in Ephesians, except in
a variant reading of 3:12; see also the "empowering" of the saints mentioned in 3:16 and 6:10. In
Romans and esp. in Galatians Paul spoke of "freedom"—but never without an added warning
against misconceptions. A sharp protest against false, i.e. proud and libertinist exploitation of the
"newness of life" (Rom 6:4) already experienced by the saints, is found not only in the Corinthian
letters and in Gal 5:13, but also in e.g. II Thess 2:2; II Tim 2:18; I Peter 2:16. See also COMMENT
IX on 1:3–14.

[145] These terms are used for a description of all Christians in Rev 1:6; 5:10; 20:4–6.

[146] If Eph 2:6 contributes to the dispute over the date of the millennium of which Rev 20
speaks, then it supports those who advocate that the millennium is the time of the church. It is
now. Cf. e.g. Augustine *de civitate Dei* xx 5–9; *enchiridion* 54–56, 84 ff.

[147] As suggested by Bengel, and by Meyer, pp. 369–70.

"to prove" in 2:7, he used a technical juridical term as a metaphor. The distinction of such realms was not as fundamental among OT and other Semitic writers, or among supposedly primitive people, as it is for western man raised in the school of Aristotelian differentiation of the various scientific fields. The sanctuary was originally the people's place of gathering for any purpose, e.g. worship, covenant and peace-making, jurisdiction, health and fertility matters, celebrations. The priest's function was correspondingly manifold. The spread of a distinction between sacred and secular realms and competence was probably connected with the rise of the monarchy and of city culture in Israel, but the reunion of the high priestly and royal function in the post-exilic periods of high priests counteracted a final separation of both. Up to the present time Jewish courts decide on matters sacred *and* profane. Paul's easy change from one set of images to another reflects the original unity of religion and life, politics and law, peace and health, honor and property.

The relatively frequent use Paul makes of the terms "demonstration" (or evidence, proof) and "to prove"[148] cannot be ascribed to immediate LXX influence, but can be explained against the background of his education in law. The study of the *Tora* included legal as well as theological training (*halacha* and *haggada*, with special emphasis on the first). A sign of Paul's concern with law is the concentration of his thought upon the righteousness of God and justification. He considers juridical imagery appropriate to the contents and meaning of the OT and to the message of Jesus Christ. In Rom 3:21 he claims that the contents of his proclamation (including the legal terminology?) were attested to in the Law and the Prophets, and he might as well have added the Psalms.[149] He may have in mind the grandiose imagery of Yahweh's "covenant lawsuit":[150] whatever the OT says about righteousness in heaven and justice on earth, or about court scenes in heaven and judgment days on earth, is concentrated and summed up in the OT visions of one world-wide day of judgment on which God will act as judge or witness, call Israel to account, and pay the Gentiles what they deserve. This lawsuit will demonstrate God's rightness and will manifest his power. Through his power he will create order in the realm of rebellion and chaos; his creation will be renewed. God holds righteous judgment for his own name and honor's sake, and by so doing acts in favor and in the best interest of all his creatures. In the OT a righteous judge is a legal aid, righteousness is an act of salvation.[151] Sometimes in the OT Israel is the object of God's litigation—in that case heaven and earth are called to the witness stand to testify against God's people, or they are invited to witness the indictment

[148] See the NOTE on "to prove" in 2:7.   [149] See e.g. Rom 3:10–20; 4:7–8.
[150] Brief descriptions of this term are given by E. Schweizer in EvTh 22 (1962), 105–7, and C. Müller, *Gottes Gerechtigkeit und Gottes Volk*, FRLANT 86 (1964), 57–72.
[151] Pss 50; 82; Isa 1:2–3, 10–20; 3:13–17; 41:21–29; Amos 1–2; 3:2; 5:18; Hosea 4; Micah 6:1–8; Jer 2:4–37, etc. II Esd 7:94; 11:37 ff: 1QS I 24–26; VIII 5–7, 10; X 19 ff, etc. In Deut 32 the logical sequence of court events is displayed: After an introduction (vss. 1–5), God's mighty acts are praised (vss. 6–14), the indictment is pronounced (vss. 15–18), the sentence is passed (vss. 19–30). Then first the poet (vss. 30–38), later God himself (vss. 39–42), give assurance of salvation and hope, and the piece ends with an invitation to the nations to praise God's mercy toward his people (vs. 43); see G. E. Wright, "The Lawsuit of God: A Form-Critical Study of Deuteronomy 32," in Fs J. Muilenburg (New York: Harper, 1962), pp. 26–27. For other pertinent literature see BIBLIOGRAPHY 13.

which God or his prophet presents.[152] But Israel is also appointed to be God's witness in confounding the nations.[153]

The same positive role, which especially in Exodus, Deuteronomy, and Second Isaiah is attributed to Israel, is according to Eph 2:7 the function of the church: the saints are destined to be God's evidence and showpiece. God has proven good to them, but the riches of his grace are not exhausted by his past and present deeds. As he was able to show his power to the Pharaoh and his wrath to unfit vessels,[154] so he will now demonstrate nothing but grace. It is the Gentiles who are now to receive good news from God: "It was God's pleasure . . . to reveal his Son in me that I announce him as good news among the nations" (Gal 1:16). OT announcements of the Messiah's honor and victories in e.g. Ps 2, included the message that he would "break them [the nations] with a rod of iron and dash them in pieces like pottery." Now a new time has dawned: the demonstration of God's grace through Jesus Christ inaugurates, continues and crowns the overflow of grace. Even the Gentiles shall now benefit from his grace—as it was earlier experienced (though also much resented) by the prophet Jonah.[155]

The manifestation of the "riches of grace" is not the novel idea of a prophet, apostle, or the congregation, and is neither their invention nor their own work: God himself delivers the proof.[156] According to Rom 3:25–26 God gives "evidence of his [own] righteousness."

By the evidence given God makes himself known to all the world. The verb "to prove" in 2:7 has a parallel in "to make known" in 3:10. In Rom 9:22 "proving" and "making known" are used as synonyms that explain one another. In creating and sustaining the church, God is, according to II Cor 3:2–3, the writer of a "letter" that is "read by all men." This does not mean that God only offers man a chance to perceive him intellectually; rather by making himself known God demonstrates his presence and his "power" (Rom 9:17) which may work out as much in "destruction" as in "salvation—and this from God" (Philip 1:28). In a Jewish court the available evidence is not used in a playful way for intellectual information only, but is used for waging the war in which justice must be carried to victory. Equally the evidence submitted to the world of the goodness shown to the saints is an instrument of God's power. God will win the battle. Other "powers" may offer resistance by claiming heavens or earth, the present or future aeons, their own spheres,[157] but God's unique power which works in Christ and in the saints[158] has proven and will prove superior to their challenge: "You are able to put up

---

[152] Deut 4:26; 30:19; 31:28; cf. G. E. Wright, *Biblical Archaeology* (Philadelphia: Westminster, 1957), pp. 100–1. It is probable that in the Pauline sermons recorded in Acts 14:15–17; 17:22–31 allusions to these passages are present, rather than a "natural theology."

[153] E.g. Isa 43:10, 12; 44:8; cf. Israel's exemplary role Exod 9:17; 19:5–6; Deut 4:6; 9:26–29 etc. See Müller *Gottes Gerechtigkeit* for parallel passages in the Jewish Apocalypses and Qumran.

[154] Rom 9:17, 22.

[155] See COMMENT II on 1:1–2 regarding the special meaning of "grace" for the Gentiles which is proclaimed by the apostle Paul. J. T. Sanders, ZNW 56 (1965), 231, believes that Ephesians is concerned with ecclesiastical hierarchy whereas Colossians stresses the world mission of the church. Eph 2:7 and 3:10, also 6:15, 19 show that he has offered a caricature of Ephesians.

[156] The middle rather than active form of the Greek verb *endeiknymi*, "to prove," emphasizes that God acts in his own interest and for his own reasons and purposes.

[157] 1:21; 2:7; 3:10, 21; 6:12–13.   [158] 1:19–20, 22; 3:16–20; 6:10.

resistance on the darkest day, to carry everything out, and to stand firm" (6:13).

Thus the church is given a decisive function in the lawsuit of God. According to Eph 2:7 God uses her as his evidence. Following 3:10 God carries out "through the church" his self-manifestation to the powers. Other Pauline passages affirm that the church itself gives proof: Gentile Christians "prove" to Jews that the "doing of the law is written in their hearts" (Rom 2:14, 15).[159] The sanctified Corinthians prove their love by their liberality and they vindicate Paul's pride before the richer churches (II Cor 8:24). The Philippians' freedom from fear in the face of their adversaries is a proof of the opponents' destruction and the saints' salvation (Philip 1:28).[160]

Many other terms besides the legal terms "to prove" or "evidence" are used in the NT to make the same point. Especially frequent are the metaphors of shining light: kindled by God the Christians are a light to the world and are appointed to shine in the darkness.[161] The "Dogmatic Constitution" *De Ecclesia* of Vatican II bears most appropriately the title, *Lumen Gentium*. It is the nature of the church to exist not for its own sake but to reflect God's glory (5:27). Her very life is God's glorification (1:6, 12, 14; 3:20–21). No one is reached by God and converted for his own benefit only. Rather, with the salvation of an individual sinner like Paul, Christ "proves his perfect patience" and makes him a "type" or example of all those who are to inherit eternal life through faith (I Tim 1:16).

The great cosmic lawsuit of God is still in progress. It reached a unique climax when Jesus was delivered by the disciple Judas into the hands of the Jewish court, by that court to the Gentiles, by the denying Peter and by Jews and Gentiles to death, and by God into final darkness, and also when Jesus Christ accepted his subjection to judgment and "delivered himself" for sinners.[162] An anticlimax followed on the spot: by raising his Son God confounded the wisdom and power of his opponents and solemnly recognized the obedience and righteousness of his Son.[163] According to Acts the lawsuit is continued not only in Jerusalem but in Hellenistic cities, far-away islands, and finally in the world's capital Rome—wherever apostles and other Christians stand up as faithful witnesses before elders, procurators, and kings.[164] Paul considers himself, his chains notwithstanding, a messenger of God's court

[159] Augustine's exegesis of this passage (which is taken up e.g. by K. Barth, *Shorter Commentary on Romans* [Richmond: Knox, 1959], pp. 38–39) identifies the "Gentiles" of Rom 2:14–15 with Gentile Christians. See also M. Barth, "Natural Law in the Teachings of St. Paul," in ed. E. Smith, *Church-State Relations in Ecumenical Perspective* (Pittsburgh; Duquesne, 1966), pp. 113–51. The Jonah story to which Jesus alludes Matt 12:41 par. is the closest parallel to Rom 2:14–15.

[160] Diogn. v 4 speaks of the proof of "the wonderful and confessedly strange character of the constitution of their own citizenship," which the Christians give "while living in Greek and Barbarian cities."

[161] Matt 5:14–16; Acts 13:47 quoting Isa 49:6; Acts 26:18, 23; Philip 2:15; I Peter 2:9; Eph 5:8.

[162] The culminating final sections of the canonical Gospels describe the trial of Jesus. The sermons contained in Acts refer to it. Paul mentions it often by using the LXX (Isa 53:12) and early church concept of "to deliver," e.g. Gal 1:4; 2:20; Rom 4:25; Eph 5:2, 25. The verses Rom 1:24, 26, 28 reveal the legal and punitive character of this term.

[163] Matt 28 par.; Acts 2:22–24, 29–36; Philip 2:9–11; Rom 4:25, etc.

[164] In Matt 10:17–18 this task and stance are anticipated; in Rev 1:1–2; 2:13; 11:3; 20:4 etc., "the faithful witness" and the martyrdom suffered in its performance are the criterion of a true Christian.

and verdict.[165] In no case is it the Christian's doing that the gospel is forcefully presented to the world, but God himself is "proving . . . his grace" (Eph 2:7) and continuing to establish his right over the earth.

This does not imply that Paul claimed for or attributed to the church the position of an institution of public law or another such establishment. What he wanted to affirm is this: God and not man has given the church the right and the task to make God's cause public. A church existing privately, for the sole benefit of its members, would not be the church described in Ephesians. This implies that everyone in the church who knows about God's kingship and goodness is a witness. Thus he cannot be silent without also being a liar.[166]

VI God's Work, Works of the Law, and Good Works

The verses Eph 2:8–10 combine references to three kinds of work: to God the creator's "work" and "gift"; to human "works" that are useless or damaging for salvation; and to "good works" prepared by God but to be done by the saints. Unless the author intended to engage in paradoxes, there must be a way to elucidate the interrelationship and connection between these key terms.[167]

A The Work of God the Creator

The apostolic mission and the building up of congregations and their memberships several times is denoted as "God's," "Christ's," or "the Lord's work." Once in the Pauline letters this work is explicitly called "good" (Philip 1:6). In Eph 1:4–10 it was affirmed that this work is not the product of a whim of God but comes out of his eternal decision to love his Son, to pour out his grace, to reveal his secret, to appoint Jesus Christ to administrate, govern, and unite all things. According to 1:19–23; 2:1–6, the work of God culminates in the resurrection of the Messiah and of the saints. God's work is a work of salvation. Eph 2:10 adds to the previous descriptions of God's work the concept of creation: "we are created." Resurrection and salvation, but also revelation and the gift of knowledge and enlightenment, missionary work and other acts of obedience receive an important qualification: in all these deeds and events God "the creator" is at work.[168] His present work recalls what he always has been, is, and will be: the creator of heaven and earth.

References to God "the creator" are repeatedly found in Pauline writings;[169] indeed, if he failed to honor God with this title the apostle would belie his Jewish upbringing, his participation in synagogue worship, and his rabbinical training. In agreement with Wisdom and contemporary theology he understood creation as *creatio ex nihilo*.[170] This does not mean that he restricted the act of creation to a past event, however. According to the OT the creator manifests himself and is in action not just in the overcoming of

[165] Rom 1:16–17; Eph 3:1; 4:1; 6:20; Philip 1:12–14, etc.
[166] Cf. 4:15; 6:14, 17, 19–20; Gal 2:5, 14 etc.   [167] See BIBLIOGRAPHY 14.
[168] See also I Cor 15:58; 16:10; Philip 1:6; 2:9–10, 13, 30; Rom 14:20; Gal 2:8.
[169] E.g. I Cor 11:9; Rom 1:20, 25; Col 1:16; Eph 3:9; I Tim 4:3–4.
[170] The specific affirmation of II Macc 7:28 (also Wisd Sol 1:14?); Philo *de specialibus legibus* IV 187 is reflected in I Cor 1:28; Rom 4:17. See also Herm. *mand.* I 1.

the *tohu-bohu* described in Gen 1 but wherever he meets and subdues the powers of darkness (sometimes called *Rahab*)—be it in the form of the Egyptian enemy, the Babylonian captivity, or personal enemies.[171] When God reminds his people of his creatorship, or when he is appealed to as the creator, the promise or expectation of mighty and marvelous help is evoked. Therefore creation is identified with salvation; as was unceasingly emphasized by the Second Isaiah, the creator is savior, the savior is creator.[172]

The close sequence of the verbs "saved" and "created" reveals Paul's awareness of the same connection. The Second Isaiah, Paul and the book of Revelation call the final salvation a "new creation." The interrelation of salvation and creation has found proper recognition in recent theological research.[173]

The creation-salvation which God alone performs from the beginning of heaven and earth to the end-time far from imposes inactivity upon man. It is the presupposition and means by which God enables his creatures to give glory and witness to him in words, deeds, and also in suffering. God blesses with all spiritual blessing of the heavens in order that those blessed bless him (Eph 1:3, 6, 12, 14).

This epistle contains explicit references to new creation, viz. to the "creation" of "one new man."[174] The designation of the resurrected saints as God's creation in 2:10, also Gal 6:15 and II Cor 5:17, implies the equation: the church is the new creation. The Christians not only witness a new creation occurring outside themselves, they are its result and evidence in person. While still living in the present evil age (1:21) and enduring evil days (5:16; 6:13), in the midst of ravaging powers (2:2, 7; 6:12), they are yet made a shining light to signal the dawn of a new heaven and a new earth. Thus they are to fulfill the Isaianic prophecies of the role of Zion for all the world, implying that they are a "new creation" not just for their own sake and benefit but as a "first fruit of all creatures." James 1:18 gives them this title, and in other terms Rom 8:19–22 and Eph 2:7 affirm the same. The Christians are not the end of God's ways, but only their beginning.[175] They are an exemplary "work" of God from which all his works will profit. God's work, in turn, calls for works which they do to God's honor.[176]

---

[171] Pss 74:12–15; 89:8–10; Exod 15:4–5; Isa 43:15–17; 51:9–10; 65:17; 66:22; Ezek 32:2–3; II Sam 22:8–20.

[172] 41:11–20; 45:7–8; 51:9–11 etc.

[173] Müller, *Gottes Gerechtigkeit;* G. von Rad, "Das theologische Problem des alttestamentlichen Schöpfungsglaubens," BhZAW 66 (1936), 138–47, repr. in *Gesammelte Studien zum Alten Testament* (München: Kaiser, 1958), pp. 136–47; R. Rendtorf, "Zur theologischen Stellung des Schöpfungsglaubens bei Deutero-Jesaia," ZTK 51 (1954), 2–13; E. Sjöberg, "Neuschöpfung in den Toten-Meer-Rollen," ST 9 (1955), 131–36; P. Stuhlmacher, "Erwägungen zum ontologischen Charakter der *kainē ktisis* bei Paulus," EvTh 27 (1967), 1–35; G. Schneider, *Neuschöpfung oder Wiederkehr*, Düsseldorf: Patmos, 1961 (ref.); G. E. Wright, and O. Michel, art. "Schöpfung im Alten Testament, im Neuen Testament," RGG, IV, 1473–77; StB, II, 421–23.

[174] 2:15; 4:24; cf. Col 3:10.

[175] In Rev 21:22 the notion of a final triumph of the church, or of a world-wide takeover by the Christians is counteracted in a unique and striking way: the seer sees in the descending holy city, Jerusalem, *no temple*. On that day neither the city nor the world, but the church will be superfluous and vanish. The church will not absorb the world. But God will be present in and to all his creatures. See also COMMENTS VI C and VII on 2:11–22 and VIII on 4:1–16.

[176] According to John 5:17, etc. Jesus saw the Father's and his own work as an inseparable unity. When the disciples asked what they were to do in order "to work the works of God" they were not condemned (e.g. as Pelagians) but frankly told by Jesus himself, "This is the work of God that you believe in him whom He has sent" (John 6:28–29).

B   The Judaizers' Works of Law

"By grace you are saved, through faith! This [was] not of your own doing
—it is a gift of God—not [as a reward] for works lest anyone boast about
himself" (2:8–9). These polemical words may well concern the same people
who are mentioned in 4:14 and 5:6. Since in these two verses the author
alludes to an existing and active opposition it ought not to be assumed[177]
that only *pro memoria* the vss. 2:8–9 refer to a fight against a non-existent
or long-defeated enemy. Even if Ephesians were written by a post-Pauline
scribe, the author would have revealed extremely poor taste and judgment
by interrupting the rhythmic sequence of vss. 4–10 with an attack on stuck
and worn-out windmills.

As little as in any other epistle does Paul give at this point a clear
picture of the beliefs and attitudes he repudiated. There appears to be some
resemblance between the opponents fought in Eph 2:9 and those refuted in
Galatians, Philippians, and Romans. Therefore the "works" of these opponents
can be more clearly defined as "works of law" to which meritorious value
was attributed,[178] rather than as human works in general. It is unlikely that the
Ephesian opposition anticipated some later Gnostic groups who openly promoted works of impurity and lawlessness as means of salvation.[179]

The similarity between Eph 2:8–9 and the message of Galatians, Philippians,
Romans consists of the following three traits: the antithesis of God's gift of
grace and man's merit;[180] the contrast between faith and boasting, or faith
and works;[181] the tendency to sing and make all Christians sing, *Sola gratia,
Soli Deo gloria*. But there are also differences: in Ephesians the verb "to
justify" and nouns such as "righteousness of God" are missing; explicit
references to Abraham and to the law are not made;[182] Christ's death and
resurrection are not mentioned together in any one single sentence as the
nucleus of salvation, and are not used to give a juridical interpretation of
justification;[183] the polemic in which Paul engages so heartily elsewhere is
cut down to utmost brevity.[184] As previously stated, such similarities and
differences are inconclusive regarding the authorship of Ephesians.

What are the "works of law" which Paul's opponents were "boasting about"?
Because their works were connected with OT commandments and Jewish
customs, and because they were obviously recommended to or imposed upon

---

[177] On the lines of the opponents of the authenticity of Ephesians.
[178] See Gal 2:16; Rom 3:28; 4:4–5; 11:6; cf. Philip 3:9; Titus 3:5, etc.
[179] That some members of the church "in Ephesus" permitted such works, is, however, suggested by
5:5–6. I Corinthians gives ample evidence of such permissiveness; the vss. Rom 6:1, 15 at least
suggest its possibility; slanderers of Paul accused him of teaching it (Rom 3:8; Philip 3:2); the
Pastoral Epistles and some of the letters collected in Rev 2–3, also Jude and II Peter outrightly
condemn antinomianism.
[180] Cf. Rom 3:23–24, 28; 4:3, etc.; cf. Titus 3:5; see also 1QM XI 4.
[181] Rom 2:17–29; 3:27; 4:2–5, etc.
[182] Still, the mention of the law in 2:15 and of the covenants of promise in 2:12 may substitute for
the long narrations and excursus of Gal 1–3, Rom 2–4, and the briefer summary of Philip 3:3–9.
[183] But see, e.g. Rom 4:25. However, the death of Christ is described in sacrificial terms in
Eph 1:7; 2:13–18; 5:2, and the resurrection of Christ in political language in 1:20–23.
[184] This fact may appear to be an un-Pauline feature of Ephesians. It is also observed in Titus
3:5. But in his Corinthian correspondence, e.g. in I Cor 1:30; II Cor 12:9, Paul proves his ability
to speak in very short and concise terms of justification and salvation.

Gentiles the adversaries of Paul are usually called "Judaizers";[185] the origin of the anti-Pauline legalism is sought among the Palestinian and the dispersed Jews, or among Jewish Christians in a conspiration of these groups. The doctrine of *self*-justification or of justification "by the law" is therefore frequently described and decried as a typically Jewish doctrine. Indeed, Paul accuses himself and Israel of seeking "righteousness in the law," or "their own righteousness from the law."[186] But he does not speak of a righteousness "by works of law" sought by the Jews for themselves. The very term "works of law" has so far not been found in the literature of the Tannaitic period; it does not occur in the LXX, the Mishna,[187] the Apocalypticists, or the Apologetes. Only in one Jewish apocalyptic book does "righteousness by law" play a certain role.[188] D. Rössler[189] has shown that in Jewish apocalyptical writings man's attitude to the law as a whole (rather than individual acts of compliance) is the condition of salvation. Unlike Apocalypticists, the rabbis put major emphasis upon indispensable single works, as for instance on the study of the law, repentance, circumcision, tithing, Sabbath-keeping, almsgiving, or upon the merits of the Fathers or suffering. Any one of these works was considered essential for pleasing God, for procuring atonement for sin, for inheriting the coming aeon.[190] But they did not call these acts "works of law," and they knew that no work in itself, but only work graciously accepted by God in his judgment was of any value or merit. E. Lohmeyer has elaborated beautifully on this trait of Jewish doctrine.[191] Still, he is as vulnerable as e.g. P. Billerbeck and G. F. Moore when he identifies what Paul calls a "work of law" with the Jewish term *mitzva*, commandment, and its theological and ethical interpretation.[192] A *mitzva* is "an opportunity to do God's will."[193] The "joy in the law"[194] celebrated on the Day of *Simchat Torah* and in the *Bar Mitzva* ceremonies has nothing to do with the term, "works of law." The sense of the term *mitzva* is caricatured when it is equated with an attempt at self-justification, pride, trust in righteousness by law. The election and privileges granted to Israel included the gift of the law to this people,[195] but Israel was given the covenant, life, and liberty before she

---

[185] The very name "Judaizer" is a misnomer. In the LXX and the NT the verb "to judaize" does not describe the action of a Jew who attempts to impose the law upon Gentiles, but the attitude of Gentiles who accept the Jewish law; see Esther 8:17 and Gal 2:14.

[186] Philip 3:6, 9; Rom 9:31; 10:3.   [187] StB, III, 160–62; Lohmeyer, *Probleme*, pp. 41, 56 f, 72.

[188] II Bar 48:22, 24; 51:2–3, 7; 61:6; 63:3; 74:1; but cf. 48:15; 67:6; 85:15.

[189] *Gesetz und Geschichte*, pp. 77–99.

[190] Important statements are collected in StB, I, 169, 362, 636–37; II, 274 ff.; III, 119 ff., 153, 160 ff., 585, 607; IV, 37 ff., 455. Circumcision as an example of fulfillment of the law will be discussed in COMMENT III on 2:11–22.

[191] *Probleme*, p. 44, "No man can pass the final decision. That is, the validity of all works is ultimately left open, in the last judgment only God can reveal them . . . *Ps Sol* 4:8, *Let God reveal the deeds of the men-pleasers, the deeds of such a one with laughter and derision.* Such statements concern the sinners first of all; but in principle they are equally valid for those righteous . . . The works are no more than they are in God's sight . . . No one knows for himself what he produces."

[192] Lohmeyer, pp. 41, 56, 72; StB, III, 161; Moore, II, 171.

[193] This amazing definition was made during a discussion by an orthodox Jewish lady. Though it appears impossible to find a similar or analogous formulation in the Jewish literature of Paul's environment or later periods, it appears that the quoted words give crisp and deep expression to the basic attitude of those Jews ancient or modern who are far from boasting about themselves or their achievements.

[194] Cf. Pss 1:2; 19; 119; H. J. Kraus, "Freude am Gesetz," EvTh 10 (1950–51), 337–51; Schoeps, *Paul*, pp. 194–98.

[195] E.g. Deut 33:3–4; Sir 24:8–12, 23–24; Baruch 3:36–37; Rom 3:2; 9:4.

was given the law. The law directed this people as to how to stay in the covenant, to keep alive, and to remain free. It was not a guarantee or way of making them alive or righteous before God.

In the NT the term "works of law" and polemics against "righteousness by
law" occur only in contexts where the imposition of some legal elements
upon the Gentiles is discussed; see especially Gal 2:11–21. In this passage
Peter's attempt to withdraw from the communion table with Gentiles is equated
with willfully forcing the Gentiles into Jewish customs (2:14), and it is
countered by a discourse on "justification by faith," not by "works of
law." The nature of "works of law" (which cannot be defined with the aid
of LXX, Qumran, Apocalypticists, Tannaites) must be elucidated by the
only group of documents in which they are mentioned, the Pauline Epistles:
these works stem from a random selection of individual commandments and
prohibitions from the bulk of Israel's legal tradition. The imposition of the
selected prescriptions upon Gentiles is rejected.[196] Of the commandments
which "some" (anonymous subjects)[197] sought to force upon Gentile Christians, the only things explicitly mentioned are circumcision, dietary laws,
observation of the Sabbath, and a festival calendar.[198]

Why did Paul reject those acts which seemed to express obedient obei-
sance to God's commandments? Not because he had become an apostate from
Judaism by becoming a Christian! For though his conviction regarding the
fulfillment of the law changed radically, he remained a Jew,[199] and loved
his people better than his own salvation (Rom 9:3). Neither did Paul reject
those works because they implied human activity. For not all acts of obedience
require activity: during his circumcision a child or man is passive, and abstinence from certain food is omission rather than commission. In turn, Paul
himself was a dynamic activist! Nor is the repudiation of the works mentioned
explained by their ceremonial and statutory, rather than ethical and voluntary,
character,[200] for the sharp distinction of cultic and moral laws is neither biblical nor Jewish nor true to the history of religions; see COMMENT IV B 2–3
on 2:11–22. Each form of obedience to God is a moral issue and is inseparably
connected with the community and worship of Israel and the church. No less
an opponent of righteousness by works than Luther emphatically emphasized
that (external) works of law are not bad in themselves.[201]

Paul was a good Jew when he rejected a random selection of some laws
and their imposition upon Gentiles. The grandeur as well as the limit of the
law forbade making legalistic tokenism—a form of hypocrisy (Gal 2:13)—

---

[196] Industrious rabbis had figured out that the whole law consisted of 613 commandments and
prohibitions. This number was believed to correspond to the addition of the number of the days of
a year and of the bones of the human body, StB, I, 900–5; III, 41–42, 542; IV, 438–39. The definitions given e.g. by Luther, Lohmeyer, Schlier of the "works of law" lack two essential features:
(a) the random selection of certain commandments and acts; (b) the imposition of the selected
elements upon Gentiles. Paul's negative attitude to "works of law" is misinterpreted whenever these
two features are neglected.

[197] Cf. Gal 1:7; 2:12; 5:10. In Gal 2:4 they are identified as (lit.) "sneaking-in, smuggled-in false
brethren."

[198] Gal 2:3–5, 12–13; 4:10; Philip 3:2; Rom 2:25; 14:13 – 15:8; Col 2:16.

[199] As Davies has shown in PRJ.

[200] Burton's commentary on Galatians is a classic example of an idealist, ethical, anti-statutory
understanding of Paul.

[201] See e.g. his first lecture on Galatians, WA, LVII, 37, 47, 63, 68 ff.

a requirement of justification. He realized that the priority of the patriarchal history over the Sinai tradition established the priority of God's love, election, and covenant of grace over all acts of human service and obedience.[202] He was aware of the absurdity of imposing the law given to the elected people of Israel alone upon nations and individuals who were not members of God's covenant. That which preserved Israel within God's custody (Gal 3:19 ff.) could not possibly be the condition of the Gentiles' admission to the covenant —least of all after they were freely promised God's blessing through Abraham! Just as rabbis spoke of Adamite or Noahite commandments[203] which permitted the nations to have life without the benefit of the Mosaic law,[204] so Paul proclaimed the freedom of the Gentiles from those laws that bound the Jews alone. In agreement with current Jewish teaching about the inseparability of circumcision from keeping the "whole law," Paul insisted that if circumcision was accepted at all, then all commandments, i.e. the "whole law," had to be observed also.[205] In harmony with orthodox Jewish teachers (cf. also Micah 6:8; Hab 2:4) he sought a way to formulate the sum of the whole law and to insist upon the fulfillment of the whole will of God (Gal 5:14; Rom 13:8–10). His opposition to sheer subservience or lip service to individual requirements is a good Jewish trait.

Certainly Paul is more radical than Peter (Acts 15:10), the Qumran community, the Apocalypticists, and many rabbis. Under the impact of Jesus Christ's crucifixion, Paul speaks not only of the factual shortcoming of the Jews' obedience to the law, but of its killing effect, even the execution of the curse threatened against its transgressor.[206] He fights a pride in the law which in Jeremiah's days was connected with the "peace" allegedly guaranteed by the temple and the law, but which could also flourish whenever (as in the diaspora) Jews relied solely on the obedience required by the law without enjoying the miracle and gift of God's presence as represented by a king of Davidic origin and the sacrifices of the temple. In no case are Paul's polemics against "works of law" directed against the Jews, their holy tradition, or their zeal as such. While in his letters he resisted distorting the meaning and fulfillment of the law, he felt free to keep the law when he was challenged to do so (I Cor 9:20–21; Acts 21:20–26). Neither did he ever urge Jews to break

[202] Gal 3; Rom 4. In the first among the Ten Commandments the reference to the liberation from Egypt plays a similar role. In the Deuteronomic sermons, the patriarchal and the Exodus motifs are combined and declared the basis of all legislation. The later rabbinic doctrine of the "merits of the Fathers," e.g. of the offering of Isaac, points in its own way in the same direction, see, e.g. Schoeps, *Paul*, pp. 141–49.

[203] For references see, e.g. Davies, PRJ, pp. 113–19. The "Apostolic Decree" (Acts 15:10, 29; 16:4; 21:25) has similar contents. But the reason which the alleged Judaizer and legalist Peter gave, according to Luke, for not imposing the Mosaic law on Gentiles (i.e. its character as an "unbearable yoke" upon the Fathers and all Jews [Act 15:10]) is never found in Pauline writings. Paul did not doubt that the law could be fulfilled and was to be completely fulfilled. Cf. Gal 1:13–14; Philip 3:6 with Rom 8:4; 13:8–10; Gal 5:14; 6:2; I Cor 9:20–21.

[204] Different opinions prevailed regarding the question whether the circumcision required of the Jews was also indispensable for Gentiles. Cf. GenR 47 (29 f); Pesiq 176a; DeutR 1 (196d); Sanh. 59a on one hand, with BQ 38a; S Lev 18:5; T. Sanh. 13:2; B Sanh. 105a; P Meq 74a, 25 on the other; see also fn. 5 to 2:11. Agreement prevails only in the requirement of circumcision for a Gentile who wants to become a Jew and keep the whole law.

[205] Gal 5:3; 6:13; Rom 2:25; see also the emphasis given to keeping "all things" in Gal 3:10.

[206] Gal 2:19; 3:13; II Cor 3:6–7; Rom 7:10; 8:3–4. Paul denies that the law gives life or righteousness (Gal 3:21)—though he knows that it was given "for life" (Rom 7:10; cf. Lev 18:5). It was and is a "law of righteousness," though Israel in seeking to fulfill it did not live up to it (Rom 9:31).

the law or to forsake it, nor did he ever agree to bring pressure against a Gentile under the law.[207]

Therefore, it is misleading (and probably nothing less than slanderous) to consider "justification by works of law" a doctrine that is distinctly and typically Jewish and basically maintained by all Jews. Jews are not, as it were by definition, Pelagians.[208] Augustine's and Luther's deep insights into Paul's doctrine of grace and the successful use they respectively made of Paul's anti-"Judaistic" utterances when condemning Pelagius and medieval concepts of meritorious works[209] have led Paul's interpreters to a caricature of "the Jews" which is not supported by historical and literary evidence.[210] "The Jews," including the early Judaeo-Christian congregation, have been falsely accused of representing a doctrine of salvation in opposition to Paul's. If Paul really intended to strike at the Jews in the polemical excursus of Eph 2:8–9, it is inconceivable that he could speak as positively of the reconciliation of Israel and the Gentiles as he does in 1:11–14; 2:11–22; 3:6.

C Indestructible Good Works

In his undisputed letters Paul speaks of two seemingly irreconcilable things, justification without works of law, and judgment according to works. Both are

[207] The circumcision of Timothy (Acts 16:1–3) does not demonstrate that Paul ever gave his consent to a Gentile Christian subjection and submission to the law. Since Timothy's mother was Jewish, this man was a Jew according to old and present Jewish application of the law. The psychological (Freudian) explanation which R. Rubinstein in *My Brother Paul*, New York: Harper, 1972, gives of Paul's rebellion against paternal authority as represented by the law is not supported by evidence in Paul's epistles. On the other hand, only a dubious variant reading of Gal 2:5 contains the information that the apostle consented on one occasion—because missionary concerns, not justification, were at stake—that a Gentile Christian associate be circumcised.

[208] The following alternatives exist to the view of the so-called "Tübingen School" (F. C. Baur and his followers), which considers *all* Jews (except Jesus and Paul) guilty of the teaching repudiated by Paul. (a) Only or primarily Paul himself was entangled in and blinded by a legalistic type of Judaism which was spread in the Hellenistic synagogues of the diaspora rather than in Jerusalem and Palestine. He fought a concept of law in which he was brought up and which contradicted the OT teaching on God's law and the proper Jewish attitude to the law (Schoeps, pp. 24–37). (b) Paul struggled against the development of certain heretical Jewish groups toward syncretism, that is, against nascent Gnosticism (Schmithals, see BIBLIOGRAPHY 2). (c) Some Gentile Christians, impressed by Paul's references to Abraham and Israel, wanted to be even truer than Paul to the OT and to Jewish traditions (Munck, PSM, pp. 87–134). The last-mentioned theory has more in its favor than either one of the others, as especially the epistle to the Galatians shows. The so-called "Judaizers" of Galatia cannot have been Jews; see E. Hirsch, "Zwei Fragen zu Galater 6," ZNW 29 (1930), 83–89; W. Michaelis, "Judaistisches Heidenchristentum," ZNW 30 (1931), 83–89. Gal 6:13 makes it probable that they were about to be circumcised, not that they had been circumcised, for the present tense "those who receive circumcision" in this verse has hardly the same meaning as the perfect tense "[having been] circumcised" (Gal 5:3 and I Cor 7:18), or the noun "circumcision" (Gal 2:7–9; Rom 2:25; Eph 2:11; etc.). Above all, the Galatian friends of circumcision asked for the circumcision of Gentiles without yet including the obligation that they fulfill all laws (Gal 5:3; 6:13; cf. Rom 2:25). There is no evidence that any orthodox Jew would ever have urged a Gentile or permitted a fellow Jew to accept circumcision without insisting that it meant submission to *all* laws. "Cursed by every one who does not abide by *all* things written in the book of law, and do them": even Paul quotes this verse from Deut 27:26 in Gal 3:10. Only after elements of apocalyptic Judaism were used to form Gnosticism and/or were absorbed in pagan Gnosticizing teaching, i.e. after A.D. 70 and in the second century, does it appear possible that a mysterious saving effect was ascribed to circumcision alone, or to circumcision in company with a few other select commandments. The "Hebrew" adversaries of Paul mentioned in II Cor 11:22 did not, as far as the evidence of II Corinthians goes, make propaganda for circumcision or "works of law."

[209] The Franciscan and the Thomist doctrines of *merita de congruo, merita de condigno*, and the *habitus* of righteousness contained important differentiations. Both schools were opposed by Duns Scotus' and W. Occam's teaching on the character of either group of the *merita* and on the interrelation between them. The Council of Trent made an attempt at reconciling the Franciscan and Thomist traditions, but failed to exclude the Pelagian tendencies of Occamism. See for a summary of the discussions W. Joest, RGG, V, 831–33.

[210] Qumran passages such as 1QS x 11 – xi 17; 1QH xi 7–8, 18, 29–31; 1QM xi 4, destroy the false image.

affirmed: justification as well as the last judgment are in the hands of the Messiah Jesus.[211] Therefore it is not wise to consider the statements on the "judgment according to works" either a residue from Paul's pre-Damascus theology, a merely hypothetical argument, or a fiction upheld because of its unquestionable value as a threat to bad conduct and an invitation to do good.[212] The doctrine of the last judgment is too deeply rooted in Paul to yield to simple eradication, contempt, or neglect. Recent works on Paul[213] state emphatically that it does not contradict his teaching on justification by grace. For the "good works" to be recognized in the last judgment are different from the "works of law" to which some "false brethren" (Gal 2:4) ascribe salvation. The eternal election of the saints by God and their salvation by grace alone are in Paul's theology the beginning rather than the end to human freedom and works done in responsibility.[214] While the omnipotent free grace rules out any value of "works" done in slavish subservience to the letter of law, to manmade tradition or to human selection, the saving grace itself opens a wide field of "good works" as "our way of life" (Eph 2:5, 8, 10). It is not one and the same thing to do or fulfill the law,[215] and to seek justification by the law or by works of law.[216] "God's work" gives man the freedom to do "good works" (Eph 2:10). Precisely because God gives the will to obey and the obedient act itself, the saints are admonished "with fear and trembling" to "work out their own salvation" (Philip 2:12–13). But the boasting or imposition of "works of law" is in opposition to the recognition of God's right over man. Therefore, it contradicts man's justification.

Eph 2:10 gives basic information on the necessity of "good works." In eternity, i.e. before the foundation of the world, when God loved his Son and elected the saints in him, he also prepared "good works" for them. If there is meaning in the term "pre-existence" at all, then the "good works" of the saints share in it.[217] Still, among the pre-existent things enumerated in the Talmud "good works" are not mentioned.[218] Thus Paul attributes to them an even higher value than do later Jewish teachers! But just like them—though mostly

---

[211] Cf. Gal 2:15 – 4:31; I Cor 1:30; II Cor 12:9; Rom 1:16–17; 3:21 – 5:11; 9:30 – 10:17; Philip 3:9 with II Thess 1:5 – 2:12; Gal 6:7–10; I Cor 3:12–15; 4:2–4; II Cor 5:1–10; Rom 2:5–16; 12:2; 13:8–10; 14:10–12; Philip 4:8; cf. Eph 6:8–9; II Tim 4:8, etc.

[212] See e.g. O. Pfleiderer, *Der Paulinismus*, 2d ed. (London: Norgate, 1891), p. 291; Lietzmann, HbNT, 8, 4th ed. (1933), 39–40; J. Knox, IB, IX, 407–9; J. Weiss, *The History of Primitive Christianity*, II (New York: Wilson-Erickson, 1937), 544. The issue is extensively discussed by H. Braun, *Gerichtsgedanke;* see also E. Jüngel, "Das Gesetz zwischen Adam und Christus," ZTK 60 (1963), 42–74; idem, *Paulus und Jesus*, pp. 66–70.

[213] Stalder, *Werk des Geistes*, pp. 258–89, 455–69; Jüngel, p. 69; Bring, *Commentary on Galatians* (Philadelphia: Muhlenberg, 1961), pp. 130–42, 241, 270–81.

[214] The impasse between determinism and freedom, absolute fate and human responsibility, in which western philosophy again and again found itself caught, is not the last word of Jewish writers about the relation between God and man. See *Pirke Aboth* III 24; Josephus *ant.* XIII 5:9. Precisely because God is "all in all" (see e.g. I Cor 15:28), man is not condemned to be "nothing." Man may be compared to a worm, to a dog, or to dust before God—he is still God's creature. He may be called "dead"—as in Eph 2:1, 5—but he is raised by God himself.

[215] See e.g. Rom 2:12–14; 8:3–4; 13:8–10.

[216] According to Bring, *Galatians*, pp. 130–42, Paul does not speak in irony when in Galatians and Romans he quotes the words of Lev 18:5 "By doing them [the statutes and ordinances] a man shall live."

[217] Cf. the "vessels of mercy prepared beforehand" (Rom 9:23) and the works mentioned in IV Ezra 8:52.

[218] See fn. 212 to 1:3–14. If the works are not mentioned nevertheless man was created for good works. See Pirke Aboth II 9, "If thou hast practiced much Torah, take no credit to thyself: for thereunto thou wast created."

with distinctive references to the judge Jesus Christ[219]—he mentions the role of works in the judgment to come. Each man will stand in God's, respectively the Lord's, judgment clothed with the works he has done during his lifetime (I Cor 5:1–3, 10). "Works are the total historical existence of man."[220] Not an idea or abstraction of man, but the real, living, historical man—i.e. the man who in his commissions and omissions is a "working" man—is elected by God, given grace, resuscitated. The life-giving Spirit was given to men dead in sins in order to make them alive and have them walk on the way of "good works." Calvin spoke of a justification of works which would follow the justification of man by the cross and resurrection of Christ,[221] but Eph 2:10 does not suggest such a double-justification doctrine. Man cannot be separated from his works, least of all a saved saint from the "good works." These works are not good by legal fiction and they are not solid because of a posthumous injection of strength. Those works that will stand in the fire of the judgment (I Cor 3:13–15) owe their durability to their eternal preparation by God.

This need not mean that every good work done by every individual saint is contained in a thought of God, written in a book of his, or pre-existent in the very existence of an angel, or in an action of an angel (as some rabbis thought). According to Eph 1:10 all things are included and secured "in the Messiah Jesus." When man was elected and created "in Christ," he was privileged to be "conformed to Christ's image" (Rom 8:29). Christ himself is the sum and epitome of the human response, obedience, and praise to God (II Cor 1:20). Those bearing his image cannot help but recognize that whatever good they do is done because of the good, is similar to the good, is judged according to the good done in and by Jesus Christ. The quality of *his* work is the origin, archetype, and standard of theirs. The eternal acceptability and pleasantness of his work includes their ability to "find out by experience" what is "good, pleasing, perfect" in God's sight (Rom 12:2; Eph 5:10). Christians do not invent or concoct good works; they are not the creators of these works. But they acknowledge and carry out by their conduct those works of trust, obedience, repentance, and praise which are revealed in Christ to be "prepared beforehand" by God himself. He who does something good receives it from the Lord (6:8). Good works are the only appropriate way to recognize, to accept, and to witness to the goodness shown in Christ.

It has been occasionally surmised that the positive attitude to "good works" displayed in Eph 2:10 is strange to Pauline theology and speaks against Pauline authorship of Ephesians. But it is certainly not strange to the way Paul lived and to the discipline he imposed upon himself. He was convinced that he carried out God's work (II Cor 5:18–20), and the term "good work" is found in his undisputed letters: Paul speaks not only of "God's good work" but also

---

[219] II Cor 5:10; I Cor 4:1–5; I Thess 4:16–17; II Thess 1:7–10; Rom 2:16; Col 3:23–25; Eph 6:8; cf. Matt 25:31–46; 7:21–24; 16:27; Mark 8:38.

[220] Lohmeyer, *Probleme*, p. 57, cf. pp. 43 and 53. Similarly Jüngel, *Paulus*, p. 69: The judgment according to works reveals that being and existence of man belong together. If God did not look upon what men have done, it would not be men upon whom he deigns to bestow his attention and grace.

[221] *Institutio* III 17:3–4; see also W. Niesel, *The Theology of Calvin* (Richmond: Knox, 1956), p. 136.

of man's.[222] Another possibility is that the singular "good work" means something different from the plural—as indeed "the *work* of the law" (Rom 2:14) done by the Gentiles is distinct from the *"works* of law" performed or required by Paul's opponents. Since the plural "good works" is found exclusively in the Pastoral Epistles,[223] a deutero-Pauline character seems to adhere to this term. Still, in genuine letters the apostle himself speaks frankly of "each good work."[224] He urges his readers to "do the good" by using four different verbs to emphasize human activity and operation.[225] The passages in which in good Greek fashion he speaks of "pleasing God" and "pleasing works,"[226] cannot be suppressed or forgotten in favor of the statements in which he denies man's ability to complete anything good or meritorious out of his own resources, or on the basis of the law alone.[227] Linguistic evidence does not prove that Eph 2:10 must be un-Pauline.

However, in Rom 4:5 it is stated, "To him who does not work but believes in Him who justifies the wicked, his faith is reckoned for righteousness." This passage, but also the condemnation of justification by "works of law" and innumerable passive forms, such as chosen, justified, sanctified, reconciled, convey the impression that man is given and receives salvation only when he is completely passive. Both Augustine and Luther praised man's passivity vis-à-vis God and thought it fit to describe "saving faith" in corresponding terms.[228] According to Ephesians this understanding of Paul is inadequate. A man behaving passively is still acting a certain way, but in 2:1, 5, man is called dead; thus his plight is beyond activity and passivity alike. Now God raises him to life with Christ, a life which is not an open possibility for either better or worse conduct, but a God-given specific life, the life of a free man on a throne, the life of a witness to the world, in brief, life led on the path of good works (2:6–7, 10). If there were no "newness of life" (Rom 6:4) given to the saints in Christ through the Spirit, there would be no life given by God worth mentioning. The gift of grace praised in 2:8–9 consists not just of a possibility of new conduct but of an actual new behavior, as the ethical chapters of Ephesians show no less than e.g. the Sermon on the Mount and the epistle of James. The Spirit of God who produces all good works and attitudes (Gal 5:22–25), does not take control over man in such a fashion that men are manipulated like puppets on strings, but he activates man and makes him a responsive partner of God's covenant.[229] "If we live by the Spirit, let us also walk by the Spirit" (Gal 5:25). "Driven by the Spirit" as they are, the children of God are "free" children, exemplifying "freedom" to all creatures.[230]

[222] Philip 1:6; Rom 2:7; Col 1:10.

[223] I Tim 2:10; 5:10; cf. II Tim 2:21; 3:17; Titus 1:16; 3:1; the equivalent, but better Greek term, "beautiful works," occurs in I Tim 3:1; 5:25; 6:18; Titus 2:7, 14; 3:8, 14; I Peter 2:12; cf. James 4:17.

[224] II Thess 2:17; II Cor 9:8; Rom 13:3.

[225] I Thess 5:15; Gal 6:10; II Cor 5:10; Rom 2:10; 9:11; 13:3; cf. Eph 4:28; 6:8. The verbs are *diōkō*, "pursue," *ergazomai*, "work," *prassō*, "accomplish," *poieō*, "do." Only in Rom 4:4–5 is *ergazomai* used with the bad connotation of working with an eye on reward.

[226] I Thess 2:15; 4:1; II Cor 5:9; Rom 12:1–2; 14:18; Philip 4:18; cf. Col 3:20; Eph 5:10.

[227] E.g. Rom 4:4–5; 7:18–24; 8:8; Philip 3:7–8.

[228] Haupt, p. 65, illustrates this assumption drastically: "Just as a drowning man through his own endeavor makes impossible his salvation and must renounce all positive cooperation, so man must deliver himself completely to divine grace."

[229] See esp. Stalder, pp. 27–50, 225–26, 235–36, 363–87.

[230] Rom 6:18; 8:14–24; Eph 2:18; 3:12; Gal 4:6, 21–31; 5:1, 13, 16–17, 22–25.

VII   Conclusion

The first ten verses of Eph 2 are replete with astonishing and seemingly contradictory doctrines. Here is a grim *anthropology* characterized by sin, death, the devil, and flesh. It is matched by the highest exaltation of man through resurrection and enthronement.

A glimpse is given into the realm of darkness which comes as near a satanology as is feasible. The inexplicable, sinister operation of evil from outside and inside man is bluntly acknowledged and no attempt is made to exempt man from his just condemnation.

Opposite the gloomy satanology a *theology* is developed which praises God as the giver of life and salvation, of honor, and of a task to fulfill. This God proves true to himself and his creatures by creating man anew so that he will live on the way prepared by God himself. No longer is mankind sold out and lost on the road of lapses and sins. God's eternal will is now realized: men are made to praise him by their works.

The history of God's victory over the devil is narrated with the help of a surprising *chronology*. Not only death, which seems to be the future of every living man, but also resurrection are described as events already accomplished. Although the devil may still exercise influence, the present and the future are yet full and to be filled with the fruit of salvation. Even though the future will still bring an attack from hostile powers, the saints are nevertheless equipped to enjoy their freedom, to render an effective testimony, and to do what is good.

In all these utterances on salvation from Satan and for God, from the past and for the future, by God's rich grace and for a responsible life of action, a definite *sociology* has become apparent. Gentile and Jewish sinners were not only described in their solidarity of sin and death, but they were also reminded of their common resurrection, their communion with the Messiah, and their task as witnesses among all creatures of God, at all times.

Just as in the former sections of Ephesians, so in 2:1–10 *Christology* forms the life nerve of and the key to all seemingly extravagant statements.

The communal and Christological *soteriology* is finally displayed in an excursus in which man is warned of his own pride and of his reliance upon any willful or slavish works. He is encouraged to rely fully upon the grace of God alone.

V PEACE THROUGH THE CROSS
(2:11–22)

2   11 Remember, then, that in the past [and] in the realm of the flesh, you, the Gentiles—called The Uncircumcision by those who call themselves The Circumcision, that handmade operation in the realm of the flesh . . . 12 [Remember] that at that time you were apart from the Messiah, excluded from the citizenship of Israel, strangers to the covenants based upon promise. In this world you were bare of hope and without God. 13 But now you are [included] in the realm of the Messiah Jesus. Through the blood of the Messiah you who in the past stood far off have been brought near. 14 For [we confess]

He is in person the peace between us.
He has made both [Gentiles and Jews] into one.
For he has broken down the dividing wall,
in his flesh [he has wiped out all] enmity.
15 He has abolished the law [, that is, only] the commandments
|expressed| in statutes.
[This was] to make peace by creating in his person
a single new man out of the two,
16 and to reconcile both to God
through the cross in one single body.
In his own person he has killed the enmity.
17 Indeed when he came he proclaimed good news:
"Peace to you who are far and peace to those near!"
18 Through him and in one single Spirit
the two [of us] have free access to the Father.

19 Accordingly you are no longer strangers and sojourners, but you are fellow citizens with the saints and members of the household of God. 20 You are built upon the foundation of the apostles and prophets, the keystone being the Messiah Jesus himself. 21 The whole construction, fitted together in him, grows in the Lord into a holy temple. 22 In him you, too, are being built together so as to be a dwelling of God in the Spirit.

NOTES

2:11. *Remember.* See the NOTE on 1:16 and the literature mentioned there. Repentance, decision, and gratitude are called for, not a mental recollection only. In the first NOTE on vs. 12 the grammatical structure of Eph 2:11–13 and the particular use of "remembering" in vs. 11 will be discussed.

in the realm of the flesh. Lit. "in the flesh." The repetition of the same phrase at the end of this verse reveals its importance. The added words, "the realm of," prepare the reader for the parallel, "in the world" (2:12), and the antitheses, "[included] in the realm of the Messiah Jesus" and "in one single Spirit" (2:13, 18). A final contrast to "the realm of the flesh" is formed by the formulae "in him," "in the Lord," "in the Spirit" (2:21–22). Paul's thought moves from men in the grip of "flesh" (2:11), over the work performed in "Christ's flesh" (2:14), to the operation of the "Spirit" (2:18). Nothing can prevent the "Spirit" from operating "in the realm of flesh." "I will pour out my Spirit upon all flesh" (Joel 3:1). Several meanings of the term "flesh" have been discussed above.[1] Among rabbis, the word "flesh" can denote the sexual organs. In 2:11 Paul may first have intended to speak only of the physical act and the visible bodily mark of circumcision, cf. Rom 2:28—without meaning to give a depreciative or ironic undertone to his mention of the external physical rite. But just as in the OT and often in Paul, the comparison of the effect of the "Spirit" (2:18) with the reality present in the "flesh" (2:11) reveals that not all is well with the "flesh." Thus "flesh" receives in 2:11 the same evil meaning as it has e.g. in Gal 3:3, 6:13; Eph 2:3. Those circumcised as well as those uncircumcised are trapped in the flesh which is as weak and perishable as grass (Gen 6:3, 12; Isa 40:6). Not despite—as the rabbis who speak of the "evil impulse" would have been willing to concede—but just because of their circumcision, Jews are included under this indictment. A prophetic OT motif is taken up in this charge: the validity of bodily circumcision has often been subjected to the criterion of the "circumcision" of the "heart" or "ear."[2]

called . . . by those who call themselves. Since in the Bible[3] the name by which a person or thing is "called" expresses its essence and dynamic presence rather than an arbitrary attribute, the translation "so-called" uncircumcision and circumcision[4] is not appropriate. The distinction between Jews and Gentiles was not nominal only, despite the phenomenal, external, and temporal character of the ceremony of circumcision (Rom 2:28). The spiteful designation of Gentiles by the term "The Uncircumcision" and the factual separation of the Jews from the Gentiles were as real as the presence or absence of the distinctive bodily mark. Paul alludes to name-calling or to a nickname, and he accepts it as fact. But he affirms that Jews who mock the uncircumcised Gentiles, even when they boast of their circumcision, are as much "in the flesh" as are the Gentiles. This does not imply that he despises circumcision as such, for

---

[1] See COMMENT II on 2:1–10; COMMENT II on 1:3–14.
[2] Jer 4:4; 6:10; 9:26[LXX 9:25]; Deut 10:16; 30:6; Ezek 44:7, 9; Lev 26:41; cf. 1QS v 5; Rom 2:29; Col 2:11.
[3] Except, e.g. Rev 3:1; also I Cor 8:5?
[4] Which is supported, e.g. by Abbott.

the same circumcision which is fleshly, external, ceremonial, which may lead to boasting (Rom 2:17, 25; Gal 6:13), and which must not be forcefully imposed upon Gentiles (Gal 2:3–5, 6:13), is never condemned or belittled for its own sake.[5] It is neither inauthentic nor wrong for Jews.[6] In Eph 2:12 and 15 Paul will show that the external distinction created by circumcision is not only human or man-made, but is the demarcation of the first elect, the Jews, from other nations. This distinction was established in the history of God with mankind and is sanctified by no less an authority than God's decision and law.

The Uncircumcision . . . The Circumcision. The translation, "The Uncircumcised . . . The Circumcised," would be almost as literal.[7] The emotional overtones of the nomenclature are obvious: uncircumcision is a terrible shame[8] and an ancient Israelite regards it with contempt.[9] It is probable that the term "circumcision" in 2:11 includes not only baptized Jews, but every Jew—be he a faithful observer of the law or a rebellious trespasser, a Pharisee or a Sadducee, orthodox or secularized.[10]

handmade. The same term is used in the LXX for idols, in the NT for the temple.[11] Its opposite is found in II Cor 5:1, "[a house] not made by hand, eternal, in heaven"; in Col 2:11, "[a circumcision] not hand-made [but performed] in the circumcision of Christ"; in Mark 14:58, "[a temple] to be built by the Messiah." The prayer, e.g. of Ps 51:18, expecting that God (himself) will rebuild the walls of Jerusalem sums up many prophecies and hopes. NT utterances on the temple to be built by God (Eph 2:20–22; Matt 16:18, etc.) are tied to this expectation. As the building of the temple by God is contrasted to the construction of temples by men, so circumcision of the heart (Rom 2:29; or the circumcision of Christ, Col 2:11) highly excels handmade circumcision. See COMMENT III.

12. [*Remember*] *that at that time you were.* It is possible that the Greek conjunction *hoti,* here translated by "that" and treated as a resumption of the

---

[5] The apostle counts circumcision among the *useful* things which constitute a privilege of Israel (Rom 2:25; 3:1). When he refers to it polemically (as in Philip 3:2; Gal 5:12), then it is because of its misuse. In refusing to have the circumcision imposed upon Gentiles as a prerequisite for participation in the coming aeon, he was eventually supported by a group of Jewish scholars. The majority opinion among the rabbis is perhaps contained in utterances like the following: Jellinek, Beth ha-Midr 5, 162, 1, "God is pleased only with Israel. What *akum* (Gentiles) do, is offense [i.e. sin; cf. Baba Bathra 106]; for it is said: for the nations to be merciful works out as sin [Prov 14:34!] . . . God loves only circumcision, for it is the seal of God, his belt, and this he loves. But the *akum* are counted for nothing, because they lack the belt; they all exist for the *gehenna.*" This view has found contradiction in the Talmud itself; see, e.g. T Sanh. 13:2; B Sanh. 105a: "There are righteous ones even among the nations who have a share in the world to come." In P Meq 74a 25, Emperor Antoninus Pius is mentioned as an example. More evidence in favor of this lenient judgment (which was earlier promoted by the book of Jonah) has been collected, e.g. by StB, II, 719–21. In StB, III, 120, and TWNTE, VI, 741 (Kuhn) the tolerant attitude is considered "not widely recognized"; "the predominant evaluation . . . is unfavourable." But see S. S. Schwarzschild, "Do Noachites have to believe in Revelation?", JQR 52 (1962), 297 ff.

[6] Cf. Robinson, pp. 56, 60, 158.

[7] In Gal 2:7–9; Rom 2:26–29 Paul follows rabbinical custom when he identifies "circumcision" with the Jews, "uncircumcision" with the Gentiles. The nouns were used to describe not only the result of circumcision and the retaining of the *praeputium* respectively, but ("metonymically") the people who had or had not been circumcised. See StB, I, 713–14; II, 705.

[8] According to a possible interpretation of Josh 5:9 it was considered a shame even by the ancient Egyptians. But it was "rolled away" by Yahweh.

[9] Judg 14:3; 15:18; I Sam 14:6; 17:26 etc.; Ezek 28:10.

[10] E. Percy, TLZ 86 (1961), 199–201, believes—as did Calvin and many others—that Eph 2:11 ff speaks of only such Jews (and Gentiles) as believe in Christ. But the word "faith" is absent from this text. The scope of the passage reaches far beyond the church. It includes all Jews and all Gentiles.

[11] Isa 2:18; 10:11, etc.; Lev 26:1, 30; LXX Dan 5:4, 23; 6:27; Judith 8:18; Mark 14:58; Acts 7:48; 17:24; Heb 9:11, 24.

hoti in vs. 11, should be translated by "because"; vs. 12 may not be a simple parallel or continuation of vs. 11, but rather a parenthesis interrupting (though supporting) the thought expressed in vss. 11 and 13: remember that you ex-Gentiles have now been brought near. In this case the subject matter to be "remembered" is the incorporation of the former aliens into Israel, rather than their past uncircumcision and strangership as such. Among the many OT and NT references to "remembering" and "remembrance," there appears to be not even one that enjoins men in so many words to remember their misdeeds, their sins, or some catastrophe of the past. Rather it is God who remembers or is asked to remember the covenant, Abraham, Zion, his people or an individual saint. When he remembers them in his faithfulness and compassion, he will set out to do a work of salvation. But when he remembers sins, it implies that he is going to punish the evildoer, or that he has not yet (fully) forgiven; see e.g. Ps 25:7; Jer 31:34; Heb 10:2–3, 17. On the other hand, God's people remember or are told to remember God, former saving acts of God, the poor, or the cucumbers eaten in Egypt. Once (in Isa 43:18; but cf. 46:9) they are commanded "not to remember the former things." Perhaps when Paul started out to write or to dictate Eph 2:11 ff, he wanted the Ephesians only to "remember" the boon of their adoption into God's house and people, and to encourage them to follow his own example, i.e. to "forget what lies behind" (Philip 3:13; cf. Eph 4:17–19). But the absence of a *hoti* at the beginning of vs. 13, that is, the distance of the *hoti* in vs. 11 from vs. 13, obfuscates this possible original intention of the apostle and makes it probable that Eph 2:11–12 is the only biblical text admonishing saved and sanctified people to remember their pernicious past. Certainly the sequence of the verbs and moods, "Remember—but now you are," is incongruous. However, the anacoluthon of vss. 11–13 contains not just a certain lack of beauty, but also makes room for the radiant and glorious crowning sentence of vs. 13: "But now you are [included] . . . you have been brought near." This sentence would lose much of its strength if converted into a dependent clause introduced by the words, "Remember that."

apart from the Messiah. So the translation of NTTEV. Moffatt translates, "outside"; Philipps, "without"; NEB, "separate from"; JB, "had no Messiah." Each of these viable versions implies the pre-existence of the Messiah in Israel.[12] The promise attached to the covenants (2:12b) with Abraham and David, and the corresponding hope that was first held by Jews (1:12), were not limited to the idea of a remote future Messiah. Rather David and other anointed servants of God anticipated the presence of the Messiah Jesus in Israel (cf. John 8:56). As long as the Gentiles lacked historic communion, e.g. with Israel's anointed priests, kings, prophets, they were deprived of communion with the Messiah to come. But their separation was yet not eternal, for according to 1:4–10 God had already before the foundation of the world, "through Jesus Christ" or "in the Messiah," predesignated both Jews *and* Gentiles to be his children. Only on the level of history and consciousness did the inclusion of the Gentiles in the Messiah's realm take place after the coming of the Messiah Jesus.

---

[12] See von Soden, p. 116. The passages I Cor 10:4; Gal 3:16; I Peter 1:11; 3:19 can be considered parallels; cf. the pre-existence texts listed in COMMENT VI on 1:3–14.

excluded from the citizenship of Israel. WBLex, 79 offers this translation. The seemingly more literal version, "alienated . . . ," suggests that there was former unity.[13] In the Aeropagus Speech (Acts 17:26) as well as in the Pauline utterances on Adam (Rom 5; I Cor 15), such original unity is presupposed. In Eph 1:4–10 also the Gentiles' eternal inclusion in God's love and election is indeed affirmed. But in Eph 2:12 Paul does not mean to argue that they have fallen out of it: falling from grace becomes a genuine threat only after the coming of Christ (Gal 5:4). In Eph 2:12 a *status* of strangership is described, not an *event* leading to estrangement. The expression "strangers and sojourners" (2:19) is the authentic interpretation of "excluded." These terms prove that the Gentiles had not been "naturalized"; Paul does not intend to say that at an earlier moment they were "expatriated." Never before have they been "fellow citizens and members" (2:19, 3:6).[14] While an Israelite may speak of himself as a "sojourner, like all my fathers" on earth, even when he dwells in the promised land,[15] all Jews are yet members of the people of God, and are therefore included among those blessed. It is true that they bear as one of their proper names the designation "Hebrews," which is related to *habiru,* a term originally denoting a member of a social or ethnic group not belonging to the resident ruling class. Non-Israelites call the children of Abraham by that name and in so doing may wish to express their contempt. But the Israelites also employ this term when addressing foreigners like the Egyptians and Philistines. The people who from the beginning understood themselves as a holy people and kingdom of priests to Yahweh (Exod 19:6) used the name "Hebrews" with pride. It served to reveal their distinction from other nations and their unity as a people among whom a man could be at home. God their king, their common history, and the promise of the coming Messiah forged them into a unit. Though more often than not divided among themselves and warring one against another, they remember the unity of the twelve tribes and are reminded of the covenant by which God granted protection and the promised land. In Ephesians the divisions running through Israel are not mentioned, e.g. between the Northern and the Southern kingdoms, or between obedient and disobedient priests, prophets, and kings. The whole of Israel as a unit, even the complete number of these children of wrath (2:3), is in the author's mind. Correspondingly, the Gentiles are described—their mutual treaties, conglomerations or occasional pacts with Israelite kings notwithstanding—as divided among themselves and separated from Israel. In vss. 13 and 17 the geographical aspect of their separation is in the foreground. They are *far* from Zion. In vs. 12 their legal status is moved into the center. There were indeed some Gentiles who were forced or willing to live in the land promised to Israel, but even they were not *near* in that they were not full citizens as long as they remained Gentiles. Geographical propinquity does not preclude legal extra-territoriality. And the opposite held equally true: Jews living abroad either by the force of circumstance or volun-

---

[13] Just as the case in Ezek 14:5, 7; LXX Ps 68[69]:8; Sir 11:34, and in today's Marxist and existentialist references to "alienation."

[14] See esp. the refutation of Bengel's opposite arguments by Robinson, pp. 158–59, and Abbott. In LXX Ps 57:4[58:3]; Eph 4:18; Col 1:21; I Clem 7:7 the same Greek verb is used to describe more than privation and separation, i.e. radical opposition and hostility, cf. C. Spicq, *Théologie morale du Nouveau Testament,* II (Paris: Gabalda, 1965), 421–22, n. 6.

[15] Pss 39:12; 119:19; Lev 25:23; I Chron 29:15; cf. Gen 23:4; Deut 26:5; Exod 16:3.

tarily were yet members of God's household and fellow citizens of the residents of Zion. Therefore the translation "citizenship"[16] with its political-legal overtone is preferable to the more geographical term, "commonwealth." The "aliens and sojourners" and their opposites mentioned in 2:19 offer, again, the author's authentic interpretation of vs. 12. An allusion to *pagani* (pagans) as uncultured people in rural places is not implied in the terms "far" and "excluded." According to Paul there are Barbarians among the Gentiles (Col 3:11), but not all Gentiles are Barbarians.

strangers to the covenants based upon promise. Lit. "strangers to the covenants of promise."[17] Several "covenants" are summarily mentioned,[18] yet all of them are denoted as unilateral contracts based upon the goodness of the "promising" God. God's promise, affirmed by a solemn oath during the covenant ceremony, is the basis of all hope (Heb 6:13–18). Promise in Eph 2:12 (as elsewhere in Paul, especially Rom 4; Gal 3) is denoted as the very blood and nerve of Israel's life and history. But is not the law—rather than promise and covenant—the living word which constitutes Israel's life (Lev 18:5; Deut 33:3–4; etc.)? Paul considers the law, e.g. the commandment of circumcision, a "seal" added to the covenant (Rom 4:11). The law gives to God's elect covenant partners directions on how to live and how to counter and avoid transgressions (Gal 3:19), but it does not annul its own presupposition and foundation: God's covenant-promise.[19] Because of the preceding reference to the Messiah, the singular "promise" may point directly to the gift of the "one seed," the Messiah (cf. Gal 3:16). However, occasionally Paul also speaks of several promises.[20] The renewal of the covenant with Israel and Judah[21] and the creation of "children of promise" among Jews and Gentiles[22] belong to the manifold specifications of God's one "promise."

In this world. Lit. "in the world"; a seemingly redundant addition. The Greek noun translated by "world" means originally the harmonious order of things, also eventually the whole universe, including the gods. The phenomenal sphere which has come into being, and the intelligible sphere (of eternal ideas) are both called "world."[23] Paul sometimes uses this elastic and often ambiguous term without any deprecating tone to denote heaven and earth, or the earth only.[24] Being God's creation, the "world" is good. However, in Eph 2:12 the addition of the article may reveal that here Paul has in mind "that well-known world" which in apocalyptic circles was considered evil and which in apocalyptic and rabbinic literature was set in opposition to the world to come (see Eph 2:2 and

---

[16] Cf. Philip 3:20; Acts 22:28 and the dictionaries; see also the discussion and literature to the Greek term *politeiā* in Spicq. *Théologie morale,* I, p. 416 ff, 452 ff, and K. L. Schmidt, *Die Polis in Kirche und Welt,* Zürich; EVZ, 1940.

[17] See BDF, 182:3 for the use of "stranger" (*xenos*) with the genitive.

[18] The covenants with Noah, Abraham, Isaac, Jacob, Moses, David, Judah, Levi are mentioned as a unit, or they are selectively enumerated, e.g. in Lev 26:42, 45; Sir 44–45; cf. Wisd Sol 18:22; II Macc 8:15. A distinction between various types of covenants, e.g. between unilateral covenants or promise and bilateral contracts stipulating certain works, as suggested by D. N. Freedman, "Divine Commitment and Human Obligation," *Interpretation* 18 (1964), 3–15, is not made in Eph 2:12, and probably not suggested by Rom 10:5–8 (Bring, *Galatians,* pp. 130–42). But see Gal 4:21–31; II Cor 3:6–11. In writing Eph 2:12 Paul appears not to have thought of the Covenant with Noah which included all of mankind (Gen 9:8 ff).

[19] Rom 4:13; 9:4; Gal 3:16–29. See M. Noth, *The Law in the Pentateuch,* Philadelphia: Westminster, 1961 (also published by Oliver & Boyd in Edinburgh, 1966); and Schlier, pp. 120–21.

[20] Gal 3:16, 21; II Cor 1:20; 7:1; Rom 9:4.

[21] Of which Hosea, Jeremiah, Ezekiel, Malachi spoke.   [22] Gal 4:28; Rom 9:8.

[23] See H. Sasse, TWNTE, III, 868–79.   [24] Rom 1:8, 20; Eph 1:4; Col 1:6; 16, etc.

1:21). This world-age (2:2) is then the Devil's sphere. Indeed Paul says else-where of "the world" (with the article) emphatically one thing only: it is subject to God's judgment![25] In Eph 2:11–12 "world" and "flesh" are practically synonyms. "The realm of the flesh," i.e. "the world," is the sphere of unreconciled humanity. But over and into both "the flesh" and "the world" the work of reconciliation done by Christ is extended.[26]

bare of hope. The same description of Gentiles is found in I Thess 4:13; however, in Isa 11:10[27] the Messiah is described as the one upon whom the Gentiles will hope, whereas in the context of Wisd Sol 15:6 the objects of the Gentiles' hope are mentioned—and ridiculed. While Bengel affirms that in Eph 2:12 the absence of the "Messianic hope" is meant, Abbott suggests the words "bare of hope" be understood "in the evident sense." Robinson sees the lack of hope among Gentiles epitomized in the yearning backward for a lost golden age. Israel's uniqueness would then exist in its orientation toward the future (see e.g. Gen 12:15; II Sam 7; Dan 7, etc.). But such a view cannot stand up to the facts since Israel cannot claim a monopoly on prospective hope; neither are Israelite writings and prayers free of retrospection and nostalgic elements. Belief in progress, perfection, the immortality of the soul, a future savior king is expressed among Gentiles as fervently as among Jews and Christians.[28] On the other hand, in the OT as well as in rabbinic teaching, Paradise, Sinai, or Zion typology were often used for describing eschatological and apocalyptic hopes; the last things were more than once expected to be like the first. Would the author of Ephesians have been so ignorant or unfair as to declare all Gentiles void of any and all hope? Unless Paul flippantly denied or dispossessed the Gentiles of any hope he must have meant a specific hope. This "hope," then, could be understood as fostered in the minds of the Jews, because it was founded and guaranteed in the heart of God or "laid up in heaven" as Col 1:5 puts it. In Eph 1:12 and 18 hope of the latter kind is meant. It is the hope for the promised Messiah from the root of David (Rom 1:1–3). But a variant reading of 4:19 supports Abbott's and Robinson's interpretation, and affirms the Gentiles' subjective despair. If Eph 2:12 does not allude to the absence of the Messianic hope but rather alludes to total despair, then this passage fits the pattern of Jewish anti-pagan polemics.[29] It would, however, fall out of the Christological orientation of Ephesians. Perhaps the designation of Gentiles by the words "bare of hope" was phrased by Paul in hidden allusion to Isa 57:10 and as antithesis to it: "You [the members of God's people] were wearied with your way, but you did not say, 'It is hopeless.'" So the prophet spoke. Cf. Ezra 10:2, "We have broken with our God . . . but even now there is hope for Israel in spite of this."

---

[25] I Cor 6:12; 11:32; Rom 3:6.
[26] E.g. II Cor 5:19; Rom 8:3; cf. John 1:14; 3:16. Sasse, TWNTE, III, 893, defines Paul's concept of the world by calling it "the sum" of the divine creation which has been shattered by the fall, which stands under the judgment of God, and in which Christ appears as the redeemer.
[27] Cf. Isa 42:4, as alluded to in Rom 15:12 and Matt 12:21.
[28] See, e.g. *Sibylline Oracles* I 167 ff. and the materials collected in M. Dibelius, "Jungfrauensohn und Krippenkind," in *Botschaft und Geschichte* I, Tübingen: Mohr, 1953; E. Rohde, *Psyche*, I–II, 5th ed., Tübingen: Mohr, 1910. In the present time Marxists, e.g. E. Bloch, *Das Prinzip Hoffnung*, 2 vols., Frankfurt: Suhrkamp, 1959, are more than others determined by hope.
[29] Cf. Wisd Sol 13:10, "their hopes set on dead things."

without God. In Greek, one single word (the adjective *atheos*) describes the ultimate reason for and the darkest aspect of the Gentiles' former status. The Greek word *atheos,* from which the English "atheist" is derived, does not occur in the LXX, the apocryphal books, or elsewhere in the NT. It denotes either a person not believing in a deity, or an impious despiser of law and tradition, or a god-forsaken man.[30] These multiple meanings made it possible for the term to be liberally used in manifold polemics. Socrates was accused of atheism; Jews and Christians used the term to describe the Gentiles; Gentiles hurled it at Jews and Christians; Christians welcomed it as a tool for confounding heretics.[31] Though in Eph 2:12 this term seems at first sight to contain no more than such a "paying back with the same coin," its place at the conclusion of the list of the Gentiles' former characteristics indicates a more important purpose. At first the difference between Jews and Gentiles was described in the ceremonial and external terms of "Circumcision" and "Uncircumcision"; then it was designated by the political, legal, sociological, and psychological concepts, "apart from the Messiah," "excluded from the citizenship of Israel," "strangers," "bare of hope." Now, at the conclusion, the difference is depicted as soteriological and theological. God himself had not shown that he cared for the Gentiles! They have been God-forsaken people. In the words of Deut 10:15, 4:19, 32:8, "The Lord set his heart in love upon your fathers and chose their dependents after them, you above all peoples . . . The sun, the moon and the stars, all the host of heaven . . . the Lord your God has allotted to all the peoples . . . He separated the sons of men." Cf. I Kings 8:53, "Thou didst separate them [i.e. Israel] from among all the peoples of the earth."

13. *But now you are [included] in the realm of the Messiah Jesus.* Lit. "in the Messiah Jesus." Regarding the addition of [included] see the NOTE on 1:13. The formula "in the Messiah" is weightier than the expression "with Christ";[32] see COMMENT V A. The contrast which is proclaimed between the time of the "past" (2:11) and the present by the triumphant words "but now" (2:3), was discussed in COMMENT IX on 1:3–14. It is equivalent to that between "flesh" and "Spirit" (2:11, 18).

Through the blood of the Messiah. See COMMENT V B.

you who . . . stood far off have been brought near. Here and in vs. 17 an allusion is made to Isa 57:19. The prophetic text originally refers not to Gentiles and Jews but to the Jews in exile and the Jews in the promised land.[33] The author of Ephesians might be accused of gross misinterpretation and misuse of the OT text—if there were no traces of a similar understanding of Isa 57 by Jewish teachers in his environment. See COMMENT II.

14–18. *For [we confess]: He is in person the peace . . . free access to*

---

[30] LSLex, s.v.; Abbott.

[31] Plato *apologia* 26 C; *Sib. Or.* VIII 395; *Martyrium Polycarpi* (henceforth *Mart. Pol.*) IX 2b; Ps.-Clem. *hom.* XV 4; Clement of Alexandria *paed.* III 11, 80. The many gods of the Gentiles were—by Jews, as in Gal 4:8; cf. I Cor 8:4–6; Rom 1:23—considered non-gods. The immoral conduct or practices of Gentiles proved that foolishness instead of the fear of God ruled among them. See, e.g. Isa 44:9–10; Wisd Sol 12:23–27; 13–15; Josephus *contra Apionem* II 148; *Mart. Pol.* III; IX 2c; Justin Martyr *apol.* I 6:1; 13:1; Ign. *Trall.* X; perhaps also III 2.

[32] Schlier, p. 122, with Calvin, against Abbott.

[33] Cf. Isa 57:14 ff with 40:1 ff; 52:7, etc.; also Jer 3:18; 24:5–7. In Theod. Dan 9:7 the same distinction is made. Cf. also NumR 8 (149d). According to Esther 9:20 Mordecai sent letters "to all the Jews . . . both near and far," i.e. in Susa and, e.g. in India and Ethiopia (1:1–2).

the Father.[34] In these five verses hymnic traits are more obvious and complete than in most other hymnodic passages of Ephesians.[35] To be enumerated are (a) the conjunctions "for" and "accordingly" which frame the hymn proper; (b) the "we"-style that interrupts the address "you" in vss. 11–13, 19–22 (but see vs. 17!); (c) the predicate "He is peace"[36] and the pointedly Christological content of the whole passage; (d) the participle forms and the relative clauses; (e) the synonyms and the parallelism of members; (f) the trinitarian conclusion; (g) the possibility or probability of interpolations.[37] G. Schille believes he can trace the origin of the hymn, reconstruct its original wording, and in the process distinguish two sets of later additions.[38] A pre-Christian (Gnostic) hymn praised in mythological terminology the reunion of the heavenly and earthly worlds, until pre-Pauline theology "reoriented" the mythological elements and put them into the service of Christology. Thus the hymn became a praise of Christ's mediation between God and (the whole of) humanity. Finally the author of Ephesians[39] added the elements that treat the unification of Jews and Gentiles. The result of this process is described by Schille in contradictory terms. The contents of the hymn are called so confused that they cannot be disentangled, and yet the same hymn is praised as an outstandingly perfect composition.[40] It is indeed probable, but not certain that earlier material was used. If 1:3–14, 20–23, 2:4–7, 10 can still be considered "psalms" composed by Paul himself (cf. 5:19; I Cor 14:26), then the formal idiosyncrasies of 2:14–18, including the simultaneous treatment of diverse topics, do not completely disprove Pauline origin. Only if decisive elements or the whole content of this passage, especially the unification of Jews and Gentiles through the death of Christ, were absent from or flatly contradictory to genuine Pauline writings, would it be

[34] For the following see besides the commentaries especially S. Hanson, *Unity*, 140 ff.; for 2:14–16, P. Feine, "Epheser 2, 14–16," TSK 72 (1899), 540–74; A. G. Lamadrid, "Ipse est pax nostra," *Estudios Biblicos* 29 (1970), 101–36, 227–66 (ref.).
[35] Already Bengel remarked *"quasi rhythmo canticum imitatur."* The modern hymnic interpretation begins with Haupt who saw in these verses an "excursus"; cf. Dibelius. Among the scholars who have elaborated upon the formal elements, the background, the *Sitz im Leben*, the parallels, and later additions that characterize the hymn found in 2:14–16 (or 2:14–17; or 2:14–18; etc.) are P. Pokorný, "Epheserbrief und gnostische Mysterien," ZNW 53 (1952), 182–83; E. Käsemann, "Epheser 2, 17–22," in *Exegetische Versuche und Besinnungen* I (Göttingen: Vandenhoeck, 1960), 280–83; Schlier, pp. 124–33; J. T. Sanders, "Hymnische Elemente in Epheser 1–3," ZNW 56 (1965), 214–32; Schille, *Hymnen*, pp. 24–31, 43; E. Testa, "Gesu pacificatore universale," *Studii Biblici Franciscani* (Liber annuus Jerusalem, 1969), 5–64 (ref.); J. Gnilka, "Christus unser Friede—ein Friedens-Erlöserlied in Epheser 2:14–17," in *Die Zeit Jesu*, Fs H. Schlier (Freiburg: Herder, 1970), pp. 190–207. The growing consensus is in an admittedly "minimal rather than definitive" fashion enriched by J. T. Sanders, *The New Testament Christological Hymns*, Society for New Testament Studies Monograph Series 15 (London University Press, 1971), 14–15, and it has not been seriously shaken by the arguments to the contrary found in e.g. R. Deichgräber, *Gotteshymnus und Christushymnus* (Göttingen: Vandenhoeck, 1967), pp. 165–67.
[36] Cf. the identical OT predications in Isa 9:5–6; see also Zech 9:10; Micah 5:4–5. Analogous Christ predications are found in I Cor 1:30; Col 1:27; 3:4, not to speak of the "I am" formulations of John 14:6, etc. Pauly-Wissowa, v, 2128 ff., gives a description of the place and function of the goddess Irene among other deities.
[37] The sudden occurrence of "you" in 2:17; according to Haupt, pp. 78–80, and Schille, p. 27, the references to "hostility" are inserted; following Sanders, ZNW 56 (1965), 217–18, and others the words "making peace" and "through the cross" are a later addition.
[38] *Hymnen*, pp. 24–31. He distinguishes a longer prehistory of the hymn than e.g. Schlier, who assumes that Paul made immediate use of pagan material.
[39] In this case Schille deviates from his inclination toward Pauline authenticity.
[40] "Unentwirrbar . . . verzüglich durchkomponiert," Schille, pp. 26 and 31. Hegermann, *Schöpfungsmittler*, pp. 145–46 endorses the negative judgment: the author of the final hymn did not succeed in combining the (original) cosmic with (his own) soteriological notions, but created confusion. Cf. N. Kehl, *Der Christushymnus Kolosser 1:12–20*, SBM 1 (1967), 132 ff.

necessary either to consider the whole of Ephesians as non-Pauline or to call the hymn of 2:14-18 a pre- or post-Pauline product. But many authentic Pauline passages affirm precisely this unification.[41]

14. *He is in person the peace between us.* Lit. "He is our peace." *Pulcherrimus titulus Christi,* says Calvin. The words "in person" were added three times in the translation of vss. 14-16; they correspond to the emphasis which the Greek pronoun "he himself" (*autos*) possesses, especially in acclamations. The translation "peace between us" is found in JB, and precludes any misunderstanding: Christ is praised here not primarily for the peace he brings to individual souls; rather the peace he brings is a social and political event (cf. COMMENT II on 1:1-2 and COMMENT V below). The "Messianic peace" here proclaimed is in Eph 4:3 distinctly called a "bond" uniting different people. In 2:14-15 this peace is first described as peace between man and fellow man, i.e. between Jew and Gentile and only then as peace between God and man (2:16-17). The same sequence of these two relationships is found in NT statements on forgiveness,[42] but it appears to be contradicted by all texts that deal with the priority of God's love and forgiveness over human and interhuman charity.[43] See COMMENT VI.

He has made both [*Gentiles and Jews*] *into one.* In Greek, the words "both" and "one" can have either masculine, feminine, or neuter forms—depending upon the gender of the nouns they modify. While in vss. 15-19 both words appear in the masculine form, in vs. 14 the neuter is used. Therefore in vs. 14 two "things" rather than two persons seem to be transformed into one "thing," not one man. This is one of the reasons why, under Schlier's inspiration, Schille and others thought they were able to discover a Gnostic *Urhymnus* that supposedly underlies Eph 2:14 ff. The myth thus spoke of the upper, spiritual world, of its conflict with the lower, material sphere, and of a wall or limit (*horos*) between both—as was outlined in COMMENT VI C on 1:15-23. Indeed, if the parallel to Eph 2:14, i.e. Col 1:20, clearly affirmed that "through the blood of the cross" peace between earthly and heavenly powers[44] was established, then the mythological understanding might be vindicated. But linguistic evidence, the interpretation of the wall contained in vss. 14-15, the context, and perhaps also Col 1:20 suggest another exposition. Philologically, the neuter "both" may be equivalent to the neuters "the foolish," "the weak," "the strong," "the ignoble," "the despised," "the not-being" in I Cor 1:27-28; in these verses Paul means men, not supramundane or earthly beings such as angels, demons, or animals.[45] In I Cor 3:8 the neuter "one" is used to describe the personal identity and oneness of two seemingly distinct persons. In either context Paul used masculine forms as well as the neuters for designating exactly the same persons.[46] Still, if the masculine of "both" and "one" would have served the same purpose as the

[41] Gal 2:11-21; 3:13-29; I Cor 1-3; 10:16-17; Rom 1:8 - 3:31; 9-11. According to Munck, PSM, this unification rather than the doctrine of justification only is the sum and apex of Paul's message. See COMMENT XIV on 1:3-14.
[42] Matt 5:23-24; 6:12, 14-15; John 20:23; cf. James 5:20.
[43] Matt 18:21-35; Rom 12:1-2; Col 3:13; I John 4:7-12, 19-21, etc.
[44] Whose internal war is described, e.g. in *Ascension of Isa* 7:9 ff; Rev 12.
[45] See BDF, 138:1; cf. 263:4.
[46] I Cor 1:25-28; Gal 3:28; Col 3:11; Heb 7:6-7; Abbott.

equivalent neuter, why did the apostle prefer the neuter forms in Eph 2:14? Perhaps the abstract metonyms, "The Uncircumcision," "The Circumcision," though they have feminine endings in Greek, influenced his diction, or he may have chosen the neuters to avoid repetition. It is certain that a sudden reference to things would crudely interrupt the context, for in 2:11–13 and 2:15b–19 Paul speaks of two groups of persons only, the Jews and the Gentiles, "those far" and "those near." Thus if the context of a passage can be considered decisive for the interpretation of one dubious individual element, then the two things made one must refer to Jews and Gentiles who are created into "a single new man" (2:15). If the meaning of the term "both" in 2:14 is to be paraphrased at all, then it must be by "Gentiles and Jews."

he has broken down. The metaphor "breaking down a wall" was used before Ephesians and phrased in different words, e.g. in Ezek 13:14. There God announces, "I will break down the wall," i.e. the deceptive visions and lies of false prophets who announce peace. In its simple or composite form (*lyō* or *katalyō*) the Greek verb used in Eph 2:14 and rendered by "to break down" occurs several times in the NT to describe the destruction of the temple[47] or the abrogation of the law.[48] The verbs "wiping out" and "removing from the middle" are used in a passage parallel to Eph 2:14, i.e. in Col 2:14, when the destruction of a document is meant. The (aorist) tense "he has broken down" reveals that Paul wants to speak of the factual, historical, completed destruction of the obstacle. Do good fences make good neighbors? "Something there is that doesn't love a wall" (Robert Frost). At this point Paul does not discuss the possibility, desirability, or necessity of the saints operating to wreck and remove the barrier. He wants to proclaim no more and no less than an event created, and a fact accomplished by Jesus Christ once and for all. All later imperatives demanding reconciliation stand upon the basis of this fact. "God has reconciled us to himself through Christ . . . He has put among us the word of reconciliation . . . Therefore we ask in Christ's name, Be reconciled with God" (II Cor 5:18–20).

the dividing wall. Lit. "the division-wall of the fence." The Greek noun *mesotoichon,* translated by the adjective "dividing," is not found in pre-Christian Greek, and nowhere in the NT except here.[49] It means a partition inside a house. The other term, *phragmos,* translated by "wall," signifies originally a fence or railing erected for protection rather than separation.[50] The combination of the two Greek nouns yields a composite sense: it is a wall that prevents certain persons from entering a house or a city (cf. 2:19), and is as much a mark of hostility (2:14, 16) as, e.g. a ghetto wall, the Iron Curtain, the Berlin Wall, a racial barrier, or a railroad track that separates the right from the wrong side of the city, not to speak of the

[47] Or of another building, Matt 24:2; 26:61; 27:40 par.; John 2:19; Acts 6:14; Gal 2:18; II Cor 5:1. For details regarding the mechanics of destroying a wall (whitewashed by prophets though it be) see the hints given in Ezek 13:10–16 and Matt 7:27. The tools of God's "wrath against the wall" are "rain," "hailstones," a "stormy wind." And the result of the wall's destruction is the laying bare of its foundation and the destruction of the people and the prophets who put it up. "The wall is no more, nor those who daubed it" (Ezek 13:15).
[48] Or of a commandment; or of Scripture, Matt 5:17; John 5:18; 7:23; 10:35.
[49] Morgenthaler, *Statistik,* pp. 175, 177.
[50] E.g. Isa 5:5; Matt 21:33.

wall between state and church. See COMMENT IV A for attempts to define the imagery of the wall.

in his flesh. Regarding form and content, this formula is a parallel, perhaps a synonym, of the formulae "in his blood," "in his person," "in one single body," "in one single Spirit" (vss. 13, 15, 16, 18). See COMMENT V for possible interpretations.

[he has wiped out all]. These words are not found in the Greek text of Ephesians. The verb "wipe out" does occur, however, in Col 2:14 and has been inserted into our translation of Ephesians for the sake of clarity. The price of the insertion is that the noun "enmity" receives an accent slightly stronger than the original wording of this verse suggests. But since "enmity" is later repeated in the hymnic text, its accentuation and generalization by the adjective "all" is in line with the author's intention.

enmity. Lit. "the enmity." This noun is perhaps in apposition to "the dividing wall," and it may have been added in order to equate the dividing wall with hostility. In this case, the "enmity" is as much the object of destruction as the wall. But another syntactical combination is equally viable: "enmity" may be the object of the verb "he abolished"; then "the law" is the appositive interpretation of "enmity." In any case, the paratactical order of "wall," "enmity," "law" is certain. Each of these terms throws light on the others; the author wants them to be considered as synonyms. The added words "[he has wiped out all]" help to avoid an arbitrary decision between the mentioned syntactic alternatives. Also they bring to light in English the rhythmic diction of the original. The sudden reference to "enmity" comes as a surprise,[51] though it fits well with the previous and following references to "peace" and the later mention of reconciling. The word "enmity" defines the separation between Jews and Gentiles more specifically: this segregation implies intolerance, and is a passionate, totalitarian, bellicose affair. While the "enmity" mentioned at the end of vs. 16 is the one-sided enmity of man against God,[52] the "enmity" of vs. 14 is mutual among men. See COMMENT IV C.

15. *He has abolished the law [, that is, only] the commandments [expressed] in statutes.* Lit. "the law [consisting] of commandments in statutes he has abolished." Greek grammar and analogous precedents in Ephesians would permit reading, "By [his] statutes he has abolished the law of commandments."[53] In this case the ordinances given by Christ would supersede OT law and commandments. However, in none of the undisputed letters does Paul call Jesus' teachings a *nova lex,* or attribute to them the function of annulling the law given to Israel.[54] Even if Ephesians was written by a

---

[51] E. Haupt who considered it an interpolation, has found many followers.

[52] Cf. Rom 8:7; Col 1:21. Consequently man only, not God, has been and is to be reconciled through Christ (II Cor 5:18–20; Rom 5:10; Col 1:21). Schille's statement, "The angry God was reconciled" (*Hymnen,* p. 29) is not supported by any Pauline texts.

[53] Bengel follows Theodore of Mopsuestia, Chrysostom, and other Greek Fathers when he understands the statutes given by Jesus Christ (e.g. the "But I say unto you . . ." statements of the Sermon on the Mount [Matt 5:20–49]) as the means by which the former law was abrogated.

[54] Abbott. In his later commentary on Galatians, M. Luther, e.g. WA 40 ɪ 50, 90, 142, 240, 248–49, 256–59, 297 ff., reacts violently against the assumption that Christ is a new legislator or another Moses. Against Luther it might be objected that Matthew's Gospel is so structured as to proclaim Jesus the anti-type of Moses. In Acts the statement "A prophet like me . . . the Lord your God will raise up to you" (Deut 18:15, 18) is interpreted as a prophetic description of Jesus Christ (Acts 3:22–23; 7:37; cf. Matt 17:5 par.). Actually neither Moses nor Jesus is in the Bible depicted

disciple of Paul, the context of Eph 2:15 reveals that for the author (as much as for Paul himself) the death of Christ rather than the promulgation of new decrees stood behind the abolition of the divisive statutes. COMMENTS IV B and V C will discuss which law or use of law was meant, how it was handled and understood, and why it deserved abolishment.

[*This was*] *to make peace by creating in his person a single new man out of the two.* Here and in vss. 16 and 18 the word "single" was added for accentuation. This sentence poses four distinct, though related, problems: (a) the equation of making peace with an act of "creation"; (b) the epitomizing of the new creation in "one man"; (c) the composition of this man "out of two" formerly divided individuals or groups; (d) finally, the location, mediation, or illustration of the new man's creation "in the person" of Christ. The first three issues will be taken up in COMMENT VI A, the last problem (together with the variant reading "in himself" and the viable translation, "in it"), in COMMENT V A.

16. *and to reconcile both to God.* The simple form of the Greek verb *allassō* means originally "to change" or "to exchange," e.g. to change money, or to turn from hostility to friendship. The passive can therefore mean "to be reconciled." Twice[55] Paul uses a composite of this verb, *kat-allassō*, which was current at his time and meant the same as the simple form, though perhaps with slightly increased emphasis. In Col 1:20, 22 and Eph 2:16 a novel composite variant of the same verb makes its appearance—a form that is not found outside Christian literature. Not one, but two prepositions are prefixed to the verb: now it has the form *apo-kat-allassō*. Some expositors fasten upon a literal meaning of the first preposition *apo* and insist that it focuses on the re-establishment of a previously existing peace and unity.[56] Others[57] consider the doubling of the prepositions an attempt at further intensification of the verb—without assuming that there is any hint of re-constituting an earlier state. Indeed, in the several cases where Paul uses or forms double composites he follows a Hellenistic trend of avoiding the simple form of the verb. In most cases the composite verb has the same, though slightly emphasized, meaning as the shortest form.[58] When an op-

---

as legislators. The Sinaitic Law passes through the hands or the mouth of Moses (cf. Gal 3:19) but is not his personal law. Jesus has come to fulfill, not to destroy (or replace) the law (Matt 5:17). He would never have been given the OT title Messiah if he had violated a basic trait of OT and intertestamental Messianic promise and hope: unlike, e.g. Hammurabi or Napoleon, a judge or king of the Jews is never depicted as a legislator—though he may, as Josiah did, rediscover the old law. In order to be different from the wicked kings on the thrones of Samaria and Jerusalem, the true king of the Jews must be subject to the law given by God, see, e.g. I Sam 10:25; Deut 17:18–20. Not even the sparse Talmudic references to a "Messianic Tora," discussed, e.g. by W. D. Davies, "Torah in the Messianic Age," JBL Monograph Series VII (1952), contradict this rule.

[55] In II Cor 5:18–20 and Rom 5:10.

[56] LSLex 201; cf. 68, 899; Chrysostom, Theophylact and other ancient interpreters; among modern scholars, e.g. H. J. Holtzmann, *Lehrbuch der Neutestamentlichen Theologie*, II (Leipzig: Mohr, 1897), 248, and B. Weiss, *Lehrbuch der Biblische Theologie*, 4th ed. (Berlin: Hertz, 1884), p. 437, support this view. While the reconciliation of Israel is a "return" into the convenant from which the people had departed (see Hosea, Jeremiah, Ezekiel) the epistle to the Ephesians excludes the idea that the Gentiles had a share in the "covenants based on promise." A "return" of the Gentiles is, therefore, not indicated.

[57] E.g. P. Feine, TSK 72 (1899), 563, 572, and Abbott. See also the commentaries on Col 1:20, 22.

[58] See Morgenthaler, *Statistik*, pp. 161–62, for a complete list of the double composites in the NT. It is clear that the prefixing of such prepositions as "before" or "with" change the meaning of composite nouns, adjectives, and verbs.

posite of reconciliation is mentioned then it is called enmity and exclusion (or estangement), but there is never an explicit reference to a former unity.[59] "Making peace" in Col 1:20–22 and Eph 2:14–16 is used as a synonym for "reconciling." The Messianic peace paid for by the blood of Christ is more than a repair of a damaged relationship. Eph 1:13; 2:1–22; and 3:5–6 describe an unheard of novelty: Jews and Gentiles, who always had been segregated in hostility, are now "reconciled" to one another and to God.

Eph 2:16 is outstanding among the parallel Pauline texts inasmuch as the Messiah rather than God is denoted as the one who reconciles. In the exposition of 1:2 and 10 it was shown why the mention of the Messiah instead of God does not imply a contradiction, inasmuch as it is God who acts in and through the Messiah appointed by him. While the "justification" terminology that prevails in Galatians, Philippians, Romans emphasizes the judgment that is being held by the king over both Jews and Gentiles, the concept of reconciliation praises the political result of the Messiah's mission and work.

through the cross. In fn. 37 it was mentioned that these words are sometimes considered a later addition to the original hymn. It is characteristic of Paul to speak of the "cross" of Christ and "Christ crucified" rather than of his "suffering" and the "wood" on which he was executed.[60] Because the "cross" is explicitly mentioned in the context of references to "blood" and "flesh" (2:13, 14), it is hardly possible to understand by blood and flesh of Christ anything else but his death. "Blood" and "flesh" designate his death as a sacrifice; see COMMENT V B. The term "cross" reveals two other marks: Christ's death is shameful among men, not honorable; it corresponds to death on the gallows. Also, it is an execution in which God's curse was borne (Gal 3:13).

in one single body. See COMMENT VI B on 1:15–23, and especially the end of COMMENT V A and the beginning of V B on 2:11–22 for the various possible meanings of "body."

In his own person he has killed the enmity. See COMMENT V A B.

17. *when he came he proclaimed good news.* The moment and place of Christ's coming and the mode of his preaching may be specified in several ways; see COMMENT V A. Eph 2:17 introduces a novel element into the context: the public announcement. The peace proclamation made by Christ is the overwhelming alternative to the hostile name-calling mentioned in 2:11. The proclamation of peace is essential to peace itself, and makes it real. The maker and the proclaimer of peace are one and the same person: it is Christ's privilege to be both the causative and the cognitive agent of peace. As the Aaronitic blessing follows upon the completed sacrifice and is pronounced by the priest who had administered it,[61] so does the announcement

---

[59] Cf. the earlier discussions of the terms "foundation of the world" (1:4); "comprehending under one head" (1:10); and "excluded . . . strangers" (2:12).

[60] The Pauline passages speaking of the crucifixion on the "cross" (Gal 3:1; 5:11; 6:12, 14; I Cor 1:13, 23; 2:2, 8; Philip 2:8; 3:18; Col 1:20; 2:14) have parallels in the Gospel accounts, in Acts 2:36; 4:10, and in Heb 12:2; Rev 11:8. The "wood" is mentioned in Acts 5:30; 10:39; 13:29; I Peter 2:24; Gal 3:13.

[61] "Purification precedes promulgation," Bengel. To say "Peace, peace where there is no peace" is according to Jer 6:14; Ezek 13:10 a travesty of the priestly and prophetic offices. See Sir 45: 15–17 for a summary of the tasks of the priest in the intertestamental period.

of peace. Christ is his own harbinger.[62] From 2:13–22 on, Paul's language contains an increasing number of cultic terms and allusions. Christ is depicted not only as a statesman appointed by God to make and announce social peace between divided groups of men, but his function and work are at the same time those of the high priest: he announces peace with God and among men and thereby bestows in full what the Aaronitic blessing (Num 6:24–26) had promised.

"Peace to you who are far and peace to those near!" Just like earlier hymnic passages of Ephesians (not to speak of the previously mentioned OT royal psalms),[63] so the hymnic praise of Christ crucified culminates in a citation which is not introduced by an explicit quotation formula. The same passage which was already alluded to in vs. 13, i.e. Isa 57:19, is now reproduced in full, though not in the wording found in the LXX editions that are in our hands today. The phrase "he proclaimed good news" does not belong in the quote,[64] and neither the Hebrew nor the Greek text of Isa 57:19 contains an equivalent. The verb "to proclaim" is taken from another text, probably from Isa 52:7. The Isa 57 quote which sums up or has inspired the whole hymn Eph 2:14–18 begins with the word "peace." "Peace upon peace to those being far and near" is a literal English version of the LXX; the Hebrew text can be translated the same way. See COMMENT II for the modification of the OT text by Paul.

18. *Through him and in one single Spirit . . . to the Father.* The conjunction "and" is not found in the Greek text; it was added for a more fluent reading. Just as in the reference to the Spirit in 1:17, so in 2:18 the "one Spirit" may at the same time mean the Holy Spirit of God (4:30) and a spirit residing in man. The human spirit in question would be the spirit of unity, reconciliation, peace—as opposed, e.g. to a spirit of strife, jealousy, superiority. What F. D. E. Schleiermacher called the *Gemeingeist,* and what in its secularized form is known as *esprit de corps,* and vulgarized in the "rah-rah spirit," is certainly an effective atmosphere and instrument for unifying and inspiring the most diverse people for the same cause with the same joy. However, Eph 2:18 does not just speak of group dynamics or common enthusiasm. In the context of the hymn to which this verse belongs, naming the Spirit in addition to the Father and the Messiah may be intentional: Ephesians contains several trinitarian statements (see, e.g. 1:4–14, 4:4–6; cf. also II Cor 13:13). It appears appropriate that the reference to the Spirit occurs in a sentence dealing with worship, as will be discussed in COMMENT VI B. Ps 51 states that the man equipped with a "new spirit," i.e. the man from whom the "Holy Spirit" is not taken away, is pure before God, can witness God's rebuilding of the walls of Jerusalem, can offer acceptable sacrifices. According to Heb 9:14 Christ's sacrifice was distinct from others in number, essence, and effect because he offered himself "through the eternal Spirit." Worship "in Spirit and in truth" is asked for in John 4:24. He who

---

[62] Eph 1:8–9 speaks of God's self-manifestation. In 1:17–18 the Spirit, in 3:5 the apostles, in 3:10 cf. 2:7 the church are the means of God's revelation.

[63] Eph 1:10, 22; Pss 110:1; 132:11–12, etc. See fn. 76 to 1:3–14, above.

[64] Nestle and GNT use boldface type for the verb translated by "to proclaim." While GNT gives the reference to Isa 52:7, Nestle omits it.

clings to the Lord is called "one spirit with him," and his "body is a temple of the Spirit," just as also the community of the saints is a "temple of the Spirit of God" (I Cor 6:16, 19; 3:16), or is built "in the Spirit" (Eph 2:22). The church cannot have Christ for a head and live as his body unless she is animated by the one Holy Spirit.[65] He inspires the community with life and unity, and makes of it a worshiping assembly.

the two [of us] have free access to the Father. Lit. "both together. . . ." This "possessive" statement resembles 1:7, "We possess forgiveness"; it will be reformulated in even more assertive terms in 3:12. At this point cultic language is used to describe the same event and status as were earlier depicted in biological and political terminology: "He raised us together and enthroned us in heaven" (2:6). The last hope, the eschaton, is already realized when no barrier keeps men separate from God. They enjoy the right of children to see their Father (cf. John 14:9). One Spirit joins them together and to him. "Access" has a transitive sense etymologically, and denotes the act of leading toward a potentate, or granting the privilege of admission. Cf. I Peter 3:18, "Christ died once for the sins, the righteous for those unrighteous, in order to lead us to God." Abbott and Gaugler believe that this transitive meaning is, in the NT occurrences of the noun "access," replaced by an intransitive sense.[66] But all pertinent passages state explicitly that the access to God is mediated "through" or "in Christ" only. An "introduction" to the Father is meant, which requires someone who introduces. The biblical book which contains the most frequent statements about "access" to God is Leviticus. While in that book the noun "access" is never used, the verb "to lead to," describes the ever new event of admission to God. After Eph 2:17 proclaimed Christ in his priestly, i.e. blessing, function, 2:18 definitely ascribes to him the decisive role in divine worship. Because *he* leads to God and gives access to the Father, "we have free access." Jesus Christ is depicted, to use the favorite term of Hebrews, as high priest. See COMMENT VI B.

19. *Accordingly*. Repeatedly the transition from a hymn to Paul's comment is indicated by a conjunction such as "accordingly." Verse 19 sums up the previous vss. 11–18; vss. 20–22 will use new imagery and will express new thoughts in which the topic will be house-building instead of the peace made between enemies and the assembly of outsiders and insiders under one ruler. The opinion of W. Nauck, that 2:19–22 contains a baptismal hymn, probably deserves less attention than other attempts to discover traditional materials in this passage.[67] As e.g. the Magnificat (Luke 1:46–55) shows, there existed hymns in honor of the Messiah that cannot be explained as baptismal.

you are no longer strangers and sojourners. The terms "strangers" and "sojourners" might as such describe two legally differentiated groups. A "stranger" could be, and sometimes was, treated as an outlaw or spy (Gen 19:1–10). A "sojourner," i.e. a resident alien, was subject only to a part of the law of the land and enjoyed only corresponding legal protection (Lev

---

[65] Robinson.   [66] I.e. in Rom 5:2; Eph 2:18; 3:12.
[67] EvTh 13 (1953), 362–71; cf. Marxsen, *Introduction*, p. 196; but see Schlier, p. 140 n. 1.

25; Deuteronomy *passim*).[68] In exceptional cases only were visiting foreigners treated with special grace: the hospitality offered to strangers by e.g. Abraham, Rahab, and Job[69] was not frequently imitated, and the reminders in Deuteronomy that Israel herself was a stranger were not followed with sufficient enthusiasm to spare the Jews the reproach of *miso-xenia* and *a-mixia* (fear and hatred of foreigners, lack of hospitality, opposition to intermarriage).[70] The various Hebrew terms that denote different degrees of strangership were confused rather than clarified by the LXX. The same Hebrew word *gēr* is sometimes translated by "stranger" (*xenos*), sometimes by "sojourner" (*paroikos*), mostly by "proselyte." *Paroikos* is used for the translation of "Gentile" (*goi*) as well as "resident alien" (*tōshāb*). The employment of the same Greek term *paroikos* to render diverse Hebrew nouns obfuscates the original distinction, e.g. between the relatively free *gēr* and the semi-serf *tōshāb* who was tied to a given piece of land. Though Paul uses two different Greek terms for the Gentiles in Eph 2:19 it is unlikely that he wanted to distinguish between two distinct socioeconomic or religious groups. The two nouns form a hendiadys to suggest all members of an out-group who were formerly segregated from a compact in-group. A stranger normally had to fend for himself; in some cases he had to "spend the night in the street" (Gen 19:2), and in extreme cases he was exposed to any abuse, including rape and murder (Gen 19:5). The Greek holy laws of hospitality were one thing, the estimate of the stranger as godless or god-forsaken (*atheos*, Eph 2:12) another. Certainly Paul did not intend to speak of a third group who might have formed an intermediate class: he does not employ the term "proselyte." Thus the possible misunderstanding is avoided that in 2:19 only such Gentiles are meant who are "God-fearers" (Acts 10:2), friends of the Jews, synagogue-builders (Luke 7:5), Sabbath-keepers (Isa 56:2–8), or persons otherwise allotted an inheritance among the tribes of Israel (Ezek 47:22–23). The Messiah's arrival would have meant nothing radically new if it had served no further purpose than to promote contemporary proselytism. Ephesians, to the contrary, affirms that even the most convinced, i.e. inimical and lawless, Gentiles have now been included among God's people. "In Christ" the whole territory is covered from farthest-out to nearest-in—and not just the last stretch of a path on which some noble Gentiles had already been proceeding. There is no evidence that the conversion of the "Ephesians" resembled that of the "God-fearing" Cornelius described in Acts 10.

but you are fellow citizens with the saints and members of the household of God. The pattern observed in vss. 12–18 is continued: first the relationship to fellow men, i.e. to the "saints" is mentioned,[71] and only then their

---

[68] See e.g. J. Horst, RGG, II, 1125–26. The principle of "one law" for all inhabitants is expressed, e.g. in Exod 12:49; Num 15:16, 29.

[69] Gen 18; Josh 2; Job 31:32.

[70] E.g. Deut 10:18–19. See W. Bousset, *Die Religion das Judentums,* 3d ed. (Tübingen: Mohr, 1926), pp. 75–76, 93–94; G. Stählin, TWNTE, V, 1–36; K. L. Schmidt, "Israels Stellung zu den Fremdlingen und Beisassen," *Judaica* 1 (1946), 269–96.

[71] See the NOTE on "saints" in 1:1. Israel as the community that worships God, i.e. Israel as God's priestly servant among the nations, is probably meant in 2:19. A reference to the angels (cf. the Qumran texts 1QH III 22; 1QS XI 7–8; IV 22; 1QSa I 9, 12–13; 1QSb IV 23, etc.) or to the Christian congregation would be equally possible—if nothing else but the various meanings of the term "saints" were to be considered. The context requires a narrow interpretation pointing to Israel only. The clause *communio sanctorum* as used in the Apostolic Creed means therefore, in the

relation to God. Not that the two were separable; one presupposes and interprets the other. Through his incorporation into Israel a Gentile finds communion with God. God himself, and not an indigenous quality or superiority, is the mystery of Israel. That man is under God's protection who submits to Israel's king and becomes a citizen of Israel. He is not only a citizen of an earthly city or state but a "member of God's household." God cares for him as a father does for his children. As the term *paroikos,* "sojourner," means in Greek etymology a man living "outside the *house*" of the native landowner, it appears to have led Paul to elaborate upon the term "house" in vss. 20–22. By speaking of members of God's "household" he denotes the church, created by Christ's work of peace and led by Christ in worship, as a house or family.[72] Beginning with the next verse the imagery of a house will become so dominant that the transition made in 2:19–22 from "house" understood as a family or community, to "house" in the sense of a building is hardly felt. An important theological transition takes place at the same time. Those who have been received into God's house are no longer described as its inhabitants in what follows; rather they are declared the building materials of a house in which God himself will dwell.

20. *built upon the foundation of the apostles and prophets.* In recent decades several scholars have discussed in detail the metaphorical use of the terms "building," "house," "temple."[73] Ephesians uses terminology that derives from several sources: ancient tales such as the building of the Tower of Babel; legendary recollections and historic accounts of the construction of the first and second Jerusalem temple; prophetic visions and warnings about building the king's house, the temple at Jerusalem; personal impressions gained from the process of building the Herodian temple; apocalyptic dreams or sectarian expectations of a true sanctuary or congregation; spiritualizing

---

light of Ephesians, the communion of Gentiles with Jews, e.g. with Abraham, Isaac, Jacob, David, Isaiah (cf. Calvin), but also with later Jews. The requirement that Christians have to limit their communion to baptized Jews is not made in Eph 2:19. Only in a derivative sense the formulation of the Creed would then also mean, "sharing in the holy things," e.g. in the blessing and inheritance given by God, and "intimate fellowship" among like-minded fellow Christians.

[72] Cf. the designation of Israel or the church as a house in Num 12:7; Heb 3:1–6; I Peter 2:5; 4:17; I Tim 3:15; see also II Cor 5:1–2 and the references to "members of the household," in Gal 6:10; I Tim 5:8. In Eph 3:14–15 and 4:6 it is made clear that God's fatherhood is not exhausted by, or limited to, his care over believers. The house rules (5:21–6:9) emphasize the ethical and missionary implications of the adoption into God's household.

[73] See H. Wenschkewitz, *Die Spiritualisierung der Kultusbegriffe,* Angelos 4, Leipzig: Pfeiffer, 1932; Schlier, *Christus,* pp. 49–60; O. Michel, TWNTE, V, 119–59, esp. 136 ff.; P. Vielhauer, *Oikodome,* Karlsruhe/Durlach: Vielhauer, 1939; M. Fraeyman, "La spiritualisation de l'idée du temple dans les épîtres pauliniennes," ETL 23 (1947), 378–412 (ref.); P. Bonnard, *Jésus-Christ édifiant son église,* Neuchatel: Delachaux, 1948; Y. Congar, *The Mystery of the Temple* (Westminster, Md: Newman Press, 1962), pp. 151–248; J. Planmatter, *Die Kirche als Bau,* Analecta Gregoriana 110, Rome, 1960 (ref.); R. J. McKelvey, *The New Temple,* London: Oxford University Press, 1969. Qumran texts such as 1QH VI 24–28; CD III 19, that speak of the "building" and the "house" of the congregation are collected, e.g. by J. Maier, *Die Texte vom Toten Meer,* II (Munich/Basel: Reinhardt, 1960), 46–47, 93–94. Dibelius, p. 71, sums up the available evidence by discerning four possible sources of the edifice imagery: (a) OT passages such as Isa 28:16; Ps 118:21–22; (b) building metaphors used to describe philosophical instruction, e.g. Epictetus *enchiridion* II 15:8; see also Heb 6:1; II Tim 2:19; (c) a fixed pre-Pauline Christian pattern of language as used e.g. in Corinth for describing religious progress, I Cor 8:1, etc.; (d) the Iranian or Mandaean notion of a heavenly city (or plantation) that exists in heaven and to which corresponds an unfinished structure on earth, see, e.g. R. Reitzenstein, *Das Iranische Erlösungsmysterium* (Bonn: Marcus, 1921), pp. 142 f. and M. Lidzbarski, *Mandäische Liturgien* (Berlin: Weidmann, 1920), p. 190 (Oxford Collection, XX 3 ff.).

tendencies of Hellenistic Jewish circles, not to speak of non-Jewish philosophical and mythological influences. In the Shepherd of Hermas the construction of the church is an ever recurring image. Finally, Gnostic and also the medieval Mandaean sources use building metaphors to denote the formation of a perfect man. Instead of mythological elements, a rich symbolism is displayed in Eph 2:20–22, and it appears that more than anything else prophetic, eschatological, perhaps also Qumranite esoteric utterances on the building and the role of God's house determined both the rhetoric and the contents of this passage.[74] The builder of the edifice described in Eph 2 is God—as the passives "built" in vss. 20, 22 and the opposite "handmade" in 2:11; II Cor 5:1, etc. show. "You are God's building" (I Cor 3:8); "I will build my church" (Matt 16:18). "The foundation of the apostles and prophets" is the basis consisting of (not laid by) specific servants of God, like Peter the rock (in Matt 16:18). The difference between Eph 2:20 and the laying of a foundation *by* the apostle mentioned in I Cor 3:10 is plain. As a comparison of Rom 4:1–16 with Gal 4:21–31 shows, Paul sometimes used the same material and imagery in different ways and adapted them to diverse purposes. See COMMENT VI C 1 for the identification of "prophets" and "apostles."

the keystone being the Messiah Jesus himself. The syntax of the Greek genitive absolute that underlies this version is highly ambiguous. At least two other translations are possible: (a) of which (sc. foundation) the Messiah Jesus is the keystone; (b) the Messiah Jesus himself being the keystone. The confusion is created by the absence of an article. The article is commonly used in Greek between the emphatic pronoun "he" (*autos*) and a proper name for emphasizing that somebody does something "in person," or "himself"; but again, before proper names the article may also be omitted.[75] For the translation "keystone" in preference to "cornerstone," see COMMENT VI C 2.

21. *The whole construction.* In Greek, just as with the English terms "building" and "construction," the same noun can possess a double meaning: (a) the process of erecting a structure; or (b) the finished edifice. Since Eph 2:21 concerns a building that is still growing, the first of these two meanings cannot be excluded from the exposition, though the second is equally present. The translation "the whole construction" presupposes that the more reliable MSS contain

---

[74] Limitations of space prohibit as extensive a discussion of the origins, variations, meanings of the building metaphors as was earlier devoted to the head-body-fullness imagery. In the following an attempt is made to use only OT precedents, promises, and expectations as a key for interpreting Eph 2:20–22, their reinterpretation by intertestamental orthodox and heterodox Judaism notwithstanding. The OT materials are easily accessible with the help of G. von Rad's chapter on Zion in his *OT Theology*, II, and G. Fohrer's and E. Lohse's article in TWNT, VII, 291–338. Ps 132:13–18 is typical of a great number of pertinent texts. Just two apocalyptical passages are to be mentioned because they take up the OT combination of hope for peace and hope for admission of Gentiles to a new temple (Isa 2:4; Micah 4:3; Isa 56:7): (a) in I Enoch 90:29–36 the "new house greater and loftier than the first," by which the Lord of the sheep replaces the "old house," is open only for the "sheep" (i.e. Israel) but also for "all the beasts of the field and all the birds of the heaven" (the nations). The sword is laid down, all their eyes are opened to see the good. "And there was no one among them that did not see. And I saw that that house was large and broad and very full." Enoch continues with a vision of the Messiah. (b) In Sib. Or. III 741–84, the gift of "great peace over all the earth," of a common law for all men, of worship of the one God in one temple are predicted in moving terms.

[75] Cf. Matt 3:4; Mark 6:17; II Cor 11:14 with Mark 12:36; Luke 3:23; 20:42; John 2:24. See BDF, 260 and 288.

a grammatical mistake[76] which was later corrected by language-conscious copyists.[77] A literal version of the more original text would say "each building." Paul would in this case affirm that several individual, i.e. local, churches are being built upon the one foundation[78]—a thought appropriate to an encyclical—or that individual Christians are each formed into a temple (of the Holy Spirit; see I Cor 6:19). As such they would be living stones in the one "temple of God" (I Cor 3:16).[79] However, these interpretations contradict the context of Eph 2: the end of 2:21 identifies the "construction" with the growth of the "holy temple"—i.e. of a temple that is but one.[80] It is not composed of side chapels, nor is there reference in Ephesians to "living stones" (but cf. I Peter 2:5). The whole epistle speaks only of the church universal. While there are passages in Paul that describe the "building" of persons and the unity necessary among several local churches,[81] Eph 2:21 cannot be counted among them. A compromise appears possible: Paul's honor as a grammarian can be saved and a literal translation of Eph 2:21 can be combined with the special message of this epistle when the suggestion of Chrysostom, von Hofmann, and Abbott[82] is accepted and the phrase is translated "all that is being built." But the indistinctness of such a version deprives it of meaning. Untenable is the opinion that two halves of the church are meant, i.e. the Judaeo- and the Gentile-Christian parts of the people of God.[83] After showing that the church exists only as a unity, that is, as one new man created out of Jews and Gentiles, the apostle does not proceed to split it into halves.

fitted together in him. Eph 2:21 and 4:16 are the earliest known instances where the verb "to fit [NEB, to bond] together" is used. The verb is derived from the Greek noun *harmos,* which generally denotes a fitting or connection. In architecture the noun describes either a joint or a junction of two stones,[84] or the sides of the stones that were so worked as to fit together. The same noun also means joints of the body, e.g. IV Macc 10:5; Heb 4:12. Eph 4:16 mixes architectural and physical imagery. The simple verb "to fit" (without the preposition "together") appears to be a non-literary word used among artisans. A mason[85] would have used this verb to describe "the whole elaborate process by which stones were fitted together," i.e. the preparation of the surfaces, including cutting and rubbing the stone and testing it with a measuring stick (*kanōn*); the preparation of bronze dowels and of dowel holes; fixing the dowels with molten lead and putting the upper stone or drum in place.[86] The com-

---

[76] So Dibelius and Schlier. The same irregularity, i.e. the omission of the Greek article which distinguishes between the meanings "whole" or "all" and "each" of the same Greek adjective *pās,* is found also in Rom 3:20 ("all flesh"); 11:26 ("all Israel"); Acts 2:26 ("the whole house of Israel"); 17:26 ("the whole surface").

[77] It is more likely that a correction was made that had the grammar fit the context, than that careless Alexandrian copyists, i.e. the writers of Ephesians in the Codices A, C and others, should have made Paul use poor Greek.

[78] Haupt; Percy, p. 463, and others chose this interpretation.   [79] Calvin.

[80] The word used for "temple," Greek *naos,* is a designation of the shrine or central building of the temple area, Luke 1:9; Matt 23:35; Mark 15:38. The NT employs frequently another noun, *hieron.* This is the case when reference is made to the entire temple precincts which included many buildings, Robinson, pp. 71-72.

[81] I Cor 8:10; 14:4-5, 17, etc.; 7:17; 11:16; II Cor 8:18; Rom 16:16, etc.

[82] Also BDF, 275:3?   [83] Jerome, Ambrosiaster, Thomas Aquinas.

[84] E.g. of drums that are placed upon one another to form a column.

[85] As is shown by inscriptions, contracts, and the formation of derived nouns, according to Robinson.

[86] Robinson, p. 262.

posite verb "to fit together" may be Paul's creation. His specific acquaintance with current technical details and diction may have been as general or vague as his knowledge of contemporary physiology and neurology. In Eph 2:21 he is concerned not with the history or processing of single stones but with the whole building; only in the next verse will he speak of the individual saints that are being "built together" and "into" the temple. The two concerns are equally combined in I Peter 2:4–8. The words translated by "in him" may also mean "on it" or "in it" (i.e. on the foundation or in the temple); or their sense may be temporal or causal: "as long" or "because." The version "in him" is to be preferred despite the duplications "in the Lord" and "in him" which follow immediately. The author never tires of pointing to Christ as the sphere, the means, the ruler, the administrator, or the one by whom the work of God is carried out (cf. 1:3–14). In COMMENT I on 1:1–2 it was shown that the transition from "in Christ" to "in the Lord" marks a shift in accent from presupposition and instrumentality to the realm of ethics and conduct.[87]

grows in the Lord into a holy temple. The verb rendered by "to grow" (cf. 4:15–16) means an increase of every kind—in size, number, age, maturity, glory, power. In classical Greek the verb is transitive, as in English, e.g. "to grow vegetables." For this reason classical writers say that a plant or a building is grown (is increased). Here in 2:21 the active form is used, but in an intransitive sense. Thus Paul puts great emphasis upon the church's responsibility for its own growth. According to the apostle, "growth" should *not* be understood just as a natural (Mark 4:27–28, "automatic") process or event; rather it is an increase involving responsibility, decision, and activity, as the Ephesian parallel to 2:21, i.e. 4:16, distinctly reveals in its somewhat clumsy diction.[88] As Paul phrases it, "The whole body . . . makes its own growth so that it builds itself up in love." We observe that the body makes its own growth; the body builds itself! Even so, growth is and remains a gift of God (I Cor 3:6–7). It comes "from the head" (Eph 4:16) and takes place "in the Lord" (2:21). Theological implications of the term "growing"[89] are discussed in COMMENT VII 2. The "holiness" attributed to the temple is according to 2:22 constituted by the presence of God in the temple. A distant or dead God could not make a building holy. Even less could the assembled multitudes perform such a miracle with their loud chanting. In Ephesians the temple is defined not in anthropological or sociological terms but theologically, "a dwelling of God in the Spirit" (2:22).

22. *built together so as to be a dwelling of God.* The verb "building together" occurs only here in the NT. Because of the contents of vss. 13–19 the metaphor must signify the mutual coordination and support of the reconciled Jews and Gentiles. The origin, continuous construction, and growth of the church are the result of the previous reconciliation—just as in OT and apocalyptical hope— the building of the new temple follows upon the gift of world-wide peace; see

[87] Robinson, p. 72, may go too far in saying that in Christ we are in heaven, in the Lord we are on earth. But cf. F. Neugebauer, NTS 4 (1957–58), 124–38.
[88] G. Bornkamm, *Das Ende des Gesetzes* (Munich: Kaiser, 1952), p. 145 (on Colossians); Pokorný, EuG, pp. 78–80.
[89] For the notion of "progress" of growth see G. T. Montague, *Growth in Christ*, Kirkwood: Mayhurst, 1961 (ref.).

fn. 74. The church herself is not reconciliation but she lives from it and manifests it. She serves the glory of God inasmuch as her members mutually assist, support, and strengthen one another. Neither Jews nor Gentiles nor any individual can independently claim after Christ's coming to offer an appropriate residence for God, but Jews and Gentiles together are now ordained by God to become his temple.

in the Spirit. It is impossible to select one single meaning for the qualification "in the Spirit" from the various possible intentions which the author may have had. The formula may grammatically belong to "God," who is the builder and inhabitant of the temple; or to those citizens of Israel and sons of God (2:19) who are "built together"; or to the building or dwelling place. (a) The "Spirit" denotes the mode of God's powerful presence.[90] No other God is meant, no presence other than the one spiritually revealed in Christ.[91] (b) The "Spirit" qualifies the building material[92] and the way it is forged into a unit. Only those Gentiles who are inspired, i.e. illuminated, purified, renewed, driven by the Spirit, are suitable stones for the temple walls. They are given a new heart and believe in God through the Messiah. They are God's spiritual building matter, as distinguished from the stones, wood, and metals used by the builders of handmade temples. "In the flesh" (cf. 2:11) or under the sway of the evil spirit (2:2) the Gentiles could not possibly be used for the holy purpose which they now serve. (c) The "Spirit" may reveal the character of the building that is being constructed.[93] Not a handmade temple (II Cor 5:1) but a "spiritual house" devoted to "spiritual sacrifices" (I Peter 2:5) is erected. Here is more than a transitory, perishable, secondary sanctuary;[94] Paul's interpretation goes beyond a merely literal reading of the Scriptures.[95] Now both the spiritual archetype and the reality are at hand as perceived by spiritual interpretation. In this case the author has not come to the notion of the holy temple not made by hand by the supererogation of an earthly sanctuary. Rather he considers the temple built by God, out of people (not of stones) and inhabited by God, as the origin of the term "temple" and the measuring stick of all earthly temples. However, since the original spiritual temple is as concrete, palpable, and historical as its stony "shadow" (Col 2:17; Heb 8:5), it is distinct from a Platonic idea. The saints in "Ephesus" and elsewhere still live "in the flesh," just as the apostle himself does (Gal 2:20). In their own persons (called their "bodies" in Rom 12:2 and I Cor 6:15), they are God's temple—they who have to be warned against prostitution and other vices (I Cor 6:15–20; Eph 4:17 ff.). The three interpretations communicate the same message: God chooses to be present in the communion of the saints. Since also elsewhere in Ephesians, especially in 1:3, 17; 2:18, the Spirit denotes simultaneously God's own nature, his gift to man, and the reality of his manifestation on earth, the various expositions cannot be mutually exclusive.

[90] Abbott; Eph 3:16–17; I Cor 3:16; 6:19; Rom 8:9 support this interpretation. Calvin speaks of the power of God as opposed to human forces and external instruments.
[91] See esp. 1:13–14; 2:18.   [92] As suggested, e.g. by Barn. XVI. See also Holtzmann.
[93] Chrysostom, Theophylact, Oecumenius.
[94] Cf. I Cor 10:2–11; Rom 5:14; Col 2:17; Heb 8:5; 9:23; 10:1; 13:10.
[95] E.g. Gal 4:21–31; I Cor 9:8–10; II Cor 3:6, 14–18; Eph 5:32 contain allegorical (pneumatic) exegesis.

COMMENTS I–VII on 2:11–22

I Structure and Summary

Eph 2:11–22 is the key and high point of the whole epistle. Its logical structure is clear, with three steps following one upon another: (a) the description of the division of mankind (vss. 11–12); (b) the praise of Christ's work of reconciliation (13–18); (c) the elaboration of the tangible result of peace, i.e. the growing church (19–22). Thus a sketch of man's sociological situation before the coming of Christ and a description of the present life of God's people frames the core, which consists of a hymn in honor of Christ crucified and his work of peace. Verses 13 and 19 indicate the transition from one step or topic to another as their opening words, "but now" and "accordingly," make evident. The contents of these two verses are almost identical—except that the reference to the Messiah in vs. 13 prepares for the stanzas on Christ the maker of peace (vss. 14–18), while mention of the "household" of God in vs. 19 introduces the subsequent building and temple metaphors.

Subsection (a) is divided into two parts. The description of the phenomenological or cultic division between Jews and Gentiles comes first (vs. 11), and is followed by a summary of the Christological, sociological, and theological aspects of their separation (vs. 12). The combination of seemingly external features with basic theological grounds for division reveals that the weight of ceremonial elements should not be belittled. Circumcision manifests much more than an incidental historical difference; the difference between Jews and Gentiles is grounded in God's own history with mankind, i.e. in the first election of Israel alone and the corresponding temporary exclusion of the Gentiles from his blessing.

Subsection (b) describes the work of the Messiah Jesus in glowing terms as elucidated and carried out in agreement with OT prophecy. Mentioned as the purpose and effect of Christ's work are peace among those formerly hostile, a new creation, reconciliation, and common access to God. The time of this work is defined by his "coming" (vs. 17); the cost and means of his intervention by the formulae "in his blood," "in his flesh," "in his person," "in one body," "through the cross," "through him," "in one Spirit"; the universal extension of his reach by the term "both" (those "near" and those "far") and the reference to the reconciliation of enemies; the publication of the new order by the verb, "he proclaimed"; the result by the nouns "peace," "a single new man," "access." The progress of thought in vss. 14–18 may also be seen as a step-by-step unfolding of the obstacles overcome, of the price Christ paid for peace, and of the reconciliation and unity effected. Most amazing is the fact that in Paul's (or the pre-Pauline hymn's) argument, peace between Jews and Gentiles precedes the description of the peace made between God and man. Verse 18 shows that both dimensions of peace are inseparable.

Subsection (c) contains, after the transitional vs. 19, three statements on the church, the house of God. Architectural metaphors reveal its foundation and the highest point toward which it is built; the building process is described as a communal event that resembles physical growth; the building and growth are seen to make sense only in terms of their purpose, i.e. to attest to the presence of God. All metaphors compiled in 2:19–22 serve to describe diverse aspects of a social event: the Gentiles naturalized in Israel and received in God's house are now living and growing together on the basis of apostolic and prophetic preaching, and with the destination to meet in and with Christ. As much as the Jews, these Gentiles are now essential members of that community which God has chosen for residence: the church. Later parts of Ephesians will show that this concept of the existence and destiny of the community is not only the presupposition of incidental moral advice, but practically identifies the church's life with the very ground and content of ethics.

II   The Quotation from Isaiah

Such key words in Eph 2:11–22 as "circumcision," "Israel," "covenants," "peace," "blood" and "flesh," "house," and "temple" are obviously used in a sense that is inspired by the OT and by OT interpretations current at Paul's time.[96] Among these terms, "circumcision" will be discussed further in the next COMMENT, "peace" has been briefly sketched in the context of 1:2, and the background of other outstanding words was at least hinted at in the NOTES.

However, verses 2:13 and 17 offer a specific problem. Here an OT text, Isa 57:19, "Peace, peace to the far and to the near, says the Lord; and I will heal him," is first alluded to and then cited directly. When Paul in both verses (or the pre-Pauline hymn in vs. 17) used only fragments of Isa 57:19 and added new words to the quotation, he probably assumed that such changes would offer an authentic interpretation of the prophetic text. Equally, unless vss. 14–16 are intended as an exposition of the Isaiah passage they would be misplaced between the two allusions to the prophet in vss. 13 and 17. But is the exegesis given in Eph 2 true to the Isaiah text, or is Paul (or the unknown author of the hymn) guilty of a gross misunderstanding? The original prophetic text referred not to Jews and Gentiles, but to Jews in exile and Jews at home in the promised land!

The use of Isa 57 in Ephesians, foremost the bold identification of "those far" with Gentiles rather than with exiled Jews, can be explained in part as a last step in a development of the Jewish exegesis that had started long before the time of Christ and Paul. The term "near" occurs also in Ps 148:14; Israel is "the people . . . near to him [the Lord]."[97] Correspondingly, in some rabbinical interpretations of Isa 57, those "far" are identified with the Gentiles— but only with such Gentiles as were proselytes.[98] As the very name "proselyte" (derived from Greek proserchomai, "to approach," "to come near") indicates, persons are meant who (from afar) "come near" the blessing and the community of Israel. They were welcomed in Israel—provided they fulfilled certain conditions that varied with the times and the status they desired or were

[96] Cf. the literature on Qumran and Pauline use of the Scriptures listed in BIBLIOGRAPHIES 3 and 4.
[97] Cf. Midr. Esther: "No nation is near to God save Israel."
[98] See StB, III, 585–87. Meuzelaar, Der Leib des Messias, pp. 61–66, 75–86, points out the distinction between Paul's and Jewish teaching: "Apparently Paul applies to the Gentiles in the church what was valid among Jews only for proselytes" (p. 75).

given.[99] Gen 17:12-14 was understood to require their circumcision, with which they became full members of the Jewish people. Exod 12:48 permits them to partake in the Passover meal, presupposing that each celebrant considers himself liberated from Egypt. Still, in Num 9:14 circumcision seems not to be a prerequisite.[100] According to Lev 17:15-16 the sojourners [LXX: the proselytes] were certainly bound by some of the dietary proscriptions observed by Israel's native sons. In Isa 56 those foreigners, including eunuchs, who "keep the Sabbath" are welcomed to the temple. According to I Kings 8:41-43, foreigners "from a far country . . . not of thy [God's] people Israel" participate in the worship offered in the temple. An ancient oracle promises that "Japheth . . . will dwell in the tents of Shem" (Gen 9:27). Isaiah (16:4) bids Israel, "let the outcasts of Moab sojourn among you." The much later text of Zech 2:11 speaks of "many nations that shall join themselves to the Lord . . . and shall be my [God's] people"; cf. Rev 21:24-26. According to Isa 59:19-20 and Ps 102:15-16, the spread of the "fear of Yahweh's name" is caused by the "coming" of Zion's redeemer and the rebuilding of Zion by his hands.

When, therefore, Paul understood Isa 57:19 to speak of the incorporation of Gentiles into God's people, such a view may already have been accepted as orthodox. He may have borrowed the quote from a liturgy (for proselytes?) that included a citation of Isa 57, but varied slightly from the original wording.

Two elements distinguish, however, his interpretation from that of Jewish texts dealing with proselytes. First, the blood of Christ, not the Gentiles' circumcision blood, is the means by which the far become near (Eph 2:13). Second, "those far" are considered the hopelessly foolish and wicked Gentiles, cf. 4:17-19—not just "God-fearers" or outstandingly pious and noble Gentiles such as Emperor Antoninus Pius. The Gentiles for whom Christ shed his blood were nothing but "dead in lapses and sins," "sons of rebellion," living in hostility against Israel and God (2:1-2, 14, 16). He died for them while they were still "godless," "sinners," "enemies" (Rom 5:6, 8, 10). Consequently neither circumcision nor Sabbath-keeping nor any other mark of distinction is now a prerequisite for their "access to God." The grace of Christ and the truth of the gospel are denied when circumcision or Sabbath-keeping or dietary restrictions are imposed.[101] The "abolition of the law . . . [expressed] in statutes" is the reason for the absence of such prerequisites according to 2:15 (see COMMENTS IV B, V C).

Another, much later rabbinical interpretation of Isa 57:19 identifies "those far" with men stricken by leprosy.[102] Indeed, the second half of that verse speaks of "healing," and Paul mentions in Eph 4:19 (Rom 1:24) the "impurity" of the Gentiles. The blood of Christ and the solemn proclamation of peace, which according to Eph 2:13-17 are the means of joining the outcasts to the life and worship of the in-group, may correspond to the sacrifice and priestly

---

[99] StB, I, 924 ff.; II, 715 ff.; III, 98 ff.; Moore, *Judaism*, I, 323 ff.; K. G. Kuhn, TWNTE, VI, 727-42.

[100] Neither is it in the NT for the meals of the Christian community, e.g. Acts 15:1, 5, 19 ff; Gal 2:3-5, 11-14, etc.

[101] Gal 2:3-5, 14; 5:2-4; 6:12-16.

[102] LevR 16 (116d), quoted in StB, IV, 751. Lepers were forced by law to keep afar from the community of the healthy.

pronouncement required for the purification of lepers (Lev 13). But since the terminology of Eph 2:14–16 is taken from the world of politics rather than hygienics, it appears unlikely that Paul alluded to this rabbinical application of Isa 57.

While the apostle (or the author of the hymn) was following the direction of contemporary scriptural interpretation, and while his results were more radical than those of some of the rabbis, he quoted the Isaiah text in a fashion that seems far from accurate. Four deviations are notable. (a) In Eph 2:17 the second mention of "peace," which in the Hebrew and Greek texts is at the beginning of the sentence, is transposed to a later position.[103] (b) The dative "to you" is inserted before "who are far." (c) The participle "being" which is found in the LXX is dropped. (d) Isa 57:19 appears to focus on the peace between God and men, be they far or near, but Paul also takes it to refer to the peace *between* those far and those near. Does not Paul press the OT text unduly with these changes? Several answers are possible. The author of Ephesians may owe the text version reproduced in 2:17 to a written Isaiah text that was worded differently from the MSS underlying the Bibles in use today. Or, he may have quoted from memory as exactly as he could. Or, he may have alluded to a paraphrase of a Targum which already contained an explicit equation of "those far" with proselytes. The words "to you" may have belonged in a paraphrased liturgical address to pagan-born God-fearers. Or Paul may have offered his own translation of the original text. Since Paul's peculiar use of Isa 57:19 in Eph 2:17 can be explained in so many plausible ways, the hermeneutics he applied to the Isaiah text need not be considered confused or tendentious.

Paul was obviously unable to imagine a peace given by God *to* those far and near which would not also be a peace *between* the two. Peace is not simply a matter of the soul or of individuals only; if it is peace from and with God, then it is also peace among men. Only by changing man's social relations does God also change man's individual life.

The importance of the quotation from Isaiah is shown by its occurrence in vss. 13 and 17, and the extended comment in vss. 14–16, 18–19. If vss. 14–18 constituted a pre-Pauline hymn, then Paul obviously regarded the quotation as of outstanding significance—otherwise he would not have alluded to it in vs. 13 to introduce the hymn. But why should he have put so much stress on a Scripture text when his topic is the recently made Messianic peace between Jews and Gentiles, which seemingly lies beyond the horizons of the Bible and tradition of Israel? H. Schlier believes that the reference to the OT served to refute an anti-Jewish tendency of the Gnostic original of the hymn.[104] The Gnostic character of the hymn is an unproven matter.[105] Perhaps in Eph 2:13 ff. Paul unwittingly anticipated a controversy which reached its culmination only after his time, in the second century and later. In this case his allusion to Isaiah emphasizes that the God who is merciful to the Gentiles is the same as Israel's God; that this God has not changed his nature and will; and that the adoption

---

[103] The repetition of "peace" is not found in the Koine and other MSS, the Syriac versions, and the texts of Ephesians used by Marcion and Origen.

[104] In Gnosticism peace is not made through the blood or cross, but through the ascension of the Redeemer, e.g. *Od. Sol.* xli 11–16. See also the exposition of Eph 4:8.

[105] See the NOTE on "He has made both [Gentiles and Jews] into one" in 2:14 and COMMENT IV A regarding the "wall."

of the Gentiles into God's house does not imply the expulsion of the Jews and the rejection of their holy writings.

III   Circumcision

The origin and meaning of circumcision can be explained in many ways.[106] Not only Israel, but the Egyptians, Edomites, Ammonites, Moabites, Ishmaelites, Syrians, and Phoenicians practiced it in the time of the OT.[107] In Egypt, since the time of the Ptolemies, the ritual was administered to priests and their offspring only. Philo exploits the latter fact to prove that Israel as a whole is a priestly people.[108] Paul assumes in Eph 2:11 that no one except the Jews practiced circumcision; he may have equated similar rites among pagans with castration.[109] Still, many non-Israelite features have left their traces in the Hebrew Bible. The main viable meanings of circumcision are the following:

a) an apotropaic sacrifice (Exod 4:24–26);

b) a horticultural or hygienic measure;[110]

c) a sacrifice for redeeming the first fruit;[111]

d) a *rite de passage*[112] for the critical age of puberty;

e) a sign of belonging to a covenant or tribe,[113] and therefore a mark of recognition and distinction comparable to other signs[114] but removed by apostates;[115]

f) a pledge of submission to the whole law[116] and thus the declaration of willingness to have the heart, the ears, the lips circumcised;[117]

---

[106] Since an extensive monographic treatment of circumcision is still missing the following description of the origin, meaning, fulfillment, appraisal of circumcision relies mainly on the articles "Circumcision" in RAC, TWNT, RGG, ERE, JE, and on the pertinent passages in Pedersen, *Israel*; StB; Moore, *Judaism*, that are accessible by means of the indices.

[107] Jer 9:25–26; Josh 5:3–9; Ezek 31:18; 32:19–32; Gen 17:23, 26; Herodotus II 104.

[108] *Spec. leg.* I 1–11.   [109] Cf. his bitter remarks in Gal 5:12; Philip 3:2.

[110] The verb, to circumcise, means originally "to cut grass" or "to trim a tree." Circumcision may specifically be a marriage ritual by which non-Israelites are purified and/or fertility is assured (Gen 34:14–17; Exod 4:24–26).

[111] The noun foreskin (*orlah*) is originally the designation of the first fruits harvested from a tree.

[112] See A. von Gennep, *The Rites of Passage*, University of Chicago Press, 1940 (French original, Paris, 1909).

[113] It appears that at the following historic moments circumcision was specifically emphasized: after the people passed through the Jordan, Josh 5; at the time of Jeremiah and the Deuteronomy, Jer 4:4; 6:10; 9:25; Deut 10:16; 30:6; in and after the exile, Gen 17; Lev 12:3; Exod 12:43 ff.; in the periods when it was outlawed, e.g. under Antiochus IV Epiphanes and Hadrian, I Macc 1:49–50, 60–61; II Macc 6:10; IV Macc 4:25. Circumcision of children and foreign house slaves is prescribed in Gen 17; Lev 12:3; Exod 12:43–48 but it does not seem to be required of all aliens resident in the land, Lev 17–18; Exod 20:10 ff.; 12:18–19; cf. Acts 15:19–20. Circumcision imposed upon more or less consenting Gentiles is attested only in Gen 34 and perhaps in Esther 8:17. An example of forcible circumcision of Gentiles by Jews is given by Josephus (*antiquitates* XIII 9:1, 254 ff.), who reports that John Hyrcanos required circumcision from the Idumaeans as a token of their acceptance of Judaism. Circumcision was enforced among Jews when it had fallen into disuse, according to I Macc 2:46. Paul resents its *par force* imposition (*anagkazō*) upon Gentiles, Gal 2:3; 6:12; cf. 2:14.

[114] Rom 2:28 alludes to the fact that circumcision is "publicly" visible (during the performance of the ritual itself, or in bathhouses and in the arena?). Similar signs borne for public display and identification are mentioned in Gen 4:15; Ezek 9:4; Lev 19:28; 21:5; Deut 14:1; Rev 13:16–17; 9:4. In Ezek 44:6–9 the admission to the sanctuary of "foreigners uncircumcised in heart and flesh" is decried as an abomination and a desecration of the temple.

[115] By the so-called *epispasmos*, i.e. an operation making the circumcision invisible and ineffective, I Macc 1:15; Josephus *ant.* XII 241; I Cor 7:18–19; StB, IV, 34.

[116] Circumcision was the last step taken by a proselyte on his long road of access to Israel. By accepting circumcision he submitted to the whole Jewish law (E. Lohse, RGG, IV, 972), i.e. to the 613 commandments and prohibitions counted by the rabbis. In Gal 5:3; 6:13; Rom 2:25; cf. I Cor 7:19, Paul insists upon the inseparability of circumcision and total obedience. As mentioned earlier, his opponents in Galatia, perhaps also in Colossae, Philippi (and Rome?), probably considered circumcision a ritual that substituted for total obedience to the whole law.

[117] Jer 4:4 etc.; Deut 10:16; 30:6; Ezek 44:7; Philo *spec. leg.* I 1–11; *migr. Abr.* 89, 92.

g) a test of complete obedience, accepted simply because it was commanded, and placed above the observance of the Sabbath.[118]

Though some of these meanings appear to bring circumcision close to a "sacrament" in the sense of Tertullian and Augustine, it is improbable that it was so understood by early orthodox rabbis. A Hebrew "sign [ōth] of the covenant" (Gen 17:11; Rom 4:11) is not automatically to be identified with, or to be treated as analogous to, a neo-Platonic and Christian sign (signum) or sacrament, or a Greek mystērion.[119] More than one opinion existed regarding the necessity of circumcision for participation in the coming age.[120]

When Paul mentions circumcision in Eph 2:11 he does not have in mind all the possible explanations and functions of the rite, but only certain specific features: he understands it as a mark of belonging to the elect people. The context refers to the opposition between the in-group that bears the sign and the out-group that does not. Because it is a distinguishing mark its effect is that of a wall or fence; while it protects, it also separates. Further, Paul takes it to imply a confession. He alludes to the self-consciousness of those "calling themselves The Circumcision" (2:11). The mention of "law" and "statutes" reveals that Paul is far from considering circumcision a human invention only. It is commanded by God's holy law and protected by statutory regulations. Finally, circumcision is characterized as something preliminary. It is "handmade" and valid only inasmuch as it confirms an act of God himself. And it is limited to the "realm of flesh," the old aeon, and will have to yield its place to that which is done "in the Spirit" (2:22; Rom 2:29).

According to Eph 2:11–15 the law of circumcision itself, or at least its statutory implications and effects, has been "abolished." See COMMENTS IV B and V C for attempts to interpret the meaning of the term "to abolish" in 2:15. The apostle intends to say that there no longer need be enmity between Jews and Gentiles because of the mark distinguishing both, i.e. circumcision. Their separation belongs to the past.

How can Paul the Jew declare this sign of the covenant antiquated without becoming not only an outright apostate from his people and its faith, but also a rebel against God and against a test and pledge of obedience required by the holy law? The clearest answer is given in Col 2:11 where Paul used an argument whose logic amounts to fighting fire with fire: "the circumcision of the Messiah" has been applied to the Gentiles and makes them "circumcised with a circumcision not made by hands." Whatever the exact sense of the formula "circumcision of the Messiah," it is clear that Paul pronounces a Messianic fulfillment and reprieve of circumcision for the benefit of Gentiles, rather than its simple contempt, disregard, or abandonment. In Christ, viz. "in his circumcision," an event has taken place which takes up, exhausts, and crowns the ritual circumcision by granting a spiritual fulfillment to both Jews and Gentiles. Therefore Paul can boldly assert that now the church is, or that "we are the circumcision" (Philip 3:3), that there exists a "hidden Jew" and a "circumcision

---

[118] Cf. John 7:22; StB, II, 487–88; IV:1, 30.
[119] See Bousset Die Religion des Judentums, p. 199; C. A. Keller, Das Wort Oth, Basel: Hoenen, 1946; the opposite opinion is represented, e.g. by Schoeps, Paul, p. 198.
[120] See the Talmud passages quoted in fn. 204 on Eph 2:1–10, and fn. 5 in this section.

of the heart in the Spirit" (Rom 2:29). The Israel of God that now exists is a "new creation" in which the presence or absence of fleshly circumcision no longer separates the Chosen People from the Nations, and those saved from those perishing (Gal 6:15–16).[121]

Eph 2 and Col 2 describe the way in which the divisiveness of fleshly circumcision was overcome. Common to these Colossian and Ephesian passages are three things: (a) The Messiah, or an event that has taken place "in Christ," has annulled the formerly valid distinction. Neither of the formerly divided groups is given the right to absorb the other on its own conditions. Rather it is the Messiah who creates a new thing, the union of the "single new man" (2:15). It is God himself who "in the Messiah" reconciles divided mankind. (b) The separation epitomized by the "handmade" circumcision has been overcome by a ceremony not made by hands. While Colossians calls the new event the "circumcision of the Messiah," the same fact is described in Ephesians by the terms "blood" and "flesh" of Christ, which point to his sacrifice. See COMMENT V B. Just as in Heb 7–10, so in Colossians and Ephesians a priestly act performed on and by the Messiah is considered unique and final. (c) The completion, consummation, and perfection "in Christ" amounts to a negation: bodily circumcision must not be required of Gentiles. In the realm of the Messiah, the Gentiles who are spiritually circumcised are as holy, as much members of God's people, and as fully blessed as were formerly only the Jews.

But there are also differences between Ephesians and Colossians. What in Colossians is described only in one verse (2:11) is in Ephesians spread over nine verses (2:11–19). On the other hand, passionate polemics against the continuation or imposition of traditional ritual practices dominate a large section of Colossians, especially 2:6–23. Ephesians, however, is irenic and states in very quiet terms that the distinction represented by circumcision is a matter of the past. Colossians introduces the novel term "circumcision of the Messiah" in order to show how the old has passed away and new things have come into being. Ephesians seems to use only traditional *sacrificial* terms for denoting the means by which the Messiah has abrogated the wall of division: "the flesh" and "the blood" of the Messiah are mentioned in 2:13–14. Further qualifications are combined in the terms "one body," "the cross," "one Spirit," the "coming" and the "proclamation" of the Messiah (2:16–18).

Does Ephesians propose a priestly or cultic action different from Colossians for abrogating the legal circumcision which created the division between Jews and Gentiles? Recently it has been argued that the "blood" mentioned in Eph 2:13 means the blood of Christ's circumcision, cf. Col 2:11.[122] Reference has already been made to the fact that "flesh" (as mentioned in 2:14) may denote the pudendum. In vss. 13–14 "blood" and "flesh" may therefore be a terminology chosen to allude to a circumcision rather than to a sacrifice. This is not to

---

[121] See also Gal 5:6; I Cor 7:19. These texts show that Paul had no objection against circumcision as such. Jews may continue to exercise it. Cf. COMMENT VI B on 2:1–10, esp. the lines to which fn. 207 is appended. But the ritual circumcision counts no longer as a separating mark between those far and those near. It is not a condition of salvation and least of all a work of law that merits justification or makes superfluous the fulfillment of the whole law (Rom 2:25; 13:8–10, etc.).

[122] G. Vermes, "Baptism and Jewish Exegesis," NTS 4 (1958), 308–19; idem, *Scripture and Tradition* (Leiden: Brill, 1961), pp. 178–92; cf. H. Sahlin, "Die Beschneidung Christi," SBU 12 (1950), 5–22.

say that in Eph 2:13–16 the ceremonial circumcision of Jesus (mentioned in Luke 2:21) is considered the means by which all circumcision was fulfilled and the wall of division, which it established, was destroyed. But it may be important for the interpretation of Eph 2:11–16 that among some rabbis, perhaps as early as in Paul's days, circumcision was understood (on the grounds of Exod 4:24–26 and other texts) to be a sacrifice and to possess the atoning effect of a sacrifice. Not only Abraham's willingness to sacrifice Isaac, but also the covenant blood of Abraham that was poured out in his circumcision was accredited to his children and children's children.[123]

In summary, the sacrificial death of Christ to which Eph 2:13–16 certainly alludes may be called metaphorically a sacrificial circumcision, as indeed the "circumcision of the Messiah" mentioned in Col 2:11 is most likely a metaphor for his death.[124] In this case, the crucifixion of Christ mentioned in Eph 2:16 is depicted in vss. 13–16 as a unique and powerful spiritual circumcision which supersedes for good and all the fleshly circumcision and its divisive effect as they were described in 2:11–12. The late date of the rabbinical texts mentioned, and the absence of unquestionable evidence for the priority of Colossians over Ephesians may be cited as reasons against this interpretation. But the logical structure of 2:11–16 supports it. As soon as Christ's death is understood as the spiritual circumcision of Jews and Gentiles alike, a connection becomes clear between the references to "circumcision" and "flesh" in Eph 2:11 and to "blood," "flesh," "body," and "cross" in 2:13–16. Only then an answer is given to both questions: Why and how did Christ's death overcome the barrier consisting of fleshly circumcision?

However, alternate ways of explaining the effect ascribed to the "blood," "flesh" and "cross" of Christ in 2:13 ff. cannot be excluded. See COMMENT V B.

IV   The Obstacle to Peace: a Legal Wall of Enmity

According to Ephesians the separation of Jews from Gentiles consists in their cultic distinction, their social and geographical segregation, and their diverse history and relation to God. The Gentiles' lack of circumcision, their exclusion from the community, the hope, and the help of Israel's God, and their aloofness are all described in precise and impressive terms (2:11–13). But Paul has more to say about the cause and effect of their segregation from Israel. Verses 14–16 add three new elements to the distinctive features already mentioned. A "wall" separating Jews and Gentiles is mentioned; reference is made to a "law" and to its application; and finally the author speaks of "enmity" against fellow man and God. Though the grammatical coordination of the three nouns "wall," "law" and "enmity" is ambiguous, it is certain that these three concepts are meant to interpret one another. The metaphor of a material "wall," the men-

---

[123] E.g. PesiqR 47 (191a–b, 18), "Abraham was circumcised on the Day of Atonement; year after year God looks upon the covenant blood of the circumcision of our father (Abraham) and creates atonement for all our sins . . . He said to you, because of your blood you shall live." ExodR 19 (81c), "The blood of the passover was mixed with the blood of circumcision. Then God went by, took each [Israelite], kissed, and blessed him . . . 'Because of the bloods you shall live.'" Mek. Exod 12, 6 (6a), "God gave them two commandments, the blood of the pass-over-lamb and the blood of circumcision in order that they occupy themselves with them for receiving redemption."

[124] See E. Lohmeyer, KEKNT, 9 (1930), 108–9. Vermes and Sahlin, however, suggest that "Christ's circumcision" be understood as a circumscription of the church's baptism.

tion of the historic (written and oral) "law," and the blunt talk of the socio-logical and psychological fact of "enmity" are used not only to clarify the meaning but also to produce an escalating effect. The strongest words and col-ors are chosen to characterize what stood in the way of peace between man and fellow man, and between man and God before the coming and work of Christ. The terms "wall" and "law" as used and qualified in 2:14–15 have been understood in widely different ways.

A   The Wall

What is meant by the "dividing wall"?[125]

1. The author of Ephesians may allude to a wall standing on the precincts of the Jerusalem temple. Or, if Ephesians was written after that temple was destroyed, a deutero-Paulinist may have capitalized upon the destruction of the sanctuary itself.[126] According to Josephus' description[127] a five-foot wall, i.e. a balustrade (called *dryphaktos lithinos*), separated the Outer Court of the Gentiles from the two stairs of fourteen and five steps that led to the platform situated above, on which the temple stood. But before the temple could be reached, the visitor had to pass through one of several gates in a high wall, and then pass in succession across the Court of Women, the Court of the Sons of Israel, and the Court of the Priests. The whole area, including all courts, walls and buildings, was called temple in the more general sense (*hieron*). Only the sanctuary proper at the far end of the Court of the Priests was called the temple in a stricter meaning (*naos*). Gentiles who brought offerings were permitted to approach the inner sanctuary as close as the small platform between those two stairs separating the Court of the Gentiles from the Court of Women. The high wall at the top of the upper stair prevented them from even looking at the Courts of Women, Israelites, and Priests. Gentiles without offerings were warned by Greek and Latin inscriptions fixed on pillars: capital punishment was imposed for trespassing even beyond the lower partition.[128] An incident reported in Acts, if it is historical, proves how sensitive the Jews were about their sanctuary: in order to placate law-abiding Jewish Christians (or, Jews, if in Acts 21:20 the words "who believed" are an interpolation), Paul had taken a vow upon himself which required frequent attendance at the temple. Jews from Asia Minor observed Paul in the temple, and in his company saw four other men whose expenses for sacrifices Paul defrayed. Previously they had seen a man from Ephesus, Trophimus, as one of Paul's companions. Supposing that the Gentile-

---

[125] For a discussion of this question see Hanson, *Unity*, pp. 143–46, and O. Betz, "The Eschatological Interpretation of the Sinai Tradition in Qumran and in the New Testament," RQum 6 (1967), 89–107.

[126] S. G. F. Brandon, *The Fall of Jerusalem and the Christian Church*, London: SPCK, 1957, collates and evaluates various early Christian attempts at a theological exploitation of the catastrophe.

[127] *Ant.* xv 417; *bellum Judaicum* v 193; cf. v 227; Philo *leg. ad Gaium* 31. In Mishna Middoth II 3 the wall is called "soreq." For detailed descriptions of the results of archeological research see the literature listed in TWNTE, III, 230–31, n. 26, and the summary given by e.g. Y. Congar, *The Mystery of the Temple* (Westminster, Md.: Newman Press, 1962), pp. 107–8.

[128] Such an inscription was discovered in 1871 by M. Clermont-Ganneau. According to Sanh. 9:6 the stranger who trespasses the *soreq* will die by the hand of God. Probably the fence built around Mount Sinai (Exod 19:12, 21–24) was considered the prototype of this temple wall, cf. O. Betz, RQum 6 (1967), 95.

born Trophimus was among Paul's fellow worshipers at the temple, they gave the alarm, assembled a crowd, and accused Paul publicly: ". . . He brought Greeks into the temple, and he has defiled this holy place!" The Jewish visitors from Asia Minor succeeded in "stirring up the whole city," and they seized Paul and dragged him out of the sanctuary. For fear of a riot the authorities had the gates of the temple shut (Acts 21:20-30). Even if this report should not be accurate in all details, it is certain that Paul could not help being aware of the practical and symbolic meanings of fence and wall in the temple precincts. If only in Eph 2:14 one of the technical names of the temple wall, *dryphaktos lithinos* or *soreq*, had been used! Then it would be certain that the balustrade or the higher wall was meant. But Paul uses a Greek formulation (*mesotoichon tou phragmou*) which suggests that his imagery may be taken from someplace else.

2. The term "dividing wall" may be a strange nomenclature for the curtain that separated the Holiest of Holies from the Holy inside the temple (*naos*). According to a tradition formulated in Mark 15:38 par., in the hour of Jesus' death on the cross that curtain was torn from top to bottom. Through this curtain, so the epistle to the Hebrews asserts, Jesus entered "in his blood, through his flesh."[129] While the fence and wall prevented the access of the Gentiles to the inner three courts of the temple (*hieron*) and thus signified the *Gentiles'* separation from both the Sons of Israel and God, the curtain marked the separation between *all men* and God. But Eph 2:14-17 mentions both separations in succession, i.e. in vss. 14-15 the inimical separation of fellow men, and in vss. 16-17 the hostile separation from God! Also, it would be hard to explain why Paul called the curtain a wall, and why he could expect the pagan-born readers of Ephesians to understand his ambiguous terminology. The "Ephesians" were not "Hebrews" who from their synagogal or Qumranite instruction, or because of pilgrimages to Jerusalem, would have known about the existence and meaning of every part of the temple.

3. The Sayings of the Fathers (*Pirke Aboth*), a rabbinical document that contains many elements taught at Paul's time, includes the commandment to "build a fence around the law."[130] Again, an allusion is probably made to the Sinai fence,[131] but here the function of the fence is protective rather than hostile.[132] Minute man-made prescriptions were supposed to prevent the breaking of God's great commandments. If e.g. the Sabbath rest is observed one hour *before* sunset, then it is certain that no one will work one second beyond the limit set by God. In post-Tannaitic rabbinic writings the fence is

---

[129] 10:19-20; cf. 4:16; 6:19-20.

[130] 1:1; cf. 3:18. See also *Letter of Aristeas* 139; I Enoch 93:6. In CD IV 19; VIII 12, 18 the term, "builders of the wall," is probably a designation of rabbinical interpreters of the law. The metaphor appears to be taken from (the indictment of false prophets in) Ezek 13:10, and the implied criticism may be directed against the "abnormal growth . . . of oral tradition" and the over-estimation of that tradition at the expense of the written Torah; see R. H. Charles, *Apocrypha and Pseudepigrapha*, II (Oxford: Clarendon, 1913), 810, 818-19, and G. F. Moore, *Judaism*, I, 258-62.

[131] Later rabbinic exegesis, e.g. Sifr. Lev 18:30 (342a) (see StB, I, 694) points to Lev 18:30.

[132] Cf. the fence built around God's vineyard (Isa 5:1-2); the role of the angels who at Mahanaim protect the promised land (Gen 31:12); the purpose of city walls. According to Betz, RQum (1967), 96, 105, the function of the boundary was changed by the rabbis. Instead of protecting from the wrath of the holy God, it became a protection from the evil world. Seen under this aspect the law has—at least "from the perspective of a Gentile Christian"—no positive force. It creates nothing but enmity.

identified with God's law itself, and to it is ascribed both a soteriological and cosmic function. Now the law is called, "the wall of the wise" or the "wall of the world."[133] In Eph 2:15 not only is the law mentioned, but also statutes and ordinances, viz. canonical statutes, as they were added by pious and learned Jewish interpreters. It is therefore possible that by "the wall" Paul means a spiritual fence consisting either of detailed biblical commandments,[134] or the additions made by scribes in their oral interpretations,[135] or both. In Gal 2:18 Paul speaks about something that must not be rebuilt once it is torn down. It may be that there as much as in Eph 2:14–15 he is thinking about divisive ceremonial laws and statutes. See the next section of this COMMENT for additional reasons supporting this theory.

4. Isa 59:2 states, "Your sins have made a separation between you and your God, your sins have hid his face before you," and Job complains bitterly about being counted as an enemy by God (19:10).[136] Some church fathers[137] identify the wall with the "flesh" (in the evil connotation of this term), or simply with enmity against God. The "works of the flesh" also include, according to Gal 5:19–21, enmity against fellow man. The futility of flesh and this double enmity are explicitly mentioned in Eph 2:11, 14, 16. Therefore "wall," "flesh," and "law" describe the effect of the "killing letter" mentioned elsewhere.[138] In this case 2:14–16 affirms that the law, the separating wall, and the resulting enmity were all killed with one stroke. Paul would then have had in mind something similar to the contents of Rom 7–8. But since this is not made explicit in Ephesians, it is difficult to imagine how pagan-born readers should have understood his cryptic allusions. In II Peter 3:16 the problem of understanding Paul's weighty doctrines is publicly recognized.

5. Schlier[139] has collected a wealth of material from Jewish and Christian heterodox writings concerning a cosmic barrier (e.g. a stream, a firewall, an ocean) that is broken up or penetrated.[140] He assumes that a common mythological background exists which shines through apocalyptic references to a cosmic wall, rabbinical descriptions of the law as a wall, and the Valentinian concept of the *horos* or limit which separates the lower world from the sphere of the divine *plērōma*. According to Schlier, in Eph 2:14 the concept "dividing wall" owes its origin to the fusion of these three: the Torah given to Israel, the cosmic order or law of the universe, and the frosty grip of fate (*heimarmenē* or *anagkē*)[141] all are mixed together by the author of Ephesians. Jewish and Christian references to legislation through

---

[133] Jer. Berakoth 6a; LevR. 76 (124a) etc. More references are given by Schoeps, *Paul*, p. 194, God will break out against those who break through it (Exod 19:24). A serpent will bite him who penetrates the wall (Eccles 10:8). O. Betz assumes that according to Eph 2 Christ became the savior by making the prohibited breakthrough but that he had to pay for it with his own life.

[134] On circumcision, diet, Sabbath keeping, etc. see Eph 2:11; Col 2:11, 21; Gal 2:11–14; 4:10.

[135] Isa 29:13; Matt 15:1–20; Col 2:8, 22–23; also Matt 5:20–48?

[136] Cf. the OT statements in Ps 106:23; Ezek 22:30 regarding the "breach" into which a mediator has to step.

[137] Victorinus, Chrysostom, Ambrosiaster, and others.

[138] Gal 2:19; 3:10–13; I Cor 15:57; II Cor 3:6; Rom 7:6, 10.

[139] *Christus*, pp. 18–26, Schlier, pp. 125–33.

[140] E.g. II Bar 54:5; I Enoch 14:9; 1QH III 26–32; *Od. Sol.* xxxix 9–12; *Acts of Thomas* 32; Eusebius HE I 13:20; the majority of Schlier's Mandaean references is selected from the Ginza.

[141] See also Jones, *Gnostic Religion*, p. 326.

angels[142] establish, so it is assumed, a connection between this law and the principalities and powers. Heterodox Jewish circles showed an increasing tendency to identify the law and the powers. When, partly under the influence of those circles, the classic second-century Gnosticism developed, law and cosmic guardians were no longer distinguished. Schlier surmises that Eph 2:14–15 presupposes their complete identification: Paul preaches the simultaneous destruction of the powers and the law. Schlier draws other far-reaching conclusions: the Jewish-Gnostic myth contains a notion of truth, and what happened in the saving Christ event must be recognized in the light of the myth. Certainly the myth is reinterpreted, for the mythical redeemer and redemption are transformed into a historical person and event. The blood and body, i.e. the cross of Christ, replace the timelessness of the Gnostic concept of redemption. But still, the mythological form given to the proclamation of Christ is an appropriate means for showing that Christ's deed, esp. the destruction of the Jewish Torah, is "an ontological and public, not just a moral event."[143] The antinomian doctrine which is thus ascribed to Paul is a result of the Gnosticizing interpretation of the wall. Whoever acknowledges and endorses a mythological background of Eph 2:14–15 may indeed have to consider the author of Ephesians an antinomian. But grave doubts concerning Schlier's and his followers' premises have been listed in section III B of the Introduction, in COMMENT VI on 1:15–23, and elsewhere. If Schlier's presuppositions are less solid than he assumes, his conclusions may be equally shaky. The Jewish apocalyptic, the Gnostic, and the Mandaean texts quoted by him are too late, too diverse, and too inconclusive to buttress his theological, philosophical, and hermeneutical results, especially his antinomianism and its counterpart in natural theology. Specific traits and accents of OT utterances on the Messiah, the wall, the temple, also some features of apocalyptic and rabbinic interpretation, suffice to demonstrate the public and cosmic character of Christ's coming and work as it is preached in Eph 2. However, the alleged Gnostic parallels are not indispensable for all of Schlier's theses. Schlier's vision of a cosmic wall and his use of mythical and other elements to interpret Eph 2:14 draw attention to the drama in this verse and are an appropriate warning against an exposition that involves petty moralizing and psychologizing.

None of the five explanations sketched for the term "wall" is so persuasive as to completely rule out the alternatives. The sources and scholarly methods available at present permit more skepticism about some than about others, but they are not sufficient for a final decision. An interpretation based on the context of Eph 2:14 still offers the safest means for finding out the author's intention. The context identifies the "wall" in four ways: it is the fact of separation between Israel and the nations; it has to do with the law and its statutes and interpretations; it is experienced in the enmity between Jews and Gentiles; it also consists of the enmity of both Jews and Gentiles against God. In every regard the essence of the wall can, if at all, be described only retrospectively. Unless it is understood as that which was "broken down"

---

[142] See LXX Deut 33:2; Ps 68:17; Acts 7:53; Gal 3:19; Heb 2:2; Josephus *ant.* xv 136; ExodR 28:1. The elements of the world mentioned in Gal 4:3, 9 and Col 2:8, 20 appear to demonstrate the identity of law and world order; but see the AB commentary on Col 2 (vol. 34B).
[143] Schlier, esp. pp. 130–33.

by Christ, it cannot be comprehended at all. In COMMENT V an attempt will be made at such a retrospective interpretation.

B   The Law

Do the words "law [, that is, only] the commandments [expressed] in statutes" in 2:15 permit a definition of the dividing wall that is independent of the coming and work of the Messiah? Again, several expositions vie for acceptance:[144]

1. If special stress is laid upon the singular *nomos* ("law") and the article before it,[145] then Paul means the "holy, perfect, righteous, spiritual" law given by God to Moses through "the hand of angels."[146] Paul's polemics against justification by the law; the contents of Gal 3:19 – 4:5 limiting the validity of the law to the time between Moses and the advent of the Messiah; the death "to the law" and "by the law" described in Gal 2:19; II Cor 3:6–7; Rom 7:1–10; the frequently suggested translation of Rom 10:4, "Christ is the end of the law"[147]—all such elements appear to suggest that the law which is "abolished" according to Eph 2:15 is the whole and holy law of God. But in Rom 3:31; 7:22; 13:8–10 Paul flatly contradicts this opinion. "Do we thus abrogate the law by faith? Far be it! On the contrary, we uphold the law . . . I delight in the law of God, in my inner man . . . He who loves his neighbor has fulfilled the law . . . Love is the fulfillment of the law."[148] Either Paul is inconsistent and his teaching paradoxical,[149] or Eph 2:15 must be understood as referring to something different from an invalidation of the revelation given to Moses on Mount Sinai.

2. It may be that instead of the singular "the law" the anarthrous interpretative plural "commandments . . . in statutes" (lit. "of commandments in statutes") bears the accent. In this case Paul does not speak of the total law, and the abrogation would then affect only a part of the law, that is, a limited number of its "commandments." It has been suggested[150] that only the ceremonial regulations have been abrogated, especially the circumcision, food, and festival laws, and that moral commandments (exemplified by the prohibition of adultery), i.e. the ethical demand of the law, were left untouched by Christ or, even better, were established in their true light and glory. Indeed, those specific legal observances are of ceremonial character which Paul calls "works of law" (or "works") and declares unfit for justification.[151] Prophets such as Amos, Hosea, Isaiah, Jeremiah denounced sheer ceremonialism and

[144] Literature dealing with Paul's attitude to the law is listed in BIBLIOGRAPHY 15.

[145] WBLex, 551–52, lists some of the literature on the use of the article. W. Bauer may be justified in beginning his article on the article by saying that hard and fast rules for the employment of the article are—in view of the Greek writers' "feeling for style" and "freedom of play" —difficult to set. P. Bläser, p. 20, has shown why this applies specifically to Paul's use of the article before *nomos;* see also E. W. Burton, pp. 454–55, and J. McKenzie.

[146] Gal 3:19; Rom 7:12, 14, 16; 9:4. Cf. also I Tim 1:8–11. "The law is good if any one uses it lawfully."

[147] Also an analogous understanding of the antitheses of Matt 5:20–48 and of Heb 7–10.

[148] Cf. the analogous sayings of Jesus in Matt 3:15; 5:17; 22:37–40.

[149] Whiteley, p. 76, speaks of the "ambivalent, love-hatred attitude of St. Paul to the law."

[150] By the medieval tradition on Eph 2:15 which stems from Origen and Jerome and was taken up e.g. by Calvin, (but cf. his exposition of Galatians, e.g. CRCO, L, 164, 194). More recent exponents of a similar exposition are e.g. E. W. Burton, *Galatians,* esp. pp. 447–48, 451–55; W. Bousset, SNT, II, on Gal 2:15–21; G. Bornkamm, pp. 92–98.

[151] See e.g. Gal 2:16; Rom 3:28; Eph 2:9; also COMMENT VI B on Eph 2:1–10.

called for total obedience to God's will. The law which according to Hebrews[152] is antiquated, senile, disappearing, and set aside, is not the total law but the institution of the Aaronitic priesthood only, including its purifications and sacrifices. And yet, the distinction between moral and ceremonial laws cannot be upheld. Neither the Bible, nor the history of religions, nor sound theological reasons support it.[153]

3. Within the description of the law given in Eph 2:15 the accent may be set upon the last term, i.e. the noun "statutes." If so, then neither the total "law" as put into writing and found in the Scriptures, nor one part of the legal "commandments," but the oral interpretation and application of the law by scribes is meant. Ezra is the prototype of these scribes and their work. The Greek word for *statutes* or decrees, *dogmata,* is not used in the LXX to denote any of the commandments, judgments, statutes, or laws of which—e.g. according to Gen 26:5—the total law consisted. But Eph 2:15 may well allude exclusively to those additional rabbinic teachings which were added as a "fence" around the law after the formation of Israel's Bible and later were collected and codified in the Mishna and the Talmud. According to rabbinical teaching the Oral Law is as much God's Law as the written Torah, and is no less God's revelation and gift. It took its start with the revelation given to the Seventy Elders on Mount Sinai, was continued through the mouths of the Prophets and the Wise Men, and is living still in the study and exposition of the law going on in the *yezivoth* (schools) as it was once in Qumran.[154] If 2:15 refers to the abrogation of the post-Scriptural additions to the law, then Jesus Christ is here proclaimed as the end of and substitution of rabbinical interpretations,[155] not to speak of sectarian exegesis. The change effected by Christ is, in this case, a change in hermeneutics. The Messiah abrogates and antiquates misinterpretations and misuse of the law rather than the holy law itself. Just as the Qumranite Teacher of Righteousness and the risen Jesus according to Luke 24:25–27, 44–46, became the source and criterion for a new exegesis that was accepted as true by their respective followers, so the teaching and work of the Messiah may

---

[152] 7:12, 18, 28; 8:13; cf. H. Windisch, *Der Brief an die Hebräer,* HbNT 14, 2d ed. (1931), 66.

[153] E.g. the exclusion of adultery and magic from Israel's cultus and life, equally the establishment of the Sabbath, but also the contents of the Apostolic Decree (Acts 15:20, 29; 21:25) can and probably must be understood at the same time as moral and ceremonial commandments. See J. H. Roper's and K. Lake's discussion of the various readings of the Apostolic Decree, in *Beginnings of Christianity,* III (London: Macmillan, 1926), 265–69; V (1933), 204–20. For the OT see von Rad, OTTh, II, 390, and A. Jepsen, "Israel und das Gesetz," TLZ 93 (1968), 85–94. Jepsen puts the distinction of Israel as a cultic and a social community in question; the *Kultgemeinde* cannot be separated from the *Lebensgemeinschaft.* Luther opposed the distinction upheld by Origen, Jerome and "the Papists." His concern was to state that the whole law, not the ceremonial commandments only, had been "killed . . . , was damned and dead, a caught thief" and was to be "torn up, thrown to the ground, . . . ignored," WA, LVII, 68 ff., 200; XL, 1, 43–44, 262, 276–77, 282, 329, etc. Calvin was occasionally willing to reject the distinction—though not for the reason given by Luther, see, e.g. CRCO, L, 154, 194–95, 200. In his interpretation of Rom 3:20 and Gal 2:16, Bengel followed the same path. Following Moore, *Judaism,* II, 6, 79, 426, the "division [is] not warranted in Scripture." Cf. also Whiteley, p. 86; Longenecker, pp. 119–20; Stalder, *Das Werk des Geistes,* pp. 309–20.

[154] See the references given in Moore, *Judaism,* I, 235 ff.; A. Wolfson, *Philo,* II (Cambridge: Harvard University Press, 1948), 36 ff.; StB, III, 554 ff.; IV, 435 ff.; O. Betz, *Offenbarung und Schriftforschung in der Qumransekte,* Tübingen: Mohr, 1960; G. Vermes, *Scripture and Tradition,* Leiden; Brill, 1961. Qumran texts, such as those referred to in fn. 130, reveal that the desert community wanted its own law interpretation to be distinct from that of the scribes.

[155] The words of Jesus presented in Matt 23:3, "Do and keep all that they say unto you," would then be contradicted by Paul, or they would have to be considered inauthentic.

be understood in Eph 2:14–15. According to Paul and other NT authors, however, Christ is more than just a teacher. Rather he is the exponent of the law's unity and is its fulfillment.[156] His obedience, proven in his death,[157] should probably be understood as the "purpose of the law" (Rom 10:4) rather than its termination. The demands and imperatives of the law are in this case "not invalidated"[158] but have a new form and sense:[159] the law has been fulfilled because the fulfiller of the law has come. Is this the meaning of 2:15? This interpretation is true enough for Galatians, Philippians, Romans, and is supported by one of the many meanings inherent in, and attributed to, the verb "to abrogate."[160] Still, in the context of Eph 2:15 the question of right or wrong interpretation is not in the foreground.

4. The formula "the law . . . the commandments . . . in statutes," may serve the purpose of identifying the law with a sentence of death. In this case only a specific function of the law is meant: its role in bringing knowledge and an increase of sin, and in inflicting a curse and death upon man.[161] It was not the original purpose of the law to exercise this function; for it was given for life, as the book of Deuteronomy, *passim*, and e.g. Lev 18:5 affirm. But even this law turned out to work for "death" (Rom 7:10). So it became a "killing letter," that is, the death sentence in writing or a "dispensation of death." Among the Qumran documents CD i 17–18; 1QS 2:16 speak of the "curses of the covenant" and the "vengeance of the covenant" which are understood to be contained in the law. The Covenant Community of Qumran teaches that the curse attached to the law will be executed solely upon the apostates and heretics in the community of Israel. In contrast to them Paul affirms that precisely the Jew who seeks to obey the law is subject to judgment and execution according to and through the law (II Cor 3:6–7). In Col 2:14 the destruction of a "document" containing "decrees against us" is explicitly mentioned—though an identification of that manuscript with the law is not made explicit. However, Eph 2:15 may presuppose that the law is to be identified with the verdict of death. While such an exposition would be suggested by other Pauline Epistles, it does not fit the context of Ephesians. This epistle is directed to former Gentiles, and these Gentiles were declared "dead in lapses and sins" without any reference to the law or statutes (2:1, 5). Death "through the law" (Gal 2:19; Rom 7:9, etc.) is the wages of sin which only befalls the Jews, according to the uncontested Pauline Epistles. Exclusively those men who have been given and who

---

[156] Cf. H. Ljungmann's interpretation of Matt 3:17; 5:17 in *Das Gesetz erfüllen*, LUA N.F. I, 50 (1954) 6, and R. Bring, *Commentary on Galatians* (Philadelphia: Muhlenberg, 1961), pp. 130 ff., 138 ff.; C. E. B. Cranfield, pp. 48–50.

[157] Gal 2:20; Philip 2:6–8; Rom 5:19; 8:3–4; 10:4.   [158] O. Betz, RQum (1967), 105.

[159] Cf. Theodoret.

[160] This verb (*katargeō*) means, according to the careful elaborations of M. E. Dahl, "The Resurrection of the Body," SBT 36 (1962), 117–19, "to render inoperative . . . fulfilled in Christ but not abolished . . . subsumed under the perfect . . . not annihilated . . . the thing put an end to is still somewhere though ineffective . . . [to] force into the service and glorification of Christ." This is certainly applicable to the invalidation of principalities and powers; for Paul explains their abrogation by speaking of "submission" rather than annihilation (I Cor 15:24–27). But in Rom 3:31, and perhaps in Eph 2:15 also, complete destruction, comparable to "breaking down" and "killing" (Eph 2:14, 16), may be meant by the same verb *katargeō*.

[161] Ezek 20:25 appears to ascribe the absence of goodness and life-giving power only to some statutes given by God. Yet Paul affirms that the law as a whole not only fails to give life but kills. See, e.g. Gal 2:19; 3:10–13; I Cor 15:56; II Cor 3:6; Rom 3:20; 4:15; 5:13, 20; 7:7–25.

"have the law," that is Israel, are judged by the law. The Gentiles who had not been given the law will perish without the law (Rom 2:12).[162] Or does Paul mean by "the law of the commandments . . . in statutes" the cosmic rule, necessity, Fate (*anagkē* or *heimarmenē*) which stipulates that "man is mortal and therefore he must die": Gnostics were led by their knowledge of the psyche and its material prison, within the framework of their metaphysics and physics, to bewail man's captivity under the law of finiteness, mortality, estrangement.[163] But the combination of the OT and rabbinical terms "law," "commandments," "statutes" in Eph 2:15 makes it most unlikely that Paul intended to speak of man's evil fate in general. Fate is not a deity, nor a master, nor an instrument of God recognized in the Bible or among its orthodox rabbinical interpreters.

5. The context of Eph 2:15 (especially the references to the exclusion of the Gentiles from the blessings of Israel; to the dividing wall; to enmity; to peace through unification and reconciliation) contains many hints showing that only one specific sense and function of the law is meant: the law has created and demonstrated a separation of the Jews from the Gentiles.[164] I Kings 8:53 affirms that God himself "separated" Israel "from among all the nations." Throughout the OT this God-willed separation is ascribed with various accents to the election of the Fathers, the liberation from Egypt, the sheer love of God, the purpose which God wanted to have fulfilled among the nations by one holy, royal, priestly people. The law which was given only to Israel (Deut 33:3–4) underscored this election, liberation, privilege and destiny. Therefore it was a legitimate and meaningful canon or limit separating those included in God's covenant from those who as yet stood outside the covenants and their promise. By the gift of the law God himself had shown how he wanted his elect people to live and to fulfill their mission. To use a prevalent church terminology, the law distinguished the "clergy" created by God for himself from the "laity" consisting of all the nations. Israel, God's priestly people (Exod 19:5–6), was to serve all the peoples of the earth. If the law was privilege and protection for those inside God's house, it also subjected the members of God's household to special discipline. Both the so-called ceremonial and moral commandments, the written codes and the ever expanding oral explications and applications, the curse threatened to the trespasser and the life promised to its observer, the legitimate use of the law and its boastful misuse, the distinction of the wise from the foolish, and the effect of proving supposedly wise men fools—such diverse aspects of the law, commandments, and statutes are suggested by the context of Eph 2:15 and

---

[162] In Deut 33:3–4; Bar 3:36–37; 4:3–4; Sir 24:3–8 the ground is laid for Paul's passionate assertions that Israel alone is under the law. The privilege granted to the chosen people by the gift of the law includes the threat that they will be measured, judged, and condemned by it, Deut 26–29, etc.; Gal 3:10–13, 19; 4:4; Rom 2:12, 17–24; 7:1–12; 9:3–4.

[163] As esp. Jonas, *Gnostic Religion*, has shown.

[164] On this point there is agreement among Cranfield, pp. 64–65; Lohmeyer, *Probleme*, pp. 54, 68–69; Bring, *Galatians*, pp. 50–51, 165–69, 177 ff; Munck, PSM *passim*. The validity of the law is not a matter of absolute principle but relative to, and contingent upon, the relation of Jews and Gentiles. For this reason it is unlikely that Eph 2:15, together with many other statements on the meaning of the law for Israel and its lack of meaning for the nations, speak only of a "misunderstood" and/or "misused" law, cf. Stalder, *Das Werk des Geistes*, pp. 334, 337, 349. Though I Tim 1:8 presupposes various "uses" of the law, this passage is not the key to Paul's authentic letters. Calvin and Robinson state emphatically that in Eph 2:15 the limits fixed by God himself are meant.

by other Pauline Epistles. Christ has abrogated the divisive function of the law—and therefore not God's holy law itself.

The translation "the law [, that is, only] the commandments [expressed] in statutes," brings out the manifold aspects of division just described, and yet shows that the law itself, along with its study and fulfillment, has not been annulled by Jesus Christ. As a barrier between Jews and Gentiles it is no longer valid; only its divisiveness was terminated when Jesus Christ died on the cross.

C The Enmity

The concept "enmity" is not as fraught with difficulties as the terms "wall" and "law" are. It is a very strong word for denoting the attitude of men to one another and to God.[165] Most amazing is the fact that in Eph 2 this term describes first (in vs. 14) the mutual hostility between Jews and Gentiles and only subsequently (in vs. 16) the enmity of man against God. The author may have in mind the contempt of Gentiles expressed by the Jews in terms such as "The Uncircumcision" (2:11), "dogs" or "pigs";[166] in catalogues of their vices;[167] by the exclusion of pagans from table communion or marriage[168]—not to speak of their legendary acts of revenge as described in the books of Esther and Judith. The Gentiles, in turn, retaliated with the denouncement of Jewish inhospitality and unwillingness to mix,[169] and with persecutions and pogroms as those described e.g. in connection with Moses' birth, Haman's rule, Pilate's revenge against zealots (Luke 13:1), and the careless way in which this Roman procurator agreed to the execution of Jesus. More than vague or incidental feelings of hatred are involved; the mutual contempt of David and Goliath and their ensuing life and death struggle exemplify the two-sided hostility. Perhaps the embittered relationship between present-day Palestinian patriots and Zionistic Jews can also serve as an illustration. However, the sum total of Jewish-Gentile relations is in Ephesians denoted by the term "enmity," not in remembrance of actual clashes between Jews and non-Jews, but because of the peace made by Jesus Christ. Solely in the light that is *now* given by the Messiah is sensitivity awakened to the horror of the total darkness that formerly covered all life and history. While from an OT point of view only "the godless have no peace" (Isa 48:22, 57:21), Ephesians affirms that neither Israel nor the nations are given peace—except when the Messiah comes to save and unite both of them.

V The Price of Peace: the Sacrifice of Jesus Christ

Verses 2:13–18 are permeated and held together by three strings of terms which describe through whom, how, by what means, or at what cost peace

---

[165] The *Heidelberg Catechism* of 1563 uses similar outspoken language for denoting man's sin and misery: "By nature I am inclined to hate God and my neighbor."

[166] Cf. Mark 7:27–28; Matt 7:6.   [167] As, e.g. Rom 1:20–32; Eph 4:17–19.

[168] While intermarriage became a crime for Jews after the exile (Ezra 9–10; Tobit 4:12), the strict prohibition of table communion, anticipated in Dan 1:8; Tobit 1:10–12; Jub 22:16; 30:7, 12–13; Acts 10:28; John 4:9; 18:28; Sanh. 63b, appears to have become canonical law in the second century A.D. only. See StB, III, 421–22; cf. IV, 374–83; Bousset *Die Religion des Judentums*, pp. 92–94.

[169] *Misoxeniā* and *amixiā* is attested to by Esther 3:8, Posidonius (ca. 100 B.C.) 87, fragment 109, and Josephus *ant*. XIII 8:3, etc. See also the second NOTE on 2:19.

was made between Jews and Gentiles, men and God. The first string consists of statements saying that peace is exclusively found "in the Messiah," "in his person," "in one body," "through him" (vss. 13, 15, 16, 18)—so much so that he alone is worthy to be acclaimed as "peace in person" (vs. 14). The peace in question is from beginning to end the Messianic peace. The second series of utterances reveal how the Messiah achieved his purpose. The information given is: "through the blood," "in his flesh," "in one body," "through the cross," "in one Spirit" (vss. 13, 14, 16, 18). A third chain is formed by the verbs that describe the Messianic actions. Though destructive to the obstacles to peace, the works of the Messiah are throughout constructive: he "came," he "made both into one," he "creates a single new man," he "reconciles with God," he "makes peace" and he "proclaims the good news"; only for this end does he "break down the wall," "abolish the law," and "kill the enmity" (vss. 14–17). Aorists, a present participle, and subjunctives with the meaning of the future, i.e. statements on the past, present, and future, are employed to describe the completed and ongoing deeds of the Messiah, their purpose and result. These three terminological strings are intertwined in the manner of a plait. The first two require intensive analysis and detailed exegesis; the third can be more briefly described.

A The Messiah in Person

According to 2:13 the opposite to the Gentiles' exclusion from Israel is their inclusion in the Messiah. The unification of Jews and Gentiles is not due to an absorption of the Gentiles in Israel or to a dispersion of and assimilation by the Jews among the Gentiles. Certainly both of these two movements were under way before and after the coming of the Messiah. Gentiles became proselytes, and proselytes became full members of Israel first by steps and finally by complete submission to the Law. Many Jews, in turn, adopted much of the philosophy, language, art and mode of living of the Hellenistic pagans. Either way might have led, without the interference of a third party, to some unification. Then one or the other of the two groups involved would have claimed the victory for itself even if peace rather than victory had become the key word. However, in Eph 2 Paul ascribes the merit for pacification neither to Israel nor to the Gentiles, but to the Messiah who cares equally for Jews and pagans. This way no one on either side of the former wall could "boast about himself" (2:9).

Yet was not the same Israel who was given the Law for her protection, and the temple with its walls for her worship, to become the "light for those living in darkness" (Isa 42:6; Rom 2:19–20, etc.)? Gal 3 takes up the question of why it is the Messiah rather than the law which makes Jews and Gentiles together children of God. There Paul's argument contains the following elements: God's promise that the blessing given to Abraham shall become a blessing for and among all nations stands firm (Gen 18:18, etc.). But sheer reliance upon "works of law" cannot bring God's blessing to the nations, for the law is given as a custodian (*paidagōgos*) only to Israel (Gal 3:24, 25). This law was given in order to be completely fulfilled; anyone not keeping it wholly was threatened with God's curse. Israel failed to render obedience, fell under the curse, and thus was unable to be the priestly nation that would bring God's blessing to the Gentiles. Finally the Messiah came and took the curse upon himself. "He redeemed us [Jews] from the legitimate curse by becoming cursed for our sake . . . God sent his son . . . who was put under the law to redeem the people under the law."[170] By his acceptance of God's judgment the Messiah Jesus became the one who could carry out Israel's commission: "In Jesus Christ Abraham's blessing was to come to the nations" (Gal 3:14). Had the seed promised to Abraham, the Messiah, not "come," that faith would not have "come" in which Jews and Greeks are now "one in Christ" (Gal 3:16, 19, 23, 28).

The exclusive role attributed by Paul to the Messiah has been anticipated in OT passages such as the following: according to Ps 2:8–9 it is God's Anointed One rather than Israel who will subjugate the rebellious nations. Following Ezek 37, especially vss. 22, 24–25, God brings reunion to the divided parts of God's people through the appointment of David as shepherd. Isa 11:12–13 speaks of the mutual jealousy between Ephraim and Judah that will be terminated by the Messiah. In Zech 9:9–10 it is promised that the king of Zion will command peace to the nations. According to John 10:16 Jesus takes up and repeats such prophetic voices when he affirms that the sheep from many folds are gathered together not because of the greater attractiveness or superiority of one flock over the others, but because of the appearance and work of "one shepherd." A difference between the pertinent OT texts and Eph 2 cannot be overlooked. In the OT it is mostly[171] the coming, enthronement, or victory of God's Anointed One that leads to unity and peace. While in Eph 1:20–23 Paul does indeed glorify the raising and enthronement of Christ in the highest terms, in Eph 2 the "coming" of the Messiah is described in different terms that point to another event. In vss. 13, 14 and 16 his "blood," his "flesh," (and the "cross") are praised as the turning point in the history of both Israel and the nations. Equally in John 10:11, 17–18 Christ is called the "good shepherd" because he "lays down his life" for the sheep. Thus the OT sings of the might, Eph 2 of the death of the Messiah.

Before the death of Christ described in the hymn (Eph 2:14–18) can be more closely scrutinized, other utterances deserve attention which ascribe unification and pacification to the Messiah alone. They also explain the title line of the hymn "He is in person the peace between us." Especially important are the references to the Messiah's coming and preaching, to his person, and to his body.

Verse 17 affirms that "when he came he proclaimed" good news: "Peace!" When did he come? How did he preach? Among the alternatives for explaining the time of Christ's coming and the mode of his proclamation the following are outstanding:[172]

---

[170] Gal 3:13; 4:4; cf. Rom 8:3–4.

[171] Except in texts such as Exod 32:30–32; Deut 9:18–19; II Sam 7:14–15; Isa 53; Zech 3:1–6; 9:9; Wisd Sol 2:12–20.

[172] To be excluded from the interpretation of Eph 2:17 is the idea of a coming and preaching of Christ before his incarnation. But I Peter 3:19–20 speaks of his "coming and preaching to the spirits in prison, in the days of Noah"; I Peter 1:10–11 speaks of the revelation through "the Spirit of the Messiah giving pre-testimony in the OT prophets"; I Cor 10:4 mentions the "spiritual rock, the Messiah," who "followed Israel" and "from whom they were drinking" in the wilderness; John 8:56 contains a reference to the "day of Christ" which "Abraham saw and enjoyed." These passages are not parallels to Eph 2:17 because this verse, no less than vss. 3:3–11, describes the unheard-of novelty of the revelation given in Christ, now, not in his pre-existence.

1. According to Chrysostom, Eph 2:17 refers to the preaching done by Jesus during the days of his ministry. One may think of his activity in "Galilee of the Gentiles" (Matt 4:15), in the half-pagan Samaria (Luke 9:51 ff.; John 4:4–42), in Judea, in Jerusalem (Mark 11–13 par.), and in the northern neighbor territories of Israel (Mark 6–8). Indeed, several NT passages state emphatically that Jesus' main commission was to preach.[173] Jesus' preaching before his crucifixion was in effect the proclamation of the kingdom of God's constitution (especially so the Sermon on the Mount) and a powerful means and demonstration of God's presence; "for God was with him" (Acts 10:38). By his word, Jesus Christ healed the sick and expelled demons. His proclamation was much more than information only; it created a new social reality. In this sense, Eph 2:17 may describe the Messiah's work, a work which consists of speaking a word of power that does what it says.

2. But the Gospels also provide another possible parallel and commentary to Eph 2:17. The Johannine tradition affirms that after his resurrection, Jesus Christ greeted his disciples with the word "Peace."[174] At the time of the writing of the Gospels, this commonplace Semitic greeting had obviously received a distinct and deep meaning, as e.g. John 14:27; 16:33 show: "I give you my peace . . . In me you have peace." In the Gospel of John, the term "coming," if applied to Jesus, means frequently the coming of the exalted one.[175]

3. The proclamation of the resurrected Christ has not stopped with the last of his appearances. The Gospels contain sayings of Jesus which affirm that peace will enter a house into which an apostle of Christ enters, and that Christ will be received where they are received: "He who hears you hears me."[176] Paul was convinced that Christ revealed himself in his messenger and spoke through the mouth of his servant.[177] Paul as well as John and Luke (cf. also Matt 10:20 par.) ascribes this presence and self-proclamation of Christ to the gift of the Spirit.

4. Though usually in the LXX and the NT the verb "to proclaim good news" denotes an act of oral proclamation, more than the mere utterance of words is meant. The authorized messenger is in person the message of peace. He not only evangelizes, but he is an evangelist.[178] When he brings the news of peace he brings peace itself; therefore his words and his very presence make for peace. Indeed, in this case, "the medium is the message." Christ's advent and person as such, including the mode of his work and death, are an act of proclamation. In the (Gnosticizing) language of Ignatius the mysteries of Jesus would have to be called "crying mysteries."[179] Or one might speak of self-

---

[173] "I must preach the good news of the kingdom of God to the other cities also; for I was sent for this purpose" (Luke 4:43); "that I may preach there also; for that is why I came out" (Mark 1:38); "such a great salvation . . . was declared at first by the Lord, and it was attested to us by those who heard him" (Heb 2:3); "you know the word which God sent to Israel, preaching good news of peace by Jesus Christ . . . the word which was proclaimed throughout all Judea" (Acts 10:36–37), in allusion to Ps 107:20, "He [God] sent forth his word." Cf. John 1:1, 14, also Barn. v 8.

[174] John 20:19, 21, 26; cf. Luke 24:36 var. lect. Similarly, Heb 7:1–3 appears to reserve the title "King of Peace" to the exalted king and priest, Christ—after the pattern of Melchizedek who was so-called "after the slaughter of the kings." In the OT cultus, the priest pronounced the Aaronitic peace-blessing only *after* the completion of the sacrifice.

[175] 14:3, 18, 28, etc. E.g. Bengel and Robinson suggest an interpretation of Eph 2:17 which is based upon the peace proclaimed by the resurrected Christ.

[176] Luke 10:16; Matt 10:13–14, 40–41; 16:19; 18:18; cf. John 20:22–23.

[177] Gal 1:16; II Cor 13:3. See also COMMENT XV on 1:3–14.

[178] See G. Friedrich, TWNTE, II, 737.   [179] *Eph.* XIX.

explanatory events, of acts and facts that speak for themselves. Either way, the birth and death of Christ, and not only the preaching about his advent and the cross, may well be the epitome of his "coming" and "preaching."

The wording of Eph 2:17 does not permit a definite decision for any of these four expositions, and H. Schlier is probably right to suggest a combination of such elements as have been listed.[180] It is fruitless to try and pin down the specific moment of the peace proclamation to one event or period of Jesus Christ's ministry before, during, or after his death. A too precise dating and placing of the proclamation might amount to a limitation of its time and place, which would contradict the universal character of the peace made. The hymn (2:14–18) praises the eternal, personal union of Christ and peace. To say Christ—that is to say peace. To speak of peace—that is to speak of Christ! "He is in person the peace" (vs. 14). This is a present, not only a past reality. Jesus Christ is still active as peacemaker. "He is not simply the means; it was in His person that this effect was produced."[181]

The formula "in his person" (lit. "in him") occurs twice, i.e. in vss. 15 and 16. The "single new man" is to be created "in his person," and the enmity (against God) was killed "in his person." This formula would offer no greater problems of interpretation than the formula "in Christ," or, "in him" in the context of 1:2, 3–10—if it did not occur within a unique syntactical structure. While in Eph 1 and elsewhere "God the Father" acts "in Christ,"[182] in 2:15–16 Christ is the subject of the action performed "in Christ"! No difficulty may be seen in the parallel statements, God delivered Christ and Christ delivered himself.[183] It is harder to understand, however, why Eph 2 states, Christ "created in himself" and Christ "killed in himself,"[184] rather than, God created in Christ, and, God killed in Christ.[185] The following choices appear open for understanding the words "creating in himself one new man":

1. Christ creates himself to be the new man, i.e., he leads such a life of total obedience, and he is in his resurrection so glorified, that in contrast to the first Adam he is true man, the real image of God.[186] Yet, if Christ is called the "firstborn of all creation," "from the dead," "among many brothers"[187] and is indeed the counterpole to Adam, these titles still do not declare him a creator, least of all of "himself!"

2. Out of himself Christ brings forth a partner. He forms this companion "from his flesh and his bones," just as God created Eve from Adam (Gen 2:21–23). This is indeed suggested by variant readings, also the Latin and

---

[180] He considers the incarnation, and the earthly ministry, and the post-Easter proclamation the means and moments of Christ's coming and preaching.

[181] Abbott, pp. 83–84, on Eph 3:6.

[182] Especially "creation" is elsewhere attributed to God only. See, e.g. 2:10; 3:9; Col 1:16, "In him all things have been created"; cf. I Cor 8:6; John 1:3.

[183] Rom 4:25; 8:32; Gal 1:4; 2:20; Eph 5:2, 25.

[184] Variant readings show the tendency to correct the grammatically uncouth original Greek "in him" by substituting "in himself."

[185] Even if the words "in him" are but a liturgical or confessional formula which sometimes may have been added to a text *ad libitum* or for filling up a rhythmic line, the question must be asked, what meaning these words possess in Eph 2:15–16? Paul may have quoted a pre-Pauline hymn precisely because it expressed that concern in Christ's own person and activity which he wanted to make the hinge of the message of Ephesians.

[186] Cf. I Cor 15:20–22, 44–47; Philip 2:6–11; Rom 5:12–21; Col 1:16. Christ himself is "the new man created after God['s image]" which has to be "put on" by the saints, Eph 4:24; Col 3:10; Rom 13:14; cf. Gal 3:27. See also Ign. *Eph.* xx.

[187] Col 1:15, 18; Rom 8:29.

Syrian versions, of Eph 5:30. Or, the words "in his person" might be equivalent to "according to his image" or "in his likeness" (cf. Col 3:10; I Cor 11:7). In either case the creation of a partner of Christ, i.e. of the bride, the Church, would be meant.[188] At other points Paul clearly affirms that the church is formed after the image of Christ and is made to conform with him.[189] Chrysostom teaches that Christ (who became man in order to die for his own people and for the Many) is the prototype of the unity of all men. Augustine's interpretation of John 19:34 has much to recommend it: the opening of the crucified Christ's side and the issue of water and blood alludes to Gen 2:21–22, and depicts the institution of the sacraments and the birth of the church.[190] A corresponding understanding of Eph 2:15 is supported by Eph 5:22–33; it confirms the earlier mentioned doctrinal parallelism between Ephesians and John; and it may resemble the contents of Col 3:10 and other passages (see COMMENT VI A 2–3). But this "plenary" interpretation is not generally accepted though its theological relevance is obvious: it emphasizes the total dependence of the church on Christ and thereby excludes an alleged triumph of ecclesiology over Christology in Ephesians.

3. The difficulties inherent in the two previous expositions are avoided when the translation of en autō in vs. 15 by "in it" (or "in which") is preferred to the version "in him" or "in his person." Indeed the dative of the Greek pronoun autos used here may be neuter rather than masculine, and those copyists of the Ephesian text who changed it to en heautō, "in himself," may have missed its genuine meaning. The thing or event "in which" the new creation took place would then be the "blood" or the "flesh" mentioned in vss. 13 and 14—though these terms are feminine in Greek—or the "one body" or the "cross" (see vs. 16). This way nothing would detract from the Christocentricity of vs. 15, but instead of the whole person of the Messiah, the hour and mode of his death would be mentioned.[191] Except for the fact that the words en autō mean in all other hymnic Christological texts "in Christ," the neuter understanding appears to solve all problems.

4. Another way to an easy solution is the following: the words "in himself," or, "in his own person," are not an indication of where or how the "one new man" was created, but describe the essential condition of newness and oneness. "If any one is in Christ he is a new creation" (II Cor 5:17); "In the Messiah Jesus all of you are one" (Gal 3:26–28). Statements like these show clearly that the one new man created by Christ is not set forth as a reality independent

---

[188] Pius' XII encyclical *Mystici Corporis* called this partner *quasi altera Christi persona*, or *veluti alter Christus*. But the Adam-Eve typology and the application of this typology to marriage in Eph 5 discourages such nomenclature. Eve is not another Adam, a wife not another husband, the creature of Christ not another creator.

[189] Gal 4:19; II Cor 3:18; 4:6; Philip 3:10, 21; Rom 8:29.

[190] Augustine *tractatus in Ioann. ev.* cxx 2. Cf. Tertullian *de anima* 43; *de jejunio* 3. Calvin, on John 19:34, declared that Christ was active when water and blood flowed from his side. A. Loisy, *Le quatrième Évangile*, 2d. ed. (Paris; Nourry, 1921), p. 492, considered the passage a *tableau symbolique* and endorsed its patristic allegorical interpretation. As to the sacramental interpretation of this text see M. Barth, *Die Taufe ein Sakrament?* (EVZ, Zurich: 1951), pp. 407–18.

[191] So, e.g. Schlier. According to Irenaeus *adv. haer.* v 14:4 "someone among the older Fathers" had given this interpretation dramatic concreteness: "By stretching out his arms on the [horizontal beam of the] cross Jesus Christ assembled the two nations to the one God." Should the reconciliation between the half-Jew Herod and the Roman Pilate (Luke 23:12) serve as an illustration of Eph 2:14–16? Hardly! For though it is a reconciliation made on the occasion of Jesus' trial, it is not described as reconciliation with God.

of him. The "one new man" remains "in the Messiah" as much as the body remains dependent upon the head. But though this interpretation makes sense and is well supported by Pauline parallels, it is discouraged by the position of the formula "in himself" in Eph 2:15, also by the parallel statement in 2:16, he killed the enmity "in his person."

The phrase "killing the enmity in his person" (vs. 16) offers problems analogous to those of vs. 15. Again, the translation "in it," this time supported by the previous mention of "one body" and "the cross," would help in avoiding lengthy discussions, but would depart from customary hymnic style. If the version "in him" or "in his own person" is maintained, then the passage speaks of a battle that took place and was decided in the Messiah himself. The "enmity" fought and defeated by Christ is in this case not an external opponent of Christ by which he is never really touched. Rather the battleground is his own person: "enmity" was fighting from within Christ against Christ! In Rom 7:14–25, cf. Gal 5:17, Paul depicts himself or every Christian as such a battleground. The NT references to Jesus' temptation, to his obedience and love, to his grief, his fear, his anticipation of final woes, to his self-delivery, his suffering—these do not resemble the reports about a hero who triumphantly runs his course to an easy victory.[192] In Rom 8:3–4 Paul states most emphatically that the Son sent by God had to perform his ministry and fulfill the requirement of the law "in the likeness of sinful flesh," so that "sin" would be "condemned in the flesh." Not as a superman but subject to the human condition, that is, "in the flesh," the Messiah had to wage his war, to overcome the enemy, and to create peace. There is a warm, passionate, admiring undertone discernible in the words, "he has killed the enmity in his own person." The Messiah who according to Matthew and Mark died in the agony of God-forsakenness and with a loud cry, was according to Paul experiencing in his own person what it means to be "made sin," i.e. to have to bear the weight and consequence of sin, and to be "accursed" (II Cor 5:21; Gal 3:13). While he was slain in person, the Messiah became the slayer of enmity. The two possible interpretations of en autō in 2:15–16, i.e. "in his person" and "on the cross" (or in his death), cannot be considered mutually exclusive alternatives. They must be held together and combined.

But there is still another formula used in Eph 2:16 which may open an additional perspective: "In one single body" the Messiah reconciles Jews and Gentiles to God. At least three interpretations have been offered:

1) This body is the body of Jesus Christ assumed in his conception and birth, suspended on the cross, and after Easter no longer found in a tomb.

2) The term "one single body" denotes the church, Christ's body.[193]

3) Both the physical as well as the so-called "mystical body" are meant, cf. I Cor 12:12–13.[194]

---

[192] See Matt 4; 6:13; 16:22–23; 24; 26:36–46; par.; Luke 22:28; 24:26, 46; Heb 2:18; 4:15; 5:7–8; Gal 1:4; 2:20; Philip 2:8; Rom 5:19; I Peter 2:21; 3:18, etc.

[193] As in Eph 1:23, etc.; I Cor 12:27. The formulation "one body" substitutes for "body of Christ" in Eph 4:4; I Cor 12:13, 20; Rom 12:5.

[194] The first interpretation is found, e.g. in Chrysostom; Theodoret; Bengel; Haupt; P. Feine, TSK 72 (1899), 570–71; Percy, Leib Christi, p. 29; Percy, pp. 280, 284, 289; Cerfaux, Le Christ, pp. 185–86. The second is upheld by Ambrosiaster; Oecumenius; Holtzmann, E. F. Scott; Abbott; Hanson, Unity, pp. 144–46; Masson. The third is Dibelius'; Schlier's; Gaugler's. Calvin assumes that

So far no safe criteria have become visible for making a decision for any of these possibilities. Because of the ambiguity of the words under review they ought not to be used for proving a direct identity of the church with the earthly historical body of Christ. While the connection between both is evident in I Cor 10:16–17 and 12:12–13, 20, 27, the emphasis laid in Ephesians on distinction between head and body, and on the partnership between Christ and his bride, the church, excludes a simple and direct equation.

Still one other exposition deserves mention: Eph 2:16 can be understood as referring to the sacramental presence of Christ's body—either in the Eucharist, or in baptism, or in both. In this case the peace-work of Christ would not be restricted to a past feat completed through his birth or "through the cross." Rather its continuation in the present and future life and worship of the church would be indicated. Several interpreters have indeed not shied away from speaking about an extension of the incarnation.[195] While 2:16 may tolerate such extensive interpretation, this verse is too ambiguous to make it imperative. Most likely the "one body" mentioned here designates the physical body of the Messiah, and more specifically, his crucified body. This interpretation must remain tentative until it is confirmed by the context to be discussed in the next section.

B   Priest and Victim

Just as Eph 1:20–23 is a hymnic praise of Christ's resurrection, so 2:14–18 is a psalm on his death and its effect. The means by which Christ made peace is identified with the price he paid. The instrument and cost of reconciliation is according to 2:13 the "blood," following 2:16, the "cross," in short, the death of the Messiah.[196] However, not all interpreters agree in this understanding of Eph 2. For it is indeed possible to combine the "blood" of vs. 13 with the "flesh" of vs. 14, perhaps also with the "body" mentioned in vs. 16, to bracket out the "cross" as a later (though typically Pauline) addition, and then to state, "blood and flesh" or "blood and body" point either to the incarnation of Christ, i.e. to the physical body of the Messiah, or to the sacrament of the eucharist. At stake is the question whether 2:14–18 proffers a theology of the cross, a theology of incarnation, or a theology of the sacrament. The various accents of these theologies need not be mutually exclusive. All or any two of them may be combined so long as they serve the purpose of extolling Jesus Christ alone and not a miraculous procedure that would shift the person, activity, obedience, and love of the Messiah himself into the background. On which, if any, of the "theologies" does the accent of Eph 2 lie?

If the "blood" in Eph 2:13 and the "cross" in 2:16 are the keys to an au-

---

Eph 2:14–16 is addressed to Jews, and supports a fourth interpretation which avoids the concreteness of the three mentioned: the words "in one body" teach the Jews that only by "practising unity with the Gentiles [believing in Christ the reconciler] can they please God." Though, e.g. Gal 2:11–21 (the account of the Antioch incident and Paul's subsequent speech on justification) prove Calvin's understanding to be genuinely Pauline, it is not a proper interpretation, but a corollary of Eph 2:14–16. For this passage is, as 2:11 and the rest of Ephesians show, addressed to Gentile Christians.

[195] See COMMENT VI on 1:15–23.

[196] Equally in Col 1:22; 2:14–15, not the resurrection but the death of Christ on the cross is described as the moment and means by which reconciliation was made, forgiveness was granted (and the powers were divested of their power).

thentic interpretation of vss. 13–15 then there is only one instrument of pacification, new creation, and reconciliation: the death of Christ. By speaking of Christ's "blood" rather than of his death, the author qualifies Christ's death in an important way[197] in that references to the "blood" of the messiah, i.e. of Jesus (Christ)[198] reveal a sacrificial understanding of Christ's death. In most cases they are found in the Pauline letters wherever the apostle takes up traditional formulations.[199] Paul identified himself fully with this traditional meaning and nomenclature of Christ's death, as shown by at least one unquestionably original Pauline phrase: "Much more we are now justified by his blood and will be saved" (Rom 5:9). While in the traditional formulations, also in Col 2:14, the personal benefit derived from the cross, i.e. forgiveness, stands in the foreground, Eph 2:13–18 stands out by stressing the social effect of Christ's death. Through the cross not only the relationship between God and each man, but also the interrelation between men belonging to different groups is radically changed. There are at least four possible ways of explaining why "blood" is called the means of the admission of the Gentiles to God and to Israel:

1. Spilled blood speaks louder than a voice. If God hears the prayers of oral petition and intercession—how much more does he hear the cry of his beloved Son, the Messiah! Blood augments the urgency of intercession.[200]

2. Blood is poured out in the making of a covenant. Just as the covenant made with Israel on Mount Sinai was sealed by "blood of the covenant," and as the covenant with Abraham was validated by an elaborate ancient sacrificial ceremony, so the "new covenant" that is made with the "Many," i.e. with the Gentiles, is made at the expense of blood. Christ's blood is now "poured out."[201] Blood affirms the establishment of intimate community and the validity of promise and oath given orally during the making of a covenant. According to I Sam 11:7 it reveals the fate threatened to him who acts disloyally. The covenant banquet presupposes that slaughtering has taken place.

3. In older traditions the blood of circumcision and of the passover lamb is credited with the power to ward off destruction. It is a sign of protection. Sometimes its function and effect are equated with those of temple sacrifices. See COMMENT III.

4. Blood is the means of making atonement and of receiving forgiveness. "Under the law almost everything is purified with blood, and without the shedding of blood there is no forgiveness" (Heb 9:22).[202]

[197] See for the following among the more recent exegetical works V. Taylor, *Jesus and His Sacrifice*, London: Macmillan, 1937; C. F. D. Moule, *The Sacrifice of Christ*, Philadelphia: Fortress, 1964. In M. Barth, "Was Christ's Death a Sacrifice?", ScotJT Occasional Papers 9, Edinburgh: Oliver, 1961; idem, *Justification* (Grand Rapids: Eerdmans, 1971), pp. 35–48, more literature is discussed.

[198] Just as the epistle to the Hebrews refers to the "blood of Jesus" and the "blood of the Messiah" without a notable distinction, e.g. 10:19; 9:14, so Paul sees no problem in speaking of the blood of the Messiah. Messiah is a title appropriate to a being that has flesh and blood. A "docetic Messiah" is a contradiction in terms.

[199] I Cor 10:16; 11:25; Rom 3:25; Col 1:20; Eph 1:7.

[200] Gen 4:10; Heb 5:7; 12:24; cf. Matt 27:50; Rom 3:25.

[201] Gen 15; Exod 24:3–11; Zech 9:11; Matt 26:28 par.; I Cor 10:16; 11:25; Heb 9:16–18.

[202] This doctrine has its seat in priestly traditions, e.g. Lev 1:4–5 etc.; 10:17–18; 17:11; Ezek 45:18–20; Eph 1:7; Heb 7–10. Rabbinic utterances stating that all sacrifices, including food offerings, serve for atonement are collected by StB III, 697 ff., esp. 699. Prophetic voices as I Sam 15:22; Hosea 6:6; Ezek 36:25–29; Ps 51, emphasize the purification of the heart by God's Spirit and by obedience, see N. Snaith, *Mercy and Sacrifice*, London: SCM, 1953. In the Epistle to the Hebrews, esp. in 4:14–16; 5:7–10; 10:5–10, the priestly and the prophetic strands are combined

While these four or more cultic functions of the shedding of blood can be discerned in the Bible and may originally reflect diverse religious beliefs, in NT times they cannot always be clearly separated. Nor are they exhaustive. As late as the time of the Maccabees, redemptive power was also attributed to the shedding of the martyrs' blood.[203] Since Eph 2:13-18 does not depict Jesus Christ as martyr, only the sacrificial-cultical meanings of the term "blood" have to be considered: he is the sacrificial victim. But because the verbs used in this context describe an activity of Christ, Christ cannot be understood as the victim only. Nor does his function correspond exactly to the content of Qumran eschatology: there Melchizedek is the prototype of a man who is only priest and ruler. According to Eph 2, Christ is—as the epistle to the Hebrews also brings to light—priest and sacrifice at the same time. Eph 5:2 makes this explicit by reproducing one of those "traditional formulations" which may well have provided inspiration for the contents of Hebrews: "The Messiah . . . has given himself for us as an offering and sacrifice whose fragrance is pleasing to God."

The reference made in 2:14 to the "flesh" of Christ and in 2:16 to "one single body" can serve as a strong support for the sacrificial interpretation of Christ's death, for Paul uses "flesh" and "body" occasionally as interchangeable synonyms.[204] The single nouns "blood," "body" or "flesh," as well as the combined nouns, "blood and flesh," or "blood and body," occur in his writings and elsewhere as designations of Christ's sacrifice.[205] Therefore it is probable that Eph 2 ascribes the making of peace to the sacrifice of Christ.

How can a sacrifice establish peace? Among the various understandings of sacrifice discernible in the OT, there is one which interprets sacrifice as an act of intercession. Isa 53 appears to take up the typology provided by Moses' intercession for the people (after they had worshiped the Golden Calf, Exod 32:30-32) and the long series of prophetic intercessions for Israel. In Isa 53 the prophetic intercession is amalgamated with that of the high priest,[206] and the result is a description of the Servant of the Lord in terms of both prophet

---

and treated as an inseparable whole. It is not the blood of goats and bulls but that of the obedient high priest who brings his offering "through the eternal Spirit," who "purifies the conscience" (9:14). After the destruction of the temple, if not earlier, rabbinical teachers ascribed atoning power to deeds of mercy, study of the law, suffering, repentance, alms-giving, the Day of Atonement, the merits of the fathers. See StB, I, 169, 636 f.; II, 274 ff.; III, 123, 153, 607; IV, 455; Moore, *Judaism* I, 497 ff.; Davies, PRJ, pp. 269 ff., and esp. E Sjöberg, *Gott und der Sünder im palästinischen Judentum*, BWANT 4:27, Stuttgart: Kohlhammer, 1939.

[203] See e.g. II Macc 7:33, 37-38; IV Macc 6:29; 17:21-22; Mark 10:45, and the discussion of the relation between cultic and martyrological ideas in E. Lohse, *Märtyrer und Gottesknecht*, Göttingen: Vandenhoeck, 1955.

[204] Gal 6:17; I Cor 6:16; II Cor 4:10-11; Eph 5:29-31. Cf. Bultmann, ThNT I, 196, 200. The conflation of the two Greek terms may be due to the fact that Hebrew *basar* and Aramaic *gûph* had several meanings and could be translated by either one of the Greek nouns, *sarx*, "flesh," or *sōma*, "body".

[205] "Blood," e.g. Rom 3:25; 5:9; "blood" and "cross," Col 1:20 ("he made peace through the blood of the cross"); "body" and "flesh," Col 1:22 ("he has reconciled you in the body of his flesh through [his] death"); "blood" and "body," I Cor 10:16; "body" and "blood," I Cor 11:24-25; Matt 26:26-28; "flesh" and "blood," John 6:51-58; I John 4:2; 5:6, 8; Heb 10:19-20, etc. Perhaps "flesh" alone (without the addition of "blood") means sacrificial meat in John 1:14, see fn. 218 below. Does "one body" in Eph 2:16 mean just one victim, or, one sacrifice?

[206] The intercessory function of the priest is revealed esp. by the inscription on the priestly garments and by the high priest's office on the Day of Atonement, Exod 28:12, 21, 29-30, 38; 29; Lev 16, but also by the atoning character ascribed to almost every sort of sacrifice, Lev 1 ff.; Ezek 43:20; 45:13-25.

and priest. This Servant is "stricken for the transgression of Israel . . . bears the transgressions of the Many . . . makes himself a sin-offering"; the complete service he renders is finally described as "intercession for transgressors" (Isa 53:8, 10–12). Whereas Moses had *offered* his life to God, and whereas the high priest *risked* his life by bearing the sin of the people inside the Holiest of Holies, the Suffering Servant of Isa 53 is the only person who actually *pays* with his life for the intercession he makes. His death is a "sin-offering" (Isa 53:10). Thus Second Isaiah understands sacrifice as an intercessory prayer. When the LXX in the great majority of cases translates the Hebrew verb "to atone" and the noun "atonement" (*kippēr* and *kippurim*) with the verb *hilasko-mai* and its derivates, it may reveal that the same concept of sacrifice has been endorsed by the translators: peace with God—unlike the pagan "appeasement" of a god or man[207]—is sought by means of "praying-out" the sinners.[208] The seven martyrs described in II Macc "give up body and soul . . . appealing to God to show mercy soon" to their nation (see 7:37–38). Their death is understood as an act of intercession. The martyr Stephen follows their example (Acts 7:60).

A great number of NT passages, e.g. Acts 8:28–35; Rom 4:25,[209] refer to various parts of Isa 53 (52:13 – 53:12) in order to proclaim that Jesus is the one anointed by God, the fulfillment of both the priestly and prophetic offices. In Rom 3:25 Paul, most likely in reference to a traditional formulation, calls Jesus Christ "the expiation"[210] set forth by God "in his [Christ's] blood." In Rom 8:34 the apostle speaks, in terms reminiscent of Heb 7:25, 9:24, of the Messiah Jesus' continued "intercession."[211] Christ is described as a sin-offering in II Cor 5:21. The motive and cost of his intercessory sacrifice are most succinctly expressed in Gal 2:20: "He loved me and gave himself for me." The beneficiaries of Christ's sacrifice are the "godless" and the "sinners" according to Rom 5:6–10. They were justified not by their conversion or their own faith, but "while they were still sinners" Christ died for them. Though they were "enemies" they were reconciled to God.

Ephesians may well contain a summary and application of the Pauline doctrine on the sacrifice of Christ. If so, it points to the mode and effect of Christ's intercession before God on behalf of Jews and Gentiles. In his prayer Jesus Christ was embracing the diverse hostile persons, groups, causes, and conditions. He brought all of them before God—including their common plight, their death in lapses and sins, their hostility against God. The method of unification, pacification, and reconciliation is in this case the prayer of Jesus Christ—a

[207] See the discussion of the difference between propitiation and expiation in C. H. Dodd, *The Bible and the Greeks* (London: Hodder, 1935), pp. 82–95; T. W. Manson, *"Hilasterion,"* JTS 46 (1945), 1–10. The opposite view is represented, e.g. by L. Morris, "The Use of *hilaskesthai* etc. in Biblical Greek," ET 62 (1951), 227–33. Cf. also J. Jeremias, *The Central Message of the New Testament* (New York: Scribner's, 1965), pp. 31–50.

[208] R. K. Yerkes, *Sacrifice in the Greek and Roman Religions and Early Judaism* (London: Black, 1952), pp. 178–82.

[209] See C. H. Dodd, *According to the Scriptures* (New York: Scribner's, 1953), esp. pp. 123–25.

[210] The Greek word used by Paul can be understood as a neuter noun, meaning atonement, or it may mean, as in the LXX, mercy seat, i.e. cover of the ark of the covenant. It can also be a masculine adjective and have the sense of "expiator."

[211] Cf. John 17. Jesus Christ's "standing" position at God's right hand (Acts 7:55) and his titles "advocate" and "faithful witness" (I John 2:1; Rev 1:5; 2:13; 3:14), point out the same function of intercession.

prayer not consisting only of words as found, e.g. in the High Priestly Prayer of John 17 and in some MSS of Luke 23:34, but a prayer, a cry magnified by the voice of "his blood" (Heb 12:24). Peace was made at the price of the Messiah who prayed himself to death. The intercession made by Christ cost him his life.

This understanding of the "blood" and sacrifice of Christ need not rule out what G. Vermes and H. Sahlin have written about the "circumcision of Christ,"[212] but their interpretation is narrower, because it thrives exclusively or primarily on the imagery of circumcision. The link with Isaiah's message is missing which, because of the Isaianic allusions and quotations in Eph 2:13, 17, ought not to be disregarded.

However, an alternative exists which may either call into question or supplement all that has been said so far about Christ's sacrifice. Eph 2:13-18 has sometimes[213] been understood as designating the incarnation rather than the sacrifice of Christ as means of reconciliation. Thomas Aquinas combined both expositions by saying that the "flesh" mentioned in 2:14 might be *caro assumpta* (Rom 8:3), or *caro immolata* (I Cor 10:16). The incarnational interpretation, in turn, permits three variants. Either *only* the miracle of Christmas is put in the foreground; the Logos entering into union with "flesh" and "blood," i.e. with all humanity,[214] has then "made peace"—long before the crucifixion. Or, as earlier mentioned, the real presence of Christ's "body" and "blood" in the eucharist is suggested, with the consequence that unification and pacification are realized by the Lord's Supper or Mass rather than by the faraway events of Bethlehem and Golgotha. Or, the term "one body" in Eph 2:16 is made the crown and criterion of the words "blood," "flesh," "cross," and the mystical body of Christ is denoted as the effective instrument for producing peace and unity. The reference to "access" to God "in one Spirit" (2:18; cf. 3:12), supports the ecclesiastical, if not the sacramental, interpretation.[215]

Since these interpretations are variants of the incarnational exposition, the question is decisive whether "flesh" and "blood" in Eph 2:13-14 refer to the assumption of humanity. Non-Pauline NT statements speak explicitly of the assumption of "flesh," or of "flesh and blood," by the Son of God and ascribe peace on earth and salvation to his very birth and name.[216] Paul probably uses pre-Pauline formulations when he refers to the Messiah's birth "from the seed of David," to the assumption of the "form of a servant," to his "likeness

---

[212] See the end of COMMENT III.   [213] E.g. by Calvin and Robinson.

[214] Calvin: "By investing himself with the nature common to all men, the Son of God consecrated in his body a perfect unity." "Flesh and blood" are, e.g. in Gal 1:16; I Cor 15:50; Heb 2:14; Matt 16:17 a metonym of mankind.

[215] These interpretations are represented esp. in some of the Anglican books listed in BIBLIOGRAPHY 12. A Gnostic background and/or an anti-Gnostic tendency of the term "flesh" are suggested by e.g. E. Käsemann, *Leib und Leib Christi* (Tübingen: Mohr, 1933), pp. 140 ff., and P. Pokorný, ZNW 53 (1962), 182.

[216] "The word became flesh," John 1:14; "Every spirit which confesses that Jesus Christ has come in the flesh is of God," I John 4:2; "Since the children share in flesh and blood, he himself likewise partook of the same . . . He took to himself the lineage [RSV: he is concerned with the descendants] of Abraham," Heb 2:14-16. See Luke 2:1-14 for the connection of the peace message with Jesus' birth, and Matt 1:21 for an etymological interpretation of the name "Jesus." Luke's genealogy of Jesus is traced back beyond the limit of Israel's forefather, Abraham, 3:23-38. The genealogy reproduced by Matthew includes two Gentile-born women, Rahab and Ruth, 1:4-5. Thus Jesus' birth is the result not only of Jewish history but sums up also the connection between Israel and Gentiles.

of men" (Rom 1:3; Philip 2:7). Paul identifies himself fully with these formulations, for also in his own language he emphasizes the meaning of the incarnation in at least two original formulations: "God sent his Son, born from a woman" (Gal 4:4); "God has done what the law weakened by the flesh could not do: He sent his own Son in the likeness of sinful flesh" (Rom 8:3). Paul's critical remark against "knowledge of Christ according to the flesh" (II Cor 5:16) has found a great number of interpretations, but the texts just quoted show that Paul by no means belittles the soteriological and epistemological relevance of the incarnation.

It is difficult, however, to maintain that according to Eph 2 the incarnation rather than the sacrifice of God's Son has effected the peace between Jews and Gentiles as well as between God and man. The incarnational interpretation would mean Eph 2:15 asserts that in Jesus two human natures—the Jewish and the Gentile flesh—were peacefully combined. Thus, in rather an odd way, this verse would become an anticipation of, or a corollary to, the Nicean and Chalcedonian doctrine of Jesus Christ's two natures. Whereas the Ecumenical Council of A.D. 451 confessed that in Jesus Christ's person the divine and the human natures were "unmixedly" but also "inseparably" united, Eph 2:15 would describe a physical union of Jewish and Gentile flesh.

Such a "two human natures doctrine" would form a strange and unique element in the NT. It is certainly not supported by the genealogies composed or transmitted by Matthew and Luke, for though they mention non-Jews or early proselytes among the ancestors of Jesus, their chief interest lies in describing Jesus as the offshoot, representative, and apex of Israel's whole history. This is confirmed by Paul: "According to the flesh" Jesus Christ is the "seed of Abraham" (Gal 3:16), the "son of David" (Rom 1:3), a native "Israelite" (Rom 9:4-5). Though in Isa 45 Cyrus is called God's Anointed, Paul's Christology presupposes and reaffirms the law of Deut 17:15 according to which a foreigner cannot be king of Israel. When Paul called Jesus "the Messiah" he affirmed the expectation of a king born from Israel. Also there is no evidence that the man called "king of the Jews" (Matt 27:38 etc.) was ever considered a half-Jew or half-Gentile as were the Samaritans or Herod the Great. Neither was he ever praised as a true Jew and a true Gentile at the same time, e.g. by analogy with the attributes "very God" and "very man" that were later used in the church's doxology and confession. Certainly Jesus shares, together with all Jews, including Abraham, a Gentile ancestry. But "according to the flesh" he is fully and only a Jew, as several NT texts unambiguously aver: "Our Lord has, as is plain, blossomed up from Judah . . . He has taken on the lineage of Abraham . . . He has been put under the law."[217] The idea of a *tertium genus* of mankind which is neither Jewish nor Gentile, or of an ideal man "beyond" the actual, good or evil, history and sociological conditions of humanity, is not mentioned in Pauline or other NT writings. According to Paul it was the chosen Jew, Jesus, who by his obedience overcame the disobedience of Adam and was established by God as the representative of all men (Rom 1:3, 5:12-21). "Salvation is from the Jews," so the Fourth Gospel affirms on the basis of the fact that "the savior of the world," that is Jesus, is a Jew (John

[217] Heb 7:14; 2:16; Gal 4:4; cf. Matt 1:1-17; Luke 1:5 - 2:80; 3:23-38.

4:9, 22, 42). Because in his authentic letters Paul confirms what appears to have been the conviction of all early Christians, it is unlikely that he himself should in Ephesians attribute the power of reconciliation to the incarnation in Jewish-Gentile flesh. Verse 2:15 is neither clear enough nor sufficient for suggesting a doctrine of two human natures of Christ.

In conclusion, the sacrificial understanding of "blood and flesh" offers the most obvious interpretation of 2:13–18 and is preferable to an incarnational or physical doctrine of atonement which would stipulate a double humanity of Christ and make his sacrificial death a mere corollary to his birth and earthly ministry.[218] It is typical of Paul to concentrate his and his readers' attention upon the cross of Christ rather than upon a mystery of Christ's human body. "We preach Christ crucified" (I Cor 1:23, 2:2).[219] This authentic summary of Paul's message does not contradict the emphasis laid on incarnation in Gal 4:4; Rom 1:3, 8:3; Philip 2:7, but it reveals a distinct accentuation which is probably also present in Eph 2:13–16.

The attempts that have been made to understand the eucharist or the church as the "body" by and in which unity and peace are established are subject to the same criticism as those just raised against the incarnational interpretation. There is also a grammatical argument against such a sacramental and/or ecclesiastical exposition: in 2:13–18 aorist verb forms prevail which usually describe a unique and completed action. The majority of aorists in 2:13 ff. most likely point to a specific and completed event (as, e.g. the incarnation or the crucifixion), rather than to repeated celebrations of the eucharist or the ongoing life and growth of the church. The epistle to the Hebrews states emphatically that Christ's sacrifice is offered "once for good and all" (*hapax* or *ephapax*, 7:27, 9:12, 26–28, 10:2) and requires no re-enactment, repetition or revalidation.

Still, the perfection of Christ's sacrifice does not preclude but establishes Christ's ongoing and eternal intercession (Heb. 7:25, 27). Equally in Eph 2:15, 16, 18 future tenses or meanings of verbal forms make it clear beyond any doubt that the peace work of Christ is not just a matter of the past, and, therefore, over and done with. After the "shedding of his blood" and "the giving of his body" (or "flesh") on a specific day,[220] Jesus Christ continues to make and to proclaim peace. The incarnation and the earthly ministry of Christ are the presupposition of his sacrificial death. Insofar as Eph 2:13–18 includes statements on the instrumental role of the incarnation, it anticipates or duplicates the contents of the four canonical Gospels. For the Gospels as much as Paul see the advent and earthly ministry of Christ as culminating in his cross. There and here, the cross itself is the very moment, means, and cost of peace. The Lord's Supper and the common life of God's people are consequential rather

---

[218] The question may be raised whether John 1:14; I John 4:2 and Heb 2:14 actually celebrate the incarnation rather than Christ's sacrifice. The "flesh" (*sarx*) mentioned in John 1:14 might not only mean "humanity" but also "sacrificial meat"—as indeed it does in John 6:51–56. According to W. Wilkens, *Die Entstehungsgeschichte des vierten Evangeliums*, Zürich: EVZ, 1958, the final redactor of the Gospel gave the *passion* of Christ supreme importance. I John 4:2; if read together with I John 5:6–8, has not only an anti-docetic ring but refutes above all those denying that Christ's death, rather than his baptism alone, brought salvation. In Heb 2:14–16 just as elsewhere in Hebrews, the "death" of Christ is the essential feature of Christ's participation in the "blood and flesh" of the "children."

[219] See fn. 60.   [220] Luke 22:19–20; I Cor 11:24–25; Eph 2:13–14.

than causative instruments of peace. They demonstrate publicly that Jesus Christ is still present to the world and that his work is not only valid but praiseworthy above all other works.

These interpretations are sufficiently strong to throw doubt on one other alternative that has been suggested for understanding Eph 2:14 ff. The supposed elucidation of this text by "Gnostic parallels" operates with the notion of a gigantic cosmic body of the Redeemer.[221] As was shown before, the figure of the Redeemed Redeemer occurs distinctly in the third century A.D. and has forerunners in the second. The pertinent myth includes the salvation of the spirits that were dispersed in the realm of matter and death by their insertion into the Redeemer's body. All those Pauline passages quoted with preference in order to establish the parallelism between the apostle's teaching and those Gnostic notions, speak of baptism: Gal 3:27; I Cor 12:13; Rom 6:3–5. It is assumed that in these texts Paul ascribes justification, or incorporation, or both to baptism.[222] However, it is impossible to make Eph 2:13–18 speak of baptism, for there is no indication that these hymnic words are a *baptismal* instruction, confession or song. As the Ephesian text stands and reads, it does not assert that through baptism the Messiah reconciled Jews and Gentiles to one another and to God. The means of pacification and unification consists solely of the sacrificial death of Christ.

In this section of Ephesians (in contrast, e.g. to Rom 3–5; Gal 3; Philip 3) the Christian's faith is never mentioned. Is faith not an instrument by which Christ's work is done and applied? Indeed, in Ephesians Paul neglects the vital function of faith as little as elsewhere.[223] But the reliance of man upon reconciliation, the loyalty shown to God and man by the united Jews and Gentiles, the common life in faith are according to Ephesians a *result* of Christ's work rather than a *means* of peacemaking. The peace described in Ephesians is a "gift" to "godless . . . sinners" and "enemies" as was already said (see 2:8 and Rom 5:6–10). Christ's peace operates from the cross and through the presence of the Lord in such fashion as to convert the unbelieving sinners, to demand their trust, obedience, compliance, to make them respond by the living holy sacrifice of their own bodies (Rom 12:1–2; Eph 4–6). The effect of peace is not less important than the making of reconciliation, but the result cannot substitute for the price paid. Otherwise the praise due to God and his Messiah would be shifted away from the giver of all good gifts and become a praise of the believers' faith.

[221] H. Hegermann, *Schöpfungsmittler*, p. 153, etc. substitutes proto-Gnostic Jewish elements for the Gnostic Redeemer myth upon which H. Schlier and E. Käsemann rely.

[222] This opinion is questionable. The image of "putting on" used in Gal 3:27 may denote not a mystic union but the taking over of a ministry or office. I Cor 12:13 speaks as little of an immersion or incorporation into Christ's body as a similarly phrased verse: I Cor 10:2 describes an immersion into, or mystical union with, Moses by means of baptism. In the latter case the "liquid" used (for immersion, if such is presupposed) is the sea, in the former, the Spirit. In both cases the liquid or its substitute is distinct from the person or fact proclaimed in "baptism"—from Moses in OT times, from Jesus Christ, the "one body" (12:12), now. The one body is as little formed by baptism as is Moses by the march through the sea. In Rom 6:5 the sudden transition from the aorist tenses of the preceding verbs to the perfect tense, "We have been united with him in a death like his," shows that implantation into Christ and his death precedes baptism. Baptism is denoted as a funeral ("through baptism we are buried") for those who have died before, and are promised life through resurrection. For details see COMMENT V C on 4:17–32, below.

[223] See Eph 1:1, 13, 15, 19; 2:8; 3:12, 17; 4:5, 13; 6:16, 23.

C   Destruction and Construction

Just as God's work is summarily described by the affirmation, "The Lord kills and brings to life" (I Sam 2:6–7), and as Jeremiah's commission is "to pluck up and to break down, to destroy and to overthrow, to build and to plant" (Jer 1:10), so Jesus Christ's peacework is in Eph 2:14–17 described in terms of destruction and construction.

While two utterances concerning destruction, the phrases "he has broken down the dividing wall" and "he has killed the enmity," have already been commented upon, the task remains to discuss the most subversive and revolutionary among the critical statements of Eph 2, the words "he has abolished the law" (2:15). When in COMMENT IV B the possible meanings of the formula, "the law . . . the commandments . . . in statutes" were compared, it became clear that there is a slight possibility of but certainly no overpowering necessity for understanding 2:15 in a subtle or crude antinomian sense. The rest of Ephesians and the Pauline letters offer sufficient evidence for affirming that Paul did not intend to treat Israel's privilege and special inheritance, the law, with contempt. It was far from him to reject God's will as revealed in his law and in the election of Israel.[224] To the contrary, the role ascribed in Eph 2:13–18 to Jesus Christ's priestly and prophetic intercession excludes and prohibits a denial of or contempt for the Law and the Prophets.[225] Jesus is given the OT title Messiah. The true Messiah is distinguished from predecessors and pretenders by the fact that he fulfills the Law and the Prophets. The love shown in his self-offering (5:2, 25; Gal 2:20) is according to Paul the way by which the law is fulfilled and the holy will of God is carried out.[226] Eph 2:15 would flatly contradict Paul's doctrine on Christ and the law, if it intended to assert that Jesus the Messiah had killed and annulled God's holy law. The verb "to abrogate," and that aspect of the law which fell victim to abrogation, do not relegate Moses and the "Books of Moses" into an abyss. As stated earlier, in the epistle to the Hebrews the "antiquation" effected by Christ's ministry concerned only the institution and the repeated sacrifices of the Aaronite priesthood. According to Ephesians only the formerly divisive effect of the law is terminated, which both split Israel as God's clergy (Exod 19:6) from the layman status of the Gentiles, and held those under the law accountable for their disobedience, by demonstrating that they were enemies of God, worthy of

---

[224] Rom 3:2, 31; 9:4; Deut 33:3–4.

[225] For illustration of the opinion refuted here see, e.g. the Luther quotations in fn. 153, but also the change of attitude visible in Schlier. In the first edition of his commentary on Galatians (KEKNT, 7, 10th ed. [1949], 108–12) Schlier arrived at some outright antinomian statements. "For Paul . . . the law is finished with Christ . . . It is not given by God neither by Christ." Just as in Gnosticism, "the Jewish God is one of those angels who stand in opposition to the Father . . . The law does not belong to the revelation of the gracious God . . . it is by no means a gift of God." These extreme statements are toned down in Schlier's re-edition of the Galatians commentary (KEKNT, 7, 13th ed. [1965], esp. the excursus on pp. 176–88," and in his exposition of Ephesians. The following quotes are from Schlier's commentary on Ephesians: One "side of the law" only—that aspect which makes it "appear to be an instrument of the powers and sin"—is destroyed. This "sense" of the law is a result of the "misuse of the Tora" for "casuistic-legalistic" purposes, i.e. for the "grace-less provocation of merit and boasting," (pp. 125–26, 130, 132, 136). The early Schlier was led by the Gnostic parallels to a radicalization of Luther's doctrine on the law; a dualistic, if not Marcionite, trend became visible. In his later commentaries Schlier deviates radically from the Gnostic understanding of law and comes near that of Calvin.

[226] Cf. Robinson, p. 69; see Rom 3:31; 8:3–4; 10:4; 13:8–10; cf. Matt 3:15; 5:17, 43–48; 12:17–21; 22:34–40, etc.

his curse. Eph 2:15 affirms, therefore, that the law has lost its validity as a barrier between insiders and outsiders and as a sentence of death. It need hardly be added that together with these two legitimate temporal functions of God's law, all arbitrary uses of the law are also condemned and abrogated. Eph 2:15 elucidates the words of Eph 2:9, "not [as a reward] for works lest anyone boast about himself." The obnoxious use made of the law by self-righteous braggers of Jewish origin and by their imitators among the Gentiles is declared invalid by the same stroke.

The verbs expressing construction, i.e. "to make one," "to make peace," "to create," "to reconcile," "to come," "to proclaim" (compare "to have access"), do not correspond directly to the terminology of destruction since the reality of the evil that is destroyed does not dictate the mode of salvation. The verbs that describe creation, pacification, and unification prevail over their opposites. Though the good news includes radical crisis and condemnation, the joyful elements of the peace message abound (cf. 1:5, 7, 8; 2:4). In Ephesians (unlike Col 2:20; Rom 6:2; 7:10; Gal 2:19, etc.) it is never stated that Jews or Gentiles "have died . . . ," or "are crucified with Christ"; rather in Ephesians it is presupposed that before Christ's coming both had been "dead in lapses and sins" (2:1, 3, 5). Salutary is only the death of Christ which was voluntarily accepted in his sacrifice on the cross. According to this epistle the "death" of enmity, the overthrowing of the wall, the abrogation of wrath and division cost no one's life except the Messiah's. For the former enemies and sinners themselves there is nothing but gain. They have come from afar and are joined to those near, and now both together have access to God. In the last section of Eph 2:11–22, vss. 20–22, the author will use a terminological anti-type to the imagery of the "broken wall" by speaking of the "building" of the walls of Zion. In all contexts his message to the Ephesians shows much more concern for construction than for destruction.

VI   The Fruit of Peace: the New Man
and the House of God

Paul uses short and precise terms to describe the peace made by Christ: the Messiah "creates a single new man out of two" (2:15). This sentence may not be free of concepts that require careful analysis, yet it is at least as perspicuous as modern utterances on the emergence of a new self-under-standing or the discovery of authentic existence. Paul evokes the image of two former enemies entering the temple together for worship, rather than praise the "warm spirit of fellowship." He talks of the foundation, growth, keystone, and inhabitants of a building and does not recommend in general terms "progress" or "process." If he talks in metaphors his imagery is nevertheless so chosen as to point out clearly the palpable results of peace. He wants to say that Christ's death on the cross was blessed with success. The effect of the cross demonstrates the reality and validity of the peace made. The three key phrases, "one new man," "access to the Father," "dwelling of God" (Eph 2:15, 18, 22) belong together but deserve individual attention. "Access to the Father" means Worship and will be treated under this heading. "The dwelling of God" will be described by reference to the constituent Elements of God's House.

A   One New Man

According to Eph 2:15 Christ "makes peace by creating in his person a single new man out of the two." Possible meanings of the formula "in his person" have been discussed in COMMENT V A. Now the three terms, "by creating," "a single new man," "out of the two," require comment:

1. The pacification carried out by Jesus Christ is an act of creation. This distinguishes it from sheer transformation or improvement, or from the unification of diverse elements by revealing or adding a common feature. Also, Christ does more than set up an ideal and a program valid for all sides. According to the Bible only God can create, and what he creates is totally new. In 3:9 God is denoted as the author of the first creation, in 2:10 he is also the artisan performing the new. In Col 1:16 and in a variant reading of Eph 3:9 Christ is designated as mediator of the (first) creation of heaven and earth. But Eph 2:15 contains a surprising and unique formulation: to Christ is attributed the dignity of "creating." This cannot mean a competition with God; it signifies rather an execution of God's decision—just as in 1:3–23 Christ was called not only the object and beneficiary of God's love and action but also the administrator of God's will and property. Eph 2:14–17 makes explicit an element that was touched upon only slightly in 1:3–10: it emphasizes Christ's own activity. Compare Philip 2:6–11: in his humiliation and death Christ is active, in his exaltation he is described as passive. According to Eph 2:15 he exerts even on the cross a power that is elsewhere attributed to God alone. On the cross the new creation begins. Out of the death of Christ comes new life. What looks like the end is in reality a beginning. According to John 19:34, living and life-giving water, together with the blood ("in which is the life,") miraculously flow from the side of the crucified.[227] Thus Christ on the cross is depicted as the source of life, although no conscious activity is ascribed to him after he has spoken his last words. Paul, however, speaks of the creative activity of the crucified Christ in Eph 2:15.[228] Thus Jesus Christ not only experiences the miracle of transition from death to life (1:20), but also has a causative role in it. He who, according to Col 1:16; John 1:3; Heb 1:3, was the mediator of the first creation, performs and completes the new creation on the cross. A similar double function was, earlier in the Bible, ascribed to Wisdom: it is active not only in the first creation but also in the salvation of man (see COMMENT X on 1:3–14). There is a difference, however: while in the first creation man was the last creature to be formed, in the new creation he is the first. In James 1:18 the church is called "a kind of first fruits of his [God's] creatures." The rest of God's creation is still "waiting for its liberation" from its present "subjection

---

[227] This verse must probably be understood in the light of John 4:14; 7:37–39; 6:53–58; Lev 17:11.
[228] As indeed, according to John too, Christ is not only the "bread of life given" by God to man (6:35), but also the "giver" of that "bread" (6:51).

to futility," according to Rom 8:18–22. Only of men (and not yet of all creatures) is it already true that they are now "in Christ" and, therefore, a "new creation" (II Cor 5:17).

2. The beginning and first fruit of the new creation is called "a single new man" (lit. "one new man"). Translations such as "new humanity,"[229] "new nature,"[230] "new personality"[231] are not to be recommended because they create the impression that out of two (old) *things*, a new *thing* was made.[232] But the text does not describe the creation of a combination of things, e.g. heaven and earth, or the production of a new concept or type of humanity or personality. It speaks only of the creation of a new person, "a single new *man*." The concern for the created new person is equally visible in the formulation of Gal 3:28, "You are all one [person, not thing; the Greek uses the masculine gender!] in Christ." Just as Christ is not a thing or concept but a person, so he creates for himself not an abstraction but a partner. When in I Cor 15:45–47 the work of God the creator is discussed, then Christ is called the last Adam, or the "Second Man."[233] Correspondingly, when in Eph 2:15 Christ is called creator and creates a person, then the term "one new man" must mean a person distinct from Christ. No other person can be meant than the "bride of Christ."[234] While this bride is never explicitly named the New Eve, she is identified as the church in 5:23–32 (cf. II Cor 11:2) or as the people or property of God in 1:14. The concept "new," especially when employed in reference to creation, denotes in the Bible a final fulfillment of God's will and work. It is an eschatological term. The Greek NT uses two terms for denoting newness: *kainos* and *neos*.[235] The word *kainos* which is found in Eph 2:15 is also chosen to describe the "new covenant" in II Cor 3:6, etc., the "new creation" in II Cor 5:17, and the "New Man" in Eph 4:24.

3. The new man is "one . . . out of the two." In Eph 2:5–6 the work of God is described as resurrection of dead people, and such resurrection is,

---

[229] NEB.

[230] So the J. Moffatt and RSV versions of Eph 4:24, etc. Cerfaux, *Le Christ*, pp. 184–85, speaks of "la nature de l'homme chrétien."

[231] According to the interpretations of C. Colpe, "Zur Leib-Christi-Vorstellung im Epheserbrief," BhZNW 26 (1960), 186, and Mussner, CAK, pp. 87, 90, Jews and Gentiles become new individuals.

[232] Schille, *Hymnen*, p. 29, goes to an extreme when (on the basis of the cosmic-mythological background of the Christ hymn, which is supposedly revealed by the neuter "both" in 2:14) he asserts: "Being reunited, the cosmos is the new man." Gal 6:15; II Cor 5:17; Rom 8:19–23; James 1:18 suggest the opposite: the new man is the beginning of the new creation, not vice versa.

[233] E. F. Scott uses the First-Second Adam typology for explaining Eph 2:15. Cf. also J. Coutts, "The relationship of Ephesians and Colossians," NTS 4 (1957–58), 205. For rabbinic parallels see, e.g. Davies, PRJ, pp. 36–57.

[234] "When Christ died the Church was created," says Augustine *hom. in Ps.* 128, 11; cf. Augustine's allegory of the creation of Eve while Adam sleeps, *hom. in Ioann.* IX 10; XV 8. This exposition was earlier suggested as the second alternative for explaining the words "Christ created in himself," see COMMENT V A. In principle, Thomas Aquinas taught that Christ himself was the "new man," and below, in COMMENT V A on 4:17–32, much will be said in favor of his interpretation, esp. in regard to 4:24. But in commenting upon 2:15 Thomas made reference to Jer 31:22, "The Lord has created a new thing on earth: a woman shall compass a man." According to the Encyclical *Mystici corporis*, the "new man" of Eph 2:15 is the church.

[235] See R. A. Harrisville, "The Concept of Newness," JBL 74 (1955), 69–79; idem, *The Concept of Newness in the New Testament*, Minneapolis: Augsburg, 1960. The first term is often used to denote qualitative newness, the second for a temporal innovation. However, passages such as I Cor 5:7; Col 3:10 reveal that both terms could be used as synonyms. Cf. the equivalent use of the two verbs meaning "to renew" (*ananeoō* and *anakainoō*) in Eph 4:23 and Col 3:10 (Rom 12:2; II Cor 4:16).

e.g. in Rom 4:17, considered a synonym for "calling non-being into being." Yet in Eph 2:15 the creator work of Jesus Christ is not designated as a *creatio ex nihilo,* because the Son of God makes use of material for the creation of the "new man." The matter out of which he creates the new man consists of Jews and Gentiles who had both been "dead in sins" and "hostile" to one another and to God. Thus the new creation is not an annihilation or replacement of the first creation but the glorification of God's work. "By grace you are saved" 2:8. The identity of the savior and bringer of peace with the creator had been emphasized especially by Second Isaiah.[236]

Among the NT books Ephesians alone calls God's covenant partner "one new man" and emphasizes that this man consists of two, that is, of Jews and Gentiles. Why are these "two" given so much weight when a reference to the totality of mankind, to the sum of all individuals, or to each single person one by one, would seem to be much more appropriate? In COMMENT V A it was observed that the incorporation of the Gentiles into Israel and the formation of one people consisting of Jews and Gentiles certainly does not mean that the Gentiles must become Jews, or the Jews Gentiles! If the Jews become "like" the others, and the Gentiles "like" the Jews (Gal 4:12)— because both live from grace alone—then the Jews are yet not paganized, and the Gentiles not "forced to judaize" (Gal 2:14) in order to be "one in Christ." Their historic distinction remains true and recognized even within their communion. According to Paul, the first may continue to observe the law as long as it is not used for a hostile division or imposition (I Cor 9:20, etc.). The Gentiles need not be forced under its "yoke"—as Paul untiringly stressed, and as Peter pointed out according to Acts 15:10. Eph 2:15 proclaims that the people of God is different from a syncretistic mixture of Jewish and Gentile elements. The members of the church are not so equalized, leveled down, or straitjacketed in a uniform as to form a *genus tertium*[237] that would be different from both Jews and Gentiles. Rather the church consists of Jews and Gentiles reconciled to one another by the Messiah who has come and has died for both. The "one new man" is by origin and constitution a community of several persons. He is not an individual, or a conglomeration of identical individuals. He is an organic body consisting of distinct members, not an amalgamation;[238] a social structure, not a shapeless mass; a continuous mutual encounter, exchange, bewildering or joyful surprise of free persons, not a boring equalitarian collective. The existence of this man is based upon liberation from deadly nationalism, religious conceit, and individualism—and upon resurrection to social behavior. Jews and Gentiles alike enjoy this liberation and resurrection in the church.

The composition of the "new man out of the two" safeguards the rights of Christians to be different from one another, to "remember" (2:11) their distinct histories, to respect priorities (Rom 3:1–2, 9:4–5), to enjoy unity in diversity

---

[236] 44:21–24; 45:7–8; 51:4–6, 9–16.

[237] See A. Harnack, *The Expansion of Christianity in the First Three Centuries,* I, (New York: Putnam, 1904), 300–52 for the use of this term by the church fathers and the reaction of their opponents. Only in I Cor 10:32 does Paul divide mankind into three groups: "Jews, Greeks and the church of God." That Christ himself is not a *genus tertium* of humanity was shown in COMMENT V B.

[238] Cf. Robinson, p. 65.

(I Cor 12; Eph 4:7, 11–12, 16). The same composition also prevents the saints from imposing the privileges or preferences of one group upon the other; it creates true tolerance. Above all, the joining of "the two" into "one new" whole reveals that neither of the two can possess salvation, peace, life without the other. Jews need Gentiles, Gentiles need Jews, man needs fellow man, if he will be saved at all. Under the rule of Christ no one "comes into heaven" except in the company of fellow men: "He [God] has in the Messiah Jesus raised and enthroned us together in the heavens" (Eph 2:6). If we were enthroned exclusively "with" the Messiah, one's fellow man might be dispensable for salvation. But "in the Messiah" and under his rule, there is no resurrection and ascension except together with one's neighbor.[239]

Is it just the like-minded, sympathetic, peaceful, believing fellow man who is given such great importance? According to Matt 5:23–24, Jesus taught that in the kingdom of God reconciliation with the neighbor "who has something against you" precedes the offering in the temple from which God's peace is expected. Love of "the enemy" is enjoined upon the disciples in Matt 5:43–48. Following Matt 6:12, 14–15, mutual forgiveness is the measure of the forgiveness granted by the heavenly Father. The parable of the Prodigal Son (Luke 15: 11–32), as much as the report on the table communion at Antioch (Gal 2:11–14), makes it clear that full communion with the Father or Lord is possible only when the hostility between older and younger brother, i.e. the segregation between Jews and Gentiles, is terminated. Eph 2 contains the same message. There is no salvation of individual souls except in the community of those confessing, "by grace" we have been "saved" (2:5, 8). There is no ideal of a Christian personality applicable to all church members alike, but there are men, women, children who because of their diverse origins, pasts, privileges, hopes, or despairs are by nature inclined to hate one another and God (Rom 5:6–10). Now they are enabled by the work and rule of Christ to contribute in common repentance and common faith their various idiosyncrasies, histories, experiences, and gifts to the peaceful common life of God's people. Later sections of Ephesians will show that this concerns not only the Jewish or Gentile provenance of the saints but also their differences in sex, age, and socioeconomic standing.

Thus the "one new man" is created to be a social being. New existence is social existence. This does not mean, however, that fellow man and the love of man replace God. The new man is still and remains totally dependent upon God. The beloved fellow man can by no means replace God and the worship of God, as is to be shown in the next paragraphs.

B Worship

All that is said about peace in Eph 2:14–17 is introduced and concluded with two sentences which speak about worship, in vss. 13 and 18. The man who is

---

[239] While, according to the Gospels, Jesus taught that the whole law is summed up in the commandments to love God and one's neighbor (Matt 22:37–40), Paul dares to sum up the same law by quoting Lev 19:18 only, i.e. by the commandment of love for one's neighbor (Rom 13:8–10; Gal 5:14). This way he states in ethical terms what is kerygmatically proclaimed in Eph 2. Without love of one's neighbor there is no love of God; cf. I John. H. von Soden's interpretation, according to which the peace between Jews and Gentiles is the central message of Eph 2:13 ff., is therefore still preferable to P. Feine's opinion. Feine followed Theodoret in saying that peace with God holds the prior rank and that peace among men is "an after-thought or consequence" (TSK 72 [1899] 540–74, esp. 549, 562, 570).

"brought near" (vs. 13) is a "foreigner who is not of the people Israel" but comes from a far country in order to "pray toward this house" (the temple) and to be "heard in heaven" (I Kings 8:41–43). The convention of those far with those near is an assembly for worship. Whereas the ancient oracle of Gen 9:27 does not state what Japheth would do once he "dwelled in the tents of Shem," the more classic OT texts describing the access of the nations announce and promise that they come to worship in Zion, i.e. to bring their gifts, to pray to the Lord, to receive God's instruction, to know him and to praise the glorification of Israel, to recognize that "the Lord is one and his name one."[240] In Eph 2:18 the effect of the peace made by Christ is summed up by the description of the "access" which Jews and Gentiles have together, "in one single Spirit . . . to the Father." The word "access" and the reference to the "Spirit" specifically suit a description of worship.

Verses 13 and 18 are not the only ones that contain terms denoting liturgical assembly. The centerpiece of the whole section, i.e. vss. 14–17, attributes the making of peace to an act of worship: Jesus Christ is high priest and victim at the same time, who by his intercession has joined Jews and Gentiles together in order to plead for them. The political, legal, and sociological terminology of Eph 2:11 ff. is, therefore, complemented by a cultic diction. Without Christ's mediation in the offering of his "blood" and "flesh" and in the peace blessing pronounced by him, there would be no political, legal, and social peace. This peace does not make superfluous the worship of God. Rather worship is the tangible result of peace, the sign of its presence, its confirmation and attestation. Rom 12:1 calls this worship "spiritual" (lit. "logical"). John 4:24 speaks of a worship in Spirit and in truth. It requires the "living sacrifice" of the saints in which they manifest that they belong to God. Similarly I Peter 2:5 mentions a "spiritual sacrifice," and Heb 13:15 specifies that such sacrifice consists of praise given to God in every possible form, specifically in oral confession.

When Jews and Gentiles worship God together, then it is because of the office fulfilled by Christ and the peace made by him: "Through him and in one single Spirit, the two [of us] have free access to the Father" (Eph 2:18). But has not Christ's own completed act of worship, his sacrifice upon Calvary, yielded so full a blessing that there is no need for further acts of worship? Are there only two choices left: i.e. either to maintain a minimum of cultic forms, with the understanding that they are post-Christian, uninspired and uninspiring; or to abandon all formal assemblies in God's name and advise the believers to concentrate upon necessary social work and other acts of brotherly love? Eph 2:18 answers the dilemma by stating that Christ is still the mediator of access to God. Equally, the Spirit must still be active if worship and sacrifice are to be spiritual rather than in the flesh. The proclamation of peace by Christ himself has to be continued lest the saints be led back to trust other officiants, and fall victim to new hostilities or pseudo-peaces. Therefore it is necessary that worship be continued in orderly fashion (cf. I Cor 14:40).

The worship of the church, described in terms of Eph 2:13–18, is this: Jesus Christ is the sole officiant. His death is the one sacrifice, in Christian terminol-

---

[240] Isa 2:2–4; 25:6–9; 55:5; 56:6–8; Micah 4:1–4; also Jer 3:17; Zech 2:10–12; 8:20–23; 14:9; Pss 48; 96:7–13; 100, etc.

ogy, the sole "sacrament," which in eternity and in time is instituted by God, accepted by God, blessed with the presence of God and with the salvation granted to the people. This sacrament gathers, forms, purifies, builds, instructs, seals, and proclaims. It is the one necessary and truly "effective sign," valid as it were *ex opere operato*. Around this sacrifice in which Christ the priest offers himself as victim to God, the one people of God is gathered. This people is manifested in the many congregations that meet at many places on earth. Compared with Christ all church members are but laymen.[241] Since Christ's sacrifice is perfect there is no need to repeat, to re-enact, or to represent him and his death;[242] rather he urges the saints in their words, deeds, and suffering to remember, proclaim, and praise God and his gift in word and deed and suffering. Therefore they participate in his worship by praying, by proclaiming his word, by intercession and mutual edification, by acts of love, and by a life that is recognizable as a praise of God among both believers and unbelievers. There is no place left for special servants who claim for themselves alone the rights or duties of priests. The special ministers who are given to the church by the risen Christ bear secular titles and do not form a clergy inside or over against the assembled saints.[243] What is more, all worshipers, whether of Jewish or Gentile origin, are "saints," i.e. they are given a priestly ministry to be exercised in and toward the world. The witness they give is dependent upon the witness they receive. By being present in the Spirit, by pouring out God's Spirit, and by communicating spiritual gifts, Jesus Christ makes the worship a sequence of appeal and response, of repentance and celebration, of concentration upon the center and of active responsibility for all men. Prayer, preaching, baptism, eucharist, mutual love and missionary zeal, suffering with, and comforting of, individuals and the whole congregation, have outstanding places in this worship. While the respect due to the Father in heaven will evoke and recommend certain forms of worship, the rights and joys given to the saints inspire them to act as free children do.[244] In such worship spontaneous outbursts of love and passion are by no means discouraged.

A similar vision of the church's worship is suggested by the epistle to the Hebrews,[245] but Ephesians combines with the concern of Hebrews the message of Matt 5:23–24; 6:6, 8, 12, 14; 25:31–46 and Luke 15:25–32: every man's cultic act in the temple is to be preceded by reconciliation with his hostile brother. Mutual forgiveness is inseparable from man's prayer for God's forgiveness. The confession of the Lord makes sense only when the least of his brethren are accepted. Unless the older brother of the Prodigal Son participates in the celebration in the Father's house, the assembly at the festival table is incomplete. Only together, in communion with former enemies, do the saints ap-

---

[241] For an opposite view regarding the nature of worship, church, ministry, see e.g. I Clem. 40 ff. In this document, which became decisive for the development of church order and liturgy after ca. A.D. 100, the repetition of sacrifices and the distinction of clergy and laity in the church are clearly demanded. In COMMENT VI on 4:1–16 the clergy-laity issue will be further discussed.

[242] Heb 13:10–16 adds two essential points: since there is "an altar" unlike the altars from which OT people received their sacrificial meals, there is no need to build and to use any other altars. Since Christ suffered "outside the gate" and "the camp" there is reason to follow him on his way of suffering in the world rather than in a sanctuary.

[243] They are called "apostles," "prophets," "evangelists," "shepherds," "teachers" (4:11). Only the title "prophet" has a partly cultic background.

[244] Cf. the NOTE on "made heirs" in 1:11; also 2:7; 3:10; Rom 8; *passim*.

[245] Esp. 4:14–16; 7–10; 12:18–28.

proach the Father under Christ's leadership (Eph 2:18). The tone in which this result of the Messianic peace is proclaimed is far from legalistic. It rings with joy and triumph: "We have free access to the Father . . . You are members of the household of God" (2:18–19).

C The Elements of God's House

In the NOTES on 2:19–22 attention was drawn to the fact that a change occurs in the use of the same image. First the Gentiles are reminded that they are received into the house of God, the community of Israel. Then the same Gentiles are reminded of the presupposition, test, and climax of their assembly in God's house: God himself will dwell in his house! First the house appeared to be ages old and complete with only Israel as its inhabitant; nevertheless, it was described as sufficiently open and wide to include the nations too (2:19). Now the foundations of the house are understood to be as recent and new as the apostles and prophets; it is presupposed that the house is unfinished, still growing toward a keystone, and still waiting for God to grace it with his presence. The transition from one concept of "house" to the other contains a double-edged warning: Jews cannot complacently claim that the house is theirs alone; Gentiles cannot presume that their arrival requires the building of a new house or an automatic completion and perfection of the old one.

In 2:20–22 three decisive parts of the building are mentioned. Since each one of them serves as a metaphor for the place and function of specific *persons,* it is clear that the whole building and each of its parts consist of persons rather than things or ideas. The "foundation" is distinguished from a "stone" placed in a key position, and "the whole construction" cannot stand and grow without the foundation and the special stone. It is now to be asked, who are the persons serving as the foundation? What is meant by calling the Messiah Jesus a "stone"? And why should all the saints understand themselves as stones joined together in one building? After these questions are answered, the next COMMENT will consider in detail the utterances of vss. 20–22 on the destiny and the growth of the building.

1. "Upon the foundation of the apostles and prophets." The titles "apostle" and "prophet" occur in the NT with both wide and narrow meanings. Sometimes the term "apostle" is filled with connotations of special election and authority; in these cases it is restricted to the twelve disciples of Jesus and Paul. On other occasions it is used in a wider sense: every witness of the resurrected Christ and anyone delegated by a church for mission work can bear the same title.[246] Most frequently the "prophets" mentioned in the NT are the well-known OT servants of God, including Moses and David. But this nomenclature is not strict. A wider meaning of "prophet" is apparent when certain charismatic figures in the early congregations are called by the same name.[247] In I Cor 12:28–29 apostles and prophets are mentioned in one breath. There "apostles" in the narrower and "prophets" in the wider NT sense are probably

---

[246] Matt 10:1–5, etc.; Gal 1:1, 17, 19; I Cor 9:1–2; 15:7; II Cor 8:23, etc. See the literature mentioned in the NOTE on 1:1; also Percy, pp. 328–42, 348.
[247] I Cor 12:10, 28–29; 14; cf. Rom 12:6; Acts 11:27; 13:1; 15:32; 21:10; Rev 16:6; 18:20, 24; 22:6, 9; *Did.* XI 3 ff.; XIII 1; XV 1–2.

meant (cf. 9:1–2, 14, 29, 32, 37). The same is true of Eph 3:5; apostles and prophets are the recipients of the revelation that was not given before the time of the Messiah's coming. Three facts make it plausible that Eph 2:20, too, speaks of prophets in the wider, and of apostles in the narrower meaning of the term: (a) the single article before the formula "apostles and prophets"; (b) the placing of "prophets" after "apostles"; (c) the contents of Eph 3:5, 4:11 and I Cor 12:28–29.

However, the recognition of these facts contradicts or complements another time-honored interpretation of Eph 2:20.[248] Based upon the assumption that this verse as much as Rom 1:1–3 connects the NT apostolate with the OT prophets, it was taught that the Old and New Testaments are the church's foundation; that these two parts of the church's Bible stand in perfect harmony; that the Christian religion is not an innovation but is as old as the world;[249] that there is no faith, and no progress in knowledge of God and his will, no criterion of faith and conduct except upon the sole ground of the Bible. Together with this exposition of Eph 2:20 went, if necessary, an anti-Marcionite thrust: Jesus Christ is confessed only when the Father is honored with him, the Father who created heaven and earth, who elected Israel, and who gave her the covenant and the law. There are abundant biblical passages in both the OT and NT which support this understanding. As shown earlier, the epistle to the Ephesians especially emphasizes the close tie between Israel and the church and makes intensive use of Israel's Bible. At the same time, 2:20 may add and emphasize something else that is worthy of attention.

It may be that only NT prophets and apostles are meant, i.e. men witnessing explicitly to Jesus Christ. If so, this verse is not only a restatement of the previously disclosed unification of Israel and the church, or of Jew and Gentile, but also a reference to the "proclamation" of peace mentioned in 2:17. The action of ongoing proclamation, called by Thomas and Calvin (ad loc.) the "doctrine," is then the foundation of the church. In 2:17 Christ was praised as the epitome of a harbinger of peace. In 2:20 those people may be mentioned who serve him and all mankind by taking up and continuing the same proclamation. In them the Spirit of Christ is at work. As I Cor 2:9–16 shows, God inspires them first—but not only them. While apostles preach and prophets prophesy, the Spirit is given to the listeners, too.[250] Thus the access to the Father which the congregation enjoys "in one Spirit" (2:18) occurs on the ground of the inspired proclamation of the "saving word of truth" (1:13) and of the inspiration of those who hear the word of peace with wisdom and understanding (1:17–18). A third fundamental feature of their access is the inspired response by hymns (5:18–20). In conclusion, the very essence of the church, which is the inspired perception of the word and the equally inspired response to it, rests upon the foundation of the inspired proclamation made by apostles and prophets.[251] Most likely the term "foundation" in 2:20 is more fully explicated by 4:7, 11; 6:19–

---

[248] See e.g. Theodore of Mopsuestia; Pelagius; J. Huby; P. Benoit; C. Masson; Ph. Vielhauer, *Oikodome*, pp. 126–27; Schlier; JB; against Origen; Chrysostom; Ambrosiaster; and others.

[249] E.g. as old as the first prophecy, i.e. the protevangel Gen 3:15.

[250] See also Gal 3:1–5; I Cor 12; 14; II Cor 3:17–18; Acts 10:34–47; John 14:16–17, 26; Matt 16:17.

[251] Evangelists and teaching shepherds are added to them in Eph 4:11.

20, i.e. by those verses in Ephesians that speak of the preaching, exhorting and warning activity of the spokesmen of God assigned to the church by Christ.[252]

The persons mentioned in 2:20a stand in this case for the function which they fulfill. Indeed, the ground upon which the church stands and relies is not the individual character of specifically outstanding apostles and prophets, their possible virtues, their persons, or their bodies (not to speak of their bones and other relics), their doctrine qua system, or their literary opus and bequest. If it were so the church would be built upon something in the past which survives up to the present in a sometimes deteriorated form. But in 4:7–13 it is presupposed that apostles and prophets are alive and at work—not because of their literary products and not in the sweet or bitter memory of later generations, but in person. The proclamation, witness, and confession for which they stand—this is the foundation of the church.[253]

The spirited, authorized, and living witness of such men keeps the church erect. The church is constituted to live from an event, i.e. from the gift of witnesses given to her by God. Doctrines, systems, and books might petrify or become incomprehensible; alone they cannot support the church though they have a necessary function to fulfill. It is the *viva vox* of the gospel as proclaimed by apostolic and prophetic figures from which the church receives stability and on which she grows. "Apostles" have been privileged to see the resurrected Christ and receive their commission from him directly. They proclaim the crucified and risen Lord and demonstrate the power he exerts. "Prophets" have the special gift of speaking to the present situation, sometimes by pointing to the near or far future. Both in their own way proclaim the *presence* of the Lord who has come and will come. The church can neither be saved, nor live, nor grow steadily without hearing their "saving word of truth" (1:13).

Since the function of "apostles and prophets" possesses this dynamic character it is devious to argue that the author of Ephesians eyes those men, as it were, from a remote distance. By calling them "the foundation" he does not depict them as people safely buried underground, surviving only in their literary products or in fading memories, and present only in their tombs, e.g. in the form of relics beneath altars.

Three things forbid ascribing Eph 2:20 (and consequently the whole of Ephesians) to the post-apostolic age: (a) Eph 4:7–12 would be meaningless if apostles and prophets were no longer "given" i.e. if they were no longer present and active in the congregation. (b) The man who wrote about living apostles in I Cor 12:28–29 and Rom 16:7 could also have easily written or dictated Eph 2:20.[254] (c) In the subapostolic age "the twelve (apostles)" rather than both "apostles

---

[252] In the case of "apostles," the writing may also be included; compare the activity of the authors of the canonical Gospels.

[253] Similarly in Rom 15:20 the preaching of Christ is called a foundation, though in this verse Paul speaks of one phase of missionary work rather than of the foundation of the church. Cf. the role of Peter's confession in his appointment as the "Rock" on which the Messiah will build his church (Matt 16:16–19). Meuzelaar, *Der Leib des Messias*, pp. 127–30, has collected an impressive array of Pauline and rabbinical passages in which "building is obviously a designation of speaking. . . . In principle there is no difference between the word of the apostles and the word of the members of the congregation. Except there is one difference: the preaching of the apostles and prophets is fundamental while the members of the congregation continue to build on the ground which the apostles and prophets have laid (I Cor 3:10; Rom 15:20; Eph 2:20)."

[254] Cf. Percy, pp. 333–42.

and prophets" would have been called the greatest authorities after Christ. Prophets were no longer highly esteemed—except among some groups that became heretical.[255] Just as Deut 18:15, 18 promised that Israel would again be given a "prophet," so the author of Ephesians cannot imagine the church living on solid ground without the service of "prophets."

2. "The keystone being the Messiah Jesus himself." The better known version "cornerstone" is upheld by the majority of translators and expositors. A reference to the cornerstone appears indeed to complement beautifully the preceding mention of the "foundation." Does not a cornerstone hold two walls together, that is, in the imagery of Eph 2, e.g. Jews and Gentiles, OT and NT, or promise and fulfillment?[256] Or does it possess a commemorative or magic function? In Ephesians its role and purpose are not spelled out. Certainly LXX Isa 28:16 uses the same term as Eph 2:20 for designating a stone laid in Zion "for a foundation." Ps 118[LXX 117]:22 speaks of a stone that was rejected by the builders but was made, as the Greek version puts it, "the head of the corner." In the Gospels this passage is quoted to illustrate Jesus' rejection by his own people.[257] Finally, Isa 8:14 mentions a stone which is set as "a trap and a snare" for Jerusalem's inhabitants; this stone is not explicitly connected with a "corner" but is presumably placed in or on the ground—otherwise it would not make people "stumble." References to "faith" are connected with the mention of the "stone" in Isa 8:14 and 28:16. These OT texts may have been combined in an early Christian collection of *testimonia*.[258] Certainly in Rom 9:32–33 (cf. 10–11) the first two, and in I Peter 2:4, 6–8 all three OT passages have been conflated. Since there is sufficient evidence that an early Christian exegetical tradition considered Christ the stone to be stumbled upon and rejected by men, but finally used by God as a firm foundation in Zion and a criterion of faith, it is possible that Eph 2:20 affirms the same: Jesus Christ is the cornerstone laid by God. These arguments for the traditional version are certainly strong.

But in a series of essays J. Jeremias has proposed an alternative:[259] the stone

---

[255] Cf. Gaugler. In *Did.* XI apostles and prophets are still mentioned together; according to J. P. Audet, *La Didaché*, Paris; Gabalda, 1958 (cf. idem, "Affinités littéraires et doctrinales du Manuel de Discipline," RB 59 [1952], 218–38; 60 [1953], 41–82) this document is older than the latest books of the NT (and to be dated ca. A.D. 75?). In Rev 18:20; 21:14; 22:6–7 prophets appear to be the successors of the passed-away apostles, cf. P. Vielhauer, RGG, V, 634. Polyc. *Phil.* VI 3 may not be the first writer who uses the term "prophet" for the OT men only. Warnings of fear of false prophets are expressed already in Matt 24:24. Herm. *mand.* XI, also Justin Martyr *dial.* 35:3; 51:2; 69:1; 82:1–2 give criteria to recognize them. If Ephesians were subapostolic and intended to defend the established church, it might well have fought foretastes of Montanism. By dropping rather than by making references to the vital role of "prophets" in the church, this purpose could have been achieved.

[256] See, e.g. Theodoret; Jerome; Thomas Aquinas; Calvin. Abbot calls this interpretation an "undue" and "unsuitable" pressing of the image: "Jews and Gentiles are now indifferently built into one building, not as if the Jews were one wall and the Gentiles another." Indeed, at least *four* cornerstones or complete corners of the building ought to be mentioned, if the idea of "holding together walls" were expressed at all.

[257] Matt 21:42; Mark 12:10; Luke 20:17; Acts 4:11.

[258] F. C. Burkitt, *The Gospel History and its Transmission* (Edinburgh: Clark, 1906), p. 126; J. R. Harris, *Testimonies*, 2 vols., Cambridge University Press, 1916, 1920; and C. H. Dodd, *According to the Scriptures* (New York: Scribner's, 1953), pp. 28–60, have developed the *testimonia* theory. They assume that before the writing of the NT books, Messianic and other OT texts were collected by Christian teachers. Such a collection or collections would as a literary genre resemble 4QTest; see J. M. Allegro, "Further Messianic References in the Qumran Literature," JBL 75 (1956), 174–87.

[259] "Der Eckstein," Angelos 1 (1925), 65–70; "*Kephalē gōniās—Akrogōniaios*," ZNW 29 (1930), 264–80; "Eckstein-Schlussstein," ZNW 36 (1937), 154–57; see also TWNTE I, 791–93; IV, 274–75. Among those accepting his view are Vielhauer, *Oikodome*, p. 127; Hanson, *Unity*, p. 131; Best,

in question is a keystone, i.e. the stone used to top an arch.[260] The following arguments support his thesis. The Greek word used in Eph 2:20 to designate the chief stone, *akrogōniaios,* is originally an adjective, not a noun. Etymologically explained it means "the one on the high corner."[261] The LXX, I Peter 2:6, and variant readings of Eph 2:20 add the noun "stone" to this word and thereby acknowledge its adjectival character. The LXX texts of Ps 118[117]:22; Isa 8:14; 28:16; also I Peter 2:6, reveal clearly that the "high-cornerstone" is considered part of the foundation. But the evidence for equating what is called a high-cornerstone in Eph 2:20 with a foundation-cornerstone has limits. It is supported only by the MT and LXX texts of Isa 28:16 and their early Christian interpretation.[262] The Peshitta version of Isa 28:16 speaks about the "head of the wall" and thereby brings this text into harmony with MT Ps 118:22 where a "pillar's head" is mentioned. Symmachus' OT mentions repeatedly the headpiece of a column.[263] A Jewish synagogal prayer mentions a keystone: i.e. the "precious cornerstone of the gates of Jerusalem."[264] Zech 4:7 speaks of the removal of a keystone,[265] and Zech 4:9 states that Zerubbabel has not only laid the foundation of the temple but will finish the building with his own hands, i.e. probably by the insertion of the keystone (cf. MT Zech 10:4). Several of the church fathers have indeed called Christ the "cornerstone at the head which supports all" or described him in similar terms.[266] The evidence brought forth by J. Jeremias against the traditional interpretation is impressive.

Further alternatives would identify the "stone" in question not just with one specific stone but with an outstandingly high corner or pinnacle of the temple,

---

One Body, pp. 155–56; Schlier; Beare. Among the outspoken opponents are Percy, pp. 330–32, 485–88; Masson; Mussner, CAK, pp. 108–9; R. J. McKelvey, "Christ the Cornerstone," NTS 8 (1962), 352–59; idem, *The New Temple,* pp. 114–15, 195–204.

[260] Whether the arch ought to be imagined as two- or three-dimensional cannot be decided. The keystone may be the top of an arched gate and carry the roof beam. It may also be the crown and centerpiece of a vaulted ceiling (cf. the cupola in the Herodium south of Jerusalem and the roof put upon the Pantheon in Rome by emperor Hadrian.) Whether or not the architect uses ribs or girders for the construction of a vault, the keystone bears all the pressure of the stones forming the arch. Its removal can cause the collapse of the whole. Jeremias (Angelos 1 [1925], 69) adds, however, a wise *caveat* to his thesis: vaulted temple buildings dating from Paul's time have not yet been found.

[261] In Ps 118:22 this stone is called "head of the corner" (*rōsh pinnā*); the LXX and NT versions use a Greek equivalent which resembles the etymological meaning of the word used in Eph 2:20.

[262] See also the variant readings of Eph 2:20; Morgenthaler, *Statistik,* p. 70; LSLex, p. 56. Robinson, p. 69, remarks that the cornerstone played no special role in Greek architecture as indeed there appears to exist no Greek *terminus technicus* for describing it. Oriental builders, e.g. Herod the Great, used cornerstones of exceptional size as parts of the walls. They were met at the corners by similar stones, and were therefore not entirely unique in a building. Perhaps they might be labelled *primi inter pares.*

[263] I Kings 7:20; II Kings 25:17; Jer 52:22; cf. Syro-Hexapla II Kings 25:17.

[264] 13 Keroba for the 9th of Ab.

[265] Perhaps the recovery of the former temple's keystone from the rubble of the temple ruins is meant; see JB note. If the removal of the keystone from its place in a complete building were in question, the metaphor would point to the destruction either of a pagan or of the pre-exilic (?) temple.

[266] Tertullian *adv. Marc.* III 7; Aphraates, see Jeremias, ZNW 29 (1930), 271, 273 ff. Jerome (PL 30, 828–29) and Augustine (PL 37, 110 ff.) combine the traditional with the more disturbing exegesis: Christ "is the foundation and the top because in him the church is founded and completed." The Vulg.'s *summus angularis lapis* has led to the English translation "chief cornerstone." Since the literal meaning of the Latin distinguishes between several cornerstones amongst which a chief stone excels, a stone that is placed on the highest spot of a building is probably meant. Origen (*comm. in Matt.* XVII 12); Hilary of Poitiers (PL 9, 1942) and others understood the stone mentioned in Ps 118:22 in this sense.

or with the rock and altar in the Jerusalem temple which was considered the groundstone or navel of the earth.[267] Consequently Eph 2:20 would describe Christ either as a most conspicuous and impressive feature of the temple, or as the ground and turning point of the new creation.

Philological and archaeological criteria alone do not decide the question. But among the competing interpretations of the chief stone mentioned in Eph 2:20, J. Jeremias' suggestion has the strongest support from the rest of Ephesians. In this letter Christ is called the "head of the body" (1:22 etc.). The body "grows to the head" (4:15); the church is still to "meet the Perfect Man" (4:13). The growth "from the head" mentioned in 4:16 hardly means a growth higher and higher up and away from Christ, the foundation stone! In I Corinthians, however, Christ is not called the head of the church, but the foundation (3:10–11). Here the building imagery is used in a sense different from Eph 2:20. There is no reason to make *par force* a tour of harmonization.

The consequences of giving preference to Jeremias' interpretation over the traditional one are considerable. Nothing need detract from the hymnic confession "The Church's One Foundation is Jesus Christ her Lord." It has solid scriptural ground in I Cor 3:10–11 (cf. Acts 4:12). But the notion that Christ supports and rules the church primarily from the past, as it were by things historical and laid beneath the ground, has to be complemented by an equally strong eschatological element. In order to be God's house the church is, according to Ephesians, still dependent upon the future gift and work of Christ. He not only has to continue giving her members and spiritual gifts, but he has to be given to her in person—just as a keystone must be fitted into an arch. Otherwise the church will collapse. In I Thess 4:17 Paul spoke in bold visionary terms of "meeting the Lord in the air." One parable and many prophecies speak of waiting for the bridegroom or Lord, of the delay experienced, and of the final arrival of the person expected.[268] The same church which is sustained solely by the Lord, who in the past has once and for all given himself for her salvation (Eph 2:13–16; 5:2, 23, 25–26), also receives her sustenance from an event that lies in the future, i.e. from the coming of the Lord. *Maranatha!*[269] To repeat Jerome's findings: Christ "is the foundation and the top because in him the church is founded and completed." Jerome thus pleads for a combination of both the traditional interpretation and that of Jeremias. It cannot be said, however, that the wording of Eph 2:20 calls for such a combination in place of a definite decision for either corner- or keystone. The verse strongly suggests that eschatology should not be neglected because of the perfect sacrifice of Golgotha. Equally, Christ's death must not be disregarded in view of his future glorious advent. It is the slaughtered lamb that will appear in glory (Rev 5).

---

[267] See, e.g. Percy's reference (*Probleme*, p. 485) to a line in Prudentius' *Dittochaeon* and R. J. McKelvey, NTS 8 (1962), 352–59. In his book *The New Temple*, R. J. McKelvey constructs out of J. Jeremias' thesis the notion of "some aerially suspended stone" which indeed he calls "unintelligible to the ancients" (p. 204). But Jeremias did not speak of a stone suspended in the fashion of Damocles' sword. "Unintelligible" is rather the theory of McKelvey saying "The building, inheres, so to speak, in the cornerstone" (p. 115). According to Herm. *sim.* IX 9:7, the finished tower (church) "appeared as if it had been hewn out of a rock, for it seemed to me to be a single stone." The idea of a monolith may have influenced McKelvey.

[268] Matt 25:1–13; 24:30–31; 26:64 f; cf. Luke 12:35–40; 21:20–28; Rev 1:7; 19:6–8, etc.

[269] I Cor 16:22; Rev 22:20; Matt 6:10.

3. "In him you, too, are being built together so as to be a dwelling of God in the Spirit." Unlike I Peter 2:5 the saints are not called "living stones" in Eph 2:22, but the same metaphor is presupposed. The saints are also compared with stones in the Shepherd of Hermas (vis. III 2:5–9; 5:1–7:6) where special stress is laid on their selection. As already stated, the building or house of which Paul speaks consists not of products from quarries or a brick kiln but of people. Earlier the OT attests to a conflict among various understandings of the term "house," e.g. through the mouth of Nathan God spurns the physical building David wants to erect. The Lord who has been "moving with all the people of Israel, moves about in a tent for his dwelling."[270] He cannot be tied down, rather he is willing to build a very special house for David, i.e. David's family and kingship. This house will be "sure for ever" (II Sam 7:5–7, 11–16). The Gospel of John clings to the tabernacle imagery when it affirms, "the Logos . . . pitched his tent among us." John of Patmos hears a voice crying from heaven, "Behold the tent of God among them, and he will pitch his tent among them, and they will be his people." The apocalyptic writer sees "no temple in the holy city of Jerusalem that descends from heaven." He speaks of "the temple of the tent of witness in heaven" and is fully supported, e.g. by Stephen's indictment of the physical temple built in Jerusalem.[271] While Paul does not take sides in the age-old struggle between the defendants of the tent and those of the temple;[272] in Ephesians he adopts imagery related to Zion and the Jerusalem temple. Yet he emphasizes that only "in one Spirit" (2:18) does worship take place and only "in the Spirit" is the church being "built up" and "growing" (2:21–22). The temple of which he speaks is, therefore, in terms of I Peter 2:5, a "spiritual house."

The spirituality of the "house" built by God of people (rather than by men of quarry stones) is not to be identified with something invisible, abstract, timeless, and placeless. The NT authors do not treat matter, time, space, and palpability as evil per se. Their fight is not for spiritualism and against materialism, or for idealism against pragmatism. The people of God who are built together and become God's house—the church—are as material, temporal, spatial, and concrete as are sticks and stones. The accent of Eph 2 lies not upon intangibleness but upon the fact that the church of God is made of people, rather than of bricks. This means it is human, not superhuman—just as the flesh which the logos assumed (John 1:14) is according to the traditional exegesis human flesh (cf. Rom 8:3). All members of the church are humans according to Eph 2:22. Angels are not built into her.[273] As long as it pleases God to dwell among his chosen people, as long as the Spirit drives them, as long as they listen and respond to the witness of the apostles and prophets, as long as they depend totally upon the support given and to be given by the Messiah—so long are they the church. Yet it can be asked, don't they need walls and buildings for their as-

[270] See M. Buber, Königtum Gottes, Heidelberg; Schneider, 1932 (3d ed., 1956) for a spirited discussion of the issues related to these words.
[271] Rev 15:5; 21:3, 22; Acts 7:44–50; also II Cor 5:1–9?
[272] The term "dwelling" might be pressed into the service of either group.
[273] In Qumran, e.g. 1QS XI 7–8; 1QH III 22, and in Revelation angels belong to the church. Eph 2:19 comes closest to the same affirmation—but the "saints" mentioned in that verse are the men of Israel, not the angels.

semblies, and in addition to them, several external signs that distinguish them from outsiders, for instance, some special rituals, traditions, books, statutes, clerics, and some glory of their own? The context of Eph 2:20–22 answers in the negative, for "the wall" was not broken down to be re-erected (cf. Gal 2:18). The covenant and tribal mark of circumcision and the correlated "name-calling" were not antiquated by Christ's sacrifice in order to be succeeded by an analogous ritual act. The divisiveness of statutes was not abrogated in order to yield to Christian canon law and tradition. Not in vain apostles and prophets are explicitly called the foundation of the church, rather than traditions or testaments. According to Eph 2 the church is real and manifest whenever and wherever Jews and Gentiles come together to receive the priestly service of Jesus Christ, to hear the testimony and to give witness to the perfection and validity of his peacework.

These assembled Jews and Gentiles, the people of God, represent all mankind. Neither the temple nor the church are built each for their own sake or only for the benefit of the officiating priestly people. Both have no other reason to exist than the glorification of God and the revelation of his presence in and for the salvation of the world. This function of the church excludes the notion that God's presence might be primarily located in the souls of individual believers. No one, not even the church and her most pious members, can possess God for himself alone.[274]

Ephesians more than other epistles insists upon the vital and indispensable role of Gentiles. Before the coming of the Messiah the nations were expected to come to Zion and take note of God's presence in Israel. Occasionally they were heartily welcomed though their presence was not of the essence of the cultus. Only in the time after the advent of Jesus Christ are they as essential as the Jews to the worship offered by the church and as witnesses to God's presence.

In the pre-Messianic period Ezekiel saw God's throne in a vision "among the exiles by the river Chebar" in Babylonia (Ezek 1:1), thus boldly announcing God's appearance far from Zion. While a theophany in the land to which Israel was exiled in punishment must have been a surprise to Ezekiel and his contemporaries, basic traditions of Israel affirmed that God had at all times proven free and willing to appear in a foreign land: the appearance to Abraham (Gen 12) is not given a location but must have taken place outside the promised land. The Sinai manifestation is connected with the tradition of Israel's deliverance from Egypt. Ephesians affirms that now, since the Messiah has come and has made and proclaimed peace, God has revealed the will and the power not only to appear, but to "dwell" (2:22) among the Gentile-born Ephesians—without ceasing to be faithful to Israel.[275]

---

[274] "Building in Paul has a cultic, soteriological meaning. It is not an individualistic concept, but one of fellowship," Hanson, *Unity*, p. 130. The doctrine proposed in Barn. XVI 1–10 is distinct from that of Ephesians. Barnabas puts all the emphasis upon the *heart* of each man: the corrupt heart of the unbelievers was a temple built by hands and serving for idolatry; man renewed by repentance, forgiveness, faith, hope is "the spiritual temple being built for the Lord." Indeed Eph 3:16–17 will refer to the inner man and to the Messiah's "dwelling in the hearts" of the saints, "through faith." However, Ephesians ascribes to the Messiah that habitation in individuals which Barnabas attributes to God.

[275] Especially McKelvey, *New Temple*, pp. 119–24, has stressed the fact that fulfillment of OT and apocalyptic hopes rather than Stoic ideas determined Paul's teaching in Eph 2:20–22.

Other temples, whether erected in Shiloh, Jerusalem, Elephantine or Leontopolis, not to speak of the Artemis temple in Ephesus,[276] were threatened with destruction and in due time actually levelled to the ground. If God was present in some of them his presence was even more transitory than their physical structure. Though built of stone and used with reverence they were not essentially superior or more enduring than Israel's sanctuary in the wilderness, the Tent of Meeting. However, in Ephesians the community of Jews and Gentiles created by the Messiah is described as a temple, not a tent. Solidly founded and expected to stand as long as the world exists, neither the saints nor God are transient guests in it. Because God will "dwell" in his house, the saints are at home in the same house.

VII Ecclesiology of Hope

While Eph 2:19–22 contains a firm and impressive doctrine of the church, still it does not promote a triumphal ecclesiology. The church described here consists of men who were dead in sins and hostile to God and one another (2:1–5, 11–16). Not they, but God and Christ alone are the object of praise. The structure and sum of 2:11–22 can be formulated in one sentence, composed of three parts, which reveals how little the church is entitled to boast about herself: (a) Into this divided world (b) Jesus Christ has come to bring peace (c) so much so that the church came into being and received the task of demonstrating to the world the accomplished reconciliation.

Since, however, the high ecclesiology of Ephesians has been a source of great joy to some interpreters, of special resentment to others, several important features of vss. 19–22 deserve special attention.

a) The triad of Spirit, Lord, and God which heads Paul's excursus on the church's structure and life in I Cor 12:4–27 is also found (though in the sequence God, Christ, Spirit) in Eph 2:19–22. The church is not described as an institution that takes the place of the "Savior" (5:23), the "Father," and the "Spirit" (2:18). Rather she confesses the Spirit, the Lord, and the Father (cf. 4:4–6)—and this not only by mouth. Under Christ's leadership the saints approach and serve the "Father" who has promised to be present, as long as they are moved by the same "Spirit." The reference to the fundamental function of "apostles and prophets" makes this church a community of listeners. The distinction of "saints" and "fellow citizens," i.e. of Jews and Gentiles who are being "joined" and "built together," characterizes the church as a representative, missionary, and intercessory group of people who behave as responsible citizens, brotherly minded children, mutually supporting stones. A church which is in this way bound to God, bound by the brotherly love of former enemies, and engaged in responsibility for the world, cannot resemble a museum, a legal institute, or a dictatorship. Neither can it be a freewheeling association of enthusiasts.

---

[276] In Egypt a Yahweh sanctuary stood in Elephantine between about 525 and 400 B.C., and in Leontopolis between ca. 160 B.C. and A.D. 73. Orthodox Jews never recognized these structures as temples. See ANET, pp. 222–23; 427–30; 491–92; RGG, II, 416–17; Pauly-Wissowa, 2d. ser. XII, 2095–96. Bengel and others believe that Eph 2:20–22 makes a tacit polemical allusion to the Artemis sanctuary mentioned in Acts 19:23–40.

b) This church "grows into a holy temple" so as "to be a dwelling place of God" (vss. 21–22). If the understanding of Christ as "keystone" is added to these teleological statements, and the verb "growing" is taken in its full weight, then the church will abstain from making any claims for herself. When in Ephesians Christ is called the keystone, then the same honor is ascribed to him as in Col 1:27 where he is called the "hope." The keystone may be called the hope of the building upon which essence and existence of the church rely. The church, in turn, must yet become what it is meant to be. If they realize their imperfection and continue "growing," the citizens of God's kingdom assembled in the church cannot become complacent, and the children of God's household cannot be spoiled children. At least four observations regarding the "growth" of the building mentioned in 2:21 are necessary:

(1) Instead of the individual growth of initiates, the growth of the community is declared decisive.[277] (2) No recommendation is given for transcending the world or fleeing earthly ties and responsibilities as a means of achieving individual or collective perfection. Instead, the church is described as a building under construction on earth, with a function from which all mankind is to benefit.[278] (3) External, numerical growth[279] and internal, personal growth in faith (cf. Col 1:6, 10) are not excluded. But though these two concepts of growth may be present somewhere under the surface of 2:21, they are certainly not in the foreground. This verse speaks of the life and promise given to the whole church, rather than of the increased number of believers or strengthened personal faith. (4) The growing church is as yet imperfect. It is still reaching out for perfection.[280] The creation of the one new man, i.e. the pacification and unification of Jews and Gentiles, is according to 2:11–19 an accomplished and perfect fact. Yet the assembly of those reconciled, the church, depends upon increment, improvement, maturation, and consummation. All this she receives from God and the Messiah, her head, alone. Unless God pleases to be present he will not inhabit his temple. Unless the keystone is added to the building, it will not last. Paul never speaks about the growth, change or improvement of God and Christ; rather he describes the church as a community founded upon a dynamic foundation. This community has to develop externally and internally and be perpetually reformed in order to grow. Paul's idea of the church's change and reform is oriented toward the future rather than to the past. Eph 2:21 can be considered a scriptural ground for the adage, *ecclesia semper reformanda*.

c) The statement "You are no longer strangers and sojourners" corresponds to several biblical passages quoted earlier, but it appears to contradict those OT and NT utterances according to which either Israel or the church,

---

[277] Individual growth is stipulated, e.g. at the end of the Mithras Liturgy as it was reconstructed by A. Dieterich. *Eine Mithrasliturgie*, 2d ed., Leipzig: Teubner, 1923; cf. G. Bornkamm, *Das Ende des Gesetzes* (München: Kaiser, 1952), p. 145, and Porkorný, EuG, pp. 78–80.

[278] Hegermann, *Schöpfungsmittler*, p. 156, discusses the following elements: growth into the measurements of the pneumatic temple in all its four dimensions (3:18); growth into her destiny as carrier of eschatological revelation (3:10–11; 2:7; cf. I Tim 3:15); growth into Christ. All of this is the opposite of a transport upward, into heaven. Cf. Schweizer, *Neotestamentica*, pp. 301, 307–9, 314.

[279] Increase in numbers is emphasized in Acts 1:13; 2:41, 47; 4:4; 5:14; 21:20.

[280] The concept *perfect* will be discussed in the last two NOTES on 4:13 and in COMMENT VII C on 4:1–16. 4:13 demonstrates that the church must be understood on the basis of her destiny.

notwithstanding God's special care or the Messiah's coming, are and remain "strangers."[281] How can Israel become a home for nomads if she herself is called a stranger? There is a difference between estrangement on earth, i.e. among all nations, and estrangement from God.[282] Precisely those who have been or are now included in God's covenant will have to accept rejection on earth—just as Paul suffers, but also bears his imprisonment in good humor.[283] Those who know and enjoy the peace given by the Messiah will not be spared the hostility of onrushing powers.[284] If the Gentiles had been removed to a far-off island of peace rather than incorporated in Israel and its dramatic history of internal and external strife, then they might presume to possess a cheap peace. But the chosen people were called to be faithful witnesses, at home and in exile, and they sought in vain to substitute cheap peace or assimilation to their pagan environment for repentance, obedience, steadfastness, and hope. The Gentiles are not incorporated into a community of flawless, faithful, and angelic OT saints. Rather they are made members of that people which lives from God's election and covenant, but is inclined to boast of fleshly circumcision or follow false prophets. It is a people that lives by God's faith and is called to live faithfully, but that at the same time tempts and provokes its Lord, is tempted by the flesh and pressed by outward enemies. This people is not holy and pure of itself. They are saved sinners, not sinless saviors. According to Eph 2:19 the church is this people of God, increased by the addition of the Gentiles under the rule of the Messiah. They depend totally upon the purification granted by the Messiah (1:7; 5:26–27). Their security is with him, not in themselves.

d) "The dwelling of God" among his people is a great miracle. Rev 21:1–5 proclaims that his indwelling is the decisive event that constitutes the new heaven and the new earth.[285] Certainly an affirmation such as "The Lord is in his holy temple, the Lord's throne is in heaven" (Ps 11:4)[286] was prone to the misunderstanding and misuse fought against in Jer 7:4, etc. Just like some priests and the prophet Jonah, so also the church might succumb to the temptation to make claims for herself on the basis of the promise and privilege given by God. But *abusus non tollit usum.* While Paul reminds his readers of God's promised presence, he does not suggest that they should pretend to possess and manage it. The church is "to be a dwelling place of God in the Spirit." Formerly the elect place, Zion, was the chosen point at which God proved by concrete acts and events his rule over heaven *and* earth (Ps 24). Now the church is the

[281] See the OT texts calling the Israelites "strangers" (*gērīm*) mentioned in the second NOTE on 2:12; also I Peter 1:1; 2:11, "To the exiles in the dispersion . . . I beseech you as aliens and exiles"; James 1:1, "To the twelve tribes in dispersion"; Heb 4:11, "Let us strive to enter that rest."
[282] Paul uses analogous dialectics, e.g. in II Cor 5:6, 8–9; 6:9–10; I Cor 7:29–31.
[283] 3:1; 4:1; 6:20.   [284] 6:10–20; also 2:7?
[285] While in Rev 21 the image of the city prevails, in Eph 2:20–22 temple imagery is finally given preference over the political metaphors of citizenship 2:12, 19. OT prophecies and hopes regarding Zion treated the rock, the temple, and the city as concentric units.
[286] Cf. Exod 15:17; LXX Ps 32[33]:13–14; LXX Ps 75:2–3[76:2]; I Kings 8:12–13, 27–30; see also the statement on God's residence "in the high and holy place, and also with him," who is of "a contrite and humble spirit" Isa 57:15. J. H. Elliott, *The Elect and the Holy,* NovT Suppl. 12 (Leiden: Brill, 1966), 70–76 shows that the Jews in Alexandria, Egypt, understood their community as the dwelling place of God, i.e. as the residence of The King. The obligation to maintain holiness and to serve as God's witnesses among the Gentiles, was included in this self-understanding, according to the version of Exod 19:6 in the LXX. Cf. I Peter 2:4–10.

sign of his mercy, his peace and his nearness to the whole world. If God can and will use people who are as tempted and weak as the Christians are, then he is certainly able and willing to exclude no one from his realm. The church lives by this hope and bears witness to it publicly.

VI COMMITMENT BY REVELATION
(3:1–13)

3 1 For this reason I, Paul, the prisoner of the Messiah Jesus for the sake of you Gentiles . . . 2 surely you have heard that I was given God's grace in order to administer it to you. 3 As I have briefly written above, the secret was made known to me by revelation. 4 Correspondingly, by reading [this] you are able to perceive how I understand the secret of the Messiah.

5 In other generations it was not made known
>to the Sons of Men

as it is now revealed through the Spirit
>to his holy apostles and prophets:

6 In the Messiah Jesus [and] through the gospel, the Gentiles are joint heirs, members in the same body, fellow beneficiaries in all that is promised. 7 Through the gift of God's grace which was given me—for his power is at work—I was made a servant of the gospel. 8 I, who am less than the least of all saints, was given the special grace to announce to the Gentiles the good news of the unfathomable riches of the Messiah 9 and to make all men see how the secret is administered [by the Messiah] that was hidden from the ages in God the creator of all things: 10 The manifold wisdom of God is now to be made known through the church to the governments and authorities in the heavens. 11 This is the design concerning the ages which God has carried out in the Messiah Jesus our Lord. 12 In him and because of his faithfulness, confidently we make use of our free access [to God]. 13 Therefore I ask [God] that you do not lose heart over the tribulations I suffer for you. For they are your glorification.

NOTES

3:1. *For this reason* . . . If these words are anything more than a meaningless transitional phrase, i.e. if they indicate a stringent logical connection with the foregoing, then an allusion is made not only to building God's house on a firm foundation, but also to the unification of Jews and Gentiles described in chapter 2. When the same phrase is resumed in 3:14, Paul refers to the contents of 3:2–13. Thus resurrection, unification, construction, and revelation together form one common reason for what follows. Paul's intention is to write about his intercession for the saints,[1] but it is not immediately carried out. The sentence which begins in 3:1 will be completed only after an extended parenthesis, i.e. an excursus describing Paul's apostolic ministry, its dependence upon the revelation of God's secret, its extension in the "cosmic" service of the church, and its confirmation by suffering and courageous endurance (3:2–13). However, the fifty-century Syriac version (the Peshitta, re-edited in the sixth and seventh centuries), Chrysostom, Beza, and others consider 3:1 an asyndeton rather than a broken sentence; they presuppose that just as elsewhere[2] a form of the verb "to be" is the proper connection between the grammatical subject and a following predicate, and they translate: "For this reason I, Paul, am a prisoner." Still, the Greek article before "prisoner" speaks against this interpretation.[3] Codex Claramontanus offers (and Calvin accepts) a variant reading based on the content of 6:19 and 3:2–13: "I, Paul, the prisoner . . . am an ambassador." The MS evidence for this variant is tenuous. Actually 3:1 is one of the numerous broken sentences to be found in most of Paul's epistles. While Origen and Jerome assumed that the thought begun in 3:1 was never completed, the intercession constituting the first main part of the epistle (1:15 ff.) is brought to a conclusion in 3:14 ff. Intercession is such an essential element of the apostolic ministry that it initiates, concludes, and thus dominates all doctrinal and narrative elements of 1:15 – 3:21. As observed in section IX of the Introduction, in Eph 1–3 the intercessory prayer practically replaces the doctrinal ("kerygmatic") first part of other Pauline epistles.

I, Paul. Carried away by the magnitude of the things for which he must thank God, Paul so far has mentioned himself only in passing.[4] The somewhat self-conscious, if not egocentric formulation "I, Paul" is found in 1:15, 4:1, 5:32, as well as in undisputed Pauline letters.[5] Invariably the formula is a display of authority. In letters addressed to people personally acquainted with him, Paul did not always bother to show reasons for his self-consciousness. But in writing (or dictating) Ephesians he seems to be aware how awkward it is to lay emphasis upon his personal authority (his *egō*), and so meets the situation with a parenthesis describing his ministry (3:2–13).[6] Why do the readers of Ephesians owe respect to him? Because a gift is given to Paul and an assignment is carried out by him, not because he possesses an individual quality inherent or presumed. Therefore the weight of Paul's *egō* is no greater and no smaller than the gift and task assigned to him "for . . . the Gentiles." Due respect for the

---

[1] See 3:13, "I ask [God]"; 3:14, "I bow my knees"; 3:16, "May he grant . . . you."
[2] Cf. the NOTES on the omission of the verbs "to be" or "to become," in 1:13; 2:13.
[3] Abbott: in 3:1 and 4:1 "prisoner" is an apposition, not a predicate.
[4] Especially in Galatians, II Corinthians, and Philippians, Paul's utterances about himself take up a good deal of space. Robinson, p. 74, observes that the apostle's reticence in speaking about himself is "strangely unlike himself"; in Ephesians Paul is "marvelously impersonal" and shows "unwanted reserve."
[5] It occurs not only in the most personal among his epistles, Galatians (5:2; cf. 1:12), but also when one or several co-authors are mentioned; I Thess 2:18; II Cor 10:1; Col 1:13; Philem 19. In Col 4:10, but not in Ephesians Paul mentions Aristarch as his fellow-prisoner. Strangely enough, this Aristarch is not called a co-author of Colossians, see Col 1:1.
[6] See the exposition of Theodore of Mopsuestia and Theodoret; cf. Dibelius.

office rather than some kind of personality cult is requested (cf. Gal 1:15–16; II Cor 3:4ff; Rom 1:5; 15:15–16).

prisoner of the Messiah Jesus. See COMMENT III C.

for the sake of you Gentiles. According to Robinson[7] "Gentile liberty had cost him [Paul] his freedom," and Jews had made him pay this price. In I Thess 2:14–16; II Cor 11:24–25 Paul confirms the reports in Acts[8] saying that the work of Paul among the Gentiles was impeded by Jews. Nevertheless it is unlikely that in Eph 3 Paul intends to combine the reminder of his suffering with an implied outburst against his Jewish brethren. For when in the excursus (3:2–13) he explains why he was made Christ's servant for the benefit of "the Gentiles," he does not capitalize on Jewish obstruction and plead for pity or admiration.

2. *surely you have heard.* The Greek language has two closely related conjunctions (*eige* and *eiper*) for introducing a justifiable assumption. In classical Greek the first indicates a higher degree of probability, the second a slightly lower one. In Eph 3:2 and 4:21 the first is used, but no conclusions can be safely drawn because in Pauline writings the difference between the two appears to be lost, if not reversed.[9] Several interpreters[10] were unable to imagine that the readers of Ephesians had only "heard" of Paul's commission. They understood the Greek verb *akouō* (to hear) in the sense of "to comprehend" or "to retain firmly." Thus the verb was interpreted in the Hebrew sense of *shama*, which includes the meanings "to obey" and "to understand." Indeed, often in the NT when the word "to hear" is used, its decisive sense appears to be not just awareness of sounds, but comprehension.[11] Yet occasionally Paul uses the same verb in the general Greek sense as the perception of a sound or rumor, which does not imply endorsement, comprehension, or obedience.[12] Eph 1:5 and 3:2 reveal that the mutual acquaintance of the apostle and the Ephesians was based on indirect information only. See section III A of the Introduction.

I was given God's grace in order to administer it to you. Lit. "the stewardship of God's grace which I was given for you." In the first NOTE on 1:10 reasons were given why in Ephesians the Greek noun *oikonomiā* probably has the same dynamic, functional sense of "stewardship" as in Paul's undisputed letters. The abstract meaning "plan" or "strategy" is attested in literature of later centuries. While in 1:10 the term *oikonomiā* was used to describe Jesus Christ as the plenipotent executor of God's decision, in 3:2 and Col 1:25[13] Paul defines his own ministry by the same word. Mitton sees a tension between Col 1:25 and Eph 3:2. He is convinced that two conflicting notions of *oikonomiā*

---

[7] Pp. 10–11, cf. 167.   [8] Esp. 16:19 ff.; 21:27 ff.

[9] See Lightfoot, *Galatians*, pp. 135–36, on Gal 3:4; and W. Sanday-A. C. Headlam, *The Epistle to the Romans*, ICC, 5th ed. (Edinburgh: Clark, 1958), p. 96, on Rom 3:30; also Abbott, on Eph 3:2.

[10] As Pelagius, Anselm of Canterbury, Grotius.

[11] Cf. the connection between hearing and believing in 1:13; Col 1:23; John 5:24; hearing and knowing, John 4:42; hearing and doing, John 7:38; Matt 7:24–27; hearing and obeying, Rom 10:14, 16; hearing and keeping, John 12:47; or the emphasis laid on hearing alone in Matt 13:9, etc. In Paul's writings, hearing of faith and obedience of faith (*akoē*, or *hypakoē pisteōs*, Gal 3:2, 5; Rom 1:5) are probably identified.

[12] Cf., e.g. Gal 4:21; I Cor 14:2 with I Cor 5:1; 11:18; II Cor 12:6; Eph 1:15; Col 1:4, 9.

[13] As in I Cor 4:1–2; 9:17; cf. COMMENT XII on 1:3–14. Calvin interprets the noun by *commissio*.

are presupposed which cannot possibly have been used by the same author at the same time. In consequence he declares Ephesians inauthentic.[14] However his argument is pointless if in Eph 3:2 as well as in 1:10 *oikonomiā* has exactly the same functional meaning as in Col 1:25 and I Cor 4:1–2; 9:17. See COMMENT III B.

3. *As I have briefly written above*. The Greek verb used here (*prographō*) possesses at least three meanings: to write above (i.e. in the same document); to write earlier (in another letter or book); to write up publicly (i.e. to announce). While the third sense is presupposed in Gal 3:1, either one of the two other meanings have been recognized in Eph 3:3. Paul may refer to Eph 1–2, that is, to the statement made in 1:9–10 about the revelation and the content of the secret, or to the description of the unification of Jews and Gentiles by the Messiah which is found in 2:11–22.[15] Or, he may remind the readers of what he wrote in some other epistles about the revelation (or the revelations; see II Cor 12:1) imparted to him.[16] If a pseudonymous author wrote Ephesians, then perhaps allusion is made to a collection of all Pauline letters.[17] Goodspeed's theory, however, which makes Ephesians a pseudonymous Introduction to the collected Pauline corpus, is in Eph 3:3 contradicted by the adverbial expression "briefly,"[18] and by the fact that to date no scroll or codex containing the collection of other epistles (to which Paul allegedly alludes) has been found that antedates Ephesians. If, however, Paul himself wrote Ephesians, how could he have presupposed that Romans and Philippians, or more specifically Galatians and II Corinthians, were in the hands of Christians in Asia Minor?[19] It is advisable to see in 3:3 an allusion to 1:9–10 or any other brief passage within Eph 1–2 which speaks about the grace and power of God, his eternal decision, revelation, the adoption of the Gentiles, the one body formed, the involvement of principalities and powers, or free access to the Father.

the secret was made known to me. COMMENT XI on 1:3–14 showed why "secret" rather than "mystery" is the proper translation for all the passages in Ephesians, Colossians, and elsewhere which concern the revelation or proclamation of that which was hidden in God. In Ephesians and Colossians the singular of the noun *mystērion* denotes an eternal decision of God which must now be proclaimed to the world, rather than a plan or doctrine which must be locked up under the *disciplina arcani*.[20] In Eph 3:4 ff. the form and sub-

[14] EE, pp. 91–94. As FBK, pp. 253–54, shows, this opinion has attained to almost canonical rank among critical scholars.

[15] Theodoret; Bengel; Robinson; Abbott; Dibelius; Gaugler.

[16] Unless he has a lost letter in mind, passages such as Gal 1:11–16 and II Cor 12:1–4 may contain the passages alluded to; cf. Calvin.

[17] E. Goodspeed, *The Meaning of Ephesians* (University of Chicago Press, 1956), pp. 41–42.

[18] A similar Greek formulation is found in I Peter 5:12; Heb 13:22; the same phrase, in Acts 26:28–29. For the latter passage, translations such as "with few words," "in a short time," "almost," have been suggested.

[19] An exchange of letters as suggested by Col 4:16, and a collection of epistles such as Rev 2–3 were feasible only when the congregations addressed lived in the same or a neighboring province. Evidence is lacking that late in the first century A.D. the complete Pauline corpus was collected, known, and used anywhere in Asia Minor or outside. Even Luke appears not to have had access to such a collection.

[20] Pokorný, EuG, p. 112. Other special problems of the "mystery" in Eph 3 are discussed by Percy, pp. 342–53; K. Sullivan, "The Mystery Revealed to Paul—Ephesians 3:1–13," BiTod 1 (1963), 246–55 (ref.); W. H. Marc, "Paul's Mystery in Ephesians 3," Bibliotheca Sacra 123 (1966), 24–31 (ref.). In some parts of the apocalyptic tradition, also in Qumranite and Gnostic writings, the opposite held true: the mysteries confided to God's elect were not to be divulged but to be kept in the heart of the seer, the initiate, or an elite among mankind.

stance of the revealed secret will be unveiled: its core is Christ and the incorporation of the Gentiles into God's people; apostles and prophets receive and proclaim its revelation; through the church not only the saints but also the principalities and powers must be informed of it.

by revelation. Instead of saying bluntly "through revelation," as in Gal 1:12, the Greek text of Eph 3:3 (also Gal 2:2 and Rom 16:25) denotes revelation as a continuous and unceasing flow of information and power. The translation "by a revelation" (NEB; JB) is not recommendable. Too easily it suggests that Paul is speaking about one specific moment of revelation[21] and about the communication of something like a dogma or march-order.[22] While the aorist "it was made known" and the many aorists in the following verses show clearly that Paul means a unique and completed event, revelation itself must not be limited to one instance only. Paul himself has gone from revelation to revelation,[23] and so do all who are chosen to see the glory of the Lord and to be transformed by it (II Cor 3:12–18; Eph 1:17). The NT mentions several means or modes by which God "reveals" himself.[24] But in Eph 3:3 the immediacy of communication between God and the apostle is emphasized, rather than the specific means by which this communication was distinct from others. See COMMENT II for a discussion of the phenomenological, soteriological, and eschatological character of revelation.

4. *Correspondingly.* Lit. "after the measure of which." A similar rather rare formulation is found in II Cor 5:10, "according to" or "with reference to" what someone did.[25]

by reading [this] you are able to perceive. The reading presupposed here is the public reading of a text in a worship service or some other assembly.[26] While Paul just as other privileged scholars may have had some scrolls or codices in his private possession (II Tim 4:13) and was able to work in libraries, according to I Cor 1:26–29 the great majority of the people to receive Pauline letters were uneducated and poor people. Thus they were dependent upon the public recital of sacred written documents. See COMMENT III D for a discussion about the relationship between the OT and apostolic writings.

how I understand. Lit. "my understanding in." In the LXX, the verbal phrase, "to be understanding in," occurs several times. Sometimes it means to be an expert in a given field; on other occasions it denotes simple understanding or ac-

---

[21] Which may be localized at Damascus or may be coincident with another single and miraculous encounter. Westcott asserts that "the general mode of communication" rather than "the specific fact" of one revelatory moment in Paul's life is meant.

[22] In his interpretation of Gal 1:12, Burton, *Galatians,* p. 42, mentions such specific propositions as the resurrection of Jesus, futility of righteousness by law, faith as the principle of life, and the justification of Gentiles without circumcision. H. Schlier, *Die Zeit der Kirche* (Freiburg: Herder, 1956), pp. 215 ff., teaches that Christ delivered himself in dogmas and is present in them. But Feuillet, *Christ Sagesse,* pp. 20–21, questions this view: it is not proven that with Paul's conversion all fundamental traits of his theology were given and present. Following P. Gaechter, *Petrus und seine Zeit* (Innsbruck: Tyrolia-Verlag, 1958), p. 338, Paul did not resemble, after his conversion, a parachutist armed with a perfect and safe piece of equipment! (ref.). See COMMENT II for alternatives.

[23] Gal 1:12, 16; 2:2; I Cor 2:6–16; Acts 16:6, 7, 9; 18:9–10; 22:17–21; 23:11; 27:23–26.

[24] By dream or vision, Acts 16:9; 18:9; 23:11; 27:23; in ecstasy, Acts 22:17; I Cor 12:1–4; by an impulse of the Spirit which need not exclude sober reflection and decision of man, Acts 13:2; 15:28; 16:6–7; 19:21; 20:22–23; I Cor 5:4; 7:40; by the voice of one or several prophets, Acts 11:27–30; I Cor 14; Rev 2–3; by the Spirit; I Cor 2:10.

[25] See WBLex, 717, 5 a–d.   [26] I Thess 5:27; Col 4:16; Matt 24:15; Rev 1:3.

ceptance.[27] In the LXX the noun "understanding," or "comprehension," is not found in conjunction with the preposition "in." Since the verb "to be understanding in," does not always imply a claim to expert knowledge, it is not necessary to assume that Eph 3:4 contains a specifically boastful affirmation of Paul's relation to the revealed secret. The version, "that I understand" (NEB), sounds too self-laudatory to fit the context—though it is grammatically possible. Whether or not Paul's perfect understanding is meant,[28] Paul urges the reader to become aware of his authority.[29] Whatever authority he has is not absolute or founded in himself, but is dependent upon the fact and substance of revelation. "Understanding" is, as was shown in a NOTE on 1:8 and in COMMENT X on 1:3–14, far from an intellectual event only. It includes the appropriate decision, action, attitude.

the secret of the Messiah. This phrase should not be interpreted to mean that there are other mysteries besides the Messianic one. In COMMENT XI on 1:3–14 it was shown that statements made in Ephesians and Colossians (except perhaps Eph 5:32, see below) on the "revelation of the secret" are distinct from those affirmations in other Pauline epistles, Qumran, and the apocalyptic literature which speak about several "mysteries," not one *mystērion.* Eph 3:4 as much as says, this secret consists of the Messiah. His place with the Father, his commission, his coming, his death, his preaching, his work, his exaltation, and his headship over the church, the world, the powers, and all things[30]—this is "The Secret" in person.[31] The one mystery is the mystery of Christ the preexistent, the revealer, the savior, the regent of church and world, the one to unite Jews and Gentiles, and the high priest leading the church to the Father. The inclusion of the Gentiles into God's people is not a further mystery added to the mystery of Jesus Christ. Neither is the equation of the mystery with "Christ among you [Gentiles]" (Col 1:27) a different interpretation of the Christ mystery. Rather to speak of the savior Messiah who includes the Gentiles in his body is to speak of the one revealed secret of God. Revelation, salvation, and unification in Christ are not only an indivisible whole. In Christ they are identified. Consequently, the secret of Christ is not just the plan or doctrine of the Gentiles' free admission, but includes the execution of God's decision on the plane of history. Ephesians and Colossians speak about this secret as it is revealed in space and time, and by no means abstractly or apart from its publication and success.

5. *In other generations . . . to his holy apostles and prophets.* That vs. 5 is probably a quote from a hymn or confession is suggested by unique elements in its form and subject matter. Its beautiful parallelism of members (which is not equally evident in the verses immediately preceding and following) deploys the contrast between the temporal concepts "in other generations" and "now," the epistemological terms "not made known" and "revealed," and the personal indirect object "to the Sons of Men" and "to his holy apostles and prophets." The terms "Sons of Men" and "his holy apostles and prophets" are strange in Pauline

---

[27] E.g. in the LXX texts of Josh 1:7; IV[II] Kings 18:7; II Chron 34:12 compared with II Esd 18[Neh 8]:8, 12.
[28] Cf. I Cor 2:6 with 13:12.   [29] Abbott.
[30] As described in 1:4–10, 20–23; 2:13–22.
[31] Just as he also is The Peace in person, 2:14; cf. I Cor 1:30; Col 1:27d.

diction.[32] The Greek sentence begins with the pronoun "which"—i.e. a relative pronoun which, usually in the masculine form "who," is typical of hymns or acclamations (I Tim 3:16, etc.). In form and content Rom 16:25–27, a passage which hardly resembles Paul's diction and thought, is a close parallel of Eph 3:5. In Col 1:26 the same affirmation is made as in Eph 3:5, although the text in Colossians appears to be a prose version of the hymnic utterance in Ephesians. The vocabulary of Eph 3:5, not of Col 1:26, differs from Paul's normal usage. Yet Paul himself may have used the quote contained in Eph 3:5 before or after rephrasing it in his own words in Col 1:26. As to subject matter: Eph 3:5 speaks about a collegium of apostles and prophets who as a community receive the same revelation; but the immediate context (Eph 3:2–4 and 7–9) describes only Paul's illumination and mission. Is vs. 5 therefore to be considered a disturbing gloss or a later addition?[33] It is safe to assume that here as elsewhere in Ephesians, also in undisputed epistles, Paul himself was able to cite a traditional text and use it as the focus for his thought. Formulations coined or used in Christian liturgies, confessions, or catechisms may have encouraged him to make bold statements regarding his own authority which, without a supporting text, might have looked extravagant. Comparable to the role which 3:5 plays in its context is the key position attributed to oracles or traditional formulations in the hymnic passages 1:4–10, 1:20–23, and in the royal Psalms. If, as we suggest, 3:5 contains a quotation, then neither its formal nor its substantial idiosyncrasies affect the question of the authenticity of Ephesians as a whole.

In other generations. This version assumes that the Greek text intends to give information about a specific time.[34] However, philological reasons permit another translation: "to other generations." The meaning of this second interpretation practically coincides with the first—if only successive generations of men are meant. However, it has been suggested that "generations" may be another name for the principalities and powers enumerated in 1:21 and for the aeons mentioned in 2:7.[35] With Reitzenstein and Dibelius, 3:9 may be interpreted as meaning, "hidden from the angelic or demonic aeons"; if this paraphrase is tenable, then also 3:5 may speak of something hidden "from" the families residing in the heavenly places. Verse 3:10 also appears to corroborate this idea, for it speaks about the task of passing on the knowledge received by revelation "to the governments and authorities in the heavens." It is possible that verses 5 and 9 contain the negative counterpart to 3:10: to the apostles and to the church is revealed that which was and still is hidden from principalities and powers. Cf. I Peter 1:12, "Things into which angels long to look" were

---

[32] When in 2:20, cf. 4:11, Paul speaks of "apostles and prophets," he may have been influenced by the text quoted in 3:5. In Luke 11:49 an unknown Wisdom book is explicitly quoted as saying, "I shall send to them prophets and apostles." Cf. Matt 23:34 where "prophets, wise men and scribes," but no apostles are mentioned.

[33] E. W. E. Reuss, *La Bible*, XIV, *Les épîtres Pauliniennes*, II (Paris: Sandoz & Fischbacher, 1878), 161–63.

[34] The widely used "dative of time" is found, e.g. in 2:12, "at that time," and is suggested in 3:5 by the parallel "in other generations—now"; cf. Rom 16:25–26: "kept silent in age-long aeons, but now revealed." In Eph 3:20–21 the terms "aeons" and "generations" have obviously an exclusively temporal meaning and do not refer to demons or angels.

[35] See the literature mentioned in the exposition of 2:7, e.g. Jonas, *Gnostic Religion*, pp. 176 ff. Jonas asserts that the "generations" of Eph 3:5 mean the same as the (second centruy A.D.) *aiōnes* spoken about in the Valentinian genealogies.

revealed to the OT prophets and are now announced to the church by evangelists. The demonological interpretation of Eph 3:5 and 9 has not only the support of I Peter, but eliminates the idea that Israel, the OT servants of God, or the OT itself were ignorant of the access given to Gentiles. However, the attractiveness of these arguments is not sufficient to rule out the alternative offered in our translation. Since vs. 5b speaks of both the time *and* the indirect object of revelation ("now," "to his holy apostles"), vs. 5a most likely also combines a separate temporal term with the distinct naming of the recipients of revelation: the "generations" denote the time, the "Sons of Men" are the beneficiaries. Not before 3:10 are angels or demons declared the indirect recipients of the knowledge conveyed by revelation. Verse 5 makes an affirmation which seems difficult to reconcile with the prophetic and Psalm quotations used in Ephesians: not even the elect men of Israel knew of the secret that is now revealed.

not made known to the Sons of Men as it is now. The archaic term "Son of Man" is treated in an abundant literature that seeks to explain its possible origin in ancient Eastern religion and anthropology, and its use in the Gospels and Acts.[36] The double plural "Sons of Men" excludes the possibility that "Sons" of a god "Man," or of God himself (cf. Dan 7:13) are meant here.[37] The term "Sons of Men" may either mean all human beings[38] or some elect men only.[39] Two things make it probable that in Eph 3:5 not all men or all members of God's people, but only specifically elect servants of God are meant. First is the statement ascribed to the Q-tradition, "Many prophets and righteous ones [or, kings] desired to see what you see and did not see it" (Matt 13:17; Luke 10:24). Second is the parallel affirmation of Eph 3:5, "revealed to his holy apostles and prophets."[40] It would be a truism to assert that not everybody was given revelation, for at all times, if God ever appeared, he "became apparent not to all the people but to the earlier elected witnesses of God" (Acts 10:41). Yet this interpretation appears flatly to contradict those OT and NT passages according to which the saints of the OT had been made aware of the calling of the Gentiles.[41] Some commentators[42] try to restore the harmony of biblical teaching by insisting upon the weight of the conjunction *hōs* ("as") in Eph 3:5b. No more is affirmed, they hold, than a *gradual* distinction of knowledge; even if OT men of God knew about the promise, they still could not know the exact means and the completed fact of the Gentiles' adoption; it was not

[36] Among the latest extensive works on this topic, H. E. Tödt, *Der Menschensohn in der synoptischen Überlieferung,* Gütersloh: Mohn, 1960, gives access to the immense literature and problems which cannot be discussed at this point. Summaries of the most recent research are given by G. Haufe, "Das Menschensohnproblem," EvTh 26 (1966), 130 ff, by J. H. Marshall, "The Synoptic Son of Man Sayings in Recent Discussion," NTS 12 (1966), 327–51, and by F. H. Borsch, *The Christian and the Gnostic Son of Man,* SBT, 2d ser. 14, 1970.

[37] The same plural, "Sons of Men," is also found in LXX Gen 11:5; LXX Ps 11:9, etc.; *Test. Levi* III 10; I Clem. 61:2. Schlier deems it possible that this is a liturgical expression.

[38] Cf. Mark 3:28 with Matt 13:31; see also Isa 51:12; Pss 8:4; 144:3. If the two Psalm passages speak about the king rather than every man, they belong in the next footnote.

[39] E.g. in Ps 80:17 the king of Israel, in Ezek 2:1, 3, 6, 8, etc. the prophet is called "Son of Man."

[40] Bengel. Abbott, however, rejects this interpretation.

[41] See among the passages quoted earlier, esp. Gen 9:27; 12:1–3; 18:18; Isa 2:2–4; 49:6, etc.; Zech 9:9–10; Jonah 4; Gal 3:8; I Peter 1:10–12.

[42] E.g. Chrysostom; Thomas Aquinas; Calvin; Th. Beza; Abbott; Dibelius.

revealed as clearly and completely then "as it is now."[43] Jerome opposed this view in a peculiar way; he simply excluded the prophets from the verdict passed on the "Sons of Men" in Eph 3:5 because they were "Sons of *God*." Neither of these simplifying expositions is acceptable. The latter, because "Sons of Men" cannot mean the plebeians as opposed to a spiritual nobility; the former, because the supposedly comparative word "as" (*hōs*) is not found in the parallel text (Col 1:26).[44] Eph 3:5 ought not therefore to be attenuated by the paraphrase, "not so clearly as . . ." Rather this verse states as distinctly as 3:9 that, compared with God's own self-manifestations in the time before the Messiah's coming, the adoption of the Gentiles into God's people through the Messiah is a novel fact. When the difference between the OT and the NT is described in terms of Ephesians, it consists of the exclusion of the Gentiles there, their full inclusion here. In Gal 4:21–31 and II Cor 3 the difference between the two "covenants" is described in different terms, but the special witness of Ephesians must not be made a victim of harmonization.[45]

revealed through the Spirit. There are several ways to analyze the function of the words "through the Spirit" (lit. "in Spirit") in the syntax of vs. 5. (a) The formula may be an attribute of the two nouns "apostles" and "prophets" (cf. 2:22; Col 1:8). The description of these men as "holy . . . in the Spirit" would amount to a tautology. Certainly such repetitions are not strange to liturgical diction, but other interpretations deserve equal attention. (b) The words "through the Spirit" may qualify only the "prophets" so as to contribute to the poetic parallelism: "Holy apostles . . . prophets by the Spirit." A specific connection between the Spirit and the prophets is seldom expressed in classic prophetic books (e.g. in Micah 3:8; Isa 61:1) but frequently after the time of the exile. (c) In addition to, rather than as a substitute for, the close association of the Spirit with the prophets, a suggestion which is offered in e.g. the NEB version of Eph 3:5b deserves consideration: "revealed by inspiration." In I Cor 2:10–16 the Spirit is extensively described as the only way and means of revelation, and Eph 1:17 speaks of the "Spirit of . . . revelation." The closest parallel to 3:5b is 3:3, "made known . . . by revelation." Our translation is determined by this parallel. The quoted words from 3:3 and their opposite in 3:5a, "not made known," make it necessary to conclude that the verbs "to make known" and "to reveal" are used as synonyms. The accent lies not upon a specific *mode* of information, but on the *fact* that a secret is "made known" to man by God himself. Or else "making known" should not have been employed as a synonym for "revealing." Though in the NT the verb "to reveal" is practically reserved for God's, the anti-Christ's, and some special servant's manifestation, other

---

[43] Compare the superiority of Priscilla's and Aquila's "more accurate" instruction in the way of God, which makes them teachers of the expert OT scholar Apollos (Acts 17:24, 26).

[44] As Schlier rightly observes.

[45] If the author of Ephesians were pressed to say whether he really wanted to deny that the prophets and psalmists of Israel knew about the Gentiles' access to God and his people, he would probably refer to his OT allusion and quotation in 2:13, 17. For him Isa 57:19 predicted the approach of the nations! But an event prophesied is for him not the same as an act of revelation. Revelation includes word and deed, announcement and performance, promise and actual salvation. Equally knowledge of revelation is, as already stated, not just intellectual perception, but includes acknowledgment and corresponding action. Such revelation and knowledge may have been foreseen by elect men of Israel, but they had not yet occurred.

verbs that are more commonly used for expressing communication can describe the same action of God. Author, content, time, and effect rather than spectacular circumstances of communication constitute the essence of revelation. See COMMENT II.

holy apostles and prophets. The adjective "holy" is not so strange or exaggerated as to exclude Pauline authorship.[46] All Christians were called "saints" and Paul reckons himself among them; the Qumran community called themselves "the saints"; "holy prophets" are mentioned in the NT, "holy presbyters" occurs in the literature of later times.[47] The adjective "holy" denotes election for God's service; it implies the respect due to persons who have been given authority and a ministry by God. Still "it does not weigh so heavily"[48] as to indicate the recognition of a higher degree of perfection achieved by a few Christians only, or as to reveal the veneration of martyrs and their tombs. Just as elsewhere in the NT[49] "the apostles" are understood to be more than a number of individuals: they form a definite group and are a collegium. Occasional disagreements and tensions among them are not belittled or denied by Paul and his admirer, Luke.[50] But Eph 3:5 agrees fully with Matthew, Acts, and Galatians in affirming that all apostles have been entrusted with the "gospel to the Gentiles" or have at least "recognized the grace" of God operating in the mission to the Gentiles (Gal 2:7, 9). The same is true of the "prophets." Eph 3:5 presupposes that all of them attest to the inclusion of Gentiles in God's people. The function which they are assigned, e.g. in Acts 9:10–18, 13:1–3, and the role they play in the Gentile Christian congregation of Corinth[51] make it possible to assume that the collegiate view of "apostles and prophets" is not the fiction of an author and age after Paul, but a conviction which was expressed in a Jewish-Hellenistic church confession or hymn, and which could be taken up by Paul (cf. Luke 11:49).

6. *In the Messiah Jesus [and] through the gospel.* In the Greek text these words are found at the end of vs. 6. Yet despite JB and NEB (in part) this position does not necessarily mean that they qualify the last statement made about the Gentiles exclusively, i.e. their participation "in all that is promised." Rather the "Messiah" and the "gospel" are emphatically pointed out as the occasion, the means, and the condition for the whole content of vs. 6. In the above translation, just as in 2:18, the conjunction "and" was added to the Greek for reasons of aesthetics and clarity. According to 2:13–16 it was exclusively the crucified Messiah who effected the access to God and the inclusion of the Gentiles among God's people. This Messiah was described as the maker as well as the harbinger of peace, not only as victim but also as priest. The prepositions "in" and "through" are found in conjunction in I Peter 1:5; Heb

---

[46] Not only conservative scholars like Robinson, Percy (pp. 335–36), Gaugler but also critical minds like Abbott, Dibelius, Schlier agree on this judgment.

[47] I Cor 6:2; Col 1:26; Eph 3:8; 1QM III 5; VI 6; Acts 3:21; Luke 1:70; Ign. *Magn.* III 1.

[48] Dibelius, p. 74.

[49] E.g. Luke 11:49; 22:14–23; Acts 2:15–26; 10:40–41; Matt 13:11, 16–17; John 17:6–19, etc.; I Cor 9:5; 15:5, 7; Rom 16:7.

[50] Gal 2:11–14; I Cor 9:1–5; II Cor 11:5, 13–15; 12:11; Acts 15. There are interpreters who find in the incident of the strange exorcist (Mark 9:38–40) a hidden reference to Paul's relation to the Twelve.

[51] I Cor 12:28; 14:1–25. In Qumran, however, viz. in CD VI 1, "the holy Annointed Ones" are the OT prophets.

5:10; and Paul sometimes uses them as synonyms.[52] In Eph 3:6; cf. 2:17 the gospel is as subordinate to the Messiah as is the act of proclaiming a message to the substance of the pronouncement. Preaching is an essential feature of the Messianic era. If the Messiah did not reveal his presence and make known his work, both his coming and death could not be called salvation. The proclaimed "word of truth" is "saving," according to 1:13.[53] "When he [the Messiah] came he proclaimed" (2:17). In 3:6 the noun "gospel" means neither a book nor a specific doctrine; rather it signifies the act of proclaiming[54] which brings the peace home to the former belligerents. This announcement—which started with Christ and is continued by him through the mouths of his servants (II Cor 13:3; cf. Heb 2:3)—belongs so closely to the event of the cross that it shares in its mediating, effective, and significant, i.e. in its truly sacramental nature. "In the Messiah" and "through the gospel, the Gentiles are joint heirs"! Eph 3:6 affirms no less than that preaching is a sacrament, an instrument and demonstration of Christ's presence and man's salvation. It is not a sacrament added to the priestly and sacrificial work of the Messiah but its radiation and application.

the Gentiles are. Lit. "the Gentiles to be." The infinitive used in the Greek can possess a wide variety of meanings: it may express an imperative, a purpose, or a consequence.[55] If (as in KJ) it is translated by "should be" then the revelation of the secret mentioned in vss. 3–5 is the pronouncement of an order, a wish or a desirable result. In that case the "gospel" would not be essentially different from a commandment or from the law expressing God's good design for men. However, according to Paul the law and its commandments are not a sacrament by which God exerts his "power . . . for salvation" or "gives life" (Rom 1:16; Gal 3:21). Rather it is the gospel which makes public what earlier was hidden, announcing more than just the possibility or desirability of the Gentiles' adoption; it proclaims their eternal inclusion in God's love (Eph 1:4–5). Now God's will is done in the Messiah's coming, death and rulership (1:13–14, 22–23; 2:11–22). Still, why should Paul use an infinitive ("to be") if a plain and straight indicative would appear to dispel all ambiguity? The infinitive found in Eph 3:6 might be a so-called expository or epexegetical infinitive,[56] employed for clarifying *what* is meant by the secret and by revelation, and for describing the work assigned to Paul, the steward of God's grace. However, no demonstrative pronoun, e.g. "this is . . . ," precedes the infinitive and justifies the epexegetical understanding. Rather the infinitive fulfills the function of a sentence that begins with "that" and describes a perception, a belief, an utterance, or a piece of information.[57] J. B. Phillips' paraphrase of Eph 3:6 is therefore appropriate: (The secret that was hidden . . .) "is simply this: that the Gentiles . . . are . . ." Paul speaks here of "the Gentiles" rather than of some or of many Gentiles. A well attested variant reading of 3:9 may

---

[52] Cf. "through baptism," "in baptism" (Rom 6:4; Col 2:12), and the frequent changes between "through faith," "through the law," and "in faith," "in the law," or "by faith," "by the law."

[53] Cf. COMMENT XV on 1:3–14.

[54] Just as in Gal 1:7–9 (cf. 1:16; 2:7; I Cor 9:16); Rom 1:1, 16–17; 15:16, etc., but unlike Gal 2:2, 5, 14, etc.

[55] For the following see BDF, 389–91, 394, 397.

[56] As in James 1:27, "This is pure religion: to visit orphans"; I Thess 4:3 and Acts 15:28, "This is the will of God, these things are necessary: to abstain from. . . ."

[57] See BDF, 397:3–4 for a host of examples.

be true to the apostle's intention: "all" (Gentiles) are meant; cf. Rom 1:5, "all the Gentiles."[58] Eph 3:6 has a universalistic ring which corresponds to the absence of any reference to faith in the immediate context.[59] Indeed, God "wills that all men be saved and come to the knowledge of truth" (I Tim 2:4). No doubt the gospel also contains God's as yet unfulfilled desire and command, including the requirement of faith, but the core of the gospel is a blunt indicative. The Messiah has come, he has made peace, and therefore he has incorporated (all) "the Gentiles" into his realm. A good and victorious king will sooner or later be trusted or respected by his subjects, though his victory over his enemies precedes his glorification by all former adversaries. Indeed, Paul thinks of Jesus Christ in terms of the victorious Messianic king who makes use of God's power over all hostile powers (1:19–23). If all the Gentiles are not yet aware of their incorporation, those who in one body, the church, already praise their resuscitation from death and sin are sufficient "proof" of God's power and goodness for all generations to come (2:7).

joint heirs, members in the same body, fellow beneficiaries in all that is promised. The Greek original is briefer: "co-heirs, con-corporate, co-partakers in the promise." The variations on the preposition *syn* ("with") had been anticipated in 2:6, "raised together," "enthroned together." While in the former passage Christ, and not only the Jews, was the person "together with" whom the Christians were exalted, in 3:6 only the Jews are meant: together with Israel the Gentiles are now "heirs, members, beneficiaries." The first among these three attributes, "joint heirs," therefore means something else here than it does in Rom 8:17. There, fellow-heirdom with Christ is in focus; here, with the Jewish people. It is the distinctive message of Ephesians that no Gentile can have communion with Christ or with God unless he also has communion with Israel. With this doctrine Ephesians does not contradict Romans or Galatians, for according to Rom 11:17 the Gentiles are grafted onto Israel. Following Galatians those Gentiles who have "put on Christ" are now "children" or "seed" of Abraham (3:7, 26–29), resembling Isaac, the son of Abraham "according to the Spirit" (4:28–29). The adjectival term "members of the same body" lit. "concorporate," is Paul's creation.[60] It is unlikely that he derived his image from a sculptor who with metal and plaster adds a missing member to an unfinished statue. Nor could he have in mind a transplantation as in the simile of the olive tree (Rom 11:17–24). If a clear image stood before him at all, it may have been the growth ("from the head," 4:16) of a formerly unknown or inoperative member; or he may have used the term "body" in its metaphorical sense, as in I Cor 12. To become a "member of the same body" is analogous to joining an army or club, or to naturalization in a city or state. Eph 2:19 supports the last interpretation, cf. 4:25. In each case the body to which the Gentiles are joined is none other than Christ's and the first members of the body are the Jews. The last term, lit. "co-partakers in the promise," harks back to 1:12–13 and 2:12, i.e. to the passages that speak of the hope first held by the Jews alone, of the "covenant of promise" from which Gentiles were excluded, and of the

---

[58] Equally passages such as Gal 1:16; 2:7, 9; Rom 15:16 permit no exclusion of any part or number of the nations from the gospel and commission entrusted to Paul.

[59] But see 1:1, 15; 2:8; 3:17; 4:5, etc.

[60] Pseudo-Aristotle (*de mundo* 396A 14) employs the passive of the verb *syssōmatopoieō*.

"earnest" or "seal" of "the promised Holy Spirit." If "promise" in 3:6 meant no more than the deed or testament by which sons or strangers are made heirs, then the term "fellow-beneficiaries" in the promise would duplicate "joint heirs." More likely the three attributes of Eph 3:6 are so arranged as to lead to a climax.[61] The last attribute is indeed a climax, if by "promise" is meant the substance and earnest of the promise, the Holy Spirit.[62] Because his presence manifests God's presence among his people, the Spirit is indeed the epitome of God's promise. The reference to inheritance emphasizes the hope for the future; the mention of the body alludes to the gift and task of an organic and social life; the endowment with the Spirit gives reason for joy and guarantees freedom. Through the Spirit the goods of the coming aeon are already tasted, cf. Heb 6:4.

7. *gift of God's grace which was given me.* What is given, the gift or grace? According to the better Greek texts grace is what was given (cf. 3:2). The Koine MSS, however, read "the gift . . . given." Both variants communicate the same idea, however, in showing that the "gift of grace" is a commission for specific work rather than a sinecure.[63] In this verse at least seven different words are used to praise God and to prepare the way for Paul's self-depreciating statements that follow: God's "power" is "at work"; it is the power of "grace"; it is a "gift"; it is "given"; Paul is a "servant"; he "was made" a servant. No loophole is left in this overly redundant diction for attributing to Paul any honor or dignity that belongs to God alone. However, as J. A. Robinson puts it, Paul is somehow "appropriating" the term "grace" to himself.[64] Does he do this because he is aware of his own extravagant sin, and concerned for his own salvation? In distinction, e.g. from Luther, he does not first of all elaborate on the gracious forgiveness of his sin and only then proclaim the validity of his experience for other men as well. Rather two things need be called to mind that have been emphasized before in the context of 1:2 and 3:2: Paul understands the "given grace" primarily as an appointment and as equipment for ministry, and he regards the calling of the Gentiles into God's fold as the essence of grace. Grace is distinctly God's own personal character and gift. It is not given to any man for personal salvation, enjoyment, and satisfaction only. According to I Tim 1:15–16 the personal salvation of Paul, the "first among the sinners," was from the beginning meant to be an example of the salvation of many. Grace is, as it were by definition, the "riches of Christ" that are to be "announced to the Gentiles" (3:8).

for his power is at work. Lit. "according to the energy of his power." The reference to the "power," viz. to "God" himself (Gal 2:8), working in Paul confirms the foregoing interpretation of grace. It would be misleading to speak at this (or any other) point of a grace poured *into* Paul, i.e. of *gratia infusa.* For according to the context the grace given to Paul makes him an instrument of God for diffusing grace. Since God's grace is communal and communicative, it

---

[61] This is e.g. Pelagius' and Jerome's judgment, but it is not shared by Abbott, Gaugler, and others.
[62] Cf. 1:13; Gal 3:14; 4:6.   [63] Col 1:24–25; I Cor 15:10; cf. COMMENT III B.
[64] P. 224; cf. the special connection between "grace," the apostle, and his ministry in Gal 1:15–16; 2:9, 21; I Cor 3:10; 15:10; II Cor 1:12; 4:15; 12:9; Rom 1:5; 12:3; 15:15; Philip 1:7.

cannot be stored in one man. By "pouring out" the "riches of his grace" (1:6–7) God manifests his royal right and power over many men. "By grace" he saves many, not just Paul (2:5, 8). This then is grace: the same power by which Jesus Christ is resurrected is also demonstrated in the resurrection of Jews and Gentiles dead in sins, and through the beginning of a new creation (2:1–10).[65] Though grace includes the "forgiveness of lapses" (1:7), it means more than just an acquittal of the sinner: it establishes God's kingship (Rom 5:21), and it equips his servants for useful activity (I Cor 3:10). Grace is that movement from God, through resurrection, through the apostle, to the Gentiles,[66] which is still going on.

I was made a servant of the gospel. Lit. "of which I was made a servant." The Greek aorist passive "I was made" (*egenēthēn*) was decried by Phrynichus, a second-century A.D. grammarian, as an idiosyncrasy of the Doric dialect.[67] In the NT this passive is used interchangeably with the middle (*egenomēn*); compare, e.g. I Thess 2:14 with John 1:3. Both forms denote creation by God rather than a deployment of man's own resources. In Gal 1:10; I Cor 4:1; Rom 15:16 Paul uses different Greek nouns for designating himself as a "servant." The term *diakonos* in Eph 3:7 describes originally a man who served at table (cf. Acts 6:2), as distinct from a slave (*doulos*) who performed inferior duties; from a steward (*oikonomos*) of a landowner; or from a public servant (*leitourgos*) of a king or tyrant. When Paul uses these terms he may not always be conscious of their original meanings. He employs the same term as in Eph 3:7 when he calls himself elsewhere a "servant" of God, of the church, or of the new covenant, and when he speaks of the "service" of the Spirit or of righteousness.[68] The multidimensional use of the respective verb and nouns ("to serve," "servant," "service") reveals that the apostle has in mind a public rather than a private function. In I Thess 3:2; Col 1:7, 4:7, etc., he calls his helpers, in Rom 13:4 Roman officials, by the same title. The designation *diakonos* ("servant") was taken from the realm of the secular and did not from the beginning carry the clerical connotation of "deacon," but passages such as Philip 1:1; cf. Acts 6:1–6, show the beginning of a specifically ecclesiastic sense of "servant."

8. *I, who am less than the least.* The first part of vs. 8, ending with the words, "the special grace," may originally have formed a parenthesis inside the large parenthesis (3:2–13); in Greek, it does not really resemble the beginning of a new sentence as in our translation. Whatever the syntactic function of 3:8a, this short sentence reveals that Paul never ceases wondering at the charge given to him. As if the superlatives "least" (among the saints) or "first" (among the sinners)[69] were too weak to express his unworthiness, in this verse he creates a novel form of a Greek adjective, which in English would be equal

[65] Among recent interpreters of Paul, especially E. Käsemann, "God's Righteousness in Paul," JTAC 1, (1965), 100–10, and P. Stuhlmacher, *Gottes Gerechtigkeit*, Göttingen: Vandenhoeck, 1966, have emphasized the indissoluble connection between God's gracious judgment and God's creative might.

[66] Schlier, p. 152.

[67] This ancient philologist may be subject to an error. For in Plato *Parmenides* 141E, the middle and passive forms occur side by side.

[68] II Cor 6:4; Col 1:23, 25; II Cor 3:6, 8–9, etc.   [69] I Cor 15:9; I Tim 1:15.

to the terms "smallester" or "leaster." In the NT only one similar formation is found, i.e., "greaterer" in III John 4. As early as Homeric Greek and among classic poets, but much more frequently in the prose writings of the Hellenistic period, such double-comparatives, or combinations of comparatives and superlatives, were used for emphasis.[70] Paul is not ashamed to place himself extremely low.

of all saints. The Chester Beatty Papyrus (P 46, third century) omits the word "saints." This reading is probably due to an error called "homoioteleuton." Since the Greek words for "all" and "saints" have the same ending, the copyist's eye may have skipped from the first to the second. If this papyrus had the more original reading, Paul would thus have declared himself the lowest among all "men"—whether Jews, Gentiles, or Christians—or the least among the collegium of apostles and prophets. While in I Cor 15:9 he admits to being the "least among the apostles," I Tim 1:15 designates him as outstanding among the sinners of the world, i.e. among all men. I Corinthians is unquestionably authentic, I Timothy is not. Therefore the more restricted comparison of I Cor 15:9 may be a closer parallel to Eph 3:8 than I Tim 1:15. The reading of Eph 3:8 presented by the great majority of MSS points in the same direction: among all Christians Paul ascribes himself to the lowest rank. The reason for such humility is not to be sought in Pauline passages such as II Cor 4:12 and Rom 7 where Paul describes the weakness of his flesh and the continued rebellion of the "old man" against the "new." Like the OT psalms of lamentation and thanksgiving, Paul considered lifelong weakness, temptation, and strife characteristic of all saints. Whenever Paul gives a reason for his specifically low and suspect place among the members of the congregation, he speaks of his outstandingly violent part in the persecution of the church.[71] The repeated explicit references to his role as a persecutor reveal indeed his consciousness of sin. But because this awareness has a specific focus, it is distinct from a possibly morbid preoccupation with himself or with sin in general. His self-humiliation is unlike the expression of hidden pride and its concomitant fishing for compliments. However low his place, on the ground of forgiveness Paul is still reckoned, and also counts himself, "among the saints" who elsewhere are called "perfect" and "blameless."[72] Just as the other "saints" he lives as a justified sinner.

the special grace. Lit. "this grace." The translation chosen follows JB. The Greek text itself suggests that God's grace may give another commission to other men (cf. Gal 2:7–9), but there is no intimation that a grace of God might be given to someone without including the gift of ministry. Even the gifts of the Spirit, the so-called *charismata* that are enumerated by Paul (I Cor 12:4–31, etc.), do not include beatific vision, undisturbed contemplation and concentration, solipsistic happiness, and the like. There are always fellow men who benefit from the gift or gifts of grace. If there be inspired men who cannot communicate and share with others (as in the case of Corinthian enthusiasts), then Paul urges that they be muzzled (I Cor 14).

to announce to the Gentiles the good news. "This is what 'this grace' consisted in";[73] cf. Rom 1:5; 15:15–16 and the first NOTE on 3:7. An interesting

---

[70] BDF, 60:2; 61:2 affirms the climactic meaning of the composite forms; Abbott denies it.
[71] Gal 1:13, 23; I Cor 15:9; Philip 3:6; cf. the analogous hints of Acts.
[72] I Cor 2:6; Philip 3:15; Eph 1:4; 5:27.   [73] Abbott.

variant which may be inspired by the parallel verse Gal 1:16[74] has "among the Gentiles" instead of "to the Gentiles." This reading recognizes that Paul cannot possibly contact more than certain representative cities, groups, and individuals of the pagan world. While OT prophets (such as Jer 46–51) pronounced oracles against the Gentiles, and OT psalms (e.g. 110:1) predicted the defeat of the nations at the hands of the Messiah, Paul is convinced that a new era has dawned with the coming of the Messiah Jesus: the era of peace for those far and those near (2:17). Paul's specific task is to announce good news to those who were far off. Whereas in 3:5 a collegial view of the NT apostles and prophets is reflected and (in agreement with Gal 2 and Acts 15) Paul assumes that all these servants of God knew about the inclusion of the Gentiles, here in 3:8 he shows that not all the apostles and prophets were actually engaged in mission work to the Gentiles. For him it is a privilege, and a burden at the same time (I Cor 9:16–17), to be entrusted with a task covering all lands, seas and islands. One man *against* the world? This sounds pretentious and is not Paul's commission. The apostle is given grace in order to be a man *for* all the Gentiles! In describing his task only in positive, constructive terms, Paul reveals that his ministry is different from that of Moses and Jeremiah; cf. II Cor 3:6–18; Jer 1:10, 18. He is not sent out to judge and to condemn. In the interpretation of 2:13–16, especially in COMMENT V C on 2:11–12, it was shown that Jesus Christ bore all condemnation in his person.[75]

the unfathomable riches of the Messiah. The "riches" of God or of his grace have been mentioned in 1:7; 2:4, 7. Eph 3:8 is the only verse in Ephesians that speaks of the *Messiah's* riches, but other Pauline texts presuppose the same riches when they point out that Christ became poor in order to enrich many.[76] The term "unfathomable" or "inscrutable," has so far not been found in non-biblical Greek, but it is used in the LXX version of the Book of Job to denote the mystery of creation,[77] and in Rom. 11:33 to describe the ways and judgments of God. The reference to inscrutability contains a warning against profanation and rationalizing. By revelation God opens and gives himself to man but does not make himself subject to man's intellectual or technical control. Revelation creates rather than annihilates wonder, awe, and respect. Neither God nor Christ can simply be grasped by man. "The god who has been comprehended . . . is always an idol."[78] The same apostle who knows that the Spirit searches all things and reveals the depth of God so as to make men "perfect" in knowledge (I Cor 2) also acknowledges freely that at present he "knows in part" only and does not yet understand fully (I Cor 13:12). True knowledge of the revealed secret does not "puff one up" (I Cor 8:1–3). While Christ's work can be admired, enjoyed, and proclaimed, it cannot be explained, deduced or induced from premises outside the mysterious unity of the Father, the Son, and the Spirit to which earlier passages of Ephesians have pointed. The unfathomableness attributed by Job to God the creator and his

---

[74] It is widely spread, and found, e.g. in the Codices Claramontanus and Boernerianus, also in the MSS of the Koine group.

[75] Cf. Gal 3:13; II Cor 5:21; Rom 3:25; 8:3.

[76] II Cor 8:9; I Cor 1:5; Philip 2:6–8. Passages such as II Cor 6:10; 8:2, 14 describe an analogous loss of riches among the saints that enriches others.

[77] Job 5:9; 9:10; 34:24; cf. 28.   [78] Gaugler, p. 140.

work is in Ephesians ascribed to the Messiah. The Messiah's work is described by the verb "he created" (2:15); and the Gentiles' adoption implies new creation (2:10). For the author of Ephesians the work done through the Messiah confirms that God is the creator (3:9; cf. John 5:17–18). More about inscrutability and the limits of knowledge will be said in Eph 3:18–19.

9. *to make all men see how the secret is administered [by the Messiah]*. This translation follows the textual tradition contained in the majority of important Greek MSS. However, the modern editions of the Greek Bible give preference to a minority reading which omits the personal object *pantas* (all men) and presupposes that the verb *phōtizō* here denotes the act of making shine, that is, of revelation as an event in its own right[79] which need not necessarily carry the sense that men are enlightened or instructed by it.[80] Perhaps H. Schlier expresses the sense of the minority reading in most striking terms when (in the language of the later M. Heidegger's writings) he speaks of the *Lichtung des Geheimnisses* (lit. "light-becoming of the secret"). Such an event can take place essentially for its own sake; only incidentally may it also be to man's benefit. The majority's reading of Eph 3:9 seems to give up this mysterious dimension. Is it a correction of the original text? Does it by rather cheap means facilitate its understanding, but demonstrate a lack of understanding far from its profound depth? Indeed, the (shorter) text of the minority emphasizes that through the apostle's vocation and ministry something happens to God's secret: it is revealed and shines in its own light. The majority puts the accent (only) upon the Gentiles who profit from the grace and commission given to Paul.[81] An analogous choice between various accents was discussed in the exposition of 1:11. However, strictly philological arguments in favor of the minority text are not available today. While Schlier and the editors of modern Greek Bibles endorse it as the *lectio difficilior*, the parallel statement on enlightenment in 1:18 also makes it possible that the shorter reading is due to a scribal error, i.e. to the inadvertent omission of the object *pantas* which stood in the original text and is still contained in the majority of the MSS. Certainly the flux of the argument in 3:1–13 is from the revealed secret itself to the many beneficiaries of God's grace; our translation has been based upon the text which expresses that movement rather than a speculative philosophical thought. In Col 1:25–26 the terms "administration," "word of

---

[79] The minority reading (found in the original script of Codex Sinaiticus, in Codex Alexandrinus, in some minuscules, in the texts used by Hilary, Jerome, Augustine, etc.; see GNT for a complete list) is supported by the sense which *phōtizō* has in I Cor 4:5: "The Lord will bring the hidden things of darkness to light," and II Tim 1:10: "He has made to shine life and incorruptibility through the Gospel." The shorter (minority) reading of Eph 3:9 can therefore be translated by "to bring the administration [or the mystery, or the plan of salvation] to light."

[80] The sense which *phōtizō* has in the majority of MSS has parallels in Eph 1:18 and John 1:9: "that he illumine the eyes of your hearts . . ."; "the true light that enlightens every man . . ." Equally in LXX Judg 13:8; IV[II] Kings 12:3; 17:27–28; Ps 118[119]:130, *phōtizō* signifies, "to give light to, to teach, to instruct." In *Corp. Herm.* XIII 19 the verb is used as a parallel or synonym of "to save," and "to inspire." Thus it can denote the initiation of a man by a cultic act into a community; see R. Reitzenstein, *Die Hellenistischen Mysterienreligionen* (henceforth HMyRel), 3d ed. (Leipzig: Teubner, 1927), pp. 44, 264, 292. For Philo's concept of enlightenment see E. R. Goodenough, *By Light, Light: The Mystic Gospel of Hellenistic Judaism* (Yale University Press, 1935), pp. 11 ff., 146 f., 166 f., etc. In the context of Eph 1:18 it was mentioned that in second-century Christian theology, if not already in Heb 6:4, baptism was sometimes called "enlightenment" (*phōtismos*).

[81] Abbott's opinion that in either case the meaning "is pretty much the same," is not beyond dispute, as especially Schlier's commentary shows.

God," and "secret" are used for identifying the task entrusted to Paul. In a similar way the apostolic proclamation, the administration, and the secret are mentioned together in Eph 3:8–9. But while in Col 1:25, cf. Eph 3:2, Paul is the steward entrusted with "administration," Eph 3:9 appears to point back to 1:10 and to speak of the stewardship of Jesus Christ (see the first NOTE on 1:10). Paul, who in I Cor 4:1 calls himself a "steward of the [many] mysteries of God," in Eph 3 (as he did in 1:10) leaves to Christ alone the honor of revealing and carrying out the one *mystērion* of God. The words "by the Messiah" have been added in our translation in order to make clear this return from Paul's subsidiary to Christ's original and plenipotentiary "administration."

hidden from the ages in God. Lit. ". . . from the aeons . . ." The preposition "from" (*apo*) and the noun "ages" (*aiōnes*) permit two interpretations that appear to be totally different, perhaps even contradictory. (*a*) The preposition *apo* can denote only duration, and *aiōn* can have the temporal meaning which was proper to this term before it became the name of a deity or of several angelic or demonic powers. If these two presuppositions are made, then Eph 3:9 speaks of a secret that was, for ages and ages, contained "in God" and known to no one. This exposition of the words *apo tōn aiōnōn* ("from the ages") is supported by the diction used in LXX Ps 40:14[41:13] (lit. "from the age to the age") and Eph 3:21 (lit. "into all generations of the age of the ages"). It is justified also on purely linguistic grounds: in good Greek the person from whom something is hidden is either in the genitive, the dative or the accusative, but the preposition "from" (*apo*) is not added to introduce him. If, therefore, Eph 3:9 is written in good Greek, a person or power from whom the secret is hidden is not mentioned but only one affirmation is made: "the past time" was the time of the "hidden *mystērion*." (*b*) If the same verse is phrased in the diction that was spread among Greek writers of Jewish origin, then the preposition "from" can mean something else; it can introduce the person who is unable to see or otherwise perceive the hidden thing.[82] Correspondingly, the *aiōnes* mentioned in this verse need not be time spans but can be angelic or demonic beings, or both. I Peter speaks of "angels" who would like to "look into" the revelation now given to the saints.[83] The very next verse in Ephesians, 3:10, affirms that God's wisdom is to be "made known" to principalities and powers. Therefore 3:9 may well assert that it was hidden "from them" and it may anticipate—Gnosticizing interpreters of Ephesians say, may reproduce —the Gnostic myth of the light messenger who penetrates a demonic wall of darkness and informs only the elect of redemption. But unlike some Gnostic streams of thought, and in tension vis-à-vis 3:5, vs. 9 may imply that the secret was hidden only from the powers, and not from elect men, e.g. the patriarchs and prophets. Rather than referring to the period of total darkness it would point out only the powers' lack of enlightenment. The tension between the two expositions sketched here is reminiscent of 2:7. There, either future periods or onrushing demons, or both, were mentioned. The late date of the so-called Gnostic parallels cannot totally preclude an interpretation of Ephesians that

[82] E.g. LXX IV Kings 4:27; Ps118[119]:19; Matt 11:27; Rev 6:16; I Clem. 56:10. The Greek *apo* reflects the Hebrew *min*, BDF, 155:3.

[83] I Peter 1:12; see also I Cor 2:8, and the literature and arguments mentioned in the interpretation of Eph 2:7 and 3:5.

resembles some Gnostic patterns of thought, for long before the classic Gnostic systems were developed, angels and demons played a major role in Jewish apocalyptic writings as possible recipients or mediators of revelation. Thus a clear-cut decision for one or the other interpretation is impossible. Most likely the very alternative—either periods of time or heavenly powers—is misleading, for there exists a close relationship between the supposedly mythical powers and the historical institutions, structures, and periods of earthly existence, as was demonstrated earlier.[84] Hiddenness "at" earlier times and hiddenness "from" the genii of the respective periods may be one and the same thing. To be excluded is, however, Marcion's tendentious interpretation of 3:9. According to him the mystery now revealed was hidden "from" the creator God himself![85] While the Codex Boerneriamus and the old Latin versions presuppose a Greek text that permits an interpretation resembling Marcion's, they should probably be understood in still another way. The Greek dative tō theō (meaning "from God") which in these MSS replaces the majority reading en tō theō ("in God") may be one of the rare NT "datives with the passive"[86] and mean "by God." Most likely Eph 3:9 does not intend to point out that the same secret which *was* hidden before its revelation still *is* hidden in God.[87] Certainly, as was stated earlier, many "mysteries," e.g. of Israel, the resurrection, certain Scripture passages, also of the trinity and incarnation etc., are known only "in part": they cannot be listed exhaustively, and those revealed are only fragmentarily understood (I Cor 13:2, 12). Yet the one secret of God of which Ephesians speaks, i.e. God's love of Jews *and* Gentiles, has been plainly revealed and is still being manifested.[88] A dialectic between revealed and yet hidden, still hidden and yet revealed, would destroy the triumphant ring of 3:2-12. It would restrict Paul's task—as if he were not to reveal too much! Actually, he has nothing else to serve but revelation; he is not appointed guardian of a truth that is partly obscure. The gospel is the full and saving "word of truth" (1:13). It can be left to Zeus "to hide all and to reveal all"![89]

the creator of all things. Lit. "who has created all things." This is the only place in which Ephesians refers to the first rather than the new creation. A variant reading supported by the Koine MSS seeks to assimilate this verse to Col 1:15-17:[90] a reference is added to Jesus Christ the mediator of creation. The Koine variant may provide valuable help for understanding the mention of "the creator." While the words, "who has created all things,"[91] or their equivalent, "who has created heaven and earth," look like no more than an almost worn-out formula taken over from Jewish prayers, it is unlikely that they served only for a pious ornament in Eph 3:9. Perhaps the author used them to protest against a Gnosticizing separation of creation and redemption, in which case he attacks the belief that the created world originated from fallen angels.[92] Since, however, no solid evidence has yet been found for dating this belief back

---

[84] See COMMENT V on 1:15-23 and the exegesis of 2:7.   [85] See Tertullian *adv. Marc.* v 18.
[86] See Matt 1:18; Luke 23:15; Rom 10:20; James 3:7; II Peter 2:19; Ps.-Clem. *hom.* 3:68; 9:21; 19:23; BDF, 191.
[87] However Schlier, p. 154, believes that "in a certain sense the hidden-ness still continues now."
[88] Eph 1:9; 3:3, 5, 9-10; 6:19; Rom 16:25-26; cf. II Cor 3:18.
[89] Orphic Fragment 168, in O. Kern, *Orphicorum Fragmenta*, Berlin: Weidmann, 1922.
[90] Cf. John 1:3; Heb 1:2.   [91] E.g. III Macc 2:3; Jub 12:19; Rev 4:11.
[92] Schlier, p. 155; see COMMENTS IV on 1:3-14 and VI C 1 on 1:15-23.

to the first century A.D., another interpretation is more appropriate. Paul wants to make clear that God has not changed and is not abandoning his first creation by forming a new creation in Christ. Salvation, life, and unity in Christ have always been the very purpose of the creation of heaven and earth.[93] The "revelation" of the secret, not the "secret" itself (that is, "all his love" with which he loves us, 2:4) is an innovation in the history of God with man. That which has now been revealed always was "in God." Revelation manifests the truth which is preexistent. It unveils that which is eternal, has no beginning, and cannot be superseded or antiquated. Just like the prologues of the Gospel of John and of Hebrews, so also Eph 3:9 contains a "supra-lapsarian" hint: even before man sinned God had decided upon the work which his Son was to carry out.

10. *The manifold wisdom of God.* The adjective "manifold" probably denoted originally the character of an intricately embroidered pattern,[94] e.g. of a cloth or flowers.[95] It does not occur in the LXX,[96] but the examples given in the excursus on Wisdom[97] demonstrate how "manifold" were the functions ascribed to her.[98] See the end of COMMENT II for other interpretations of the adjective "manifold."

to be made known through the church to the governments and authorities in the heavens. See COMMENT IV below for a discussion of the mediating and cosmic role thus ascribed to the church. It is unlikely that the words "in the heavens" belong to the verb "to make known" and affirm that the church fulfills its function outside the present world of space and time. Although according to 2:6 the saints are "enthroned in the heavens," their residence is on earth in Zion, cf. the location of the Messianic king's throne. See COMMENT IV on 2:1–10. The spiritual character of the powers is described by the attribute "in the heavens," cf. 2:2 and 6:12. It is also improbable that in 3:10 Paul proposes "a perfectly satisfying philosophy of history" for justifying God's ways.[99] Paul is a practical theologian who speaks about the specific task of the church. He is not a speculating philosopher or a contemplative mystic who deals with the course of the world in general.

11. *the design concerning the ages.* Lit. "the plan of the aeons." Three interpretations deserve consideration:

a) The translation presented here suggests (*1*) that both aeons, the "period of the hidden secret" before the Messiah's advent and the "period of revelation" inaugurated by him, have been preconceived by God. Even the past, when Israel was separated from the Gentiles and the Gentiles were excluded from God's people, is thus designated as a time created, given, filled by God. The

[93] Robinson; also K. Barth, *Church Dogmatics*, III:1 (1958), 94–329: the covenant of grace is the internal basis of creation; creation is the external basis of the covenant.

[94] Robinson, p. 80; e.g. Euripides *Iphigenia of Taurus* 1149.

[95] Abbott, referring to Eubulus Comicus (fourth century B.C.) *ap. Athen.* 15, 679d.

[96] Though the attribute "consisting of many parts" (*polymeros*) comes near it. The latter adjective is used in Wisd Sol 7:22, together with many others, to describe the spirit of Wisdom. In Heb 1:1 the "many parts" and "many modes" of the prophetic attestation to God are compared with the final revelation through the Son.

[97] COMMENT X on 1:3–14.

[98] Wisdom is creator, judge, life-giver, the basis of knowledge and science. She is guide, savior, revealer, the key to nature, but also bride, virgin and mother. See Noth, Wilckens, Arvedson, von Rad and others in BIBLIOGRAPHY 8.

[99] As Robinson suggests.

same God has "in the Messiah" Jesus created the past and the present. (2) Reference may be made either to the present and the future aeons (1:21) or to subdivisions of the passing aeon and the new era. Paul may allude to the age of the patriarchs, the exodus, David, the exile, and to the various time spans of Jesus' earthly ministry, the first eyewitnesses, the later proclamation (Heb 2:3), the final woes, and the judgment.[100] (3) Eph 3:11 may in its own way rephrase what in Ps 31:15 is formulated in the words, "My times are in thy hand"; perhaps the author intends to present a theological and Christological re-interpretation of Eccles 3:1–8, "For everything there is a season . . . a time to be born and a time to die . . ." Ephesians would then reproduce here a reflection on the contradictory nature of all times and their inevitable passing. However, nowhere else in the NT is the noun "plan" or "design" (*prothesis*) followed by a genitive of content as is presupposed in this interpretation. The wording of Eph 3:11 also permits, and perhaps urgently suggests two entirely different versions.

b) It may be that the author wants to speak of a divine purpose that runs like a golden thread through the ages[101] in order to lead to the "days of fulfillment" (1:10). This interpretation is mandatory if the Greek phrasing is explained as a Hebraism in form and contents.

c) Or the genitive, "of the aeons," may here be equivalent to the adjective, "eternal" (*aiōnios*); cf. Rom 16:25.[102] Then it points out that God's decision was made "before all times"[103] and is "eternal."

These three interpretations need not be mutually exclusive, but in Eph 1:4 and 10 the concerns expressed by the second and third were already clearly stated. Eph 3:5 and 9 add a new element: they give explicit mention to the time and condition of the hiddenness which prevailed before the time of the Messiah's coming. It is more likely that 3:11 refers to the contents of 3:5 and 9, protects them from misunderstanding, and puts them into sharp focus, than that it repeats earlier utterances. The author probably wants to affirm that even the time of hiddenness was God's time.

God has carried out. Lit. "which he made."[104] In this verse, the term, "to make a design" or "plan," can have two meanings:

a) "Making a plan" may be identified with "planning." The longer form of diction could be equivalent to the Latinism, "to make a counsel" (Mark 3:6) and therefore signify to form or to conceive a plan.[105] In the context of Eph 3:11 the phrase then means that God's eternal design, his predestination (1:4 ff.), was focused upon the Messiah Jesus.[106] Therefore it was not an impersonal, cold, absolute, and eternal decree, resembling predetermination by a blind fate. However, linguistic evidence does not support a version such as, "the design . . . which God has conceived," or, "the plan . . . which God has made." For when the author of Ephesians uses periphrastic diction (e.g. in 1:16, lit. "I make remembrance" instead of "I remember," or in 4:16, "the body makes its growth" in place of "the body grows"), he uses the middle

---

[100] W. Michaelis, *Die Versöhnung des Alls,* (Gümlingen; Siloah, 1950), p. 43.
[101] Robinson; Abbott.   [102] Dibelius; Gaugler.
[103] See I Cor 2:7; II Tim 1:9; Titus 1:2; cf. Eph 1:4; 3:9; Col 1:26.
[104] Origen, Jerome, Theophylact, Chrysostom, Victorinus consider wisdom or the church the object of "making." But it is much more likely that the text speaks of an action related to the noun, design, plan (*prothesis*).
[105] Calvin; Th. Beza; Bengel; Abbott; Schlier; Gaugler.
[106] As discussed in COMMENT V on 1:3–14.

rather than the active form of the verb "to make."[107] Since in Eph 3:11 the active is used, the phrase "making a plan" may not serve as a periphrasis of the simpler form "planning."

b) "Making" may mean "performing" or "carrying out"; cf. J. Moffatt's version, RSV, NEB, NTTEV. This translation is supported by the analogous phrase, "to do the will," or, "to carry out the decision."[108] After the eternal decision was stressed in 1:4–5, 10, chapters 2 and 3 of Ephesians describe the execution of God's will.

in the Messiah Jesus our Lord. This pleonastic formulation[109] reveals the author's special interest in Jesus Christ as the center and plenipotent agent of God's will. Christ has not been dethroned or retired because of the instrumentality attributed to the church in 3:10; rather what the church is to do in relation to the powers has its ground, measure, and force "in" the execution of God's plan through "Christ." The name "Jesus" may be added to the titles Messiah and Lord in order to draw attention to the ministry of the incarnate and crucified (cf. 2:13–18) rather than to the function of the preexistent.[110]

12. *In him and because of his faithfulness.* Lit. "In him . . . through the faith of him." The conjunction "and" is not found in the Greek text, but the placement of the words "in him" at the beginning, and "through his faithfulness" at the end gives these formulae an almost pathetic weight, which justifies the English version given. Biblical reasons and scholarly literature supporting the translation "his faithfulness" rather than "faith in him" have been mentioned in the NOTE on "faith" in 2:8.[111] Since in 2:18, in the closest parallel to 3:12, Christ alone is described as the mediator of the Jews' and Gentiles' access to God, and since (except in 1:1, 15, 19; 2:8) the faith of the believing church members has not yet been explicitly mentioned, it is unlikely that Paul should suddenly attribute to "their" faith alone a mediating function.[112] A man may approach God in good faith, that is, "in confidence," as a literal translation of 3:12 indeed would state (cf. Rom 5:2), but such confidence alone is not an instrument but an accompaniment of access. In the interpretation of "access" in 2:18 it was shown that the NT writers put all emphasis upon him who made the "introduction," i.e. Jesus Christ the mediator.

confidently we make use of our free access [to God]. Lit. "We possess boldness and access in confidence." Among the parallel NT statements that mention "boldness" or "access to God,"[113] Eph 3:12 is outstanding for the combination

[107] Robinson, p. 171.
[108] See, e.g. LXX III Kings 5:8; Isa 44:28; Eph 2:3; Matt 21:3; John 6:38. The verb "to make" has the sense "to carry out," also in phrases such as "to do mercy," "to create justice," Luke 1:72; 10:37; 18:7. Cf. Rom 4:21.
[109] Instead of, or combined with "the Messiah," the title "Lord" is used, e.g. in Ps 110:1; Acts 2:36. See the literature mentioned in the third NOTE on 1:1.
[110] The combination of both titles, "Messiah" and "our Lord," with the name "Jesus" is also found in I Cor 15:31; Rom 6:23; 8:39; Philip 3:8. See COMMENT IV on 4:17–32 for a discussion of the emphatic reference to "Jesus."
[111] The presence of the article in the formula, "through his faithfulness" distinguishes 3:12 from the parallel passages Gal 2:16; 3:22; Rom 3:22; Philip 3:9. These texts speak of the "faith of Christ" which was earlier (in 2:13–18) described as the means to open the door to God. In that case the words, "through his faithfulness" are synonyms for "in Christ's blood," "in his flesh," "in one body," "through the cross," "in one Spirit" in 2:13–18; cf. Heb 9:14; 10:19–20.
[112] On grammatical grounds, it is certainly possible to interpret "faith of him" by "faith in him," see, e.g. Mark 11:22; James 2:1. Paul, however, is wont to speak of "faith into" or "upon" Christ (*eis Christon, epi Christō*) when he discusses the believers' faith in him. Cf. the NOTE on the words *faithful to the Messiah* in 1:2.
[113] Rom 5:2; Eph 2:18; Heb 3:6; 4:16; 10:19, 35; I John 2:28; 3:21; 4:17; 5:14.

of both nouns. Other texts contain but one. "Free access" was discussed in 2:18.[114] "Boldness" (*parrhēsia*) means, etymologically, "free or frank speech," including either impertinence, courage, or special clarity (John 16:29, 18:20). Its opposite is an attitude determined by fear or shame. The original *Sitz im Leben* for demonstrating such "freedom of speech" was an appearance before the throne of a ruler or the bar of a judge,[115] but the meaning of the word was soon broadened beyond the confines of its etymology. It began to signify the right to stand with uplifted head before a potentate (cf. Luke 21:28), and it is in this sense that it is used in Eph 3:12. In Acts 2:29, 4:13 etc., also in Eph 6:19–20 and on some other occasions in NT writings, *parrhēsia* has lost the connotation of appearing before a mighty one. It can simply mean the presence of high spirits and the lack of fear. The words "[to God]" have been added to the Greek text in order to point out that in Eph 3:12 the original image is retained, i.e. access, with uplifted head, to the highest ruler. The noun *pepoithēsis* ("confidence") is a late Greek formation found in the LXX (in IV Kings 18:19 only) but also in Philo and Josephus. The original Greek script of the sixth-century Codex Claramontanus[116] contains the variant, "liberation" through faithfulness. This variant may be dependent on Rom 8 where the "freedom" of the saints is closely connected with their secure stand before the loving judge. The variant offers a fine exegesis of Eph 3:12 and avoids the ambiguous term "confidence," but it has no claim to authenticity.

13. *Therefore.* The logical referent is the preceding description of the great cause for which Paul was appointed and equipped. If he were suffering for a smaller reason the saints might consider his imprisonment (3:1) a trivial or frustrating matter.

I ask [*God*] *that you* . . . Two other translations are also possible. (a) The version which has the strongest support from old and new interpreters is "I ask you not to lose heart."[117] This interpretation is subject to doubt because in the NT epistles and in the Fourth Gospel the verb "to ask" more frequently means "to ask God," than "to ask something of men."[118] (b) Equally possible on philological grounds is the translation, "I ask God that I may not . . ."[119] This alternative is not recommendable, for the end of 3:13 shows that Paul is concerned less with his own peace of mind than with the glorification of the Ephesians. In 3:13 Paul gives an example of how free access and the right to speak to God are to be used: a prayer for oneself is hardly the first step! It is probable that Paul sees in intercession the proper exercise of the privilege granted to God's children. In short, the intercession contained in 3:14[16]–19 would look strange if it limped after a petition addressed in 3:13 either to the Ephesians, or to God, on Paul's own behalf.

---

[114] Free access is the privilege of a worshiper to offer a sacrifice; of a plaintiff or defendent to get a hearing from the judge; of an ambassador to see the king to whom he is accredited.

[115] Dibelius, referring to an essay by E. Peterson; also Schlier. In Philip 1:20; I John 2:28; 4:17 references to the absence of shame and to a judgment are found in the context of "boldness."

[116] Cf. the replacement of "access" by "freedom" on the Latin side of the same Codex and in Ambrosiaster.

[117] See the Syriac versions; Chrysostom; Theodoret; Jerome; Thomas Aquinas; Bengel; Robinson, p. 173; von Soden; de Wette; J. Huby; Dibelius; RSV; NEB; JB.

[118] See, e.g. Eph 3:20 and the parallelism between "praying" and "asking" in Col 1:9. Five times in James and equally often in I John the verb means to pray to God, but cf., e.g. Matt 5:42; John 4:9; Acts 3:2; I Cor 1:22; I Peter 3:15.

[119] Origen; Theodore of Mopsuestia; Jerome; and, e.g. Goodspeed.

not lose heart. The temptation to become tired, lazy, despondent, and desperate is mentioned and fought in several Pauline epistles.[120] Though the author of Hebrews does not use the same word as Paul, he addresses himself to the same danger. He exhorts the readers to "hold fast" the confession of hope, and urges them not to forsake the congregation. Thus he meets the phenomena of dwindling strength and increasing stupor.[121] Equally the Gospel of John contains the admonition to abide with Christ and to keep his word.[122] It is possible that in these writings, just as in the parable of the Ten Virgins (Matt 25:5) and in II Peter 3:9, the delay of the Lord's glorious advent was the ultimate cause of despair. However, unless it can be demonstrated that in Eph 4:13 the parousia of Christ is explicitly mentioned,[123] a direct connection between threatening despair and delayed parousia cannot be ascertained. The next words in Eph 3:13 show that the saints in Ephesus were troubled by the apostle's condition (his captivity) rather than by sufferings of their own endured in a time of affliction that appeared to have no end. Not until 5:16 and 6:10 ff. will Paul turn to a discussion of the sufferings of all the saints in the end-time.[124]

over the tribulations I suffer for you. The noun translated by "tribulations" occurs in Ephesians only here, but frequently elsewhere in the NT. It denotes temptations from inside, persecutions from outside, discouragement among the Christians, and the general horrors which God's chosen have to suffer in the last days.[125] These sufferings are compared to the birth pangs of a woman and sometimes described by the term "woes."[126] Since on occasion[127] Paul compares himself with a father or mother who "gives birth" to the saints, it is not totally impossible that a similar idea underlies Eph 3:13. However, elsewhere the bold analogy is used by the apostle only in writing to Christians converted by him and specifically dear to him. Since the Ephesians were not personally known to the apostle, it is unlikely that by implication he should call them "his" children.[128] The Colossian parallel to Eph 3:13 speaks about "sufferings" for the church and proves that the temptation, persecution, and passion connected with Paul's apostolic ministry were not always described in gynecological terms. The main emphasis of Eph 3:13 rests upon the ministerial and eschatological character of Paul's affliction. "If we are afflicted then it is for your consolation and salvation" (II Cor 1:6). A fuller discussion of the representative, if not vicarious, suffering of the apostle "for the church" belongs in the exposition of Col 1:24, cf. also II Tim 2:10.[129]

For they are your glorification. Lit. "which is your glory." This is a surprising way to explain the preceding prayer and admonition.[130] The feminine singular relative pronoun used in the Greek text is a sophisticated "attraction of the rel-

[120] II Thess 3:13; Gal 6:9; II Cor 4:1, 16; cf. Luke 18:1.
[121] Heb 3:1, 6; 6:12; 10:23–25, 32–36; 12:2–6, 12–13.   [122] John 6:66–67; 8:51; 12:26; 14:23, etc.
[123] Just as in I Thess 4:14 ff.; I Cor 7:29; Philip 4:4–6; Col 3:4; Heb 9:28; 10:37–39, etc.
[124] The persecution of *all* the saints is among the primary causes why, e.g. Matthew, I Peter, Revelation, and James have been written.
[125] Schlier, TWNTE, III, 139–48; see, e.g. I Thess 3:3, 7; Matt 24:21, 29; Acts 14:22; Rev 7:14.
[126] John 16:21, 33; I Thess 5:3; Matt 24:8.   [127] Gal 4:19; I Cor 4:15; Philem 10.
[128] Instead, he calls them, "[God's] beloved children" (5:1; cf. 1:5).
[129] G. H. P. Thompson, "Ephesians 3:13 and II Timothy 2:10 in the Light of Colossians 1:24," ET 71 (1960), 187–89, emphasizes the Messianic-eschatological character of the apostolic tribulations.
[130] Abbott suggests the version *quippe qui,* viz. in as much.

ative." The Jewish-Greek meaning of the noun "glory" (*doxa*) includes the dynamic meaning of glorification (cf. 1:6, 12, 14; 3:21). The seeming paradox, my tribulations are your glory, is called by Robinson "a logic which we can hardly analyze" and a product of "the language of the heart." An attempt to explain Paul's reasoning will be made in COMMENT III C.

COMMENTS I–IV on 3:1–13

I   Structure and Summary

The core of Eph 3:1–13 contains an excursus on the commission given to Paul by God. The centerpiece is bracketed at the beginning and at the end by utterances concerning Paul's self-consciousness, i.e. by reference to his captivity or suffering, and by two formulae meaning "for you" (*eis hymās* and *hyper hymōn*). The whole passage explains why Paul dares identify his personal history with an event from which the Gentiles benefit.[131]

The heart of this section is one of the NT's key statements on revelation. This topic is unfolded in a climactic way, in which narrative elements prevail over doctrinal assertions.

a) Verses 2–4: the saints have heard and can verify by reading what Paul has written that this man has been given authority to do two things, to grasp the secret which God has revealed to him, and to fulfill a commission in the service of God's grace.

b) Verses 5–6: a new aeon has dawned because it has pleased God to terminate the time of hiding and ignorance. He has disclosed to the apostles and prophets the incorporation of the Gentiles into his people.

c) Verses 7–9: this disclosure was an act of sheer grace—but not a grace that makes man inactive. From the beginning grace and revelation meant for Paul, the unworthiest of all Christians, commitment to a specific task. He was given the power to preach to the nations the gospel of the Gentiles' inclusion in the realm of the Messiah.

d) Verses 10–12: the Gentiles, in turn, were not to become the final beneficiaries of revelation. Rather through the proclamation addressed to them, the people of God composed of Jews and Gentiles are given an assignment for the benefit of the whole world. By its very existence the church proves to good and evil creaturely powers how splendid and wise God is in crowning his former history with mankind by his full revelation. In the end his decision to give peace to all men through Jesus, the Messiah, is carried out. Thanks to the Messiah, man stands free and confident before God.

Other subdivisions of this section are equally feasible.[132] All attempts at reconstructing the clear progress of Paul's thought are hampered by the fact that

---

[131] A brief parallel is found in Philip 1:12: "What has happened to me has really served to advance the gospel."

[132] E.g. (a) personal puzzles of Paul's existence (vss. 1–4) are (b) explained by reference to the recent revelation of the formerly hidden secret, the Gentiles' inclusion, vss. 5–6. (c) This revelation is to be spread abroad, vss. 7–11. (d) It has the double result of confident access to God, and of suffering among men, vss. 12–13. Or shorter, revelation to Paul, vss. 2–7; revelation through Paul, vss. 8–13 (Schlier). Or again, salvation is for the Gentiles, vss. 2–6; Paul has to proclaim this, vss. 7–12 (Gaugler).

main elements are anticipated and repeated in several subsections. Yet neither such duplications nor the insertion of a quote (vs. 5) from a hymn or confession and of a parenthesis within the parenthesis (vs. 8a) obscure a continuous train of thought in the maze of this passage. Paul's history and his personal relevance for all nations are based upon something which happened to him. By the knowledge and commission given to him he became a signal which indicated a turn in the history of mankind: he stands for the inclusion of the Gentiles in God's love and God's people. Paul has to tell the Gentiles the same secret that was revealed to all apostles and prophets, and the church has to demonstrate it to all powers of the world. Since nothing less than the cause of the Messiah is at stake, it is worthwhile for Paul and good for many that he pays for it with the price of imprisonment.

The themes of revelation, apostleship, and the servant role of the church need further clarification at this point.

II   Unique and Manifold Revelation

Access to the rich literature dealing with revelation is given by articles in theological wordbooks and by monographs.[133] The Greek and Latin (including the French, English, etc.) terms used to describe "revelation" (apokalyptō and revelare) are in substance cognates. The manifestation of the divine is circumscribed by terms originally denoting the "removal of a veil." Whether the idea of "unveiling" has its common root in some phase of Indo-European culture, or in a liturgical act in which the image of a deity was laid bare of its cover, cannot be discussed here. Certainly the Hebrew verb (gālāh), which in most cases underlies the LXX passages that speak about revelation, has little or nothing to do with the religious imagery mentioned. In the LXX the noun "revelation" and the verb "reveal" designate the uncovering e.g. of the head only in a minority of cases.[134] More frequent is their metaphorical usage for the exposure (to the eye) of land formerly hidden by a flood, or for the manifestation (to the mind) of a hidden thought or a secret: revelation is always the means and the act of exposing something which is present and true. Paul seems no longer to have the etymological meaning in mind, for when he mentions a veil and its removal[135] he does not employ the verb "to reveal" or even the noun "revelation." In non-biblical and in NT Greek three other verbs, i.e. "to appear" (epiphainō), "to make apparent" (phaneroō), and "to make known" (gnōrizō) and their cognate nouns are almost synonyms of "to reveal" and "revelation" (apokalyptō and apokalypsis).[136] However, the synonyms may accentuate slightly varying features. The first emphasizes the suddenness of a bright appearance; the second, the visibility attained, i.e. the result of the first;[137] the third alludes to the

[133] E.g. A. Oepke, TWNTE, III, 563–92; G. S. Hendry, Theological Wordbook of the Bible, ed. A. Richardson, 5th ed. (New York: Macmillan, 1956), pp. 195–200; H. Schulte, Der Begriff der Offenbarung im Neuen Testament, BEvTh 13 (1949); D. Lührmann, Das Offenbarungsverständnis bei Paulus und in den paulinischen Gemeinden, WAATNT 16 (1966), esp. 113–40.
[134] LXX Ezek 16:36; 23:18: "to uncover the shame." J. Moltmann, "Offenbarung und Wahrheit," in Parrhesia, Fs K. Barth (Zurich; EVZ, 1966), pp. 149–72, interprets revelation as the start of a new event and history, that is, as an act of transformation (II Cor 3:18).
[135] In II Cor 3:13–16; I Cor 11:5–6.
[136] See Rom 1:17–19; 3:21; 8:18; I Cor 2:10; II Cor 4:10–11; Col 3:4; Eph 1:9; 3:3–10.
[137] Ophthē, lit. "he was seen," has in the Bible the meaning "he appeared," and is the technical term for the risen Jesus' appearances, see, e.g. I Cor 15:5–8; Luke 24:34; but cf. ephanerōthē in the spurious ending of Mark (16:12, 14).

realm of the intellect, and in the Bible points also to action and conduct fitting such insight. The verb *apokalyptō* (reveal) can comprehend each of the elements special to the synonyms.[138]

In classic Greek the manifestation of something divine is not called "revelation" but "proof," "omen," "indication" (*endeixis, sēmainō*). In Greek oracles —provided they are properly interpreted—the self-manifestation of the deity is not in the foreground, but an announcement is made of something that is going to happen, or that is to be done or not to be done. The term *apokalyptō* ("to reveal") or a synonymous designation of divine self-manifestation does not play a great role earlier than in Hellenistic religious magical writings, especially in the Corpus Hermeticum. Corresponding terminology was perhaps embraced among the Corinthians addressed by Paul (I Cor 1–2), and it is certain that it became a favorite among the Gnostics.[139] H. Schulte is convinced that the revelation terminology in the NT was dictated by the anti-Gnostic fight waged by the NT authors; in facing this opposition, the apostles and evangelists have allegedly succumbed to the notions and imagery of their opponents. Miss Schulte concludes that the concepts used in the NT for revelation became a "cuckoo's egg" and a snare for all later Christian theology.[140] The post-NT date of the main sources upon which this theory is built limits the value of the conclusion drawn from it.

One question, however, remains essential for the interpretation of Ephesians: does this epistle deviate from the concept of revelation presented elsewhere in the Bible, and enunciate a special, if not unique, notion of revelation? First we list some important features common to Ephesians and other biblical books:

a) God himself is the subject *and* object of revelation: he alone gives revelation, and he reveals himself. It is his good pleasure and favor not only to perform astonishing things but also to inform men of his identity, of himself as the creator of all things and events, and of the good and wise purpose fulfilled by his actions. God himself is the interpreter of the decisive events that immediately affect man. Thus it is he who by revelation makes the events meaningful and memorable. Revelation constitutes the difference between bare facts and a history that is worthy of praise because of its creator; see e.g. Amos 3:7 and II Isaiah.

b) What God reveals about himself and about the origin and goal of his deeds pertains to the salvation of many. "I shall be your God and you shall be my people" (Lev 26:12; Jer 7:23; 11:4; 24:7 etc.). The grace of revelation includes salvation, and vice versa. He who is led from darkness to light, from ignorance to knowledge of God, experiences more than a mere chance to see and to understand: his life is saved, he will and can live. In brief, revelation is salvation.

c) The revelation or epiphany of God, sometimes called theophany, is addressed to specifically chosen people. It makes them new men and opens a new

---

[138] Burton, *Galatians*, pp. 49–50, 433, may not be correct in ascribing to revelation only the character of internal, subjective manifestation. See, e.g. Matt 10:26; 11:25–27; 13:11; 16:17; Luke 8:17; 12:2; cf. TWNTE, III, 564.

[139] Cf. especially Marcion's beautiful statement: "*Deus . . . naturaliter ignotus nec usquam nisi in evangelio revelatus.* See H. Schulte, *Der Begriff der Offenbarung im Neuen Testament*, p. 26, n. 1.

[140] Pp. 21 ff., 42, 64, 69, 72 ff.

era, for by revelation they are committed to be God's witnesses before many and, at the same time, representatives of the many before God. Thus revelation is far from a merely noetic or intellectual event. Always it transforms the total person and changes the whole life of its recipient—and not only him: a great people, if not all the nations and the whole world, are affected by it. While revelation is not dependent on, or subsequent to, faith, it calls forth faith and actions of faith. On the other hand, those chosen to receive revelation are tempted more and suffer more severely than others. Outstanding men like Moses, Jeremiah, and Paul partake both in God's suffering for his rebellious people and in the suffering which Israel and the church have to bear.

d) The modes of revelation show great variety. The dreams, visions, (also auspices?) and casting of lots mentioned in the early strata of the OT resemble Canaanite and priestly means of obtaining information about the will of a deity. In the NT dreams, visions, ecstasy, an impulse of the Spirit, and the voice of prophets or angels are among the means of revelation.[141] During the period of Israel's classic prophets, but also in NT times, these several modalities are challenged, judged or confirmed. Their usefulness and validity are tested by personal appearances of God, by prophets who claim to stand in God's counsel, and by apostles who have enjoyed extended communion with Jesus Christ from the days of his baptism to his appearances after the resurrection. Since not even Paul knows whether he was "in the body" or "out of the body" when he "heard things that cannot be told" (II Cor 12:2–4), his interpreters certainly cannot know more than he about the mode of true revelation. Not only the appearances of the resurrected Jesus Christ, but also his activity during his Galilean and Judaean ministry, and finally the mission work done by his disciples and followers—all these modes of revelation make clear that sensory perception, i.e. hearing, seeing, touching, is not excluded from being used and reached by revelation (cf. I John 1:1–3).

e) If any criteria for discerning true from false revelation are given at all, they are not uniform. Among those mentioned are: (1) fulfillment or non-fulfillment of a prediction; (2) a prophet's simple compulsion and the absence of a personal motif of gain; (3) acknowledgment of God's judgment as opposed to the proclamation of peace at any price.[142] "All these tests are provisional."[143] Actually there is no criterion for revelation apart from revelation itself. By nature the revelation of God is unique and incomparable. It is God's appearance, Christ's advent and activity, the Spirit's manifold operation and not an extraordinary mode of communication that give revelation its special and unique character. If extraordinary modes of experience were the marks of revelation, Canaanite priests and Egyptian soothsayers, persons endowed with mystic and ecstatic gifts, and probably all those who have founded religions would have to be credited as recipients of God's revelation. Most of them did not simply dream up what they passionately affirmed, but were inspired by some *mysterium tremendum*. The only criterion of revelation is that God re-

---

[141] Gospels, *passim;* I Cor 5:4; 12:1–4; 14; Rev, *passim;* Acts 11:27–30; 13:2; 15:28; 16:6–7, 9; 18:9; 19:21?; 20:22–23; 22:17–21; 23:11; 27:23–24.
[142] (1) I Sam 3:19; Deut 18:21–22; Isa 41:22; 43:9, etc.; (2) Amos 3:8; 7:14–16; Micah 3:11; Jer 29; (3) II Kings 22:13; Jer 6:14; 28:8–9; Ezek 13:10, 16.
[143] Hendry, in *Theological Wordbook of the Bible*, p. 200.

veals himself. In the Bible revelation is the event in which the God of Abraham, Isaac, and Jacob proves his presence, goes into action, and equips man with a task for the salvation of his chosen ones and, ultimately, for the glorification of God's name in the world. Revelation is not limited to so-called "religious" issues, it pertains to all realms of life. It establishes God's Lordship over all persons, things, and conditions.

f) Since by his revelation God terminates a period of ignorance, of despair, or of preparation, it is not just one of many historical happenings but a culmination and conclusion. Particularly in post-OT Jewish and in Christian literature revelation is an eschatological event.[144] For this reason the book of Revelation may have been placed at the end of the church's canon. As long as revelation received earlier is considered glorious and yet not conclusive, references to future revelation will complement reminders of past manifestations and present knowledge.[145] By revelation God's final judgment and action regarding Christ, the angels, Israel, the Gentiles, and the whole world are disclosed.

g) Revelation makes use of sociological, psychological, auditory, visionary, and other means of communication. It contains traditional and revolutionary elements, stereotyped speech, worn-out clichés, and screaming novelties and paradoxes. But it is, especially in Gal 1:11–12, contrasted with the human way of transmitting knowledge, e.g. with law, doctrine, commandments, statutes. The life and work of Scribes, Wise Men, Pharisees such as Ezra, Koheleth, and Gamaliel need by no means be spurned in the name of revelation. However, by revelation God has given much more to man than just insight, doctrine, tradition, or commandments; he has given himself. The Lord is not just "heard of" but "seen" (cf. Job 42:5). Under the impact of such revelation the recipient of God's self-manifestation ventures to challenge tradition, to contradict established religious patterns, to reinterpret ancient events and texts, and to point out a new way. Revelation stands not in absolute but often in factual contradiction to tradition. It leads to praising the glory of God with a new song.

These seven points may be augmented, but they suffice to establish a background against which three specific elements of Eph 3:3–11 can be discerned.

First, the time of revelation is now and its substance is the Gentiles' inclusion in God's people. In Ephesians revelation is treated as an unheard-of novelty which goes beyond the gifts given to men like Abraham, Moses, David, Isaiah. This seems to contradict I Peter 1:10–12, the passage which emphatically states that OT prophets had received revelation by the Spirit regarding the Messiah's suffering and subsequent glorification, but the contradiction is not total. I Peter discusses the sequence of suffering and glory that was predicted earlier and is experienced in the analogous histories of Noah, Christ, and the Christian congregation (3:13 – 4:6). Ephesians unfolds the secret now manifest: the Gentiles who are now included in God's people have always been loved by God. In I Peter revelation is presented as a sequence of seemingly opposite events with Jesus Christ crucified and raised at the center. In Ephesians revelation is one specific event seen from different angles. Its core is the coming of Jesus Christ, which establishes his universal rule and demonstrates God's love of Jews and

---

[144] Oepke, TWNTE, III, 576–77 and 584–86, emphasizes the inseparability of revelation from eschatology.
[145] Deut 18:15, 18; compare Gal 3:23; I Cor 2:10–12; Rom 1:17–18; Philip 3:15; Eph 3:5 with II Thess 2:3, 8; I Cor 3:13; Rom 8:18.

Gentiles alike. I Peter is not concerned with past revelation only (1:12); the epistle is representative of the majority of NT books which repeatedly point toward future revelation.[146] In Ephesians only the present is depicted as the time, the product, the glorification of revelation. Equally in Rom 1:17–18; 3:21, Paul placed all emphasis upon the here and now. Since according to I Peter revelation is complete only when all suffering is swallowed up in glory, revelation must still be given, but following Ephesians the secret of God has already been fully manifested and is still gloriously manifested by the creation and witness of the one people of God consisting of Jews and Gentiles; thus nothing essentially new will ever be added to revelation. As was shown earlier, the "days of fulfillment" (1:10) are not just the end of time but the extended end-time in which the church lives. Just as these days are not yet finished, revelation is not yet complete. And yet the substance and glory of revelation are complete. God's revelation presupposes and signals his presence among the nations and for their benefit. God is now revealed as the present savior. The statement, Revelation Now, cannot be separated from the confession, God Here and Now.

Second, in Eph 3 the modality of revelation, e.g. dreams, auditions, visions, or the transfiguration of Jesus, the appearance of the resurrected Lord, the mode of outpouring of the Spirit are not even mentioned—except for the one important mention of "the Spirit" in vs. 5, cf. 1:17–18. Instead of the modes of revelation, the persons touched upon, changed, charged, and informed by God's revelation are placed in the foreground. Apostles and (NT) prophets receive the revelation first. They receive it as a unit—though nothing is said as to whether they have all received it at the same moment or by the same means. The substance of revelation is the assembly of Jews and Gentiles in Christ. The creative and engaging character of revelation is exemplified by Paul: this unworthy man could not help but become overwhelmed by grace. An equal change is effected upon Jews and Gentiles. By the revelation which they receive through the preaching of the gospel they are not only enlightened, saved, and created to be a growing body, rather they are also made into carriers of revelation. As a lighthouse of God (cf. 5:8) they shine brightly among the powers of the world and prove God's goodness to them (2:7; 3:10). In fulfilling this mission they are not left empty. The missionary church is a worshiping church; all its members have free access to God. Worship, the last-mentioned effect of revelation, is described here not as one of the many duties of the church but as the privilege which underlies and crowns her very existence.

Third, in Eph 3 the content of revelation is given a name which occurs nowhere else in the NT, and which in the history and thought of the western church has hardly played any role—except in some mystic or theosophic circles. In 3:10 it is called "the manifold wisdom of God." It is unlikely that this term is employed to contradict or correct all that was said about the one substance and unique gift and time of revelation. Obviously it is used to hint at the riches of revelation. What exactly does it mean?

Schlier is not satisfied with an interpretation derived from Jewish Wisdom literature alone[147] (see the first NOTE on Eph 3:10). He presents evidence col-

---

[146] I Peter 1:5, 7, 13; 4:13; 5:1. Since all these passages point to specific things to be revealed in the one coming revelation, they cannot be legitimately used for justifying the many and arbitrary revelations of new things claimed by Mani (*Kephalaia* I 14 ff.) and by the Montanists.

[147] *Christus*, pp. 60–65; Schlier, pp. 157–66.

lected from Gnostic and other writings. More or less dependent upon pagan and late Jewish-heterodox notions, the adduced literature tends to identify the all-permeating and all-present power of a creator-deity with a moon goddess (the partner of the sun god) and with wisdom. Using a somewhat surprising amalgamation of diverse statements and elements, Schlier attempts to demonstrate that the mystery of God, the wisdom of God, and the church are practically identified. He believes that the "manifold wisdom" mentioned in Eph 3:10 reflects the multiformity attributed to the moon goddess. He surmises that the author of Ephesians first took up the notions contained in pagan and Gnostic-Jewish "premonitions" and then gave Jews and Gentiles the right "answer" in their own diction: the wisdom manifested by creation, in Christ, and through the church is one and the same; the church herself is "revelation of God's secret in action."

Schlier's argument appears rather far-fetched and is connected with his questionable theory regarding the endorsement by Ephesians of syzygies (pairwise copulations).[148] Only those theological conclusions deserve to be regarded as reliable which are independent of the material Schlier has unearthed from diverse religious movements of later periods and pressed in the service of his theology. In 3:10 there is no trace of a simple identification of the mystery or wisdom of God with the church; neither is there any explicit endorsement of Stoic or other "natural" theology. Rather the church is assigned no more than a servant role in the public manifestation of God's secret and wisdom. Eph 4:12 provides the term "service." In COMMENT IV a more detailed description of the church's function will be given.

Yet another explanation of the "manifold wisdom" was suggested by Gregory of Nyssa. For him the text describes the paradoxes of the Christian message concerning life created by death, the attainment of glory by dishonor, of blessing by curse, of power by weakness, and more.[149] However, the beauty of this interpretation does not make it more solid than the exposition based on the many functions ascribed to wisdom in the Proverbs and Wisdom of Solomon and elsewhere (see COMMENT X on 1:3–14). "Manifold" does not necessarily point to the presence of a paradox. Still it admittedly includes the essence of that love which according to 3:19 transcends rational comprehension. This love is manifested in ever new and surprising, i.e. in "manifold," ways. It is inventive, full of originality, and proves rich enough to meet and match most diverse circumstances. Human knowledge is but "a minute door"[150] through which man may peep at the riches of God's inexhaustible wisdom.

III   The Chained Apostle's Ministry

Four outstanding features mark the way in which Paul speaks about himself in Eph 3:1–13:[151] it appears to be full of paradoxes; it ties together grace, revelation, apostlehood, and the nations into a tightly woven unit; it connects

---

[148] In COMMENT VII A B on 5:21–33 this problem is treated more fully.

[149] *Hom.* VIII *in Cant.;* cf. Theophylact and Oecumenius. The contrast between "God's" wisdom and the "wisdom of the world" (I Cor 1:18–2:8), esp. the term "scandal of the cross," can be quoted in support of their interpretation.

[150] Calvin.

[151] See the literature on the term, apostle, quoted in the exposition of Eph 1:1, and commentaries and monographs, esp. on Col 1:24.

captivity and suffering with glory; it reveals more than a trifle of authoritative self-consciousness. Each of these four traits deserves special attention.

A   Paradoxical Existence

Eph 3:1–13 is replete with seeming contradictions. Self-consciousness, a tone of authority, and conviction of the Self's importance are combined with an almost artificial self-humiliation. The "prisoner of Christ" is at the same time proud and ashamed of himself. He is the instrument of "God's grace for all the Gentiles," the exponent of a new era—but still he is "less than the least of all the saints." While he claims to possess no more than a share in the revelation given all "the apostles and prophets" together, he shows great concern in having his own comprehension of the revealed secret duly recognized. Even when he ascribes all his missionary effort to God's grace alone, he is rather self-centered. He is at the same time a man of the Spirit and a man concerned with cultural and social questions: revelation given by the Spirit counts more than centuries of past religious and spiritual quest and insight; in the light of the revelation now given the whole past looks dark, and it appears as if all tradition must be scorned. But the apostle also expects and commands that the one specific revelation now given be accepted, that the church ask for none other, that she make it known everywhere, at all times, to all powers. He requires that this one revelation be accepted as The Tradition binding all. Thus he combines concentration upon one person and one event (Jesus Christ's coming, death, resurrection, spiritual manifestation) with concern not only for all people that dwell on earth but also for all heavenly powers. Finally he realizes what temptation may befall his readers when they realize that he is suffering imprisonment; yet he ventures to affirm that his own tribulations are a crown on their heads.

This man is certainly not the exponent of one idea only, and what he reveals of his character includes blatant contradictions. As is true of every person, so in his case the man is formed by the unique combination of elements standing in mutual tension or contradiction. He is convinced that he does not want to be praised for his own sake, be it simply as an individual like others, or as a genius outstanding among them.[152] Just when, e.g. in II Cor 10–13, he puts his own self into the foreground in almost shocking fashion, he intends to praise nothing but the ministry entrusted to him; what the apostle concedes about himself is certainly also to be admitted by his interpreters: "Though the will to do what is good is in me, the performance is not" (Rom 7:19 JB).

Together with other factors it may have been certain contradictory traits in Paul's character, self-consciousness, and self-defense that led to conflicts in his relationship with the Corinthian church and with Jerusalem. Nevertheless, at least one undisputed Pauline passage reveals that in spite of the contradictions in the man Paul the unity of the apostolic ministry was "officially" recognized. According to Gal 2:8–9 the leaders of the Jerusalem church, including those who had been apostles before Paul, acknowledged that the same grace worked in all apostles. While specific fields of responsibility and mission were delineated, the sameness of the apostolic task which underlies all personal distinctions was solemnly recognized; see also Luke's report on an apostolic con-

---

[152] Cf. S. Kierkegaard's distinction between a genius and an apostle.

ference (Acts 15). Eph 3 stresses, in agreement with Gal 2 and Acts 15, the full harmony of all apostles (and NT prophets). They all live by the same revelation and for the same service. Everything written by Paul in Ephesians about himself is to be understood as an intended glorification of the whole and undivided apostolic ministry.

The effect of this ministry is twofold: it helps to spread a revolution, and at the same time it contributes to a new establishment. The revolution which over-throws traditional statutes, barriers, frontiers was started when God sent his Son to make all the outcasts of the pagan world share in the privileges of his one favorite son, Israel. He who is overpowered by God's revolutionary reve-lation is an apostle of Jesus Christ; he has to go out and make its effect felt everywhere. It is not as if apostles were to make their own revolutions—they are but the voice, the sign, the agents of the new era that has dawned, and their task is to preach reconciliation (II Cor 5:18–20). Inasmuch as they announce the termination and futility of existing segregation, they can, however, be re-garded as peace-breakers and a danger to traditional society and its time-hon-ored order (see, e.g. Acts 19:23 ff.; 21:27 ff.). And yet the hostile reaction they may encounter does not make them enemies of law and order, or of all struc-tures of communal and individual existence. They work *for* the humanity of men and not *against* it in proclaiming the priority of reconciliation over all other issues and interests. Thus their intention and effect are far from destruc-tive. According to Paul a new community, called "the new man" (Eph 2:15) and consisting of insiders and outsiders, of high and low people combined in unity, is built upon, and grows from, the work of the apostles. This community is a new establishment, and more than this: a new creation. Certainly Paul does not claim that he and his like can improve the world, but he powerfully attests the formation of one human community within the world in which, by defini-tion and constitution, God is to dwell, peace is to rule, divisions are overcome, and proof is given to all mankind and all powers of the triumph of God's good-ness. The constructive task of the apostolic ministry consists in serving as the foundation of the church (2:20) and showing the church that each of her mem-bers is entrusted with a world-wide missionary ministry (3:8, 10).

B   Stewardship of Grace for the Nations

It was shown above that in Pauline diction the term "grace" frequently means the specific favor shown to the Gentiles by God in the present Messianic era.[153] According to Eph 3:2, 7, 8 the same grace of God which is given to all the saints[154] is given to the apostle for the sake of all Gentiles. In Col 1:25, a parallel to Eph 3:2, Paul speaks of the "administration" rather than the grace that was "given." Since in other, unquestionably authentic letters Paul also speaks of both the grace and the ministry entrusted to him, there cannot be an absolute contrast between the two affirmations.[155] In Rom 1:5 "grace" and "apostlehood" are probably used as synonyms. The Pauline parallels to Eph 3:2, 7, 8 make it certain that in these verses Paul is not thinking primarily of

---

[153] See the interpretation of 1:2 and 2:5.   [154] 1:2, 7; 2:5, 7–8; 4:7; 6:24.
[155] Cf. Gal 2:9; Rom 15:15; Eph 4:7 with Rom 1:5; 15:16; Col 1:25; II Tim 1:9–11.

God's personal favor[156] toward him but of the ministry he was given. Grace does not make men passive! It is the gift of an assignment. To serve in the salvation of the nations—this is the grace experienced and praised by Paul, rather than the consciousness of his own salvation. "By God's grace I am what I am, and his grace toward me was not in vain: But I worked more than all others—still, not I, but God's grace that is with me" (I Cor 15:10).[157] Paul's own intimations in Gal 1 regarding his conversion and the reports of Acts 9, 22, 26 confirm this interpretation. I Tim 1:16, however, shows that the personal element need not be suppressed or excluded by the ministerial: "If mercy has been shown to me, it is because Jesus Christ meant to make me the greatest evidence of his inexhaustible patience for all the other people who would later have to trust in him to come to eternal life" (JB). Whether Paul himself or one of his secretaries wrote these lines, they beautifully combine the private and the ministerial character of God's gift. Similarly, an altruistic and missionary essence is ascribed to "the goodness of God shown to" all the saints (Eph 2:7).

Does this mean that a public ministry of grace is a desirable *consequence* of the grace given? According to Eph 3 the connection between the personal and official element is much more intimate. As earlier observed, not infusion but diffusion of grace stands in the foreground, as if to put to shame all theological discussions about *gratia infusa*. Grace is according to 3:2, 7–9 nothing but an entrusted good. Paul affirms, "I was given God's grace in order to administer it to you" i.e. *only* for distribution among the Gentiles! For this reason he declares himself in Rom 1:14 a "debtor" of the "Greeks and Barbarians." His own election and appointment by God do not resemble a Catholic or Protestant "consecration" or "ordination" of a clergyman which is eventually followed by an "installation" in a specific parish. The gift of grace to Paul is not a dignity or character which he first receives independent of a specific charge, neither is it a generally valid diploma or brevet. Rather it calls the former enemy of Christ and the church to fulfill a function among all who were hostile to God and to one another (2:15–16). The gift of grace is "for you Gentiles" (3:1, 2, 8).

C Captivity, Suffering, and Glory

In 3:1 (cf. 4:1) Paul calls himself "the prisoner of the Messiah Jesus for the sake of you Gentiles." A prisoner can either be subject to his own or public condemnation, contempt, and pity, or he can (as did Socrates) make a virtue of his plight and become lionized for his conviction, courage, and endurance. Acceptance of the legal establishment's judgment is the presupposition of the first attitude, martyrdom for a noble cause is the basis of the second. A martyr easily gains an authority which exceeds that of a tyrant or a perfectly respectable office-holder.

Eph 3 presupposes neither of these two reactions. Verses 3:2–13 are Paul's

---

[156] In 1:5, 9 this "favor" is denoted by a noun other than "grace" (*charis*) i.e. by the Greek *eudokia*.

[157] Cf. Gal 2:7–9. Dibelius speaks of *Amtsgnade* (office-grace), Gaugler of *Gnadenamt* (office of grace) as opposed to *persönliche Heilsgnade* (grace of personal salvation). Robinson, p. 75, makes a similar distinction: "Not a spiritual endowment for his own personal life, but the Gospel of God's mercy to the Gentile world."

own commentary on 3:1. He explains why he undauntedly endures captivity, why he is conscious of his Self, and why his fate is beneficial for the Gentiles. Already 3:1 contains preliminary expository hints regarding his imprisonment. Why is he in chains? Instead of a condemnable deed of his own, or an eternal and noble cause, he mentions persons, i.e. the Messiah Jesus and the Gentiles. The apostle is standing in *his* service and he is serving *them*—this is how Paul wants his captivity to be understood.

The term "prisoner" itself is used in a double, i.e. a literal and a metaphorical, sense: it denotes physical incarceration, probably in a Roman building. According to the book of Acts, Jewish and eventually Gentile obstruction of Paul's missionary work led to several arrests.[158] If he had not worked in the service of Jesus Christ "among" and "for the Gentiles," he might never have seen a prison from the inside. Among the letters of captivity, only Philippians contains specific information on the mode and consequences of his confinement.[159]

Paul shows no trace of sentimentality or self-pity. Just as Philippians rings with joy and Acts 16:25 reports that the apostle's fellow prisoners became witnesses of loud prayer and hymn singing, so Ephesians is a document of Paul's courage and good cheer. Imprisonment not only failed to impede the progress of Paul's mission work and lessen the concern of congregations for him, but it contributed to the progress of the gospel and confidence in salvation (Philip 1:12–26). With a touch of good humor Paul calls himself an "ambassador in chains" (Eph 6:20). To say it in the words of I Peter 4:15–16: because he was not held for robbery, theft, or another immoral and illegal deed, but "as a Christian," he was not ashamed of himself but "praised God in this [Christ's] name." While suffering evil *as if* he were a felon, he yet knew that he suffered for the manifestation of the life of Jesus in the saints (II Cor 4:10). "Prisoner" was for him an honorary title as long as the Messiah Jesus and the Gentiles entrusted to him were the cause of his captivity.

The second, metaphorical, sense of "prisoner" is best illustrated either by the parallel term "servant of the Messiah Jesus" (Rom 1:1, etc.), or by the analogy of Israel's temporary custody behind the walls of the law (Gal 3:22 – 4:5). No self-respecting, religious Greek or Roman would have considered himself the "slave" of his deity,[160] but Paul was not ashamed to import into the West the oriental notion of a slave's relationship with his lord. Because his concept of "service" was based upon the redemption through Christ and the liberation from slavery to sin and death,[161] it was distinct from empty rhetoric. Paul considered it a privilege to be Jesus Christ's property; if his ministry was a necessity laid upon him, making him aware of his unworthiness and weakness,[162] it was also his pride and joy. Since he was in the service of the crucified Lord he did not resent being even more closely joined to his Lord by suffering. For this reason he may vary his self-description slightly in Eph 3:1 and 4:1, "The prisoner *of* the Messiah Jesus" calls himself in the latter passage a "prisoner *in*

---

[158] In section VII of the Introduction it was mentioned why Caesarea, Ephesus, and Rome are considered the possible locations of the prison from which the Captivity Letters were written.
[159] See esp. the commentaries on Philip 1:12 ff.; 4:12.
[160] See the article *doulos* by K. H. Rengstorf in TWNTE, II, 261–80.
[161] I Cor 7:22–23; Rom 7:25 – 8:2.   [162] I Cor 9:16; II Cor *passim.*

the Lord."[163] His fetters are "chains of the gospel" (Philem 13). While according to Acts 15:10 Peter called the law a "yoke" imposed upon the Jews, and while Paul was aware of the custody in which Israel had been placed between Moses and Christ (Gal 3:17 ff.), Paul never described his service to Christ as a humiliating tutelage. Nor did the apostle envisage a time when he or anybody else would serve Jesus Christ without being conformed to his passion.

The closest analogy to this combination of external and internal captivity is probably the suffering endured by the prophet Jeremiah in the course and as a part of his ministry.[164] It does not seem probable that the seclusion or imprisonment endured by pagan initiates in a temple (or experienced, according to Greek thought, by the soul of man in the physical body[165]) in order to attain "perfection" is the pattern which Paul followed in magnifying his captivity.

Paul's sober acceptance of his imprisonment was a challenge to fears or suspicions that may have been fostered in the Christian congregations (see esp. II Corinthians). Since Paul wants the saints to be as much at ease as he is, he goes so far as to declare his "tribulations" their very "glorification" (3:13). This bold affirmation need not be an expression of an inscrutable, irrational, perhaps mystical, feeling. Among the interpretations proposed the following appear to be most logical:

(1) The apostle's suffering intensified his communion with Christ;[166] surely the saints can profit from events which make Paul glad and fill him with pride.[167] (2) For the benefit and salvation of many, God delivered his son into suffering and death. A servant who suffers with his Lord gives the saints a credible witness of how highly God esteems them. God himself provides his chosen servants with credibility when he gives them courage and endurance in their sufferings. (3) Paul deems the saints so worthy that for them he pays the price of being slandered and persecuted by Jews and Gentiles. He does it for their glory and they can be proud of it; it confirms their faith.[168] (4) Eschatological tribulations are a foretaste of eschatological glory.[169] What looks like failure before men is a diadem and scepter before God. (5) Through God's providence, Paul's imprisonment and trials create new missionary contacts; they contribute to a spreading of the gospel that could otherwise not be anticipated (Philip 1:12–13). (6) The fact that the saints do not tire is their glory.[170]

The number of interpretations that have more or less explicit support (especially in II Corinthians and Philippians) reveal that there is probably no one connection between apostolic afflictions and the glorification of church members which in the interpretation of Eph 3:13 can exclude or dominate all others.

[163] Cf. also the related passages Philip 1:7, 13–14; II Tim 1:8; 2:9.
[164] Gaugler. It is, however, noteworthy that except in Rom 7:24 there are no "lamentations of Paul" resembling, e.g. Jer 20:7–18; Num 11:11–15; Ps 22.
[165] See Reitzenstein, HMyRel, p. 314.
[166] Philip 1:29; 3:10; II Cor 12:9.   [167] Col 1:24; II Cor 12:9–10; Philip 2:17–18.
[168] Philip 1:14, cf. Calvin on 3:13.
[169] Revelation, passim. Schlier, pp. 166–67; according to G. H. P. Thompson, ET 71 (1960), 187–89, and others the apostle's suffering reduces the amount of Messianic or eschatological suffering still to be endured before final liberation can come.
[170] Theodoret. A more extensive discussion of the apostle's suffering will be found in the context of Col 1:24.

Each of them reveals that suffering is as essential a characteristic of the apostolic ministry as is proclamation.[171]

D   The Authority of Apostolic Writing

Paul affirms in I Cor 5:3–4 and Col 2:5 that he can be "spiritually present" in the midst of a congregation while he is "bodily absent." How are the saints confronted with his authority when the apostle is physically absent? By reading and heeding the letters he writes! His written words substitute, at least temporarily, for his bodily presence and his spoken words (cf. II Cor 13:10). "By reading [what I have written] you are able to perceive how I understand the secret of the Messiah" (Eph 3:4). Just as according to I Cor 2:12–16 a "spiritual" man can recognize an inspired teacher, so he "who deems himself to be a spiritual prophet shall acknowledge that what I write to you is the Lord's command. If any one does not recognize this, he is not recognized" (I Cor 14:37–38). The importance Paul attributed to his letters corresponds to the authority of the OT scriptures which he quotes. He subjects not only others but himself, too, to scriptural authority. In II Cor 3:7–18 he compared his own ministry to that of Moses, and in Eph 3:5, 9 he claims a knowledge that was formerly not available. While occasionally he distinguishes between the "word of the Lord" and his own "opinion," he expects that the Spirit speaking through him will always be obeyed.[172] In the name of the Lord he gives blunt commands,[173] he praises those who receive his word as "God's word,"[174] and he scolds those who assume that there might be another gospel besides the one preached by him.[175] Thus he appears to canonize his own doctrine and writings.

In the earliest days of the church, public reading in worship was from OT books only;[176] but in Eph 3:4 Paul presupposes that his epistle is "read" to the worshiping assembly, and in Col 4:16 he instructs the recipients of his letter to share it with the congregation in Laodicea, and after that to have it sent to Colossae, too. Thus Paul himself prepared the way for the formation of the Christian canon which would be composed of prophetic OT and apostolic NT books.[177] It appears natural that only toward the end of or after the apostolic period would OT and NT writings really be placed on the same level.

Does the emphasis placed upon Paul's "writing" in Eph 3:3–4 demonstrate the post-apostolic origin of Ephesians? Actually these verses—the only ones in Ephesians that allude to apostolic literature—attribute relatively little weight to what Paul "has briefly written above." For what is to be gained from reading his letter? No more, so 3:4 states, than an insight into his understanding of

---

[171] In II Cor 12:12, cf. Gal 3:5, but not in Ephesians, miracles are also mentioned as a sign of the apostolate. E. Güttgemanns, *Der leidende Apostel und sein Herr* (Göttingen; Vandenhoeck, 1966), esp. pp. 102–12, demonstrates why a mystical interpretation of Paul's suffering is inappropriate in the light of Paul's own testimony.

[172] I Cor 7:6, 10, 12, 25, 40; 9:14.   [173] I Thess 4:11; II Thess 3:4, 6, 10.

[174] I Thess 2:13; II Cor 13:3.   [175] Gal 1:8–9.

[176] See, e.g. Matt 24:15; II Tim 3:15–16. Cf. the role of OT quotations and allusions esp. in Matthew, Luke, John, Paul, I Peter, Revelation. The canonical collection (or collections) presupposed by various NT writers was different from the Roman Catholic and the Protestant churches' OT canons; see Luke 11:49; I Cor 2:9; 15:45; John 7:38; James 4:5; Jude 9, 14, etc.

[177] In the exposition of Eph 2:20 it was pointed out that the "apostles and prophets" mentioned there were sometimes understood to represent the OT and NT, and that the text itself makes another interpretation more persuasive.

God's secret! Paul's literary product is recommended as appropriate evidence of his attitude to the revelation granted to him; but the high claims made for the gospel itself in Rom 1:16–17 are not repeated when Paul speaks of his own writing in Ephesians. The preached "word of truth" (rather than a written document) is the "message that saves you" (1:13). The restricted function ascribed in Eph 3:4 to Paul's writing suggests either an author who wanted to belittle the authority of Paul's letters, or Paul's own awareness of the limits of his literary effectiveness. The first alternative is not supported by the context: the author is fully aware of the unique place and task of an apostle. The second supports the assumption that Paul himself wrote Ephesians.[178] But while reference to written materials can easily amount to legalistic overemphasis, in Eph 3:3–4, Paul does not suggest that his literary works be used as a book of law. The criterion of his letters is the clarity of insight which they convey into God's secret. Paul the servant of the Messiah knows better than to attribute to his writings the character of dictatorial edicts.

IV   The Servant Church

One of the several amazing features of Eph 3:10 is the occurrence of the formula "through the church" which is found nowhere else in Pauline or other NT writings.[179] Because this statement ascribes a mediating role to the church, it seems to imply that in Ephesians the doctrine of the church (ecclesiology) is exaggerated at the expense of Christology. In addition, because 3:10 relates the church's mediation not to the souls of men but to the spiritual powers, nothing less than a cosmic function of the church appears to be stipulated.[180]

Surely the author of Ephesians is not willing to make the church a competitor of Christ—otherwise he would explicitly negate the unique function of Jesus Christ described in the two foregoing chapters! Actually the church's mediatory function is infinitely smaller than that of Christ, the "one mediator between God and man" and the mediator of "all creation."[181] He alone makes peace by being king, priest, victim, and prophet at the same time (2:14–18); he alone sits above all governments and authorities (1:20–22). This is not denied by 3:10, for here the church's function is limited to taking up and extending Jesus Christ's prophetic ministry.[182] Her *raison d'être* lies in the cognitive rather than the causative realm: she is destined to "make known."

This does not mean that the church serves no higher purpose than that of disseminating intellectual information or emotional propaganda. Just like the wisdom described in OT and apocryphal books, so also the knowledge which the church is given (1:17–18) is a knowledge that saves men and makes them re-

---

[178] II Peter 3:15–16 offers an example of how high and how low a post-apostolic author from Asia Minor rated the Pauline writings.

[179] The "church" is explicitly mentioned twenty-three times in I Corinthians, but less often in Ephesians, i.e. in 1:22; 3:10, 21, and six times in 5:23–32. Thus the instrumental function attributed to her in 3:10 is puzzling. Schlier's assumption that the words "through all" in 4:6 constitute a parallel has to be questioned. The OT or Stoic "omnipotence formula" reflected in 4:6 suggests that in this verse "all" refers to much more than the members of the church only.

[180] See, e.g. R. M. Grant, *Historical Introduction to the New Testament* (London: Collins, 1963), p. 201, and sections IV–VI of the Introduction.

[181] I Tim 2:5; cf. Heb 8:6; 9:15; 12:24; Col 1:15–20; John 1:3.

[182] Cf. K Barth, *Church Dogmatics* IV:3 (1961).

spect the order of the universe, including the proper place assigned to its various forces and features.[183] Since God's own wisdom according to OT and NT utterances penetrates the universe and upholds it (even before God's elect were given wisdom and knowledge), the church does not add wisdom to the world. Still, she is to proclaim it.

Since the verbs "making known" and "revealing" are used as synonyms in this context, the church is described here as an agent of revelation. According to Rom 1:16–17; Eph 3:6, the gospel and the apostolate were instruments of God's self-revelation. In Eph 3:10 the church is instructed to participate in that authentic "proclamation of peace" which was commenced and is still continued by Jesus Christ himself (2:17). The church of which Paul speaks is therefore by definition "evangelic and apostolic." Otherwise she would not be the church built and growing "in the Lord . . . into God's temple . . . on the foundation of the apostles and prophets" (2:20–21). In other words, the church is not an end in itself but a functional outpost of God's kingdom.

Eph 3:10 does not specify how the church is to convey knowledge. The reference to the word of truth, the gospel that saves (1:13), and the emphasis with which Paul identifies his main apostolic task with preaching[184] suggest that Paul has verbal proclamations in mind.[185] But vs. 2:7, the closest parallel of 3:10, reveals clearly that more is meant than oral and written statements only.[186] By its very existence the church is called and equipped to be the "theater of God's works."[187] In her total being, that is, as founded and ruled by the Messiah; as composed of Jews and Gentiles formerly dead in sins and divided in hostility; as a people daring to live on the basis of forgiveness; as a community boldly looking into God's face and speaking to him; as a suffering and struggling, poor and yet enriched nation—this way the church *is* God's display, picture window, legal "proof" (2:7), lighthouse (5:8), for the benefit of the world. If she failed to proclaim with words what she is given to know, or if she condoned division and sin, she would belie her essence and function, and she would grieve "the holy Spirit of God" (4:30) from which she lives. Then by her faithlessness she would attempt to abrogate God's faithfulness and commission (cf. Rom 3:3). But as established, maintained, and sent out by God, the church is an instrument through which he reveals himself. She is, in brief, by her very existence the "revelation of God's secret in action . . . the manifestation of the wisdom of God."[188] He who would despise or belittle God's church would blaspheme against God's temple. He would reject God himself and his ongoing self-revelation.

But why are "governments and authorities in the heavens" rather than men

---

[183] See COMMENT X on 1:3–14.   [184] I Cor 1:17; Gal 1:16; Eph 6:19–20.

[185] What in today's churches is called preaching, teaching, liturgy, cure of souls, fraternal consolation, a pastoral letter, a public declaration, and intervention on political or economic scenes, may be an example or extension of Paul's intention as long as Christ and the gospel are the center of all proclamations.

[186] For the following see esp. Calvin and Schlier.

[187] Bengel. Cf. Abbott, p. 89, "The Church is the phenomenon which by its existence is a proof and exhibition of the Divine Wisdom."

[188] Schlier, pp. 156–57. If Schlier's way of arguing for these conclusions is cumbersome and unconvincing (see the end of COMMENT II), there is yet no reason to throw out his findings along with his method. In COMMENT V on 2:1–10, i.e. in the discussion of the covenant lawsuit pattern taken up by Paul, an alternative has been offered to Schlier's Gnosticizing arguments.

inside and outside the church called the recipients of the revelation given "through the church" (3:10)? The mention of these powers is a key factor in the disdain in which some critical interpreters hold the so-called "cosmic ecclesiology" of Ephesians. Indeed, if Colossians excels for its cosmic Christology then Ephesians adds to such Christology a corresponding ecclesiology.[189] Eph 3:10 illustrates and perhaps corrects certain implications of the modern term "cosmic." The church is given an assignment among intangible powers that make their spiritual dominion felt from their "heavenly" places.[190] She is to be an example to all creation.[191] Following this verse the church would unduly limit her task if she cared only for the souls of men or for an increase in membership. Rather she has to be a sign and proof of a change that affects the institutions and structures, patterns and spans of the bodily and spiritual, social and individual existence of all men. The power of filling, subjugating, and dominating "all things," including these powers, is reserved to God and Christ alone.[192] But the function of demonstrating God's dominion and love is entrusted to the church. She is appointed and equipped to be a public exponent of grace and unity. Political and social, cultural and religious forces, also all other institutions, traditions, majorities, and minorities are exposed to her testimony.[193] Barbarous dictatorships and nations that enjoy orderly democratic processes; rampant prejudices and heroic fighters for civil rights; savage and tender expressions of man's sexuality; devastating effects of civilization and highest achievements of culture alike—all these and other powers are given a unique chance by God: they are entitled to see in their midst the beginning of a new heaven and a new earth. To let God's light shine—this is the servant task ascribed to the church in Eph 3:10. The secret yearning of some ecclesiastic personnel for world dominion is not supported by this verse.

Chapters 4–6 will describe in some detail the conduct by which the church "without word," i.e. by sheer good conduct, shall excel among people and powers outside the church.[194] In 6:10–18 this stance of the church among the heavenly powers is equated not with an attack against them but with an appropriate and feasible resistance to their onrush, cf. Rev 12–13. According to Rom 13:1–7 not all "powers" are vicious enemies of God and opponents of the church, even political officials are assigned by God to be "servants of God" and have the right to be honored, respected, obeyed, and supported by the members of the church; even they are to be treated as fellow servants, that is, as colleagues of the apostle and all Christians. The end of this passage in Romans shows that the proper attitude toward the powers is not a matter of demonizing or idolizing institutions, laws, and a given order, but of appropriate

---

[189] See esp. 1:20–23; 2:7; 3:10, 21; 6:10–20.

[190] COMMENT V on 1:15–23 made a tentative identification of the essence, appearance, and quality of these powers on the grounds of Paul's own occasional specifications. In commenting on 2:7 and 3:10 Schlier affirms that the church is given by God the right: (a) to act as a public institution (*Öffentlichkeitsanspruch*), (b) to be rather a document of God's grace than a leaf thrown about by the whims of given periods (*Zeitgeist*), (c) to belong to the realm of politics.

[191] Cf. the predicate, "first fruit of the creatures," James 1:18; see also Gal 6:15; Rom 8:19–23; II Cor 5:17, and the discussions on new creation in the context of 2:10 and 15.

[192] 1:22–23; 4:10; Colossians, *passim;* I Cor 15:24–27; see COMMENTS V and VI C on 1:15–23.

[193] Bengel and Gaugler agree in stating that in Eph 3:10 both good and evil principalities and powers are meant.

[194] Just like the women addressed in I Peter 3:1; cf. 2:12.

communication with the persons (rulers, officials, employees) who represent the intangible structures. Following Rom 13 the church is indebted to these men— no less than Paul is indebted to Greeks and Barbarians (Rom 1:14)! By paying their debt and by resisting vicious attacks Christians "make known" the revolutionary peace of Christ.

VII PRAYER FOR PERFECTION
(3:14–21)

3 14 For this reason I bow my knees before the Father 15 from whom each family in heaven and on earth receives its name: 16 Rich as he is in glory may he grant that through his Spirit you be fortified with power [to grow] toward the Inner Man 17 [i.e.] that through faith the Messiah may dwell in your hearts. Stand firm on the root and foundation of love. 18 May you be strong enough to grasp together with all the saints what is the breadth, the length, the height, the depth, 19 and to know the love of Christ though it surpasses knowledge. May you become so perfect as to attain to the full perfection of God.

20 To him who by the power exerted in us
is able to outdo superabundantly
all that we ask or imagine—

21 Glory to him in the church and in the Messiah Jesus
from generation to generation,
for ever and ever! Amen.

NOTES

3:14. *For this reason.* The "reason" mentioned here and the relation of this verse to 3:1 are discussed in the first NOTE on 3:1.

I bow my knees. For the background and meaning of this extraordinary attitude of prayer see COMMENT II.

before the Father. Other NT occurrences of the attribute "Father" have been discussed in COMMENT II on 1:1–2. The reference to "the Father"[1] lacks here and in 2:8 the frequently found specification "God our Father" or "Father of our Lord Jesus Christ." Although a variant reading does contain the latter formula, philological and material reasons advise against its endorsement. The next verse gives a surprising and unique explication of the term "Father." See COMMENT III A.

15. *each family in heaven and on earth.* The Greek noun translated by "fam-

---

[1] Cf. the references for the absolute use of (God the) "Father" collected from Philo, Josephus, the NT, the Apostolic Fathers, etc. in WBLex, 641–42, and TWNTE, V, 951–59, 978–82.

ily" (*patriā*) means, just like its older and shorter form (*patrā*), "lineage," "descent from a common father." It may also mean "clan." In the LXX this noun is never used to denote the abstract concept "fatherhood," but always means a specific, concrete group of people, i.e. a family, a clan, a tribe, or a nation.[2] The question of which families Paul has in mind when he adds "heavenly" to "earthly" clans is discussed in COMMENT III B.

receives its name. Lit. "is named." The same verb (*onomazō*) was used in 1:21 and translated there by "to bestow a title." It can also mean "to utter or to use a name," "to call after," "to address by name," "to invoke," "to nominate for," or "to install in a position," "to make famous."[3] Ordinary and exceptional events in familial, professional, and institutional life, but especially in cultic and magic realms, are the *Sitz im Leben* for this verb. The various possible meanings of the term in 3:15 will be discussed in COMMENT III C.

16–19. Rich as he is in glory . . . the full perfection of God. Paul unfolds the content of his intercession in these verses, which in the Greek text form one long and complicated sentence running from vs. 14 to vs. 19. In the translation this sentence has been broken up. Paul does not begin vs. 16 with the words "I ask," but he treats the statement "I bow my knees . . . that" as an equivalent to "I pray that" (1:16–17); cf. the combination of "bowing the knees" and "praying" in Acts 9:40, 20:36. Three petitions may be discerned in what follows. (a) Intercession for the inner fortification of the saints; this is unfolded in the prayer that Christ reside in their hearts (vss. 16–17). (b) Supplication for their strong perception of all the dimensions of God's will; this supplication is interpreted by a request for knowledge of Christ's love (vss. 18–19a). (c) Petition for perfection with God's perfection (vs. 19b). While the three clauses beginning in our translation with "may" (lit. three times, "that") can be understood to set apart the three main elements of Paul's prayer, it is also possible that the Greek conjunction "that" has different meanings in the same long sentence: perhaps only vss. 16–17 contain Paul's prayer. In this case the apostle asks for fortification and indwelling by the Spirit, as well as for steadfast love. Verses 18–19 would then describe three consequences of the gifts granted: i.e. invigoration, knowledge, and perfection. Either way, elements typical of the language of prayer defy a strictly logical analysis. At this point Paul's thinking follows the form of devotion and meditation rather than that of deduction, induction, careful subordination or coordination.

16. Rich as he is in glory. Lit. "according to the riches of his glory." In 3:14–15 the title of Father pointed out God's stable love, and the reference to "all

---

[2] "Fatherhood" is designated in Greek by a derivative from *patēr*, such as *patrotēs* (in Latin: *paternitas*). The Syriac and Vulg. versions, and among the expositors Athanasius *c. Arianum* I 23; Theodoret; Severianus *Catenae* VI 159; Robinson, pp. 83–84; K. Barth, e.g. *Credo* (London; Stoughton, 1936) esp. p. 24; Percy, pp. 276–78, suggest that in Eph 3:15 *patriā* means *paternitas*; but others, e.g. Dibelius and Gaugler, point out that there is no philological evidence for this exposition. The dictionaries contain no examples of an abstract meaning of *patriā*. As long as there are meaningful ways to understand Eph 3:15 without ascribing to Paul—as in the case of 1:10— a willful change in a word's meaning, they are to be preferred.

[3] See LSLex, 1232–33; WBLex, 577. In the LXX and the NT the verb, "to call" (*kaleō*), occurs more frequently than "to name" (*onomazō*), but the meaning of both are to a wide extent synonymous; see e.g. Gen 21:12; Hosea 2:1, 25 as quoted in Rom 9:7, 25–26. An act of election and creation is denoted by "calling," as a NOTE on 1:18 and COMMENT II on 4:1–16 show. Correspondingly the verb "to name" may mean in Eph 3:15 much more than "to address," "to tag," or "to label": the term includes the recognition, exertion, or conveyance of power.

families" stressed God's universal power. The inexhaustible "glory" of God is the third and final presupposition of Paul's prayer. The triad "love," "power," "glory" and the reference to "riches" were also found in 1:3–23. In remembering the "riches" and "glory" of the Father, Paul is convinced that God need not change or lose anything by granting the requests made to him. God is expected to act according to his nature, his character, i.e. his radiating love and power.[4]

through his Spirit . . . fortified with power. This pleonastic diction reflects the baroque description of God's "power" in 1:19;[5] but only in 3:16 is the "Spirit" explicitly mentioned. In 3:18, again, a reference to reinforcement will be made: strength is necessary to comprehend the dimensions of God's wisdom. Spirit, wisdom, knowledge, and power were also linked in 1:17–19 as they are in Wisdom literature (see COMMENT X on 1:3–14). In Eph 3 these nouns are so arranged as to make it clear that man must be invigorated by God's Spirit before he is able to grasp God's manifold wisdom and hold onto it in knowledge. Paul would hardly affirm in general terms, that knowledge is power. Rather he avers that through his Spirit God empowers man to know things that are beyond the human mind, eye, ear (I Cor 2:9–16).

[*to grow*] *toward the Inner Man.* The words "to grow" are not in the Greek text but are borrowed from 2:21 and 4:15–16. Because the literal version of 3:16, as "fortified toward [or into] the inner man," makes as little sense in English as, e.g. in the Vulgate and Calvin translations, a verb expressing movement is necessary for clarity. Versions and commentaries that fail to make clear the movement "toward the inner man," and instead point to the strengthening "of the inner man," or the increase of strength "in" him, are not doing justice to the Greek text. Verse 2:20 mentions a keystone toward which the building must grow if it is to grow at all "into" a holy temple. Verse 4:15 describes the growth "toward him who is the head." Verse 4:13 promises the saints that they will meet the one Perfect Man. Equally in 3:16 "the inner man" is a goal rather than a quality or possession of the saints. The saints, not the "inner man," have to grow strong. Who or what is this "inner man"? Is this term used in Ephesians as a title for Jesus Christ? Or does it denote an *alter ego* of natural man, corresponding, e.g. to the subconscious, to a higher level, or a projection of personal existence?[6] Verse 6:10 contains the appeal, "become strong in the Lord." If this command is a parallel to the prayer contained in 3:16, then "the Lord" is the aim, focus, and source of gathering strength—he, and not some innate self that resides in the nature of man and constitutes his individual quality.[7]

17. [*i.e.*] *that.* Since in the Greek text no conjunction whatever connects the

---

[4] Schlier, p. 168, writes movingly, "What the apostle asks for his Christians of Gentile origin originates from, and corresponds to, the radiating power of God: it is a little bit (*ein bisschen*) of power and light from his fullness."

[5] See fn. 39 to 1:15–23 for indications of the different accents inherent in the various nouns denoting "power."

[6] See COMMENT IV for a discussion of the alternatives.

[7] While 6:10 ff. describes the opponents *against* whom the saints are to be fortified, 3:16 treats their fortification *for* the right goal. There the armor of God provides their strength; here, as vss. 16–17 show, the presence of the Spirit and of Christ gives force. In both cases power is continually communicated to the saints, as it were from outside. A sheer hardening of their hearts against blows from the outside, or an increased inflammation of their spirits alone are apparently not sufficient for the war they are to wage. The fortification of man is in 3:14–17 directly related to the presence and work of the Father, the Son, and the Spirit.

two aorist infinitives "to be fortified" and "to dwell," it is more likely that the second verb and the clause governed by it interpret the first verb and vs. 16, than that they contain different thoughts and petitions.[8] Thus the addition of "[i.e.]" serves to express the intimate connection between vss. 16 and 17. "Spirit" and "faith" are assigned parallel instrumental functions. The "fortification" of the saints is unthinkable without the "indwelling" of the Messiah in their hearts, and their movement "toward the inner man" depends upon the Messiah's movement "into their hearts." These parallels between vss. 16 and 17 support the conclusion tentatively reached at the end of the previous NOTE: the Messiah himself is meant by the "inner man." He is at the same time the goal (vs. 16) and the source (vs. 17) of the saints' strength. Verses 4:15–16 contain analogous statements: the church grows "toward" and (lit.) "from" Christ the head (in our translation, "He enables the body to make its own growth"). The designations of Christ as foundation and keystone contain the same dialectic.

through faith. See the NOTE on the same words in 2:8. The instrumentality ascribed to faith excludes the idea that the indwelling Christ and the person in whom he dwells might ultimately melt into one and lose all distinctive traits. Each of them has and retains his personality. Faith—whether God's, the Messiah's, or the saints'—presupposes a covenant relationship between at least two persons in which one partner trusts and is faithful to the other without trying to absorb him and remain alone on the field. The parallel words "through the Spirit" (3:16) show that faith is understood as a gift of the Spirit (cf. 2:8–9; Gal 5:22–23).

the Messiah may dwell in your hearts. The closest Pauline parallel to this amazing statement is Gal 2:20, "The life I now live is not my life but the life which Christ lives in me" (NEB). See COMMENT IV B for the mystical meaning found in analogous NT statements.[9] The verb "to dwell" denotes permanent habitation as opposed to sojourning, pitching a tent, or an occasional visit.[10] The "heart" is in biblical diction man's total identity and existence described under the aspect of his vitality, intelligence, will, decision.[11] In the OT and NT the bowels rather than the heart are the seat of emotion. When in II Cor 6:11–12 Paul intends to speak of the emotive capacity of the heart he adds a reference to "bowels" (or "compassion"). More frequently he mentions joy or sorrow without locating them in the "heart."[12] The term "heart" can also denote an essential trait of human existence hidden to the eye; Paul is as much aware as OT writers that not everything human is apparent on the surface. In Eph 3:17 he may have in mind not only Christ's rulership over man's reason, will, and decision, but also the hidden quality of a Christian's existence. It is far from evident to every onlooker that Christ fills and directs the saints. Ac-

---

[8] Abbott; Schlier.

[9] Barn XVI 1–10 spoke of "God" dwelling in the hearts of the believers. It is not certain whether the end of Eph 4:6 ("God in all") and 3:17 inspired his thoughts.

[10] Cf. Gen 37:1; II Cor 5:1–9; Eph 2:19, 21.

[11] See the biblical wordbooks and esp. W. Eichrodt, *Theology of the Old Testament,* II (Philadelphia; Westminster, 1967), 142–45; Bultmann, ThNT, I, 220–27. In e.g. Jer 31:33; 32:39; Rom 2:15; Philip 4:7, "the heart" is mentioned in connection with man's thought and the fulfillment of God's will.

[12] II Cor 7:9–11; I Cor 7:30; 13:6; Rom 12:15.

cording to Acts 2 those inspired were considered drunk. Bultmann[13] defines the "heart" in this special sense as "the interior in contrast to the exterior, the real self in contrast to what a man appears to be." However, this possible connotation of the term "heart" is hardly reason enough to consider the "heart" and the "inner man" synonyms.[14] If this were so, 3:16–17 would suggest that around Christ, the "indwelling" core, first the inner man, then the outer man, then perhaps the church, the earth, and the heavens form concentric circles. Nowhere in any Pauline letter is such a notion expressed, and 3:16–17 far from affirms it unambiguously. Unlike later Gnostics Paul did not forge a *Weltanschauung* and force it upon his readers. Schlier sees a parallel to 3:17 in a Mandaean text[15] and uses it to attribute Christ's indwelling to baptism. But the parallel is too remote to make his suggestion persuasive.

Stand firm on the root and foundation of love. Lit. "in love being rooted and founded." The reference to "love" may belong to the preceding statement;[16] "love," together with "faith," would then be the manner in which, and the means by which, Christ inhabits the heart. In this case vs. 17 would say nothing at all about the soil and ground in which the saints are "rooted and founded." In the Colossian parallels, however, there is always a reference to such a ground.[17] Therefore, it is probable that in Eph 3:17 love is designated as the soil upon which the seedling can grow. The same love is also the ground upon which the building is to be constructed.[18] Yet there is still another possibility: style-conscious ancient writers were less afraid than are modern authors to mix diverse metaphors,[19] and Paul appears not to have felt at all restricted in this regard. Thus he may have added to the two combined images of "rooting" and "founding," or planting and building,[20] a third picture, i.e. a reference to the father-child, or the bridegroom-bride relationship. Most likely in 3:17 as well as in 4:16 no other "love" is in Paul's mind than that of God and Christ which is reflected in man's love of God and his neighbor.[21] God's and man's love are not alternatives in the interpretation of these verses.

The whole clause, lit. "rooted and founded in love," stands in relatively loose syntactical connection with the surrounding statements. So-called "absolute participles" are used in the Greek text and seem to interrupt the smooth flow of thought. The perfect participles "rooted" and "founded" fit poorly the preceding and following Greek subjunctives and infinitives that contain Paul's several petitions. The nominative case of these participles clashes with the dative and genitive cases of the pronoun "you," for it suits neither the indirect

---

[13] ThNT, I, 222; cf. the context, pp. 220–27. He refers to I Thess 2:17; I Cor 4:5; 14:25; II Cor 5:12; Rom 2:28–29. See also, e.g. I Sam 16:7; Jer 17:9–10.

[14] In Rom 7:22–23 the terms "inner man" and "mind" are equivalents.

[15] *Book of John* 57 (212), ed. M. Lidzbarski, *Das Johannesbuch der Mandäer* (Giessen; Töpelmann, 1915), p. 204, lines 11–14.

[16] NEB; cf. the NOTE on the words "by love" in 1:4.

[17] In Col 1:23 the foundation "in" or "by faith"; in Col 2:7 the rooting "in Christ" is mentioned separately.

[18] While e.g. Abbott and Gaugler agree on this, their ways part when they define "love." Gaugler speaks of "the love of God in Christ," cf. 3:19; Abbott, of "the grace of love in general as the fundamental principle of the Christian character," cf. 4:2, 32.

[19] See Abbott, p. 98, for examples from Cicero and Lucianus. In Eph 4:16 the intermingling process reaches a climax.

[20] The first two metaphors are also combined, e.g. in I Cor 3:9; Col 2:7; Eph 4:16.

[21] See 4:2; 5:25; 6:24 for the mutual love of the saints, the love of the husband, and the love of the Lord respectively. The verses 1:4, 6; 2:4; 5:1–2, 25 ff. describe God's and Christ's love.

(dative) object "you" nor the possessive genitive (hearts) "of yours" in vss. 16–17a. In 1:18 Paul employs an accusative rather than a nominative participle for describing the subject matter of his intercession. Certainly the Greek forms "rooted" and "founded" describe the result, not the process, of rooting and founding.[22] What is the exact meaning of these disturbing participles? It is probable that in 3:17 as much as elsewhere they possess the character and force of imperatives.[23] Instead of a third petition, a prayer for stability, they may contain an exhortatory digression. This exhortation would concern the maintenance of an attained status, described by the perfect tenses of the Greek text. In our translation the words "stand firm on" have been added in order to convey the imperative sense related to the status, and the nouns "root" and "foundation" were chosen to express as literally as possible the meaning of the forms "rooted" and "founded" in the Greek text.

18. *May you be strong enough to grasp.* The term "grasping" belongs to the vocabulary describing a fight against a strong opponent, cf. 1:19, 6:10; strength is required to seize an opponent or to sack an acropolis.[24] However, in 3:18 the verb "to grasp" is used in a metaphorical sense, which was at least as common as the physical: here it means to comprehend, to acknowledge a fact.[25] Dibelius's suggestion that this term be considered a mystical *terminus technicus* on the basis of Philip 3:12 is not convincing.[26] Paul points out that knowledge of the full dimensions of God's secret cannot be easily mastered; it requires a strength only God can give. According to I Cor 2:13–15 spiritual things are adjudicated by spiritual things only: solely "the spiritual man has a judgment on all things and is himself judged by no one." Eph 1:18 contains a

---

[22] As Origen and Chrysostom point out clearly.

[23] This is the case in II Cor 6:3–10; 9:11, 13; Rom 12:9–13; Col 2:2; 3:13, 16; Eph 4:2–3; 5:21; also 4:25?; cf. I Peter 2:18; 3:1, 7–9. See D. Daube, in Selwyn, *First Peter* (London: Macmillan, 1947), pp. 467–88; idem, "Haustafeln," in *The New Testament and Rabbinic Judaism* (London: Athlone, 1956), pp. 90–105; BDF, 468:2; Davies, PRJ, pp. 130–31, 329; H. G. Meecham, "The Use of the Participle for the Imperative in the New Testament," ET 58 (1947), 207–8 (evidence from Greek papyri); C. F. D. Moule, *An Idiom Book of New Testament Greek*, 2d ed. (Cambridge University Press, 1963), pp. 31, 179–80; Abbott, p. 164. However, J. H. Moulton, *A Grammar of the New Testament Greek* (Edinburgh: Clark, 1906), p. 182, treats the participles of Eph 3:17 as substitutes for optatives, i.e. as expressions of a petition, and Dibelius follows his example. Again a different interpretation is suggested by E. Norden, *Agnostos Theos* (Leipzig: Teubner, 1913), p. 251, n. 1. The evidence collected and interpreted by D. Daube in his essays is striking: the participles are a post-prophetic, typically rabbinic form of legislation. They do not make the claim of containing a divine command, but rather express considered opinion and experience regarding "the right thing to do." They are not found in the *Pirke Aboth*, but are frequent in the *derek-eretz* literature, i.e. those second-century and later Jewish tractates which invite the members of the elect community to follow the right way. A quasi-enthusiastic description is given of the conduct adopted by a chosen *élite*. The admonition is an appeal to their pride. Daube assumes that the early Christians used available Hebrew codes of duties, and that both Paul and I Peter were dependent on them. A direct dependence of the formulations of the ethics of I Peter upon Paul need therefore no longer be stipulated. Even in Hebrew legislation, participle forms equal negative imperatives.

[24] The other verb used in 3:18, "to be able" (*epischyo*), may belong to the same *Sitz im Leben*: it denotes originally not the potential in opposition to the actual (in the Aristotelian sense of these terms), but the presence and display of sufficient power to carry out what is planned, promised, necessary (see LSLex, 452)—even against opposition by adverse men or circumstances. Cf. *dynamai* in Eph 6:10, 11, 13, 16. As Robinson, p. 176, comments on 3:18, this verse "suggests the difficulty of the task, which calls for all their [the saints'] strength."

[25] Cf. Acts 4:13; 10:34; 25:25; Abbott. It is less evident that the completeness, clarity, certainty, and existential application of understanding (Schlier) is also implied by the verb, "to grasp." The accent of Eph 3:18–19 lies on the vastness of the material to be comprehended rather than upon the intensity or completeness of perception. A different accent is set in Col 2:2 where "fullness" of understanding is emphasized.

[26] See J. A. Dyer, "The Unappreciated Light," JBL 79 (1960), 170–71, and W. Nagel, "Die Finsternis hat's nicht begriffen (Joh 1, 5)," ZNW 50 (1959), 132–37, for details.

petition for the spiritual strength of insight, rather than for a mystical exclusion of reason.

the breadth, the length, the height, the depth. Lit. "what is the breadth," etc. These terms have been understood to refer to the heavenly heritage or city, to the wisdom or love of God, to the arms of the cross and their meaning, or to other specified things. See COMMENT VI. NEB may be right to identify them with the dimensions of Christ's love. "Love" is explicitly mentioned in the preceding and following verses.

19. *to know the love of Christ though it surpasses knowledge*. A statement such as this is called an oxymoron by Greek philologists: Paul makes a seemingly absurd combination of opposites in order to emphasize a particular point (cf. Philip 4:7, "The peace of God surpassing all understanding").[27] Former statements in Ephesians on the revelation of God's secret would exclude the affirmation, "Christ's love surpasses God's revelation," for God's revelation is complete and clear. It cannot be surpassed—its continuing spread among the Gentiles notwithstanding. God laid his heart bare when he showed that from eternity the Gentiles are included in his love and in the Messiah's realm,[28] but the saints' knowledge and understanding of the secret is still "imperfect" (I Cor 13:12, JB). They, not revelation, still labor under imperfection.[29] Whatever inkling of God's "thoughts" and "ways" men have already received, God's counsel remains as superior to low and high theology as are the heavens above the earth (Isa 55:8–9).[30] The Corinthians' claim to be perfect and to possess perfect knowledge (I Cor 1:18–2:16; 8:1–2, etc.) anticipates the claim of later Gnostic elites. But as Isa 55 and Wisdom passages such as Job 28; 38–42:6 show, long before the rise of Gnosticism there existed people and trends in need of the restriction given in I Corinthians and Eph 3:19.[31]

May you become so perfect as to attain to the full perfection of God. Lit. "in order that you be filled into (or, toward) all the fullness of God." Just as in 3:16, so also in 3:19 (cf. 4:12–13) the teleological and eschatological meaning of the Greek preposition "into," or "toward" (*eis*), ought not to be allowed to disappear in the translation. While Col 1:19 and 2:9 speak of the "indwelling" of "the whole fullness of God" in Christ and the church, and describe it as an accomplished fact, it is (despite all elements of "realized eschatology") characteristic of Ephesians to speak of "filling" as a process still going on. For people on earth, fullness is a promise and hope that has still to be realized and com-

[27] Such statements may be characteristic of modest theologians. Still, the use of oxymora or paradoxa as such is not sufficient proof of the theological (or of the truly modest) character of a given thought. Even reason that belittles itself, acknowledges its limits, and expresses itself in paradoxical statements, may claim to be autonomous. Biblical statements on the limits of human reason are, as in the case of Eph 3:19–20, found in the context of prayer to God, or of speech in the name of God.
[28] 1:4–12; 3:3–11; cf. COMMENT XI on 1:3–14.
[29] E.g. in Eph 1:17–18; Col 1:9, Paul intercedes for an increase in their knowledge, and in Gal 2:16; 4:9; I Cor 3:16; Rom 6:2, 9, etc. he appeals to a knowledge that ought to be there but appears neglected. As the content and mode of God's revelation are God's love, only a life in love can be an adequate recognition and acknowledgement of revelation. Only love knows love. Only the one who is known by God can know him. Not before the last day will God's and Christ's perfection be fully reflected by man's full knowledge and perfection, Gal 4:9; I Cor 8:3; 13:12–13; II Cor 5:11, 14–15; II Tim 2:19; John 10:14–15; I John 3:1–3, 19–20; Eph 4:13.
[30] "The love of Christ is a mystery in the sense that it is known and yet remains the great mystery," Gaugler.
[31] Cf. the texts attesting to a futuristic eschatology, as discussed in COMMENT IX on 1:3–14.

pleted.[32] A simple identification or conflation of God, Christ, and the church is prevented by eschatological suspension. In our translation, the verb "to attain to" was interpolated into 3:19; it may help to make the reader aware of the eschatological flavor of this verse. In order to show that God's "fullness" and "filling" possess a qualitative and dynamic character rather than only a quantitative and spatial nature,[33] the noun *plērōma* is in our version rendered by "perfection," and the verb *plēroō* by "to make perfect." Gaugler denounces versions that speak of "perfection"; he considers them "old" and "insufficient."[34] Yet the cultic OT meaning of this term and the function of "filling" ascribed to Christ in his relation to the church and all things (1:23; 4:10) require a translation which reveals rather than hides the mode in which God's presence, glory, and power operate. In OT diction an ordained priest assigned to one of the cultic tasks "fills his hands" or has his hands "filled." This "filling" signifies authority to perform a holy office. Eph 3:19 may intend to say that the saints shall be the sanctuary of God filled by his glory; cf. 2:21–22. The variant reading[35] that the whole fullness of God be filled, suggests that some contribution to God may be made through man's knowledge. Indeed the acquisition of a people as God's property and his glorification by them contribute to his glory (1:6, 11, etc.); God is not an unmoved mover. But the study of the terms "fullness" and "to fill" made in the context of 1:23 has shown that in the Bible these terms do not denote the complementation or implementation of God.[36] God's glory is radiated when man is made his perfect "image" (cf. Gen 1:26–27; Col 3:10). This God and his glory "create" a "resplendent" (lit. "glorious") partner of Christ (Eph 2:15; 5:27), yet God's glory is not created by the human partner. Rather it is acknowledged and reflected.

20–21. *To him who . . . is able . . . for ever and ever.* The last two verses of Eph 3 make use of a liturgical pattern which is probably not Paul's own creation.[37] The specific wording of 3:20–21, however, may still be Paul's.

20. *who . . . is able.* The ability mentioned here is distinct from mere potential, and denotes not the possibility but the power to carry something out.[38]

---

[32] 1:23; 2:22; 4:10. See COMMENT VI C on 1:15–23 for a discussion of the OT and other possible background of the notion of "filling," and especially for the rendering of "fullness" by "perfection."

[33] According to the OT God "fills" the sanctuary and the earth with his presence and glory.

[34] Such interpretations are found, e.g. in the Catena; in Calvin's commentary; in P. Ewald, *Kommentar zum Neuen Testament*, ed. Th. Zahn, 10th (Leipzig: Deichert, 1905), 173–74; in H. Oltramare, *Commentaire sur les épîtres de saint Paul aux Colossiens, Éphésiens, Philemon*, Paris: Fischbacher, 1891–92, on 1:23; 4:13 (ref.). Abbott considers II Peter 1:4, "participants of God's nature," rather than Matt 5:48, "You shall be perfect as your heavenly Father is perfect," a parallel of Eph 3:19. Thomas Aquinas speaks of full participation in all God's gifts. But it appears that Matt 5:48 stands specifically close to Eph 3:19, for this verse combines the same cultic and ethical meanings of fullness and filling (cf. Lev 19:2; Exod 31:13; Deut 32:4; Luke 6:36) which are also made explicit in a variant reading of Col 4:12: In that verse the words "perfect" and "filled" are probably combined to interpret each other mutually. The phrase, "filled with the fruit of righteousness" (Philip 1:11), is a parallel of the adjective "perfect" that is used in Philip 3:15. The criterion and main support for the equation of fullness and perfection are contained in Eph 4:13, see COMMENT VII C on 4:1–16.

[35] In the Chester Beatty Papyrus, the Vatican Codex, and the important Minuscule 33.

[36] Cf. Feuillet, *Christ Sagesse*, p. 285, etc.; Gaugler.

[37] Dibelius. Though the similarly constructed doxologies of Rom 16:25–27; Jude 24–25; *martyrium Polcarpi* XX:2, are probably post-Pauline, the common beginning with a reference to God's ability and their common ending reveal a pattern that may have been in synagogal and church use long before the writing of Ephesians. Until clear texts are produced that prove this assumption, there is, however, no certainty available.

[38] Calvin. Cf. fn. 24.

Therefore the omnipotence shown in specific actions, and not the idea of an omnipotent being, is described.

by the power exerted in us. In the Greek text, the verb translated by "exerted" may be in the middle rather than the passive form.[39] The two forms are indistinguishable in the Greek present tense. Most versions and commentaries reproduce the sense of the middle, translating "the power which is at work," or "which operates in us," and thus make "the power" appear to be a relatively free agent. But it is more probable that the text speaks of the Holy Spirit by which God himself works effectively and irresistibly in the saints. Because of this power exerted in man, God is praised as omnipotent. The Greek text of 3:20 contains a play on words which cannot be reproduced in English: The term "by the power" (*kata dynamin*) takes up the verb rendered by "who is able" (*tō dynamenō*). The wordplay helps justify the minority's interpretation, "exerted."

to outdo superabundantly all that we ask or imagine. This statement buttresses our NOTE on the oxymoron in 3:19. The limited knowledge mentioned there includes the limitation of man's will, desire, prayer, and performance. Such double-compounds as "superabundantly" are favorites with Paul.[40]

21. *Glory to him in the church and in the Messiah Jesus.* This statement is puzzling and hard to explain for two reasons. Two widely different terms: "the church" and "the Messiah" are accorded parallel, if not equal, dignity. Both are mentioned in the same place as the locus or the means of God's glorification—as if no sharp distinction were made elsewhere between the people of God and their head! The sequence of the terms "in the church" and "in the Messiah Jesus" is also startling.[41] Why is the Messiah not mentioned before his people? Unequivocal readings of 3:21 found in third-, fourth-, and fifth-century MSS (the Ch. Beatty Papyrus and the Codices Sinaiticus, Vaticanus and Ephraemi) follow this perplexing coordination and sequence. However, the variant readings of the Koine Group, the ninth-century Codices Angelicus and Porfirianus, and other MSS as well as Oecumenius and Theophylact omit the conjunction "and" between "the church" and "the Messiah." They suggest the version, "in the church through Christ."[42] The first script of the sixth-century Codex Claramontanus, the ninth-century Boernerianus, also Ambrosiaster and other fathers, reverse the order of "the church" and "Christ." The Vulgate, by inserting a comma after "the church," perhaps intends to indicate that temporal praise is given to God "in the church," while eternal praise is offered "in Christ." The reading "in the church and in the Messiah Jesus" is harder to explain than the others.[43] Because it is the *lectio difficilior,* and because of its age and spread, it is to be preferred to the variants contained in the other groups, and to the version of the Vulgate, which look distinctly like well-meant simplifications. Indeed, even the oldest reading of 3:21 can be shown to

---

[39] Robinson (cf. G. Estius) has compiled reasons for favoring the passive interpretation. The pertinent article in LSLex, 564 reveals that passive meanings (such as, to be actualized, to be object of an action) were much more widespread than those of the middle (e.g. to be at work, to be effective, to work out). See also G. Bertram, TWNTE, II, 652–54.

[40] Morgenthaler, *Statistik,* pp. 161–62.   [41] Robinson, p. 288.

[42] So, e.g. Calvin. The opposite way is chosen by J. Bengel: "through the church [cf. 3:10], in Christ."

[43] Dibelius.

harmonize with Pauline teaching. In II Thess 1:12 and Philip 1:11 (cf. Eph 1:6, 12, 14) Paul speaks of God's glorification in the church. In Eph 4:4–6 Paul mentions the church first because he starts from the actual locus of God's praise. Then he adds a reference to the Messiah Jesus to designate the basis of that praise. The existence and manifestation of God's glory *in the church* is and remains dependent upon glorification of God through the Son.[44] The secret of God is indeed now known only to the church, but it was revealed in Christ for the benefit of the whole world. In the confessional summary of Eph 4 the author follows the same procedure as in 3:21; he mentions what is most important at the end, not at the beginning.

from generation to generation, for ever and ever. Lit. "into all generations of the aeon of the aeons." Nowhere in the LXX or the NT is exactly the same formulation found.[45] It is most unlikely that in Eph 3:21 the nouns "generation" and "aeon" possess the same angelic or demonic meaning which they may have in 2:7, 3:5, 9. Here, as in most pre-Gnostic documents, they denote time spans, eventually eternity. The liturgical formulation appears not to allude to quasi-personal "powers" but makes it possible that here and elsewhere in Ephesians the same nouns have a primarily temporal meaning. Several interpreters[46] oppose the translation "for ever and ever," or a similar version, and see in the formula "the aeon [singular!] of the aeons" a specific message—as though the author wanted to say: the present aeon comprehends all former generations and periods into one; or, the present is the beginning of the eternal (perpetual) aeon. Any reference to a still future aeon (cf. 1:21) or to aeons still coming (2:7) would in this case detract from the presence of the eternity that is confessed in the church's Christological doxology. However, since in analogous doxologies (see LXX I Esdras 4:38; Theod. Dan 7:18) the same phrase, "the aeon of the aeons," is found, it need not be considered a typically Christian coinage and ought not to be overloaded with secret meanings.

Amen. The addition of the "Amen" by the same person who has pronounced the prayer, doxology, or benediction is strange to synagogal practice but is found several times in Pauline writings.[47] It cannot be stated with certainty whether this addition has to do with a practice of Jesus who, according to the canonical Gospels, was wont to open given statements with a single or double "Amen." However, when the apostle himself says the "Amen" he apparently speaks as a spokesman of the congregation addressed—as will be explained further in COMMENT II.

---

[44] Cf. Philip 2:6–11; John 17:1, 4, 5; Matt 11:25–30; Luke 2:14. While Eph 3:21 indicates the necessary connection between the praising church and the praising Christ, it does not justify any reading that assumes their identity. Indeed *in* or through *Christ* man's "Amen" is offered to God, II Cor 1:20. If he is God's glory in person, II Cor 4:6, then the church is the lighthouse which serves to radiate his light, Eph 2:7; 3:10; 5:8. Still, the distinction of an outer and an inner or a temporal and an eternal sphere of glorification should not be superimposed upon Eph 3:21. Also a church mysticism, corresponding to an alleged personal mysticism of 3:17, would hardly express the apostle's intention. See COMMENT IV B below, and the discussion on the head-body metaphor in COMMENT VI on 1:15–23.

[45] But Exod 40:15; Pss 9[10]:6; 105[106]:31; Dan 6:27; Tobit 1:4; Gal 1:5; Rom 16:27; Philip 4:20; I Tim 1:17; II Tim 4:18; Rev 20:10, etc. come near the pleonasm of Eph 3:21.

[46] E.g. Bengel; Schlier; Gaugler.

[47] Gal 1:5; Rom 15:33; Philip 4:20; I Tim 1:17, etc.

COMMENTS I–VI on 3:14–21

I Structure and Summary

Eph 3:14–21 contains three clearly distinguishable parts. (a) Verses 14–15 begin by describing the mode of Paul's prayer, but turn immediately to a description of the fatherly majesty of him to whom Paul lifts his voice. (b) Verses 16–19 contain the prayer itself. It is a prayer for the work of the Spirit, the presence of Christ, and manifestation of God's glory in the saints. Above all it asks for strength and knowledge. It seems to be composed of three petitions, followed by comments on the first and the second, with a parenthetical exhortation separating the two. Or Paul may first pronounce three petitions and then enumerate three hoped-for consequences of God's hearing the prayer. The various structural possibilities have been discussed in the NOTE on vss. 16–19. Characteristic of Paul's prayer is the combination of trinitarian theological elements with a passionate concern for the faith, comprehension, growth of each of the saints, and the intimate connection of certainty, humility, and hope. The man who was able to put himself as much into the foreground as 1:15; 3:1, 13; 4:1 indicate, was also so totally immersed in the service of God and the Spiritual welfare of the saints that he could forget himself completely: vss. 16–19 are strictly intercessory. Paul does not ask for a concession of God in favor of the saints. He petitions for the manifestation of God's very essence. If God is true to himself, to his glory, then he will hear Paul's prayer and be good to the saints. (c) Verses 20–21 utter such praise of God as befits the congregation. Just as Paul admitted the limits of human knowledge and yet asked for more, so he now acknowledges the insufficiency of human prayer and confesses the conviction that God will grant all that is necessary, for his own eternal glory's sake.

E. Haupt called this passage the highlight of Ephesians. Mitton[48] considered it one of the gems of the epistle. The same may be said of John 17 in the context of the whole Fourth Gospel: the reader is shown that praying stands above all reasoning, even theological.

II Kneeling

The OT as a whole and the writers and redactors of its individual parts attest to a rich variety of Israelite forms of worship. No one stance, attitude, or mode of prayer appears to have been required, recommended, or accepted at the expense of others. Amazing liberty and spontaneity prevailed in Israel's history and cult. All the more surprising is the fact that OT literature contains only a few references to prayers spoken by persons on their knees. Perhaps only in exceptional cases did individuals or the whole congregation kneel down for prayer.[49] It may well be that for a long time genuflection was considered an act strange to the ritual of a Yahweh sanctuary, if not also to a court in Israel. Kneeling is attributed to the priests and adherents of Baal, but the remnant of

---

[48] EE, p. 236.
[49] A late OT text states that Solomon was kneeling when he dedicated the temple by prayer, I Kings 8:54. David made the whole congregation kneel before the Lord, I Chron 29:20. Daniel prayed on his knees, Dan 6:10.

Israel who refused Baal worship seemed to ignore the form of that worship[50] together with its object. To emphasize the universal role of the Lord, the OT and Paul occasionally point out that the Lord will be revered by adoration offered by men on their knees.[51] When Luke mentions that Jesus, Stephen, Paul, or the congregation was kneeling, and when Mark reports on the soldiers mockworshiping Jesus, they use a Latinism.[52] Thus kneeling looks more like a non-Israelite form of prayer than a genuinely Hebrew tradition.[53] A story as rich in Hebrew colors as that of the Prodigal Son does not mention genuflection; both the Pharisee and the publican are *standing* in the temple while they offer their prayers (Luke 18:11, 13).

In Romans, Philippians, and Ephesians Paul uses terminology which is employed twice in the LXX for kneeling Gentiles, and once for the attitude of the congregation assembled in the temple. Only in Eph 3:14 does he mention that he himself is kneeling in prayer. Why should he draw attention to this in this particular letter? Perhaps because Ephesians was addressed exclusively to Gentile-born readers. Paul may have intended to show the former Gentiles how much he had "become like them" (Gal 4:12). "To those without the law [I have become] like one without the law, not as a trespasser of God's law, but bound by the law of the Messiah" (I Cor 9:21). By assuming or endorsing an originally pagan form of worship, Paul gave vivid testimony to the unification of Jews, Gentiles, and the whole world (cf. Eph 1:10, 22–23, etc.). Indeed, according to a prophetic oracle this form of worship was expected to be universally adopted by all powers in heaven, on earth, and under the earth (Philip 2:10–11). Certainly it was adopted by some Jews several centuries before the NT was written (I Chron 29:20; Dan 6:10).

The specific form of kneeling presupposed by Paul was most likely different from that used today in western churches. When Jesus "bent his knees" to pray in Gethsemane (Luke 22:41), he, according to Matt 26:39, "fell upon his face," and, following Mark 14:35, "fell upon the earth." I Chron 29:20 and Mark 15:19 identify "bending of the knees" and "approaching in dog-like fashion."[54] In Paul's time Hellenistic rulers, creditors, masters, and on occasion the Lord Jesus, but also several gods or deities, even Satan and devilish beings, were worshiped in this manner. Bending one's knees was the initial step in approach-

[50] I Kings 19:18, quoted in Rom 11:4.
[51] Isa 45:23, cited in Philip 2:10 and in Rom 14:11. In the Amarna Age kneeling involved prostrating oneself face down seven times and on one's back seven times before the suzerain. Such an attitude was certainly an eastern rather than a western rite, see Robinson, p. 83. Kneeling was the approach, e.g. of the Persians to their king, but occasionally also the attitude of Greeks before a deity, e.g. of women in Athens (see J. Leipoldt, *Die Frau in der antiken Welt und im Urchristentum* 3d ed. (Leipzig: Koehler, 1965), p. 39. As the Talmud passages in StB, I, 78; II, 260–61 show, early and late rabbis mentioned kneeling among other attitudes of prayer. But there appears to be no evidence that they required or recommended kneeling for special occasions or prayers. Bowing, however, was prescribed, e.g. for the Eighteen [Petitions] Prayers.
[52] Luke 22:41; Acts 7:60; 20:3; 21:5; Mark 15:19: *tithēmi gonata*, rendering, *ponere genua* DBF 5, 3b; LXX and Paul: *kamptō gony*, or *gonata*. In a spiritualized sense the latter terminology reoccurs also in I Clem 57:1, "bending the knees of your hearts." The employment of the verb, "to crouch" (*oklazō*) describing Solomon's attitude (LXX III [I] Kings 8:54) is unique.
[53] E.g. Mark 11:25; Matt 6:5; Luke 18:11, 13 show that in Jesus' time standing was the normal attitude of prayer. Eusebius HE v 5 appears to be the first to assert that among Christians kneeling was customary.
[54] The latter is a literal etymological rendition of the Greek verb (*proskyneō*) usually rendered by "to [fall down and] worship"; see WBLex, 723–24. The corresponding Hebrew verb is *hishtahaweh* ("to prostrate oneself").

ing the person worshiped; further movements included embracing his feet and/ or kissing the hem of his garment or the ground. It is rather unusual that I Kings 8:54 assumes Solomon was kneeling "with hands outstretched to heaven." According to I Kings 8:22, Solomon "stood" when he prayed this way. In Eph 3:14 Paul is most likely thinking of the crouching position, that is, of utter humiliation before God.

III   The Father and the Families

Eph 3:14–15 makes amazing use of the term "father." Also, a reference occurs here to "families in heaven and on earth" which is unique in the NT. Mention of the father and of families is combined with the concept of "naming." Each of these three terms, but also the relevance of their combination, requires special discussion.

A   The Father

There are at least three ways to explain the absolute term, "The Father."

1. The title "Father" may be derived from the address, "Abba," "Father" (Gal 4:6; Rom 8:15).[55] In this case it is equivalent to "our Father,"[56] and God is called upon as the Father of the Jews and Christians who are his beloved and faithful children and are joined together in one house, that is, the church (2:13–22). This narrow interpretation clearly contradicts the contents of Eph 3:14–15.

2. The term "Father" may possess a much wider sense. He who is called in Ephesians the "one God and Father of all, over all, through all, and in all" (4:6) or, elsewhere, the "Father of the lights" (James 1:17) and the "Father of the spirits" (Heb 12:9) is obviously the Father also of men and power who do not, or do not yet, believe in him. Thus the term "father" may possess a cosmic significance. This meaning need not imply that in a literal or metaphorical way creation is understood as an act of physical procreation by God. For in biblical books the physical aspect of fatherhood is but one of many essential elements, and perhaps not the dominant characteristic. A man becomes "father" or is called "father" when he adopts a foreign-born person, when he fills a legally superior or honorary position (e.g. as a leader), or when he is considered a prototype.[57] When Greek thinkers designated time or war as the "father of all things" they may have extended and spiritualized a relationship which originally was understood as a physical bond only. However, in biblical language the terms "father" and "son" denote basically an economic, legal, moral, educational or religious relationship which may or may not be based on common blood. Philo and Josephus use the nouns "father" and "creator" as equiva-

---

[55] Cf. G. Kittel, TWNTE, I, 5–6; J. Jeremias, "The Prayers of Jesus," SBT, Second Series 6 (1967), 11–65; G. Schrenk and G. Quell, TWNTE, V, 945–1014. Dibelius guesses that "Father of all families" may have been "a Jewish-Hellenistic prayer-address of God."

[56] Isa 63:16; 64:8; Matt 6:9; Luke 11:2 var. lect.; cf. Mal 2:10.

[57] See e.g. II Kings 2:12; Matt 23:9; I John 2:13–14; I Cor 4:15; Rom 4:11–12, 16–17. Gaugler regards the Father title as founded not upon an alleged progenitorship of the creator, but upon his capacity as Lord and Trustee who combines supreme power and love, and exerts them over men and angels alike. Cf. also the idiom, "son of . . ." which in many cases has nothing to do with physical descendence.

lents.[58] Not only the unity of Israel or of mankind, but also of the whole universe is guaranteed by the unwavering direction, care, and dominion exerted over all things by the one God, the Father. Classic Greek writers, Stoics, members of the Mystery Cults, and later also the Gnostics spoke of spiritual fathers or of a cosmic "Father of all." Since in Eph 3:15 it is explicitly stated that all families "in heaven and on earth" are affected by God's fatherhood, a cosmic understanding of the term "father" is required by the context of 3:14.

3. A widespread and fairly well-attested variant reading excludes neither of the two foregoing expositions, but adds to them a formula which belongs to indisputable Pauline tradition.[59] The variant reads, "the Father of our Lord Jesus Christ." The attribute "of our Lord Jesus Christ" anticipates the trinitarian tenor of 3:14–19 and brings vs. 14 into harmony with the opening formula of Paul's epistles (1:3; II Cor 1:3, etc.). It also seems to solve an enigma of 3:15: not from God the Father immediately, but from or after Jesus Christ the families in heaven and upon earth take their name.[60] However, the superior MS attestation to the shorter reading, the Greek play on the words, "Father-family," in vss. 14–15,[61] and the tendency of the variant to simplify, if not eliminate, a unique and disturbing element of vs. 14—these facts advise against acceptance of the variant reading.[62] Once again the more difficult text is to be heeded in its own right.

Preference is probably to be given to the second of the three expositions sketched. If scholarly terms contribute to understanding Paul at all, it must be stated that the Cosmic Christology of 1:4–23 and the Cosmic Ecclesiology of 2:7, 10; 3:10, are crowned by a Cosmic Theology or Patrology in 3:14–15. In the following two sections evidence for or against this hypothesis will have to be weighed.

B The Families

As a translation of several different Hebrew terms, the LXX frequently uses the word "family" (*patriā*) to denote Jewish groups "narrower than a tribe, wider than a house."[63] Sometimes reference is made to the "families of the

[58] E.g., Plato *spec. leg.* I 96; II 6; *de ebrietate* 30; 81; Josephus *ant.* I 20, 230; II 152; IV 262; VII 380. It is possible that the identification of father with creator narrows down rather than expands religious meanings of the term "father." For example in the Canaanite pantheon the chief God El is called "father" because he is the progenitor, lord, master, chief practitioner or principal exemplar of all things, see M. H. Pope, *El in the Ugaritic Texts*, Suppl. VT II, Leiden: Brill, 1955. On pp. 102 ff. limitations of El are mentioned. Unlike the "high god" he could not establish some sort of monotheism; Baal was able to displace him. Ps 29 illustrates the use made in Israel of Canaanite religious terminology.

[59] See the old Latin and three Syriac versions, the third correction in the Codex Sinaiticus, the Codices Claramontanus and Boernerianus, the MSS of the so-called Antiochian family; Origen partly, Ambrosiaster, Victorinus, Ephraem, Basilius of Caesarea, Chrysostom, Theodore, Theodoret.

[60] Calvin suggests that the Jews were named after Abraham; Jesus Christ's name is decisive for Jews, Gentiles and angels. Others think of baptism in the name of Christ, of the name, "Christians," or of the title, "sons," which is borne by the members of the church on earth and in heaven. Bengel states, *fundamentum omnis filiationis est in Jesu Christo*. Still, in Eph 3:14–15 no explicit reference to sonship or the title, Christian, is made.

[61] Which is not visible in our translation. See the first NOTE on vs. 15 for the reason why the seemingly appropriate pair father-fatherhood could not be used.

[62] Though they hardly warrant Robinson's designation of the added words as "a mischievous gloss," p. 174. Actually, the expansion may be attributed to the unconscious influence of other Pauline passages upon a copyist. Perhaps he understood the word "Father" as an abbreviation of the longer expression.

[63] Abbott; e.g. Exod 6:14–15; 12:3; Num 1:2, 4, 16, etc.

earth" or the "families of the Gentiles,"[64] or the term "the nations of the earth" substitutes as a synonym.[65] In the NT the noun "family" occurs only in Luke-Acts[66] and in Ephesians. If by the term "each family in heaven and upon earth" (Eph 3:15) the Jews and the Gentiles are meant, then neither mankind as a whole nor the church in particular is depicted as an amorphous mass. Rather both groups, separately or in combination within the church, are seen as societies with certain structures—even the structures of "families." The created world does not only consist of men and things; to its substance belong some systems, structures, and institutions. He who names these powers intends to include "all things" (ta panta) under their sway. In COMMENT V on 1:15–23 it was shown how (and why) the term "all things" is sometimes replaced by a reference to principalities and powers. When Paul speaks of families "in heaven and upon earth" (3:15) he is certainly not thinking only of Jewish and Gentile persons and groups. The invisible angelic or demonic powers of history, procreation or dependence, tradition and law; the influence of geographical locations, of opportunities offered in a given period, of exploits, of defeats; perhaps also the magic of nationalism and a hundred other isms, or of naked nihilistic power or tyrannical ideologies may be in the apostle's mind. There is not one among them that has not been idolized and misused. Dibelius and Schlier especially have emphasized that the "families in heaven" mentioned in 3:15 mean angels corresponding to the principalities and powers, aeons and generations to which Ephesians referred earlier.[67] Eph 3:15 as the analogy of Eph 4:6 may proclaim that God himself is their originator and sustainer. They are not created by, and freely at the disposition of, a deity or fate opposed to God (as assumed in later Gnosticism).

Three other interpretations are to be mentioned only in passing:

1. If it is presupposed that 3:15 contains the same grammatical mistake as 2:21, i.e. the omission of the article before the noun qualified by pās ("each," "all," or "whole"), then 3:15 can be translated with the American Version as referring to the one "whole" family that embraces heaven and earth. But the Greek text of all MSS speaks, correctly translated, of "each family," not of "the whole family." The emotionally appealing notion of a single family (comprehending angels, demons, all things, and all men under the fatherhood of God) is too weakly supported if it rests solely upon the assumption of a grammatical error in Eph 3:15.

2. C. L. Mitton[68] refers to 2:21 for another purpose. Assuming that the author of Ephesians did not violate sound grammar in that verse but rather intended to speak—the idea of one church and church unity notwithstanding —of individual local congregations, he suggests that in 3:15 "family" means local congregation. The families "in heaven" are identified by Mitton either with the members of the church that have already passed out of earthly hard-

---

[64] E.g. Gen 12:3; Ps 21[22]:28; I Chron 16:28.
[65] E.g. Gen 22:18; 26:4.
[66] In Luke 2:4 as equivalent of a Jewish "house;" in Acts 3:25 as a designation for the Gentiles.
[67] Their exposition is supported, e.g. by the reference made to angelic families in I Enoch 69: 3–4; 71:1; 106:5; cf. StB, III, 594. Mark 12:25 expresses the conviction that such heavenly families do not persist because of fleshly procreation. It is, therefore, not necessary to assume that in Eph 3:15 Paul thinks primarily of units formed by blood-relationship.
[68] EE, pp. 237–39.

ship—"one of the first examples of the line of thought which led to the doctrine of the Church as both triumphant and militant"—or with the guardian angels of local churches mentioned in Rev 2-3. The name given these congregations from the common Father would then be (except for the play on words mentioned earlier), "brotherhood." Mitton is probably right in dating the formation of such ideas toward the end of the first century. He is less convincing when he finds them already in Eph 3:15 and declares this verse irreconcilable with Pauline authorship. There is no evidence that Paul was thinking here specifically either of brotherhood, or of the perpetual survival of "house" churches or rural and urban congregations, or of the "green pastures" of heaven.

3. The idea that Paul might have in mind those two families that form the church, i.e. the Jews and the Gentiles who confess Christ, seems to have some support in all Ephesian passages which stress their unification, especially in 2:11-22. But since in the church Jews and Gentiles are "members of the same household" (2:19), and since a vertical division ("in heaven and on earth") between them would as much contradict the message of Ephesians as would a horizontal wall of separation, this interpretation is not to be recommended.

C The Naming

In view of the wide variety of meanings inherent in the word "to name" (see the second NOTE on 3:15), at least four interpretations appear possible:

1. The heavenly and earthly families mentioned in 3:15 have been named after God—just as indeed names of men such as Isaiah or Zedekiah, and names of angels such as Michael or Gabriel in themselves contain the name of God.[69] The phrase "to name after" (*ek*) occurs in classical Greek (but not in LXX) and may be used in Eph 3:15 in the classical sense.[70] However, not all men and angelic or demonic powers have been given and bear such names. Therefore this understanding is contradicted by the present tense used in 3:15: each family "takes" its name.

2. A "nomenclature" and exposition conflicting with the actual names borne by heavenly and earthly tribes or powers is avoided when the translation "fatherhood" is given preference over "family."[71] Then 3:15 answers an ontological and an epistemological question at the same time. God is the archetype of a father, the creator of all fatherhood; and, he bears the name "Father" in an exemplary way: the earthly concept and word "father" is formed after the precedent set by God. The ontic and noetic aspects of this etiology and their combination in an indivisible unit may well correspond to an intention of the biblical creation stories and other passages that include hermeneutical information.[72] But since, as was stated earlier, there is no linguistic evidence available from Paul's time showing that *patriā* means an abstract "fatherhood" (*paternitas*) rather than a concrete "family," this beautiful exposition can at best be considered a homiletical corollary to 3:15.

---

[69] See, e.g. the etymologies given in Isa 12:2; Jer 23:6 (Isaiah=Yahweh is my salvation; Zedekiah=Yahweh is our righteousness); all proper names ending with -*el*, or with -*yah*, -*yahu* can be given corresponding interpretations.
[70] E.g. Homer *Iliad* x 68; Sophocles *Oedipus Tyrannus* 1036. Gaugler.
[71] See fn. 2.   [72] See, e.g. I Cor 2:9-16; II Cor 3:12-18; 5:16.

3. The giving of a name amounts, e.g. in the case of the twelve apostles and Peter, to the exertion of power and the conveyance of an authority which is to be recognized by man.[73] The act of "naming" or "calling" has in Semitic and other cultures more than just a nominal or descriptive meaning. It gives a person or thing identity, essence, function. He over whom God's name is called out is put under God's protection and judgment,[74] just as the naming of animals by man is synonymous with man's dominion over them.[75] Perhaps the term "instituted by God" (Rom 13:1–2) is equivalent to "named . . . from God." Eph 3:15 shows that Paul does not prostrate himself before one of the many gods and lords called upon (or, with RSV, "so-called gods . . .") "in heaven and upon earth" but before the one God who is "God of gods," "King of kings," "Lord of lords," "the King, the Lord of hosts," "the God and Father" "over, through, in all."[76] A monotheistic creedal formulation is coined or used by Paul. The history of Israel in OT times demonstrates that even before "the Hellenistic synagogue" was founded, sufficient reasons existed to use such formulae. The doxological character of 3:15 is a warning against shifting attention away from God himself to visible and invisible powers that do not deserve adoration.[77] Though this interpretation makes good sense, it is not beyond doubt. For it is not certain whether "named . . . from God" can really be identified with "named by God," or "instituted by God," or, "subjugated under God"—or whether it means, as the parallel of I Cor 8:5 would suggest, "named by men," i.e. falsely attributed divine honor. The Greek wording is not yet sufficiently elucidated to permit a clear decision.

4. All preceding sections of Ephesians have in one way or another pointed out that God rules not only over Israel but also over the Gentiles and all the powers that be. Specifically the term "all families" was in Gen 12 and in the Psalms understood to denote the Gentiles. In turn, these Gentiles are always described as nations who are subject to their gods. Therefore it is possible that "each family in heaven and on earth," while not excluding Israel, denotes specifically the Gentiles, including the structures and supposed deities to whom they were subject. In this case Eph 3:15 complements 3:14. According to 3:14 Paul adopted a predominantly pagan form of prayer; he was praying with and for the Gentiles. In 3:15 he gives the reason for this liberty: by the revelation and ministry described in 3:2–13 (which includes baptism) God has put his name upon the Gentile world. His name, "Father," was reflected already in the nomenclature "sons of God," attributed to heavenly beings (Gen 6:2). Now it will be exalted by the "adoption" of Gentiles into God's house (Gal 3–4; Rom 8), and by the submission of all principalities and powers (Eph 1:19–23). Paul worships God in the extraordinary form of crouching

---

[73] Mark 3:14 var. lect.; Luke 6:13–14; Matt 10:1, 13; 16:18–19, etc. Cf. W. Heitmüller, *Im Namen Jesu*, Göttingen: Vandenhoeck, 1903; J. Pedersen, *Israel*, I–II, 252 f., III–IV, 649; G. van der Leeuw, *Religion in Essence and Manifestation* (Gloucester: Smith, 1967), pp. 147–58.

[74] E.g. in baptism or in an act of intercession, healing or discipline, Matt 28:19; Acts 3:6; 19:13; I Cor 5:4–5; James 2:7.

[75] Gen 2:19; 1:26; Ps 8:6.

[76] Cf. I Kings 18:39; Dan 2:27; Deut 10:17; Rev 19:16; Isa 6:5; Second Isaiah, *passim;* Eph 4:6; I Cor 8:5–6; I Tim 1:17.

[77] In Col 2:8, 18, 23; Heb 1:5–13; also in apocalyptic literature, e.g. Rev 19:10; 22:8–9, angel worship is explicitly ruled out.

before him because he has to give thanks for the revolutionary, universal manifestation of God's power and love (cf. Dan 6).

Each of the interpretations above can be questioned, but none can simply be ruled out. Until new materials or deeper reflection award priority to one of them or to an alternative not yet mentioned, they have to be left standing as complementary. Eph 3:15 may serve as an example that there are multiple literal senses of certain biblical passages, just as is the case, e.g. in the parables of Jesus.

IV   Spiritual Anthropology

Eph 3:16–19 deals with man's inner life. Certainly the apostle has touched upon man's personal hope, faith, and love earlier in the epistle. He has mentioned forgiveness, life from the dead, peace, access to God. He has spoken of knowledge and comprehension, also of works to be done and a mission to be carried out.[78] What he wrote of himself, his history, his ministry, his prayer, his suffering, has demonstrated that the gospel does not destroy personality, the life of the soul, or one's individual responsibility. Still, in the first two chapters of Ephesians the social character of the gospel has been emphasized more strongly than the impact of the good news upon the individual believer. In other epistles the accents appear reversed; a personal element prevails though the social one is never completely missing. The former is epitomized by Rom 7:24, "Wretched man that I am! Who will deliver me from this body of death?"; the latter, e.g. by Rom 12:5, "We, though many, are one body in Christ." In Ephesians the gospel's nucleus, its internal moving power, and its external manifestation consist of the gathering of Jews and Gentiles into one flock, of the peace made between both groups, of their common worship and its effect upon the whole world.[79] The church rather than the individual is called a new "creation" and a "new man."[80] Those political, ideological, or religious movements and organizations[81] in which the individual is more or less completely lost in the community appear to have a parallel, or competition, in the message of Ephesians. The communal, i.e. ecclesiastical, character of the message of Ephesians is readily recognized by Roman, Anglican, and Presbyterian "high-church" theologians; it is acknowledged for different reasons by a social (if not Marxist) interpretation of Ephesians; and it is conceded and scornfully evaluated by those who consider Ephesians a product of "early Catholicism."[82]

However, together with certain elements of Eph 1–3, vss. 3:16–19 provide

---

[78] 1:1, 7, 12, 13, 15, 19; 2:1–3, 5–6, 8, 10, 12, 16, 18; 3:10.

[79] The message of Ephesians embraces not only an in-group but also all those alienated and excluded from the holy community (2:11–19). It is by definition good news not only for the church, but also for the world. As shown on many occasions, in this epistle the church is the exponent of God's will toward all men, all powers exerting domination over the creatures, and all things. The Gentiles, in turn, are representatives of the cosmic powers and all other created things.

[80] Eph 2:10, 16. In II Cor 5:17, "new creation" may be understood in a more personal sense; in Gal 6:15 the same term may describe both the new person and the new community. Eph 4:13, 22–24 combine both concerns. See esp. COMMENT VII on 4:1–16 and V on 4:17–32.

[81] As, e.g. Communism, Religious Socialism, certain pioneering congregations and religious orders.

[82] The names of Schlier, L. S. Thornton, T. F. Torrance, Pokorný, Käsemann represent these five groups of expositors.

a necessary correction. The gospel proclaimed in Ephesians is distinct from many variants of secular and religious collectivism by the vital concern shown for the enrichment, strength, stability, love, knowledge, growth, and perfection of each member of the community and, virtually, of every man. If this concern is honest and adequate, and if it does justice to the condition and disposition, the yearning and trembling, the confinement and the outreach of individual man and his "soul," then this epistle contains a vital contribution to the problem of "community and personality." It does not leave a complete void at the point where personal life, experience, understanding, and counseling are at stake—even in those realms focused upon by the research of anthropology, psychology, and psychiatry.

Two questions may be posed in order to study the possible relevance of Eph 3:16–19 for these fields. (a) Does the word "mysticism" aptly describe the antidote supplied by this passage (or other texts of the epistle) against sheer collectivism? (b) Do these verses propose a general anthropology as a precondition of conversion and faith, or do they contain traces of a specific anthropology and psychology on the ground of the gospel of Jesus Christ? Both questions will be treated separately.

A Mysticism?

Among the doctrines and individual assertions that have contributed to labeling Paul's theology "mystical," the following are outstanding:[83]

1. Many or all clauses containing the formulae "in Christ" and "Christ in me" or "in you."[84]

2. Paul's doctrine of "dying" and "rising with Christ," his teaching on baptism and the Lord's Supper, and his concept of union with (or in) Christ.[85]

3. Utterances such as, "It is no longer I who lives, but Christ who lives in me . . .";[86] "I worked harder . . . though it was not I but the grace of God that is with me . . ."; "God revealed it to us through the Spirit." Cf. the various references to his knowledge, to his visions, and to revelation received.[87]

4. An outright mystical statement which crowns all evidence: "In everything and all things I am initiated" (*memyēmai*, Philip 4:12).

Though a "God-mysticism" that is traceable also in Jewish writings may be discerned within the distinctly Christian (Pauline and Johannine) "Christ-mysticism" and "Spirit-mysticism," the distinction of these several "mysticisms" contributes little to an understanding of Paul. In his theology the presence of God and the working of his grace cannot be separated from the indwelling of

---

[83] The literature relevant for the following is listed in BIBLIOGRAPHY 16. The exclusion of a mystical interpretation of Paul's suffering by E. Güttgemanns, *Der leidende Apostel und sein Herr* (Göttingen: Vandenhoeck, 1966), pp. 102–12, was mentioned earlier.

[84] See COMMENTS I on 1:1–2 and V on 1:3–14; Gal 2:20; Rom 8:9–10; Col 1:27, etc.

[85] Gal 3:26–28; I Cor 10:16–17; 12:12–13; Col 3:11; Rom 6:3–5; II Cor 4:10–12, etc.

[86] Lam 4:20 may be the most authentic and helpful parallel: "The Lord's Anointed . . . the breath of our nostrils." Calvin's exegesis of Eph 3:17 corresponds to that text: "Those err who hope to receive God's Spirit by other means than by accepting Christ . . . The Spirit is found nowhere else but in Christ."

[87] Gal 2:20; I Cor 15:10; 1:18 – 2:16; II Cor 3:18; 12:2–4, 9. Parallel non-Pauline statements are found, e.g. in Luke 17:21, "The kingdom of God is in the midst of you," and in the Fourth Gospel, e.g. 14:10, 20, 23, "I am in the Father and the Father is in me . . . The Father who remains in me does his work . . . I am in my Father and you are in me and I in you . . . [My Father and I] we shall come and stay with him who loves me."

Christ and the work of the Spirit in man. Nor is a differentiation advisable between individual (personal) and church (collective) mysticism. Paul understands all experiences pertaining to himself as relevant to the public proclamation and spread of the gospel.[88] Certainly he is aware of privileges granted to him by revelation and of the uniqueness of the apostolic ministry, but he treats his commission and his very existence as a servant of Christ as typical of the destiny of the whole congregation. And this is not enough: things concerning him concern the whole world; see e.g. Gal 6:14. He expects that God the Father, the Son, and the Spirit will be as near the church, and that the church in turn will be as near and dear to God, as God is to him and he to God. The church, in turn, is the showpiece of God's will regarding the world (Eph 2:7, 3:10). Therefore, the problem of a possible church mysticism does not require separate consideration. The question is essential, however, whether "mysticism" is in any sense a fitting explanation of, and label for, Paul's religion, and a key to his anthropology.

If the term mysticism is used to point to one of the following features, it may serve a good purpose: (1) something greater is at work than a power that can be defined by human reason and controlled by an enlightened intellect; (2) God is nearer and more mysteriously at work than cultic manipulations can achieve or express; (3) man is judged and determined by deeds of God that defy control and repetition by laboratory, psychological, or sociological methods. If one or several of these tenets is meant by "mysticism," then this concept conveys no more than a certain negative information on Paul's thought, experience, and teaching. But, frequently the concept "mysticism," is meant to give a positive and substantial description of given facts and methods:

1. In popular diction mysticism is sometimes bluntly, either with appreciation or depreciation, identified with religion. Whoever relies upon the impact and success of an extraordinary experience, mood, or destiny rather than upon the dictates of logic, natural science, history, ethics, etc., may be called a mystic. The experience of any and each *mysterium tremendum* may be ascribed to mysticism.

2. Or, mysticism is the reaction of certain religious people against the piety of others. It seeks to replace the rigorous demands of prophetic zeal and tradition as well as the rule of organized (priestly) religion.[89] It upholds the right of the individual to possess an immediate relationship to the deity (viz. to the ground of being), and it refuses to submit itself to the verbalization, universalization, moralization, organization, and intolerance of formalized religion. Individualism, pantheism or panentheism (as opposed to the notion of a personal God); lack of concern for any history except the soul's; rejection of dogmatic and legalistic formulations; predilection for negative, if not paradoxical statements on the deity and on man; emphasis upon the unspeakable and unmanageable; glorification of man's passivity; concentration upon an inner circle of initiates and imitators; practice of paralogical techniques—such are the characteristics of mystic groups and individuals. Prayer, silence, intuition, ecstasy, aloofness, or asceticism are among their most sacred tenets and conspicuous marks.

---

[88] See esp. Gal 1:15–24; Philip 1:12–14; cf. I Tim 1:15–16.   [89] See F. Heiler, *Prayer*.

3. Or, mysticism seeks to overcome tragic divisions by realizing the idea of oneness, by seeking means of unification, and by expressing the hidden unity of all things.[90] The underlying belief in the unity of all with the deity can be based upon the conviction that the immeasurable deity is present in the confines of the finite. It may lead to the demand, "Escape from finitude!" and to the promise of a transfer into the realm of transcendence. Assured of the ascension of the soul, a mystic can stand the torments of the present world. Even when the dualistic tension between the carnal and the spiritual worlds appears to become unbearable, and when the seeming contradiction between immanentism and transcendentalism defies any explanation or mitigation, the idea of incarnation (understood as a perpetual process) offers relief and a solution to the insoluble problem. The celebration of the One who fills all by his omnipresence can be amalgamated and expressed in a confidence founded upon individual experience, self-knowledge, rebirth, transformation, and deification.

Scholarly definitions of mysticism in general and the selection of its salient points seldom agree. There is a corresponding variety of reasons why Paul was called a mystic. Jewish and Greek mysticisms were jointly or alternatively considered precedents of Paul's thought and language.[91] Sacramental mysticism was combined with, or distinguished from, the mysticism of conversion to God and conversation with God. Active or passive, objective or subjective elements of Paul's mysticism were moved into the foreground. While it is undeniable that Paul uses formulations that resemble pagan or Jewish diction, the distinctly prophetic and doctrinal tone of most of his writings gives little encouragement to calling his total theology mystical. E.g. in Gal 2:16–20; Philip 3:6–14; Rom 8:9–18, mystical, narrative, and juridical diction are so intertwined that it is impossible to separate from Paul's prophetic and historical theology of revelation a distinct, a historical, and mystical system of thought in which the identification of God and man formed the center.[92] Paul did not say and could never have said to God, to the Messiah, or to the Holy Spirit, "You are I and I am you."[93] Paul's theology is in every aspect related to Christ crucified and risen—rather than to a transhistorical deity that is either a captive of its transcendence or trapped by its immanence in the universe. Union with

[90] Cf. the summary given by J. Amstutz in JR 41 (1961), 248. R. Reitzenstein, *Poimandres* (Leipzig: Teubner, 1904), p. 21, quotes from a Greek papyrus the words of a magical prayer addressed to Hermes: "I am you and you are I." Such identification is typical of one strand of mysticism.

[91] Apocalyptic, cultic, speculative, ascetic, etc. variants exist in Jewish mysticism. Mystery Religions and early forms of Gnosticism are among the Hellenistic elements that may have influenced Paul.

[92] Dibelius admits that in discussing the reality, presence, and transforming power of Christ, and in describing the new life given by the Spirit, the apostle makes use of the language and thought pattern of mystical piety. But when Dibelius discusses the words "I am initiated" (Philip 4:12), he asks, "What kind of mysticism is that?" He decides to allocate Paul to an essentially prophetic type of piety and to describe his method of theologizing as essentially *heilsgeschichtlich* (related to the history of salvation). See *Botschaft und Geschichte*, II, 122, 151, 159; also E. Schweizer, EvTh 26 (1966), 250 ff.

[93] This formulation is found in the London Papyrus 122:36. K. Barth, *Church Dogmatics*, I:2 (1956), 319–20, considers the tendency toward identification the core of mysticism. R. Bultmann, ThNT, I, 311, 328, agrees with Dibelius in rejecting a mystical interpretation of the "in Christ" formula, for this formula cannot be rightly understood unless the Pauline statements about walking "in the flesh" are also taken seriously. Even the "in Christ" formula implies that the earthly pilgrimage of the saints is still being continued. Therefore it means the opposite of an escape from earthly bondage and historical responsibility, whereas in his ecstasy an enthusiastic mystic is wholly transformed and transposed into another world. But Paul knows that he is righteous and a sinner at the same time. Even while Christ is in him, the apostle still walks "in the flesh" (Gal 2:20).

Christ is not taught at the expense of respect for the difference between God and man, Christ and the saints, the Spirit and the people of God. There is no trace of man's deification or of *fruitio Dei* in beatific vision. Instead of being an escape from history, salvation means to enter "an objective event that is going on" (Dibelius): it means to be sent out with a mission into the world and to hurry forward toward a goal that is not yet reached. Though Paul was given knowledge, auditions, and visions, and though he experienced ecstasy, he played down and belittled these moments (I Cor 13:1–3; 14:18–19; II Cor 12:2–4, 9). All that he says about the personal God's righteous judgment, about the beginning of the new aeon in the midst of history, about mission, action, and obedience, and all his concern for the most diverse congregations, for their hope, and for their unfinished search for faith and growth in perfection, distinguish his theology from the esoteric, perfectionistic, timeless, and identification-happy traits of mysticism.[94] In short, all the mystical elements or parallels that appear in his life and writings are under the safe control of historical and practical, if not pragmatic, arguments.

Therefore the term mysticism is either too vague or outright misleading as a description of Paul's piety and theology.[95] It is an equally improper way to characterize the basis of his anthropology.

B   Humanity by Partnership

Just as the dwelling of God in his holy temple was the highlight of Paul's doctrine of the church (2:22), so the inhabitation of Christ in each of the saints is decisive for his anthropology (3:17). By joining Jews and Gentiles together in peace and by leading them to the Father, Jesus Christ founded the church. By dwelling in the hearts of the saints he keeps the church and its members alive and makes them grow from him and toward him (cf. 4:15–16). By using the metaphors of "head," "body," and "filling," Paul describes the dominion and care exerted by Christ over his body. Terms denoting inhabitation and filling are used to designate God's presence in the church and the perfection to which he leads her members (2:22, 3:19). Eph 3:17 and the supposedly mystical passages quoted in the preceding section reveal how Jesus Christ, the head, in carrying out the ministry entrusted to him, is not only ruler of the cosmos and the church, but also a gift of God to individual man. Jesus Christ is proclaimed as being present not only for man and amongst men, but also *in* man.

Does there exist in man a place, a potential or a function that is equipped to form an entryway and a domicile for Christ? Among modern scholars R. Bultmann has shown the greatest concern for Paul's anthropology and has come out with the most serious results elaborating upon it.[96] His findings are: even before God reveals himself to man and before faith is born, man is so constituted that he can be reached and transformed by a power outside himself. The potential for dialogue is innate in man and demonstrates his openness to

---

[94] Dibelius, *Botschaft und Geschichte*, II, 155–58, 105–11.

[95] Bultmann, RGG, IV, 1243–46, has come to similar conclusions regarding the alleged mysticism of the Fourth Gospel. Regarding Paul's mysticism see also Davies, PRJ, esp. pp. 13 f., and Best, *One Body*, p. 23.

[96] See ThNT, I, 191–227. A comparison of the anthropology ascribed by Bultmann to Paul, with the anthropological views of, e.g. M. Heidegger and P. Tillich reveals striking analogies.

the influence of a transcendental power.[97] Among the criticisms uttered against this picture of Pauline anthropology is the charge of individualism.[98] If Bultmann were right, Paul would consider every person perfectly constituted in himself, a particle in an amorphous collective, ultimately alone with himself and a transcendent power. Even if man's openness and disposition for experience from beyond prevents him from being simply autonomous or self-supporting, he is yet depicted as being in himself as complete as a radio set, equipped with all necessary mechanisms for action and reaction, including a powerful antenna for receiving signals from the outer world. Revelation, the gospel, decisions of obedience and faith may activate and perfect his potentials, but they inform, form, or reform his humanity and do not exert a creative and constitutive power. Man as depicted by Bultmann possesses a humanity that is independent of God. He seems to be fully human apart from God's revelation, the creation in Christ, the word addressed to him, and the response evoked. (Therefore the first part of Bultmann's reconstruction of Paul's doctrine is called "Man Prior to the Revelation of Faith."[99])

Is this view supported by Eph 3:16–19? Whether or not Ephesians is accepted as authentically Pauline, this passage will either support or call into question Bultmann's anthropology. While other Pauline texts offer their own criteria for a critical assessment of the picture just sketched, the special contribution of Eph 3 is just as important. What is meant by the "inner man," and what does Paul expect to happen to him or through him?

The key words of 3:16 have been translated in various ways. JB has: "for your inner self to grow strong"; NEB: "strength and power . . . in your inner being"; RSV: "strengthened with might in the inner man"; NTTEV: "power

[97] Bultmann argues the following way: each of the terms "body, soul, spirit, mind, conscience, heart," etc. describe the total man. As was quoted earlier, "man does not have a body; he is a body" (ThNt, I, 194, 209, 213, 221). OT evidence, the Semiticizing anthropological passages in the NT, and also some rabbinical sources support this view. On the basis of the foregoing data Bultmann makes his decisive step: each of the named "anthropological concepts" denotes man in a potential dialogue situation. The "body" is man "in respect to his being able to make himself the object of his own action or to experience himself as the subject to whom something happens" (p. 195). The "inner man" mentioned in Rom 7:22; II Cor 4:16 is for all practical purposes identified with the "soul," the "spirit," or, the "life" of man. "Inner man" is "man's real self," i.e. "a person who lives in his intentionality, his pursuit of some purpose, his willing and knowing. This state of living to some goal . . . belongs to man's very nature and in itself is neither good nor bad" for it "offers the possibility of choosing one's goal, of deciding for good or evil, for or against God" (p. 203). "Mind" means "the possibility of heeding or rejecting God's demand" and "the self that makes itself the object of its own judging" (pp. 213, 215). Conscience "too, denotes a relationship of man to himself," i.e. "knowledge about one's own conduct in respect to a requirement" (pp. 216–17). "Paul understands man's self as the specific self. This self is realized whenever I [and no one else; in German: wenn je ich] assume the responsibility for the life handed to me from beyond myself . . . My self is constituted as my own specific self when my conscience responds to a power which transcends the conscience" (p. 219, my revised translation). The "heart" is "the intending, purposing self—which decides within itself or is moved from without," or it is the "hidden" existence "of the self's intent" (pp. 221–22). Bultmann sums up his findings by stating, "The ontological structure of human existence, as Paul sees it, . . . affords the presuppositions for his ontic statements about man," i.e. about sin and redemption (p. 277).

[98] E.g. Stalder, Das Werk des Geistes, pp. 58–59, remarks that in Pauline diction the term "body" denotes more than only man's relation to himself. It implies man's involvement in history and his relationship to his fellowman. According to R. Jewett, Paul's Anthropological Terms, Arbeiten zur Geschichte des Judentums und des Urchristentums 10 (Leiden: Brill, 1971), p. 249, "when the word soma [body] is used in the individual sense, it implies not relationship to oneself but communication with the world." Similar observations could be made if the Pauline terms "soul," "heart," etc., were explained more explicitly in the light of the communal OT anthropology and psychology which is most pointedly discussed by Pedersen, Israel, I–II, 99–181.

[99] The quote is the title of chapter IV in ThNT, I, 190–269. Bultmann corrects himself when he states that Paul "sees man always in his relation to God" and that "the eye of faith" alone contributes "transparency to man's existence prior to faith" (ThNT, I, 191, 270).

. . . to be strong in your inner selves"; Phillips: "strength of . . . inner reinforcement."[100]

A linguistic observation, classical Greek and Hellenistic parallels, and the logic of Paul's argument appear to favor such versions and a corresponding exposition:

1. In Hellenistic Greek, and therefore in the NT, too, the local preposition "in" (*en* with following dative) is frequently replaced by "into" (*eis* with accusative).[101] Therefore our translation, "fortified with power [to grow] toward the inner man" may overemphasize a literal meaning of the preposition *eis* (into, toward) which need not have been in the mind of the author of Ephesians.

2. Though the pre-history of the term "inner man" is still "not perspicuous,"[102] some interpreters[103] believe that its origin must be traced to Platonic thought.[104] They define the "inner man" as a thinking, morally disposed being; as the higher, moral, and rational nature of man as distinct from his baser fleshly attributes; as the reason which in essence, constitution, and function harmonizes with the divine law; or as humanity in its godward, immortal dimension. They do admit that in Pauline theology there is no human being or nature left unharmed by Adam's fall. Therefore it is conceded that at least in II Cor 4:16, though perhaps not in Rom 7:22, the meaning of the term has been slightly changed by Paul: even the "inner man" must be renewed day by day. Paul cannot be credited with belief in an undefiled good core in man—otherwise the devastating statements made about man's "mind" in Rom 1:20 ff., also in Eph 4:17 (cf. 23) cannot be taken at their face value and their intent is belied. Calvin indeed identifies the inner man with man's *anima* ("soul")—but he does not add a statement saying that the soul is *naturaliter christiana*. Thus the interpreters who believe that Paul took over a pagan term make it clear that under Paul's hands its pagan meaning was either lost or so altered that the original dualistic anthropological sense is no longer in the foreground.

3. It appears to make good sense that an inner self of man is strengthened in order to withstand the obstruction coming from that other self which (in the very context of two Pauline utterances on the inner man) is denoted by the nouns "my members," "this body of death," "the outward man." The inner man "enjoys God's law" and is also called "my mind"; the other man follows "another law," i.e. the "law of sin" or "flesh." The first determines the "willing," the second the "performing" (Rom 7:14-24). In II Cor 4:16 the apostle speaks correspondingly of the "inner" man who is "renewed day by day" while the "outer man is perishing." The first may also be identified with "the light" or

---

[100] ZB: "mit Kraft gestärkt zu werden am inwendigen Menschen." Similarly Dibelius; Schlier; Conzelmann.

[101] More often than others Luke exchanges them; see 4:23; 11:7; Acts 2:5; 14:25, etc. In modern Greek *eis* has absorbed *en*. See BDF, 2, n. 1; 205-6; 208; I. de la Potterie, "L'emploi dynamique de *eis* dans Saint Jean . . . ," *Biblica* 43 (1962), 366-87.

[102] Schlier. Bultmann, too, reveals uncertainty when he says: this expression "appears to be derived from the anthropology of Hellenistic dualism," ThNT, I, 203. In his book, *Christus*, p. 35, n. 2, Schlier was still satisfied with explaining Eph 3:16-17 as a parallel to Gnostic, esp. Mandaean, texts.

[103] Abbott; von Soden; Gaugler.

[104] See, e.g. Plato *resp.* IV 439D; IX 589A; *Corp. Herm.* I 15, 18, 21; the Naassene Sermon in Hippol. *ref.* V 7, 35 ff; Plotinus *ennead* V 1:10. Abbott is inclined to find its background rather in the Aristotelian teaching on *energeiā*. He assumes that the concept was mediated to Paul by means of the rabbinic term, impulse (*yēṣer*).

the "Spirit of faith" at work in those created anew by God, the second is in this case characterized by the "earthly tent" that will be destroyed, or by the "flesh and blood" that cannot inherit God's kingdom.[105] The former is called a "vessel" and it is "visible," the second is a "treasure" which is "invisible" (II Cor 4:7, 18). One is public, the other is still "hidden" (Rom 2:28–29; cf. I Peter 3:3–4). The idea that something inside man that may be called "inner man" should be strengthened or renewed is certainly compatible with Paul's teaching.

But four other arguments also deserve consideration:

4. Not all NT authors exercise the prerogative of replacing *en* (in) by *eis* (into). Matthew and the author of Revelation never do so, and nowhere in the NT letters, except the ending of I Peter (5:12), is there a clear example of this exchange. Would Paul (or an imitator of the apostle) have yielded to sloppy (Koine) grammar just in Eph 3:16? Perhaps he did. But just the fact that here *eis* (into) with accusative may perhaps have the meaning of *en* (in) with the dative does not provide a solid enough basis for developing a doctrine of man. Actually the preposition *eis* occurs frequently in Ephesians and has a pronounced teleological and eschatological meaning.[106] As long as an eschatological interpretation of 3:16 makes any good sense, it is preferable to the translations quoted above. The danger of substituting an immanent process of growth (e.g. psycho-dynamics) for an eschatological event is then avoided. The Greek text says nothing of a strengthening "of" the "inner man," or of a fortification that takes place "in" the "inner man." But it speaks of becoming strong, that is, of growth, "toward" him.

5. It is far from self-evident that in II Cor 4:16; Rom 7:22; Eph 3:16 the concept "inner man" has exactly the same sense.[107] As observed earlier, Paul did not carry a wordbook around with him containing exact definitions of terms either picked up from his environment or coined personally. He—or if Ephesians should be unauthentic, someone imitating the master or developing his thought—may have used the words "inner man" with a unique connotation in this epistle, that is, as a title of Christ. Later in the exposition of 4:24 it will be shown that the term "new man" may equally be a designation of Christ himself. "Put on Christ . . . put on the new man" (Gal 3:27; Col 3:10, etc.).[108] In that case the words "inner man" must, by analogy with the titles Messiah or Son of God, be capitalized.

6. The verse which follows the reference to the "inner man," i.e. 3:17 is an interpretive comment on the foregoing rather than a new and additional thought. Paul asks for the inhabitation of Christ in the hearts of the saints. According to this verse Christians need not grope for stars or establish, out of their own resources, contacts with transcendental spheres in order to be strengthened. The movement which really interests Paul is God's movement toward man. When the Messiah comes and dwells in the saints, then the spiritual strengthening mentioned in vs. 16 will take place. He is their strength in

---

[105] II Cor 4:6, 13; 5:1; I Cor 15:50. [106] 1:6, 12, 14; 2:1, 21–22; 4:12–13, etc.

[107] Bultmann, ThNT, I, 203, elaborates on the different meanings in II Cor 4:16 and Rom 7:22. While the inner man in Romans appears not to be under sin, and stands in opposition to the sinful body, the inner man of II Corinthians needs daily renewal and contrasts with the finitude, not the sinfulness, of bodily life. A third sense may prevail in Eph 3:16.

[108] The question whether the "inner man" is, therefore, identified with the "new man" of Eph 4:24 or 2:15 (so Schlier, *Christus*, p. 35, n. 2) will be discussed in the context of 4:24.

person. As the "breath in their nostrils" (Lam 4:20) he alone can make them strong. Therefore, "Be strong in the Lord" (6:10). When "the head fills the body," the body becomes "full." What is said of the church in 1:23 is applied to each saint in 3:16–19. The "strengthening" (vs. 16) and the "indwelling" (vs. 17) are described in vs. 18 by the verb "to grasp" and in vs. 19 by the verbs "to know" and (lit.) "to be filled." Instead of describing an element or process in natural man or in "man prior to . . . faith," the context of vs. 16 speaks about the impact and effect of the Messiah's coming. There is not only an advent of Christ among mankind and a presence of Christ in the congregation, he also comes into individual men in order to dwell there (3:17). He proves present and effective by creating faith, love, and knowledge.

7. The diction of 1:23, 4:15–16, and the Colossian parallels include physiological metaphors; see COMMENT VI A 3 and C 3 on Eph 1:15–23. It is possible that some of the terms used in 3:16–19 are technical terms of psychology contemporary to Paul. But not only psychological diction may be present: since in 4:13 and 5:22 ff. metaphors and comparisons from erotic life are included in Paul's argument, the same may be true of 3:16–19. A "Freudian" understanding of any one of the words "fortifying," "inner man," "indwelling," "grasping," "knowing," "filling," "love" cannot simply be excluded. The many metaphorical expressions may be held together by the repeated mention of "love." It is possible that at least some of them allude to sexual union. Employment of such imagery may be obnoxious to western theologians—except for Count N. L. Zinzendorf, the eighteenth-century founder of the Unity of Brethren, and other exponents of bride mysticism—but it is not strange to a rabbi such as Paul, see e.g. Rom 4:19–21. If elements of the sexual imagery are accepted, then they certainly point to the encounter of the church with another person: Christ.

If any of these four points, not to speak of their cumulative evidence, is stronger than the three arguments previously listed, the conclusion is inevitable: the "inner man" of Eph 3:16 is Jesus Christ himself, rather than a part or function of each man's individual self. In this case the strengthening of man does not depend upon man's relation to himself, upon the dialogue between a higher and a baser Ego,[109] or upon man's openness to the influence of certain transcendental powers. Rather the intimate meeting with a specific partner who comes from outside is decisive. The partner is according to 3:16–19 Jesus Christ who through the Spirit acts in God's power and makes man strong. Man's self is now determined by the encounter, the conversation, the contact with Christ—and not by a dialogue which man, potentially or actually, always carried on with himself and with some impersonal transcendental force. Instead of an *esprit vitale* innate in every man there is the Holy Spirit. Instead of a superego in man, a real *alter ego* to man—Jesus Christ—is declared the es-

---

[109] Such a dialogue is mentioned in Rom 7:7–25, also in Rom 2:15 where Paul speaks of "accusing and also excusing thoughts in man." Both passages probably describe a dialogue taking place in the saints, "after the revelation of faith" (against Bultmann). Therefore they ought not be considered an anticipation of the modern concepts of self-consciousness, self-understanding, or awareness of the *nihil* or of death. Paul's anthropology is not based upon a covenant of man with himself from which God may be excluded, but on the covenant, peace, and reconciliation between God and man. Nor is a "covenant [and a corresponding dialogue] with death" (see Isa 28: 15, 18) envisaged by Paul as a viable alternative.

sence of man's humanity. According to Eph 3:16–19 Christology is the nerve and criterion of man's humanity and of anthropology. A psychology or doctrine of man that antedates or overlooks the Messiah's coming cannot occupy the key position of Christology in Paul's thinking.

Can the contents of this passage be applied to all men? In Eph 3 Paul speaks only of the saints. This text and other anthropological statements of this epistle (e.g. in 2:1–3, 4:17–19) do not disclose Paul's view of humanity in general. Eph 2:11–22 suggests that even those farthest away from the holy community are already included in it by the Messiah. In Rom 3:13–16 picturesque imagery from the animal world is employed for describing the abnormal, as it were inhuman, behavior of sinners. According to Ps 73:22 (cf. Dan 4:25–34), a man estranged from God is "like a beast" (rather than still a true man). In all Pauline letters the most decisive positive statements about the function of heart and soul, tongue, feet, and hands are made in descriptions of the saints or exhortations addressed to them. However, the Pauline epistles appear not to contain material from which to reconstruct a general Pauline anthropology. What the apostle says about man is said in relation to Christ and faith.

What makes the Christian a strong and genuine man is according to Eph 3:16–19 not a noble capability implanted in him at the first creation and surviving the lapse into sin, but his ongoing visitation and strengthening by God. When God's Spirit supplies strength—and when man grows toward the Messiah who is his very life—then he will live as a true man. A one-sided dynamic prevails. Man's humanity depends on the partner who cares for him. In being "fortified," "in-dwelt," "rooted," "founded," "made perfect," or "filled," man is a recipient. But the purpose and result of the onrushing and overwhelming divine dynamics does not lie in the obliteration or extinction of man as a grappling, searching, thinking, deciding, acting, growing individual being. Paul asks God to make men strong; he encourages men to stand firm; he expects that in view of the overwhelming disclosure of God's wisdom they will not abandon clear thought but come to know and obey the love shown in Christ. He finally expects and requests for man nothing less than perfection (3:18–19). Elsewhere he calls the perfect work done by God a new creation.[110] Because Paul relies on God's faithfulness, Christ's love, and the Spirit's power, his view of man (his so-called anthropology) possesses a bright and optimistic character. Although he certainly has not forgotten what he has said in 2:1–3 about sin, death, the devil, the flesh, and their control over every man, he demonstrates in 3:16–19 that he was serious in his earlier proclamation of man's resuscitation, salvation, enthronement, new creation, reconciliation, and access to God (2:5–18). Paul attests to an unconditional miracle.

However, do not the terms "faith," "love," and "knowledge" which occur at prominent places in 3:16–19 qualify this miracle? It is not likely, for they are not found in conditional clauses but describe the mode in which the saints are made perfect. Each of these nouns presupposes, as it were by definition, that two persons are joined together by a solid bond: he who is faithful and has confidence, and he who is trusted; the lover and the beloved; the knower and the one acknowledged. Man's humanity is solidly founded when in matters

---

[110] 2:10, 15; II Cor 4:6; Col 3:10; Gal 6:15.

of creativity, authority, and majesty an irreversible order is maintained. God does more than merely initiate or recognize the constitution of true man. He alone is and remains its giver, guarantor, judge, and perfector.

It was said earlier that according to Ephesians human existence is a social existence. The term "social" was used to denote the character and dimension of Christ's peace work, i.e. the resurrection and reconciliation of Jews and Gentiles, those near and those far. In 2:13–18 (cf. 1:7) it became clear that peace among men is impossible without peace with God. What might be called the "vertical-social relation" to God could not be separated from the horizontal peace with fellow man. In Eph 3:16–19 Paul has given specific attention to the partnership of God and man without which human partnership is impossible. The association of the Gentiles with Israel is according to Paul the demonstration of man's association with God himself.

Thus Eph 3:16–19 is a beautiful illustration of the concept "enthronement in the heavens" (2:6): here is testimony to the enthronement of man, and to his highest possible elevation. Through the Father, the Messiah, and the Spirit, humanity is not only created, saved, and created anew, but also glorified. This passage in fact constitutes a creed to man: Man shall be strong! More power to man—from God!

V   Ecumenical Theology

It would appear that the disclosure of a secret, the perception of another person's love, the surprise of mutual affection, and the birth of knowledge are highly private and personal events which can take place only when man is removed from the eyes of onlookers and witnesses, aloof from the madding crowd. There is no reason to doubt that Paul was aware of this fact,[111] but in Eph 3:18 he states that the dimensions of God's attitude and work are to be "grasped together with all the saints." Thus he asserts that the "secret" fostered by God the creator and now revealed (3:9), the "manifold wisdom" of God (3:10), and the "unfathomable riches of Christ" lavished upon the Gentiles (3:6, 8) cannot be understood in separation from one's fellow man. The social orientation of Eph 2 is not forgotten during the discussion of God's relationship to every saint. He who searches for love and knowledge is warned by the words "together with all the saints" against insulating himself from those Jews and Gentiles who are engaged in the same quest. The men already filled with "hope for the Messiah" and those who "have heard the word of truth" (1:12–13) are indispensable companions for each love-and-knowledge-hungry Christian.

In 3:16–19 Paul does not explicitly say why he considers the birth or increase of knowledge a social rather than a private event. But the contents of Eph 2 and 3 supply a reason: the mode of gaining knowledge is determined by that which is to be known. The secret revealed is that the outsider has been included together with the insider in God's love and the Messiah's realm. The revelation of the secret is not just an act of intellectual information but takes

---

[111] The three years spent "in Arabia" (Gal 1:17) may have been devoted to reflection and meditation—though other possibilities cannot be excluded. Paul never complains about the solitude imposed upon him, at least temporarily, by his imprisonment.

place in the actual salvation and unification of Jews and Gentiles. The result and celebration of the revealed secret consists in the worship offered to God by Jews and Gentiles together, and by the evidence which their peaceful community gives the world. Therefore the very act of knowledge cannot take place except when the saving knowledge also granted to one's fellow man is gladly recognized, endorsed, and celebrated.

As was earlier shown, in Paul's thought the connection is indissoluble between the secret that is known and to be made known, on one side, and the gaining of knowledge, on the other. The reference to "all saints" in 3:18 points out a consequence: either worship, theological work, and spiritual insight are ecumenical events or they have nothing to do with the knowledge and proclamation of God. According to 3:18 all theology is communal, ecclesiastical, and ecumenical at the same time.[112] This does not make a simple majority or the shining excellence of certain opinions the criterion of truth. The adage, *Ecclesia suadet, Spiritus sanctus persuadet* (the church—that is, the fathers, the tradition, a consensus, or spirited individuals—recommends; the Holy Spirit convinces) would have been approved by Paul. God who fills, Christ who inhabits, and the Spirit who strengthens exert an authority unequaled by that of the saints, according to 3:16–19. But "access" to God who is fully present and revealed in the man Jesus Christ (Col 1:19, 2:9) is granted solely in the company of fellow saints (Eph 2:18). If imprisonment or other events impose upon man months or years of isolated existence, the remembrance of other saints, of their faith and love, mutual intercession, and also the exchange of news and letters, will "maintain" the indispensable "unity of the Spirit through the bond of peace" (4:3), as Paul's own example clearly shows.[113]

In turn, knowledge of the revealed secret and its dimensions is not restricted to a selected number of saints or to the occupants of a specific office. Only in later times was true and full knowledge (*gnōsis*) considered the privilege of an elite, i.e. of those "perfect" among the Gnostics. According to Paul the lowliest member of the church may deserve the greatest honor (I Cor 12:23); "he who holds the place of an uneducated man" will be able to understand the communication of spiritual men, if God's revelation and love rather than human conceit dominates the congregation (I Cor 14:16). The "knowledge" of which Eph 3:18–19 speaks "is neither a private nor a conventicle knowledge . . . it belongs to its essence that it is shared with others."[114]

VI   The Four Dimensions

The "breadth, length, height, depth," which in 3:18 are the object of man's comprehension, have been interpreted in most diverse ways:[115]

a) Ambrosiaster considered the four terms a circumscription of the spheric, i.e. perfect, shape of God.

---

[112] To be specific, e.g. the writing of a biblical commentary cannot have the form of a dialogue between the interpreter and the Bible text alone. Respectful attention to the voices of fathers and brothers in faith is a *conditio sine qua non*—though technical problems prevent an equal heeding of *all saints* among past and present expositors!

[113] 1:12, 15 ff.; 3:1–3, 14–21; Philip *passim*.   [114] Schlier, p. 170.

[115] Surveys or an extensive discussion are given, e.g. by Haupt; Meyer, pp. 148–149; Feuillet, *Christ Sagesse*, pp. 292–317.

b) Chrysostom, Theodoret, Beza, and others assumed that the mystery of God was so denoted.[116]

c) According to D. J. Dupont the whole universe is meant—that universe which is "one and all" (*hen kai pān*) and therefore essentially not distinct from God.[117]

d) Reitzenstein thinks of the space or domicile created for the deity, according to magic texts, by the light of revelation.[118]

e) Bengel, Dibelius, Schlier refer to the cubic form of the heavenly city as mentioned in Rev 21:16.[119]

f) A seemingly unbroken line of interpretation runs from Origen,[120] by way of Thomas Aquinas and Calvin, to T. K. Abbott and the NEB version: taking their clue from the reference to the "love of Christ" that is to be known by the saints "though it surpasses knowledge" (3:19), they see in the dimensions mentioned in 3:18 a description of the extent of Christ's love.

g) A special form of the same exposition equates the four dimensions with the four arms of Christ's cross.[121]

h) Some interpreters find in Eph 3:18 a reference to the Gnostic Prime-Anthropos and his cosmic body. The body of the crucified Christ is in this case denoted as a body that fills the world in all dimensions.[122]

i) There are innumerable interpretations that venture to equate each of the four dimensions with a specific reality or virtue. The nations, the aeons, sin, and glory; good angels, bad angels, men on the steep way upward, and humanity on the broad way; the divinity and the humanity of Christ, the length and breadth of apostolic preaching; the virtues of love, hope, patience, and humility—quartets such as these have been formed to explain the hidden meaning of the four dimensions in Eph 3:18.[123] The pungent statement made by Calvin (in his interpretation of this verse) about Augustine's exegesis of this text is appropriate to many, if not all, of these interpretations: they come to a result "that is pleasant because of its subtlety. But what has it to do with Paul's intention?"

Feuillet[124] is aware of the difficulties inherent in these attempts to elucidate Eph 3:18. The expositors who refer to the cubic form of the heavenly city or tower (as taught by some apocalypticists and rabbis) presuppose that Eph

---

[116] Percy, p. 310, speaks of "the divine counsel of salvation." Gaugler assumes that an originally Gnostic notion appears here in a form purified by *Heilsgeschichte* and without the restriction of knowledge to an elite.

[117] Dupont, *Gnosis* (Louvain: Neuvelaerts, 1949), pp. 476–89, quotes Stoic texts, e.g. Plutarch *de facie in orbe lunae* 25 (939A).

[118] *Poimandres* (Leipzig: Teubner, 1904), p. 25. Texts such as *Corp. Herm.* x 25; also Papyrus IV in K. Preisendanz, *Griechische Zauberpapyri*, I (Leipzig: Teubner, 1928), pp. 106–7, lines 968–72, appear to support his view.

[119] See Herm. *vis.* III 2:5, for the square shape of the heavenly tower, and the rabbinic passages collected in StB, III, 849–50, regarding the cubic form of Jerusalem. Cf. also E. Peterson, *Heis Theos* (Göttingen: Vandenhoeck, 1926), p. 250, n. 3.

[120] *Catenae* VI 162; also Chrysostom and Theodore of Mopsuestia.

[121] Augustine *epistulae* CXII 14; CXX 36; *tract. in Ioann.* CXVIII; *de doctrina Christiana* II 41; see also G. Estius.

[122] Schlier supports his view with quotes from the martyrologies of Andrew and Peter, the *Acts of Andrew* 14, the *Acts of Peter* 38, Irenaeus *adv. haer.* v 17:4. Conzelmann also mentions Gnostic parallels, and emphasizes that the exoteric proclamation of the mystery in 3:18 contradicts the originally narrow esoteric meaning of the language used here.

[123] See e.g. Jerome, Augustine, Oecumenius, Severianus, Bengel.

[124] *Christ Sagesse*, esp. pp. 297 ff.

3:18 speaks of three dimensions—those of height, depth, breadth—as they are usually distinguished in geometry. But while "the Greeks distinguished three dimensions only, not four," Ephesians mentions four. Where, Feuillet asks, are four dimensions ever enumerated in Paul's environment or in literature known to him?[125] He answers, in OT Wisdom books and related sources! According to Wisdom thought, the search for wisdom goes on in the four dimensions of heaven, earth, water, and a depth "deeper than Sheol."[126] These four dimensions are usually mentioned when an author wants to point out that God and his wisdom cannot be traced but remain inscrutable—"a perfect antithesis to the Gnostic theme which treats knowledge of the cosmos as equivalent to the knowledge of God."[127] Since Ephesians is replete with borrowings from Wisdom tradition, Eph 3:18 may reflect the same influence. In this case Paul wants to show in 3:18 how impossible it is ever to grasp fully the manifold wisdom of God. Compare variant (b) in the expositions given above. Abbott has come to an analogous result: in the apostle's mind is "not so much the thoroughness of comprehension as the vastness of the thing to be comprehended." This interpretation is buttressed by the verse that follows 3:18: the object of knowledge, Christ's love, is called "surpassing knowledge." Feuillet's interpretation recommends itself as the least fantastic and the one best supported by the context. Even when Paul asks God for more knowledge, he remembers the "depth of the riches and wisdom and knowledge of God" and the impossibility of exploring and tracing "his judgments and ways" (Rom 11:33).

[125] Magic Papyri and findings of modern physics are not included among the sources which Feuillet traces to explain Ephesians.
[126] Job 11:7–9; cf. 28:12–14, 21–22; Amos 9:2–3; Ps 139:8–9; Isa 7:11; 40:12–14; Rom 8:37–39; Rev 5:13.
[127] Feuillet, Christ Sagesse, pp. 301, cf. 310.

BIBLIOGRAPHIES

I COMMENTARIES AND SPECIAL STUDIES

Note: The works listed in this bibliography are cited by abbreviation—see individual entries—throughout both volumes, 34 and 34A.

Abbott, T. K. *The Epistles to the Ephesians and to the Colossians.* ICC. 5th ed. London: Clark, 1946. *Cited as* Abbott.

Ambrosiaster. *Commentaria in epistolan B. Pauli ad Ephesios.* PL 16, 371–404. *Cited as* Ambrosiaster.

Beare, F. W. *The Epistle to the Ephesians.* IB, X, 597–749. *Cited as* IB, X.

Bengel, J. A. *Gnomon Novi Testamenti.* Tübingen: Schramm, 1742. *Cited as* Bengel.

Benoit, P. *Les Épîtres de saint Paul aux Philippiens, à Philémon, aux Colossiens, aux Éphésiens.* 2d ed. Paris: Du Cerf, 1953. *Cited as* Benoit.

Calvin, J. *Commentarius in epistolam ad Ephesios.* CRCO 15, 1895. Columns 141–240. *Cited as* Calvin.

Catenae. See below, Cramer, J. A.

Chrysostom. *Homiliae in epistolam ad Ephesios.* PG 62, 7–176. *Cited as* Chrysostom.

Conzelmann, H. *Der Brief an die Epheser.* NTD 8, 1965. *Cited as* Conzelmann.

Cramer, J. A., ed. *Catenae Graecorum Patrum in Novum Testamentum,* 6. Oxford: Typographia Academica, 1834. Pages 100–225. Cited as *Catenae.*

Cross, F. L., ed. *Studies in Ephesians.* London: Mowbray, 1956. *Cited as* Cross.

Dahl, N. A. *Das Volk Gottes.* SNVA 2, 1941; reprinted 1962. *Cited as* Dahl.

Dibelius, M. and Greeven, H. *An die Kolosser, Epheser, an Philemon.* HbNT 12. 3d ed. Tübingen: Mohr, 1953. *Cited as* Dibelius.

Eadie, J. *A Commentary on the Greek Text of the Epistle of Paul to the Ephesians.* 2d ed. New York: Carter, 1861. *Cited as* Eadie.

Ephraim the Syrian. *Commentarii in Epistolas D. Pauli.* Venice: Typographia Sancti Lazari, 1893. Pages 140–56. *Cited as* Ephraem.

Erasmus of Rotterdam. *In Novum Testamentum Annotationes.* Basel: Froben, 1519. Pages 413 ff. Reprinted 1540. Pages 591 ff. Etc. *Cited as* Erasmus.

Gaugler, E. *Der Epheserbrief.* ANS 6, 1966. *Cited as* Gaugler.

Goodspeed, E. J. *The Meaning of Ephesians.* University of Chicago Press, 1933. *Cited* as Goodspeed.

Grotius, Hugo. *Annotationes in Novum Testamentum,* II. 1646. Reprinted Leipzig: Tetzscher, 1757. *Cited as* Grotius.

Hanson, S. *The Unity of the Church in the New Testament, Colossians and Ephesians*. ASNU 14. Uppsala: Almquist, 1946. Cited as *Unity*.

von Harless, G. C. A. *Commentar über den Brief Pauli an die Epheser*. 2d ed. Erlangen: Heider, 1834. *Cited as* von Harless.

Haupt, E. *Der Brief an die Epheser*. KEKNT 8. 7th rev. ed. 1902. *Cited as* Haupt.

von Hofmann, J. C. K. *Der Brief Pauli an die Epheser*. HSNT 6:1, 1870. *Cited as* von Hofmann.

Holtzmann, H. J. *Kritik der Epheser- und Kolosserbriefe*. Leipzig: Engelmann, 1872. *Cited as* Holtzmann.

Jerome. *Commentaria in epistolam ad Ephesios*. PL 26, 459–554. *Cited as* Jerome.

Kirby, J. C. *Ephesians, Baptism and Pentecost*. McGill University Press, and London: SPCK, 1968. *Cited as* EBP.

Lueken, W. "Der Brief an die Epheser," in SNT 2. 2d ed. 1908. Pages 348–72. *Cited as* Lueken.

Mackay, J. A. *God's Order*. New York: Macmillan, 1953. *Cited as* Mackay.

Masson, C. *L'épître de S. Paul aux Éphésiens*. CNT 9. Neuchâtel: Delachaux, 1953. *Cited as* Masson.

Meyer, H. A. W. *Critical and Exegetical Handbook to the Epistle to the Ephesians*. New York: Funk and Wagnalls, 1884. KEKNT 9, 1859. 3d German ed. *Cited as* Meyer from the German edition.

Mitton, C. L. *The Epistle to the Ephesians: Its Authorship, Origin and Purpose*. Oxford: Clarendon Press, 1951. *Cited as* EE.

Oecumenius. *Pauli apostoli ad Ephesios epistola*. PG 118, 1170–1266. *Cited as* Oecumenius.

Pelagius. See below, Souter, A.

Percy, E. *Die Probleme der Kolosser- und Epheserbriefe*. Lund: Gleerup, 1946. *Cited as* Percy.

Pokorný, P. *Der Epheserbrief und die Gnosis*. Berlin: Evangelische Verlagsanstalt, 1965. *Cited as* EuG.

Robinson, J. A. *St. Paul's Epistle to the Ephesians*. 2d ed. London: Clark, 1922. *Cited as* Robinson.

Schlier, H. *Der Brief an die Epheser*. 2d ed. Düsseldorf: Patmos, 1958. *Cited as* Schlier.

——— *Christus und die Kirche im Epheserbrief*. BHTh 6, 1930; repr. 1966. Cited as *Christus*.

Scott, E. F. *The Epistles of Paul to the Colossians, to Philemon, and to the Ephesians*. MNTC 11, 1930. *Cited as* Scott.

von Soden, H. *Der Brief an die Epheser*. HCNT 3, 1891. Pages 79–153. *Cited as* von Soden.

Souter, A., ed. *Pelagius' Exposition of the Thirteen Epistles of St. Paul*. Cambridge University Press, 1922. Pages 344–80. *Cited as* Pelagius.

Synge, F. C. *St. Paul's Epistle to the Ephesians*. London: SPCK, 1954. *Cited as* Synge.

Theodore of Mopsuestia. *In Epistolas B. Pauli Commentarii*. H. B. Swete, ed. Cambridge University Press, 1880. I, 112–96. *Cited as* Theodore of Mopsuestia.

Theodoret. *Interpretatio epistolae ad Ephesios.* PG 82, 508–58. *Cited as* Theodoret.

Theophylact. *Commentarius in epistolam ad Ephesios.* PG 124, 1031–1138. *Cited as* Theophylact.

Thomas Aquinas. *Commentary on Saint Paul's Epistle to the Ephesians.* M. L. Lamb, trans. Albany: Magi Books, 1966. *Cited as* Thomas Aquinas.

Westcott, B. F. *St. Paul's Epistle to the Ephesians.* London: Macmillan, 1906. Reprinted Grand Rapids: Eerdmans, n.d. *Cited as* Westcott.

de Wette, W. M. L. *Kurze Erklärung der Briefe an die Kolosser, an Philemon, an die Epheser und Philipper.* Kurzgefasstes exegetisches Handbuch zum Neuen Testament, II 4. Leipzig: Weidmann, 1847. *Cited as* de Wette.

II SECTIONAL BIBLIOGRAPHIES

BIBLIOGRAPHY 1

> *Note:* The works listed in this and succeeding sectional bibliographies are cited by abbreviation, sometimes the author's name only, in the section specified parenthetically in the subheading.

(INTRODUCTION, II)

Hymnic, Confessional and Catechetical Formulations

Debrunner, A. "Grundsätzliches zur Kolometrie im Neuen Testament," TB 5 (1926), 231–33.

Deichgräber, R. *Gotteshymnus und Christushymnus in der frühen Christenheit.* SUNT 5, 1967. Cited as *Gotteshymnus.*

Jörns, K.-P. *Das hymnische Evangelium.* Gütersloh: Mohn, 1971.

Lohmeyer, E. "Das Proömium des Epheserbriefs," TB 5 (1926), 120–25.

Maurer, C. "Der Hymnus von Epheser 1 als Schlüssel zum ganzen Brief," EvTh 11 (1951–52), 151–72.

Norden, E. *Agnostos Theos.* Leipzig: Teubner, 1913. Pages 141–276, 380–87.

Rese, M. "Formeln und Lieder im Neuen Testament," *Verkündigung und Forschung* 15 (Munich: Kaiser, 1970), 75–95.

Robinson, J. M. "Die Hodajoth-Forme in Gebet und Hymnus des Frühchristentums," in *Apaphoreta,* Fs E. Haenchen, BhZNW 30 (1964), 194–235.

Sanders, J. T. "Hymnic Elements in Eph. 1–3," ZNW 56 (1965), 214–32.

——— *The New Testament Christological Hymns.* Society for NTS Monograph 15, Cambridge University Press, 1971.

Schille, G. *Frühchristliche Hymnen.* Berlin: Evangelische Verlagsanstalt, 1965. Cited as *Hymnen.*

Stanley, D. M. "Carmenque Christo quasi Deo Dicere," CBQ 20 (1958), 173–91.

BIBLIOGRAPHY 2

(INTRODUCTION, III B)

Gnosticism in Ephesians

Bartsch, H. W. *Gnostisches Gut und Gemeindetradition bei Ignatius von Antiochien*. Gütersloh: Bertelsmann, 1940.

Bianchi, U., ed. *The Origins of Gnosticism, Colloquium of Messina*. Leiden: Brill, 1967.

Bieder, W. "Das Geheimnis des Christus nach dem Epheserbrief," TZ 11 (1955), 329–43.

Böhlig, S. *Mysterion und Wahrheit*. Leiden: Brill, 1968 (ref.).

Bousset, W. *Hauptprobleme der Gnosis*. FRLANT 10, 1907.

Bultmann, R. *Theology of the New Testament*. 2 vols. New York: Harper, 1951, 1955. *Cited as* ThNT.

———— *Primitive Christianity*. London: Thames, 1956. Pages 162–71.

Burkitt, F. C. *Church and Gnosis*. Cambridge University Press, 1932.

Colpe, C. *Die religionsgeschichtliche Schule*, I. FRLANT 78, 1961. *Cited as* RelgS.

———— "Zur Leib-Christi-Vorstellung im Epheserbrief," in *Judentum-Urchristentum Kirche*, Fs J. Jeremias. BhZNW 26 (1960), pp. 172–87.

Dupont, D. J. *Gnosis*. Louvain: Nouvelaerts, 1949. Esp. ch. VII.

Eltester, W., ed. *Christentum und Gnosis*. BhZNW 37, 1969.

Grant, R. M. *Gnosticism and Early Christianity*. Columbia University Press, 1959.

———— *Gnosticism*. New York: Harper, 1961.

van Groningen, G. *First Century Gnosticism*. Leiden: Brill, 1967 (ref.).

Haardt, R. *Die Gnosis*. Salzburg: O. Müller Verlag, 1967.

Hegermann, H. *Die Vorstellung vom Schöpfungsmittler*. TU 82, 1961. Cited as *Schöpfungsmittler*.

Jonas, H. *Gnosis und spätantiker Geist*. 2 vols. FRLANT 33, 1934, and 45, 1954.

———— *The Gnostic Religion*. Boston: Beacon, 1959; rev. ed. 1963.

Käsemann, E. *Leib und Leib Christi*. BHTh, 9, 1933.

———— "Epheserbrief," in RGG. 3d ed. II (1958), 517–20.

Koester, H. "Gnomai Diaphorai," HTR 58 (1965), 279–318.

Kraeling, G. H. *Anthropos and Son of Man*. Columbia University Press, 1927. Pages 38–54.

Langerbeck, H. *Aufsätze zur Gnosis*. Göttingen: Vandenhoeck, 1967.

Munck, J. "The New Testament and Gnosticism," in *Current Issues in New Testament Interpretation*, Fs O. R. Piper. London: SCM, 1962, Pages 224–38.

Norden, E. *Agnostos Theos*. Leipzig / Berlin: Teubner, 1913. Pages 56–115.

Pokorný, P. *Der Epheserbrief und die Gnosis*. Berlin: Evangelische Verlagsanstalt, 1965. *Cited as* EuG.

———— "Epheserbrief und gnostische Mysterien," ZNW 53 (1962), 160–94.

Quispel, G. *Gnosis als Weltreligion.* Zürich: Origo, 1951.

———— "Neue Funde zur Valentinianischen Gnosis," ZRG 6 (1954), 289–305.

———— "Christliche Gnosis und jüdische Heterodoxie," EvTh 14 (1954), 474–84.

———— "Der gnostische Anthropos und die jüdische Tradition," EJb 22 (1953), 195–234.

Reitzenstein, R. *Poimandres.* Leipzig: Teubner, 1904.

———— *Das iranische Erlösungsmysterium.* Bonn: Marcus, 1921. Cited as *Erlösungsmysterium.*

———— and H. H. Schaeder. *Studien zum antiken Synkretismus.* Leipzig: Teubner, 1926.

Schenke, H.-M. *Der Gott "Mensch" in der Gnosis.* Göttingen: Vandenhoeck, 1962. Cited as GMG.

Schlier, H. *"kephalē,"* in TWNTE, III, 673–82.

———— *Religionsgeschichtliche Untersuchungen zu den Ignatiusbriefen.* BhZNW 8, 1929.

Schmithals, W. *Gnosticism in Corinth.* Nashville: Abingdon, 1971.

———— *Das kirchliche Apostelamt.* FRLANT 79, 1961.

———— *Paul and the Gnostics.* Nashville: Abingdon, 1972.

Schoeps, H. J. *Urgemeinde-Judenchristentum-Gnosis.* Tübingen: Mohr, 1965.

van Unnik, W. C. *Newly Discovered Gnostic Writings.* SBT 30, 1960.

Wilson, R. McL. *The Gnostic Problem.* London: Mowbray, 1958.

———— *Gnosis and the New Testament.* Philadelphia: Fortress, 1968.

BIBLIOGRAPHY 3

(INTRODUCTION, III C)

Qumran Materials in Ephesians

Benoit, P. "Qumran and the New Testament," in *Paul and Qumran,* ed. J. Murphy-O'Connor. Chicago: Priory Press, 1968. Pages 1–30, esp. 17.

Betz, O. *Offenbarung und Schriftforschung in der Qumransekte.* Tübingen: Mohr, 1960.

———— "The Eschatological Interpretation of the Sinai Tradition in Qumran and in the New Testament," RQum 6 (1967), 89–107.

Bieder, W. "Das Geheimnis des Christus nach dem Epheserbrief," TZ 11 (1955), 329–43.

Braun, H. *Qumran und das Neue Testament.* 2 vols. Tübingen: Mohr, 1956. Esp. I, 215–25. Cited as QuNT.

———— "Rom. 7:7–25 und das Selbstverständis des Qumranfrommen," ZThK 56 (1959), 1–18.

———— "Spätjüdisch-häretischer und frühchristlicher Radikalismus," BHTh 24 (1957), 1–25.

Brown, R. E. "The Pre-Christian Semitic Concept of Mystery," CBQ 20 (1958), 417–43.

———— "The Semitic Background of the New Testament *mystērion*," *Biblica* 39 (1958), 426–48; 40 (1959), 70–87.

———— *The Semitic Background of the Term "Mystery" in the New Testament.* Philadelphia: Fortress, Facet Books, 1968.

Cambier, J. "Le grand mystère concernant le Christ et son église. Éph. 5, 22–33," *Biblica* 47 (1966), 43–90, 223–42.

Cerfaux, L. "L'influence des 'Mystères' sur les épîtres de saint Paul aux Colossiens et aux Éphésiens," in *Sacra Pagina.* 2 vols. Paris / Gembloux, 1959. II, 373–79 (ref.).

Coppens, J. "Le 'mystère' dans la théologie paulinienne et ses parallèles Qumrâniens," in *Littérature et théologie pauliniennes,* ed. A. Descamps. RecB 5 (1960), 142–65.

Daniel, C. "Une mention paulienne des Esséniens de Qumran," RQum 5 (1966), 553–67.

Ellis, E. E. "A Note on Pauline Hermeneutics," NTS 2 (1955–56), 121–33.

Hegermann, H. *Die Vorstellung vom Schöpfungsmittler.* TU 82, 1961. Cited as *Schöpfungsmittler.*

Johnson, S. "Paul and the Manual of Discipline," HTR 48 (1955), 157–65.

Kuhn, K. G. "Der Epheserbrief im Lichte der Qumrantexte, NTS 7 (1960–61), 334–46. Eng. tr. in *Paul and Qumran,* ed. Murphy-O'Connor. (See also the essays by F. Mussner and J. Coppens on Ephesians and Qumran, in the same volume.)

Murphy-O'Connor, J. "Who Wrote Ephesians?" BiTod 18 (1965), 1201–9 (ref.).

Mussner, F. "Beiträge aus Qumran zum Verständnis des Epheserbriefes," in *Neutestamentliche Aufsätze,* Fs J. Schmid. Regensburg: Pustet, 1963. Pages 185–97. Article reprinted in *Praesentia Salutis.* Düsseldorf: Patmos, 1967. Pages 197–211.

Reicke, Bo. "Traces of Gnosticism in the Dead Sea Scrolls?" NTS 1 (1954–55), 137–51.

Rigaux, B. "Revelation des Mystères et Perfection à Qumran et dans le Nouveau Testament," NTS 4 (1957–58), 237–62.

Ryrie, C. C. "The Mysteria in Eph. 3," Bibliotheca Sacra 123 (Dallas, 1966), 24–31.

Schubert, K. "Der gegenwärtige Stand der Erforschung der in Palästina neu gefundenen hebräischen Handschriften," TLZ 78 (1953), 495–506.

Schulz, S. "Zur Rechtfertigung aus Gnade in Qumran und bei Paulus," ZTK 56 (1959), 155–85.

Stendahl, K., ed. *The Scrolls and the New Testament.* New York: Harper, 1957. *Cited as* SaNT.

Vogt, E. "Mysteria in textibus Qumran," *Biblica* 37 (1956), 247–57.

Wilson, R. McL. "Gnostic Origins," VigChr 9 (1957), 193–211.

———— "Simon, Dositheus and the Dead Sea Scrolls," ZRG 9 (1956), 21–30.

BIBLIOGRAPHY 4

(INTRODUCTION, III E)

Paul's Use of the Old Testament

Bonsirven, J. *Exégèse rabbinique et exégèse paulinienne.* Paris: Beauchesne, 1939.

Dietzfelbinger, C. "Paulus und das Altes Testament," *Theologische Existenz heute*, N.F. 95, Munich: Kaiser, 1961.

Dodd, C. H. *According to the Scriptures.* New York: Scribner's, 1953.

—————— *The Old Testament in the New.* London: Athlone, 1952.

Ellis, E. E. "A Note on Pauline Hermeneutics," NTS 2 (1955–56), 127–33.

—————— *Paul's Use of the Old Testament.* Edinburgh: Oliver & Boyd, 1957.

Lietzmann, H. *An die Galater*, HbNT XI (1930), 34–36.

Lindars, B. *New Testament Apologetic.* Philadelphia: Westminster, 1962. Pages 222–50.

Michel, O. *Paulus und seine Bibel.* Gütersloh: Bertelsmann, 1929.

Schmid, J. "Die AT Zitate bei Paulus und der sensus plenior," BZ 3 (1959), 161–73.

Strack, H. L. *Einleitung in Talmud und Midrasch.* Munich: Beck, 1930. III, 95–109.

Tasker, R. V. G. *The Old Testament in the New.* 2d ed. London: SCM, 1954. Pages 80–102.

Ulousska, H. *Paulus und das Alte Testament.* Münster: Rotraprint, 1964.

BIBLIOGRAPHY 5

(INTRODUCTION V–VI)

The Question of Authorship

Albertz, M. *Die Botschaft des Neuen Testamentes.* Zollikon-Zürich: EVZ, 1952. I, 2, 165–68.

Allan, J. A. "The 'in Christ' Formula in Ephesians," NTS 5 (1958–59), 54–62.

Asting, *Die Heiligkeit im Urchristentum.* FRLANT 45, N.F. 29, 1930. Pages 4–5.

Baur, F. C. *Paulus der Apostel Jesu Christi.* Stuttgart: Becker & Müller, 1845. Pages 449–55.

Benoit, P. *Éphésiens.* DB Suppl. VII (1961), 195–211.

—————— "L'horizon paulinien de l'épître aux Éphésiens," RB 46 (1937), 342–61, 506–25. Reprinted in *Exégèse et théologie.* Paris: Du Cerf, 1961, II, 53–96.

Brandon, S. G. F. *The Fall of Jerusalem.* London: SPCK, 1957. Pages 215–16.

Cadbury, H. J. "The Dilemma of Ephesians," NTS 5 (1958–59), 91–102.

Cerfaux, L. "En faveur de l'authenticité des épîtres de la captivité," in RecB 5 (1960), 60–71.

——— in *Introduction to the New Testament*, eds. A. Robert and A. Feuillet. New York: Desclée, 1965. Pages 502–3.

——— *The Spiritual Journey of Saint Paul*. New York: Sheed & Ward, 1968.

Erasmus of Rotterdam. *In Novum Testamentum Annotationes*. Basel: Froben, 1519. Page 413.

——— *Opera omnia*, VI, Lugduni Batavorum, 1705. Column 831.

Evanson, E. *The Dissonance of the four generally received Evangelists and the Evidence of their respective Authenticity examined*. Ipswich, 1792 (ref.).

Feine, P., J. Behm, and W. G. Kümmel. *Introduction to the New Testament*. Nashville: Abingdon, 1965. *Cited as* FBK.

Goguel, M. "Esquisse d'une solution nouvelle du problème de l'épître aux Éphésiens," RHPR 111 (1935), 254–85; 112 (1936), 73–99.

Goodspeed, E. J. *The Meaning of Ephesians*. University of Chicago Press, 1956.

Grant, R. M. *Historical Introduction to the New Testament*. London: Collins, 1963.

Harnack, A. "Die Adresse des Epheserbriefes des Paulus," SbPA 37 (21. Juli 1910), 696–709.

Harrison, P. N. "The Author of Ephesians," TU 87 (1964), 595–604.

Holtzmann, H. J. *Kritik der Epheser- und Kolosserbriefe*. Leipzig: Englemann, 1872.

Hort, F. J. A. *Prolegomena to St. Paul's Epistles to the Romans and Ephesians*. London: Macmillan, 1895. Pages 65–125.

Jülicher, A. *Introduction to the New Testament*. London: Smith, 1904. Pages 127–47.

Käsemann, E. "Epheserbrief," in RGG. 3d ed., 1958. II, 517–20.

Klijn, A. F. L. *An Introduction to the New Testament*, Leiden: Brill, 1967. Pages 103–4.

Knox, J. *Chapters in a Life of Paul*. Nashville: Abingdon, 1950. Page 19.

Knox, W. L. *St. Paul and the Church of the Gentiles*. Cambridge University Press, 1939. Pages 182–203.

Marxsen, W. *Introduction to the New Testament*. Philadelphia: Fortress, 1968. Pages 187–98.

Michaelis, W. *Einleitung in das Neue Testament*. Bern: BEG, 1946.

Mitton, C. L. *The Epistle to the Ephesians*. Oxford: Clarendon Press, 1951. *Cited as* EE.

Murphy-O'Connor, J. "Who Wrote Ephesians?" BiTod 18 (1965), 1201–9 (ref.).

Nineham, D. E. "The Case against Pauline Authorship," in *Studies in Ephesians*, ed. F. L. Cross. London: Mowbray, 1956. Pages 21–35. *Cited as* Cross.

Paley, W. *Horae Paulinae*. London: C. Baldwin reprint, 1822 (ref.).

Percy, E. *Die Probleme der Kolosser- und Epheserbriefe*. 2d rev. ed. Lund: Gleerup, 1964. *Cited as* Percy.

——— "Zu den Problemen der Kolosser und Epheserbriefe," ZNW 43 (1950–51), 178–94.

Robert, A., and Feuillet, A. *Introduction to the New Testament.* New York: Desclée, 1965. Pages 501–4.

Roller, O. *Das Formular der Paulinischen Briefe.* BWANT IV, 6, 1933.

Sanders, J. N. "The Case for Pauline Authorship," in *Studies in Ephesians,* ed. F. L. Cross. London: Mowbray, 1956. Pages 9–20. *Cited as* Cross.

Schille, G. "Der Autor des Epheserbriefes," TLZ 82 (1957), 325–34.

Schmid, J. "Der Epheserbrief des Apostels Paulus," BiSt 22, 1928 (ref.).

Schweizer, E. "Zur Frage der Echtheit der Kolosser- und Epheserbriefe," ZNW 47 (1956), 287. Reprinted in *Neotestamentica.* Zürich: Zwingli, 1963. Page 429.

Scott, E. F. *The Epistles of Paul to the Colossians, to Philemon, and to the Ephesians.* MNTC 11. New York: Harper, 1930. *Cited as* Scott.

Usteri, L. *Die Entwicklung des paulinischen Lehrbegriffs.* Zürich: Orell Füssli, 1824. Pages 2–8.

Wagenführer, M. A. *Die Bedeutung Christi für Kirche und Welt.* Leipzig: Wigand, 1941 (ref.).

Weiss, J. *History of Primitive Christianity.* 2 vols. New York: Wilson-Erikson, 1931. I, 150; II, 684.

de Wette, W. M. L. *Lehrbuch des Neuen Testamentes.* Berlin: Reimer, 1826. Pages 254–65.

Wikenhauser, *New Testament Introduction.* New York: Herder, 1958. Pages 423–30.

Zahn, T. *Introduction to the New Testament,* I. London: Clark, 1909. Pages 499–522.

BIBLIOGRAPHY 6

(COMMENTS I and II on 1:1–2)

The Pauline Phrase "in Christ"

Allan, J. A. "The 'in Christ' Formula in Ephesians," NTS 5 (1958–59), 54–62.

Bouttier, M. *En Christ.* Paris: EHPR Presses, 1962.

———— "La condition chrétienne selon saint-Paul," *N.S. théologique* 16. Geneva: Labor et Fides, 1964.

Büchsel, F. "In Christo," ZNW 42 (1949), 141–58.

Deissmann, A. *Die neutestamentliche Formel 'in Christo Jesu'.* Marburg: Friedrich, 1892.

Grossouw, W. *In Christ.* Westminster, Md.: Newman Press, 1952.

Lohmeyer, *Grundlagen paulinischer Theologie.* Tübingen: Mohr, 1929. Pages 139–40.

Neugebauer, F. *In Christus.* Göttingen: Vandenhoeck, 1961.

———— "Das paulinische 'In Christo'," NTS 4 (1957–58), 124–38.

Parisius, H. L. "Uber die forensische Deutungsmöglichkeit des paulinischen *en Christo*," ZNW 49 (1958), 285–88.

Reid, J. K. S. "The Phrase 'In Christ'," TT 17 (1960), 353–65.

Schmauch, W. *In Christus*. Gütersloh: Bertelsmann, 1935.
Schweitzer, A. *The Mysticism of Paul the Apostle*. New York: Holt 1931.

BIBLIOGRAPHY 7

(Notes on 1:3 and Comments I–II on 1:3–14)

Origin and Form of the Benediction

Cambier, J. "La bénédiction d'Éphésiens 1, 3–14," ZNW 54 (1963), 58–104.
Coutts, J. "Eph. 1:3–14 and I Pet. 1:3–12," NTS 3 (1956–57), 115–27.
Dahl, N. A. "Adresse und Proömium des Epheserbriefes," TZ 7 (1951), 241–64.
Deichgräber, R. *Gotteshymnus und Christushymnus in der frühen Christenheit*. SUNT 5, 1967. Cited as *Gotteshymnus*.
Innitzer, T. "Der Hymnus in Eph. 1:3–14," ZKT 28 (1904), 612–21 (ref.).
Kramer, H. "Zur sprachlichen Form der Eulogie Eph. 1, 3–14," *Wort und Dienst*, N.F. 9 (1967), 34–46 (ref.).
Lyonnet, S. "La bénédiction de Eph. 1:3–14 et son arrière plan judaïque," in Fs A. Gelin. Paris: Le Puy, 1961. Pages 341–52 (ref.).
Maass, E. "Segnen, Weihen, Taufen," AR 21 (1922), 241–81.
Robinson, J. M. "Die Hodajoth-Formel in Gebet und Hymnus des Frühchristentums," in *Apophoreta*, Fs E. Haenchen. BhZNW 30 (1964), 194–235.

BIBLIOGRAPHY 8

(Note on 1:8 and Comment X on 1:3–14)

Wisdom

Arvedson, T. *Das Mysterium Christi*. Uppsala: Wretmans, 1937.
Christ, F. *Jesus Sophia*. ATANT 57, 1970.
Conzelmann, H. "Paulus und die Weisheit," NTS 12 (1965–66), 231–44.
Davies, W. D. *Paul and Rabbinic Judaism*. London: SPCK, 1955. Pages 147–76. *Cited as* PRJ.
Feuillet, A. *Le Christ Sagesse de Dieu d'après les épîtres pauliniennes*. Paris: Études bibliques, Lecoffre, 1966. Cited as *Christ Sagesse*.
Gerstenberger, E. "Zur alttestamentlichen Weisheit," Verkündigung und Forschung 14 (Munich: Kaiser, 1969), 28–44.
Jacob, E. *Theology of the Old Testament*. New York: Harper, 1958. Pages 118–20, 251–53.
Murphy, R. E. *Introduction to the Wisdom Literature of the Old Testament*. Collegeville, Minn.: Liturgy Press, 1965.
——— *Seven Books of Wisdom*. Milwaukee: Bruce, 1960.

Noth, M., and Thomas, D. W., eds. *Wisdom in Israel and in the Ancient Near East*, Fs H. H. Rowley. VTS 3, 1955.

von Rad, G. *Old Testament Theology*. 2 vols. New York: Harper, 1962. I, 418–53. *Cited as* OTTh.

———— *Weisheit in Israel*. Neukirchen: Neukirchener Verlag, 1970.

Ringgren, H. *Word and Wisdom*. Lund: Ohlssons, 1947. Pages 89–171.

Rylaarsdam, C. *Revelation in Jewish Wisdom Literature*. University of Chicago Press, 1951.

Schlier, H. *Der Brief an die Epheser*. 2d ed. Düsseldorf: Patmos, 1958. Pages 159–67. *Cited as* Schlier.

Schmidt, H. H. *Wesen und Geschichte der Weisheit*. BhZAW 101, 1967.

Schweizer, E. "Aufnahme und Korrektur jüdischer Sophiatheologie im Neuen Testament," in *Neotestamentica*. Zürich: Zwingli, 1963. Pages 110–21.

Strack, H. L., and P. Billerbeck. *Kommentar zum Neuen Testament aus Talmud und Midrasch*. 6 vols. Munich: Beck, 1922–61. II, 353–58. *Cited as* StB.

Wilckens, U. *Weisheit und Torheit*. BHTh 26, 1959.

Zimmerli, W. "The Place and Limit of Wisdom in the Framework of Old Testament Theology," ScotJT 17 (1964), 146–58.

———— "Die Weisheit Israels," EvTh 31 (1971), 680–95.

BIBLIOGRAPHY 9

(Last NOTE on 1:10)

Recapitulation

ab Alpe, A. "Instaurare omnia in Christo," VD 23 (1943), 97–103 (ref.).

Burney, C. F. "Christ as the ΑΡΧΗ of Creation," JTS 27 (1926), 160–77.

Cazelles, H. "Instaurare omnia in Christo," *Biblica* 40 (1959), 342–54.

Dufort, J. M. "La recapitulation paulinienne dans l'exégèse des pères," ScEccl 12 (1960), 21–38 (ref.).

Hanson, S. *Unity*. Pages 123–26.

Michaelis, W. *Versöhnung des Alls*. Gümligen-Berne: Siloah, 1950.

Staerck, W. "Anakephalaiosis," RAC I (1950), 411–14.

BIBLIOGRAPHY 10

(COMMENT IV on 1:15–23)

Resurrection

Barr, R. R. "The Soteriological Value of Resurrection," AER 146 (1962), 304–14.

Barth, C. *Die Errettung vom Tode*. Zürich: EVZ, 1947.

Barth, K. *The Resurrection of the Dead.* London: Hodder, 1933.

―――― *Church Dogmatics,* IV 1–3. Edinburgh: Clark, 1956, 1958, 1961.

Barth, M. *Die Taufe ein Sakrament?* Zürich: EVZ, 1951. Pages 283–306.

―――― *Justification.* Grand Rapids: Eerdmans, 1971. Pages 51–60.

―――― and Fletcher, V. *Acquittal by Resurrection.* New York: Holt, 1964.

Bonnard, P. "Mourir et vivre avec Jesus-Christ," RHPR 36 (1956), 101–12.

Bonsirven, J. *L'évangile de Paul.* Paris: Aubier, 1948. Pages 160–62.

Branton, R. "Resurrection in the Early Church," in *Early Christian Origins,* Fs H. R. Willoughby. Chicago: Quadrangle Press, 1961. Pages 35–47.

Bultmann, R. *Theology of the New Testament,* I. New York: Harper, 1951. Pages 292–306. *Cited as* ThNT, I.

Cerfaux, L. *Le Christ dans la théologie de saint Paul.* Paris: Du Cerf, 1964. Pages 57–93.

Clark, N. *Interpreting the Resurrection.* Philadelphia: Westminster, 1967.

Cullmann, O. *Immortality of the Soul, or Resurrection of the Dead?* New York: Macmillan, 1958.

Dahl, M. E. *The Resurrection of the Body.* SBT 36, 1962.

Davies, J. G. *He Ascended into Heaven.* London: Lutterworth, 1958.

Davies, W. D. *Paul and Rabbinic Judaism.* London: SPCK, 1955. Pages 285–320. *Cited as* PRJ.

Durwell, F. X. *The Resurrection.* New York: Sheed and Ward, 1960.

Ehrhardt, A. "Ein antikes Herrscherideal," EvTh 8 (1948–49), 101–10.

Faw, C. E. "Death and Resurrection of Christ in Paul," JBL 27 (1959), 291–98.

Filson, F. V. *Jesus Christ the Risen Lord.* Nashville: Abingdon, 1956.

Goguel, M. *La foi à la résurrection de Jésus.* Paris: Leroux, 1933.

Goppelt, L. *The Easter Message Today.* New York: Nelson, 1964.

Hahn, W. T. *Mitsterben und Mitauferstehen mit Christus.* Gütersloh: Bertelsmann, 1937.

Holtz, F. "La valeur sotériologique de la résurrection du Christ d'après saint Thomas," ETL 29 (1953), 609–45.

Hooke, S. H. *The Resurrection of Christ as History and Experience.* London: Darton, Longman and Todd, 1967.

Hulsbosch, A. "Resurrectio Christi in doctrina soteriologica S. Pauli," *Divus Thomas* 47–49 (1944–46), 193–227 (ref.).

Künneth, W. *The Theology of the Resurrection.* St. Louis: Concordia, 1965.

Leipoldt, J. *Sterbende und auferstehende Götter.* Leipzig: Deichert, 1923.

Lyonnet, S. "La valeur sotériologique de la résurrection du Christ selon saint Paul," *Gregorianum* 39 (1958), 295–318.

Martin-Achard, R. *From Death to Life.* Edinburgh: Oliver, 1960.

Marxsen, W. *The Resurrection of Jesus of Nazareth.* Philadelphia: Fortress, 1970.

McCasland, S. V. *The Resurrection of Jesus.* New York: Nelson, 1937.

Moule, C. F. D., ed. *The Significance of the Message of the Resurrection for Faith in Jesus Christ.* SBT, 2d ser. 8, 1968.

Murphy, F. X. "History and the Resurrection," AER 140 (1959), 152–58.

Niebuhr, R. R. *Resurrection and Historical Reason.* New York: Scribner, 1959.

Nikolainen, A. T. *Der Auferstehungsglaube in der Bibel und ihrer Umwelt.* 2 vols. AFAW 49:3, 1944; 59:3, 1946.

Noetscher, F. *Altorientalischer und alttestamentlicher Auferstehungsglauben.* Würzburg: Becker, 1926.

Prat, F. *La théologie de saint Paul,* II. 43d ed. Paris: Beauchesne, 1961. Pages 250–56.

Ramsey, A. M. *The Resurrection of Christ.* London: Bles, 1950; reprinted Philadelphia: Westminster, 1956.

Rohde, E. *Psyche,* II Tübingen: Mohr, 1921. Pages 27 ff., 130, 143 ff., 263 ff., 282, 298 ff., 393 ff., English tr. London: Routledge, 1925.

Schmitt, J. *Jésus résuscité dans la prédication apostolique.* Paris: Gabalda, 1949. Esp. pages 217–40.

Schubert, K. "Die Entwicklung der Auferstehungslehre von der nachexilischen bis zur frührabbinischen Zeit," BZ N.F. 6 (1962), 177–214 (ref.).

Stanley, D. M. *Christ's Resurrection in Pauline Soteriology,* AnBib 13, 1961. StB, III. Pages 474 f., 827 ff.; IV, 971 ff., 1017 ff., 1166 ff.

Tillich, P. *Systematic Theology,* II. University of Chicago Press, 1957. Pages 156–58.

Vawter, B. "Resurrection and Redemption," CBQ 15 (1953), 11–23.

Wagner, G. *Das religionsgeschichtliche Problem von Römer 6, 1–11,* ATANT 39, 1962.

Westcott, B. F. *The Gospel of the Resurrection,* 7th ed. London: Macmillan, 1891.

BIBLIOGRAPHY 11

(COMMENT V on 1:15–23)

Principalities and Powers

Aulen, G. *Christus Victor.* New York: Macmillan, 1945.

Barth, K. *Church Dogmatics,* III 3. Edinburgh: Clark, 1961. Pages 369–531.

Berkhof, H. *Christ and the Powers.* Scottdale, Pa.: Herald, 1962.

Caird, G. B. *Principalities and Powers.* Oxford: Clarendon, 1956.

Cullmann, O. *The State in the New Testament.* New York: Scribner, 1956.

Dahl, M. E. "The Resurrection of the Body," SBT 36 (1962), 117–19.

Dibelius, H. *Die Geisterwelt im Glauben des Paulus.* Göttingen: Vandenhoeck, 1909.

Everling, E. *Paulinische Angelologie und Dämonologie.* Göttingen: Vandenhoeck, 1888 (ref.).

Galloway, A. D. *The Cosmic Christ.* New York: Harper, 1951. Pages 24 ff.

van den Heuvel, A. H. *These Rebellious Powers.* New York: Friendship, 1965.

Kallas, J. G. *A Satanward View.* Philadelphia: Westminster, 1966.

Langton, E. *Angel Teaching of the New Testament.* London: Clarks, n.d. (ref.).

Lee, J. Y. "Interpreting the Demonic Powers in Pauline Thought," NovT 12 (1970), 54–69.

Lightfoot, J. B. *St. Paul's Epistles to the Colossians and to Philemon.* London: Macmillan, 1875. Pages 217–20.

MacGregor, G. H. C. "Principalities and Powers: the Cosmic Background of Paul's Thought," NTS 1 (1954), 17–28.

Maurer, C. "Die Begründung der Herrschaft Christi über die Mächte nach Kol. 1, 15–20," WoDie N.S. 4 (1955), 79–93.

Morrison, C. "The Powers That Be," SBT 29, 1960.

Percy, E. *Die Probleme der Kolosser- und Epheserbriefe.* Lund: Gleerup, 1946. Pages 149–69. *Cited as* Percy.

Rupp, E. G. *Principalities and Powers.* New York: Abingdon, 1952.

Schlier, H. *Principalities and Powers in the New Testament.* New York: Herder, 1961.

Schmidt, K. L. "Natur- und Geisteskräfte im paulinischen Erkennen und Glauben," EJb 14 (1946), 87–143.

StB, IV, 501–35.

Whiteley, D. E. H. *The Theology of St. Paul.* Philadelphia: Fortress, 1964. Pages 19–31.

———— "Expository Problems: Eph. 6:12: Evil Powers," ET 68 (1957), 100–3.

Wilder, A. "Kerygma, Eschatology and Social Ethics," in *The Background of the New Testament and Its Eschatology,* Fs C. H. Dodd. Cambridge University Press, 1957. Pages 509–36, esp. 527 ff.

BIBLIOGRAPHY 12

(COMMENT VI on 1:15–23)

Head, Body, and Fullness

Aalen, S. "Begreped plerome i Kolosser- och Efeserbrevet," TTK 23 (1952), 49–67 (ref.).

Barth, K. *Church Dogmatics,* IV 1–3. Edinburgh: Clark, 1956, 1958, 1961. Esp. 1, pages 660–62; 2, pages 621–27; 3, pages 752–57, 790–92.

Bedale, S. F. B. "The Theology of the Church," in Cross.

Benoit, P. "Corps, tête et plérôme dans les épîtres de la captivité," RB 63 (1956), 5–44; reprinted in *Exégèse et théologie,* II. Paris: Du Cerf, 1961. Pages 107–53. Quoted from RB.

Best, E. *One Body in Christ.* London: SPCK, 1955.

———— "The Body of Christ," EcuR 9 (1957), 122–28.

Burtness, J. H. "All the Fulness," *Dialog* 3 (Minneapolis, 1964), 257–63.

Cerfaux, L. *The Church in the Theology of St. Paul.* New York: Herder, 1959.

———— *La théologie de l'église suivant saint Paul.* Unam Sanctam 54, rev. ed. Paris: Du Cerf, 1965. Especially pages 223–319. Cited as *Église.*

Chavasse, C. *The Bride of Christ.* London: Faber, 1940.

Colpe, C. "Zur Leib-Christi-Vorstellung im Epheserbrief," in Fs J. Jeremias, BhZNW 26 (1960), 172–87.

Dacquino, P. "De Christo capite et ecclesia eius corpore secundum S. Paulum," VD 40 (1962), 81–88 (ref.).

Dahl, N. A. *Das Volk Gottes*. SNVA 2, 1941, reprinted 1962.

Deimel, L. *Der Leib Christi*. Wiesbaden: Herder, 1940.

Delling, G. art. *"plērēs,"* etc. TWNTE, VI, 283–311.

Dillistone, F. W. "How is the Church Christ's Body?" TT 2 (1945), 56–68.

Dubarle, A. M. "L'origine dans l'Ancient Testament de la notion paulinienne de l'église corps du Christ," AnBib 17–18, I (1963), 231–40.

Ernst, J. *Pleroma und pleroma Christi*. Regensburg: Pustet, 1970.

Feuillet, A. "L'église plérôme du Christ d'après Éphés. 1, 23," NRT 78 (1956), 449–72, 593–610.

———— *Le Christ Sagesse de Dieu d'après les épîtres pauliniennes*. Paris: Gabalda, 1966. Pages 275–319. Cited as *Christ Sagesse*.

Fowler, F. "Ephesians 1:23," ET 76 (1965), 294.

Gabathuler, H. J. *Jesus Christus, Haupt der Kirche—Haupt der Welt*, ATANT 45, 1965.

Gewiess, J. "Die Begriffe *pleroun* und *pleroma* im Kolosser- und Epheserbrief," in *Vom Wort Des Lebens*, Fs M. Meinertz. Münster: Aschendorff, 1951. Pages 128–41.

Goossens, W. *L'Église, corps du Christ, d'après S. Paul*. Paris: Gabalda, 1949.

Grant, R. M. *Gnosticism*. New York: Harper, 1961. Pages 163–81.

Grossouw, W. *In Christ*. Westminster, Md.: Newman, 1952.

Hanson, S. *The Unity of the Church in the New Testament, Colossians and Ephesians*. ASNU 14. Uppsala: Almquist, 1946. Cited as *Unity*.

Hebert, A. G. *Liturgy and Society*. London: Faber, 1944.

Huby, J. *St. Paul, Les épîtres de la captivité*. Paris: Beauchesne, 1947. Pages 167–70 (ref.).

Jewett, R. *Paul's Anthropological Terms*. Leiden: Brill, 1971. Pages 200–30.

Jonas, H. *The Gnostic Religion*. Boston: Beacon, 1963. Pages 40–46, 177–205.

Käsemann, E. *Leib und Leib Christi*. Tübingen: Mohr, 1933.

———— "Unity and Diversity in New Testament Ecclesiology," NovT 6 (1963), 290–97.

———— "The Theological Problem Presented by the Motif of the Body of Christ," in *Perspectives on Paul*. Philadelphia: Fortress, 1971. Pages 102–21.

Kehl, N. *Der Christushymnus Kol 1, 12–20*, SBM 1 (1967), 109–25.

Lightfoot, J. B. *St. Paul's Epistles to the Colossians and to Philemon*, London: Macmillan, 1875. Especially pages 223, 264–67, 323–39.

Linton, O. *Das Problem der Urkirche in der neueren Forschung*, Uppsala: Almquist, 1932; reprinted Frankfort: Minerva, 1957.

de Lubac, H. "Corpus Mysticum," RCR 29 (1939), 257–302, 429–80; 30 (1940), 40–80, 191–225.

Malevez, L. "L'église, corps du Christ," RSR 32 (1944), 27–94.

Mascall, E. L. *Christ, the Christian and the Church*. London: Longmans, 1946.

McGlasham, A. R. "Ephesians 1:23," ET 76 (1965), 132–33.

Merklinger, H. A. "Pleroma and Christianity," ConcTM 36 (1965), 739–40.

Mersch, E. *The Whole Christ*. Milwaukee: Bruce, 1938.

Meuzelaar, J. J. *Der Leib des Messias*. Assen: Van Gorcum, 1961.

Minear, P. *Images of the Church in the New Testament.* Philadelphia: Westminster, 1960. Pages 173–220.

Mitton, C. L. *The Epistle to the Ephesians: Its Authorship, Origin and Purpose.* Oxford: Clarendon, 1951. Pages 94–97. *Cited as* EE.

Moule, C. F. D. *The Epistles of Paul the Apostle to the Colossians and to Philemon.* Cambridge University Press, 1957. Pages 164–69.

Münderlein, G. "Die Erwählung durch das Pleroma—Bemerkungen zu Kol. 1, 19," NTS 8 (1962), 264–76.

Mussner, F. *Christus, das All und die Kirche.* Trier: Paulus Verlag, 1955, reprinted 1968. *Cited as* CAK.

Nelson, J. R. "Many Images of the Church," EcuR 9 (1957), 105–13.

Nygren, A. *Christ and His Church.* Philadelphia: Westminster, 1956.

Percy, E. *Der Leib Christi.* Lund: Universitets Arsschrift, 1942.

——— *Die Probleme der Kolosser- und Epheserbriefe.* Lund: Gleerup, 1946. Pages 75–78.

Pius XII. *Mystici Corporis.* Acta Apostolicae Sedis 35 (1943), 193–248.

Pokorný, P. *Der Epheserbrief und die Gnosis.* Berlin: Evangelische Verlagsanstalt, 1965. *Cited as* EuG.

——— "Soma Christou im Epheserbrief," EvTh 20 (1960), 456–64.

Prat, F. *La théologie de saint Paul.* 43d ed. Paris: Beauchesne, 1961. I, 355–70; II, 331–73.

Rawlinson, E. J. "Corpus Christi," in *Mysterium Christi,* ed. G. K. A. Bell and A. Deissmann. London: Longmans, 1930. Pages 225–44.

Reuss, J. "Die Kirche als der Leib Christi," BZ 26 (1958), 103–27.

Robinson, J. A. *St. Paul's Epistle to the Ephesians.* 2d ed. London: Clark, 1922. Pages 42–45, 255–59.

Robinson, J. A. T. "The Body," SBT 5, 1952.

Schlier, H. *Christus und die Kirche im Epheserbrief.* BHTh 6, 1930; repr. 1966. Cited as *Christus.*

——— "*kephalē,*" TWNTE, III, 673–82.

Schlink, E. "Christ and the Church," ScotJT 10 (1957), 1–23.

Schmidt, K. L. art. "*ekklēsiā,*" TWNTE, III, especially 509–13.

Schmidt, T. *Der Leib Christi.* Leipzig/Erlangen: Deichert, 1919.

Schnackenburg, R. *The Church in the New Testament.* New York: Herder, 1966.

——— "Gestalt und Wesen der Kirche nach dem Epheserbrief," *Catholica* 15 (1961), 104–20.

——— "Wesenzüge und Geheimnis der Kirche nach dem Neuen Testament," in *Mysterium Kirche,* I, ed. F. Holböck and Th. Sartory. Salzburg: Otto Müller Verlag, 1962. Pages 89–199.

Schweizer, E. "The Church as the Missionary Body of Christ," NTS 8 (1961), 1–11; reprinted in *Neotestamentica,* 1963. Pages 317–29.

——— "Die Kirche als Leib Christi . . . ," TLZ 86 (1961), 161–74, 241–56; reprinted in *Neotestamentica,* 1963. Pages 272–316.

——— art. "*sōma,*" TWNTE, VII, 1024–91.

——— *The Church as the Body of Christ.* Richmond: Knox, 1964.

Soiron, T. *Die Kirche als der Leib Christi.* Düsseldorf: Patmos, 1951.

Thornton, L. S. *The Common Life of the Body of Christ.* London: Dacre, 1942.

———— "The Body of Christ in the New Testament," in *The Apostolic Ministry,* ed. K. E. Kirk. 2d ed. New York: Morehouse, 1947. Pages 53–111.

Torrance, T. F. *Royal Priesthood.* ScotJT Occasional Papers 3, 1955.

Tromp, S. "Caput influit sensum et motum, Col. 2, 19 et Eph. 4, 16 in luce traditionis," *Gregorianum* 39 (1958), 353–66.

a Vallisoleto, H. A. "Christi pleroma juxta Pauli conceptionem," VD 14 (1934) 49–55 (ref.).

Wikenhauser, A. *Die Kirche als der mystische Leib des Christus nach dem Apostel Paulus.* 2d ed. Münster: Aschendorff, 1940.

Williamson, L. *God's Work of Art.* Richmond: CLC, 1971.

BIBLIOGRAPHY 13

(Comment V on 2:1–10)

The Covenant Lawsuit

Boecker, H. J. "Anklagereden und Verteidigungsreden im Alten Testament," EvTh 20 (1960), 398–412.

———— *Redeformen des Rechtslebens im AT,* WMANT 40, 1964.

Cross, F. M. "The Council of Yahwe in Second Isaiah," JNES 12 (1953), 274–77.

Gemser, B. "The *Rib* or Controversy-Pattern in Hebrew Mentality," in *Wisdom in Israel and in the Ancient Near East,* VTS 3 (1955), 120–37.

Gunkel, H. and Begrich, J. *Einleitung in die Psalmen.* Göttingen: Vandenhoeck, 1933. Pages 75, 365 ff.

Holladay, W. L. "Jeremiah's Lawsuit with God," *Interpretation* 17 (1963), 280–87.

Huffmon, H. B. "The Covenant Lawsuit in the Prophets," JBL 78 (1959), 285–95.

Jackson, J. J. "Yahweh vs. Cohen et al.", *Pittsburgh Perspective* 7 (1966), 28–32.

Jepsen, A. "Zdq und zdqh im AT," in *Gottes Wort und Gottes Land,* Fs H.-W. Hertzberg. Göttingen: Vandenhoeck, 1965. Pages 78–89.

Koch, K. *SDQ im AT.* Diss. Heidelberg, 1953 (ref.).

Preiss, T. *Life in Christ,* SBT 13. London: SCM, 1954. Pages 48–60.

von Rad, G. *Old Testament Theology,* I. New York: Harper, 1962. Pages 371 ff.

de Vaux, R. *Ancient Israel.* New York: McGraw-Hill, 1961. Ch. X.

Wright, G. E. "The Lawsuit of God: A Form-Critical Study of Deuteronomy 32," Fs J. Muilenburg. New York: Harper, 1962. Pages 26–67.

BIBLIOGRAPHY 14

(COMMENT VI on 2:1–10)

The Work of God and the Works of Man

Barrett, C. K. *A Commentary on the Epistle to the Romans.* New York: Harper, 1957. Pages 46–48.

Barth, K. *Church Dogmatics* IV 2 (1958), 584–98.

Bertram, G. *"ergon,"* etc., TWNTE II, 635–55.

Braun, H. *Gerichtsgedanke und Rechtfertigungslehre bei Paulus.* Leipzig: Hinrichs, 1930.

Burton, E. W. *The Epistle to the Galatians.* ICC. 5th ed., 1956. Especially page 120.

Crowther, C. "Works, Work and Good Works," ET 81 (1970), 66–71.

Descamps, A. *Les justes et la justice.* Gembloux: Duculot, 1950.

Jüngel, E. *Paulus und Jesus.* 2d ed. Tübingen: Mohr, 1964. Pages 17–70.

Lohmeyer, E. "Gesetzeswerke," ZNW 28 (1929), 177–207. Reprinted in *Probleme paulinischer Theologie.* Stuttgart: Kohlhammer, n.d. Pages 31–74.

Luther, M. Commentaries on Galatians in WA II, 436–618; XL 1, 2; LVII 2, 1–108.

Moore, G. F. *Judaism.* Harvard University Press, 1954. II, 170–74.

Quell, G. and Schrenk, G. art. *"dikē,"* etc., TWNTE II, 174–225.

Rössler, D. *Gesetz und Geschichte.* Neukirchen: Neukirchener Verlag, 1960.

Schlier, H. *Der Brief an die Galater,* KEKNT 7. Rev. ed. (1965), 91–95, 176–88.

Schoeps, H.-J. *Paul.* Philadelphia: Westminster, 1961. Pages 168–218.

Stalder, K. *Das Werk des Geistes in der Heiligung bei Paulus.* Zürich: EVZ, 1962. Especially pages 455 ff., 464 f.

StB, III, 160–62.

Stendahl, K. "Justification and Last Judgment," LuthW 8 (1961), 1–7.

BIBLIOGRAPHY 15

(COMMENT IVB on 2:11–22)

The Law in Paul

Barth, K. "Gospel and Law," in *Community, State and Church.* New York: Doubleday, 1960. Pages 71–100.

Bläser, P. *Das Gesetz bei Paulus.* NTAbh 19, 1941.

Bornkamm, G. "Wandlungen im alt- und neutestamentlichen Gesetzesverständnis," in *Geschichte und Glaube,* II. BEvTh, 1971, 73–119.

Bring, R. *Christus und das Gesetz.* Leiden: Brill, 1969.

Buber, M. *Two Types of Faith.* New York: Harper, 1961.

Bultmann, R. *Theology of the New Testament*, I. New York: Harper, 1951. Pages 259–69. *Cited as* ThNT, I.

——— "Christus des Gesetzes Ende," in R. Bultmann and H. Schlier, *Christus des Gesetzes Ende*. BEvTh I (1940), 3–27.

Burton, E. W. *The Epistle to the Galatians*. ICC. 5th ed., 1956. Pages 443–60.

Cranfield, C. E. B. "St. Paul and the Law," ScotJT 17 (1964), 43–68.

Davies, W. D. *Paul and Rabbinic Judaism*. London: SPCK, 1955. Pages 147–226.

von Dülmen, A. *Die Theologie des Gesetzes bei Paulus*. Stuttgart: Katholisches Verlagswerk, 1968.

Ebeling, G. "Reflections on the Doctrine of the Law," in *Word and Faith*. 2d ed. Philadelphia: Fortress, 1964. Pages 247–81.

Howard, G. E. "Christ the End of the Law," JBL 88 (1969), 331–37.

Jepsen, A. "Israel und das Gesetz," TLZ 93 (1968), 85–94.

Jüngel, E. "Das Gesetz zwischen Adam und Christus," ZTK 60 (1963), 42–74.

Kraus, H.-J. "Freude am Gesetz," EvTh 10 (1950–51), 337–51.

Longenecker, R. N. *Paul Apostle of Liberty*. New York: Harper, 1964. Pages 147–55.

Maurer, C. *Die Gesetzeslehre bei Paulus*. Zollikon: EVZ, 1941.

McKenzie, J. "Natural Law in the New Testament," BiRes 9 (1964), 3–13.

Moore, G. F. *Judaism*, I. Harvard University Press, 1954. Pages 235–80.

Noth, M. *The Laws in the Pentateuch and Other Studies*. Philadelphia: Westminster, 1961. Also published by Oliver and Boyd in Edinburgh, 1966.

von Rad, G. *Theology of the Old Testament*. 2 vols. New York: Harper, 1962, 1965. I, 187–279; II, 388–409.

Rössler, D. *Gesetz und Geschichte*. Neukirchen: Neukirchener Verlag, 1960.

Schlier, H. *Der Brief an die Galater*. KEKNT 7. 13th ed., 1965. Especially pages 176–88.

Schneider, E. E. "Finis legis Christus," TZ 20 (1964), 410–22.

Schoeps, H. J. *Paul of Tarsus*. Philadelphia: Westminster, 1961. Pages 38, 52–53, 168–218.

Whiteley, D. E. H. *The Theology of St. Paul*. Philadelphia: Fortress, 1964. Pages 83–86.

Wyschogrod, M. "The Law, Jews and Gentiles—a Jewish Perspective," *Lutheran Quarterly* 21 (1969), 405–15.

BIBLIOGRAPHY 16

(COMMENT IVA on 3:14–21)

Mysticism

Abelsen, J. *Jewish Mysticism*. London: Bell, 1913.

Amstutz, J. "Origin and Types of Existentialism," JR 41 (1961), 248–62.

Baeck, L. "Jewish Mysticism," JJS 2 (1949–50), 3–16.

Bousset, W. *Kyrios Christos*. Nashville: Abingdon, 1970. Pages 153–210.

Bultmann, R. art. "Mystik im NT," RGG, IV. 3d ed. Tübingen: Mohr, 1960. Columns 1243–48.

Conzelmann, H. "Current Problems in Pauline Research," *Interpretation* 22 (1968), 171–86.

Davies, W. D. *Paul and Rabbinic Judaism*. London: SPCK, 1955. Especially pages 13–16, 86–110. *Cited as* PRJ.

Deissmann, A. *Paul*. Torchbook 15. New York: Harper, 1957.

Dibelius, M. "Glaube und Mystik bei Paulus," in *Botschaft und Geschichte*, II. Tübingen: Mohr, 1956. Pages 94–116.

————— "Paulus und die Mystik," in *Botschaft und Geschichte*. II, 134–59.

Heiler, F. *Prayer*. Oxford University Press, 1932. Pages 135 ff.

Heitmüller, W. *Im Namen Jesu*. FRLANT 12, 1903. Especially pages 153 f., 164, 169 f., 303 ff.

Inge, W. R. *Christian Mysticism*. New York: Scribner, 1899. Pages 59–72.

————— "St. Paul," in *Outspoken Essays*, First Series. New York: Longmans, 1919. Pages 205–29.

James, W. *Varieties of Religious Experience*. London-New York: Longmans, 1919. Pages 205–29.

Lohmeyer, E. *Urchristliche Mystik*. Darmstadt: Gentner, 1956.

Odeberg, H. *Third Enoch, or The Hebrew Book of Enoch*. Cambridge University Press, 1928.

Otto, R. *The Idea of the Holy*. Oxford University Press, 1957.

Reitzenstein, R. *Die Hellenistischen Mysterienreligionen*. 3d ed. Leipzig: Teubner, 1927. *Cited as* HMyRel.

Schneider, J. *Die Passionsmystik des Paulus*. Leipzig: Hinrichs, 1929.

Scholem, G. G. *Major Trends in Jewish Mysticism*. New York: Schocken, 1946.

Schweitzer, A. *The Mysticism of Paul the Apostle*. New York: Holt, 1931.

Schweizer, E. "Die Mystik des Sterbens und Auferstehens mit Christus bei Paulus," EvTh 26 (1966), 234–57.

Stewart, J. S. *A Man in Christ*. New York: Harper, 1963.

Underhill, E. *Mysticism*. New York: Noonday, 1955. Especially pages 71–124.

KEY TO THE TEXT